THIRD EDITION

A First Book of C++

From Here to There

Gary J. Bronson
Fairleigh Dickinson University

COURSE TECHNOLOGY
CENGAGE Learning™

Australia • Brazil • Japan • Korea • Mexico • Singapore • Spain • United Kingdom • United States

COURSE TECHNOLOGY
CENGAGE Learning™

A First Book of C++: From Here to There, Third Edition
Gary J. Bronson

Senior Product Manager: Alyssa Pratt

Executive Editor: Mac Mendelsohn

Production Editor: Jennifer Harvey,
  Pre-Press Company

Senior Marketing Manager: Karen Seitz

Associate Product Manager: Mirella
  Misiaszek

Editorial Assistant: Jennifer Smith

Senior Manufacturing Coordinator:
  Laura Burns

Cover Designer: Laura Rickenbach

Compositor: Pre-Press Company, Inc.

For product information and technology assista nce, contact us at
Cengage Learning Customer & Sales Support, 1-800-354-9706

For permission to use material from this text or product,
submit all requests online at **cengage.com/permissions**
Further permissions questions can be emailed to
permissionrequest@cengage.com

ISBN-13: 978-0-534-49281-6

ISBN-10: 0-534-49281-9

Course Technology
25 Thomson Place
Boston, MA, 02210
USA

Cengage Learning is a leading provider of customized learning solutions with office locations around the globe, including Singapore, the United Kingdom, Australia, Mexico, Brazil, and Japan. Locate your local office at:
international.cengage.com/region

Cengage Learning products are represented in Canada by
Nelson Education, Ltd.

Visit our corporate website at **www.cengage.com**

Printed in Canada
5 6 7 8 9 09

Contents

Preface

"...in the long term to get the most out of something like C++ you will need to use it in an object-oriented manner. You need to use object-oriented programming and to do object-oriented design. However, you also have to get from here to there."[1]

The primary goal of this third edition of *A First Book of C++* has remained the same as that of previous editions: to introduce, develop, and reinforce well-organized programming skills using C++. All topics are presented in a clear, unambiguous, and accessible manner to beginning students. Students should be familiar with fundamental algebra, but no other prerequisites are assumed.

To remain up-to-date with the current ANSI/ISO C++ standard, the third edition has a number of significant changes and added features. These include the following:

- Use of the ANSI/ISO C++ iostream library and namespace mechanism in all programs
- The presentation of exception handling in a complete section, with practical applications of exception handling presented throughout the text.
- Presentation of the new C++ string class
- A thorough discussion of input data validation and functions to both check the numerical data type of an input item and provide for re-entry of invalid numerical types
- A completely new chapter devoted to the Standard Template Library (STL)

Even with these additions, the central elements of the prior editions remain essentially unchanged in this new edition. Thus, all of the topics, examples, explanations, and figures in the prior editions, aside from being updated to the current ANSI standards, will be found in this edition.

Distinctive Features of This Text

Writing Style. I firmly believe that introductory texts do not teach students— professors teach students. An introductory textbook, if it is to be useful, must be the primary "supporting actor" to the "leading role" of the professor. Once the professor sets the stage, however, the textbook must encourage, nurture, and assist the student in acquiring and "owning" the material presented in class. To

---

[1] "Interview with Bjarne Stroustrup," *C++ Journal*, Vol. 1, no. 3, pp. 16-25, 1991.

accomplish this, the text must be written in a manner that makes sense to the student. My primary concern, and one of the distinctive features of this book, is that it is written for the student. Thus, first and foremost, I feel the writing style used to convey the concepts presented is the most important aspect of the text.

Software Engineering. Rather than simply introduce students to programming in C++, this text introduces students to the fundamentals of software engineering, from both a procedural and object-oriented viewpoint. This begins with a discussion of these two programming approaches in Section 1.1 and is reinforced throughout the text.

Introduction to References and Pointers. One of the unique features of my previous text, *A First Book of ANSI C*, was the early introduction of pointer concepts. This was done by displaying the addresses of variables and then using other variables to store these addresses. This approach always seemed a more logical and intuitive method of understanding pointers than the indirection description in vogue at the time *A First Book of ANSI C* was released.

I have since been pleased to see that the use of an output function to display addresses has become a standard way of introducing pointers. Although this approach is no longer a unique feature of this book, I am very proud of its presentation, and continue to use it in this text. Additionally, references are also introduced early, in Chapter 2.

Program Testing. Every C++ program in this text has been successfully compiled, run, and Quality Assurance tested using Microsoft Visual C++ .NET. Source code for all programs can be found on the Course Technology Web site (http://www.course.com) This will permit students to both experiment and extend the existing programs and more easily modify them as required by a number of end-of-section exercises.

Pedagogical Features

To facilitate the goal of making C++ accessible as a first level course, the following pedagogical features have been incorporated into the text:

Programming Notes. A set of shaded boxes that highlight important concepts, useful technical points, programming tips, and programming tricks used by professional programmers.

End of Section Exercises. Almost every section in the book contains numerous and diverse skill builder and programming exercises. Additionally, solutions to selected odd-numbered exercises are provided in an appendix.

Pseudocode Descriptions. Pseudocode is stressed throughout the text. Flowchart symbols are presented, but are only used in visually presenting flow-of-control constructs.

Common Programming Errors and Chapter Review. Each Chapter ends with a section on common programming errors and a review of the main topics covered in the chapter.

Appendices

An expanded set of appendices are provided. These include appendices on Operator Precedence, ASCII codes, and Bit Operations. Additionally, Course Technology provides a number of tutorials for using various C++ compilers. These tutorials can be located on the text's catalog page at http://www.course.com.

Supplemental Materials

The following supplemental materials are available when this book is used in a classroom setting.

Electronic Instructor's Manual. The Instructor's Manual that accompanies this textbook includes:

- Additional instructional material to assist in class preparation, including suggestions for lecture topics.

ExamView®. This textbook is accompanied by ExamView, a powerful testing software package that allows instructors to create and administer printed, computer (LAN-based), and Internet exams. ExamView includes hundreds of questions that correspond to the topics covered in this text, enabling students to generate detailed study guides that include page references for further review. These computer-based and Internet testing components allow students to take exams at their computers, and save the instructor time because each exam is graded automatically.

PowerPoint Presentations. This book comes with Microsoft PowerPoint slides for each chapter. These are included as a teaching aid for classroom presentations, either to make available to students on the network for chapter review, or to be printed for classroom distribution. Instructors can add their own slides for additional topics that they introduce to the class.

Distance Learning. Course Technology is proud to present online courses in WebCT and Blackboard to provide the most complete and dynamic learning experience possible. When you add online content to one of your courses, you're adding a lot: Topic Reviews, Practice Tests, Review Questions, Assignments, PowerPoint presentations, and, most of all, a gateway to the 21st century's most important information resource. For more information on how to bring distance learning to your course, contact your local Course Technology sales representative.

Source Code. The source code for this text is available at www.course.com and is also available on the Teaching Tools CD-ROM.

Solution Files. The solution files for all programming exercises are available at www.course.com, and are also available on the Teaching Tools CD-ROM.

Acknowledgments

The writing of this third edition is a direct result of the success (and limitations) of the first two editions. In this regard, my most heartfelt acknowledgment and appreciation is to the instructors and students who found these editions to be of service to them in their respective quests to teach and learn C++.

Next, I would like to thank Alyssa Pratt, Senior Product Manager at Course Technology. In addition to her continuous faith and encouragement, her ideas and partnership were instrumental in creating this text. Once the development process was completed, the task of turning the final manuscript into a textbook depended on many people other than myself. For this I especially want to thank my Production Editor, Jennifer Harvey of the Pre-Press Company, Inc., my copy-editor Cheryl Hauser, interior designer Lisa Devenish, and Nicole Ashton who created the solution files. The dedication of this team of people was incredible and very important to me. As always, any errors in the text rest solely on my shoulders.

Finally, the direct encouragement and support of Fairleigh Dickinson University is also gratefully acknowledged. Specifically, this includes the constant encouragement, support, and positive academic climate provided by Dr. Kenneth Greene, the Provost, my Dean, Dr. David Steele, and my Chairperson, Dr. Paul Yoon. Without their support, this text could not have been written.

Finally, I deeply appreciate the patience, understanding, and love provided by my friend, wife, and partner, Rochelle.

Gary Bronson

DEDICATED TO

Rochelle, David, Matthew, and Jeremy

PART I

Fundamentals

CHAPTER 1

Getting Started

1.1   Introduction to Programming

A computer is a machine, and like other machines, such as automobiles and lawn mowers, it must be turned on and then driven, or controlled, to do the task it was meant to do. In an automobile, control is provided by the driver, who sits inside of and directs the car. In a computer, control is provided by a computer program. More formally, a **computer program** is a structured combination of data and instructions that is used to operate a computer. Another term for a computer program is **software**, and we will use both terms interchangeably throughout the text.

Programming is the process of writing a computer program in a language that the computer can respond to and that other programmers can understand. The set of instructions, data, and rules that can be used to construct a program is called a **programming language**.

Programming languages are usefully classified by level and orientation. Languages that use instructions resembling written languages, such as English, are referred to as **high-level languages**. Visual Basic, C, C++, and Java are all examples of high-level languages.[1] The final program written in such languages can be run on a variety of computer types, such as those manufactured by IBM, Apple, and Hewlett-Packard. In contrast, **low-level languages** use instructions that are directly tied to one type of computer.[2] Although programs written in low-level languages are limited in that they can be run only on the type of computer they were written for, they do permit using special features of the computer that are different from other machines. They can also be written to execute faster than programs written in high-level languages.

In addition to classifying programming languages as high or low-level, they are also classified by orientation, as either procedural or object-oriented. In a **procedural language** the available instructions are used to create self-contained units, referred to as **procedures**. The purpose of a procedure is to accept data as input and transform the data in some manner to produce a specific result as an output. Initially, high-level programming languages were predominately procedural.

At a very basic level, the purpose of almost all high-level programs is to process data to produce one or more specific results. In a procedural language, such programs are constructed from sets of instructions, with each set referred to

---

[1] C++ is sometimes classified as a middle-level language to convey the fact that although C++ is written as a high-level language, it can also take advantage of machine features that historically could be accessed only with low-level languages.

[2] In actuality, the low-level language is defined for the processor around which the computer is constructed.

as a procedure, as noted previously. Effectively, each procedure moves the data one step closer to the final desired output along the path shown in Figure 1.1.

FIGURE 1.1 *Procedure-Oriented Program Operations*

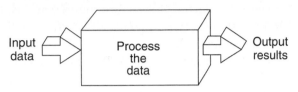

It is interesting to note that the programming process illustrated in Figure 1.3 directly mirrors the input, processing, and output hardware units that are used to construct a computer. This was not accidental, because high-level programming languages were initially designed to match and, as optimally as possible, directly control corresponding hardware units. In C++ a procedures is formally referred to as a **function**.

Currently, a second approach, object orientation, has taken center stage. One of the motivations for **object-oriented languages** was the development of graphical screens and support for graphical user interfaces (GUIs) capable of displaying multiple windows containing both graphical shapes and text. In such an environment, each window on the screen can conveniently be considered an object with associated characteristics, such as color, position, and size. Using an object-oriented approach, a program must first define the objects it will be manipulating, which includes describing both the general characteristics of the objects themselves and specific operations to manipulate them, such as changing size and position and transferring data between objects. Equally important is the fact that object-oriented languages tend to more easily support reusing existing code, which removes the necessity for revalidating and retesting new or modified code. C++, which is classified as an object-oriented language, contains features found in both procedural and object-oriented languages.

The reason for C++'s dual nature is that it began as an extension to C, which is a procedural language developed in the 1970s at AT&T Bell Laboratories. In the early 1980s, Bjarne Stroustrup (also at AT&T) used his background in simulation languages to develop C++. A central feature of simulation languages is that they model real-life situations as objects that respond to stimuli in well-defined ways. This object orientation, along with other procedural improvements, was combined with existing C language features to form the C++ language.

Algorithms and Procedures

Because algorithms are central to C++'s procedural side, it will serve us well to understand what an algorithm is. From a procedural point of view, before writing a program, a programmer must clearly understand what data is to be used, the desired result, and the procedure to be used to produce this result. The procedure to be used is referred to as an algorithm. More precisely defined, an **algorithm** is a step-by-step sequence of instructions that describes how a computation is to be performed.

Only after we clearly understand the data that we will be using and the algorithm (the specific steps required to produce the desired result) can we write the program. Seen in this light, procedure-oriented programming is the translation of a selected algorithm into a language that the computer can use.

To illustrate an algorithm, we shall consider a simple problem. Assume that a program must calculate the sum of all whole numbers from 1 through 100. Figure 1.2 illustrates three methods we could use to find the required sum. Each method constitutes an algorithm.

Most people would not bother to list the possible alternatives in a detailed step-by-step manner, as we did in Figure 1.2, and then select one of the algorithms to solve the problem. But then, most people do not think algorithmically; they tend to think heuristically. For example, if you had to change a flat tire on your car, you would not think of all the steps required—you would simply change the tire or call someone else to do the job. This is an example of heuristic thinking.

Unfortunately, computers do not respond to heuristic commands. A general statement such as "Add the numbers from 1 through 100" means nothing to a computer, because the computer can respond only to algorithmic commands written in an acceptable language such as C++. To program a computer successfully, you must clearly understand this difference between algorithmic and heuristic commands. A computer is an "algorithm-responding" machine; it is not an "intuition-responding" machine. You cannot tell a computer to change a tire or to add the numbers from 1 through 100. Instead, you must give the computer a detailed, step-by-step sequence of instructions that, collectively, forms an algorithm. For example, the sequence of instructions

$$\textit{Set n equal to 100}$$
$$\textit{Set a = 1}$$
$$\textit{Set b equal to 100}$$
$$\textit{Calculate sum} = \frac{n * (a + b)}{2}$$

constitutes a detailed method, or algorithm, for determining the sum of the numbers from 1 through 100. Note that these instructions are not a computer program.

FIGURE 1.2　*Summing the Numbers from 1 through 100*

Method 1. *Columns:* Arrange the numbers from 1 to 100 in a column and add them:

$$
\begin{array}{r}
1 \\
2 \\
3 \\
4 \\
\cdot \\
\cdot \\
\cdot \\
98 \\
99 \\
+100 \\
\hline
5050
\end{array}
$$

Method 2. *Groups:* Arrange the numbers in convenient groups that sum to 100. Multiply the number of groups by 100 and add any unused numbers to the total:

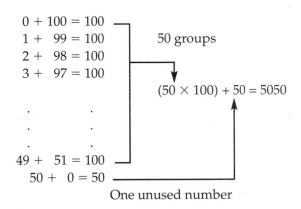

Method 3. *Formula:* Use the formula

$$
\text{Sum} = \frac{n(a + b)}{2}
$$

where

n = number of terms to be added (100)
a = first number to be added (1)
b = last number to be added (100)

$$
\text{Sum} = \frac{100\,(1 + 100)}{2} = 5050
$$

Unlike a program, which must be written in a language the computer can respond to, an algorithm can be written or described in various ways. When English-like phrases are used to describe the algorithm (the processing steps), as in this example, the description is called **pseudocode**. When mathematical equations are used, the description is called a **formula**. When diagrams that employ the symbols shown in Figure 1.3 are used, the description is referred to as a **flowchart**. Figure 1.4 illustrates the use of these symbols in depicting an algorithm for determining the average of three numbers.

Because flowcharts are cumbersome to revise and can easily support unstructured programming practices, they have fallen out of favor among professional programmers, except for visually describing extremely simple program structures. In their place, pseudocode has gained increasing acceptance. In describing an algorithm with pseudocode, we use short English phrases. For example, acceptable pseudocode for describing the steps needed to compute the average of three numbers is

> *Input the three numbers into the computer*
> *Calculate the average by adding the numbers*
>   *and dividing the sum by 3*
> *Display the average*

Only after an algorithm has been selected and the programmer understands the steps required can the algorithm be written using computer-language statements. The writing of an algorithm using computer-language statements is called **coding** the algorithm (see Figure 1.5).

Classes and Objects

We live in a world full of objects—planes, trains, cars, cell phones, books, computers, and so on. It should not seem surprising then that programming languages themselves would eventually be based on objects. The most basic objects used in object-oriented C++ programming are data objects. A *data object* is a set of one or more values that are packaged together as a single unit; as such it can be considered as a packet of data values. For example, a student's name and grade point average can be considered as a data object; in this case the object consists of two pieces of data. Similarly, a name, street address, city, state, and zip code can also be packaged as an object, one that would be useful for a program that must print address labels. Lastly, a multiplication table, such as the tens table, can be considered a data object, in this case a specific instance of one table out of a set of multiplication tables.

FIGURE 1.3 *Flowchart Symbols*

SYMBOL	NAME	DESCRIPTION
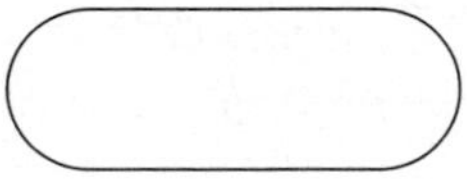	Terminal	Indicates the beginning or end of an algorithm
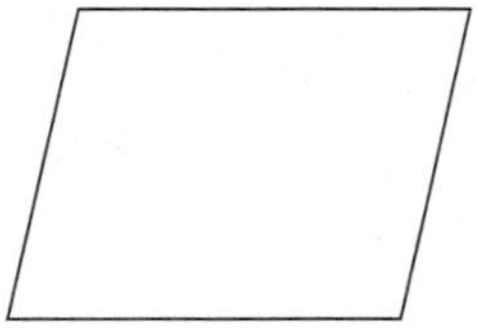	Input/output	Indicates an input or output operation
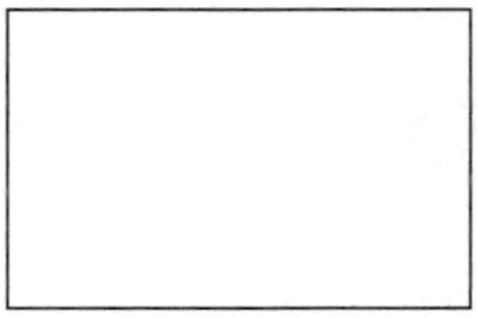	Process	Indicates computation or data manipulation
	Flow lines	Used to connect the flowchart symbols and indicate the logic flow
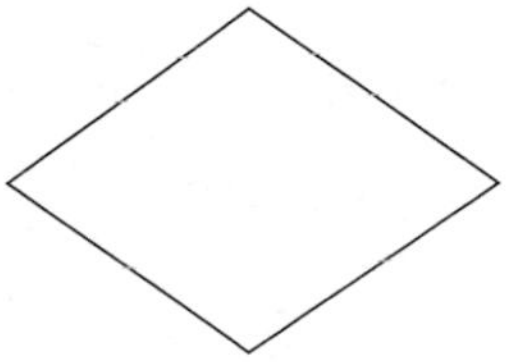	Decision	Indicates a decision point in the algorithm
	Loop	Indicates the initial, final, and increment values of a loop
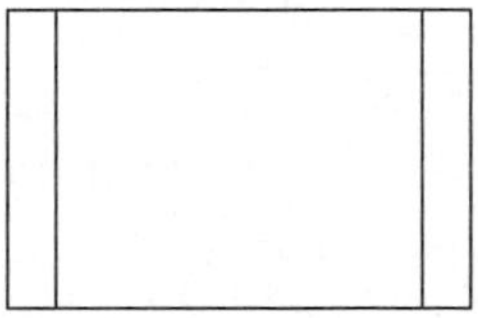	Predefined process	Indicates a predefined process, as in calling a sorting process
	Connector	Indicates an entry to, or exit from another part of the flowchart

FIGURE 1.4   *Flowchart for Calculating the Average of Three Numbers*

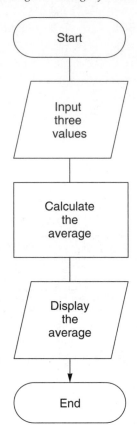

FIGURE 1.5   *Coding an Algorithm*

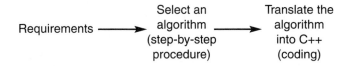

A central concept in all object-oriented programming languages is the differ-ence between a particular object and the larger set of which it is a member. To make this clearer, consider any automobile. From an object viewpoint, a specific car is simply a particular instance, or object, of a more general class of car. Thus, a particular Ford Taurus with its own specific attributes of color, engine size, body type, and so on, can be considered as one object, in this case a car object, from the broader class of all possible Ford Tauruses that could have been built. Similarly, a BMW 525 can be considered as one object from the broader class of all possible BMW 525s that could have been built. The plan for building a particular car is held by the respective manufacturers. Only when such a plan is put into action and a car is actually built, does a specific object come into existence. The concept of creating a particular object from a larger defining set, or class, of object types is fundamental to all object-oriented programming languages, such as C++. It is from the object type, or more accurately speaking, from a class, that any one specific object is created.

In this text we will present both aspects of the C++ language: its procedural and object-oriented aspects. Initially we start with its procedural aspects. The reason for this is that because C++ is based on the procedural language C, you cannot write a C++ program without relying on some procedural code. In fact, many very useful programs can be written entirely as procedural programs. Once you have established a firm grasp of C++'s procedural elements, you can then extend these elements to create object-oriented programs using classes and objects.

Although we will create our own classes and objects as we become more fluent in C++. We will see shortly that two objects, named cin and cout, have been provided in C++ for the input and output, respectively, of data values. We will use these two objects extensively in our early work.

Program Translation

Once an algorithm or class is written in C++, it still cannot be executed on a computer without further translation. This is because the internal language of all computers consists of a series of 1s and 0s, called the computer's **machine language**. To generate a machine-language program that can be executed by the computer requires that the C++ program, which is referred to as a **source program**, be translated into the computer's machine language (see Figure 1.6).

FIGURE 1.6 *Source Programs Must Be Translated*

The translation into machine language can be accomplished in two ways. When each statement in the source program is translated individually and executed immediately, the programming language used is called an **interpreted language**, and the program doing the translation is called an **interpreter**.

When all of the statements in a source program are translated before any one statement is executed, the programming language used is called a **compiled language**. In this case, the program doing the translation is called a **compiler**. C++ is a compiled language. Here, the source program is translated as a unit into machine language. The output produced by the compiler is called an object program. An **object program** is simply a translated version of the source program that can be executed by the computer system with one more processing step. Let us see why this is so.

Most C++ programs contain statements that use preprogrammed routines for input and output and for finding such quantities as square roots, absolute values, and other commonly encountered mathematical calculations. Additionally, a large C++ program may be stored in two separate program files. In such a case, each file can be compiled separately. However, both files must be combined to form a single program before the program can be executed. In both of these cases, it is the task of a linker program, which is often called automatically by the compiler, to combine all of the preprogrammed routines and individual object files into a single program ready for execution. This final program is called an **executable program**.

▌ EXERCISES 1.1

1. Define the following terms:
   a. computer program
   b. programming language
   c. programming
   d. algorithm
   e. pseudocode
   f. flowchart
   g. procedure
   h. object
   i. method
   j. message
   k. response
   l. class
   m. source program
   n. compiler
   o. object program
   p. executable program
   q. interpreter

2. Determine a step-by-step procedure (list the steps) to do each of the following tasks. *Note:* There is no one single correct answer for each task. The exercise is designed to give you practice in converting heuristic commands into equivalent algorithms and understanding the differences among the thought processes involved.
   a. Fix a flat tire.

        b. Make a telephone call.
        c. Go to the store and purchase a loaf of bread.
        d. Roast a turkey.

3. Determine and write an algorithm (list the steps) to interchange the contents of two cups of liquid. Assume that a third cup is available to hold the contents of either cup temporarily. Each cup should be rinsed before any new liquid is poured into it.

4. Write a detailed set of instructions, in English, to calculate the dollar amount of money in a piggybank that contains h half-dollars, q quarters, n nickels, d dimes, and p pennies.

5. Write a set of detailed, step-by-step instructions, in English, to find the smallest number in a group of three integer numbers.

6. *a.* Write a set of detailed, step-by-step instructions, in English, to calculate the least number of dollar bills needed to pay a bill of amount TOTAL. For example, if TOTAL were $98, the bills would consist of one $50 bill, two $20 bills, one $5 bill, and three $1 bills. For this exercise assume that only $100, $50, $20, $10, $5, and $1 bills are available.
    b. Repeat Exercise 6a, but assume the bill is to be paid only in $1 bills.

7. *a.* Write an algorithm to locate the first occurrence of the name JEANS in a list of names arranged in random order.
    b. Discuss how you could improve your algorithm for Exercise 7a if the list of names were arranged in alphabetical order.

8. Determine and write an algorithm to sort three numbers in ascending (from lowest to highest) order. How would you do this problem heuristically?

9. Define an appropriate class for each of the following specific objects:
    a. the number 5
    b. a square that measures 4 inches by 4 inches
    c. this C++ textbook
    d. a 1955 Ford Thunderbird car
    e. the last ballpoint pen that you used

10. *a.* What operations should the following objects be capable of doing?
        i.   a 1955 Ford Thunderbird car
        ii. the last ballpoint pen that you used
    b. Do the operations determined for Exercise 10a apply only to the particular object listed, or are they more general and applicable to all objects of the type listed?

1.2   Function and Class Names

A well-designed program is constructed by using a design philosophy similar to that used in constructing a well-designed building; it doesn't just happen but depends on careful planning and execution for the final design to accomplish its intended purpose. Just as an integral part of the design of a building is its structure, the same is true for a program.

    Programs whose structure consists of interrelated segments arranged in a logical order to form an integrated and complete unit are referred to as **modular programs** (Figure 1.7). Modular programs are easier to develop, correct, and modify than programs constructed otherwise. In general programming terminology, the smaller segments used to construct a modular program are referred to as **modules**. In C++ the modules can be either classes or functions. A function, as we have seen, is the name given to a procedure in C++. It is composed of a sequence of C++ language instructions.

FIGURE 1.7   *A Well-Designed Program Is Built Using Modules*

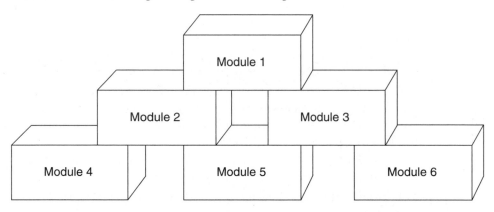

It helps to think of a function as a small machine that transforms the data it receives into a finished product. For example, Figure 1.8 illustrates a function that accepts two numbers as inputs and multiplies the two numbers to produce a result.

FIGURE 1.8   *A Multiplying Function*

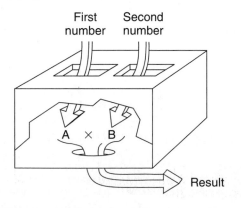

As illustrated in Figure 1.8, the interface to the function is its inputs and results. How the inputs are converted to results is both encapsulated and hidden within the function. In this regard, the function can be thought of as a single unit providing a special-purpose operation. A similar analogy is appropriate for a class. A class, which encapsulates both data and operations, can be thought of as a small processing plant contains all the raw materials (which corresponds to the data being operated on) and the machines required for the input, output, and processing of the raw materials.

One important requirement for designing a good function or class is to give it a name that conveys to the reader some idea about what the function or class does. The names permissible for functions and classes are also used to name other elements of the C++ language, and they are collectively referred to as identifiers. **Identifiers** can be made up of any combination of letters, digits, and underscores (_) selected according to the following rules:

1. The first character of an identifier must be a letter or underscore (_).
2. Only a letter, digit, or underscore may follow the initial letter. Blank spaces are not allowed; separate words in an identifier consisting of multiple words are indicated by capitalizing the first letter of one or more of the words. (Although underscores may also be used for this purpose, they are increasingly being used only for compiler-dependent identifiers.)
3. An identifier cannot be one of the keywords listed in Table 1.1. (A **keyword** is a word that is set aside by the language for a special purpose and should only be used in a specified manner.)[3]

Examples of valid C++ identifiers are

grosspay	taxCalc	addNums	degToRad
multByTwo	salestax	netpay	bessel

Examples of invalid identifiers are

4ab3	(begins with a number, which violates Rule 1)
e*6	(contains a special character, which violates Rule 2)
while	(is a keyword, which violates Rule 3)

Besides conforming to C++'s identifier rules, a good function or class name should also be a mnemonic. A **mnemonic** is a word or name designed as a memory aid. For example, the name degToRad would be a mnemonic if it were the

---

[3] Keywords in C++ are also reserved words, which means they must be used only for their specified purpose. Attempting to use them for any other purpose will generate an error message.

TABLE 1.1 *C++ Keywords*

auto	default	goto	public	this
break	do	if	register	template
case	double	inline	return	typedef
catch	else	int	short	union
char	enum	long	signed	unsigned
class	extern	new	sizeof	virtual
const	float	overload	static	void
continue	for	private	struct	volatile
delete	friend	protected	switch	while

name of a function that converts degrees to radians. Here, the name itself helps to identify what is being done.

Examples of valid identifiers that are not mnemonics are

easy   c3po   r2d2   theForce   mike

Nonmnemonic identifiers should not be used, because they convey no information about their purpose.

Note that all identifiers have been typed almost exclusively in lowercase letters. This is traditional in C++, although it is not absolutely necessary. Initial capitals are conventionally used to indicate class names and the use of all uppercase letters are usually reserved for symbolic constants, a topic covered in Chapter 3, and intermediate capitals are used for distinguishing words in multiword identifiers such as degToRad. Furthermore, C++ is a *case-sensitive* language. This means that the compiler distinguishes between uppercase and lowercase letters. In C++, therefore, TOTAL, total, and TotaL represent three distinct and different names.

The `main` Function

A distinct advantage of using functions and classes in C++ is that the overall structure of the program, in general, and of individual modules, in particular, can be planned in advance; this includes provision for testing and verifying each module's operation. Each function and class can then be written to meet its intended objective.

To provide for the orderly placement and execution of modules, each C++ program must have one and only one function named `main`. The `main` function is referred to as a *driver function* because it drives the other modules, or tells them the sequence in which they are to execute (Figure 1.9).[4]

FIGURE 1.9   *The* `main` *Function Directs All Other Modules*

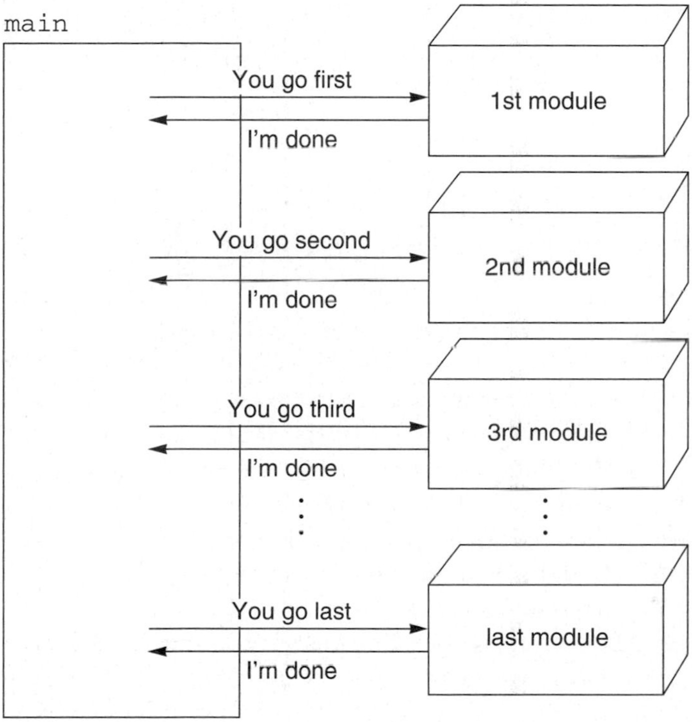

Figure 1.10 illustrates a structure for the `main` function. The first line of the function, in this case `int main()`, is referred to as a function header line. A *function header line*, which is always the first line of a function, contains three pieces of information: [5]

---

[4] Modules executed from `main` may, in turn, execute other modules. Each module, however, always returns to the module that initiated its execution. This is true even for `main`, which returns control to the operating system that was in effect when `main` was initiated.

[5] As we will see in Chapter 12, a class must also begin with a header line that adheres to these same rules.

FIGURE 1.10 *The Structure of a* `main()` *Function*

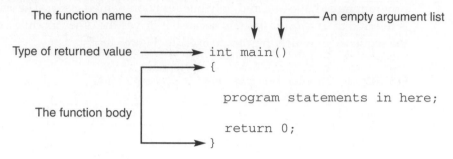

1. What type of data, if any, is returned from the function
2. The name of the function
3. What type of data, if any, is sent into the function

The keyword before the function name defines the type of value the function returns when it has completed operation. When placed before the function's name, the keyword `int` (see Table 1.1) indicates that the function will return an integer value. Similarly, when the parentheses following the function name are empty, it signifies that no data will be transmitted into the function when it is run. (Data transmitted into a function at run time are referred to as **arguments** of the function.) The braces, `{` and `}`, determine the beginning and end of the function body and enclose the statements making up the function. The statements inside the braces determine what the function does. Each statement inside the function must end with a semicolon (`;`).

You will be naming and writing many of your own C++ functions. In fact, the rest of this book is primarily about the statements required to construct useful functions and how to combine functions and data into useful classes and programs. Each program, however, must have one and only one `main` function. Until we learn how to pass data into a function and return data from a function (the topics of Chapter 6), the header line illustrated in Figure 1.10 will serve us for all the programs we need to write. Until they are explained more fully, it is useful simply to regard the first two lines

```
int main()
{
```

as indicating that "the program begins here" and to regard the last two lines

```
    return 0;
}
```

as designating the end of the program. Fortunately, many useful functions and classes have already been written for us. We will now see how to use an object created from one of these classes to create our first working C++ program.

▌ EXERCISES 1.2

1. State whether the following are valid identifiers. For each that is valid, state whether it is a mnemonic name. A mnemonic identifier conveys some idea about its intended purpose. For each invalid identifier, state why it is invalid.

```
1m1234        newBal        abcd          A12345    1A2345
power         absVal        invoices      do        while
add5          taxes         netPay        12345     int
newBalance    a2b3c4d5      salesTax      amount    $taxes
```

2. Assume that functions with the following names have been written.

```
retrieveOldBal    enterSoldAmt    calcNewBal    report
```

    a. From the functions' names, what do you think each function might do?
    b. In what order do you think a `main` function might execute these functions (based on their names)?

3. Assume that the following functions have been written.

```
inputBill    calcSalestax    calcBalance
```

    a. From the functions' names, what do you think each function might do?
    b. In what order do you think a `main` function might execute these functions (based on their names)?

4. Determine names for functions that
    a. find the maximum value in a set of numbers
    b. find the minimum value in a set of numbers
    c. convert a lowercase letter to an uppercase letter
    d. convert an uppercase letter to a lowercase letter
    e. sort a set of numbers from lowest to highest
    f. alphabetize a set of names

5. Just as the keyword `int` can be used to signify that a function will return an integer, the keywords `void`, `char`, `float`, and `double` can be used to signify that a function will return no value, a character, a floating-point number, and a double-precision number, respectively. Using this information, write header lines for a `main` function that will receive no arguments but will return
    a. no value
    b. a character
    c. a floating-point number
    d. a double-precision number

1.3   The cout Object

One of the most versatile and commonly used objects provided in C++ is cout (pronounced "see out"). This object, whose name was derived from Console OUTput, is an output object that sends data given to it to the standard output display device. For most systems this display device is a video screen. The cout object displays, on the monitor, whatever is passed to it. For example, if the data Hello there world! is passed to cout, this data is printed (or displayed) on the terminal screen. The data Hello there world! is passed to the cout object by simply putting the insertion ("put to") symbol, <<, before the message and after the object's name, as shown in Figure 1.11.

Now let's put all this together into a working C++ program that can be run on your computer. Consider Program 1.1.

FIGURE 1.11 *Passing a Message to* cout

```
cout << "Hello there world!";
```

Program 1.1

```
#include <iostream>
using namespace std;

int main()
{
  cout << "Hello there world!";

  return 0;
}
```

The first line of the program,

```
#include <iostream>
```

is a preprocessor command that uses the reserved word include. Preprocessor commands begin with a pound sign, (#), and perform some action before the compiler translates the source program into machine code. Specifically, the #include preprocessor command causes the contents of the named file, in this case the iostream file, to be inserted wherever the #include command appears in the program. The iostream is a part of the standard library that contains, among other code, two classes named *istream* and *ostream*. These two classes provide the data declarations and methods used for data input and output, respectively. The iostream file is referred to as a **header file** because a reference to it is always placed at the top, or head, of a C++ program using the #include command. You may be wondering what the iostream file has to do with this simple program. The answer is that the cout object is created from the ostream class. Thus, the iostream header file must be included in all programs that use cout. As indicated in Program 1.2, preprocessor commands do not end with a semicolon.

Following the preprocessor include command is a statement containing the reserved word using. The statement

```
using namespace std;
```

tells the compiler where to look to find the header files in the absence of any further explicit designation. You can think of a namespace as a file that is accessed by the compiler when it is looking for prewritten classes or functions. Because the iostream header file is contained within a file named std, the compiler will automatically use the iostream's cout object from this namespace whenever cout is referenced. Using namespaces effectively permits you to create your own classes and functions with the same names as those provided by the standard library, and place them in differently named namespaces. We can then tell the program which class or function to use by indicating the namespace where we want the compiler to look for the class or function.

The using statement is followed by the start of the program's main() function. This function begins with the header line developed at the beginning of this section. The body of the function, enclosed in braces, consists of only two statements. The first statement in main() passes one message to the cout object. The message is the string "Hello there world!".

Because cout is an object of a prewritten class, we do not have to write it; it is available for use, and all we need to do is activate it correctly. Like all C++ objects, cout can perform only certain well-defined actions. For cout, that action is to assemble data for output display. When a string of characters is passed to cout, the object sees to it that the string is correctly displayed on the monitor, as shown in Figure 1.12.

FIGURE 1.12   *The Output from Program 1.1*

```
Hello there world!
```

PROGRAMMING NOTES

What Is Syntax?

A programming language's *syntax* is the set of rules for formulating grammatically correct language statements. In practice, this means that a C++ statement with correct syntax has the proper form specified for the compiler. Accordingly, the compiler will accept the statement and not generate an error message.

It should be noted that an individual statement or program can be syntactically correct and still be logically incorrect. Such a statement or program would be correctly structured but would produce an incorrect result. This is similar to an English statement that is grammatically correct but makes no sense. For example, although the sentence "The tree is a ragged cat" is grammatically correct, it makes no sense.

Strings in C++ are any combination of letters, numbers, and special characters enclosed in double quotes (`"string in here"`). The double quotes are used to delimit (mark) the beginning and ending of the string; they are not considered part of the string. Thus the string of characters making up the message sent to `cout` must be enclosed in double quotes, as we have done in Program 1.1.

Let us write another program to illustrate `cout`'s versatility. Read Program 1.2 to determine what it does.

Program 1.2

```
#include <iostream>
using namespace std;

int main()
{
  cout << "Computers, computers everywhere";
  cout << "\n  as far as I can C";

  return 0;
}
```

When Program 1.2 is run, the following is displayed:

```
Computers, computers everywhere
   as far as I can C
```

You might be wondering why the \n did not appear in the output. The two characters \ and n, when used together, are called a **newline escape sequence**. They tell cout to instruct the display device to move to a new line. In C++, the backslash (\) character provides an "escape" from the normal interpretation of the character that follows it by altering the meaning of the next character. If the backslash were omitted from the second cout statement in Program 1.2, the n would be printed as the letter n, and the program would print

```
Computers, computers everywheren  as far as I can C
```

Newline escape sequences can be placed anywhere within the message passed to cout. See whether you can determine what display Program 1.3 produces.

 Program 1.3

```cpp
#include <iostream>
using namespace std;

int main()
{
    cout << "Computers everywhere\n as far as\n\nI can see";

    return 0;
}
```

The output for Program 1.3 is

```
Computers everywhere
 as far as

I can see
```

▌ EXERCISES 1.3

1. *a.* Using cout, write a C++ program that prints your name on one line, your street address on a second line, and your city, state, and zip code on the third line.

b. Run the program you wrote for Exercise 1a on a computer. (*Note:* You must understand the procedures for entering and running a C++ program on the particular computer installation you are using.)

2. *a.* Write a C++ program to print out the following verse:

```
Computers, computers everywhere
  as far as I can see
I really, really like these things,
  Oh joy, Oh joy for me!
```

b. Run the program you wrote for Exercise 2a on a computer.

3. *a.* Indicate how many cout statements you would use to print out the following:

PART NO.	PRICE
T1267	$6.34
T1300	$8.92
T2401	$65.40
T4482	$36.99

b. What is the minimum number of cout statements that could be used to print the table in Exercise 3a?

c. Write a complete C++ program to produce the output illustrated in Exercise 3a.

d. Run the program you wrote for Exercise 3c on a computer.

4. In response to a newline escape sequence, cout positions the next displayed character at the beginning of a new line. This positioning of the next character actually represents two distinct operations. What are they?

5. *a.* Most computer operating systems allow the operator to redirect the output produced by cout either to a printer or directly to a floppy or hard disk file. Read the first part of Appendix D for a description of this redirection capability.

b. If your computer supports output redirection, run the program written for Exercise 2a using this feature. Have your program's display redirected to a file named poem.

c. If your computer supports output redirection to a printer, run the program you wrote for Exercise 2a using this feature.

1.4   Programming Style

C++ programs start execution at the beginning of the main() function. Because a program can have only one starting point, every C++ language program must contain one and only one main() function. As we have seen, all of the statements that make up the main() function are then included within the braces { } following the function name. Although the main() function must be present in every C++ program, C++ does not require that the word main, the parentheses

( ), or the braces { } be placed in any particular form. The form used in the last section,

```
int main()
{
   program statements in here;

   return 0;
}
```

was chosen strictly for clarity and ease in reading the program. If one of the program statements uses the cout object, the iostream header file must be included, as well as the statement using namespace std;. For example, the following general form of a main() function would also work.

```
int main
  (
  ) { first statement;second statement;
           third statement;fourth
statement;
return 0;}
```

Note that more than one statement can be put on a line, or one statement can be written across lines. Except for strings, double quotes, identifiers, and keywords, C++ ignores all **white space** (white space is any combination of one or more blank spaces, tabs, or new lines). For example, changing the white space in Program 1.1 and making sure not to split the string Hello there world! across two lines results in the following valid program:

```
#include <iostream>
using namespace std;

int main
(
){
cout <<
"Hello there world!";
 return 0;
}
```

Although this version of `main()` does work, it is an example of extremely poor programming style. It is difficult to read and understand. For readability, the `main()` function should always be written in standard form:

```
int main()
{
   program statements in here;

   return 0;
}
```

In this standard form, the function name starts in column 1 and is placed, with the required parentheses, on a line by itself. The opening brace of the function body follows on the next line and is placed under the first letter of the line that contains the function name. Similarly, the closing function brace is placed by itself in column 1 as the last line of the function. This structure serves to highlight the function as a single unit.

Within the function itself, all program statements are indented at least two spaces. Indentation is another sign of good programming practice, especially if the same indentation is used for similar groups of statements. Review Program 1.2 and note that the same indentation was used for both `cout` object calls.

As you progress in your understanding and mastery of C++, you will develop your own indentation standards. Just keep in mind that the final form of your programs should be consistent and should always serve as an aid to the reading and understanding of your programs.

Comments

Comments are explanatory remarks made within a program. When used carefully, comments can be helpful in clarifying what the complete program is about, what a specific group of statements is meant to accomplish, or what one line is intended to do. C++ supports two types of comments: line and block. Both types of comments can be placed anywhere within a program, and neither has any effect on program execution. The computer ignores all comments—they are there strictly for the convenience of anyone reading the program.

A **line comment** begins with two slashes (//) and continues to the end of the line. For example, the following lines are all line comments.

```
// this is a comment
// this program prints out a message
// this program calculates a square root
```

The symbols //, with no white space between them, designate the start of the line comment. The end of the line on which the comment is written designates the end of the comment.

A line comment can be written either on a line by itself or at the end of the same line that contains a program statement. Program 1.4 illustrates the use of line comments within a program.

Program 1.4

```
// this program displays a message
#include <iostream>
using namespace std;

int main()
{
  cout << "Hello there world!"; // this produces the display

  return 0;
}
```

The first comment appears on a line by itself at the top of the program and describes what the program does. This is generally a good place to put a short comment describing the program's purpose. If more comments are required, they can be added, one per line. When a comment is too long to be contained on one line, it can be separated into two or more line comments, with each separate comment preceded by the double-slash symbol set (//). The comment

```
// this comment is invalid because it
   extends over two lines
```

will result in a C++ error message on your computer. This comment is correct when written as follows:

```
// this comment is used to illustrate a
// comment that extends across two lines
```

Comments that span across two or more lines are, however, more conveniently written as **block comments** than as multiple-line comments. Such comments begin with the symbols /* and end with the symbols */. For example,

```
/* This is a block comment that
   spans
   across three lines */
```

In C++, a program's structure is intended to make the program readable and understandable, rendering the use of extensive comments unnecessary. This is reinforced if function, class, and variable names, described in the next chapter, are carefully selected to convey their meaning to anyone reading the program. However, if the purpose of a function, class, or statement is still not clear from its structure, name, or context, it is important to include additional comments where clarification is needed. Obscure code with no comments is a sure sign of bad programming. Excessive comments are also a sign of bad programming, because they imply that insufficient thought was given to making the code self-explanatory. Typically, any program that you write should begin with a set of initial program comments that includes a short program description, your name, and the date that the program was last modified. To save space, and because all programs in this text were written by the author, initial comments will be used for short program descriptions only when they are not provided as part of the accompanying descriptive text.

▌ EXERCISES 1.4

1. *a.* Will the following program work?

```
#include <iostream>
using namespace std;
int main(){cout << "Hello there world!"; return 0;}
```

b. Why is the program given in Exercise 1a not a good program?

2. Rewrite the following programs to conform to good programming practice.

a.
```
#include <iostream>
using namespace std;
int main(
){
cout            <<
"The time has come"
; return 0;}
```

b.
```
#include <iostream>
using namespace std;
int main
(     ){cout << "Newark is a city\n";cout <<
"In New Jersey\n"; cout <<
"It is also a city\n"
; cout << "In Delaware\n"
; return 0;}
```

c.
```
#include <iostream>
using namespace std;
int main(){cout << Reading a program\n";cout <<
"is much easier\n"
;cout << "if a standard form for main is used\n"
;cout
<<"and each statement is written\n";cout
<<          "on a line by itself\n"
; return 0;}
```

d.
```
#include <iostream>
using namespace std;
int main
(    ){cout << "Every C++ program"
;cout
<<"\nmust have one and only one"
;
cout << "main function"
;
cout <<
"\n the escape sequence of characters"
;cout <<
 "\nfor a newline can be placed anywhere"
;cout
<<"\n within the message passed to cout"
; return 0;}
```

3. a. When used in a message, the backslash character alters the meaning of the character immediately following it. If we wanted to print the backslash character, we would have to tell cout to escape from the way it normally interprets the backslash. What character do you think is used to alter the way a single backslash character is interpreted?

b. Using your answer to Exercise 3a, write the escape sequence for printing a backslash.

4. a. A *token* of a computer language is any sequence of characters that as a unit, with no intervening characters or white space, has a unique meaning. Using this definition of a token, determine whether escape sequences, function names, and the keywords listed in Table 1.2 are tokens of the C++ language.

b. Discuss whether adding white space to a message alters the message. Discuss whether messages can be considered tokens of C++.

c. Using the definition of a token given in Exercise 4a, determine whether the following statement is true: "Except for tokens of the language, C++ ignores all white space."

1.5   Common Programming Errors

Part of learning any programming language is making the elementary mistakes commonly encountered as you begin to use the language. These mistakes tend to be frustrating, because each language has its own set of common programming errors lying in wait for the unwary. The errors commonly made when initially programming in C++ include

1. Omitting the parentheses after `main`
2. Omitting or incorrectly typing the opening brace { that signifies the start of a function body
3. Omitting or incorrectly typing the closing brace } that signifies the end of a function
4. Misspelling the name of an object or function—for example, typing `cot` instead of `cout`
5. Forgetting to close a string sent to `cout` with a double-quote symbol
6. Omitting the semicolon at the end of each statement
7. Forgetting the `\n` to indicate a new line

Our experience is that the third, fifth, and sixth errors in this list tend to be the most common. We suggest that you write a program and specifically introduce each of these errors, one at a time, to see what error messages your compiler produces. Then, when these error messages appear as a result of inadvertent errors, you will have had experience in understanding the messages and correcting the errors.

1.6   *Chapter Summary*

1. A C++ program consists of one or more modules. One of these modules must be the function `main()`. The `main()` function identifies the starting point of a C++ program.
2. The simplest C++ program consists of the single function `main` and has the form

```
#include <iostream>
using namespace std;

int main()
{
    program statements in here;

    return 0;
}
```

This program consists of a preprocessor `#include` statement, a `using` statement, a header line for the `main()` function, and the body of the `main()` function. The body of the function begins with the opening left-facing brace, {, and ends with the terminating right-facing brace, }.

3. All C++ statements within a function body must be terminated by a semicolon.

4. Many functions and classes are supplied in a standard library provided with each C++ compiler. One such set of classes, which are used to create input and output capabilities, is defined in the header file `<iostream>`.

5. The `cout` object is used to display text or numerical results. A stream of characters can be sent to `cout` by enclosing the characters in double quotes and using the insertion ("put to") operator, `<<`, as in the statement `cout << "Hello World!";`. The text in the string is displayed directly on the screen and may include newline escape sequences for format control.

Data Types, Declarations, and Displays

C++ programs can process different types of data in different ways. For example, calculating the bacteria growth in a polluted pond requires mathematical operations on numerical data, whereas sorting a list of names requires comparison operations using alphabetical data. In this chapter we introduce C++'s elementary data types and the operations that can be performed on them. We also show how to use the `cout` object to display the results of these operations.

2.1   Data Types

The objective of all programs is ultimately to process data, be it numerical, alphabetical, audio, or video. Central to this objective is the classification of data into specific types. For example, calculating the interest due on a bank balance requires mathematical operations on numerical data, while alphabetizing a list of names requires comparison operations on character-based data. Additionally, some operations are not applicable to certain types of data. For example, it makes no sense to add names together. To prevent the programmer from attempting to perform an inappropriate operation, C++ allows only certain operations to be performed on certain types of data.

The types of data permitted and the appropriate operations defined for each type are referred to as a data type. Formally, a **data type** is defined as a set of values *and* a set of operations that can be applied to these values. For example, the set of all integer (whole) numbers constitutes a set of values, as does the set of all real numbers (numbers that contain a decimal point). These two sets of numbers, however, do not constitute a data type until a set of operations is also included. These operations, of course, are the familiar mathematical and comparison operations. The combination of a set of values plus operations becomes a true data type.

C++ categorizes data types into one of two fundamental groupings: built-in data types and class data types. A **class data type**, which is referred to as a class, for short, is a programmer-created data type. This means that the set of acceptable values and operations is defined by a programmer, using C++ code.

A **built-in data type** is one that is provided as an integral part of the C++ compiler and requires no external C++ code. Thus, a built-in data type can be used without recourse to supplementary language additions, such as that provided by the `iostream` header file needed for the `cout` object. Built-in data types, which are also referred to as **primitive** types, consist of the basic numerical types shown in Figure 2.1 and the operations listed in Table 2.1. As seen in this table, the majority of operations for built-in types are provided as symbols. This is in contrast to class types, where the majority of operations are provided as functions.

FIGURE 2.1   *Built-In Data Types*

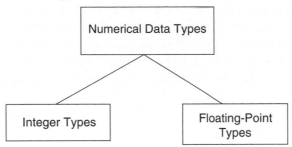

In introducing C++'s built-in data types, we will make use of literals. A **literal** is an acceptable value for a data type. The term "literal" reflects the fact that such a value explicitly identifies itself. (Another name for a literal is a **literal value,** or **constant**.) For example, all numbers, such as 2, 3.6, and –8.2, are referred to as literal values because they literally display their values. Text, such as `"Hello World!"` is also referred to as a literal value because the text itself is displayed. You have been using literal values throughout your life and have commonly referred to them as numbers and words. In Section 2.4 you will see some examples of non-literal values—that is, values that do not display themselves but are stored and accessed using identifiers.

TABLE 2.1   *Built-In Data Type Operations*

Built-in Data Types	Operations
Integer	+, −, *, /, %, =, ==, !=, <=, >=, sizeof(), and bit operations (see Sec. 17.4)
Floating Point	+, −, *, /, =, ==, !=, <=, >=, sizeof()

Integer Data Types

C++ provides nine built-in integer data types, as shown in Figure 2.2. The essential difference among the various integer data types is the amount of storage used for each type, which directly affects the range of values that each type is capable of representing. The three most important integer types that are used almost exclusively in the majority of applications are the `int`, `char`, and `bool` types. The reason for the remaining types is essentially historical, as they were originally provided to accommodate special situations (a very small or a very large range of numbers). This permitted a programmer to maximize memory usage by selecting a data type that used the smallest amount of memory consistent with an application's requirements. When computer memories were both very small relative to today's computers and extremely expensive, this was a major concern. Although no longer a concern for the vast majority of programs, it still provides a programmer the ability to optimize memory usage when necessary. Typically these situations occur in engineering applications, such as control systems used in home appliances and automobiles.

FIGURE 2.2   *C++ Integer Data Types*

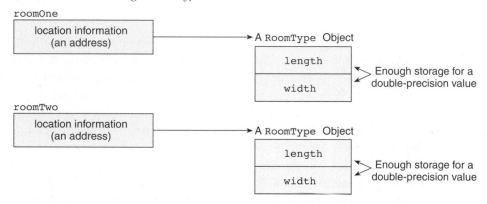

The `int` Data Type

The set of values supported by the `int` data type are whole numbers, which are mathematically known as integers. An integer value consists of digits only and can optionally be preceded by either a plus (+) or minus (−) sign. Thus, an integer value can be the number zero or any positive or negative numerical value without a decimal point. Examples of valid integers are:

$$0 \quad 5 \quad -10 \quad +25 \quad 1000 \quad 253 \quad -26351 \quad +36$$

As these examples illustrate, integers may contain an explicit sign. No commas, decimal points, or special symbols, such as the dollar sign, are allowed. Examples of invalid integers are:

$$\$255.62 \quad 2{,}523 \quad 3. \quad 6{,}243{,}892 \quad 1{,}492.89 \quad +6.0$$

Different compilers have their own internal limit on the largest (most positive) and smallest (most negative) integer values that can be stored in each data type.[1]

---

[1] The limits imposed by the compiler can be found in the `limits` header file and are defined as the hexadecimal constants `int_max` and `int_min`.

PROGRAMMING NOTE

Atomic Data

An **atomic data value** is a value that is considered a complete entity by itself and cannot be decomposed into a smaller data type. For example, although an integer can be decomposed into individual digits, C++ does not have a numerical digit type. Rather, each integer is regarded as a complete value by itself and, as such, is considered atomic data. Similarly, because the integer data type supports only atomic data values, it is said to be an **atomic data type**. As you might expect, all of the built-in data types are atomic data types.

The most common storage allocation is four bytes for the int data type, which restricts the set of values permitted in this data type to represent integers in the range of –2,147,483,648 to 2,147,483,647.[2]

The char Data Type

The char data type is used to store individual characters. Characters include the letters of the alphabet (both uppercase and lowercase), the ten digits 0 through 9, and special symbols such as + $. , - !. A single character value is any one letter, digit, or special symbol enclosed by single quotes. Examples of valid character values are:

```
'A'    '$'    'b'    '7'    'y'    '!'    'M'    'q'
```

Character values are typically stored in a computer using either the ASCII or Unicode codes. ASCII, pronounced AS-KEY, is an acronym for American Standard Code for Information Interchange. The ASCII code provides codes for an English-language-based character set plus codes for printer and display control, such as new line and printer paper-eject codes. Each character code is contained within a single byte, which provides for 256 distinct codes. Table 2.2 lists the ASCII byte codes for uppercase letters.

Additionally, C++ provides for the newer Unicode character set that uses two bytes per character and can represent 65,536 characters. This code is used for international applications by providing other language character sets in addition to English. As the first 256 Unicode codes have the same numerical value as the 256 ASCII codes (the additional byte is simply coded with all 0s), you need not concern yourself with which storage code is used when using English language characters.

---

[2] It is interesting to note that in all cases the magnitude of the most negative integer number is always one more than the magnitude of the most positive integer. This is due to the twos complement method of integer storage, which is described in Section 2.7.

TABLE 2.2   *The ASCII Uppercase Letter Codes*

Letter	ASCII Code	Letter	ASCII Code
A	01000001	N	01001110
B	01000010	O	01001111
C	01000011	P	01010000
D	01000100	Q	01010001
E	01000101	R	01010010
F	01000110	S	01010011
G	01000111	T	01010100
H	01001000	U	01010101
I	01001001	V	01010110
J	01001010	W	01010111
K	01001011	X	01011000
L	01001100	Y	01011001
M	01001101	Z	01011010

Using Table 2.2, we can determine how the characters 'W', 'E', 'S', 'T', 'B', and 'Y', for example, are stored inside a computer that uses the ASCII character code. This sequence of six characters requires six bytes of storage (one byte for each letter) and would be stored as illustrated in Figure 2.3.

FIGURE 2.3   *The Letters WESTBY Stored Inside a Computer*

01010111	01000101	01010011	01010100	01000010	01011001
W	E	S	T	B	Y

The Escape Character

One character that has a special meaning in C++ is the backslash, \, which is referred to as the **escape character**. When this character is placed directly in front of a select group of characters, it tells the compiler to escape from the way these characters would normally be interpreted. The combination of a backslash and these specific characters is called an **escape sequence**. We have already encountered an example of this in the newline escape sequence, \n, in Chapter 1. Table 2.3 lists C++'s most common escape sequences.

TABLE 2.3 *Escape Sequences*

Escape Sequence	Character Represented	Meaning	ASCII Code
\n	Newline	Move to a new line	00001010
\t	Horizontal tab	Move to next horizontal tab setting	00001001
\v	Vertical tab	Move to next vertical tab setting	00001011
\b	Backspace	Move back one space	00001000
\r	Carriage return	(Moves the cursor to the start of the current line— used for overprinting)	00001101
\f	Form Feed	Issue a form feed	00001100
\a	Alert	Issue an alert (usually a bell sound)	00000111
\\	Backslash	Insert a backslash character (this is used to place an actual backslash character within a string)	01011100
\?	Question mark	Insert a question mark character	00111111
\'	Single quotation	Insert a single quote character (this is used to place an inner single quote within a set of outer single quotes)	00100111
\"	Double quotation mark	Insert a double quote character (this is used to place an inner double quote within a set of outer double quotes)	00100010
\nnn	Octal number	The number *nnn* (*n* is a digit) is to be considered an octal number	–
\xhhhh	Hexadecimal number	The number *hhhh* (*h* is a digit) is to be considered a hexadecimal number	–
\0	Null character	Insert the Null character, which is defined as having the value 0	00000000

Although each escape sequence listed in Table 2.3 is made up of two distinct characters, the combination of the two characters, with no intervening white space, causes the compiler to create the single code listed in the ASCII Code column of Table 2.3.

PROGRAMMING NOTE

The Character `'\n'` *and the String* `"\n"`

Both `'\n'` and `"\n"` are recognized by the compiler as containing the newline character. The difference is in the data types being used. Formally, `'\n'` is a character literal, while `"\n"` is a string literal. From a practical standpoint both cause the same thing to happen: a new line is forced on the output display. In encountering the character value `'\n'`, however, the compiler translates it using the single byte code 00001010 (see Table 2.3). In encountering the string value `"\n"`, the compiler translates this string using the correct character code, but also adds a string termination character, which is `'\0'`.

Good programming practice requires that you end the last output display with a newline escape sequence. This ensures that the first line of output from one program does not end up on the last line displayed by the previously executed program.

The `bool` Data Type

In C++, the `bool` data type is used to represent Boolean (logical) data. As such, this data type is restricted to one of two values: `true` or `false`. This data type is most useful when a program must examine a specific condition and, as a result of the condition being either true or false, take a prescribed course of action. For example, in a sales application, the condition being examined might be "is the total purchase for $100 or more." Only when this condition is true is a discount applied. The fact that the Boolean data type uses an integer storage code, however, has very useful implications that are exploited by almost all professional C++ programmers. The practical uses of Boolean conditions is considered in Chapter 4, so we defer further discussion of Boolean data until then.

Determining Storage Size

A unique feature of C++ is that it permits you to see where and how values are stored. As an example, C++ provides an operator named `sizeof()` that provides the number of bytes used to store values for any data type name included within the operator's parentheses. (Review Section 2.7 if you are unfamiliar with the concept of a byte.) Notice that this is a built-in operator that does not use an arithmetic symbol to perform its operation. Program 2.1 uses this operator to determine the amount of storage reserved for the `int`, `char`, and `bool` data types.

Program 2.1

```
#include <iostream>
using namespace std;

int main()
{
  cout << "\nData Type  Bytes"
       << "\n---------  -----"
       << "\nint         " << sizeof(int)
       << "\nchar        " << sizeof(char)
       << "\nbool        " << sizeof(bool)
       << '\n';

  return 0;
}
```

In reviewing Program 2.1 notice that a single character value is inserted into cout by enclosing it within single quotes, as is the escape sequence '\n' insertion at the end of the last cout statement. Within the first five displayed lines this character is simply included within each output string. Each time the compiler encounters the newline escape sequence, either as a single character or as part of a string, it is translated as a single character that forces the display to start on a new line. Although double quotes can be used for the final newline insertion, as "\n", this would designate a string. As such, storage for the string would include not only the character code for the newline escape sequence, but also adds a standard string termination character, which is '\0'. Because only a single character is being transmitted, and to emphasize that single characters are designated using single quotes, we have used '\n' in place of "\n". From a practical standpoint, however, both notations will force a new line in the display.

The output of Program 2.1 is compiler dependent. That is to say, each compiler will correctly report the amount of storage that it provides for the data type under consideration. When run on the author's computer, which uses Microsoft's current Visual C++.net compiler, the following output was produced:

```
Data Type    Bytes
---------    -----
int            4
char           1
bool           1
```

PROGRAMMING NOTE

Object-Oriented and Procedural Programs

Except for the Boolean type, all of C++'s built-in data types are direct carryovers from the C procedural language. It should not be surprising, therefore, that programs using only individual built-in types will not be object-oriented programs. Rather, as in Program 2.1, they become procedural programs; that is, a program primarily based on procedures, such as main().

It is only when built-in types are bundled together to form a packet of data, which becomes an object, can an object-oriented program come into existence. How this is accomplished is explained in Chapter 12.

For this output, which is the typical storage provided by almost all current C++ compilers, we can determine the range of values that can be stored in each of these int data types. To do so, however, requires understanding the difference between a signed and unsigned data type.

Signed and Unsigned Data Types

A **signed data type** is defined as one that permits storing negative values in addition to zero and positive values. As such, the int data type is a signed data type. An **unsigned data type** is one that provides only for non-negative (that is, zero and positive) values. Both the char and bool data types are unsigned data types, which means that they have no codes for storing negative values.

There are applications that only require unsigned numerical values. For example, many date applications store dates in the numerical form *yearmonthday* (thus, the date 12/25/2007 would be stored as 20071225) and are only concerned with dates after 0 CE. For such applications, which will never require a negative value, an unsigned data type could be used.

All unsigned integer types, such as unsigned int, provide a range of positive values that is, for all practical purposes, double the range provided for its signed counterpart. This extra positive range is made available by using the negative range of its signed version for additional positive numbers.

With the understanding of the difference between a signed and unsigned data type, Table 2.4 can be used to determine the range of integer values supported by current C++ compilers.

One item to notice in Table 2.4 is that a long int uses the same amount of storage (four bytes) as an int. The only requirement of the ANSI C++ standard is that an int must provide at least as much storage as a short int, and that a long int must provide at least as much storage as an int. On the first desktop computer systems (1980s), which were limited in their memory capacity to thousands of bytes, a `short int` typically used one byte of storage, an `int` two bytes, and a `long int` four bytes. Because this storage limited the range of `int` values from –32,768 to +32,767, while the use of an `unsigned int` provided a range of values from 0 to 65,535, the doubling of possible positive values was significant. With the current range of `int` values in the –2 to +2 billion range, the doubling of positive values is rarely a consideration. Additionally, using a `long int` becomes unnecessary, because it is now uses the same storage capacity as an `int`.

TABLE 2.4   *Integer Data Type Storage*

Name of Data Type	Storage Size (in bytes)	Range of Values
char	1	256 characters
bool	1	true (which is considered as any positive value) and false (which is a zero)
short int	2	–32,768 to +32,767
unsigned short int	2	0 to 65,535
int	4	–2,147,483,648 to +2,147,483,647
unsigned int	4	0 to 4,294,967,295
long int	4	–2,147,483,648 to +2,147,483,647
unsigned long int	4	0 to 4,294,967,295

Floating-Point Types

A **floating-point number**, which is also called a **real number**, can be the number zero or any positive or negative number that contains a decimal point. Examples of floating-point numbers are:

```
+10.625  5.  -6.2  3251.92  0.0  0.33  -6.67  +2.
```

Notice that the numbers 5., 0.0, and +2. are classified as floating-point values, but the same numbers written without a decimal point (5, 0, +2) would be integer values. As with integer values, special symbols such as the dollar sign and the comma are not permitted in real numbers. Examples of invalid real numbers are:

```
5,326.25    24    6,459    $10.29    7.007.645
```

C++ supports three floating point data types: `float`, `double`, and `long double`. The difference between these data types is the amount of storage that a

PROGRAMMING NOTE

What Is Precision?

In numerical theory, the term **precision** typically refers to numerical accuracy. In this context, a statement such as "this computation is accurate, or precise, to the fifth decimal place" is used. This means that the fifth digit after the decimal point has been rounded, and the number is accurate to within ±0.00005.

In computer programming, precision can refer either to the accuracy of a number or the amount of significant digits in the number, where significant digits are defined as the number of clearly correct digits plus 1. For example, if the number 12.6874 has been rounded to the fourth decimal place, it is correct to say that this number is precise (that is, accurate) to the fourth decimal place. In other words, all of the digits in the number are accurate except the fourth decimal digit, which has been rounded. Similarly, it can be said that this same number has a precision of six digits, which means that the first five digits are correct and the sixth digit has been rounded. Another way of saying this is that the number 12.6874 has six significant digits.

Notice that the significant digits in a number need not have any relation to the number of displayed digits. For example, if the number 687.45678921 has five significant digits, it is only accurate to the value 687.46, where the last digit is assumed to be rounded. In a similar manner, dollar values in many very large financial applications are frequently rounded to the nearest hundred-thousand dollars. In such applications, a displayed dollar value of $12,400,000, for example, is not accurate to the closest dollar. If this value is specified as having three significant digits, it is only accurate to the hundred-thousands digit.

compiler uses for each type. Most compilers use twice the amount of storage for doubles than for floats, which allows a double to have approximately twice the precision of a `float`. For this reason, a `float` value is sometimes referred to as a **single-precision** number and a `double` value as a **double-precision** number. The actual storage allocation for each data type, however, depends on the particular compiler. The ANSI C++ standard only requires that a `double` has at least the same amount of precision as a `float` and that a `long double` has at least the same amount of storage as a `double`. Currently, most C++ compilers allocate four bytes for the `float` data type and eight bytes for both `double` and `long double` data types. This produces the range of numbers listed in Table 2.5.

TABLE 2.5 *Floating-Point Data Types*

Type	Storage	Absolute Range of Values (+ and −)
`float`	4 bytes	1.40129846432481707e−45 to 3.40282346638528860e+38
`double` and `long double`	8 bytes	4.94065645841246544e−324 to 1.79769313486231570e+308

In compilers that use the same amount of storage for `double` and `long double` numbers, these two data types become identical. (The `sizeof()` operator that was used in Program 2.1 can always be used to determine the amount of storage reserved by your compiler for these data types.) A `float` literal is indicated by appending either an f or F after the number and a `long double` is created by appending either an l or L to the number. In the absence of these suffixes, a floating point number defaults to a `double`. For example:

> 9.234 indicates a double literal
> 9.234F indicates a float literal
> 9.234L indicates a long double literal

The only difference in these numbers is the amount of storage the computer may use to store them. If you require numbers having more than six significant digits to the right of the decimal point, this storage becomes important, and you should use double-precision values.

Exponential Notation

Floating-point numbers can also be written in exponential notation, which is similar to scientific notation and is commonly used to express both very large and very small values in compact form. The following examples illustrate how numbers with decimals can be expressed in exponential and scientific notation.

Decimal Notation	Exponential Notation	Scientific Notation
1625.	1.625e3	1.625×10^3
63421.	6.3421e4	6.3421×10^4
.00731	7.31e–3	7.31×10^{-3}
.000625	6.25e–4	6.25×10^{-4}

In exponential notation, the letter e stands for exponent. The number following the e represents a power of 10 and indicates the number of places the decimal point should be moved to obtain the standard decimal value. The decimal point is moved to the right if the number after the e is positive or moved to the left if the number after the e is negative. For example, the $e3$ in 1.625e3 means move the decimal place three places to the right so that the number becomes 1625. The e–3 in 7.31e–3 means move the decimal point three places to the left so that 7.31e–3 becomes .00731.

▌ EXERCISES 2.1

1. Determine data types appropriate for the following data.
   a. the average of four grades
   b. the number of days in a month
   c. the length of the Golden Gate Bridge
   d. the numbers in a state lottery
   e. the distance from Brooklyn, NY, to Newark, NJ

2. Convert the following numbers into standard decimal form.

   6.34e5   1.95162e2   8.395e1   2.95e–3   4.623e–4

3. Convert the following decimal numbers into exponential notation.

   126.   656.23   3426.95   4893.2   .321   .0123   .006789

4. Using the system reference manuals for your computer, determine what character code your computer uses.

5. a. Using the ASCII codes, determine the number of bytes required to store the letters KINGSLEY.
   b. Show how the letters KINGSLEY would be stored inside a computer that uses the ASCII codes. That is, draw a figure similar to Figure 2.3 for the letters KINGSLEY.

6. a. Repeat Exercise 5a using lowercase ASCII letter codes.
   b. Repeat Exercise 5b using lowercase ASCII letter codes.

7. a. Repeat Exercise 6a using the letters of your own last name.
   b. Repeat Exercise 6b using the letters of your own last name.

8. Because most computers use different amounts of storage for integers, floating-point numbers, double-precision numbers, and character values, discuss how a program might alert the computer to the amount of storage needed for the various data types in the program.

Note: For the following exercise, the reader should understand basic computer storage concepts. Specifically, if you are unfamiliar with the concept of a byte, refer to Section 2.7 before doing the next exercise.

9. Although the total number of bytes varies from computer to computer, memory sizes of 65,536 to more than several million bytes are not uncommon. In computer language, the letter K is used to represent the number 1024, which is 2 raised to the 10th power, and M is used to represent the number 1,048,576, which is 2 raised to the 20th power. Thus a memory size of 640K is really 640 times 1024, or 655,360 bytes, and a memory size of 4M is really 4 times 1,048,576, which is 4,194,304 bytes. Using this information, calculate the actual number of bytes in
   a. a memory containing 128M bytes
   b. a memory containing 256M bytes
   c. a memory containing 512M bytes
   d. a memory containing 256M words, where each word consists of 2 bytes
   e. a memory containing 256M words, where each word consists of 4 bytes
   f. a floppy diskette that can store 1.44M bytes

2.2   Arithmetic Operators

Integers and real numbers may be added, subtracted, divided, and multiplied. Although it is usually better not to mix integers and real numbers when performing arithmetic operations, predictable results are obtained when different data types are used in the same arithmetic expression. Somewhat surprising is the fact that character data can also be added to and subtracted from both character and integer data to produce useful results.

The operators used for arithmetic operations are called **arithmetic operators**. The operators are:

Operation	Operator
Addition	+
Subtraction	−
Multiplication	*
Division	/
Modulus	%

Don't be concerned at this stage if you don't understand the term "modulus division." You'll learn more about this operator later in this section.

These operators are referred to as **binary operators**. This term reflects the fact that the operator requires two operands to produce a result. An **operand** can be either a literal value or an identifier that has a value associated with it. A **simple binary arithmetic expression** consists of a binary arithmetic operator connecting two literal values in the form:

```
literalValue  operator  literalValue
```

Examples of simple arithmetic expressions are

$$3 + 7$$
$$18 - 3$$
$$12.62 + 9.8$$
$$.08 * 12.2$$
$$12.6 / 2.$$

The spaces around the arithmetic operators in these examples are inserted strictly for clarity and may be omitted without affecting the value of the expression. When evaluating simple arithmetic expressions, we determine the data type of the result by applying the following rules:

1. If both operands are integers, the result is an integer.
2. If any operand is a floating-point value, the result is a floating-point value.

An expression that contains only integer operands is called an **integer expression,** and the result of the expression is an integer value (Rule 1). Similarly, an expression that contains only floating-point operands is called a **floating-point expression,** or **real expression,** and the result of the expression is a floating-point value (Rule 2). An arithmetic expression that contains both integer and noninteger operands is called a **mixed-mode expression**. The result of a mixed-mode expression is always a floating-point value (Rule 2).

It is worth noting that the arithmetic operations of addition, subtraction, multiplication, and division are implemented differently for integer and floating-point values. Specifically, whether an integer or a floating-point arithmetic operation is performed depends on what types of operands (integer or floating-point) are contained in the arithmetic expression. In this sense, the arithmetic operators are considered to be overloaded. More formally, an **overloaded operator** is a symbol that represents more than one operation and whose execution depends on the types of operands encountered. Although the overloaded nature of the arithmetic operators is rather simple, we will encounter the concept of overloading many more times in our journey through C++.

Integer Division

The division of two integers can produce results that seem rather strange to the unwary. For example, dividing the integer 15 by the integer 2 yields an integer result. Because integers cannot contain a fractional part, a result such as 7.5 cannot be obtained. In C++, the fractional part of the result obtained when two integers are divided is dropped (truncated). Thus the value of 15/2 is 7, the value of 9/4 is 2, and the value of 17/5 is 3.

Often, however, we may need to retain the remainder of an integer division. To do this, C++ provides an arithmetic operator having the symbol %. This operator, called both the **modulus** and **remainder operator**, captures the remainder when an integer number is divided by an integer (using a noninteger value with the modulus operator results in a compiler error). For example,

9 % 4 is 1   (that is, the remainder when 9 is divided by 4 is 1)
17 % 3 is 2   (that is, the remainder when 17 is divided by 3 is 2)
15 % 4 is 3   (that is, the remainder when 15 is divided by 4 is 3)
14 % 2 is 0   (that is, the remainder when 14 is divided by 2 is 0)

More precisely, the modulus operator first determines the integer number of times that the dividend, which is the number following the % operator, can be divided into the divisor, which is the number before the % operator. It then returns the remainder.

Negation

Besides the binary operators for addition, subtraction, multiplication, and division, C++ also provides unary operators. One of these unary operators uses the same symbol that is used for binary subtraction (–). The minus sign used in front of a single numerical operand negates (reverses the sign of) the number.

Table 2.6 summarizes the six arithmetic operations we have described so far and lists the data type of the result produced by each operator on the basis of the data type of the operands involved.

TABLE 2.6   *Summary of Arithmetic Operators*

Operation	Operator	Type	Operand	Result
Addition	+	Binary	Both integers	Integer
			One operand not an integer	Double-precision
Subtraction	–	Binary	Both integers	Integer
			One operand not an integer	Double-precision
Multiplication	*	Binary	Both integers	Integer
			One operand not an integer	Double-precision
Division	/	Binary	Both integers	Integer
			One operand not an integer	Double-precision
Remainder	%	Binary	Both integers	Integer
Negation	–	Unary	Integer	Integer
			Double-precision	Double-precision

Operator Precedence and Associativity

Besides such simple expressions as 5 + 12 and .08 * 26.2, we frequently need to create more complex arithmetic expressions. C++, like most other programming languages, requires that we follow certain rules when writing expressions that contain more than one arithmetic operator. These rules are:

1. Two binary arithmetic operator symbols must never be placed side by side.
For example, 5 * % 6 is invalid because the two operators * and % are placed next to each other.

2. Parentheses may be used to form groupings, and all expressions enclosed within parentheses are evaluated first.
For example, in the expression (6 + 4) / (2 + 3), the 6 + 4 and 2 + 3 are evaluated first to yield 10 / 5. The 10 / 5 is then evaluated to yield 2.

3. Sets of parentheses may also be enclosed by other parentheses. For example, the expression (2 * (3 + 7)) / 5 is valid. When parentheses are used within parentheses, the expressions in the innermost parentheses are always evaluated first. The evaluation continues from innermost to outermost parentheses until the expressions in all the parentheses have been evaluated. The number of right-facing parentheses, (, must always equal the number of left-facing parentheses,) , so that there are no unpaired sets.

4. Parentheses cannot be used to indicate multiplication; the multiplication operator, *, must be used.
For example, the expression (3 + 4) (5 + 1) is invalid. The correct expression is (3 + 4) * (5 + 1).

Parentheses should specify logical groupings of operands and indicate clearly, to both the compiler and programmers, the intended order of arithmetic operations. Although expressions within parentheses are always evaluated first, expressions containing multiple operators, both within and without parentheses, are evaluated by the priority, or **precedence**, of the operators. There are three levels of precedence:

- P1—All negations are done first.
- P2—Multiplication, division, and modulus operations are computed next. Expressions containing more than one multiplication, division, or modulus operator are evaluated from left to right as each operator is encountered. For example, in the expression 35 / 7 % 3 * 4, the operations are all of the same pri-

ority, so the operations will be performed from left to right as each operator is encountered. Thus, the division is done first, yielding the expression 5 % 3 * 4. The modulus operation is performed next, yielding a result of 2. And finally, the value of 2 * 4 is computed to yield 8.

- P3—Addition and subtraction are computed last. Expressions containing more than one addition or subtraction are evaluated from left to right as each operator is encountered.

In addition to precedence, operators have an **associativity**, which is the order in which operators of the same precedence are evaluated, as described in rule P2. For example, does the expression 6.0 * 6 / 4 yield 9.0, which is (6.0 * 6)/4, or 6.0, which is 6.0 * (6/4)? The answer is 9.0, because C++'s operators use the same associativity as in general mathematics, which evaluates multiplication from left to right, as rule P2 indicates. Table 2.7 lists both the precedence and associativity of the operators considered in this section. As we have seen, the precedence of an operator establishes its priority relative to all other operators. Operators at the top of Table 2.7 have a higher priority than operators at the bottom of the table. In expressions with multiple operators of different precedence, the operator with the higher precedence is used before an operator with lower precedence. For example, in the expression 6 + 4 / 2 + 3, since the division operator has a higher precedence (P2) than addition, the division is done first, yielding an intermediate result of 6 + 2 + 3. The additions are then performed, left to right, to yield a final result of 11.

TABLE 2.7 *Operator Precedence and Associativity*

Operator	Associativity
unary −	right to left
* / %	left to right
+ −	left to right

Finally, let us use either Table 2.7 or the precedence rules to evaluate an expression containing operators of different precedence, such as 8 + 5 * 7 % 2 * 4. Because the multiplication and modulus operators have a higher precedence than the addition operator, these two operations are evaluated first (P2), using their left-to-right associativity, before the addition is evaluated (P3). Thus, the complete expression is evaluated as:

$$8 + 5 * 7 \% 2 * 4 =$$
$$8 + 35 \% 2 * 4 =$$
$$8 + 1 * 4 =$$
$$8 + 4 = 12$$

▌ EXERCISES 2.2

1. Following are algebraic expressions and incorrect C++ expressions corresponding to them. Find the errors and write corrected C++ expressions.

	Algebra	*C++ Expression*
a.	(2)(3) + (4)(5)	(2)(3) + (4)(5)
b.	$\dfrac{6 + 18}{2}$	6 + 18 / 2
c.	$\dfrac{4.5}{12.2 - 3.1}$	4.5 / 12.2 − 3.1
d.	4.6(3.0 + 14.9)	4.6(3.0 + 14.9)
e.	(12.1 + 18.9)(15.3 − 3.8)	(12.1 + 18.9)(15.3 − 3.8)

2. Assuming that amount = 1, $m = 50$, $n = 10$, and $p = 5$, evaluate the following expressions.

a. $n / p + 3$

b. $m / p + n - 10 *$ amount

c. $m - 3 * n + 4 *$ amount

d. amount $/ 5$

e. $18 / p$

f. $18 \% p$

g. $-p * n$

h. $-m / 20$

i. $-m \% 20$

j. $(m + n) / (p +$ amount$)$

k. $m + n / p +$ amount

3. Repeat Exercise 2, assuming that amount = 1.0, $m = 50.0$, $n = 10.0$, and $p = 5.0$.

4. Determine the value of the following integer expressions.

a. $3 + 4 * 6$

b. $3 * 4 / 6 + 6$

c. $2 * 3 / 12 * 8 / 4$

d. $10 * (1 + 7 * 3)$

e. $20 - 2 / 6 + 3$

f. $20 - 2 / (6 + 3)$

g. $(20 - 2) / 6 + 3$

h. $(20 - 2) / (6 + 3)$

5. Determine the value of the following floating-point expressions.

a. $3.0 + 4.0 * 6.0$

b. $3.0 * 4.0 / 6.0 + 6.0$

c. $2.0 * 3.0 / 12.0 * 8.0 / 4.0$

d. $10.0 * (1.0 + 7.0 * 3.0)$

e. $20.0 - 2.0 / 6.0 + 3.0$

f. $20.0 - 2.0 / (6.0 + 3.0)$

g. $(20.0 - 2.0) / 6.0 + 3.0$

h. $(20.0 - 2.0) / (6.0 + 3.0)$

6. Evaluate each of the following expressions and list the data type of the result. In evaluating the expressions, be aware of the data types of all intermediate calculations.

a. $10.0 + 15 / 2 + 4.3$

b. $10.0 + 15 \% 2 + 4.3$

c. $10.0 + 15.0 / 2 + 4.3$

d. $3.0 * 4 / 6 + 6$

e. $3.0 * 4 \% 6 + 6$

f. $3 * 4.0 / 6 + 6$

g. $20.0 - 2 / 6 + 3$

h. $10 + 17 \% 3 + 4$

i. $10 + 17 \% 3 + 4.$

j. $10 + 17 / 3. + 4$

2.3   **Numerical Output Using cout**

In addition to displaying strings, the cout object allows us to display, on the standard output device, the numerical result of an expression. To do this we must pass the desired value to cout. For example, the statement

```
cout << (6 + 15);
```

yields the display 21. Strictly speaking, the parentheses surrounding the expression 6 + 15 are not necessary to indicate that it is the value of the expression, which is 21, that is being placed on the output stream.[3]

In addition to displaying a numerical value, a string identifying the output can also be displayed by passing the string to cout as we did in Chapter 1. For example, the statement

```
cout << "The total of 6 and 15 is " << (6 + 15);
```

causes two pieces of data to be sent to cout: a string and a value. Individually, each set of data is sent to the cout preceded by its own insertion symbol (<<). Here the first data sent to the stream is the string "The total of 6 and 15 is ", and the second item stream is the value of the expression 6 + 15. The display produced by this statement is

```
The total of 6 and 15 is 21
```

Note that the space between the word is and the number 21 is caused by the space placed within the string passed to cout. As far as cout is concerned, its input is simply a set of characters that are then sent on to be displayed in the order in which they are received. Characters from the input are queued, one behind the other, and sent to an output stream for display. Placing a space in the input causes this space to be part of the output stream that is ultimately displayed. For example, the statement

```
cout << "The sum of 12.2 and 15.754 is " << (12.2 + 15.754);
```

---

[3] This is because the + operator has a higher precedence than the << operator so that the addition is performed before the insertion.

yields the display

```
The sum of 12.2 and 15.754 is 27.954
```

Note that insertion of data into the output stream can be made over multiple lines and is terminated only by a semicolon. Thus the prior display is also produced by the statement

```
cout << "The sum of 12.2 and 15.754 is "
     << (12.2 + 15.754);
```

The requirements for using multiple lines are that a string contained within double quotes cannot be split across lines and that the terminating semicolon must appear only on the last line. Within a line, multiple insertion symbols can be used.

As the last display indicates, floating-point numbers are displayed with sufficient digits to the right of the decimal place to accommodate the fractional part of the number. This is true if the number has six or fewer significant digits. If the number has more than six significant digits, the fractional part is rounded to six significant digits, and if the number has no decimal digits, neither a decimal point nor any decimal digits are displayed.[4]

Character data can also be displayed using cout. For example, the statement

```
cout << "The first letter of the alphabet is an " << 'a';
```

results in the display

```
The first letter of the alphabet is an a
```

Program 2.2 illustrates using cout to display the results of an expression within the statements of a complete program. In reviewing this program, note the use of the term endl as the last item to be inserted into the output stream. The keyword endl is an example of a C++ **manipulator**, which is an item used to manipulate how the output stream of characters is displayed. In particular, the endl manipulator first causes a newline character ('\n') to be added to the output stream and then forces an immediate display of the output stream. When used with the cout object, this has the effect of ensuring an immediate display of the data on the terminal. (Additional manipulators are listed in Table 2.8.)

---

[4] Note that none of this output is defined as part of the C++ language. Rather, it is defined by a set of classes and routines provided with each C++ compiler.

Program 2.2

```cpp
#include <iostream>
using namespace std;

int main()
{
 cout << "15.0 plus 2.0 equals " << (15.0 + 2.0) << endl
      << "15.0 minus 2.0 equals " << (15.0 - 2.0) << endl
      << "15.0 times 2.0 equals " << (15.0 * 2.0) << endl
      << "15.0 divided by 2.0 equals " << (15.0 / 2.0) << endl;

 return 0;
}
```

The output of Program 2.2 is

```
15.0 plus 2.0 equals 17
15.0 minus 2.0 equals 13
15.0 times 2.0 equals 30
15.0 divided by 2.0 equals 7.5
```

Formatted Output

Besides displaying correct results, it is extremely important for a program to present its results attractively. Most programs are judged, in fact, on the perceived ease of data entry and the style and presentation of their output. For example, displaying a monetary result as 1.897 is not in keeping with accepted report conventions. The display should be either $1.90 or $1.89, depending on whether rounding or truncation is used.

The format of numbers displayed by cout can be controlled by field width manipulators included in each output stream. Table 2.8 lists the most commonly used manipulators available for this purpose.

TABLE 2.8 *Commonly Used Stream Manipulators*

Manipulator	Action
`setw(n)`	Set the field width to n.
`setprecision(n)`	Set the floating-point precision to n places. If the `fixed` manipulator is designated, n specifies the total number of displayed digits after the decimal point; otherwise n specifies the total number of significant digits displayed (integer plus fractional digits).
`setfill('x')`	Set the default leading fill character to x. (The default leading fill character is a space, which is output to fill the front of an output field whenever the width of the field is larger than the value being displayed.)
`setiosflags(flags)`	Set the format flags (see Table 2.10 for flag settings).
`scientific`	Set the output to display real numbers in scientific notation.
`showbase`	Display the base used for numbers. A leading 0 is displayed for octal numbers and a leading 0x for hexadecimal numbers.
`showpoint`	Always display 6 digits in total (combination of integer and fractional parts). Fill with trailing zeros, if necessary. For larger integer values revert to scientific notation.
`showpos`	Display all positive numbers with a leading + sign.
`boolalpha`	Display Boolean values as true and false, rather than as 1 and 0.
`dec`	Set output for decimal display (this is the default).
`endl`	Output a newline character and display all characters in the buffer.
`fixed`	Always show a decimal point and use a default of 6 digits after the decimal point. Fill with trailing zeros, if necessary.
`flush`	Display all the characters in the buffer.
`left`	Left justify all numbers.
`hex`	Set output for hexadecimal display.
`oct`	Set output for octal display.
`uppercase`	Display hexadecimal digits and the exponent in scientific notation in uppercase.
`right`	Right justify all numbers (this is the default).
`noboolalpha`	Display Boolean values as 1 and 0, rather than as true and false.
`noshowbase`	Do not display octal numbers with a leading 0 and hexadecimal numbers with a leading 0x.
`noshowpoint`	Do not use a decimal point for real numbers with no fractional parts, do not display trailing zeros in the fractional part of a number, and display a maximum of 6 decimal digits only.

TABLE 2.8 *(continued)*

Manipulator	Action
noshowpos	Do not display leading + signs (this is the default).
nouppercase	Display hexadecimal digits and the exponent in scientific notation in lowercase.

For example, the statement

```
cout << "The sum of 6 and 15 is" << setw(3) <<  21;
```

creates this printout:

```
The sum of 6 and 15 is 21
```

The setw(3) field width manipulator included in the stream of data passed to cout is used to set the displayed field width. The 3 in this manipulator sets the default field width for the next number in the stream to be three spaces wide. This field width setting causes the 21 to be printed in a field of three spaces, which includes one blank and the number 21. As illustrated, integers are right-justified within the specified field.

Field width manipulators are useful in printing columns of numbers so that the numbers in each column align correctly. For example, Program 2.3 illustrates how a column of integers would align in the absence of field width manipulators.

 Program 2.3

```cpp
#include <iostream>
using namespace std;

int main()
{
  cout << 6 << endl
       << 18 << endl
       << 124 << endl
       << "---\n"
       << (6+18+124) << endl;

  return 0;
}
```

The output of Program 2.3 is

```
6
18
124
---
148
```

Since no field width manipulators are included in Program 2.3, the cout object allocates enough space for each number as it is received. To force the numbers to align on the units digit requires a field width wide enough for the largest displayed number. For Program 2.3, a width of three would suffice. The use of this field width is illustrated in Program 2.4.

Program 2.4

```cpp
#include <iostream>
#include <iomanip>
using namespace std;

int main()
{
  cout << setw(3) << 6 << endl
       << setw(3) << 18 << endl
       << setw(3) << 124 << endl
       << "---\n"
       << (6+18+124) << endl;

  return 0;
}
```

The output of Program 2.4 is

```
  6
 18
124
---
148
```

Notice that the field width manipulator must be included for each occurrence of a number inserted into the data stream sent to cout, and that this particular manipulator only applies to the next insertion of data immediately following it. The other manipulators remain in effect until they are changed.

When a manipulator requiring an argument is used, the iomanip header file must be included as part of the program. This is accomplished by the preprocessor command #include <iomanip>, which is listed as the second line in Program 2.4

Formatted floating-point numbers completely requires the use of three field width manipulators. The first manipulator sets the total width of the display, the second manipulator forces the display of a decimal point, and the third manipulator determines how many significant digits will be displayed to the right of the decimal point. For example, the statement

```
cout << "|" << setw(10) << fixed << setprecision(3) << 25.67 << "|";
```

causes the printout

```
|    25.670|
```

The bar symbol, |, in the example is used to delimit (mark) the beginning and end of the display field. The setw manipulator tells cout to display the number in a total field of 10, the fixed manipulator explicitly forces the display of a decimal point and designates that the setprecision manipulator is used to designate the number of digits to be displayed after the decimal point. In this case, a display of 3 digits after the decimal point is specified by setprecision. Without the explicit designation of a decimal point (which can also be designated as setiosflags(ios::fixed)), the setprecision manipulator specifies the total number of displayed digits, which includes both the integer and fractional parts of the number.

For all numbers (integers, single-precision, and double precision), cout ignores the setw manipulator specification if the total specified field width is too small, and allocates enough space for the integer part of the number to be printed. The fractional part of both single-precision and double-precision numbers is displayed up to the precision set with the setprecision manipulator (in the absence of a setprecision manipulator, the default precision is set to six decimal places). If the fractional part of the number to be displayed contains more digits than called for in the setprecision manipulator, the number is rounded to the indicated number of decimal places; if the fractional part contains fewer digits than specified, the number is displayed with the fewer digits. Table 2.9 illustrates the effect of various format manipulator combinations. Again, for clarity, the bar symbol, |, is used to clearly delineate the beginning and end of the output fields.

TABLE 2.9 *Effect of Format Manipulators*

Manipulators	Number	Display	Comments
`setw(2)`	3	| 3|	Number fits in field
`setw(2)`	43	|43|	Number fits in field
`setw(2)`	143	|143|	Field width ignored
`setw(2)`	2.3	|2.3|	Field width ignored

`setw(5)`
`fixed`
`setprecision(2)`
	2.366	| 2.37|	Field width of 5 with 2 decimal digits

`setw(5)`
`fixed`
`setprecision(2)`
	42.3	|42.30|	Number fits in field with specified precision

`setw(5)` `setprecision(2)`	142.364	|1.4e+002|	Field width ignored and scientific notation used with the `setprecision` manipulator specifying the total number of significant digits (integer plus fractional)

`setw(5)`
`fixed`
`setprecision(2)`
	142.364	|142.36|	Field width ignored but precision specification used. Here the `setprecision` manipulator specifies the number of fractional digits

`setw(5)`
`fixed`
`setprecision(2)`
	142.366	|142.37|	Field width ignored but precision specification used. Here the `setprecision` manipulator specifies the number of fractional digits. (Note the rounding of the last decimal digit)

`setw(5)`
`fixed`
`setprecision(2)`
	142	| 142|	Field width used, `fixed` and `setprecision` manipulators irrelevant, because the number is an integer

In addition to the `setw` and `setprecision` manipulators, a field justification manipulator is also available. As we have seen, numbers sent to `cout` are normally displayed right-justified in the display field, while strings are displayed left-justified. To alter the default justification for a stream of data, the `setflags` manipulator can be used. For example, the statement

```
cout << "|" << setw(10) << setiosflags(ios::left) << 142 << "|";
```

P R O G R A M M I N G   N O T E

What Is a Flag?

In current programming usage the term **flag** refers to an item, such as a variable or argument, that sets a condition usually considered as either active or nonactive. Although the exact origin of this term in programming is not known, it probably originates from the use of real flags to signal a condition, such as the Stop, Go, Caution, and Winner flags commonly used at car races.

In a similar manner, each flag argument for the `setiosflags()` manipulator function activates a specific condition. For example, the `ios::dec` flag sets the display format to decimal, while the flag `ios::oct` activates the octal display format. Since these conditions are mutually exclusive (that is, only one condition can be active at a time), activating one such flag automatically deactivates the other flags.

Flags that are not mutually exclusive, such as `ios::dec`, `ios::showpoint`, and `ios::fixed` can all be set to on at the same time. This can be done using three individual `setiosflags()` calls or combining all arguments into one call as follows:

```
cout << setiosflags(ios::dec | ios::fixed | ios::showpoint);
```

causes the following left-justified display

```
|142        |
```

As we have previously seen, since data passed to cout may be continued across multiple lines, the previous display would also be produced by the statement

```
cout << "|" << setw(10)
     << setiosflags(ios::left)
     << 142 << "|";
```

As always, the field width manipulator is only in effect for the next single set of data displayed by cout. Right-justification for strings in a stream is obtained by the manipulator `setiosflags(ios::right)`. The symbol `ios` in both the function name and the `ios::right` argument comes from the first letters of the words "input output stream."

In addition to the left and right flags that can be used with the `setiosflags()` manipulator, other flags may also be used to affect the output. The most commonly used flags for this manipulator are listed in Table 2.10. Notice that the flags in this table effectively provide an alternate way of setting the equivalent manipulators previously listed in Table 2.8.

Because the flags in Table 2.10 are used as arguments to the `setiosflags()` manipulator method, and the terms argument and parameter are synonymous,

Formatting cout Stream Data

Floating-point data in a cout output stream can be formatted in precise ways. One of the most common format requirements is to display numbers in a monetary format with two digits after the decimal point, such as 123.45. This can be done with the following statement:

```
cout << setiosflags(ios::fixed)
     << setiosflags(ios::showpoint)
     << setprecision(2);
```

The first manipulator flag, ios::fixed, forces all floating-point numbers placed on the cout stream to be displayed in decimal notation. This flag also prevents the use of scientific notation. The next flag, ios::showpoint, tells the stream to always display a decimal point. Finally, the setprecision manipulator tells the stream to always display two decimal values after the decimal point. Instead of using manipulators, you can also use the cout stream methods setf() and precision(). For example, the previous formatting can also be accomplished using the code:

```
cout.setf(ios::fixed);
cout.setf(ios::showpoint);
cout.precision(2);
```

Note the syntax here: the name of the object, cout, is separated from the method with a period. This is the standard way of specifying a function and connecting it to a specific object. Which style you select is a matter of preference.

Additionally, the flags used in both the setf() function and the setiosflags() manipulator can be combined using the bitwise Or operator, | (explained in Appendix D). Using this operator, the following two statements are equivalent.

```
cout << setiosflags(ios::fixed | ios::showpoint);
cout.setf(ios::fixed | ios::showpoint);
```

Which style you select is a matter of preference.

another name for a manipulator method that uses arguments is a **parametrized manipulator**. The following is an example of parameterized manipulator methods:

```
cout << setiosflags(ios::showpoint) << setprecision(4);
```

This forces all subsequent floating point numbers sent to the output stream to be displayed with a decimal point and four decimal digits. If the number has fewer than four decimal digits it will be padded with trailing zeros.

TABLE 2.10   *Format Flags for Use with* `setiosflags()`

Flag	Meaning
`ios::fixed`	Always show the decimal point with 6 digits after the decimal point. Fill with trailing zeros, if necessary. This flag takes precedence if it is set with the `ios::showpoint` flag.
`ios::scientific`	Use exponential display on output.
`ios::showpoint`	Always display a decimal point and 6 significant digits in total (combination of integer and fractional parts). Fill with trailing zeros after the decimal point, if necessary. For larger integer values revert to scientific notation unless the `ios::fixed` flag is set.
`ios::showpos`	Display a leading + sign when the number is positive.
`ios::left`	Left-justify output.
`ios::right`	Right-justify output.

In addition to outputting integers in decimal notation, the `oct` and `hex` manipulators permit conversions to octal and hexadecimal, respectively. Program 2.5 illustrates the use of these flags. Because decimal is the default display, the `dec` manipulator is not required in the first output stream.

 Program 2.5

```cpp
// a program that illustrates output conversions
#include <iostream>
using namespace std;

int main()
{
  cout << "The decimal (base 10) value of 15 is " << 15 << endl;
  cout << "The octal (base 8) value of 15 is "
       << showbase << oct << 15 << endl;
  cout << "The hexadecimal (base 16) value of 15 is "
       << showbase << hex << 15 << endl;

  return 0;
}
```

The output produced by Program 2.5 is:

```
The decimal (base 10) value of 15 is 15
The octal (base 8) value of 15 is 017
The hexadecimal (base 16) value of 15 is 0xf
```

The display of integer values in one of the three possible number systems (decimal, octal, and hexadecimal) does not affect how the number is actually stored inside a computer. All numbers are stored using the computer's own internal codes. The manipulators sent to cout simply tell the object how to convert the internal code for output display purposes.

Besides displaying integers in octal or hexadecimal form, integer constants can also be written in a program in these forms. To designate an octal integer constant, the number must have a leading zero. The number 023, for example, is an octal number in C++. Hexadecimal numbers are denoted using a leading 0x. The use of octal and hexadecimal integer constants is illustrated in Program 2.6.

Program 2.6

```cpp
#include <iostream>
using namespace std;

int main()
{
  cout << "The decimal value of 025 is " << 025 << endl
       << "The decimal value of 0x37 is "<< 0x37 << endl;

  return 0;
}
```

The output produced by Program 2.6 is

```
The decimal value of 025 is 21
The decimal value of 0x37 is 55
```

The relationship between the input, storage, and display of integers is illustrated in Figure 2.4.

Finally, the manipulators specified in Tables 2.8 and 2.9 can also be set using the ostream class methods listed in Table 2.11.

FIGURE 2.4   *Input, Storage, and Display of Integers*

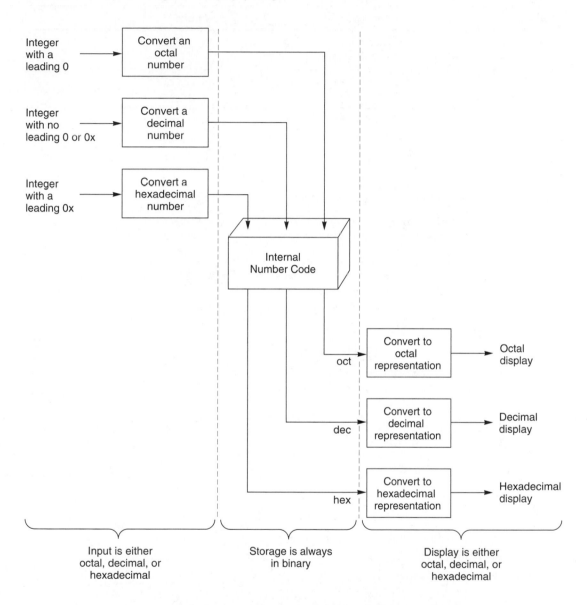

Note that in the Examples column of Table 2.11 the name of the object, `cout`, is separated from the method with a period. As noted above, this content now is later in the book. This is the standard way of calling a class method and providing it with the object it is to operate on.

TABLE 2.11   ostream *Class Methods*

Method	Comment	Example
precision(*n*)	Equivalent to setprecision()	cout.precision(2)
fill('*x*')	Equivalent to setfill()	cout.fill('*')
setf(ios::fixed)	Equivalent to setiosflags(ios::fixed)	cout.setf(ios::fixed)
setf(ios::showpoint)	Equivalent to setiosflags(ios::showpoint)	cout.setf(ios::showpoint)
setf(ios::left)	Equivalent to left	cout.setf(ios::left)
setf(ios::right)	Equivalent to right	cout.setf(ios::right)
setf(ios::flush)	Equivalent to endl	cout.setf(ios::flush)

▍ EXERCISES 2.3

1. Determine the output of the following program.

```
#include <iostream>
using namespace std;

int main()    // a program illustrating integer truncation
{
   cout << "answer1 is the integer " << 9/4
        << "answer2 is the integer " << 17/3 << endl;

   return 0;
}
```

2. Determine the output of the following program.

```
#include <iostream>
using namespace std;

int main()    // a program illustrating the % operator
{
   cout << "The remainder of 9 divided by 4 is " << 9 % 4
        << "\nThe remainder of 17 divided by 3 is " << 17 % 3
        << endl;

   return 0;
}
```

3. Write a C++ program that displays the results of the expressions 3.0 * 5.0, 7.1 * 8.3 – 2.2, and 3.2 / (6.1 * 5). Calculate the value of each expression manually to verify that the displayed values are correct.

4. Write a C++ program that displays the results of the expressions 15 / 4, 15 % 4, and 5 * 3 – (6 * 4). Calculate the value of these expressions manually to verify that the display produced by your program is correct.

5. Determine the errors in each of the following statements.

   a. `cout << "\n << " 15)`

   b. `cout << "setw(4)" << 33;`

   c. `cout << "setprecision(5)" << 526.768;`

   d. `"Hello World!" >> cout;`

   e. `cout << 47 << setw(6);`

   f. `cout << set(10) << 526.768 << setprecision(2);`

6. Determine and write out the display produced by the following statements.

   a. `cout << "|" << 5 << "|";`

   b. `cout << "|" << setw(4) << 5 << "|";`

   c. `cout << "|" << setw(4) << 56829 << "|";`

   d. `cout << "|" << setw(5) << setiosflags(ios::fixed)`
       `<< setprecision(2) << 5.26 << "|";`

   e. `cout << "|" << setw(5) << setiosflags(ios::fixed)`
       `<< setprecision(2) << 5.267 << "|";`

   f. `cout << "|" << setw(5) << setiosflags(ios::fixed)`
       `<< setprecision(2) << 53.264 << "|";`

   g. `cout << "|" << setw(5) << setiosflags(ios::fixed)`
       `<< setprecision(2) << 534.264 << "|";`

   h. `cout << "|" << setw(5) << setiosflags(ios::fixed)`
       `<< setprecision(2) << 534. << "|";`

7. Write out the display produced by the following statements.

   a. `cout << "The number is " << setw(6) << setiosflags(ios::fixed)`
       `<< setprecision(2) << 26.27 << endl;`
    `cout << "The number is " << setw(6) << setiosflags(ios::fixed)`
       `<< setprecision(2) << 682.3 << endl;`
    `cout << "The number is " << setw(6) << setiosflags(ios::fixed)`
       `<< setprecision(2) << 1.968 << endl;`

   b. `cout << setw(6) << setiosflags(ios::fixed)`
       `<< setprecision(2) << 26.27 << endl;`
    `cout << setw(6) << setiosflags(ios::fixed)`
       `<< setprecision(2) << 682.3 << endl;`
    `cout << setw(6) << setiosflags(ios::fixed)`
       `<< setprecision(2) << 1.968 << endl;`
    `cout << "------\n";`

```
     cout << setw(6) << setiosflags(ios::fixed)
          << setprecision(2) << 26.27 + 682.3 + 1.968 << endl;

c.   cout << setw(5) << setiosflags(ios::fixed)
          << setprecision(2) << 26.27 << endl;
     cout << setw(5) << setiosflags(ios::fixed)
          << setprecision(2) << 682.3 << endl;
     cout << setw(5) << setiosflags(ios::fixed)
          << setprecision(2) << 1.968 << endl;
     cout << "-------\n";
     cout << setw(5) << setiosflags(ios::fixed)
          << setprecision(2) << 26.27 + 682.3 + 1.968 << endl;

d.   cout << setw(5) << setiosflags(ios::fixed)
          << setprecision(2) << 36.164 << endl;
     cout << setw(5) << setiosflags(ios::fixed)
          << setprecision(2) << 10.003 << endl;
     cout << "------" << endl;
```

8. The following table lists the correspondence between the decimal numbers 1 through 15 and their octal and hexadecimal representations.

Decimal:	1	2	3	4	5	6	7	8	9	10	11	12	13	14	15
Octal:	1	2	3	4	5	6	7	10	11	12	13	14	15	16	17
Hexadecimal:	1	2	3	4	5	6	7	8	9	a	b	c	d	e	f

Using this table, determine the output of the following program.

```cpp
#include <iostream>
#include <iomanip>
using namespace std;

int main()
{
  cout << "\nThe value of 14 in octal is " << oct << 14
       << "\nThe value of 14 in hexadecimal is " << hex << 14
       << "\nThe value of 0xA in decimal is " << dec << 0xA
       << "\nThe value of 0xA in octal is " << oct << 0xA
       << endl;

  return 0;
}
```

2.4   Variables and Declarations

All integer, floating-point, and other values used in a computer program are stored in and retrieved from the computer's memory unit. Conceptually, individual memory locations in the memory unit are arranged like the rooms in a large hotel. Like hotel rooms, each memory location has a unique address ("room number"). Before high-level languages such as C++ existed, memory locations were referenced by their addresses. For example, to store the integer values 45 and 12 in the memory locations 1652 and 2548 (see Figure 2.5), respectively, required instructions equivalent to

Put a 45 in location 1652
Put a 12 in location 2548

To add the two numbers just stored and save the result in another memory location—for example, at location 3000—required a statement comparable to

Add the contents of location 1652
to the contents of location 2548
and store the result into location 3000

Clearly this method of storage and retrieval is a cumbersome process. In high-level languages like C++, symbolic names are used in place of actual memory addresses. These symbolic names are called variables. A **variable** is simply a name the programmer uses to refer to computer storage locations. The term variables is used because the value stored in the variable can change, or vary. The computer keeps track of the actual memory address that corresponds to each name the programmer assigns. In our hotel room analogy, this is equivalent to putting a name on the door of a room and referring to the room by this name, such as the Blue Room, rather than using the actual room number.

FIGURE 2.5 *Enough Storage for Two Integers*

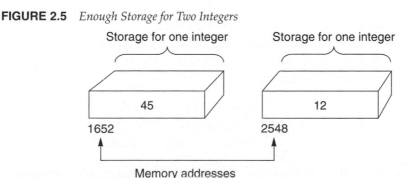

FIGURE 2.6 *Naming Storage Locations*

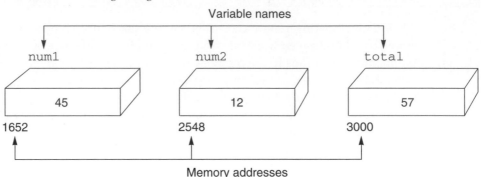

In C++ the selection of variable names is left to the programmer, as long as the following rules are observed.

1. The variable name must begin with a letter or underscore (_) and may contain only letters, underscores, or digits. It cannot contain any blanks, special symbols such as ()&$#.!\?, or commas. It uses initial capital letters to separate names that consist of multiple words.

2. A variable name cannot be a keyword (see Table 1.2).

These rules are similar to those used for selecting function names. Like function names, variable names should be mnemonics that give some indication of the variable's use. For example, a good name for a variable used to store a value that is the total of some other values would be sum or total. Variable names that give no clue to the type of value stored, such as r2d2, linda, bill, and getum, should not be selected. Like function names, variable names can be typed in uppercase and lowercase letters.

Now assume that the first memory location illustrated in Figure 2.5, which has address 1652, is given the name num1. Also assume that memory location 2548 is given the variable name num2 and that memory location 3000 is given the variable name total, as illustrated in Figure 2.6.

With these variable names, the operation of storing 45 in location 1652, storing 12 in location 2548, and adding the contents of these two locations is accomplished by the C++ statements

```
num1 = 45;
num2 = 12;
total = num1 + num2;
```

Each of these three statements is called an **assignment statement** because it tells the computer to assign a value to (store it in) a variable. Assignment statements always have an equals (=) sign and one variable name immediately to the left of this sign. The value on the right of the equals sign is determined first, and this value is assigned to the variable on the left of the equals sign. The blank spaces in the assignment statements are inserted for readability. We will have much more to say about assignment statements in the next chapter, but for now we will just use them to store values in variables.

A variable name is useful because it frees the programmer from concern over where data are physically stored inside the computer. We simply use the variable name and let the compiler worry about where the data are actually stored in memory. However, C++ requires that before we store a value in a variable, we clearly declare the type of data that is to be stored in it. We must tell the compiler, in advance, the names of the variables that will be used for characters, the names that will be used for integers, and the names that will be used to store the other C++ data types.

Declaration Statements

Naming a variable and specifying the data type that can be stored in it are accomplished by using declaration statements. A **declaration statement** has the general form

$$dataType \; variableName;$$

where `data-type` designates a valid C++ data type and `variable-name` is a user-selected variable name. For example, variables used to hold integer values are declared using the keyword `int` to specify the data type and have the form

$$\texttt{int} \; variableName;$$

Thus the declaration statement

```
int sum;
```

declares `sum` as the name of a variable capable of storing an integer value.

In addition to the reserved word `int` used to specify an integer, the reserved word `long` is used to specify a long integer.[6] For example, the statement

```
long datenum;
```

---

[6] Additionally, the reserved words `unsigned int` are used to specify an integer that can store only nonnegative numbers, and the reserved words `short int` are used to specify a short integer.

declares `datenum` as a variable that will be used to store a long integer. When using the long qualifier, we can include the keyword `int`. Thus the previous declaration can also be written as

```
long int datenum;
```

Variables used to hold single-precision values are declared using the keyword `float`, whereas variables that will be used to hold double-precision values are declared using the keyword `double`. For example, the statement

```
float firstnum;
```

declares `firstnum` as a variable that will be used to store a single-precision number. Similarly, the statement

```
double secnum;
```

declares that the variable `secnum` will be used to store a double-precision number.

Although declaration statements may be placed anywhere within a function, most declarations are typically grouped together and placed immediately after the function's opening brace. In all cases, however, a variable must be declared before it can be used, and like all C++ statements, declaration statements must end with a semicolon. If the declaration statements are placed after the opening function brace, a simple `main()` function containing declaration statements would have the general form

```
#include <iostream>
using namespace std;

int main()
{
  declaration statements;

  other statements;

  return 0;
}
```

Program 2.7 illustrates this form in declaring and using four double-precision variables, with the `cout` object used to display the contents of one of the variables.

Program 2.7

```cpp
#include <iostream>
using namespace std;

int main()
{
   double  grade1;   // declare grade1 as a double variable
   double grade2;    // declare grade2 as a double variable
   double total;     // declare total as a double variable
   double average;   // declare average as a double variable

   grade1 = 85.5;
   grade2 = 97.0;
   total = grade1 + grade2;
   average = total/2.0; // divide the total by 2.0
   cout << "The average grade is " << average << endl;

   return 0;
}
```

The placement of the declaration statements in Program 2.7 is straightforward, although we will see that the four individual declarations can be combined into a single declaration. When Program 2.7 is run, the following output is displayed:

The average grade is 91.25

Note that when a variable name is sent to cout, the value stored in the variable is placed on the output stream and displayed.

Just as integer and real (single-precision, double-precision, and long-double) variables must be declared before they can be used, a variable used to store a single character must also be declared. Character variables are declared by using the reserved word char. For example, the declaration

char ch;

declares ch to be a character variable. Program 2.8 illustrates this declaration and the use of cout to display the value stored in a character variable.

Program 2.8

```
#include <iostream>
using namespace std;

int main()
{
  char ch;      // this declares a character variable

  ch = 'a';    // store the letter a into ch
  cout << "The character stored in ch is " << ch << endl;
  ch = 'm';    // now store the letter m into ch
  cout << "The character now stored in ch is "<< ch << endl;

  return 0;
}
```

When Program 2.8 is run, the output produced is

```
The character stored in ch is a
The character now stored in ch is m
```

Note in Program 2.8 that the first letter stored in the variable ch is a and the second letter stored is m. Because a variable can be used to store only one value at a time, the assignment of m to the variable automatically causes a to be overwritten.

Multiple Declarations

Variables that have the same data type can always be grouped together and declared by using a single declaration statement. The common form of such a declaration is

dataType variableList;

For example, the four separate declarations used in Program 2.7,

```
double grade1;
double grade2;
double total;
double average;
```

can be replaced by the single declaration statement

```
double grade1, grade2, total, average;
```

Similarly, the two character declarations

```
char ch;
char key;
```

can be replaced by the single declaration statement

```
char ch, key;
```

Note that declaring multiple variables in a single declaration requires that the data type of the variables be given only once, that all the variables' names be separated by commas, and that only one semicolon be used to terminate the declaration. The space after each comma is inserted for readability and is not required.

Declaration statements can also be used to store an initial value in declared variables. For example, the declaration statement

```
int num1 = 15;
```

both declares the variable num1 as an integer variable and sets the value of 15 in the variable. When a declaration statement is used to store a value in a variable, the variable is said to be **initialized**. Thus, in this example, it is correct to say that the variable num1 has been initialized to 15. Similarly, the declaration statements

```
double grade1 = 87.0;
double grade2 = 93.5;
double total;
```

declare three floating-point variables and initialize two of them. Good programming practice dictates that when initializations are used, each initialized variable be declared on a line by itself. Constants, expressions using only constants (such as 87.0 + 12 – 2), and expressions using constants and previously initialized variables can all be used as initializers within a function. For example, Program 2.7 with declaration initialization becomes Program 2.7a.

Program 2.7a

```
#include <iostream>
using namespace std;

int main()
{
  double grade1 = 85.5;
  double grade2 = 97.0;
  double total, average;

  total = grade1 + grade2;
  average = total/2.0; // divide the total by 2.0
  cout << "The average grade is " << average << endl;

  return 0;
}
```

Note the blank line after the declaration statement. Inserting a blank line after the variable declarations placed at the top of a function body is good programming practice. It improves both a program's appearance and its readability.

An interesting feature of C++ is that variable declarations may be freely intermixed and even contained within other statements; the only requirement is that a variable must be declared prior to its use. For example, the variable `total` in Program 2.7a could have been declared when it was first used by using the statement `float total = grade1 + grade2`. In very restricted situations (such as debugging, described in Section 4.7, or in a `for` loop, described in Section 5.3), declaring a variable at its point of use can be helpful. In general, however, it is preferable not to disperse declarations but rather to group them, in as concise and clear a manner as possible, at the top of each function.

Reference Variables[7]

Once a variable has been declared, it may be given additional names. This is accomplished by using a reference declaration, which has the form

$$dataType\ \&newName\ =\ existingName;$$

---

[7] This section may be omitted on first reading without loss of subject continuity.

For example, the reference declaration

```
double &sum = total;
```

equates the name sum to the name total—both now refer to the same variable, as illustrated in Figure 2.7.[8]

Once another name has been established for a variable by using a reference declaration, the new name, which is referred to as an **alias,** can be used in place of the original name. For example, consider Program 2.9.

Program 2.9

```
#include <iostream>
using namespace std;

int main()
{
  double total = 20.5;   // declare and initialize total
  double &sum = total;   // declare another name for total

  cout << "sum = " << sum << endl;
  sum = 18.6;                // this changes the value in total
  cout << "total = " << total << endl;
  return 0;
}
```

The following output is produced by Program 2.9:

```
sum = 20.5
total = 18.6
```

Because the variable sum is simply another reference to the variable total, it is the value stored in total that is obtained by the first cout statement in Program 2.9. Changing the value in sum then changes the value in total, which is displayed by the second call to cout in Program 2.9.

---

[8] Knowledgeable C programmers should not confuse the use of the ampersand symbol, &, in a reference declaration with the address operator or with the use of a reference variable as a pointer. A reference variable simply equates two variable names.

FIGURE 2.7   *sum Is an Alternative Name for* `total`

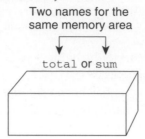

Two names for the
same memory area

`total` or `sum`

In constructing references, two considerations must be kept in mind. First, the reference must be of the same data type as the variable it refers to. For example, the sequence of declarations

```
int num = 5;
double& numref = num;   // INVALID - CAUSES A COMPILER ERROR
```

does not equate `numref` to `num`; rather it causes a compiler error. Secondly, a compiler error is also produced when an attempt is made to equate a reference to a constant. For example, the declaration

```
int& val = 5;   // INVALID - CAUSES A COMPILER ERROR
```

is also invalid.

Once a reference name has been correctly equated to one variable name, the reference cannot be changed to refer to another variable.

As with all declaration statements, multiple references may be declared in a single statement as long as each reference name is preceded by the ampersand symbol. Thus the declaration

```
double &sum = total, &mean = average;
```

creates two reference variables named `sum` and `mean`.[9]

---

[9] Reference declarations may also be written in the form `dataType& newName = existingName;`, where a space is placed between the ampersand symbol and the reference variable name. This form, however, becomes prone to error when multiple references are declared in the same declaration statement and the ampersand symbol is inadvertently omitted after the first reference name is declared. In order to accommodate multiple references in the same declaration more easily and mark a variable clearly as a reference, we will adhere to the convention of placing the ampersand directly in front of each reference variable name.

As we learn more about C++, we will have occasion to use reference variables in more detail, primarily as function arguments or as a function return type. Reference variables used in this manner are described in Section 6.3.

Specifying Storage Allocation

The declaration statements we have introduced perform both software and hardware tasks. From a software perspective, declaration statements always provide a list of all variables and their data types. In this software role, variable declarations also help to control an otherwise common and troublesome error caused by the misspelling of a variable's name within a program. For example, assume that a variable named `distance` is declared and initialized using the statement

```
int distance = 26;
```

Now assume that this variable is inadvertently misspelled in the statement

```
mpg = distnce / gallons;
```

In languages that do not require variable declarations, the program would treat `distnce` as a new variable and either assign an initial value of zero to the variable or use whatever value happened to be in the variable's storage area. In either case, a value would be calculated and assigned to `mpg`, and finding the error could be extremely troublesome (one might not even be aware that an error had occurred). Such errors are impossible in C++, because the compiler would flag `distnce` as an undeclared variable. The compiler cannot, of course, detect when one declared variable is typed in place of another declared variable.

In addition to their software role, declaration statements can also perform a distinct hardware task. Because each data type has its own storage requirements, the computer can allocate sufficient storage for a variable only after it knows the variable's data type. Variable declarations provide this information, so they can be used to force the compiler to reserve enough physical memory storage for each variable. Declaration statements used for this hardware purpose are also called *definition statements* because they define, or tell the compiler, how much memory is needed for data storage.

All the declaration statements that we have encountered so far have also been definition statements. Later, we will see cases of declaration statements that do not cause any new storage to be allocated and are used simply to declare, or alert the program to, the data types of variables that are created elsewhere in the program.

FIGURE 2.8a   *Defining the Integer Variable Named* total

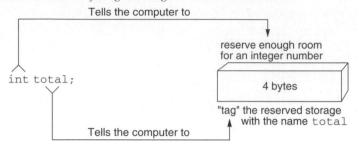

FIGURE 2.8b   *Defining the Floating-Point Variable Named* firstnum

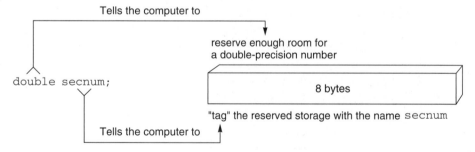

FIGURE 2.8c   *Defining the Double-Precision Variable Named* secnum

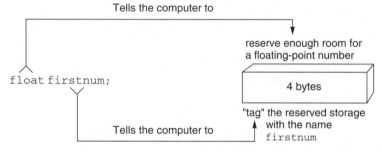

FIGURE 2.8d   *Defining the Character Variable Named* key

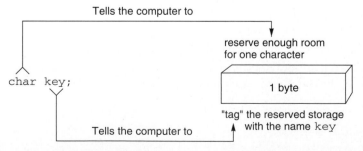

Figures 2.8(a–d) illustrate the series of operations set in motion by declaration statements that also perform a definition role. The figures show that definition statements (or, if you prefer, declaration statements that also cause memory to be allocated) "tag" the first byte of each set of reserved bytes with a name. This name is, of course, the variable's name and is used by the computer to locate correctly the starting point of each variable's reserved memory area.

Within a program, after a variable has been declared it is typically used by a programmer to refer to the contents of the variable (that is, the variable's value). Where in memory this value is stored generally matters little to the programmer. The compiler, however, must be concerned with where each value is stored and with correctly locating each variable. In this task the computer uses the variable name to locate the first byte of storage previously allocated to the variable. Knowing the variable's data type then allows the compiler to store or retrieve the correct number of bytes.

▌ EXERCISES 2.4

1. State whether each of the following variable names is valid. For those that are invalid, give the reason why.

```
prod_a    c1234     abcd       _c3       12345
newbal    while     $total     new bal   a1b2c3d4
9ab6      sum.of    average    grade1    finGrad
```

2. State whether each of the following variable names is valid. For those that are invalid, give the reason why. Also indicate which of the valid variable names should not be used because they convey no information about the variable.

```
salestax    a243     r2d2      firstNum    cca1
harry       sue      c3p0      average     sum
maximum     okay     a         awesome     goforit
3sum        for      tot.a1    c$five      netpay
```

3. a. Write a declaration statement to declare that the variable count will be used to store an integer.
b. Write a declaration statement to declare that the variable grade will be used to store a floating-point number.
c. Write a declaration statement to declare that the variable yield will be used to store a double-precision number.
d. Write a declaration statement to declare that the variable initial will be used to store a character.

4. Write declaration statements for the following variables.
   a. `num1`, `num2`, and `num3` used to store integer numbers
   b. `grade1`, `grade2`, `grade3`, and `grade4` used to store floating-point numbers
   c. `tempa`, `tempb`, and `tempc` used to store double-precision numbers
   d. `ch`, `let1`, `let2`, `let3`, and `let4` used to store character types

5. Write declaration statements for the following variables.
   a. `firstnum` and `secnum` used to store integers
   b. `price`, `yield`, and `coupon` used to store floating-point numbers
   c. `maturity` used to store a double-precision number

6. Rewrite each of these declaration statements as three individual declarations.
   a. `int month, day = 30, year;`
   b. `double hours, rate, otime = 15.62;`
   c. `float price, amount, taxes;`
   d. `char in_key, ch, choice = 'f';`

7. a. Determine what each statement causes to happen in the following program.

```cpp
#include <iostream>
using namespace std;
int main()
{
  int num1, num2, total;

  num1 = 25;
  num2 = 35;
  total = num1 + num2;
  cout << "The total of" << num1 << " and "
       << num2 << " is " << total << endl;
  return 0;
}
```

   b. What is the output that will be printed when the program listed in Exercise 7a is run?

8. Write a C++ program that stores the sum of the integer numbers 12 and 33 in a variable named `sum`. Have your program display the value stored in `sum`.

9. Write a C++ program that stores the integer value 16 in the variable `length` and the integer value 18 in the variable `width`. Have your program calculate the value assigned to the variable `perimeter`, using the assignment statement

`perimeter = 2 * length + 2 * width;`

and print out the value stored in the variable `perimeter`. Be sure to declare all the variables as integers at the beginning of the `main()` function.

10. Write a C++ program that stores the integer value 16 in the variable `num1` and the integer value 18 in the variable `num2`. (Be sure to declare the variables as integers.) Have your program calculate the total of these numbers and their average. Store the total in an integer variable named `total` and the average in an integer variable named `average`. (Use the statement `average = total/2.0;` to calculate the average.) Use the `cout` object to display the total and average.

11. Repeat Exercise 10, but store the number 15 in num1 instead of 16. With a pencil, write down the average of num1 and num2. What do you think your program will store in the integer variable that you used for the average of these two numbers? How can you ensure that the correct answer will be printed for the average?

12. Write a C++ program that stores the number 105.62 in the variable `firstnum`, 89.352 in the variable `secnum`, and 98.67 in the variable `thirdnum`. (Be sure to declare the variables first as either float or double.) Have your program calculate the total of the three numbers and their average. The total should be stored in the variable `total` and the average in the variable `average`. (Use the statement `average = total /3.0;` to calculate the average.) Use the `cout` object to display the total and average.

13. Every variable has at least two items associated with it. What are these two items?

14. a. A statement used to clarify the relationship between squares and rectangles is "All squares are rectangles but not all rectangles are squares." Write a similar statement that describes the relationship between definition and declaration statements.

    b. Why must a variable be defined before any other C++ statement that uses the variable?

Note for Exercises 15 through 17: Assume that a character requires one byte of storage, an integer four bytes, a single-precision number four bytes, and a double-precision number eight bytes and that variables are assigned storage in the order in which they are declared (review Section 2.7 if you are unfamiliar with the concept of a byte).

15. a. Using Figure 2.9 and assuming that the variable named `rate` is assigned to the byte that has memory address 159, determine the address that corresponds to each variable declared in the following statements. Also fill in the appropriate bytes with the initialization data included in the declaration statements (use letters for the characters, not the computer codes that would actually be stored).

```
double rate;
char ch1 = 'B', ch2 = Lo', ch3 = Ow', ch4 = 'T';
double taxes;
int num, count = 0;
```

    b. Repeat Exercise 15a, but substitute the actual byte patterns that a computer employing the ASCII code would use to store the characters in the variables ch1, ch2, ch3, and ch4. (*Hint:* Use Table 2.2.)

16. a. Using Figure 2.9 and assuming that the variable named `cn1` is assigned to the byte at memory address 159, determine the address that corresponds to each variable declared in the following statements. Also, fill in the appropriate bytes with the initialization data included in the declaration statements (use letters for the characters, not the computer codes that would actually be stored).

```
char cn1 = 'A', cn2 = 'N', cn3 = Pb', cn4 = Pu', cn5 = Pn';
char cn6 = 'L', cn7 = 'E', key = '\\', sch = '\'', inc = 'O';
char inc1 = 'F';
```

    b. Repeat Exercise 16a, but substitute the actual byte patterns that a computer employing the ASCII code would use to store the characters in each of the declared variables. (*Hint:* Use Tables 2.2 and 2.3.)

17. Using Figure 2.9 and assuming that the variable named `miles` is assigned to the byte at memory address 159, determine the address that corresponds to each variable declared in the following statements.

```
double miles;
int count, num;
double dist, temp;
```

FIGURE 2.9   *Memory Bytes for Exercises 15, 16, and 17*

Address:	159	160	161	162	163	164	165	166

Address:	167	168	169	170	171	172	173	174

Address:	175	176	177	178	179	180	181	182

Address:	183	184	185	186	187	188	189	190

2.5   Common Programming Errors

The common programming errors associated with the material presented in this chapter are

1. Forgetting to declare all the variables used in a program. This error is detected by the compiler, and an error message is generated for all undeclared variables.
2. Attempting to store one data type in a variable declared for a different type. This error is not detected by the compiler. Here, the value is converted to the data type of the variable it is assigned to.

3. Using a variable in an expression before a value has been assigned to the variable. Here, whatever value happens to be in the variable will be used when the expression is evaluated, and the result will be meaningless.

4. Dividing integer values incorrectly. This error is usually disguised within a larger expression and can be troublesome to detect. For example, the expression

$$3.425 + 2/3 + 7.9$$

yields the same result as the expression

$$3.425 + 7.9$$

because the integer division of $2/3$ is 0.

5. Mixing data types in the same expression without clearly understanding the effect produced. C++ allows mixed-mode expressions, so it is important to be clear about the order of evaluation and the data type of all intermediate calculations. The rules for evaluating the result of a numeric expression follow:
   a. If all operands are integers, the result is an integer.
   b. If any operand is a floating-point value, the result is a floating-point value.

   As a general rule, it is better not to mix data types in an expression unless a specific effect is desired.

6. Forgetting to separate individual data streams passed to `cout` with an insertion ("put to") symbol, `<<`.

2.6   *Chapter Summary*

1. The four basic types of data recognized by C++ are integer, floating-point, character, and Boolean data. Each of these types of data is typically stored in a computer using different amounts of memory.

2. The `cout` object can be used to display all of C++'s data types.

3. Every variable in a C++ program must be declared as to the type of value it can store. Declarations within a function may be placed anywhere within the function, although a variable can be used only after it is declared. Variables may also be initialized when they are declared. Additionally, variables of the same type may be declared by using a single declaration statement. Variable declaration statements have the general form

   dataType variableName(s);

4. Reference variables can be declared that associate a second name to an existing variable. The reference variable, which is also called an alias, is simply another name for the existing variable. Reference declarations have the form

   dataType &referenceName = existingName;

5. A simple C++ program containing declaration statements typically has the following form:

```
#include <iostream>
using namespace std;
int main()
{
  declaration statements;

  other statements;

  return 0;
}
```

Although declaration statements may be placed anywhere within the function's body, a variable may be used only after it is declared.

6. Declaration statements always play a software role, informing the compiler of a function's valid variable names. When a variable declaration also causes the computer to set aside memory locations for the variable, the declaration statement is also called a definition statement. (All the declarations we have used in this chapter have also been definition statements.)

7. The `sizeof()` operator can be used to determine the amount of storage reserved for variables.

2.7   Chapter Supplement: Bits, Bytes, Addresses, and Number Codes

The physical components used in manufacturing a computer require that the numbers and letters inside its memory unit are not stored using the same symbols that people use. The number 126, for example, would not be stored using the symbols 1, 2, and 6. Nor is the letter that we recognize as A stored using this symbol. In this section, we will see why this is so and how computers store numbers.

The smallest and most basic data item in a computer is called a **bit**. Physically, a bit is really a switch that can be either open or closed. The convention we will follow is that the open and closed positions of each switch are represented as 0 and 1, respectively.[10]

---

[10] This convention, unfortunately, is rather arbitrary, and you frequently will encounter the reverse correspondence, where the open and closed positions are represented as 1 and 0, respectively.

A single bit that can represent the values 0 and 1, by itself, has limited usefulness. All computers, therefore, group a set number of bits together, both for storage and for transmission. The grouping of eight bits to form a larger unit is an almost universal computer standard. Such groups are commonly referred to as **bytes**. A single byte consisting of eight bits, where each bit is either 0 or 1, can represent any one of 256 distinct patterns. These consist of the pattern 00000000 (all eight switches open), the pattern 11111111 (all eight switches closed), and all possible combinations of 0s and 1s in between. Each of these patterns can be used to represent a letter of the alphabet, other single characters (such as a dollar sign, a comma, or a single digit), or numbers containing more than one digit. The patterns consisting of 0s and 1s used to represent letters, single digits, and other single characters are called **character codes** (one such code ASCII was presented in Section 2.1). The patterns used to store numbers are called **number codes,** one of which is presented at the end of this section.

Words and Addresses

One or more bytes may themselves be grouped into larger units, called *words*, which facilitate faster and more extensive data access. For example, retrieving from a computer's memory a word that consists of four bytes results in more information than retrieving a word that consists of a single byte. Such a retrieval is also considerably faster than four individual byte retrievals. This increase in speed and capacity, however, is achieved by increasing the computer's cost and complexity.

Early personal computers, such as the Apple IIe, internally stored and transmitted words consisting of single bytes. The first IBM-PCs used word sizes consisting of two bytes, and more current PCs store and process words consisting of four and eight bytes each.

The arrangement of words in a computer's memory can be compared to the arrangement of suites in a large hotel, where each suite is made up of rooms of the same size. Just as each suite has a unique room number to locate and identify it, each word has a unique numeric address. In computers that allow each byte to be individually accessed, each byte has its own address. Like room numbers, word and byte addresses are always unsigned whole numbers that are used for location and identification purposes. And like hotel rooms with connecting doors for forming larger suites, words can be combined to form larger units for the accommodation of different-sized data types.

Twos Complement Numbers

The most common number code for storing integer values inside a computer is called the **twos complement** representation. With this code, the integer equivalent of any bit pattern, such as 10001101, is easy to determine and can be found for either positive or negative integers with no change in the conversion method. For convenience, we will assume byte-sized bit patterns consisting of a set of eight bits each, although the procedure carries directly over to bit patterns of larger sizes.

The easiest way to determine the integer represented by each bit pattern is first to construct a simple device called a value box. Figure 2.10 illustrates such a box for a single byte. Mathematically, each value in the box illustrated in Figure 2.10 represents an increasing power of 2. Because twos complement numbers must be capable of representing both positive and negative integers, the leftmost position, in addition to having the largest absolute magnitude, also has a negative sign.

FIGURE 2.10   *An Eight-Bit Value Box*

$-(2^7)$	(2^6)	(2^5)	(2^4)	(2^3)	(2^2)	(2^1)	(2^0)
−128	64	32	16	8	4	2	1

Conversion of any binary number—for example, 10001101—simply requires inserting the bit pattern in the value box and adding the values that have 1s under them. Thus, as illustrated in Figure 2.11, the bit pattern 10001101 represents the integer number −115.

FIGURE 2.11   *Converting 10001101 to a Base-10 Number*

−128	64	32	16	8	4	2	1
1	0	0	0	1	1	0	1

−128 + 0 + 0 + 0 + 8 + 4 + 0 + 1 = −115

The value box can also be used in reverse, to convert a base 10 integer number into its equivalent binary bit pattern. Some conversions, in fact, can be made by inspection. For example, the base 10 number −125 is obtained by adding 3 to −128. Thus the binary representation of −125 is 10000011, which equals −128 + 2 + 1. Similarly, the twos complement representation of the number 40 is 00101000, which is 32 plus 8.

Although the value box conversion technique is deceptively simple, the technique is directly related to the underlying mathematical basis of twos complement binary numbers. The twos complement code was originally called the **weighted-sign** code, which correlates directly with the value box. As the name weighted sign implies, each bit position has a weight, or value, of 2 raised to a power and a sign. The signs of all bits except the leftmost bit are positive, and the sign of the leftmost bit is negative.

In reviewing the value box, it becomes evident that any twos complement binary number with a leading 1 represents a negative number and that any bit pattern with a leading 0 represents a positive number. Using the value box, it is easy to determine the most positive and the most negative values capable of being stored. The most negative value that can be stored in a single byte is the decimal number −128, which has the bit pattern 10000000. Any other nonzero bit will simply add a positive amount to the number. It is also clear that a positive number must have 0 as its leftmost bit. From this you can see that the largest positive eight-bit twos complement number is 01111111, or 127.

Assignment and Interactive Input

In the last chapter we introduced the concept of data storage, variables, and their associated declaration statements. We also presented the use of cout for formatted output. This chapter continues our introduction to C++ by discussing the proper use of both constants and variables in constructing expressions and statements and the use of the cin object for entering data interactively while a program is running.

3.1   Assignment Operators

We have already encountered simple assignment statements. In Chapter 2, we saw that assignment statements are the most basic C++ statements for both assigning values to variables and performing computations. This statement has the syntax

variable = expression;

The simplest expression in C++ is a single constant. In each of the following assignment statements, the operand to the right of the equals sign is a constant.

```
length = 25;
width = 17.5;
```

In each of these assignment statements, the value of the constant to the right of the equals sign is assigned to the variable to the left of the equals sign. It is important to note that the equals sign in C++ does not have the same meaning as an equals sign in algebra. The equals sign in an assignment statement tells the computer first to determine the value of the operand to the right of the equals sign and then to store (or assign) that value in the locations associated with the variable to the left of the equals sign. In this regard, the C++ statement length = 25; is read "length is assigned the value 25." The blank spaces in the assignment statement are inserted for readability only.

Recall that a variable can be initialized when it is declared. If an initialization is not done within the declaration statement, the variable should be assigned a value with an assignment statement before it is used in any computation. Subsequent assignment statements can, of course, be used to change the value assigned to a variable. For example, assume that the following statements are executed one after another and that total was not initialized when it was declared.

```
total = 3.7;
total = 6.28;
```

The first assignment statement assigns the value of 3.7 to the variable named total.[1] The next assignment statement causes the computer to assign a value of 6.28 to `total`. The 3.7 that was in `total` is overwritten with the new value of 6.28 because a variable can store only one value at a time. It is sometimes useful to think of the variable to the left of the equals sign as a temporary parking spot in a huge parking lot. Just as an individual parking spot can be used by only one car at a time, each variable can store only one value at a time. The "parking" of a new value in a variable automatically causes the computer to remove any value that has previously been parked there.

In addition to being a constant, the operand to the right of the equals sign in an assignment statement can be a variable or any other valid C++ expression. An *expression* is any combination of constants and variables that can be evaluated to yield a result. Thus the expression in an assignment statement can be used to perform calculations via the arithmetic operators introduced in Section 2.2. Here are some examples of assignment statements using expressions that contain these operators:

```
sum = 3 + 7;
diff = 15 - 6;
product = .05 * 14.6;
tally = count + 1;
newtotal = 18.3 + total;
taxes = .06 * amount;
totalWeight = factor * weight;
average = sum / items;
slope = (y2 - y1) / (x2 - x1);
```

As always in an assignment statement, the computer first calculates the value of the expression to the right of the equals sign and then stores this value in the variable to the left of the equals sign. For example, in the assignment statement `totalWeight = factor * weight;` the arithmetic expression `factor * weight` is first evaluated to yield a result. This result, which is a number, is then stored in the variable `totalWeight`.

---

[1] Because this is the first time a value is explicitly assigned to this variable, it is frequently referred to as an initialization. This stems from historical usage that said a variable was initialized the first time a value was assigned to it. Under this usage, it is correct to say that "`total` is initialized to 3.7." From an implementation viewpoint, however, this latter statement is incorrect. This is because the assignment operation is handled differently by the C++ compiler than an initialization performed when a variable is created by a declaration statement. This difference is important only when we are using C++'s class features and is explained in detail in Section 12.1.

In writing assignment expressions, you must be aware of two important considerations. The expression to the right of the equals sign is evaluated first, so all variables used in the expression must previously have been given valid values if the result is to make sense. For example, the assignment statement `totalWeight = factor * weight;` causes a valid number to be stored in `totalWeight` only if the programmer first takes care to assign valid numbers to `factor` and `weight`. Thus the sequence of statements

```
factor = 1.06;
weight = 155.0;
totalWeight = factor * weight;
```

ensures that we know the values being used to obtain the result that will be stored in `totalWeight`.

The second consideration to keep in mind is that because the value of an expression is stored in the variable to the left of the equals sign, there must be a variable listed immediately to the left of the equals sign. For example, the assignment statement

```
amount + 1892 = 1000 + 10 * 5
```

is invalid. The expression on the right-hand side of the equals sign evaluates to the integer 1050, which can be stored only in a variable. Because `amount + 1892` is not a valid variable name, the computer does not know where to store the calculated value. Program 3.1 illustrates the use of assignment statements in calculating the area of a rectangle.

When Program 3.1 is run, the output obtained is

```
The length of the rectangle is 27.2
The width of the rectangle is 13.6
The area of the rectangle is 369.92
```

Consider the flow of control that the computer uses in executing Program 3.1. Program execution begins with the first statement and continues sequentially, statement by statement, until the closing brace of `main()` is encountered. This flow of control is true for all programs. The computer works on one statement at a time, executing that statement with no knowledge of what the next statement will be. This explains why all operands used in an expression must have values assigned to them before the expression is evaluated.

Program 3.1

```cpp
// this program calculates the area of a rectangle
//    given its length and width

#include <iostream>
using namespace std;

int main()
{
  double length, width, area;

  length = 27.2;
  width = 13.6;
  area = length * width;
  cout << "The length of the rectangle is " << length << endl;
  cout << "The width of the rectangle is " << width << endl;
  cout << "The area of the rectangle is " << area << endl;

  return 0;
}
```

When the computer executes the statement area = length * width; in Program 3.1, it uses whatever values are stored in the variables length and width at the time the assignment is executed. If no values have been specifically assigned to these variables before they are used in the expression length * width, the computer uses whatever values happen to occupy these variables when they are referenced. The computer does not "look ahead" to see that you might assign values to these variables later in the program.

It is important to realize that in C++ the equals sign, =, used in assignment statements is itself an operator, *which differs from the way most other high-level languages process this symbol*. In C++ (as in C), the = symbol is called the *assignment operator*, and an expression using this operator, such as interest = principal * rate, is an assignment expression. Because the assignment operator has a lower precedence than any other arithmetic operator, the value of any expression to the right of the equals sign is evaluated first, prior to assignment.

Like all expressions, assignment expressions themselves have a value. The value of the complete assignment expression is the value assigned to the variable on the left of the assignment operator. For example, the expression a = 5 both assigns a value of 5 to the variable a and results in the expression itself having a value of 5. The value of the expression can always be verified by using a statement such as

```
cout << "The value of the expression is " << (a = 5);
```

Here, the value of the expression itself is displayed, not the contents of the variable a. Although both the contents of the variable and the expression have the same value, it is worthwhile to realize that we are dealing with two distinct entities.

From a programming perspective, it is the actual assignment of a value to a variable that is significant in an assignment expression; the final value of the assignment expression itself is of little consequence. However, the fact that assignment expressions have a value has implications that must be considered when C++'s relational operators are presented.

Any expression that is terminated by a semicolon becomes a C++ statement. The most common example of this is the assignment statement, which is simply an assignment expression terminated with a semicolon. For example, terminating the assignment expression a = 33 with a semicolon results in the assignment statement a = 33; which can be used in a program on a line by itself.

Because the equals sign is an operator in C++, multiple assignments are possible in the same expression or in its equivalent statement. For example, in the expression a = b = c = 25, all the assignment operators have the same precedence. The assignment operator has a right-to-left associativity, so the final evaluation proceeds in the sequence

```
c = 25
b = c
a = b
```

In this case, this has the effect of assigning the number 25 to each of the variables individually, and it can be represented as

```
a = (b = (c = 25))
```

Appending a semicolon to the original expression results in the multiple assignment statement

```
a = b = c = 25;
```

This latter statement assigns the value 25 to the three individual variables equivalent to the following order:

```
c = 25;
b = 25;
a = 25;
```

Coercion

One thing to keep in mind when working with assignment statements is the data type assigned to the values on both sides of the expression, because data type conversions take place across assignment operators; that is, the value of the expression on the right side of the assignment operator will be converted to the data type of the variable to the left of the assignment operator. This type of conversion is referred to as a coercion, because the value assigned to the variable on the left side of the assignment operator is forced into the data type of the variable it is assigned to. An example of a coercion occurs when an integer value is assigned to a real variable; this causes the integer to be converted to a real value. Similarly, assigning a real value to an integer variable forces conversion of the real value to an integer, which always results in the loss of the fractional part of the number because of truncation. For example, if temp is an integer variable, the assignment temp = 25.89 causes the integer value 25 to be stored in the integer variable temp.[2]

Another example of data type conversions, which includes both mixed-mode and assignment conversion, is the evaluation of the expression

$$a = b * d$$

where a and b are integer variables and d is a double-precision variable. When the mixed-mode expression b * d is evaluated,[3] the value of b used in the expression is converted to a double-precision number for purposes of computation (it is important to note that the value stored in b remains an integer number, and the resulting value of the expression b * d is a double-precision number). Finally, data type conversion across the assignment operator comes into play. The left side of the assignment operator is an integer variable, so the double-precision value of the expression (b * d) is truncated to an integer value and stored in the variable a.

Assignment Variations

Although only one variable is allowed immediately to the left of the equals sign in an assignment expression, the variable to the left of the equals sign can also be used to the right of the equals sign. For example, the assignment expression sum = sum + 10 is valid. Clearly, if this were an algebra equation, sum could

---

[2] Clearly, the correct integer portion is retained only when it is within the range of integers allowed by the compiler.

[3] Review the rules given in Table 2.7 (Section 2.2) for the evaluation of mixed-mode expressions, if necessary.

P R O G R A M M I N G   N O T E

lvalues *and* rvalues

You will encounter the terms `lvalue` and `rvalue` frequently in almost all programming languages that define assignment using an operator that permits multiple assignments in the same statement. The term `lvalue` refers to any quantity that is valid on the left side of an assignment operator. An `rvalue` refers to any quantity that is valid on the right hand side of an assignment operator.

For example, each variable we have encountered so far can be either an `lvalue` or `rvalue` (that is, a variable, by itself, can appear on both sides of an assignment operator), while a number can only be an `rvalue`. More generally, any expression that yields a value can be an `rvalue`. Not all variables, however, can be used as either lvalues or rvalues. For example, an array type, which is introduced in Chapter 8, cannot be either an `lvalue` or an `rvalue`, while individual array elements can be both.

never be equal to itself plus 10. But in C++, the expression `sum = sum + 10` is not an equation—it is an expression that is evaluated in two major steps. The first step is to calculate the value of `sum + 10`. The second step is to store the computed value in `sum`. See whether you can determine the output of Program 3.2.

 ## Program 3.2

```cpp
#include <iostream>
using namespace std;

int main()
{
  int sum;

  sum = 25;
  cout << "The number stored in sum is " << sum << endl;
  sum = sum + 10;
  cout << "The number now stored in sum is " << sum << endl;

  return 0;
}
```

The assignment statement `sum = 25;` tells the computer to store the number 25 in `sum`, as shown in Figure 3.1.

FIGURE 3.1 *The Integer* 25 *Is Stored in* sum

The first cout statement causes the value stored in sum to be displayed by the message The number stored in sum is 25. The second assignment statement in Program 3.2, (sum = sum + 10;) causes the program to retrieve the 25 stored in sum and add 10 to this number, yielding the number 35. The number 35 is then stored in the variable on the left side of the equals sign, which is the variable sum. The 25 that was in sum is simply overwritten with the new value of 35, as shown in Figure 3.2.

FIGURE 3.2 sum = sum + 10; *Causes a New Value to Be Stored in* sum.

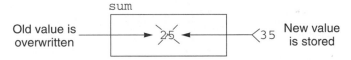

Assignment expressions such as sum = sum + 25, which use the same variable on both sides of the assignment operator, can be written by using the following **shortcut assignment operators:**

$$+= \quad -= \quad *= \quad /= \quad \%=$$

For example, the expression sum = sum + 10 can be written as sum += 10. Similarly, the expression price *= rate is equivalent to the expression price = price * rate.

In using these shortcut assignment operators it is important to note that the variable to the left of the assignment operator is applied to the *complete* expression on the right. For example, the expression price *= rate + 1 is equivalent to the expression

price = price * (rate + 1), not to price = price * rate + 1

Accumulating Assignment expressions like sum += 10 or its equivalent, sum = sum + 10, are very common in programming. These expressions are required in accumulating subtotals when data is entered one number at a time. For example, if we want to add the numbers 96, 70, 85, and 60 in calculator fashion, we could use the following statements:

Statement	Value in sum
sum = 0;	0
sum = sum + 96;	96
sum = sum + 70;	166
sum = sum + 85;	251
sum = sum + 60;	311

The first statement initializes sum to 0. This removes any number ("garbage value") stored in sum that would invalidate the final total. As each number is added, the value stored in sum is increased accordingly. After completion of the last statement, sum contains the total of all the added numbers.

Program 3.3 illustrates the effect of these statements by displaying sum's contents after each addition is made.

 Program 3.3

```cpp
#include <iostream>
using namespace std;

int main()
{
  int sum;

  sum = 0;
  cout << "The value of sum is initially set to " << sum << endl;
  sum = sum + 96;
  cout << " sum is now " << sum << endl;
  sum = sum + 70;
  cout << " sum is now " << sum << endl;
  sum = sum + 85;
  cout << " sum is now " << sum << endl;
  sum = sum + 60;
  cout << " The final sum is " << sum << endl;

  return 0;
}
```

The output displayed by Program 3.3 is

```
The value of sum is initially set to 0
  sum is now 96
  sum is now 166
  sum is now 251
The final sum is 311
```

Although Program 3.3 is not a practical program (it is easier to add the numbers by hand), it does illustrate the subtotaling effect of the repeated use of statements that have the form

```
variable = variable + newValue;
```

We will find many uses for this type of statement when we become more familiar with the repetition statements introduced in Chapter 5.

Counting

An assignment statement that is very similar to the accumulating statement is the counting statement. **Counting statements** have the form

```
variable = variable + fixedNumber;
```

Here are some examples of counting statements:

```
i = i + 1;
n = n + 1;
count = count + 1;
j = j + 2;
m = m + 2;
kk = kk + 3;
```

In each of these examples, the same variable is used on both sides of the equals sign. After the statement is executed, the value of the respective variable is increased by a fixed amount. In the first three examples, the variables i, n, and count have all been increased by 1. In the next two examples, the respective variables have been increased by 2, and in the final example, the variable kk has been increased by 3.

For the special case in which a variable is either increased or decreased by 1, C++ provides two unary operators. Using the **increment operator**,[4] ++, we can

---

[4] As an historical note, the ++ in C++ was inspired by the increment operator symbol. It was used to indicate that C++ was the next increment to the C language.

replace the expression `variable = variable + 1` by either the expression `variable++` or the expression `++variable`. Examples of the increment operator follow.

Expression	Alternative
`i = i + 1`	`i++` or `++i`
`n = n + 1`	`n++` or `++n`
`count = count + 1`	`count++` or `++count`

Program 3.4 illustrates the use of the increment operator.

Program 3.4

```cpp
#include <iostream>
using namespace std;

int main()
{
  int count;

  count = 0;
  cout << "The initial value of count is " << count << endl;
  count++;
  cout << " count is now " << count << endl;
  count++;
  cout << " count is now " << count << endl;
  count++;
  cout << " count is now " << count << endl;
  count++;
  cout << " count is now " << count << endl;

  return 0;
}
```

The output displayed by Program 3.4 is:

```
The initial value of count is 0
 count is now 1
 count is now 2
 count is now 3
 count is now 4
```

When the ++ operator appears before a variable, it is called a **prefix increment operator;** when it appears after a variable, it is called a **postfix increment operator.** The distinction between a prefix increment operator and a postfix increment operator is important when the variable being incremented is used in an assignment expression. For example, the expression k = ++n does two things in one expression. Initially the value of n is incremented by 1, and then the new value of n is assigned to the variable k. Thus the statement k = ++n; is equivalent to the two statements

```
n = n + 1;   // increment n first
k = n;       // assign n's value to k
```

The assignment expression k = n++, which uses a postfix increment operator, reverses this procedure. A postfix increment operates after the assignment is completed. Thus the statement k = n++; first assigns the current value of n to k and then increments the value of n by 1. This is equivalent to the two statements

```
k = n;       // assign n's value to k
n = n + 1;   // and then increment n
```

In addition to the increment operator, C++ also provides a **decrement operator,** --. As you might expect, the expressions variable-- and --variable are both equivalent to the expression variable = variable - 1.

Examples of the decrement operator are

Expression	Alternative
i = i - 1	i-- or --i
n = n - 1	n-- or --n
count = count - 1	count-- or --count

When the -- operator appears before a variable, it is called a **prefix decrement operator.** When the decrement appears after a variable, it is called a **postfix decrement operator.** For example, the expressions n-- and --n both reduce the value of n by 1. These expressions are equivalent to the longer expression n = n - 1. As with the increment operator, however, the prefix and postfix decrement operators produce different results when used in assignment expressions. For example, the expression k = --n first decrements the value of n by 1 before assigning the value of n to k, whereas the expression k = n-- first assigns the current value of n to k and then reduces the value of n by 1.

The increment and decrement operators can often be used advantageously to reduce program storage requirements and increase execution speed. For example, consider the following three statements:

```
count = count + 1;
count += 1;
count++;
```

All perform the same function; however, when these instructions are compiled for execution on an IBM personal computer, the storage requirements for the instructions are 9, 4, and 3 bytes, respectively.[5] Using the assignment operator, =, instead of the increment operator results in using three times as much storage space for the instruction, with an accompanying decrease in execution speed.

▍ EXERCISES 3.1

1. Determine and correct the errors in the following programs.

   a.
   ```
   #include <iostream>
   using namespace std;
   int main()
   {
     width = 15
     area = length * width;
     cout << "The area is " << area
     return 0;
   }
   ```

   b.
   ```
   #include <iostream>
   using namespace std;
   int main()
   {
     int length, width, area;
     area = length * width;
     length = 20;
     width = 15;
     cout << "The area is " << area;
   ```

---

[5] This is obviously a compiler-dependent result.

c.
```
#include <iostream>
using namespace std;
int main()
{
   int length = 20; width = 15, area;
   length * width = area;
   cout << "The area is " , area;
   return 0;
}
```

2. *a.* Write a C++ program to calculate and display the average of the numbers 32.6, 55.2, 67.9, and 48.6.
   b. Run the program written for Exercise 2a on a computer.

3. *a.* Write a C++ program to calculate the circumference of a circle. The equation for determining the circumference of a circle is *circumference = 2 * 3.1416 * radius*. Assume that the circle has a radius of 3.3 inches.
   b. Run the program written for Exercise 3a on a computer.

4. *a.* Write a C++ program to calculate the area of a circle. The equation for determining the area of a circle is *area = 3.1416 * radius * radius*. Assume that the circle has a radius of 5 inches.
   b. Run the program written for Exercise 4a on a computer.

5. *a.* Write a C++ program to calculate the volume of a pool. The equation for determining the volume is *volume = length * width * depth*. Assume that the pool has a length of 25 feet, a width of 10 feet, and a depth of 6 feet.
   b. Run the program written for Exercise 5a on a computer.

6. *a.* Write a C++ program to convert temperature in degrees Fahrenheit to temperature in degrees Celsius. The equation for this conversion is *Celsius = 5.0/9.0 * (Fahrenheit − 32.0)*. Have your program convert and display the Celsius temperature corresponding to 98.6 degrees Fahrenheit.
   b. Run the program written for Exercise 6a on a computer.

7. *a.* Write a C++ program to calculate the dollar amount contained in a piggy bank. The bank currently contains 12 half-dollars, 20 quarters, 32 dimes, 45 nickels, and 27 pennies.
   b. Run the program written for Exercise 7a on a computer.

8. *a.* Write a C++ program to calculate the distance, in feet, of a trip that is 2.36 miles long. One mile is equal to 5280 feet.
   b. Run the program written for Exercise 8a on a computer.

9. *a.* Write a C++ program to calculate the elapsed time it took to make a 183.67-mile trip. The equation for computing elapsed time is *elapsed time = total distance / average speed*. Assume that the average speed during the trip was 58 miles per hour.
   b. Run the program written for Exercise 9a on a computer.

10. *a.* Write a C++ program to calculate the sum of the numbers from 1 to 100. The formula for calculating this sum is *sum = (n/2) * (2*a + (n − 1)*d)*, where *n* = number of terms to be added, *a* = the first number, and *d* = the difference between each number and the next.
    b. Run the program written for Exercise 10a on a computer.

11. Determine why the expression a − b = 25 is invalid but the expression a − (b = 25) is valid.

3.2   Mathematical Library Functions

As we have seen, assignment statements can be used to perform arithmetic computations. For example, the assignment statement

```
totalPrice = unitPrice * amount;
```

multiplies the value in `unitPrice` times the value in amount and assigns the resulting value to `totalPrice`. Although addition, subtraction, multiplication, and division are easily accomplished using C++'s arithmetic operators, no such operators exist for raising a number to a power, finding the square root of a number, or determining trigonometric values. To facilitate such calculations, C++ provides standard preprogrammed functions that can be included in a program.

Before using one of C++'s mathematical functions, you need to know

- The name of the desired mathematical function
- What the mathematical function does
- The type of data required by the mathematical function
- The data type of the result returned by the mathematical function

To illustrate the use of C++'s mathematical functions, consider the mathematical function named `sqrt()`, which calculates the square root of a number. The square root of a number is computed using the expression

```
sqrt(number)
```

where the function's name, in this case `sqrt`, is followed by parentheses containing the number for which the square root is desired. The purpose of the parentheses after the function name is to provide a funnel through which data can be passed to the function (see Figure 3.3). The items that are passed to the function through the parentheses are called **arguments** of the function and constitute its input data. For example, the following expressions are used to compute the square root of the arguments 4., 17.0, 25., 1043.29, and 6.4516, respectively.

```
sqrt(4.)
sqrt(17.0)
sqrt(25.)
sqrt(1043.29)
sqrt(6.4516)
```

Note that the argument to the `sqrt` function must be a real value. This is an example of C++'s overloading capabilities. Function overloading permits the same function name to be defined for different argument data types. In this case there are really three square root functions named sqrt—defined for `float`, `double`, and `long-double` arguments. The correct sqrt function is called, depending on the type of value given it. The `sqrt` function determines the square root of its argument and returns the result as a double. The values returned by the previous expressions are

Expression	Value Returned
sqrt(4)	
sqrt(17.0)	4.12311
sqrt(25)	
sqrt(1043.29)	32.3
sqrt(6.4516)	2.54

FIGURE 3.3 *Passing Data to the* sqrt() *Function*

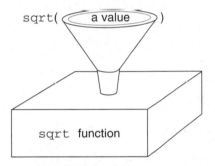

Table 3.1 lists the more commonly used mathematical functions provided in C++. To access these functions in a program requires that the mathematical header file named `cmath`, which contains appropriate declarations for the mathematical function, be included with the function. This is done by placing the following preprocessor statement at the top of any program using a mathematical function:

        #include <cmath> ◄——— no semicolon

Although some of the mathematical functions listed require more than one argument, all functions, by definition, can directly return at most one value. Furthermore, all of the functions listed are overloaded: This means the same function name can be used with integer and real arguments. Table 3.2 lists the values returned by selected functions in response to sample arguments.

TABLE 3.1 *Common C++ Functions*

Function Name	Description	Returned Value
abs(x)	absolute value	same data type as argument
pow(x1,x2)	x1 raised to the x2 power	data type of argument x1
sqrt(x)	square root of x	double
sin(x)	sine of x (x in radians)	double
cos(x)	cosine of x (x in radians)	double
tan(x)	tangent of x (x in radians)	double
log(x)	natural logarithm of x	double
log10(x)	common log (base 10) of x	double
exp(x)	e raised to the x power	double

Each time a mathematical function is used, it is called into action by giving the name of the function and passing any data to it within the parentheses following the function's name (see Figure 3.4).

The arguments that are passed to a function need not be single constants. An expression can also be an argument, provided that the expression can be computed to yield a value of the required data type. For example, the following arguments are valid for the given functions:

```
sqrt(4.0 + 5.3 * 4.0)        abs(2.3 * 4.6)
sqrt(16.0 * 2.0 - 6.7)       sin(theta - phi)
sqrt(x * y - z/3.2)          cos(2.0 * omega)
```

TABLE 3.2 *Selected Examples of Functions*

Example	Returned Value
abs(-7.362)	7.362
abs(-3)	3
pow(2.0,5.0)	32
pow(10,3)	1000
log(18.697)	2.92836
log10(18.697)	1.27177
exp(-3.2)	

FIGURE 3.4 *Using and Passing Data to a Function*

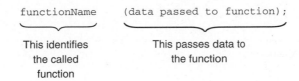

The expressions in parentheses are first evaluated to yield a specific value. Thus, values would have to be assigned to the variables theta, phi, x, y, z, and omega before their use in the foregoing expressions. After the value of the argument is calculated, it is passed to the function.

Functions may be included as part of larger expressions, as in the following example:

```
1 * sqrt(1.5 * 10.0 - 9.0) - 2.0 =
        4 * sqrt(36.0) - 2.0 =
             4 * 6.0 - 2.0 =
                 24.0 - 2.0 = 22.0
```

The step-by-step evaluation of an expression such as

```
3.0 * sqrt(5 * 33 - 13.71) / 5
```

is

Step	Result
1. Perform multiplication in argument	`3.0 * sqrt(165 - 13.71) / 5`
2. Complete argument calculation	`3.0 * sqrt(151.29) / 5`
3. Return a function value	`3.0 * 12.3 / 5`
4. Perform the multiplication	`36.9 / 5`
5. Perform the division	`7.38`

Program 3.5 illustrates the use of the sqrt function to determine the time it takes a ball to hit the ground after it has been dropped from an 800-foot tower. The mathematical formula used to calculate the time, in seconds, that it takes to fall a given distance, in feet, is

$$time = sqrt(2 * distance / g)$$

where g is the gravitational constant, which is equal to 32.2 ft/sec^2.

Program 3.5

```cpp
#include <iostream> // this line may be placed second instead of first
#include <cmath>    // this line may be placed first instead of second
using namespace std;

int main()
{
  int height;
  double time;

  height = 800;
  time = sqrt(2 * height / 32.2);
  cout << "It will take " << time << " seconds "
       << "to fall " << height << " feet.\n";
  return 0;
}
```

The output produced by Program 3.5 is:

```
It will take 7.04907 seconds to fall 800 feet.
```

As used in Program 3.5, the value returned by the `sqrt` function is assigned to the variable `time`. In addition to being assigned to a variable, a function's returned value may be included within a larger expression or even used as an argument to another function. For example, the expression

```
sqrt(pow(abs(num1),num2))
```

is valid. Because parentheses are present, the computation proceeds from the inner pair of parentheses to the outer pair. Thus the absolute value of `num1` is computed first and used as an argument to the `pow()` function. The value returned by the `pow()` function is then used as an argument to the `sqrt()` function.

Casts

We have already seen the conversion of an operand's data type within mixed-mode arithmetic expressions (Section 2.2) and across assignment operators (Section 3.1). In addition to these implicit data type conversions that are automatically made within mixed-mode arithmetic and assignment expressions, C++ also provides for explicit user-specified type conversions. The operator used to force the conversion of a value to another type is the **cast** operator. C++ provides both a compile-time and run-time cast operator.

The compile-time cast is a unary operator having the syntax

$$dataType(expression)$$

where *dataType* is the desired data type that the *expression* within parentheses will be converted to. For example, the expression

```
int (a * b)
```

ensures that the value of the expression a * b is converted to an integer value.[6]
In a run-time cast, the requested type conversion is checked at run-time, and is only applied if the conversion results in a valid value. Although four different types of run-time casts are available, the most commonly used cast and the one corresponding to the compile-time cast has the syntax

```
staticCast<dataType>(expression)
```

For example, the run-time cast staticCast<int>(a*b) is equivalent to the compile-time cast int(a * b).

▌ EXERCISES 3.2

1. Write function calls to determine each of the following:
   a. the square root of 6.37
   b. the square root of $x - y$
   c. the sine of 30 degrees
   d. the sine of 60 degrees
   e. the absolute value of $a^2 - b^2$
   f. the value of e raised to the third power
2. For $a = 10.6$, $b = 13.9$, and $c = -3.42$, determine the value of each of the following:
   a. int(a)
   b. int(b)
   c. int(c)
   d. int(a + b)
   e. int(a) + b + c
   f. int(a + b) + c
   g. int(a + b + c)
   h. double(int (a)) + b
   i. double(int (a + b))
   j. abs(a) + abs(b)
   k. sqrt(abs(a - b))

---

[6] The C type cast syntax, in this case (int)(a*b), where the parentheses are placed around the keyword int, also works in C++.

3. Write C++ statements for the following:

a. $c = \sqrt{a^2 + b^2}$

b. $p = \sqrt{|m - n|}$

c. $sum = \dfrac{a(r^n - 1)}{r - 1}$

4. Write, compile, and execute a C++ program that calculates and returns the fourth root of the number 81, which is 3. When you have verified that your program works correctly, use it to determine the fourth root of 1,728.896400. Your program should make use of the sqrt function.

5. Write, compile, and execute a C++ program that calculates the distance between two points whose coordinates are (7, 12) and (3, 9). Use the fact that the distance between two points having coordinates $(x1, y1)$ and $(x2, y2)$ is $distance = sqrt([x1 - x2]^2 + [y1 - y2]^2)$. When you have verified that your program works correctly by calculating the distance between the two points manually, use your program to determine the distance between the points (−12, −15) and (22, 5).

6. A model of worldwide population after 2000, in billions of people, is given by the equation

$$Population = 6.0e^{.02\,[Year\,-\,2000]}$$

Using this formula, write, compile, and execute a C++ program to estimate the worldwide population in the year 2010. Verify the result displayed by your program by calculating the answer manually. After you have verified that your program is working correctly, use it to estimate the world's population in the year 2020.

7. Although we have been concentrating on integer and real arithmetic, C++ allows characters and integers to be added or subtracted. This can be done because C++ always converts a character to an equivalent integer value whenever a character is used in an arithmetic expression (the decimal value of each character can be found in Appendix B). Thus characters and integers can be freely mixed in arithmetic expressions. For example, if your computer uses the ASCII code, the expression 'a' + 1 equals 98 and 'z' - 1 equals 121. These values can be converted back into characters by using the cast operator. Thus char ('a' + 1) = 'b' and char ('z' - 1) = 'y'. Similarly, char ('A' + 1) is 'B' and char ('Z' - 1) is 'Y'. With this as background, determine the character results of the following expressions (assume that all characters are stored using the ASCII code).

a. char ('m' - 5)   e. ('b' - 'a')
b. char ('m' + 5)   f. ('g' - 'a' + 1)
c. char ('G' + 6)   g. ('G' -'A' + 1)
d. char ('G' - 6)

8. a. The table in Appendix B lists the integer values corresponding to each letter stored using the ASCII code. Note that in this table, the uppercase letters consist of contiguous codes starting with an integer value of 65 for the letter A and ending with 90 for the letter Z. Similarly, the lowercase letters begin with the integer value of 97 for the letter a

and end with 122 for the letter z. With this as background, determine the character value of the expressions char ('A' + 32) and char ('Z' + 32).

b. Using Appendix B, determine the integer value of the expression 'a' – 'A'.

c. Using the results of Exercises 8a and 8b, determine the character value of the following expression, where *uppercase letter* can be any uppercase letter from A to Z.

```
char (uppercase letter + 'a' - 'A')
```

3.3   Interactive KeyBoard Input

Data for programs that are going to be executed only once may be included directly in the program. For example, if we wanted to multiply the numbers 30.0 and 0.05, we could use Program 3.6.

Program 3.6

```cpp
#include <iostream>
using namespace std;

int main()
{
  double num1, num2, product;

  num1 = 30.0;
  num2 = 0.05;
  product = num1 * num2;
  cout << "30.0 times 0.05 is " << product << endl;

  return 0;
}
```

The output displayed by Program 3.6 is

```
30.0 times 0.05 is 1.5
```

Program 3.6 can be shortened, as illustrated in Program 3.7. Both programs, however, suffer from the same basic problem: They must be rewritten in order to multiply different numbers. Neither program allows us to enter different numbers to be operated on.

Program 3.7

```cpp
#include <iostream>
using namespace std;

int main()
{

   cout << "30.0 times 0.05 is " << 30.0 * 0.05 << endl;

   return 0;
}
```

Except that they give the programmer practice in writing, entering, and running the program, programs that do the same calculation only once, on the same set of numbers, are clearly not very useful. After all, it is simpler to use a calculator to multiply two numbers than to enter and run either Program 3.6 or Program 3.7.

This section presents the `cin` object, which is used to enter data into a program while it is executing. Just as the `cout` object displays a copy of the value stored inside a variable, the `cin` object allows the user to enter a value at the terminal (see Figure 3.5). The value is then stored directly in a variable.

When a statement such as `cin >> num1;` is encountered, the computer stops program execution and accepts data from the keyboard. When a data item is typed, the `cin` object stores the item in the variable listed after the extraction ("get from") operator, `>>`. The program then continues execution with the next statement after the call to `cin`. To see this, consider Program 3.8.

FIGURE 3.5 *cin Is Used to Enter Data; cout Is Used to Display Data*

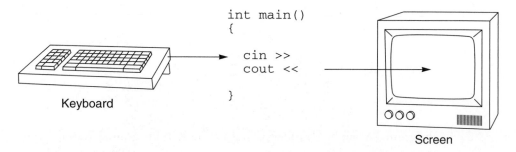

INT MAIN()
{

cout << "Jeffrey Perkin";
cout << "2701 Homestead Rd.), Apt 104"
cout << "Chapel Hill, NC"

cout << left << setw(10) << "Name:" << _____
cout << left << setw(10) << "Address:" <<
cout << left << setw(10) << "City"
        "State"
        "Zip Code"
        "Gender"

Pg 23-24 1a, 2a, 3a

• bj. symbol

Output

cout << "name: ____ ";

address: "

city:

state:

zipcode:

gender:

1a #include <iostream>
    using namespace std;

p 28-29 1a 2a 2b 2c

Program 3.8

```cpp
#include <iostream>
using namespace std;

int main()
{
  double num1, num2, product;

  cout << "Please type in a number: ";
  cin  >> num1;
  cout << "Please type in another number: ";
  cin  >> num2;
  product = num1 * num2;
  cout << num1 << " times " << num2 << " is " << product << endl;

  return 0;
}
```

The first cout statement in Program 3.8 prints a string that tells the person at the terminal what should be typed. When an output string is used in this manner, it is called a **prompt.** In this case the prompt tells the user to type a number. The computer then executes the next statement, which is a call to cin. The cin object puts the computer into a temporary pause (or wait) state for as long as it takes the user to type a value. Then the user signals the cin object that the data entry is finished by pressing the return key after the value has been typed. The entered value is stored in the variable to the right of the extraction symbol, and the computer is taken out of its paused state. Program execution then proceeds with the next statement, which in Program 3.8 is another cout activation. This call causes the next message to be displayed. The second cin statement again puts the computer into a temporary wait state while the user types a second value. This second number is stored in the variable num2.

The following sample run was made using Program 3.8.

```
Please type in a number: 30
Please type in another number: 0.05
30 times 0.05 is 1.5
```

In Program 3.8, each time cin is invoked, it is used to store one value in a variable. The cin object, however, can be used to enter and store as many values as there are extraction symbols, >>, and variables to hold the entered data. For example, the statement

```
cin >> num1 >> num2;
```

results in two values being read from the terminal and assigned to the variables num1 and num2. If the data entered at the terminal were

```
0.052    245.79
```

the variables num1 and num2 would contain the values 0.052 and 245.79, respectively. Note that when we are entering numbers such as 0.052 and 245.79, there must be at least one space between the numbers. The space between the entered numbers clearly indicates where one number ends and the next begins. Inserting more than one space between the numbers has no effect on cin.

The same spacing is applicable to entering character data; that is, the extraction operator, >>, will skip blank spaces and store the next nonblank character in a character variable. For example, in response to the statements

```
char ch1, ch2, ch3; // declare three character variables
cin >> ch1 >> ch2 >> ch3; // accept three characters
```

the input

```
a     b  c
```

causes the letter a to be stored in the variable ch1, the letter b to be stored in the variable ch2, and the letter c to be stored in the variable ch3. Because a character variable can be used only to store one character, the input

```
abc
```

can also be used.

Any number of statements using the cin object may be made in a program, and any number of values may be input using a single cin statement. Program 3.9 illustrates using the cin object to input three numbers from the keyboard. The program then calculates and displays the average of the numbers entered.

The following sample run was made using Program 3.9.

```
Enter three integer numbers: 22 56 73
The average of the numbers is 50.3333
```

Program 3.9

```cpp
#include <iostream>
using namespace std;

int main()
{
    int num1, num2, num3;
    double average;

    cout << "Enter three integer numbers: ";
    cin  >> num1 >> num2 >> num3;
    average = (num1 + num2 + num3) / 3.0;
    cout << "The average of the numbers is " << average << endl;

    return 0;
}
```

Note that the data typed at the keyboard for this sample run consist of the input

$$22 \quad 56 \quad 73$$

In response to this stream of input, Program 3.9 stores the value 22 in the variable num1, the value 56 in the variable num2, and the value 73 in the variable num3 (see Figure 3.6). Because the average of three integer numbers can be a floating-point number, the variable average, which is used to store the average, is declared as a double-precision variable. Note also that the parentheses are needed in the assignment statement average = (num1 + num2 + num3) / 3.0;. Without these parentheses, the only value that would be divided by 3 would be the integer in num3 (because division has a higher precedence than addition).

The cin extraction operation, like the cout insertion operation, is "clever" enough to make a few data type conversions. For example, if an integer is entered in place of a double-precision number, the integer will be converted to the correct data type.[7] Similarly, if a double-precision number is entered when an integer is expected, only the integer part of the number will be used. For example, assume the following numbers are typed in response to the statement

---

[7] Strictly speaking, what comes in from the keyboard is not any data type, such as an int or a double, but is simply a sequence of characters. The extraction operation handles the conversion from the character sequence to a defined data type.

`cin >> num1 >> num2 >> num3;` where `num1` and `num3` have been declared as double-precision variables and `num2` is an integer variable.

56   22.879   33.923

The 56 will be converted to 56.0 and stored in the variable `num1`. The extraction operation continues extracting data from the input stream sent to it, expecting an integer value. As far as `cin` is concerned, the decimal point after the 22 in the number 22.879 indicates the end of an integer and the start of a decimal number. Thus the number 22 is assigned to `num2`. Continuing to process its input stream, `cin` takes the .879 as the next double-precision number and assigns it to `num3`. As far as `cin` is concerned, 33.923 is extra input and is ignored. If, though, you do not initially type enough data, the `cin` object will continue to make the computer pause until sufficient data have been entered.

FIGURE 3.6 *Inputting Data into the Variables* `num1`, `num2`, *and* `num3`

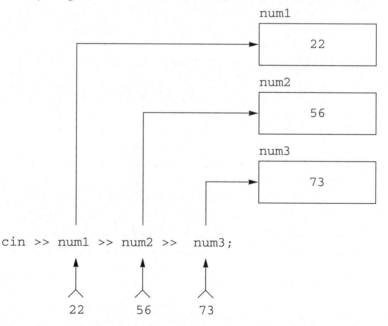

A First Look at User-Input Validation

A well-constructed program should validate user input and ensure that a program does not either crash or produce nonsensical output due to unexpected input. The term **validate** means checking that the entered value matches the data type of the variable that the value is assigned to within a `cin` statement, and that the value is within an acceptable range of values appropriate to the application. Programs that detect and respond effectively to unexpected user input are formally referred to as **robust programs** and informally as "bullet-proof" programs. One of your jobs as a programmer is to produce such programs. As written, both Programs 3.8 and 3.9 are not robust programs. Let's see why.

The first problem with these programs becomes evident when a user enters a non-numerical value. For example, consider the following sample run using Program 3.9.

```
Enter three integer numbers: 10 20.68 20
The average of the numbers is -2.86331e+008
```

This output occurs because the conversion of the second input number results in the integer value 20 assigned to num2 and the value –858993460 assigned to num3. This last value corresponds to an invalid character, the decimal point, being assigned to an expected integer value. The average of the numbers 10, 20, and –858993460 is then computed correctly as –286331143.3, which is displayed in scientific notation with six significant digits as –2.86331e+008. As far as the average user is concerned, this will be reported as a program error. This same problem occurs whenever a noninteger value is entered for either of the first two inputs (it does not occur for any numerical value entered as the third input, because the integer part of the last input is accepted and the remaining input ignored). As a programmer your initial response may be "The program clearly asks you to enter integer values." This, however, is the response of a very inexperienced programmer. Professional programmers understand that it is their responsibility to ensure that a program anticipates and appropriately handles any and all input that a user can possibly enter. This is accomplished by both thinking about what can go wrong with your own program as you develop it and then having another person or group thoroughly test the program.

The basic approach to handling invalid data input is referred to as **user-input validation**, which means validating the entered data either during or immediately after the data have been entered, and then providing the user with a way of re-entering any invalid data. User-input validation is an essential part of any commercially viable program, and if done correctly, it will protect a program from attempting to process data that can cause computational problems. We will see how to provide this type of validation after C++'s selection and repetition statements have been presented in Chapters 4 and 5, respectively.

▌ EXERCISES 3.3

1. For the following declaration statements, write a statement using the `cin` object that will cause the computer to pause while the appropriate data are typed by the user.
  a. int firstnum;
  b. double grade;

c. `double secnum;`

d. `char keyval;`

e. `int month, years;`
   `double average;`

f. `char ch;`
   `int num1, num2;`
   `double grade1, grade2;`

g. `double interest, principal, capital;`
   `double price, yield;`

h. `char ch, letter1, letter2;`
   `int num1, num2, num3;`

i. `double temp1, temp2, temp3;`
   `double volts1, volts2;`

2. Write, compile, and execute a C++ program that displays the following prompt:

`Enter the radius of a circle:`

After accepting a value for the radius, your program should calculate and display the area of the circle. (**Note:** *area = 3.1416 * radius².*) For testing purposes, verify your program by using a test input radius of 3 inches. After manually determining that the result produced by your program is correct, use your program to complete the following table:

Radius (in.)	Area (sq. in.)
1.0	
1.5	
2.0	
2.5	
3.0	
3.5	

3. *a.* Write a C++ program that first displays the following prompt:

`Enter the temperature in degrees Celsius:`

Have your program accept a value entered from the keyboard and convert the temperature entered to degrees Fahrenheit, using the formula *Fahrenheit = (9.0 / 5.0) * Celsius + 32.0.* Your program should then display the temperature in degrees Celsius, using an appropriate output message.

b. Compile and execute the program written for Exercise 3a. Verify your program by calculating, by hand and then using your program, the Fahrenheit equivalent of the following test data:

Test data set 1:   0 degrees Celsius
Test data set 2:   50 degrees Celsius
Test data set 3:   100 degrees Celsius

When you are sure your program is working correctly, use it to complete the following table:

Degrees Celsius	Degrees Fahrenheit
45	
50	
55	
60	
65	
70	

4. a. Write a C++ program that displays the following prompts:

```
Enter the length of the room:
Enter the width of the room:
```

After each prompt is displayed, your program should use a `cin` object call to accept data from the keyboard for the displayed prompt. After the width of the room is entered, your program should calculate and display the area of the room. The area displayed should be calculated using the equation *area = length * width* and should be included in an appropriate message.

b. Check the area displayed by the program written for Exercise 4a by calculating the result manually.

5. a. Write, compile, and execute a C++ program that displays the following prompts:

```
Enter the miles driven:
Enter the gallons of gas used:
```

After each prompt is displayed, your program should use an input statement to accept data from the keyboard for the displayed prompt. After the "gallons of gas used" number has been entered, your program should calculate and display the miles per gallon obtained. This value should be calculated using the equation *miles per gallon = miles / gallons used* and should be included in an appropriate message. Verify your program using the following test data:

Test data set 1:   Miles = 276, Gas = 10 gallons
Test data set 2:   Miles = 200, Gas = 15.5 gallons

When you have completed your verification, use your program to complete the following table:

Miles Driven	Gallons Used	Miles per Gallon
250	16.00	
275	18.00	
312	19.54	
296	17.39	

b. For the program written for Exercise 5a, determine how many verification runs are required to ensure that the program is working correctly, and give a reason supporting your answer.

6. *a.* Write a C++ program that displays the following prompts:

```
Enter the length of the swimming pool:
Enter the width of the swimming pool:
Enter the average depth of the swimming pool:
```

After each prompt is displayed, your program should use a cin object call to accept data from the keyboard for the displayed prompt. After the depth of the swimming pool is entered, your program should calculate and display the volume of the pool. The volume should be calculated using the equation *volume = length * width * average depth* and should be included in an appropriate message.

b. Check the volume displayed by the program written for Exercise 6a by calculating the result manually.

7. *a.* Write a C++ program that displays the following prompts:

```
Enter a number:
Enter a second number:
Enter a third number:
Enter a fourth number:
```

After each prompt is displayed, your program should use a cin object call to accept a number from the keyboard for the displayed prompt. After the fourth number has been entered, your program should calculate and display the average of the numbers. The average should be included in an appropriate message.

b. Check the average displayed for the program written in Exercise 7a by calculating the result manually.

c. Repeat Exercise 7a, making sure that you use the same variable name, number, for each number input. Also use the variable sum for the sum of the numbers. (*Hint:* To do this, you must use the statement sum = sum + number; after each number is accepted. Review the material on accumulating presented in Section 3.1.)

8. Write a C++ program that prompts the user to type in a number. Have your program accept the number as an integer and immediately display the integer using a cout object call. Run your program three times. The first time you run the program enter a valid integer number, the second time enter a number that contains a decimal point, and the third time enter a character. Using the output display, see what number your program actually accepted from the data you entered.

9. Repeat Exercise 8, but have your program declare the variable used to store the number as a double-precision variable. Run the program three times. The first time enter an integer, the second time enter a number that has a decimal point, and the third time enter a character. Using the output display, keep track of what number your program actually accepted from the data you typed in. What happened, if anything, and why?

10. Repeat Exercise 8, but have your program declare the variable used to store the number as a double-precision variable. Run the program four times. The first time enter an integer, the second time enter a decimal number that has fewer than six decimal places, the third time enter a number that has more than six decimal places, and the fourth time enter a character. Using the output display, keep track of what number your program actually accepted from the data you typed in. What happened, if anything, and why?

11. a. Why do you think successful application programs contain extensive data input validity checks? (*Hint:* Review Exercises 8, 9, and 10.)

  b. What do you think is the difference between a data type check and a data reasonableness check?

  c. Assume that a program requests that a month, day, and year be entered by the user. What are some checks that could be made on the data entered?

12. Program 3.8 prompts the user to input two numbers, where the first value entered is stored in num1 and the second value is stored in num2. Using this program as a starting point, write a program that swaps the values stored in the two variables.

3.4   Symbolic Constants

Literal data are any data within a program that explicitly identify themselves. For example, the constants 2 and 3.1416 in the assignment statement

```
circum = 2 * 3.1416 * radius;
```

are literal data, or literals, for short, because they are literally included directly in the statement. Additional examples of literals are contained in the following C++ assignment statements. See if you can identify them.

```
perimeter = 2 * length * width;
        y = (5 * p) / 7.2;
 salestax = 0.05 * purchase;
```

The literals are the numbers 2, 5 and 7.2, and 0.05 in the first, second, and third statements, respectively.

Quite frequently, literal data used within a program have a more general meaning that is recognized outside the context of the program. Examples of these types of constants include the number 3.1416, which is π accurate to four decimal places; 32.2 ft/sec^2, which is the gravitational constant; and the number 2.71828, which is Euler's number accurate to five decimal places.

The meanings of certain other constants that appear in a program are defined strictly in the context of the application being programmed. For example, in a program used to determine bank interest charges, the interest rate would typically appear in a number of different places throughout the program. Similarly, in a program used to calculate taxes, the tax rate might appear in many individual instructions. Programmers refer to numbers such as these as **magic numbers.** By themselves the numbers are ordinary, but in the context of a particular application they have a special ("magical") meaning. Frequently, the same magic number appears repeatedly within the same program. This recurrence of the same constant throughout a program is a potential source of error should the constant have to be changed. For example, if either the interest rate or the sales tax rate changed, as such rates are likely to do, the programmer would have the cumbersome task of changing the value everywhere it appeared in the program. Such multiple changes are subject to error: If just one value is overlooked and remains unchanged, the result obtained when the program is run will be incorrect, and the source of the error will be difficult to locate.

To avoid the problem of having a magic number spread throughout a program in many places, and to permit clear identification of more universal constants, such as π, C++ allows the programmer to give these constants their own symbolic names. Then, instead of the number being used throughout the program, the symbolic name is used instead. If the number ever has to be changed, the change need only be made once, at the point where the symbolic name is equated to the actual number value. Equating numbers to symbolic names is accomplished by means of a `const` declaration qualifier. The `const` qualifier specifies that the declared identifier can only be read after it is initialized; it cannot be changed. Here are three examples using this qualifier:

```
const float PI = 3.1416f;
const double SALESTAX = 0.05;
const int MAXNUM = 100;
```

The first declaration statement creates a floating-point variable named `PI` and initializes it with the value 3.1416. The second declaration statement creates the double-precision constant named `SALESTAX` and initializes it to 0.05. Finally, the third declaration creates an integer constant named `MAXNUM` and initializes it with the value 100.

Once a `const` identifier is created and initialized, *the value stored in it cannot be changed.* Thus, for all practical purposes, the name of the constant and its value are linked together for the duration of the program that declares them.

Although we have typed the `const` identifiers in uppercase letters, lowercase letters could have been used. It is customary in C++, however, to use uppercase letters for `const` identifiers to make them easy to identify. Then, whenever a programmer sees uppercase letters in a program, he or she knows that the value of the constant cannot be changed within the program.

Once declared, a `const` identifier can be used in any C++ statement in place of the number it represents. For example, the assignment statements

```
circum = 2 * PI * radius;
amount = SALESTAX * purchase;
```

are both valid. These statements must, of course, appear after the declarations for all their variables and constants. Because a const declaration effectively equates a constant value to an identifier, and the identifier can be used as a direct replacement for its initializing constant, such identifiers are commonly referred to as **symbolic constants** or **named constants.** We shall use these terms interchangeably.

Placement of Statements

At this stage we have introduced a variety of statement types. The general rule in C++ for statement placement is simply that a variable or symbolic constant must be declared before it can be used. Although this rule permits both preprocessor directives and declaration statements to be placed throughout a program, doing so results in a very poor program structure. As a matter of good programming form, the following statement order should be used:

```
preprocessor directives

int main()
{
   symbolic constants
   variable declarations
   other executable statements

   return value
}
```

As new statement types are introduced, we will expand this placement structure to accommodate them. Note that comment statements can be freely intermixed anywhere within this basic structure.

Program 3.10 illustrates the use of a symbolic constant to calculate the sales tax due on a purchased item.

The following sample run was made using Program 3.10:

```
Enter the amount purchased: 36.00
The sales tax is 1.80
The total bill is 37.80
```

Although we have used the const qualifier to construct symbolic constants, we will encounter this data type once again in Chapter 13, where we will show that it is useful as a function argument in ensuring that the argument is not modified within the function.

Program 3.10

```cpp
#include <iostream>
#include <iomanip>
using namespace std;

int main()
{
  const double SALESTAX = 0.05;
  double amount, taxes, total;

  cout << "\nEnter the amount purchased: ";
  cin  >> amount;
  taxes = SALESTAX * amount;
  total = amount + taxes;
  cout << setiosflags(ios::fixed)
       << setiosflags(ios::showpoint)
       << setprecision(2);
  cout << "The sales tax is " << setw(4) << taxes << endl;
  cout << "The total bill is " << setw(5) << total << endl;

  return 0;
}
```

▌ EXERCISES 3.4

Determine the purpose of the programs given in Exercises 1 through 3. Then rewrite each program using a symbolic constant for the appropriate literals.

1.
```cpp
#include <iostream>
using namespace std;
int main()
{
  double radius, circum;

  cout << "Enter a radius: ";
  cin  >> radius;
  circum = 2.0 * 3.1416 * radius;
  cout << "\nThe circumference of the circle is " << circum << endl;

  return 0;
}
```

2.
```cpp
#include <iostream>
using namespace std;
int main()
{
  double prime, amount, interest;

  prime = .08;  // prime interest rate
  cout << "Enter the amount: ";
  cin  >> amount;
  interest = prime * amount;
  cout << "The interest earned is " << interest << endl;

  return 0;
}
```
3.
```cpp
#include <iostream>
using namespace std;
int main()
{
  double fahren, celsius;

  cout << "Enter a temperature in degrees Fahrenheit: ";
  cin  >> fahren;
  celsius = (5.0/9.0) * (fahren - 32.0);
  cout << "The equivalent Celsius temperature is "
       << celsius << endl;

  return 0;
}
```

3.5   Common Programming Errors

In using the material presented in this chapter, be aware of the following possible errors.

1. Forgetting to assign or initialize values for all variables before the variables are used in an expression. Such values can be assigned by assignment statements, initialized within a declaration statement, or assigned interactively by entering values using the cin object.

2. Applying either the increment or the decrement operator to an expression. For example, the expression

$$(count + n)++$$

is incorrect. The increment and decrement operators can be applied only to individual variables.

3. Forgetting to separate all variables passed to `cin` with an extraction symbol, `>>`.

4. A more exotic and less common error occurs when the increment and decrement operators are used with variables that appear more than once in the same expression. This error occurs because C++ does not specify the order in which operands are accessed within an expression. For example, the value assigned to `result` in the statement

```
result = i + i++;
```

is computer-dependent. If your computer accesses the first operand, `i`, first, this statement is equivalent to

```
result = 2 * i;
i++;
```

However, if your computer accesses the second operand, `i++`, first, the value of the first operand will be altered before it is used the second time, and the value $2i + 1$ is assigned to `result`. As a general rule, therefore, do not use either the increment or the decrement operator in an expression when the variable it operates on appears more than once in the expression.

3.6   Chapter Summary

1. An expression is a sequence of one or more operands separated by operators. An operand is a constant, a variable, or another expression. A value is associated with an expression.

2. Expressions are evaluated according to the precedence and associativity of the operators used in the expression.

3. The assignment symbol, `=`, is an operator. Expressions using this operator assign a value to a variable, and the expression itself also takes on a value. Because assignment is an operation in C++, multiple uses of the assignment operator are possible in the same expression.

4. The increment operator, `++`, adds 1 to a variable, whereas the decrement operator, `--`, subtracts 1 from a variable. Both of these operators can be used as prefixes or postfixes. In prefix operation, the variable is incremented (or decremented) before its value is used. In postfix operation, the variable is incremented (or decremented) after its value is used.

5. C++ provides library functions for performing square root, logarithmic, and other mathematical computations. Each program that uses one of these mathematical functions must either include the statement `#include c<math>` or have a function declaration for the mathematical function before it is called.

6. Every mathematical library function operates on its arguments to calculate a single value. To use a library function effectively, you must know what the function does, the name of the function, the number and data types of the arguments expected by the function, and the data type of the returned value.

7. Data passed to a function are called arguments of the function. Arguments are passed to a library function by including each argument, separated by commas, within the parentheses following the function's name. Each function has its own requirements for the number and data types of the arguments that must be provided.

8. Functions may be included within larger expressions.

9. The `cin` object is used for data input. This object accepts a stream of data from the keyboard and assigns the data to variables. The general form of a statement using `cin` is

```
cin >> var1 >> var2 . . . >> varn;
```

The extraction symbol, >>, must be used to separate the variable names.

10. When a `cin` statement is encountered, the computer temporarily suspends statement execution until sufficient data have been entered for the number of variables contained in the `cin` function.

11. It is good programming practice to display, prior to a `cin` statement, a message that alerts the user to the type and number of data items to be entered. Such a message is called a prompt.

12. Values can be equated to a single constant by using the `const` keyword. This creates a named constant that is read-only after it is initialized within the declaration statement. This declaration has the form

```
const dataType constantName = initialValue;
```

and permits the constant to be used instead of the initial value anywhere in the program after the declaration. Generally, such declarations are placed before a program's variable declarations.

Selection

The term **flow of control** refers to the order in which a program's statements are executed. Unless directed otherwise, the normal flow of control for all programs is sequential. This means that the statements are executed in sequence, one after another, in the order in which they are placed within the program.

Both selection and repetition statements allow the programmer to alter the normal sequential flow of control. As their names imply, selection statements make it possible to select which statement, from a well-defined set, will be executed next, and repetition statements make it possible to go back and repeat a set of statements. In this chapter we present C++'s selection statements. Because selection requires choosing between alternatives, we begin this chapter with a description of C++'s selection criteria.

4.1   Relational Expressions

Besides providing addition, subtraction, multiplication, and division capabilities, all computers have the ability to compare numbers. Because many seemingly "intelligent" decision-making situations can be reduced to the level of choosing between two values, a computer's comparison capability can be used to create a remarkable intelligence-like facility.

The expressions used to compare operands are called **relational expressions**. A **simple relational expression** consists of a relational operator connecting two variable and/or constant operands, as shown in Figure 4.1. The relational operators available in C++ are given in Table 4.1. These relational operators may be used with integer, Boolean, double, or character data, but they must be typed exactly as given in Table 4.1. Thus the following examples are all valid:

```
age > 40          length <= 50          temp > 98.6
   3 < 4             flag == done       idNum == 682
day != 5            2.0 > 3.3           hours > 40
```

FIGURE 4.1   *Anatomy of a Simple Relational Expression*

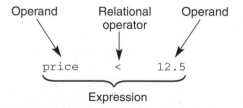

TABLE 4.1   *Relational Operators in C++*

Relational Operator	Meaning	Example
<	less than	`age < 30`
>	greater than	`height > 6.2`
<=	less than or equal to	`taxable <= 20000`
>=	greater than or equal to	`temp >= 98.6`
==	equal to	`grade == 100`
!=	not equal to	`number != 250`

The following are invalid:

```
length =< 50    // incorrect symbol
2.0 >> 3.3      // invalid relational operator
flag = = done   // spaces are not allowed
```

Relational expressions are sometimes called **conditions**, and we will use both terms to refer to these expressions. Like all C++ expressions, relational expressions are evaluated to yield a numerical result.[1] *A condition that we would interpret as true evaluates to an integer value of 1, and a false condition results in an integer value of 0.* For example, because the relationship 3 < 4 is always true, this expression has a value of 1, and because the relationship 2.0 > 3.3 is always false, the value of the expression itself is 0. This can be verified by using the statements

```
cout << "The value of 3 < 4 is " << (3 < 4);
cout << "\nThe value of 2.0 > 3.0 is " << (2.0 > 3.0);
```

which result in the display

```
The value of 3 < 4 is 1
The value of 2.0 > 3.0 is 0
```

The value of a relational expression such as `hours > 40` depends on the value stored in the variable `hours`.

In a C++ program, a relational expression's value is not so important as the interpretation C++ places on the value when the expression is used as part of a

---

[1] In this regard, both C and C++ differ from other high-level programming languages that yield a Boolean (true, false) result.

selection statement. In these statements, which are presented in the next section, we will see that a zero value is used by C++ to represent a false condition and that any nonzero value is used to represent a true condition. The selection of which statement to execute next is then based on the value obtained.

In addition to numerical operands, character data can also be compared by using relational operators. For example, in the ASCII code the letter 'A' is stored using a code that has a lower numerical value than the letter 'B', the code for a 'B' is lower in value than the code for a 'C', and so on. For character sets coded in this manner, the conditions listed in the following table are evaluated as shown.

Expression	Value	Interpretation
'A' > 'C'	0	false
'D' <= 'Z'	1	true
'E' == 'F'	0	false
'g' >= 'm'	0	false
'b' != 'c'	1	true
'a' == 'A'	0	false

Comparing letters is essential in alphabetizing names or using characters to select a particular choice in decision-making situations.

Logical Operators

In addition to using simple relational expressions as conditions, we can create more complex conditions by using the logical operations AND, OR, and NOT. These operations are represented by the symbols &&, ||, and !, respectively.

When the AND operator, &&, is used with two simple expressions, the condition is true only if both individual expressions are true by themselves. Thus the compound condition

```
(age > 40) && (term < 10)
```

is true (has a value of 1) only if age is greater than 40 and term is less than 10. Because relational operators have a higher precedence than logical operators, the parentheses in this logical expression could have been omitted.

The OR operator, ||, is also applied between two expressions. When using the logical OR operator, the condition is satisfied if either one of the two expressions is true or both are true. Thus the compound condition

$$(age > 40) \mid\mid (term < 10)$$

is true if age is greater than 40, if term is less than 10, or if both conditions are true. Again, the parentheses around the relational expressions are included to make the expression easier to read. Because relational operators have a higher precedence than logical operators, the same evaluation would be made even if the parentheses were omitted.

For the declarations

```
int i,j;
double a,b,complete;
```

the following represent valid conditions:

```
a > b
(i == j) || (a < b) || complete
(a/b > 5) && (i <= 20)
```

Before these conditions can be evaluated, the values of a, b, i, j, and complete must be known. For the assignments

```
        a = 12.0;
        b = 2.0;
        i = 15;
        j = 30;
complete = 0.0;
```

the previous expressions yield the following results:

Expression	Value	Interpretation
a > b	1	true
(i == j) || (a < b) || complete	0	false
(a/b > 5) && (i <= 20)	1	true

The NOT operation is used to change an expression to its opposite state; that is, if the expression has any nonzero value (true), then !expression produces a zero value (false). If an expression is false to begin with (has a zero value), then !expression is true and evaluates to 1. For example, if the number 26 is stored in the variable age, then the expression (age > 40) has a value of zero (it is false), and the expression !(age > 40) has a value of 1. Because the NOT operator is used with only one operand, it is a unary operator.

The relational and logical operators have a hierarchy of execution similar to that of the arithmetic operators. Table 4.2 shows the precedence of these operators in relation to the other operators we have used.

TABLE 4.2   *Precedence of Relational and Logical Operators*

Operator	Associativity
! unary - ++ --	right to left
* / %	left to right
+ -	left to right
< <= > >=	left to right
== !=	left to right
&&	left to right
||	left to right
= += -= *= /=	right to left

The following example illustrates the use of an operator's precedence and associativity to evaluate relational expressions, assuming these declarations:

```
char key = 'm';
int i = 5, j = 7, k = 12;
double x = 22.5;
```

Expression	Equivalent Expression	Value	Interpretation
i + 2 == k - 1	(i + 2) == (k - 1)	0	false
3 * i - j < 22	((3 * i) - j) < 22	1	true
i + 2 * j > k	(i + (2 * j)) > k	1	true
k + 3 <= -j + 3 * i	(k + 3) <= ((-j) + (3*i))	0	false
'a' + 1 == 'b'	('a' + 1) == 'b'	1	true
key - 1 > 'p'	(key - 1) > 'p'	0	false
key + 1 == 'n'	(key + 1) == 'n'	1	true
25 >= x + 1.0	25 >= (x + 1.0)	1	true

As with all expressions, parentheses can be used to alter the assigned operator priority and to improve the readability of relational expressions. By evaluating the expressions within parentheses first, we find that the following compound condition is evaluated as shown.

```
(6 * 3 == 36 / 2)  || (13 < 3 * 3 + 4)  && !(6 - 2 < 5)
        (18 == 18) ||     (13 < 9 + 4)  && !(4 < 5)
                 1 ||       (13 < 13)    && !1
                 1 ||           0        &&  0
                 1 ||           0
                 1
```

A Numerical Accuracy Problem

A subtle numerical accuracy problem related to floating-point and double-precision numbers can occur with C++'s relational expressions. Because of the way computers store these numbers, tests for equality of single-precision and double-precision values and variables using the relational operator == should be avoided.

The reason for this is that many decimal numbers, such as 0.1, cannot be represented exactly in binary using a finite number of bits. Thus, testing for exact equality for such numbers can fail. When equality of noninteger values is desired, it is better to require that the absolute value of the difference between operands be less than some extremely small value. Thus, for real operands, the general expression

$$operand\_1 == operand\_2$$

should be replaced by the condition

$$abs(operand\_1 - operand\_2) < EPSILON$$

where EPSILON can be a named constant set to any acceptably small value, such as 0.0000001.[2] Thus, if the difference between the two operands is less than the value of EPSILON, the two operands are considered essentially equal. For example, if x and y are floating-point variables, a condition such as

$$x/y == 0.35$$

---

[2] Using the abs() function requires inclusion of the cmath file. This is done by placing the preprocessor statement #include <cmath> either immediately before or immediately after the #include <iostream> preprocessor statement. Unix-based systems also require specific inclusion of the math library at compile time with a -lm command line argument.

should be programmed as

$$\text{abs}(x/y - 0.35) < \text{EPSILON}$$

This latter condition ensures that slight inaccuracies in representing noninteger numbers in binary do not affect evaluation of the tested condition.

▌ EXERCISES 4.1

1. Determine the values of the following expressions. Assume a = 5, b = 2, c = 4, d = 6, and e = 3.

   a. a > b   *f.* a * b

   b. a != b   *g.* a % b * c

   c. d % b == c % b   *h.* c % b * a

   d. a * c != d * b   *i.* b % c * a

   e. d * b == c * e

2. Using parentheses, rewrite the following expressions to indicate the correct order of evaluation. Then evaluate each expression, assuming a = 5, b = 2, and c = 4.

   a. a % b * c && c % b * a

   b. a % b * c || c % b * a

   c. b % c * a && a % c * b

   d. b % c * a || a % c * b

3. Write relational expressions to express the following conditions (use variable names of your own choosing).

   a. A person's age is equal to 30.

   b. A person's temperature is greater than 98.6.

   c. A person's height is less than 6 feet.

   d. The current month is 12 (December).

   e. The letter input is m.

   f. A person's age is equal to 30 and the person is taller than 6 feet.

   g. The current day is the 15th day of the 1st month.

   h. A person is older than 50 or has been employed at the company for at least 5 years.

   i. A person's identification number is less than 500 and the person is older than 55.

   j. A length is greater than 2 feet and less than 3 feet.

4. Determine the value of the following expressions, assuming a = 5, b = 2, c = 4, and d = 5.

   a. a == 5

   b. b * d == c * c

   c. d % b * c > 5 || c % b * d < 7

4.2   The **if-else** Statement

The if-else statement directs the computer to select a sequence of one or more instructions on the basis of the result of a comparison. For example, if a New Jersey resident's income is less than $20,000, the applicable state tax rate is 2 percent. If the person's income is greater than $20,000, a different rate is applied to the amount over $20,000. The if-else statement can be used in this situation to determine the actual tax on the basis of whether the income is less than or equal to $20,000. The general form of the if-else statement is

```
if (expression) statement1;
else statement2;
```

The expression is evaluated first. If the value of the expression is nonzero, statement1 is executed. If the value is zero, the statement after the keyword else is executed. Thus, one of the two statements (either statement1 or statement2) is always executed, depending on the value of the expression. Note that the tested expression must be put in parentheses and that a semicolon is placed after each statement.

For clarity, the if-else statement is generally written on four lines, using the form

```
if (expression)  ◄──────────  no semicolon here
    statement1;
else  ◄──────────────────  no semicolon here
    statement2;
```

The form of the if-else statement that is selected typically depends on the lengths of statements 1 and 2. However, when using the second form, do not put a semicolon after the parentheses or the keyword else. The semicolons are placed only at the end of each statement.

As an example, let us write an income tax computation program containing an if-else statement. As previously described, a New Jersey state income tax is assessed at 2 percent of taxable income for incomes less than or equal to $20,000. For taxable incomes greater than $20,000, state taxes are 2.5 percent of the income that exceeds $20,000, plus a fixed amount of $400. The expression to be tested is whether taxable income is less than or equal to $20,000. An appropriate if-else statement for this situation follows.[3]

---

[3] Note that in actual practice, the numerical values in this statement would be defined as named constants.

```
            if (taxable <= 20000.0)
               taxes = 0.02 * taxable;
            else
               taxes = 0.025 * (taxable - 20000.0) + 400.0;
```

Here we have used the relational operator <= to represent the relation "is less than or equal to." If the value of taxable is less than or equal to 20000.0, the condition is true (has a value of 1) and the statement taxes = 0.02 * taxable; is executed. If the condition is not true, the value of the expression is zero, and the statement after the keyword else is executed. Program 4.1 illustrates the use of this statement in a complete program.

 Program 4.1

```cpp
#include <iostream>
#include <iomanip>
using namespace std;

int main()
{
  float taxable, taxes;

  cout << "Please type in the taxable income: ";
  cin  >> taxable;

  if (taxable <= 20000.0)
    taxes = 0.02 * taxable;
  else
    taxes = 0.025 * (taxable - 20000.0) + 400.0;

  cout << setiosflags(ios::fixed)
       << setprecision(2)
       << "Taxes are $ " << taxes << endl;

  return 0;
}
```

Here we inserted a blank line before and after the if-else statement to highlight it in the complete program. We will continue to do this throughout the text to emphasize the statement being presented.

To illustrate selection in action, we ran Program 4.1 twice with different input data. The results were:

```
Please type in the taxable income: 10000.
Taxes are $ 200.00
```

and

```
Please type in the taxable income: 30000.
Taxes are $ 650.00
```

Observe that the taxable income input in the first run of the program was less than $20,000, and the tax was correctly calculated as 2 percent of the number entered. In the second run, the taxable income was more than $20,000, and the else part of the if-else statement was used to yield a correct tax computation of

$$0.025 * (\$30,000. - \$20,000.) + \$400. = \$650.$$

Although any expression can be tested by an if-else statement, only relational expressions are generally used. However, statements such as

```
if (num)
    cout << "Bingo!";
else
    cout << "You lose!";
```

are valid. Because num, by itself, is a valid expression, the message Bingo! is displayed if num has any nonzero value, and the message You lose! is displayed if num has a value of zero.

Compound Statements

Although only a single statement is permitted in both the if part and the else part of the if-else statement, this statement can be a single compound statement. A **compound statement** is any number of single statements contained between braces, as shown in Figure 4.2.

The use of braces to enclose a set of individual statements creates a single block of statements, which may be used anywhere in a C++ program in place of a single statement. The next example illustrates the use of a compound statement within the general form of an if-else statement.

```
              {
                statement1;
                statement2;
                statement3;

                    .

                    .

                    .

                last statement;
              }
```

FIGURE 4.2 *A Compound Statement Consists of Individual Statements Enclosed Within Braces*

```
if (expression)
{
  statement1;    // as many statements as necessary
  statement2;    // can be put within the braces
  statement3;    // each statement must end with a ;
}
else
{
  statement4;
  statement5;

     .

     .

     .

  statementn;
}
```

Program 4.2 illustrates the use of a compound statement in an actual program. This checks whether the value in tempType is f. If the value is f, the compound statement that corresponds to the if part of the if-else statement is executed. Any other letter results in execution of the compound statement that corresponds to the else part. A sample run of Program 4.2 follows.

```
Enter the temperature to be converted: 212
Enter an f if the temperature is in Fahrenheit
   or a c if the temperature is in Celsius: f

The equivalent Celsius temperature is 100.00
```

Program 4.2

```cpp
#include <iostream>
#include <iomanip>
using namespace std;

// a temperature conversion program
int main()
{
  char tempType;
  double temp, fahren, celsius;

  cout << "Enter the temperature to be converted: ";
  cin  >> temp;
  cout << "Enter an f if the temperature is in Fahrenheit";
  cout << "\n or a c if the temperature is in Celsius: ";
  cin  >> tempType;

    // set output formats
  cout << setiosflags (ios::fixed)
       << setiosflags (ios::showpoint)
       << setprecision(2);

  if (tempType == 'f')
  {
    celsius = (5.0 / 9.0) * (temp - 32.0);
    cout << "\nThe equivalent Celsius temperature is " << celsius
         << endl;
  }
  else
  {
    fahren = (9.0 / 5.0) * temp + 32.0;
    cout << "\nThe equivalent Fahrenheit temperature is " << fahren
         << endl;
  }

  return 0;
}
```

The Boolean Data Type

Before the current ANSI/ISO C++ standard, C++ did not have a built-in Boolean data type with its two Boolean values, true and false. Because this data type was not originally part of the language, a tested expression could not evaluate to a Boolean value. Thus, the syntax

```
if(Boolean expression is true)
```

was not a part of the C++ language. Rather, C++ used the more encompassing syntax

```
if(expression)
    execute this statement;
```

where *expression* is any expression (relational, logical, or numeric) that evaluates to a numeric value. If this value were nonzero, it was considered true, and only a zero value was considered false.

As specified by the ANSO standard, C++ has a built-in Boolean data type, **bool**, containing the two values true and false. As currently implemented, the actual values represented by the bool values, true and false, are the integer values 1 and 0, respectively. For example, consider the following program, which declares two Boolean variables.

```cpp
#include <iostream>
using namespace std;

int main()
{
  bool t1, t2;
  t1 = true;
  t2 = false;

  cout << "The value of t1 is " << t1
       <<  "\n and the value of t2 is " << t2 << endl;

  return 0;
}
```

The output displayed by this method is:

```
The value of t1 is 1 and
 the value of t2 is 0
```

As can be seen by this output, the Boolean values true and false are represented by the integer values 1 and 0, respectively. To see Boolean values displayed as true and false, you can insert the manipulator boolalpha into the cout stream prior to displaying Boolean values.

(continued on next page)

> *(continued from previous page)*
>
> Boolean values have the following relationships:
>
> ```
> !true  = false
> !false = true
> ```
>
> Additionally, applying either a postfix or prefix increment (`++`) operator to a variable of type **bool** sets the Boolean value to `true`. The postfix and prefix decrement operators (`--`) cannot be applied to a Boolean variable.
>
> Boolean values can also be compared. For example, if `flag1` and `flag2` are two Boolean variables, the relational expression `flag1 == flag2` is valid. Lastly, assigning any nonzero value to a Boolean variable results in the variable being set to `true` (that is, a value of 1), and assigning a zero to a Boolean variable results in the variable being set to `false` (that is, a value of 0).

Block Scope

All statements contained within a compound statement constitute a single block of code, and any variable declared within such a block has meaning only between its declaration and the closing braces that define the block. For example, consider the following section of code, which consists of two blocks of code.

```cpp
{   // start of outer block
    int a = 25;
    int b = 17;

    cout << "The value of a is " << a << " and b is " << b << endl;

    {     // start of inner block
      double a = 46.25;
      int c = 10;

      cout << "a is now " << a
           << " b is now " << b
           << " and c is " << c << endl;
    }    // end of inner block

    cout << "a is now " << a << " and b is "<< b << endl;

}   // end of outer block
```

The output that is produced by this section of code is

```
The value of a is 25 and b is 17
a is now 46.25 b is now 17 and c is 10
a is now 25 and b is 17
```

PROGRAMMING NOTE

Placement of Braces in a Compound Statement

A common practice for some C++ programmers is to place the opening brace of a compound statement on the same line as the `if` and `else` statements. If this convention were used, the `if` statement in Program 4.2 would appear as shown below. This placement is a matter of preference. Both styles are used, and both are acceptable.

```
if (tempType == 'f') {
    celsius = (5.0 / 9.0) * (temp - 32.0);
    cout << "/nThe equivalent Celsius temperature is "
        << celsius << endl;
}
else {
    fahren = (9.0 / 5.0) * temp + 32.0;
    cout << "/nThe equivalent Fahrenheit temperature is "
        << fahren << endl;
}
```

This output is produced as follows: The first block of code defines two variables named a and b, which may be used anywhere within this block after their declaration, including within any block contained inside it. Within the inner block, two new variables named a and c have been declared. At this stage, then, we have created four different variables, two of which have the same name. Any referenced variable first results in an attempt to access a variable correctly declared within the block that contains the reference. If no variable is defined within the block, then an attempt is made to access a variable in the next immediate outside block, and so on until a valid access results.

Thus the values of the variables a and c referenced within the inner block use the values of the variables a and c declared in that block. Because no variable named b was declared inside the inner block, the value of b displayed from within the inner block is obtained from the outer block. Finally, the last cout object, which is outside the inner block, displays the value of the variable a declared in the outer block. If an attempt were made to display the value of c anywhere in the outer block, the compiler would issue an error message stating that c is an undefined symbol.

The location within a program where a variable can be used is formally referred to as the **scope** of the variable, and we will have much more to say on this subject in Chapter 6.

One-Way Selection

A useful modification of the `if-else` statement involves omitting the `else` part of the statement altogether. In this case, the `if` statement takes the shortened and frequently useful form

$$if \ (expression)$$
$$statement;$$

The statement following the `if (expression)` is executed only if the expression has a nonzero value (a true condition). As before, the statement may be a compound statement.

This modified form of the `if` statement is called a **one-way if statement**. It is illustrated in Program 4.3, which checks a car's mileage and prints a message if the car has been driven more than 3000.0 miles.

Program 4.3

```cpp
#include <iostream>
using namespace std;

int main()
{

  const double LIMIT = 3000.0;
  int idNum;
  double miles;

  cout << "Please type in car number and mileage: ";
  cin  >> idNum >> miles;

  if(miles > LIMIT)
    cout << " Car " << idNum << " is over the limit." << endl;

  cout << "End of program output." << endl;

  return 0;
}
```

To illustrate the one-way selection criteria in action, Program 4.3 was run twice, each time with different input data. Only the input data for the first run causes the message `Car 256 is over the limit` to be displayed.

```
Please type in car number and mileage: 256 3562.8
  Car 256 is over the limit.
End of program output.
```

and

```
Please type in car number and mileage: 23 2562.3
End of program output.
```

Problems Associated with the `if-else` Statement

Two of the most common problems that programmers encounter when first using C++'s `if-else` statement are

1. Misunderstanding the full implications of what an expression is

2. Using the assignment operator, =, in place of the relational operator, ==

Recall that an expression is any combination of operands and operators that yields a result. This definition is extremely broad and is more encompassing than is initially apparent. For example, all of the following are valid C++ expressions:

```
age + 5
age = 30
age == 40
```

Assuming that the variables are suitably declared, each of these expressions yields a result. The following section of code uses the `cout` object to display the value of these expressions when age is initially assigned the value 18.

```
age = 18;
cout << "The value of the first expression is " << (age + 5) << endl;
cout << "The value of the second expression is " << (age = 30) << endl;
cout << "The value of the third expression is " << (age == 40) << endl;
```

The display produced by this section of code is

```
The value of the first expression is 23
The value of the second expression is 30
The value of the third expression is 0
```

As this output illustrates, each expression, by itself, has a value associated with it. The value of the first expression is the sum of the variable age plus 5, which is 23. The value of the second expression is 30, which is also assigned to the variable age. The value of the third expression is zero, because age is not equal to 40, and a false condition is represented in C++ with a value of zero. If the value in age were 40, the relational expression a == 40 would be true and would have a value of 1.

Now assume that the relational expression age == 40 was intended to be used in the if statement

```
if (age == 40)
    cout << "Happy Birthday!";
```

but was mistyped as age = 40, resulting in

```
if (age = 40)
    cout << "Happy Birthday!";
```

Because the mistake results in a valid C++ expression, and any C++ expression can be tested by an if statement, the resulting if statement is valid and will cause the message Happy Birthday! to be printed regardless of what value was previously assigned to age. Can you see why?

The condition tested by the if statement does not compare the value in age to the number 40 but rather assigns the number 40 to age. That is, the expression age = 40 is not a relational expression at all, but an assignment expression. At the completion of the assignment, the expression itself has a value of 40. Because C++ treats any nonzero value as true, the cout statement is executed. Another way of looking at this is to realize that the if statement is equivalent to the following two statements:

```
age = 40;     // assign 40 to age
if (age)      // test the value of age
cout << "Happy Birthday!";
```

Because a C++ compiler has no means of knowing that the expression being tested is not the desired one, you must be especially careful when writing conditions.

EXERCISES 4.2

1. Rewrite Program 4.1 using the following statements:

```
const double LIMIT = 20000.0;
const double REGRATE = 0.02;
const double HIGHRATE = 0.025;
const double FIXED = 400.0;
```

(If necessary, review Section 3.4 for the use of symbolic constants.)

2. *a.* If money is left in a particular bank for more than 5 years, interest is paid by the bank at a rate of 4.5 percent; otherwise, the interest rate is 3.0 percent. Write a C++ program that uses the `cin` object to accept the number of years into the variable `numYears` and display the appropriate interest rate, depending on the value input into `numYears`.

b. How many runs should you make for the program written in Exercise 2a to verify that it is operating correctly? What data should you input in each of the program runs?

3. *a.* In a pass/fail course, a student passes if the grade is greater than or equal to 70 and fails if the grade is lower. Write a C++ program that accepts a grade and prints the message `A passing grade` or `A failing grade`, as appropriate.

b. How many runs should you make for the program written in Exercise 3a to verify that it is operating correctly? What data should you input in each of the program runs?

4. *a.* Write a C++ program to compute and display a person's weekly salary as determined by the following expressions:

If the number of hours worked is less than or equal to 40, the person receives $8.00 per hour; otherwise, the person receives $320.00, plus $12.00 for each hour worked over 40 hours.

The program should request the hours worked as input and should display the salary as output.

b. How many runs should you make for the program written in Exercise 4a to verify that it is operating correctly? What data should you input in each of the program runs?

5. *a.* A senior salesperson is paid $500 a week, and a junior salesperson is paid $300 a week. Write a C++ program that accepts as input a salesperson's status in the character variable `status`. If status equals `'s'`, the senior person's salary should be displayed; otherwise, the junior person's salary should be output.

b. How many runs should you make for the program written in Exercise 5a to verify that it is operating correctly? What data should you input in each of the program runs?

6. *a.* Write a C++ program that displays either the message `I feel great today!` or `I feel down today #$*!` depending on the input. If the character u is entered in the variable `ch`, the first message should be displayed; otherwise, the second message should be displayed.

b. How many runs should you make for the program written in Exercise 6a to verify that it is operating correctly? What data should you input in each of the program runs?

7. *a.* Write a program to display the following two prompts:

```
Enter a month: (use a 1 for Jan, etc.)
Enter a day of the month:
```

Have your program accept and store a number in the variable month in response to the first prompt and, in response to the second prompt, accept and store a number in the variable day. If the month entered is not between 1 and 12, inclusive, print a message informing the user that an invalid month has been entered. If the day entered is not between 1 and 31, print a message informing the user that an invalid day has been entered.

b. What will your program do if the user types a number with a decimal point for the month? How can you ensure that your `if` statements check for an integer number?

8. Write a C++ program that accepts a character using the `cin` object and determines whether the character is a lowercase letter. A lowercase letter is any character that is greater

than or equal to 'a' and less than or equal to 'z'. If the entered character is a lowercase letter, display the message The character just entered is a lowercase letter. If the entered letter is not lowercase, display the message The character just entered is not a lowercase letter.

9. Write a C++ program that first determines whether an entered character is a lowercase letter (see Exercise 8). If the letter is lowercase, determine and print out its position in the alphabet. For example, if the entered letter is c, the program should print out 3, because c is the third letter in the alphabet. (*Hint:* If the entered character is in lowercase, its position can be determined by subtracting 'a' from the letter and adding 1.)

10. Repeat Exercise 8 to determine whether the character entered is an uppercase letter. An uppercase letter is any character greater than or equal to 'A' and less than or equal to 'Z'.

11. Write a C++ program that first determines whether an entered character is an uppercase letter (see Exercise 10). If the letter is uppercase, determine and print its position in the alphabet. For example, if the entered letter is G, the program should print out 7, because G is the seventh letter in the alphabet. (*Hint:* If the entered character is in uppercase, its position can be determined by subtracting 'A' from the letter and adding 1.)

12. Write a C++ program that accepts a character using the cin object. If the character is a lowercase letter (see Exercise 8), convert the letter to uppercase and display the letter in its uppercase form. (*Hint:* Subtracting the integer value 32 from a lowercase letter yields the code for the equivalent uppercase letter. Thus, 'A' = char('a' - 32).)

13. The following program displays the message Hello there! regardless of the letter input. Determine where the error is and why the program always causes the message to be displayed.

```cpp
#include <iostream>
int main()
using namespace std;

{
  char letter;

  cout << "Enter a letter: ";
  cin  >> letter;
  if (letter = 'm')
    cout << "Hello there!" << endl;

  return 0;
}
```

14. Write a C++ program that asks the user to input two numbers. After your program accepts these numbers using one or more cin object calls, have your program check the numbers. If the first number entered is greater than the second number, print the message The first number is greater; otherwise, print the message The first number is not greater than the second. Test your program by entering the numbers 5 and 8 and then using the numbers 11 and 2. What will your program display if the two numbers entered are equal?

4.3   Nested `if` Statements

As we have seen, an `if-else` statement can contain simple or compound statements. Any valid C++ statement can be used, including another `if-else` statement. Thus, one or more `if-else` statements can be included within either part of an `if-else` statement. For example, substituting the one-way `if` statement

```
if (hours > 6)
  cout << "snap";
```

for `statement1` in the `if` statement

```
if (hours < 9)
  statement1;
else
  cout << "pop";
```

results in the nested `if` statement

```
if (hours < 9)
{
  if (hours > 6)
    cout << "snap";
}
  else
    cout << "pop";
```

The braces around the inner one-way `if` are essential, because in their absence, C++ associates an `else` with the closest unpaired `if`. Thus, without the braces, the foregoing statement is equivalent to

```
if (hours < 9)
  if (hours > 6)
    cout << "snap";
  else
    cout << "pop";
```

Here the `else` is paired with the inner `if`, which destroys the meaning of the original `if-else` statement. Note also that the indentation is irrelevant as far as the compiler is concerned. Whether the indentation exists or not, the statement is compiled by associating the last `else` with the closest unpaired `if`, unless braces are used to alter the default pairing.

The process of nesting `if` statements can be extended indefinitely, so the `cout << "snap";` statement could itself be replaced by either a complete `if-else` statement or another one-way `if` statement.

The if-else Chain

Generally, the case in which the statement in the if part of an if-else statement is another if statement tends to be confusing and is best avoided. However, an extremely useful construction occurs when the else part of an if statement contains another if-else statement. This takes the form

```
if (expression_1)
    statement1;
else
    if (expression_2)
        statement2;
    else
        statement3;
```

As with all C++ programs, the indentation we have used is not required. In fact, the foregoing construction is so common that it is typically written using the following arrangement:

```
if (expression_1)
    statement1;
else if (expression_2)
    statement2;
else
    statement3;
```

This construction is called an if-else chain and is used extensively in programming applications. The conditions are evaluated in order, and if any condition is true, the corresponding statement is executed and the remainder of the chain is terminated. The final else statement is executed only if none of the previous conditions is satisfied. This serves as a default or catch-all case that is useful for detecting an impossible or error condition.

The chain can be continued indefinitely by repeatedly making the last statement another if-else statement. Thus the general form of an if-else chain is

```
if (expression_1)
    statement1;
else if (expression_2)
    statement2;
else if (expression_3)
    statement3;
            .
            .
            .
```

(continued on next page)

(continued from previous page)

```
else if (expression_n)
    statement_n;
else
    last_statement;
```

As with all C++ statements, each individual statement can be a compound statement bounded by the braces { and }. To illustrate the if-else chain, Program 4.4 displays a person's marital status corresponding to a letter input. The following letter codes are used:

Marital Status	Input Code
Married	M
Single	S
Divorced	D
Widowed	W

 Program 4.4

```cpp
#include <iostream>
using namespace std;

int main()
{
  char marcode;

  cout << "Enter a marital code: ";
  cin  >> marcode;

  if (marcode == 'M')
    cout << "Individual is married." << endl;
  else if (marcode == 'S')
    cout << "Individual is single." << endl;
  else if (marcode == 'D')
    cout << "Individual is divorced." << endl;
  else if (marcode == 'W')
    cout << "Individual is widowed." << endl;
  else
    cout << "An invalid code was entered." << endl;

  return 0;
}
```

As a final example illustrating the if-else chain, let us calculate the monthly income of a salesperson by using the following commission schedule:

Monthly Sales	Income
greater than or equal to $50,000	$375 plus 16% of sales
less than $50,000 but greater than or equal to $40,000	$350 plus 14% of sales
less than $40,000 but greater than or equal to $30,000	$325 plus 12% of sales
less than $30,000 but greater than or equal to $20,000	$300 plus 9% of sales
less than $20,000 but greater than or equal to $10,000	$250 plus 5% of sales
less than $10,000	$200 plus 3% of sales

The following if-else chain can be used to determine the correct monthly income, where the variable monthlySales is used to store the salesperson's current monthly sales.

```
if (monthlySales >= 50000.00)
   income = 375.00 + .16 * monthlySales;
else if (monthlySales >= 40000.00)
   income = 350.00 + .14 * monthlySales;
else if (monthlySales >= 30000.00)
   income = 325.00 + .12 * monthlySales;
else if (monthlySales >= 20000.00)
   income = 300.00 + .09 * monthlySales;
else if (monthlySales >= 10000.00)
   income = 250.00 + .05 * monthlySales;
else
   income = 200.000 + .03 * monthlySales;
```

Note that this example makes use of the fact that the chain is stopped once a true condition is found. This is accomplished by checking for the highest monthly sales first. If the salesperson's monthly sales are less than $50,000, the if-else chain continues checking for the next highest sales amount until the correct category is obtained.

Program 4.5

```cpp
#include <iostream>
#include <iomanip>
using namespace std;

int main()
{
  double monthlySales, income;

  cout << "Enter the value of monthly sales: ";
  cin  >> monthlySales;
  if (monthlySales >= 50000.00)
    income = 375.00 + .16 * monthlySales;
  else if (monthlySales >= 40000.00)
    income = 350.00 + .14 * monthlySales;
  else if (monthlySales >= 30000.00)
    income = 325.00 + .12 * monthlySales;
  else if (monthlySales >= 20000.00)
    income = 300.00 + .09 * monthlySales;
  else if (monthlySales >= 10000.00)
    income = 250.00 + .05 * monthlySales;
  else
    income = 200.00 + .03 * monthlySales;

  cout << setiosflags(ios::showpoint)
       << setiosflags(ios:: fixed)
       << setprecision(2)
       << "The income is $" << income << endl;

  return 0;
}
```

Program 4.5 uses this if-else chain to calculate and display the income that corresponds to the value of monthly sales that is input to the cin object.

A sample run using Program 4.5 follows.

```
Enter the value of monthly sales: 36243.89
The income is $4674.27
```

▌ EXERCISES 4.3

1. A student's letter grade is calculated according to the following schedule:

Numerical Grade	Letter Grade
greater than or equal to 90	A
less than 90 but greater than or equal to 80	B
less than 80 but greater than or equal to 70	C
less than 70 but greater than or equal to 60	D
less than 60	F

Write a C++ program that accepts a student's numerical grade, converts the numerical grade to an equivalent letter grade, and displays the letter grade.

2. The interest rate paid on funds deposited in a bank is determined by the amount of time the money is left on deposit. For a particular bank, the following schedule is used:

Time on Deposit	Interest Rate
greater than or equal to 5 years	.045
less than 5 years but greater than or equal to 4 years	.04
less than 4 years but greater than or equal to 3 years	.035
less than 3 years but greater than or equal to 2 years	.025
less than 2 years but greater than or equal to 1 year	.02
less than 1 year	.015

Write a C++ program that accepts the time that funds are left on deposit and displays the interest rate that corresponds to the time entered.

3. Write a C++ program that accepts a number followed by one space and then a letter. If the letter following the number is f, the program is to treat the number entered as a temperature in degrees Fahrenheit, convert the number to the equivalent temperature in

degrees Celsius, and print a suitable display message. If the letter following the number is c, the program is to consider the number entered as a Celsius temperature, convert the number to the equivalent Fahrenheit temperature, and print a suitable display message. If the letter is neither f nor c, the program is to print a message that the data entered is incorrect and then terminate. Use an if-else chain in your program and make use of the conversion formulas

```
Celsius = (5.0 / 9.0) * (Fahrenheit - 32.0)
Fahrenheit = (9.0 / 5.0) * Celsius + 32.0
```

4. Using the commission schedule from Program 4.5, the following program calculates monthly income.

```cpp
#include <iostream>
#include <iomanip>
using namespace std;

int main()
{
  double monthlySales, income;

  cout << "Enter the value of monthly sales: ";
  cin  >> monthlySales;
  if (monthlySales >= 50000.00)
    income = 375.00 + .16 * monthlySales;
  if (monthlySales >= 40000.00 && monthlySales < 50000.00)
    income = 350.00 + .14 * monthlySales;
  if (monthlySales >= 30000.00 && monthlySales < 40000.00)
    income = 325.00 + .12 * monthlySales;
  if (monthlySales >= 20000.00 && monthlySales < 30000.00)
    income = 300.00 + .09 * monthlySales;
  if (monthlySales >= 10000.00 && monthlySales < 20000.00)
    income = 250.00 + .05 * monthlySales;
  if (monthlySales > 10000.00)
    income = 200.00 + .03 * monthlySales;

  cout << setiosflags(ios::showpoint)
       << setiosflags(ios:: fixed)
       << setprecision(2)
       << "\n\nThe income is $" << income << endl;

  return 0;
}
```

a. Will this program produce the same output as Program 4.5?

b. Which program is better? Why?

5. The following program was written to produce the same result as Program 4.5.

```cpp
#include <iostream>
#include <iomanip>
using namespace std;

int main()
{
  double monthlySales, income;

  cout << "Enter the value of monthly sales: ";
  cin  >> monthlySales;

  if (monthlySales < 10000.00)
    income = 200.00 + .03 * monthlySales;
  else if (monthlySales >= 10000.00)
    income = 250.00 + .05 * monthlySales;
  else if (monthlySales >= 20000.00)
    income = 300.00 + .09 * monthlySales;
  else if (monthlySales >= 30000.00)
    income = 325.00 + .12 * monthlySales;
  else if (monthlySales >= 40000.00)
    income = 350.00 + .14 * monthlySales;
  else if (monthlySales >= 50000.00)
    income = 375.00 + .16 * monthlySales;

  cout << setiosflags(ios::showpoint)
       << setiosflags(ios:: fixed)
       << setprecision(2)
       << "The income is $" << income << endl;

  return 0;
}
```

a. Will this program run?
b. What does this program do?
c. For what values of monthly sales does this program calculate the correct income?

4.4   The switch Statement

The if-else chain is used in programming applications where one set of instructions must be selected from many possible alternatives. The switch statement provides an alternative to the if-else chain for cases that compare the value of an integer expression to a specific value. The general form of a `switch` statement is

```
switch (expression)
{                            // start of compound statement
   case value_1: ←————————— terminated with a colon
      statement1;
      statement2;
            .
            .
            .
      break;
   case value_2: ←————————— terminated with a colon
      statementm;
      statementn;
            .
            .
            .
      break;
            .
            .
            .
   case value_n: ←————————— terminated with a colon
      statementw;
      statementx;
            .
            .
            .
      break;
   default: ←————————————— terminated with a colon
      statement_aa;
      statement_bb;
}                            // end of switch and compound statement
```

The `switch` statement uses four new keywords: `switch`, `case`, `default`, and `break`. Let's see what each of these words does.

The keyword `switch` identifies the start of the `switch` statement. The expression in parentheses following this word is evaluated, and the result of the expression is compared to various alternative values contained within the compound statement. The expression in the `switch` statement must evaluate to an integer result; otherwise, a compilation error results.

Internal to the switch statement, the keyword case is used to identify or label individual values that are compared to the value of the switch expression. The switch expression's value is compared to each of these case values, in the order in which these values are listed, until a match is found. When a match occurs, execution begins with the statement immediately following the match. Thus, as illustrated in Figure 4.3, the value of the expression determines where in the switch statement execution actually begins.

FIGURE 4.3   *The Expression Determines an Entry Point*

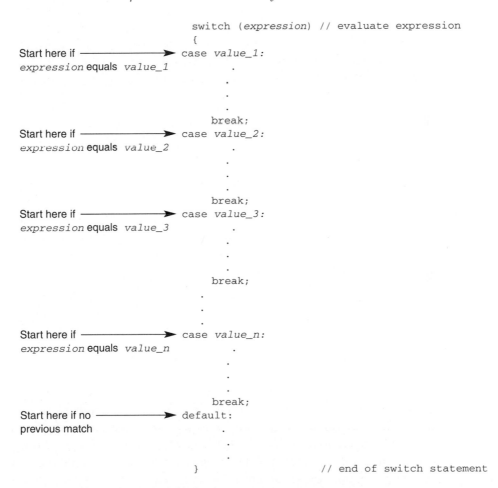

Any number of case labels may be contained within a switch statement, in any order. If the value of the expression does not match any of the case values, however, no statement is executed unless the keyword default is encountered. The keyword `default` is optional and operates the same as the last `else` in an `if-else` chain. If the value of the expression does not match any of the `case` values, program execution begins with the statement following the word `default`.

Once an entry point has been located by the `switch` statement, all further case evaluations are ignored, and execution continues through the end of the compound statement unless a `break` statement is encountered. This is the reason for the `break` statement, which identifies the end of a particular `case` and causes an immediate exit from the `switch` statement. Thus, just as the word `case` identifies possible starting points in the compound statement, the `break` statement determines terminating points. If the `break` statements are omitted, all `cases` following the matching `case` value, including the `default case`, are executed.

In writing a `switch` statement, we can use multiple case values to refer to the same set of statements; the `default` label is optional. For example, consider the following:

```
switch (number)
{
   case 1:
     cout << "Have a Good Morning" << endl;
     break;
   case 2:
     cout << "Have a Happy Day" << endl;
     break;
   case 3: case 4: case 5:
     cout << "Have a Nice Evening" << endl;
}
```

If the value stored in the variable `number` is 1, the message `Have a Good Morning` is displayed. Similarly, if the value of `number` is 2, the second message is displayed. Finally, if the value of `number` is 3 or 4 or 5, the last message is displayed. Because the statements to be executed for these last three `cases` are the same, the `cases` for these values can be "stacked together," as shown in the example. Also, because there is no `default`, no message is printed if the value of `number` is not one of the listed `case` values. Although it is good programming practice to list `case` values in increasing order, this is not required by the `switch` statement. A `switch` statement may have any number of `case` values, in any order; we need to list only the values being tested.

Program 4.6 uses a `switch` statement to select the arithmetic operation (addition, multiplication, or division) to be performed on two numbers, depending on the value of the variable `opselect`.

Program 4.6

```cpp
#include <iostream>
using namespace std;
int main()
{
  int opselect;
  double fnum, snum;

  cout << "Please type in two numbers: ";
  cin  >> fnum >> snum;
  cout << "Enter a select code: ";
  cout << "\n        1 for addition";
  cout << "\n        2 for multiplication";
  cout << "\n        3 for division : ";
  cin  >> opselect;

  switch (opselect)
  {
    case 1:
      cout << "The sum of the numbers entered is " << fnum+snum << endl;
      break;
    case 2:
      cout << "The product of the numbers entered is " << fnum*snum << endl;
      break;
    case 3:
      cout << "The first number divided by the second is " << fnum/snum << endl;
      break;
  }      // end of switch

  return 0;
}    // end of main()
```

Program 4.6 was run twice. The resulting display clearly identifies the case selected. The results were

```
Please type in two numbers: 12 3
Enter a select code:
        1 for addition
        2 for multiplication
        3 for division : 2
The product of the numbers entered is 36
```

and

```
        Please type in two numbers: 12 3
        Enter a select code:
                1 for addition
                2 for multiplication
                3 for division : 3
        The first number divided by the second is 4
```

In reviewing Program 4.6, note the break statement in the last case. Although this break is not necessary, it is good practice to terminate the last case in a switch statement with a break. This prevents a possible program error later, if an additional case is subsequently added to the switch statement. With the addition of a new case, the break between cases becomes necessary; having the break in place ensures that you will not forget to include it at the time of the modification.

Because character data types are always converted to integers in an expression, a switch statement can also be used to "switch" on the basis of the value of a character expression. For example, assuming that choice is a character variable, the following switch statement is valid:

```
switch(choice)
{
  case 'a': case 'e': case 'i': case 'o': case 'u':
    cout << "\nThe character in choice is a vowel" << endl;
    break;
  default:
    cout << "\nThe character in choice is not a vowel" << endl;
    break; // this break is optional
}    // end of switch statement
```

▩ EXERCISES 4.4

1. Rewrite the following if-else chain using a switch statement:
```
if (letGrad == 'A')
  cout << "The numerical grade is between 90 and 100";
else if (letGrad == 'B')
  cout << "The numerical grade is between 80 and 89.9";
else if (letGrad == 'C')
  cout << "The numerical grade is between 70 and 79.9";
```

```
else if (letGrad == 'D')
  cout << "How are you going to explain this one" << endl;
else
{
  cout << "Of course I had nothing to do with my grade." << endl;
  cout << "\nThe professor was really off the wall." << endl;
}
```

2. Rewrite the following `if-else` chain using a `switch` statement:

```
if (bondType == 1)
{
  inData();
  check();
}
else if (bondType == 2)
{
  dates();
  leapYr();
}
else if (bondType == 3)
{
  yield();
  maturity();
}
else if (bondType == 4)
{
  price();
  roi();
}
else if (bondType == 5)
{
  files();
  save();
}
else if (bondType == 6)
{
  retrieve();
  screen();
}
```

3. Rewrite Program 4.4 in Section 4.3 using a `switch` statement.

4. Determine why the `if-else` chain in Program 4.5 cannot be replaced with a `switch` statement.

5. Repeat Exercise 3 in Section 4.3 using a `switch` statement instead of an `if-else` chain.

6. Rewrite Program 4.6 using a character variable for the select code.

7. Each disk drive in a shipment is stamped with a code from 1 to 4, where the codes indicate the following drive manufacturers:

Code	Disk Drive Manufacturer
1	3M Corporation
2	Maxell Corporation
3	Sony Corporation
4	Verbatim Corporation

Write a C++ program that accepts the code number as an input and, on the basis of the value entered, displays the correct disk drive manufacturer.

4.5 Common Programming Errors

There are three programming errors that are commonly made in C++'s selection statements. Let us briefly consider each.

1. Using the assignment operator, =, in place of the relational operator, ==. This can cause an enormous amount of frustration because any expression can be tested by an if-else statement. For example, the statement

```
if (opselect = 2)
   cout << "Happy Birthday";
else
   cout << "Good Day";
```

always results in the message Happy Birthday being printed, regardless of the initial value in the variable opselect. This is because the assignment expression opselect = 2 has a value of 2, which is considered a true value in C++. The correct expression to determine the value in opselect is opselect == 2.

2. Assuming that the if-else statement is selecting an incorrect choice when the problem is really the values being tested. This is a typical debugging problem in which the programmer mistakenly concentrates on the tested condition as the source of the problem rather than on the values being tested. For example, assume that the following correct if-else statement is part of your program.

```
if (key == 'F')
{
   contemp = (5.0/9.0) * (intemp - 32.0);
   cout << "Conversion to Celsius was done";
```

```
    }
    else
    {
      contemp = (9.0/5.0) * intemp + 32.0;
      cout << "Conversion to Fahrenheit was done";
    }
```

This statement will always display `Conversion to Celsius was done` when the variable `key` contains an `F`. Therefore, if this message is displayed when you believe `key` does not contain `F`, investigation of `key`'s value is called for. As a general rule, whenever a selection statement does not act as you think it should, be sure to test your assumptions about the values assigned to the tested variables by displaying their values. If an unanticipated value is displayed, you have at least traced the source of the problem to the variables themselves, rather than the structure of the `if-else` statement. From there you will have to determine where and how the incorrect value was obtained.

3. Using nested `if` statements without including braces to indicate clearly the desired structure. Without braces, the compiler defaults to pairing `else`s with the closest unpaired `if`s, which sometimes destroys the original intent of the selection statement. To avoid this problem and to create code that is readily adaptable to change, it is useful to write all `if-else` statements as compound statements in the form

```
    if (expression)
    {
      one or more statements in here
    }
    else
    {
      one or more statements in here
    }
```

Using this form maintains the original integrity and intent of the `if` statement, no matter how many statements are added later.

4.6   *Chapter Summary*

1. Relational expressions, which are also called conditions, are used to compare operands. If a relational expression is true, the value of the expression is the integer 1. If the relational expression is false, it has an integer value

of 0. Relational expressions are created by using the following relational operators:

Relational Operator	Meaning	Example
<	less than	`age < 30`
>	greater than	`height > 6.2`
<=	less than or equal to	`taxable <= 20000`
>=	greater than or equal to	`temp >= 98.6`
==	equal to	`grade == 100`
!=	not equal to	`number != 250`

2. More complex conditions can be constructed from relational expressions by using C++'s logical operators, `&&` (AND), `||` (OR), and `!` (NOT).

3. `if-else` statements are used to select between two alternative statements on the basis of the value of an expression. Although relational expressions are generally used for the tested expression, any valid expression can be used. In testing an expression, `if-else` statements interpret a nonzero value as true and a zero value as false. The most common form of an `if-else` statement is

```
if (expression)
    statement1;
else
    statement2;
```

This is a two-way selection statement. If the expression has a nonzero value, it is considered as true, and `statement1` is executed; otherwise, `statement2` is executed.

4. `if-else` statements can contain other `if-else` statements. In the absence of braces, each `else` is associated with the closest unpaired `if`.

5. The `if-else` chain is a multiway selection statement that has the general form

```
if (expression_1)
    statement_1;
else if (expression_2)
    statement_2;
else if (expression_3)
    statement_3;
```

```
                   .
                   .
                   .
        else if (expression_m)
          statement_m;
        else
          statement_n;
```

The expressions are evaluated in the order in which they appear in the chain. Once an expression is true (has a nonzero value), only the statement between that expression and the next `else if` or `else` is executed, and no further expressions are tested. The final `else` is optional, and the statement corresponding to the final `else` is executed only if none of the previous expressions were true.

6. A compound statement consists of any number of individual statements enclosed within the brace pair `{` and `}`. Compound statements are treated as a single block and can be used anywhere a single statement is called for.

7. Variables have meaning only within the block where they are declared, which includes any inner blocks contained within the declaring block.

8. The `switch` statement is a multiway selection statement. The general form of a `switch` statement is

```
switch (expression)
{                          // start of compound statement
case value_1:  ←────────────── terminated with a colon
  statement1;
  statement2;
     .
     .
     .
  break;
case value_2:  ←────────────── terminated with a colon
  statementm;
  statementn;
     .
     .
     .
  break;
     .
     .
     .
```

(continued on next page)

(continued from previous page)

```
        case value_n:  ◄─────────────── terminated with a colon
            statementw;
            statementx;

                .

                .

                .

            break;
        default:  ◄─────────────────── terminated with a colon
            statement_aa;
            statement_bb;

                .

                .

                .

        }                    // end of switch and compound statement
```

For this statement, the value of an integer expression is compared to a number of integer or character constants or constant expressions. Program execution is transferred to the first matching case and continues through the end of the switch statement unless an optional break statement is encountered. cases in a switch statement can appear in any order, and an optional default case can be included. The default is executed if none of the other cases is matched.

4.7   Chapter Supplement: Errors, Testing, and Debugging

The ideal in programming is to produce readable, error-free programs that work correctly and can be modified or changed with a minimum of testing. You can work toward this ideal by keeping in mind the different types of errors that can occur, when they are typically detected, and how to correct them.

An error can be detected:

1. Before a program is compiled
2. While the program is being compiled
3. While the program is being run
4. After the program has been executed and the output is being examined

In some cases, an error may not be detected at all. The method for detecting errors before a program is compiled is called **desk checking**. Desk checking, which typically is performed while sitting at a desk with the code in front of you, refers to the process of checking the actual program code for syntax and logic errors.

Errors detected by the compiler are formally referred to as **compile-time errors,** and errors that occur while the program is running are formally referred to as **run-time errors.** Other names for compile time errors are **syntax errors** and **parse errors,** terms that emphasize the type of error being detected by the compiler.

By now, you have probably encountered numerous compile-time errors. Although beginning programmers tend to be frustrated by them, experienced programmers understand that the compiler is doing a lot of valuable checking, and that it is usually quite easy to correct any errors the compiler does detect. In addition, because these errors occur while the program is being developed, and not while a user is attempting to perform an important task, no one but the programmer ever knows they occurred; you fix them and they go away.

Run-time errors are much more troubling because they occur while a user is executing the program, and in most commercial systems the user is not the programmer. Although there are a number of error types that can cause a run-time error, such as a failure in the hardware, from a programming standpoint the majority of run-time errors are referred to as **logic errors**; that is faulty logic, which encompasses not fully thinking out what the program should do or not anticipating how a user can make the program fail, is at fault. For example, if a user enters data that results in an attempt to divide a number by zero, a run-time error occurs. As a programmer, the only way to protect against run-time errors is to sufficiently anticipate everything a person might do to cause errors and submit your program to rigorous testing. Although beginning programmers tend to blame a user for an error caused by entering obviously incorrect data, professionals don't. They understand that a run-time error is a flaw in the final product that additionally can cause damage to the reputation of both program and programmer.

There are ways to detect errors both before a program is compiled and after it has been executed. In terms of preventing compile and run-time errors it is more fruitful to distinguish these errors based on what causes them. As has been noted, compile errors are also named syntax errors, which refer to errors in either the structure or spelling of a statement. For example the statements

```
cout << "There are four syntax errors here\n
cot " Can you find tem";
```

contain four syntax errors. These errors are:

1. A closing quote is missing in line 1.
2. A terminating semicolon (;) is missing in line 1.
3. The keyword cout is misspelled in line 2.
4. The insertion symbol, <<, is missing in line 2.

All of these errors will be detected by the compiler when the program is compiled. This is true of all syntax errors because they violate the basic rules of C++; if they are not discovered by desk checking, the compiler detects them and displays an error message.[4] In some cases, the error message is clear and the error is obvious; in other cases, it takes a little detective work to understand the error message displayed by the compiler. Because syntax errors are the only type of error that can be detected at compile time, the terms compile-time errors and syntax errors are used interchangeably. Strictly speaking, however, compile-time refers to when the error was detected and syntax refers to the type of error detected.

Note that the misspelling of the word them in the second statement is not a syntax error. Although this spelling error will result in an undesirable output line being displayed, it is not a violation of C++'s syntactical rules. It is a simple case of a **typographical error**, commonly referred to as a "typo."

A logic error can either cause a run-time error or produce incorrect results. Such errors are characterized by erroneous, unexpected, or unintentional output that is a direct result of some flaw in the program's logic. These errors, which are never caught by the compiler, may be detected by desk checking, by program testing, by accident when a user obtains an obviously erroneous output while the program is executing, or not at all. If the error is detected while the program is executing, a run-time error can occur that results in an error message being generated or premature program termination (or both).

The most serious logic error is caused by an incorrect understanding of the full requirements that the program is expected to fulfill. This is true because the logic contained within a program is always a reflection of the logic upon which it is coded. For example, if the purpose of a program is to calculate a mortgage payment on a house or the load bearing strength of a steel beam, and the programmer does not fully understand how the calculation is to be made, what inputs are needed to perform the calculation, or what special conditions exist (such as what happens when someone makes an extra payment on a mortgage or how temperature effects the beam), a logic error will occur. Because such errors are not detected by the compiler and frequently even may go undetected at run time, they are always more difficult to detect than syntax errors. If they are detected, a logic error typically reveals itself in one of two predominant ways. In one instance, the program executes to completion but produces obviously incorrect results. Generally, logic errors of this type are revealed by:

- **No output**—This is caused either by an omission of an output statement or a sequence of statements that inadvertently bypasses an output statement.
- **Unappealing or misaligned output**—This is caused by an error in an output statement.

---

[4] They may not, however, all be detected at the same time. Frequently, one syntax error masks another error, and the second error is only detected after the first error is corrected.

- **Incorrect numerical results**—This is caused by incorrect values assigned to the variables used in an expression, the use of an incorrect arithmetic expression, an omission of a statement, a round-off error, or the use of an improper sequence of statements.

A second way that logic errors reveal themselves is by causing a run-time error. Examples of this type of logic error are attempts to divide by zero or to take the square root of a negative number.

Testing and Debugging

In theory, a comprehensive set of test runs would reveal all logic errors and ensure that a program will work correctly for any and all combinations of input and computed data. In practice, this requires checking all possible combinations of statement executions. Because of the time and effort required, that is impossible for all but extremely simple programs. Let us see why this is so. Consider Program 4.7.

Program 4.7 has two paths that can be traversed from when the program is run to when the program reaches its closing brace. The first path, which is executed when the input number is 5, is in the sequence

```
cout << "Enter a number: ";
cin  >> num;
cout << "Bingo!" << endl;
```

Program 4.7

```cpp
#include <iostream>
using namespace std;

int main()
{
  int num;

  cout << "Enter a number: ";
  cin  >> num;

  if (num == 5)
    cout  << "Bingo!" << endl;
  else
    cout  << "Bongo!" << endl;

  return 0;
}
```

The second path, which is executed whenever any number except 5 is input, includes the sequence of instructions

```
cout << "Enter a number: ";
cin  >> num;
cout << "Bongo!" << endl;
```

To test each possible path through Program 4.7 requires two runs of the program, with a judicious selection of test input data to ensure that both paths of the if statement are exercised. The addition of one more if statement in the program increases the number of possible execution paths by a factor of 2 and requires four (2^2) runs of the program for complete testing. Similarly, two additional if statements increase the number of paths by a factor of 4 and require eight (2^3) runs for complete testing, and three additional if statements produce a program that requires sixteen (2^4) test runs.

Now consider a modest-size application program consisting of only ten modules, each module containing five if statements. Assuming that the modules are always called in the same sequence, there are 32 possible paths through each module (2 raised to the fifth power) and more than 1,000,000,000,000,000 (2 raised to the 50th power) possible paths through the complete program (all modules executed in sequence). The time needed to create individual test data to exercise each path and the actual computer run time required to check each path make the complete testing of such a program impossible.

Our inability to test fully all combinations of statement execution sequences has led to the programming proverb "There is no error-free program." It has also led to the realization that any testing that is done should be well thought out to maximize the chances of locating errors. Also, keep in mind that *although a single test can reveal the presence of an error, it does not verify the absence of another error.* That is, the fact that one error is revealed by testing does not indicate that another error is not lurking somewhere else in the program; furthermore, *the fact that one test revealed no errors does not mean there are no errors.*

Once you discover an error, however, the programmer must locate where the error occurs and then fix it. In computer jargon, a program error is referred to as a **bug**, and the process of isolating, correcting, and verifying the correction is called **debugging**.[5]

Although there are no hard-and-fast rules for isolating the cause of an error, some useful techniques can be applied. The first of these is a preventive technique.

---

[5] The derivation of this term is rather interesting. When a program stopped running on the MARK I computer at Harvard University in September 1945, the malfunction was traced to a dead insect that had gotten into the electrical circuits. The programmer, Grace Hopper, recorded the incident in her logbook as, "First actual case of bug being found."

Frequently, many errors are introduced by the programmer in the rush to code and run a program before fully understanding what is required and how the result is to be achieved. A symptom of this haste to get a program entered into the computer is the lack of an outline of the proposed program or the lack of a detailed understanding of what is actually required. Many errors can be eliminated simply by desk checking a copy of the program before it is ever entered or compiled.

A second useful technique is to imitate the computer and execute each statement by hand, as the computer would. This means writing down each variable as it is encountered in the program and listing the value that should be stored in the variable as each input and assignment statement is encountered. Doing this also sharpens your programming skills because it requires that you fully understand what each statement in your program causes to happen. Such a check is called **program tracing**.

A third and very powerful debugging technique is to include some temporary code in your program that displays the values of selected variables. If the displayed values are incorrect, you can then determine what part of your program generated them, and make the necessary corrections.

In the same manner, you could add temporary code that displays the values of all input data. This technique is referred to as **echo printing**, and it is useful in establishing that the program is correctly receiving and interpreting the input data.

The most powerful of all debugging and tracing techniques is to use a special program called a **debugger**. A debugger program controls the execution of a C++ program, can interrupt the C++ program at any point in its execution, and can display the values of all variables at the point of interruption.

Finally, no discussion of debugging is complete without mentioning the primary ingredient needed for successful isolation and correction of errors. This is the attitude and spirit you bring to the task. After you write a program, it's natural to assume it is correct. It is extremely difficult to back away and honestly test and find errors in your own software. As a programmer, you must constantly remind yourself that just because you think your program is correct does not make it so. Finding errors in your own programs is a sobering experience, but one that will help you to become a master programmer. It can also be exciting and fun if approached as a detection problem with you as the master detective.

Repetition

The programs examined so far have been useful in illustrating the correct structure of C++ programs and in introducing fundamental C++ input, output, assignment, and selection capabilities. By now you should have gained enough experience to be comfortable with the concepts and mechanics of the C++ programming process. It is time to move up a level in our knowledge and abilities.

The real power of most computer programs resides in their ability to repeat the same calculation or sequence of instructions over and over, each time using different data, without the necessity of rerunning the program for each new set of data values. In this chapter we explore the C++ statements that make this possible. These statements are the while, for, and do-while statements.

5.1   The while Statement

The while statement is a general repetition statement that can be used in a variety of programming situations. The general form of the while statement is

while (*expression*)
    statement;

The expression contained within the parentheses is evaluated in exactly the same manner as an expression contained in an if-else statement; the difference is how the expression is used. As we have seen, when the expression is true (has a nonzero value) in an if-else statement, the statement following the expression is executed once. In a while statement, the statement following the expression is executed repeatedly as long as the expression retains a nonzero value. This naturally means that somewhere in the while statement there must be a statement that alters the value of the tested expression. As we will see, this is indeed the case. For now, however, when we consider just the expression and the statement following the parentheses, the process used by the computer in evaluating a while statement is

1. **test the expression**
2. **if the expression has a nonzero (true) value**
       a. **execute the statement following the parentheses**
       b. **go back to step 1**
   else
       exit the while statement

Note that step 2b forces program control to be transferred back to step 1. This transfer of control back to the start of a while statement in order to reevaluate the expression is what forms the program loop. The while statement literally loops back on itself to recheck the expression until it evaluates to zero (becomes false). This naturally means that somewhere in the loop, provision must be made for the value of the tested expression to be altered. As we will see, this is indeed the case.

This looping process produced by a while statement is illustrated in Figure 5.1. A diamond shape is used to show the entry and exit points required in the decision part of the while statement.

To make this a little more tangible, consider the relational expression count <= 10 and the statement cout << count;. Using these, we can write the following valid while statement:

```
while (count <= 10)
    cout << count;
```

FIGURE 5.1   *Anatomy of a* while *Loop*

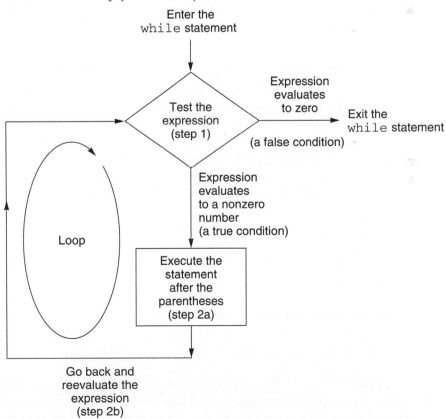

Although this statement is valid, the alert reader will realize that we have created a situation in which the cout object either is called forever (or until we stop the program) or is not called at all. Let us see why this happens.

If count has a value less than or equal to 10 when the expression is first evaluated, a call to cout is made. The while statement then automatically loops back on itself and retests the expression. Because we have not changed the value stored in count, the expression is still true and another call to cout is made. This process continues forever, or until the program containing this statement is prematurely stopped by the user. However, if count starts with a value greater than 10, the expression is false to begin with and the cout object call is never made.

How do we set an initial value in count to control what the while statement does the first time the expression is evaluated? The answer, of course, is to assign values to each variable in the tested expression before the while statement is encountered. For example, the following sequence of instructions is valid:

```
count = 1;
while (count <= 10)
   cout << count;
```

Using this sequence of instructions, we have ensured that count starts with a value of 1. We could assign any value to count in the assignment statement—the important thing is to assign *some* value. In practice, the assigned value depends on the application.

We must still change the value of count so that we can finally exit the while statement. To do this requires an expression such as count++ to increment the value of count each time the while statement is executed. The fact that a while statement provides for the repetition of a single statement does not prevent us from including an additional statement to change the value of count. All we have to do is replace the single statement with a compound statement. Here is an example:

```
count = 1;                    // initialize count
while (count <= 10)
{
   cout << count;
   count++;                   // increment count
}
```

Note that, for clarity, we have placed each statement in the compound statement on a separate line. This is consistent with the convention adopted for compound statements in the last chapter. Let us now analyze the foregoing sequence of instructions.

The first assignment statement sets count equal to 1. The while statement is then entered, and the expression is evaluated for the first time. The value of count is less than or equal to 10, so the expression is true and the compound statement is executed. The first statement in the compound statement is a call to the cout object to display the value of count. The next statement adds 1 to the value currently stored in count, making this value equal to 2. The while statement now loops back to retest the expression. Because count is still less than or equal to 10, the compound statement is executed again. This process continues until the value of count reaches 11. Program 5.1 illustrates these statements in an actual program.

 ## Program 5.1

```
#include <iostream>
using namespace std;

int main()
{
  int count;

  count = 1;                 // initialize count
  while (count <= 10)
  {
    cout << count << " ";
    count++;                 // increment count
  }

  return 0;
}
```

The output produced by Program 5.1 is

1 2 3 4 5 6 7 8 9 10

There is nothing special about the name count used in Program 5.1. Any valid integer variable could have been used.

Before we consider other examples of the while statement, two comments concerning Program 5.1 are in order. First, the statement count++ can be replaced with any statement that changes the value of count. A statement such as count = count + 2, for example, would cause every second integer to be displayed. Second, it is the programmer's responsibility to ensure that count is changed in a way that ultimately leads to a normal exit from the while. For example, if we replace the expression count++ with the expression count--, the value of count will never reach 10, and an infinite loop will be created. An *infinite loop* is a loop that never ends. The computer will not tap you on the shoulder and say, "Excuse me, you have created an infinite loop." It just keeps displaying numbers until you realize that the program is not working as you expected.

Now that you have some familiarity with the while statement, see whether you can read and determine the output of Program 5.2.

Program 5.2

```
#include <iostream>
using namespace std;

int main()
{
  int i;

  i = 10;
  while (i >= 1)
  {
    cout << i << " ";
    i--;                  // subtract 1 from i
  }

  return 0;
}
```

The assignment statement in Program 5.2 initially sets the int variable i to 10. The while statement then checks whether the value of i is greater than or equal to 1. While the expression is true, the value of i is displayed by the cout object and the value of i is decremented by 1. When i finally reaches zero, the expression is false and the program exits the while statement. Thus the following display is obtained when Program 5.2 is run:

10   9   8   7   6   5   4   3   2   1

To illustrate the power of the while statement, consider the task of printing a table of numbers from 1 to 10 with their squares and cubes. This can be done with a simple while statement, as illustrated by Program 5.3.

Program 5.3

```cpp
#include <iostream>
#include <iomanip>
using namespace std;

int main()
{
  int num;
  cout << "NUMBER    SQUARE    CUBE\n"
       << "------    ------    ----\n";

  num = 1;
  while (num < 11)
  {
    cout << setw(3) << num << "          "
         << setw(3) << num * num << "       "
         << setw(4) << num * num * num << endl;
    num++;     // increment num
  }

  return 0;
}
```

When Program 5.3 is run, the following display is produced:

NUMBER	SQUARE	CUBE
1	1	1
2	4	8
3	9	27
4	16	64
5	25	125
6	36	216
7	49	343
8	64	512
9	81	729
10	100	1000

Note that the expression used in Program 5.3 is num < 11. For the integer variable num, this expression is exactly equivalent to the expression num <= 10. The choice of which to use is entirely up to you.

If we want to use Program 5.3 to produce a table of 1000 numbers, all we do is change the expression in the `while` statement from `num < 11` to `num < 1001`. Changing the 11 to 1001 produces a table of 1000 lines—not bad for a simple five-line `while` statement.

All the program examples illustrating the `while` statement are examples of fixed-count loops, because the tested condition is a counter that checks for a fixed number of repetitions. A variation on the fixed-count loop can be made where the counter is not incremented by 1 each time through the loop but is incremented by some other value. For example, consider the task of producing a Celsius-to-Fahrenheit temperature-conversion table. Assume that Fahrenheit temperatures corresponding to Celsius temperatures ranging from 5 to 50 degrees are to be displayed in increments of 5 degrees. The desired display can be obtained with the following series of statements:

```
celsius = 5;      // starting Celsius value
while (celsius <= 50)
{
   fahren = (9.0/5.0) * celsius + 32.0;
   cout << setw(4) << celsius
        << setw(13) << fahren << endl;
   celsius = celsius + 5;
}
```

As before, the `while` statement consists of everything from the word `while` through the closing brace of the compound statement. Prior to entering the `while` loop, we have made sure to assign a value to the counter being evaluated, and there is a statement to alter the value of the counter within the loop (in increments of 5) to ensure an exit from the `while` loop. Program 5.4 illustrates the use of similar code in a complete program.

The display obtained when Program 5.4 is executed is

```
DEGREES   DEGREES
CELSIUS   FAHRENHEIT
-------   ----------
   5         41.00
  10         50.00
  15         59.00
  20         68.00
  25         77.00
  30         86.00
  35         95.00
  40        104.00
  45        113.00
  50        122.00
```

Program 5.4

```cpp
#include <iostream>
#include <iomanip>
using namespace std;

// a program to convert Celsius to Fahrenheit
int main()
{

  const int MAXCELSIUS = 50;
  const int STARTVAL = 5;
  const int STEPSIZE = 5;
  int celsius;
  double fahren;

  cout << "DEGREES    DEGREES\n"
       << "CELSIUS   FAHRENHEIT\n"
       << "-------   ----------\n";

  celsius = STARTVAL;

    // set output formats for floating point numbers only
  cout << setiosflags(ios::showpoint) << setiosflags(ios::fixed)
       << setprecision(2);

  while (celsius <= MAXCELSIUS)
  {
   fahren = (9.0/5.0) * celsius + 32.0;
   cout << setw(4) << celsius
        << setw(13) << fahren << endl;
   celsius = celsius + STEPSIZE;
  }

  return 0;
}
```

EXERCISES 5.1

1. Rewrite Program 5.1 to print the numbers 2 to 10 in increments of 2. The output of your program should be

2   4   6   8   10

2. Rewrite Program 5.4 to produce a table that starts at a Celsius value of –10 and ends with a Celsius value of 60, in increments of 10 degrees.

3. a. For the following program, determine the total number of items displayed. Also, determine the first and last numbers printed.

```cpp
#include <iostream>
using namespace std;

int main()
{
  int num = 0;
  while (num <= 20)
  {
    num++;
    cout << num << " ";
  }

  return 0;
}
```

b. Enter and run the program from Exercise 3a on a computer to verify your answers to the exercise.

c. How would the output be affected if the two statements within the compound statement were reversed (that is, if the cout call were made before the num++ statement)?

4. Write a C++ program that converts gallons to liters. The program should display gallons from 10 to 20 in 1-gallon increments and the corresponding liter equivalents. Use the relationship that 1 gallon of liquid is equivalent to 3.785 liters.

5. Write a C++ program that converts feet to meters. The program should display feet from 3 to 30 in 3-foot increments and the corresponding meter equivalents. Use the relationship that there are 3.28 feet to a meter.

6. A machine purchased for $28,000 is depreciated at a rate of $4,000 a year for 7 years. Write and run a C++ program that computes and displays a depreciation table for 7 years. The table should have the form

YEAR	DEPRECIATION	END-OF-YEAR VALUE	ACCUMULATED DEPRECIATION
1	4000	24000	4000
2	4000	20000	8000
3	4000	16000	12000
4	4000	12000	16000
5	4000	8000	20000
6	4000	4000	24000
7	4000	0	28000

7. An automobile travels at an average speed of 55 miles per hour for 4 hours. Write a C++ program that displays the distance, in miles, that the car has traveled after 0.5, 1.0, 1.5, etc., hours until the end of the trip.

5.2   cin within a while Loop

Combining interactive data entry with the repetition capabilities of the while statement produces very adaptable and powerful programs. To understand the concept involved, consider Program 5.5, where a while statement is used to accept and then display four user-entered numbers, one at a time. Although it employs a very simple idea, the program highlights the flow-of-control concepts needed to produce more useful programs.

Program 5.5

```cpp
#include <iostream>
using namespace std;

int main()
{
  const int MAXNUMS = 4;
  int count;
  double num;

  cout << "\nThis program will ask you to enter "
       << MAXNUMS << " numbers.\n";
  count = 1;

  while (count <= MAXNUMS)
  {
    cout << "\nEnter a number: ";
    cin  >> num;
    cout << "The number entered is " << num;
    count++;
  }
  cout << endl;

  return 0;
}
```

The following is a sample run of Program 5.5. The italicized items were input in response to the appropriate prompts.

```
This program will ask you to enter 4 numbers.

Enter a number: 26.2
The number entered is 26.2
Enter a number: 5
The number entered is 5
Enter a number: 103.456
The number entered is 103.456
Enter a number: 1267.89
The number entered is 1267.89
```

Let us review the program so that we clearly understand how the output was produced. The first message displayed is caused by execution of the first `cout` object call. This call is outside and before the `while` statement, so it is executed once before any statement in the `while` loop.

Once the `while` loop is entered, the statements within the compound statement are executed `while` the tested condition is true. The first time through the compound statement, the message `Enter a number:` is displayed. The program then calls `cin`, which forces the computer to wait for a number to be entered at the keyboard. Once a number is typed and the Return or Enter key is pressed, the `cout` object displays the number. The variable `count` is then incremented by 1. This process continues until four passes through the loop have been made and the value of `count` is 5. Each pass causes the message `Enter a number:` to be displayed, one call to `cin` to be made, and the message `The number entered is` to be displayed. Figure 5.2 illustrates this flow of control.

Rather than simply displaying the entered numbers, Program 5.5 can be modified to use the entered data. For example, let us add the numbers entered and display the total. To do this, we must be very careful about how we add the numbers. Because the same variable, `num`, is used for each number entered, the entry of a new number in Program 5.5 automatically causes the previous number stored in `num` to be lost. Thus each number entered must be added to the total before another number is entered. The required sequence is

Enter a number
Add the number to the total

How do we add a single number to a total? A statement such as `total = total + num` does the job perfectly. This is the accumulating statement introduced in Section 3.1. After each number is entered, the accumulating statement adds the number into the total, as illustrated in Figure 5.3. The complete flow of control required for adding the numbers is illustrated in Figure 5.4.

FIGURE 5.2 *Flow-of-Control Diagram for Program 5.5*

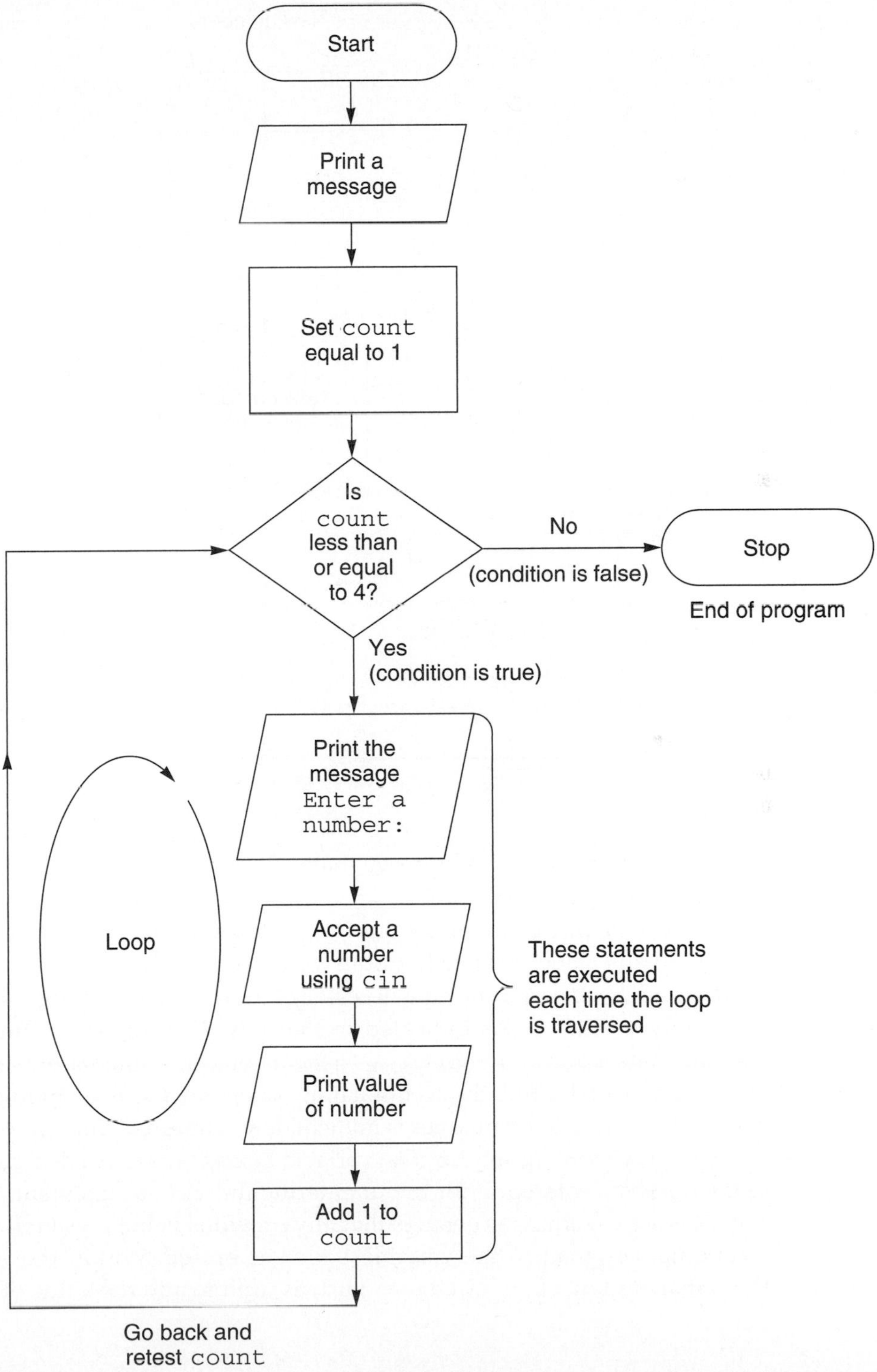

FIGURE 5.3   *Accepting and Adding a Number to a Total*

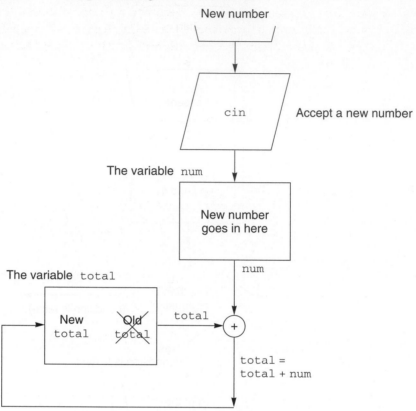

In reviewing Figure 5.4, observe that we have made a provision for initially setting the total to zero before the while loop is entered. If we were to clear the total inside the while loop, it would be set to zero each time the loop was executed, and any value previously stored would be erased.

Program 5.6 incorporates the necessary modifications to Program 5.5 to total the numbers entered. As indicated in the flow diagram shown in Figure 5.4, the statement total = total + num; is placed immediately after the cin object statement. Putting the accumulating statement at this point in the program ensures that the entered number is immediately "captured" into the total.

Let us review Program 5.6. The variable total was created to store the total of the numbers entered. Prior to our entering the while statement, the value of total is set to zero. This ensures that any previous value present in the storage location(s) assigned to the variable total is erased. Within the while loop, the statement total = total + num; is used to add the value of the entered number into total. As each value is entered, it is added into the existing total to create a new total. Thus total becomes a running subtotal of all the values entered. Only when all numbers are entered does total contain the final sum of all the numbers. After the while loop is finished, a cout statement is used to display this sum.

FIGURE 5.4   *Accumulation Flow of Control*

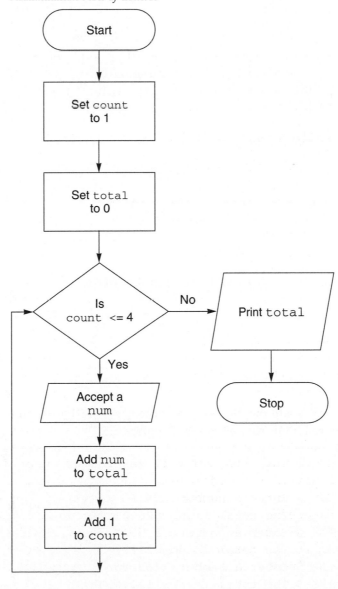

Program 5.6

```cpp
#include <iostream>
using namespace std;

int main()
{
  const int MAXNUMS = 4;
  int count;
  double num, total;

  cout << "\nThis program will ask you to enter "
       << MAXNUMS << " numbers.\n";
  count = 1;
  total = 0;

  while (count <= MAXNUMS)
  {
    cout  << "\nEnter a number: ";
    cin   >> num;
    total = total + num;
    cout  << "The total is now " << total;
    count++;
  }

  cout    << "\n\nThe final total is " << total << endl;

  return 0;
}
```

We made the following sample run of Program 5.6 using the same data we entered in the sample run for Program 5.5.

```
This program will ask you to enter 4 numbers.

Enter a number: 26.2
The total is now 26.2
Enter a number: 5
The total is now 31.2
Enter a number: 103.456
The total is now 134.656
```

```
Enter a number: 1267.89
The total is now 1402.546

The final total is 1402.546
```

Having used an accumulating assignment statement to add the numbers entered, we can now go further and calculate the average of the numbers. Where do we calculate the average, within the while loop or outside of it?

In the case at hand, calculating an average requires that both a final sum and the number of items in that sum be available. The average is then computed by dividing the final sum by the number of items. Now we must ask, "At what point in the program is the correct sum available, and at what point is the number of items available?" In reviewing Program 5.6, we see that the correct sum needed for calculating the average is available after the while loop is finished. In fact, the whole purpose of the while loop is to ensure that the numbers are entered and added correctly to produce a correct sum. After the loop is finished, we also have a count of the number of items used in the sum. However, because of the way the while loop was constructed, the number in count (5) when the loop is finished is 1 more than the number of items (4) used to obtain the total. Knowing this, we simply subtract 1 from count before using it to determine the average. With this as background, see whether you can read and understand Program 5.7.

Program 5.7 is almost identical to Program 5.6, except for the calculation of the average. We have also removed the constant display of the total within and after the while loop. The loop in Program 5.7 is used to enter and add four numbers. Immediately after the loop is exited, the average is computed and displayed. A sample run of Program 5.7 follows.

```
This program will ask you to enter 4 numbers.

Enter a number: 26.2
Enter a number: 5
Enter a number: 103.456
Enter a number: 1267.89

The average of the numbers is 350.637
```

Sentinels

All of the loops we have created thus far have been examples of fixed-count loops, where a counter has been used to control the number of loop iterations. By means of a while statement, variable-condition loops may also be constructed.

Program 5.7

```cpp
#include <iostream>
using namespace std;

int main()
{
  const int MAXNUMS = 4;
  int count;
  double num, total, average;

  cout << "\nThis program will ask you to enter "
       << MAXNUMS << " numbers.\n\n";
  count = 1;
  total = 0;

  while (count <= MAXNUMS)
  {
    cout << "Enter a number: ";
    cin  >> num;
    total = total + num;
    count++;
  }

  count--;
  average = total / count;
  cout << "\nThe average of the numbers is " << average << endl;

  return 0;
}
```

For example, when entering grades, we may not want to count the number of grades that will be entered but may prefer to enter the grades continuously and, at the end, type in a special data value to signal the end of data input.

In computer programming, data values used to signal either the start or the end of a data series are called **sentinels**. The sentinel values must, of course, be selected so as not to conflict with legitimate data values. For example, if we were constructing a program to process a student's grades, and assuming that no extra credit is given that could produce a grade higher than 100, we could use any grade higher than 100 as a sentinel value. Program 5.8 illustrates this concept. In Program 5.8, data is continuously requested and accepted until a number larger than 100 is entered. Entry of a number higher than 100 alerts the program to exit the `while` loop and display the sum of the numbers entered.

Program 5.8

```cpp
#include <iostream>
using namespace std;

int main()
{
  const int HIGHGRADE = 100;
  double grade, total;

  grade = 0;
  total = 0;
  cout << "\nTo stop entering grades, type in any number";
  cout << "\n greater than 100.\n\n";
  cout << "Enter a grade: ";
  cin  >> grade;

  while (grade <= HIGHGRADE)
  {
    total = total + grade;
    cout << "Enter a grade: ";
    cin  >> grade;
  }

  cout << "\nThe total of the grades is " << total << endl;

  return 0;
}
```

We show a sample run using Program 5.8 below. As long as grades less than or equal to 100 are entered, the program continues to request and accept additional data. When a number less than or equal to 100 is entered, the program adds this number to the total. When a number greater than 100 is entered, the loop is exited and the sum of the grades that were entered is displayed.

```
To stop entering grades, type in any number
 greater than 100.

Enter a grade: 95
Enter a grade: 100
Enter a grade: 82
Enter a grade: 101

The total of the grades is 277
```

break and continue Statements

Two statements useful in connection with repetition statements are the break and continue statements. We have encountered the break statement in relation to the switch statement. The syntax of this statement is

```
break;
```

A break statement, as its name implies, forces an immediate break, or exit, from switch, while, and the for and do-while statements presented in the next sections.

For example, execution of the following while loop is immediately terminated if a number greater than 76 is entered.

```
while(count <= 10)
{
  cout << "Enter a number: ";
  cin  >> num;
  if (num > 76)
  {
    cout << "You lose!\n";
    break;        // break out of the loop
  }
  else
    cout << "Keep on truckin!\n";
  count++;
}
// break jumps to here
```

The break statement violates pure structured programming principles because it provides a second, nonstandard exit from a loop. Nevertheless, the break statement is extremely useful and valuable for breaking out of loops when an unusual condition is detected. The break statement is also used to exit from a switch statement, but this is because the desired case has been detected and processed.

The continue statement is similar to the break statement but applies only to loops created with while, do-while, and for statements. The general format of a continue statement is

```
continue;
```

When continue is encountered in a loop, the next iteration of the loop is immediately begun. For while loops, this means that execution is automatically transferred to the top of the loop, and reevaluation of the tested expression is initiated. Although the `continue` statement has no direct effect on a `switch` statement, it can be included within a `switch` statement that itself is contained in a loop. Here the effect of `continue` is the same: The next loop iteration is begun.

As a general rule, the `continue` statement is less useful than the `break` statement, but it is convenient for skipping over data that should not be processed while remaining in a loop. For example, invalid grades are simply ignored in the following section of code, and only valid grades are added to the total.[1]

```
while (count < 30)
{
  cout << "Enter a grade: ";
  cin  >> grade;
  if(grade < 0 || grade > 100)
    continue;
  total = total + grade;
  count++;
}
```

The Null Statement

All statements must be terminated by a semicolon. A semicolon with nothing preceding it is also a valid statement, called the **null statement**. Thus the statement

```
;
```

is a null statement. This is a do-nothing statement that is used where a statement is syntactically required but no action is called for. Null statements typically are used with either `while` or `for` statements. An example of a `for` statement that uses a null statement is found in Program 5.9c in the next section.

---

[1] Although this section of code is useful in illustrating the flow of control provided by the `continue` statement, it is not the preferred way of achieving the desired result. Rather than using an `if` and a `continue` statement to exclude invalid data, a better method is to include valid data using the statement

```
if (grade >= 0 && grade <= 100)
{
  total = total + grade;
  count++;
}
```

▌ EXERCISES 5.2

---

1. Rewrite Program 5.6 to compute the total of eight numbers.

2. Rewrite Program 5.6 to display the prompt

```
Please type in the total number of data values to be added:
```

In response to this prompt, the program should accept a user-entered number and then use this number to control the number of times the while loop is executed. Thus, if the user enters 5 in response to the prompt, the program should request the input of five numbers and display the total after five numbers have been entered.

3. a. Write a C++ program to convert Celsius degrees to Fahrenheit. The program should request the starting Celsius value, the number of conversions to be made, and the increment between Celsius values. The display should have appropriate headings and should list the Celsius value and the corresponding Fahrenheit value. Use the relationship *Fahrenheit = (9.0 / 5.0) * Celsius + 32.0.*

b. Run the program written in Exercise 3a on a computer. Verify that your program starts at the correct starting Celsius value and contains the exact number of conversions specified in your input data.

4. a. Modify the program written in Exercise 3 to request the starting Celsius value, the ending Celsius value, and the increment. Thus, instead of the condition checking for a fixed count, the condition will check for the ending Celsius value.

b. Run the program written in Exercise 4a on a computer. Verify that your output starts at the correct beginning value and ends at the correct ending value.

5. Rewrite Program 5.7 to compute the average of ten numbers.

6. Rewrite Program 5.7 to display the prompt

```
Please type in the total number of data values to be averaged:
```

In response to this prompt, the program should accept a user-entered number and then use this number to control the number of times the while loop is executed. Thus, if the user enters 6 in response to the prompt, the program should request the input of six numbers and display the average of the next six numbers entered.

7. By mistake, a programmer put the statement average = total / count; within the while loop immediately after the statement total = total + num; in Program 5.7. Thus the while loop became

```
while (count <= 4)
{
  cout << "\nEnter a number: ";
  cin  >> num;
  total = total + num;
  average = total / count;
  count++;
}
```

Will the program yield the correct result with this `while` loop? From a programming perspective, which `while` loop is better to use, and why?

8. *a.* Modify Program 5.8 to compute the average of the grades entered.

   b. Run the program written in Exercise 8a on a computer and verify the results.

9. *a.* A bookstore summarizes its monthly transactions by keeping the following information for each book in stock:

> Book identification number
> Inventory balance at the beginning of the month
> Number of copies received during the month
> Number of copies sold during the month

Write a C++ program that accepts this data for each book and then displays the book identification number and an updated book inventory balance using the relationship

> New balance = Inventory balance at the beginning of the month
> + Number of copies received during the month
> – Number of copies sold during the month

Your program should use a `while` statement with a fixed-count condition so that information on only three books is requested.

   b. Run the program written in Exercise 9a on a computer. Review the display produced by your program and verify that the output produced is correct.

10. Modify the program you wrote for Exercise 9 to keep requesting and displaying results until a sentinel identification value of 999 is entered. Run the program on a computer.

5.3   The `for` Statement

The `for` statement performs the same functions as the `while` statement but uses a different form. In many situations, especially those with a fixed-count condition, the `for` statement format is easier to use than its `while` statement equivalent. The general form of the `for` statement is

```
for (initializing list; expression; altering list)
    statement;
```

Although the `for` statement looks a little complicated, it is really quite simple if we consider each of its parts separately. Within the parentheses of the `for` statement are three items separated by semicolons. Each of these items is optional and can be described individually, but the semicolons must always be present. As we shall see, the items in parentheses correspond to the initialization, expression evaluation, and altering of expression values that we have already used with the `while` statement.

The middle item in the parentheses, the expression, is any valid C++ expression, and there is no difference in the way for and while statements use this expression. In both statements, as long as the expression has a nonzero (true) value, the statement following the parentheses is executed. This means that prior to the first check of the expression, initial values for the tested expression's variables must be assigned. It also means that before the expression is reevaluated there must be one or more statements that alter these values. Recall that the general placement of these statements using a while statement follows the pattern

```
initializing statements;
while (expression)
{
   loop statements;
         .

         .

         .
   expression-altering statements;
}
```

The need to initialize variables or make some other evaluations prior to entering a repetition loop is so common that the for statement allows all the initializing statements to be grouped together as the first set of items within the for's parentheses. The items in this initializing list are executed only once, before the expression is evaluated for the first time.

The for statement also provides a single place for all expression-altering statements. These items can be placed in the altering list, which is the last list contained within the for's parentheses. All items in the altering list are executed by the for statement at the end of the loop, just before the expression is reevaluated. Figure 5.5 shows the for statement's flow-of-control diagram.

The following section of code illustrates the correspondence between the while and for statements:

```
count = 1;
while (count <= 10)
{
   cout << count;
   count++;
}
```

The for statement corresponding to this section of code is

```
for (count = 1; count <= 10; count++)
   cout << count;
```

FIGURE 5.5   *The* `for` *Statement's Flow of Control*

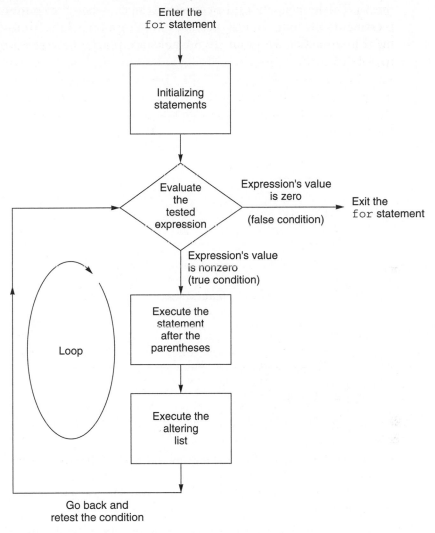

As this example shows, the only difference between the `for` statement and the `while` statement is the placement of equivalent expressions. The grouping together of the initialization, expression test, and altering list in the `for` statement is very convenient, especially when they are used to create fixed-count loops. Consider the following `for` statement:

```
for (count = 2; count <= 20; count = count + 2)
    cout << count;
```

In this statement all the loop control information is contained within the parentheses. The loop starts with a count of 2, stops when the count exceeds 20, and increments the loop counter in steps of 2. Program 5.9 illustrates this `for` statement in an actual program. Two blanks are placed between output values for readability.

Program 5.9

```
#include <iostream>
using namespace std;

int main()
{
  int count;

  for (count = 2; count <= 20; count = count + 2)
    cout << count << "  ";

  return 0;
}
```

The output of Program 5.9 is

2 4 6 8 10 12 14 16 18 20

The `for` statement does not require that any of the items in parentheses be present or that they be used for initializing or altering the values in the expression statements. However, the two semicolons must be present within the `for`'s parentheses. For example, the construction `for ( ; count <= 20;)` is valid.

If the initializing list is missing, the initialization step is omitted when the `for` statement is executed. This, of course, means that the programmer must provide the required initializations before the `for` statement is encountered. Similarly, if the altering list is missing, any expressions needed to alter the evaluation of the tested expression must be included directly within the statement part of the loop. The `for` statement ensures only that all expressions in the initializing list are executed once, before evaluation of the tested expression, and that all expressions in the altering list are executed at the end of the loop before the tested expression is rechecked. Thus Program 5.9 can be rewritten in any of the three ways shown in Programs 5.9a, 5.9b, and 5.9c.

Program 5.9a

```cpp
#include <iostream>
using namespace std;

int main()
{
  int count;

  count = 2;     // initializer outside for statement
  for ( ; count <= 20; count = count + 2)
    cout << count << " ";

  return 0;
}
```

Program 5.9b

```cpp
#include <iostream>
using namespace std;

int main()
{
  int count;

  count = 2;    // initializer outside for loop
  for( ; count <= 20; )
  {
    cout << count << " ";
    count = count + 2;     // alteration statement
  }

  return 0;
}
```

In Program 5.9a, count is initialized outside the for statement, and the first list inside the parentheses is left blank. In Program 5.9b, both the initializing list and the altering list are removed from within the parentheses. Program 5.9b also uses a compound statement within the for loop, with the expression-altering statement included in the compound statement. Finally, Program 5.9c has included all items within the parentheses, so there is no need for any useful statement following the parentheses. Here the null statement satisfies the syntactical requirement of one statement to follow the `for`'s parentheses. Observe also in Program 5.9c that the altering list (the last set of items in parentheses) consists of two items and that a comma has been used to separate these items. The use of commas to separate items in both the initializing list and the altering list is required if either of these two lists contains more than one item. Finally, note the fact that Programs 5.9a, 5.9b, and 5.9c are all inferior to Program 5.9. The `for` statement in Program 5.9 is much clearer, because all the expressions that pertain to the tested expression are grouped together within the parentheses.

 Program 5.9c

```
#include <iostream>
using namespace std;

int main()    // all expressions within the for's parentheses
{
  int count;

  for (count = 2; count <= 20; cout << count << " ", count = count + 2);

  return 0;
}
```

Although the initializing and altering lists can be omitted from a `for` statement, omitting the tested expression results in an infinite loop. For example, such a loop is created by the statement

```
for (count = 2; ; count++)
  cout << count;
```

Like the `while` statement, both `break` and `continue` statements can be used within a `for` loop. The `break` forces an immediate exit from the `for` loop, as it does from the `while` loop. The `continue`, however, forces control to be passed to the altering list in a `for` statement, after which the tested expression is reevaluated. This differs from the action of a `continue` in a `while` statement, where control is passed directly to the reevaluation of the tested expression.

Finally, many programmers use the initializing list of a `for` statement to both declare and initialize the counter variable and any other variables used primarily within the `for` loop. For example, in the `for` statement

---

PROGRAMMING NOTE

Where to Place the Opening Braces

Two styles of writing `for` loops are used by professional C++ programmers. These styles come into play only when the `for` loop contains a compound statement. The style illustrated and used in the text takes the form

```
for (expression)
{
   compound statement in here
}
```

An equally acceptable style that is used by many programmers places the initial brace of the compound statement on the first line. In this style, a `for` loop appears as

```
for (expression) {
   compound statement in here
}
```

The advantage of the first style is that the braces line up under one another, making it easier to locate brace pairs. The advantage of the second style is that it makes the code more compact and saves a line, permitting more code to be viewed in the same display area. Both styles are used, but they are almost never intermixed. As always, the indentation used within a compound statement (two or four spaces, or a tab) should also be consistent throughout all of your programs. If the choice is yours, select whichever style appeals to you and be consistent in its use. If a style is dictated by the company or course in which you are programming, find out what the style is and be consistent in following it.

```
for(int count = 0; count < 10; count++)
   cout << count << endl;
```

the variable `count` is both declared and initialized from within the `for` statement. As always, having been declared, the variable `count` can now be used anywhere following its declaration within the body of the function that contains the declaration.

To understand the enormous power of the `for` statement, consider the task of printing a table of numbers from 1 to 10, including their squares and cubes, using this statement. In Program 5.3, we saw the use of a `while` statement to produce such a table. You may wish to review Program 5.3 and compare it to Program 5.10 to get a further sense of the equivalence between the `for` and `while` statements.

Program 5.10

```cpp
#include <iostream>
#include <iomanip>
using namespace std;

int main()
{
  const int MAXNUMS = 10;
  int num;
  cout << endl;      // print a blank line
  cout << "NUMBER    SQUARE    CUBE\n"
       << "------    ------    ----\n";

  for (num = 1; num <= MAXNUMS; num++)
    cout << setw(3) << num << "        "
         << setw(3) << num * num << "      "
         << setw(4) << num * num * num << endl;

  return 0;
}
```

When Program 5.10 is run, the display produced is

NUMBER	SQUARE	CUBE
------	------	----
1	1	1
2	4	8
3	9	27
4	16	64
5	25	125
6	36	216
7	49	343
8	64	512
9	81	729
10	100	1000

Simply changing the number 10 in the for statement of Program 5.10 to 100 creates a loop that is executed 100 times and produces a table of numbers from 1 to 100. As with the while statement, this small change produces an immense increase in the processing and output provided by the program. Note also that the expression num++ was used in the altering list in place of the equivalent num = num + 1.

cin within a for Loop

Using the cin object inside a for loop produces the same effect as using this object within a while loop. For example, in Program 5.11 a cin object is used to input a set of numbers. As each number is input, it is added to a total. When the for loop is exited, the average is calculated and displayed.

Program 5.11

```cpp
#include <iostream>
using namespace std;

// This program calculates the average
// of MAXCOUNT user-entered numbers
int main()
{
  const int MAXCOUNT = 5;
  int count;
  double num, total, average;

  total = 0.0;

  for (count = 0; count < MAXCOUNT; count++)
  {
    cout << "Enter a number: ";
    cin  >> num;
    total = total + num;
  }

  average = total / count;
  cout << "The average of the data entered is " << average
       << endl;

  return 0;
}
```

The for statement in Program 5.11 creates a loop that is executed five times. The user is prompted to enter a number each time through the loop. After each number is entered, it is immediately added to the total. Although total was initialized to zero before the for statement, this initialization could have been included with the initialization of count, as follows:

```cpp
for (total = 0.0, count = 0; count < MAXCOUNT; count++)
```

PROGRAMMING NOTE

Do You Use a *for* or a *while* Loop?

Beginning programmers often ask whether they should use a `for` or a `while` loop. This is a good question, because both of these loop structures are pretest loops that, in C++, can be used to construct both fixed-count and variable-condition loops.

In many other computer languages, the answer is relatively straightforward because the `for` statement can be used only to construct fixed-count loops. Thus, in these languages, `for` statements are used to construct fixed-count loops and `while` statements are generally used only to construct variable-condition loops.

In C++, this easy distinction does not hold, inasmuch as each statement can be used to create each type of loop. The answer in C++, then, is that it's really a matter of style. Because `for` loops and `while` loops are interchangeable in C++, either loop is appropriate. Some professional programmers always use a `for` statement for every pretest loop they create and almost never use a `while` statement; others always use a `while` statement and rarely use a `for` statement. A third group tends to retain the convention used in other languages: A `for` loop is generally used to create fixed-count loops, and a `while` loop is used to create variable-condition loops. In C++ it is a matter of preference, and you will encounter all three styles in your programming career.

Additionally, the declarations for both `total` and `count` could have been included with their initializations from within the initializing list, as follows:

```
for (double total = 0.0, int count = 0; count < MAXCOUNT; count++)
```

Any one of these for constructs represents good programming practice. Which one you choose is simply a matter of your own programming style.

Nested Loops

In many situations it is very convenient to have a loop contained within another loop. Such loops are called **nested loops**. A simple example of a nested loop is

```
for(i = 1; i <= 5; i++)              // start of outer loop  <-----+
{                                    //                             |
  cout << "\ni is now " << i << endl; //                            |
                                     //                             |
  for(j = 1; j <= 4; j++)            // start of inner loop         |
    cout << " j = " << j;            // end of inner loop           |
}                                    // end of outer loop    <-----+
```

The first loop, controlled by the value of i, is called the **outer loop**. The second loop, controlled by the value of j, is called the **inner loop**. Note that all statements in the inner loop are contained within the boundaries of the outer loop and that we have used a different variable to control each loop. For each single trip through the outer loop, the inner loop runs through its entire sequence. Thus, each time the i counter increases by 1, the inner `for` loop executes completely. This situation is illustrated in Figure 5.6.

FIGURE 5. 6   *For Each i, j Loop*

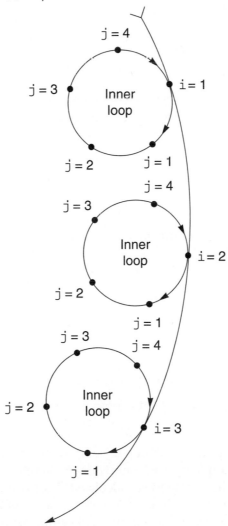

Program 5.12 includes the foregoing code in a working program.

Program 5.12

```cpp
#include <iostream>
using namespace std;

int main()
{
  int i,j;

  for(i = 1; i <= 5; i++)          // start of outer loop <----+
  {                                //                          |
    cout << "\ni is now " << i << endl;    //                  |
                                   //                          |
    for(j = 1;  j <= 4; j++)       // start of inner loop      |
      cout << " j = " << j;        // end of inner loop        |
  }                                // end of outer loop    <----+

  return 0;
}
```

Following is the output of a sample run of Program 5.12.

```
i is now 1
    j = 1  j = 2  j = 3  j = 4
i is now 2
    j = 1  j = 2  j = 3  j = 4
i is now 3
    j = 1  j = 2  j = 3  j = 4
i is now 4
    j = 1  j = 2  j = 3  j = 4
i is now 5
    j = 1  j = 2  j = 3  j = 4
```

Let us use a nested loop to compute the average grade for each student in a class of 20 students. Each student has taken four exams during the course of the semester. The final grade is calculated as the average of these examination grades.

The outer loop in our program will consist of 20 passes. Each pass through the outer loop is used to compute the average for one student. The inner loop will consist of 4 passes. One examination grade is entered in each inner-loop pass.

As each grade is entered, it is added to the total for the student, and at the end of the loop, the average is calculated and displayed. Program 5.13 uses a nested loop to make the required calculations.

Program 5.13

```cpp
#include <iostream>
using namespace std;

int main()
{

  const int NUMGRADES = 4;
  const int NUMSTUDENTS = 20;
  int i,j;
  double grade, total, average;

  for (i = 1; i <= NUMSTUDENTS; i++)         // start of outer loop
  {
    total = 0;                     // clear the total for this student
    for (j = 1; j <= NUMGRADES; j++)          // start of inner loop
    {
      cout << "Enter an examination grade for student: " << j << ":";
      cin  >> grade;
      total = total + grade;     // add the grade into the total
    }                            // end of the inner for loop
    average = total / NUMGRADES;             // calculate the average
    cout << "\nThe average for student " << i
         << " is " << average << "\n\n";
  }                                    // end of the outer for loop

  return 0;
}
```

In reviewing Program 5.13, pay particular attention to the initialization of `total` within the outer loop, before the inner loop is entered. `total` is initialized 20 times, once for each student. Also note that the average is calculated and displayed immediately after the inner loop is finished. Because the statements that compute and print the average are also contained within the outer loop, 20 averages are calculated and displayed. The entry and addition of each grade within the inner loop use techniques we have seen before, which should now be familiar to you.

▍ EXERCISES 5.3

1. Determine the output of the following program:

```
#include <iostream>
using namespace std;

int main()
{
  int i;

  for (i = 20; i >= 0; i -= 4)
  cout << i;

  return 0;
}
```

2. Modify Program 5.10 to produce a table of the numbers 0 through 20 in increments of 2, with their squares and cubes.

3. Modify Program 5.10 to produce a table of numbers from 10 to 1, instead of from 1 to 10 as it currently does.

4. Write and run a C++ program that displays a table of 20 temperature conversions from Fahrenheit to Celsius. The table should start with a Fahrenheit value of 20 degrees and should be incremented in values of 4 degrees. Recall that *Celsius = (5.0/9.0) * (Fahrenheit – 32.0)*.

5. Modify the program written for Exercise 4 to request initially the number of conversions to be displayed.

6. Write a C++ program that converts Fahrenheit to Celsius temperature in increments of 5 degrees. The initial value of Fahrenheit temperature and the total conversions to be made are to be requested as user input during program execution. Recall that *Celsius = (5.0/9.0) * (Fahrenheit – 32.0)*.

7. Write and run a C++ program that accepts six Fahrenheit temperatures, one at a time, and converts each value entered to its Celsius equivalent before the next value is requested. Use a `for` loop in your program. The conversion required is *Celsius = (5.0/9.0) * (Fahrenheit – 32.0)*.

8. Write and run a C++ program that accepts ten individual values of gallons, one at a time, and converts each value entered to its liter equivalent before the next value is requested. Use a `for` loop in your program. There are 3.785 liters in 1 gallon of liquid.

9. Modify the program written for Exercise 8 to request initially the number of data items that will be entered and converted.

10. Is the following program correct? If it is, determine its output. If it is not, determine the error and correct it so that the program will run.

```cpp
#include <iostream>
using namespace std;

int main()
{

  for(int i = 1; i < 10; i++)
    cout << i << '\n';

  for (int i = 1; i < 5; i++)
    cout << i << endl;

  return 0;
}
```

11. Write and run a C++ program that calculates and displays the amount of money available in a bank account that initially has $1000 deposited in it and that earns interest at the rate of 8 percent a year. Your program should display the amount available at the end of each year for a period of 10 years. Use the relationship that the money available at the end of each year equals the amount of money in the account at the start of the year plus .08 times the amount available at the start of the year.

12. a. Modify the program written for Exercise 11 to prompt the user for the amount of money initially deposited in the account.
b. Modify the program written for Exercise 11 to prompt the user for both the amount of money initially deposited and the number of years that should be displayed.
c. Modify the program written for Exercise 11 to prompt the user for the amount of money initially deposited, the interest rate to be used, and the number of years to be displayed.

13. A machine purchased for $28,000 is depreciated at a rate of $4,000 a year for 7 years. Write and run a C++ program that computes and displays a depreciation table for 7 years. The table should have the form

```
                  DEPRECIATION SCHEDULE
                  ----------------------

                                END-OF-YEAR        ACCUMULATED
  YEAR        DEPRECIATION          VALUE          DEPRECIATION
  ----        ------------       ------------      ------------
   1              4000              24000              4000
   2              4000              20000              8000
   3              4000              16000             12000
   4              4000              12000             16000
   5              4000               8000             20000
   6              4000               4000             24000
   7              4000                  0             28000
```

14. A well-regarded manufacturer of widgets has been losing 4 percent of its sales each year. The annual profit for the firm is 10 percent of sales. This year the firm has had

$10 million in sales and a profit of $1 million. Determine the expected sales and profit for the next 10 years. Your program should complete and produce a display as follows:

```
                  SALES AND PROFIT PROJECTION
                  ---------------------------


   YEAR                EXPECTED SALES            PROJECTED PROFIT
   ----                --------------            ----------------
    1                  $10000000.00                $1000000.00
    2                  $ 9600000.00                $ 960000.00
    3                       .                           .
    .                       .                           .
    .                       .                           .
    .                       .                           .
   10                       .                           .
   -----------------------------------------------------------------
   Totals:          $       .                   $       .
```

15. Four experiments are performed, each experiment consisting of six test results. The results for each experiment follow. Write a C++ program using a nested loop to compute and display the average of the test results for each experiment.

1st experiment results:	23.2	31.5	16.9	27.5	25.4	28.6
2nd experiment results:	34.8	45.2	27.9	36.8	33.4	39.4
3rd experiment results:	19.4	16.8	10.2	20.8	18.9	13.4
4th experiment results:	36.9	39.5	49.2	45.1	42.7	50.6

16. Modify the program written for Exercise 15 so that the number of test results for each experiment is entered by the user. Write your program so that a different number of test results can be entered for each experiment.

17. **a.** A bowling team consists of five players. Each player bowls three games. Write a C++ program that uses a nested loop to enter each player's individual scores and then computes and displays the average score for each bowler. Assume that each bowler has the following scores:

1st bowler:	286	252	265
2nd bowler:	212	186	215
3rd bowler:	252	232	216
4th bowler:	192	201	235
5th bowler:	186	236	272

b. Modify the program written for Exercise 17a to calculate and display the average team score. (*Hint:* Use a second variable to store the total of all the players' scores.)

18. Rewrite the program written for Exercise 17a to eliminate the inner loop. To do this, you will have to input three scores for each bowler rather than one at a time. Each score must be stored in its own variable name before the average is calculated.

19. Write a C++ program that calculates and displays the yearly amount available if $1000 is invested in a bank account for 10 years. Your program should display the amounts available for interest rates from 6 percent to 12 percent, inclusive, in 1 percent increments. Use a nested loop, with the outer loop having a fixed count of 7 and the inner loop a fixed count of 10. The first iteration of the outer loop should use an interest rate of 6 percent and display the amount of money available at the end of the first 10 years. In each subsequent pass through the outer loop, the interest rate should be increased by 1 percent. Use the relationship that the money available at the end of each year equals the amount of money in the account at the start of the year plus the interest rate times the amount available at the start of the year.

5.4   The do Statement

Both the `while` statement and the `for` statement evaluate an expression at the start of the repetition loop. In some cases, however, it is more convenient to test the expression at the end of the loop. For example, suppose we have constructed the following `while` loop to calculate sales taxes:

```
cout << "Enter a price: ";
cin  >> price;
while (price != SENTINEL)
{
   salestax = RATE * price;
   cout << "The sales tax is $" << salestax;
   cout << "\nEnter a price: ";
   cin >> price;
}
```

Using this `while` statement requires either duplicating the prompt and `cin` statement before the loop and then within the loop, as we have done, or resorting to some other artifice to force initial execution of the statements within the `while` loop.

The do statement, as its name implies, allows us to execute some statements before an expression is evaluated. In many situations, this approach can be used to eliminate the duplication illustrated in the previous example. The general form of the do statement is

```
do
   statement;
while (expression);  ◄────────── don't forget the final  ;
```

As with all C++ programs, the single statement in the do may be replaced with a compound statement. Figure 5.7 is a flow-of-control diagram illustrating the operation of the do statement.

FIGURE 5.7   *The* do *Statement's Flow of Control*

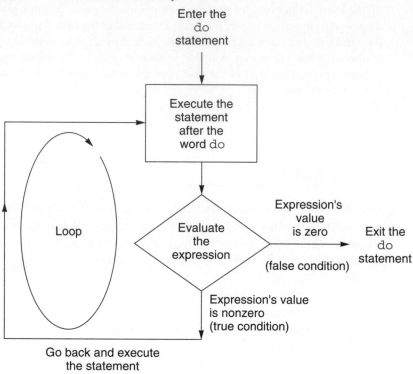

As shown in Figure 5.7, all statements within the do statement are executed at least once before the expression is evaluated. Then, if the expression has a nonzero value, the statements are executed again. This process continues until the expression evaluates to zero. For example, consider the following do statement:

```
do
{
  cout << "\nEnter a price: ";
  cin  >> price;
  if ( abs(price - SENTINEL) < 0.0001 ) break;
  salestax = RATE * price;
  cout << "The sales tax is $" << salestax;
}
while (price != SENTINEL);
```

Observe that only one prompt and cin statement are used here, because the tested expression is evaluated at the end of the loop.

As with all repetition statements, the do statement can always replace or be replaced by an equivalent while or for statement. The choice of which statement to use depends on the application and on the style the programmer prefers. In general, the while and for statements are preferred because they clearly let anyone reading the program know what is being tested "right up front" at the top of the program loop.

Validity Checks

The do statement is particularly useful in filtering user-entered input and providing data validity checks. For example, assume that an operator is required to enter a valid customer identification number between the numbers 100 and 1999. A number outside this range is to be rejected and a new request for a valid number made. The following section of code provides the necessary data filter to verify the entry of a valid identification number.

```
do
{
  cout << "\nEnter an identification number: ";
  cin  >> idNum;
}
while (idNum < 100 || idNum > 1999);
```

Here, a request for an identification number is repeated until a valid number is entered. This section of code is "bare bones" in that it neither alerts the operator to the cause of the new request for data nor allows premature exit from the loop if a valid identification number cannot be found. An alternative that removes the first drawback is

```
do
{
  cout << "\nEnter an identification number: ";
  cin  >> idNum;
  if (idNum < 100 || idNum > 1999)
  {
    cout  << "\n An invalid number was just entered"
          << "\nPlease check the ID number and re-enter";
  }
  else
    break;      // break if a valid id number was entered
} while(1);    // this expression is always true
```

Here we have used a break statement to exit from the loop. Because the expression being evaluated by the do statement is always 1 (true), an infinite loop has been created that is exited only when the break statement is encountered.

▌ EXERCISES 5.4

1. *a.* Using a do statement, write a C++ program to accept a grade. The program should request a grade continuously as long as an invalid grade is entered. An invalid grade is any grade less than 0 or greater than 100. After a valid grade has been entered, your program should display the value of the grade entered.
   b. Modify the program written for Exercise 1a so that the user is alerted when an invalid grade has been entered.
   c. Modify the program written for Exercise 1b so that it allows the user to exit the program by entering the number 999.
   d. Modify the program written for Exercise 1b so that it automatically terminates after five invalid grades are entered.

2. *a.* Write a C++ program that continuously requests a grade to be entered. If the grade is less than 0 or greater than 100, your program should print an appropriate message informing the user that an invalid grade has been entered; otherwise, the grade should be added to a total. When a grade of 999 is entered, the program should exit the repetition loop and compute and display the average of the valid grades entered.
   b. Run the program written in Exercise 2a on a computer and verify the program using appropriate test data.

3. *a.* Write a C++ program to reverse the digits of a positive integer number. For example, if the number 8735 is entered, the number displayed should be 5378. (*Hint:* Use a do statement and continuously strip off and display the units digit of the number. If the variable num initially contains the number entered, the units digit is obtained as (num % 10). After a units digit is displayed, dividing the number by 10 sets up the number for the next iteration. Thus (8735 % 10) is 5 and (8735 / 10) is 873. The do statement should continue as long as the remaining number is not zero.)
   b. Run the program written in Exercise 3a on a computer and verify the program using appropriate test data.

4. Repeat any of the exercises in Section 5.3 using a do statement rather than a for statement.

5.5   Common Programming Errors

Six errors are commonly made by beginning C++ programmers when they are using repetition statements. The most troublesome of these for new programmers is the "off by one" error, where the loop executes either one too many or one too

few times than was intended. For example, the loop created by the statement
`for(i = 1; i < 11; i++)` executes 10 times, not 11, even though the number
11 is used in the statement. Thus an equivalent loop can be constructed using the
statement `for(i = 1; i <= 10; i++)`. However, if the loop is started with
an initial value of i = 0, using the statement `for(i = 0; i < 11; i++)`, the
loop will be traversed 11 times, as will a loop constructed with the statement
`for(i = 0; i <= 10; i++)`. Thus, in constructing loops, you must pay particular attention to both initial and tested conditions used to control the loop to
ensure that the number of loop traversals is not off by one, resulting in either one
too many or one too few executions.

The next two errors pertain to the tested expression and have already been encountered with the `if` and `switch` statements. The first is the inadvertent use of
the assignment operator, =, for the equality operator, ==, in the tested expression.
An example of this error is typing the assignment expression a = 5 instead of the
desired relational expression a == 5. Because the tested expression can be any
valid C++ expression, including arithmetic and assignment expressions, this error
is not detected by the compiler.

As with the `if` statement, repetition statements should not use the equality
operator, ==, when testing double-precision operands. For example, the expression fnum == 0.01 should be replaced by a test requiring that the absolute
value of fnum - 0.01 be less than an acceptable amount. The reason for this is
that all numbers are stored in binary form. Given that we are limited to a finite
number of bits, decimal numbers such as .01 have no exact binary equivalent, so
tests requiring equality with such numbers can fail.

The next two errors are specific to the `for` statement. The more common is to
place a semicolon at the end of the `for`'s parentheses, which frequently produces
a do-nothing loop. For example, consider the statements

```
for(count = 0; count < 10; count++);
    total = total + num;
```

Here the semicolon at the end of the first line of code is a null statement. This has
the effect of creating a loop that is executed ten times with nothing done except
the incrementing and testing of count. This error tends to occur because C++
programmers are used to ending most lines with a semicolon.

The next error occurs when commas, instead of the required semicolons, are
used to separate the items in a `for` statement. An example of this is the statement

```
for (count = 1, count < 10, count++)
```

Commas must be used to separate items within the initializing and altering lists,
and semicolons must be used to separate these lists from the tested expression.

The last error we want to point out occurs when the final semicolon is omitted from the do statement. This error is usually made by programmers who have learned to omit the semicolon after the parentheses of a while statement and carry over this habit when the reserved word while is encountered at the end of a do statement.

5.6   *Chapter Summary*

1. The while, for, and do repetition statements create program loops. These statements evaluate an expression and, on the basis of the resulting expression value, either terminate the loop or continue with it. Each pass through the loop is referred to as a repetition or iteration. The tested condition must always be explicitly set prior to its first evaluation by the repetition statement. Within the loop there must always be a statement that permits altering of the condition so that the loop, once entered, can be exited.

2. The while statement checks its expression before any other statement in the loop. This requires that any variables in the tested expression have values assigned before the while is encountered. Within a while loop there must be a statement that either alters the tested expression's value or forces a break from the loop. The general form of a while statement is

```
while (expression)
    statement;
```

If the statement contained within a while statement is a compound statement, the while statement takes the form

```
while (expression)
{
    any number of statements in here;
}
```

3. The for statement is extremely useful in creating loops that must be executed a fixed number of times. Initializing expressions (including declarations), the tested expression, and expressions that affect the tested expression can all be included in parentheses at the top of a for loop. Any other loop statement can also be included within the for's parentheses as part of its altering list. The general form of a for statement is

```
for(initializing list; expression; altering list)
    statement;
```

If the statement contained within a `for` statement is a compound statement, the `for` statement takes the form

```
for(initializing list; expression; altering list)
{
    any number of statements in here;
}
```

4. The do statement checks its expression at the end of the loop. This ensures that the body of a do loop is executed at least once. Within a do loop there must be at least one statement that either alters the tested expression's value or forces a break from the loop. The general form of a do statement is

```
do
    statement;
while (expression);
```

If the statement contained within a do statement is a compound statement, the do statement takes the form

```
do
{
    any number of statements in here;
}
while (expression);
```

Modularity Using Functions

Professional programs are designed, coded, and tested very much like hardware, as a set of modules that are integrated to form a completed whole. A good analogy for this is an automobile, where one major module is the engine, another is the transmission, a third the braking system, a fourth the body, and so on. All of these modules are linked together and ultimately placed under the control of the driver, who is comparable to a supervisor or main program module. The whole now operates as a complete unit able to do useful work, such as driving to the store. During the assembly process, each module is individually constructed, tested, and found to be free of defects (bugs) before it is installed in the final product.

In this analogy, each of a car's major systems can be compared to a function. For example, the driver calls on the engine when the gas pedal is pressed. The engine accepts inputs of fuel, air, and electricity to turn the driver's request into a useful product—power—and then sends this output to the transmission for further processing. The transmission receives the output of the engine and converts it to a form that can be used by the drive axle. An additional input to the transmission is the driver's selection of gears (drive, reverse, neutral, and so on).

In each case, the engine, transmission, and other modules only "know" the universe bounded by their inputs and outputs. You, as the car's driver, need never know how the engine, transmission, air-conditioning, brakes, steering, and other modules work internally. You simply need to know what each system does and how to "call" on each system when that component's output is required. Communication between components is restricted to passing needed inputs to each module as that module is called on to perform its task, and each module operates internally in a relatively independent manner. Programmers employ this same modular approach to create and maintain reliable C++ programs using functions.

As we have seen, each C++ program must contain a `main()` function. In addition to this required function, C++ programs may also contain any number of additional functions. In this chapter we learn how to write these additional functions, pass data to them, process the passed data, and return a result.

6.1   Function and Parameter Declarations

In creating C++ functions we must be concerned with both the function itself and how it interacts with other functions, such as `main()`. This includes correctly passing data into a function when it is called and returning values from a function. In this section we describe the first part of the interface, passing data to a function and having the function correctly receive, store, and process the transmitted data.

FIGURE 6.1   *Calling and Passing Data to a Function*

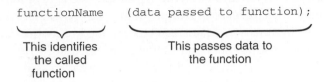

functionName   (data passed to function);

This identifies   This passes data to
the called   the function
function

As we have already seen with mathematical functions, a function is called, or used, by giving the function's name and passing any data to it, as arguments, in the parentheses following the function name (see Figure 6.1).

The called function must be able to accept the data passed to it by the function doing the calling. Only after the called function successfully receives the data can the data be manipulated to produce a useful result.

To clarify the process of sending and receiving data, consider Program 6.1, which calls a function named findMax(). The program, as shown, is not yet complete. Once the function findMax() is written and included in Program 6.1, the completed program, consisting of the functions main() and findMax(), can be compiled and executed.

Program 6.1

```cpp
#include <iostream>
using namespace std;

void findMax(int, int);  // the function declaration (prototype)

int main()
{
  int firstnum, secnum;

  cout << "\nEnter a number: ";
  cin  >> firstnum;
  cout << "Great! Please enter a second number: ";
  cin  >> secnum;

  findMax(firstnum, secnum);  // the function is called here

  return 0;
}
```

Let us examine the declaration and calling of the function `findMax()` from `main()`. We will then write `findMax()` to accept the data passed to it and determine the largest or maximum value of the two passed values.

The function `findMax()` is referred to as the **called function** because it is called or summoned into action by its reference in `main()`. The function that does the calling, in this case `main()`, is referred to as the **calling function**. The terms **called** and **calling** come from standard telephone usage, where one party calls the other on a telephone. The party initiating the call is referred to as the calling party, and the party receiving the call is referred to as the called party. The same terms describe function calls. The called function, in this case `findMax()`, is declared as a function that expects to receive two integer numbers and to return no value (a void) back to `main()`. This declaration is formally referred to as a function prototype. The function is then called by the last statement in the program.

Function Prototypes

Before a function can be called, it must be declared to the function that will do the calling. The declaration statement for a function is referred to as a **function prototype**. The function prototype tells the calling function the type of value that will be formally returned, if any, and the data type and order of the values that the calling function should transmit to the called function. For example, the function prototype used in Program 6.1,

```
void findMax(int, int);
```

declares that the function `findMax()` expects two integer values to be sent to it and that this particular function formally returns no value (`void`). Function prototypes may be placed with the variable declaration statements of the calling function, above the calling function name, as in Program 6.1, or in a separate header file that will be included using a `#include` preprocessor statement. Thus the function prototype for `findMax()` could have been placed either before or after the statement `#include <iostream>`, prior to `main()`, or within `main()`. (The reasons for the choice of placement are presented in Section 6.3.) The general form of function prototype statements is

```
returnDataType functionName(list-of-parameter-data-types);
```

where the `returnDataType` refers to the data type of the value that will be formally returned by the function. Examples of function prototypes are

```
int fmax(int, int);
double swap(int, char, char, double);
void display(double, double);
```

In the first example, function prototype for fmax() declares that this function expects to receive two integer arguments and will formally return an integer value. The function prototype for swap() declares that this function requires four arguments, consisting of an integer, two characters, and a double-precision argument, in this order, and that it will formally return a double-precision number. Finally, the function prototype for display() declares that this function requires two double-precision arguments and does not return any value. Such a function might be used to display the results of a computation directly, without returning any value to the called function.

The use of function prototypes permits error checking of data types by the compiler. If the function prototype does not agree with data types defined when the function is written, an error message will occur when the program is compiled and linked. The prototype also performs another task: It ensures conversion of all arguments passed to the function to the declared parameter data type when the function is called.

Calling a Function

Calling a function is a rather easy operation. The only requirements are that the name of the function be used and that any data passed to the function be enclosed within the parentheses following the function name, using the same order and type as declared in the function prototype. The items enclosed within the parentheses are called **arguments** of the called function (see Figure 6.2).

FIGURE 6.2   *Calling and Passing Two Values to* findMax()

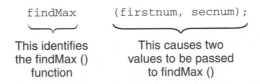

findMax	(firstnum, secnum);
This identifies the findMax () function	This causes two values to be passed to findMax ()

If a variable is one of the arguments in a function call, the called function receives a copy of the value stored in the variable. For example, the statement findMax(firstnum, secnum); calls the function findMax() and causes the values currently residing in the variables firstnum and secnum to be passed to findMax(). The variable names in parentheses are arguments that provide values to the called function. After the values are passed, control is transferred to the called function.

As illustrated in Figure 6.3, the function findMax() *does not receive the variables named* firstnum *and* secnum *and has no knowledge of these variable*

FIGURE 6.3 `findMax()` *Receives Actual Values*

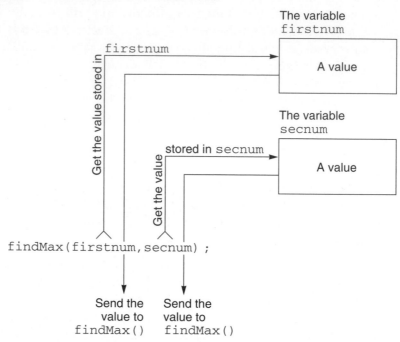

names.[1] The function simply receives the values in these variables and must itself determine where to store these values before it does anything else. Although this procedure for passing data to a function may seem surprising, it is really a safety procedure for ensuring that a called function does not inadvertently change data stored in a variable. The function gets a copy of the data to use. It may change its copy and, of course, change any variables declared inside itself. However, unless specific steps are taken to enable it to do so, a function is not allowed to change the contents of variables declared in other functions.

Now we will begin writing the function `findMax()` to process the values passed to it.

Defining a Function

A function is defined when it is written. Each function is defined once (that is, written once) in a program and can then be used by any other function in the program that suitably declares it.

---

[1] In Section 6.3 we will see how C++, using reference variables, also permits direct access to the calling function's variables.

FIGURE 6.4   *General Format of a Function*

```
function header line    ◄─────  Function header
{
    C++ statements;          ⎫
                             ⎬   Function body
}                            ⎭
```

Like the `main()` function, every C++ function consists of two parts, a **function header** and a **function body**, as illustrated in Figure 6.4. The purpose of the function header is to identify the data type of the value returned by the function; provide the function with a name; and specify the number, order, and type of arguments expected by the function. The purpose of the function body is to operate on the passed data and directly return, at most, one value back to the calling function. (We will see, in Section 6.3, how a function can be made to return multiple values using its arguments.)

The function header is always the first line of a function and contains the function's returned value type, its name, and the names and data types of its arguments. Because `findMax()` will not formally return any value and is to receive two integer arguments, the following header line can be used:

```
void findMax(int x, int y)    ◄────────── no semicolon
```

The argument names in the header are referred to as **formal parameters** of the function.[2] Thus the parameter x will be used to store the first value passed to `findMax()`, and the parameter y will be used to store the second value passed at the time of the function call. The function does not know where the values come from when the call is made from `main()`. The first part of the call procedure executed by the computer involves going to the variables `firstnum` and `secnum` and retrieving the stored values. These values are then passed to `findMax()` and ultimately stored in the parameters x and y (see Figure 6.5).

The function name and all parameter names in the header (in this case `findMax`, x, and y) are chosen by the programmer. Any names selected according to the rules used to choose variable names can be used. All parameters listed in the function header line must be separated by commas and must have their individual data types declared separately.

Now that we have written the function header for the `findMax()` function, we can construct its body. Let us assume that the `findMax()` function selects and displays the larger of the two numbers passed to it.

---

[2] The portion of the function header that contains the function name and parameters is formally referred to as a function declarator.

FIGURE 6.5 *Storing Values into Parameters*

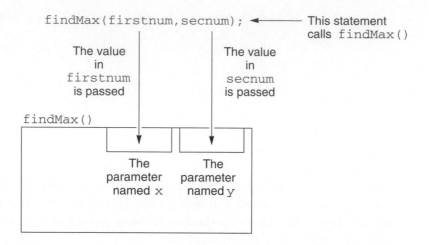

As illustrated in Figure 6.6, a function body begins with an opening brace, {, contains any necessary declarations and other C++ statements, and ends with a closing brace, }. This should be familiar to you because it is the same structure used in all the main() functions we have written. This should not be a surprise; main() is itself a function and must adhere to the rules that govern the construction of all legitimate functions.

In the body of the function findMax(), we will declare one variable to store the maximum of the two numbers passed to it. We will then use an if-else statement to find the maximum of the two numbers. Finally, a cout statement will be used to display the maximum. The complete function definition for the findMax() function is

```
void findMax (int x, int y)
{                       // start of function body
  int maxnum;           // variable declaration

  if (x >= y)           // find the maximum number
    maxnum = x;
  else
    maxnum = y;

  cout << "\nThe maximum of the two numbers is " << maxnum << endl;
}   // end of function body and end of function
```

Note that the parameter declarations are made within the header line and that the variable declaration is made immediately after the opening brace of the function's body. This is in keeping with the concept that parameter values are passed

P R O G R A M M I N G   N O T E

Function Definitions and Function Prototypes

A **function definition** defines a function. Thus, when you write a function, you are really writing a function definition. Each definition begins with a header line that includes a parameter list, if any, enclosed in parentheses and ends with the closing brace that terminates the function's body. The parentheses are required whether or not the function uses any parameters. A commonly used syntax for a function definition is

```
return-data-type function-name(parameter list)
{
    constant declarations
    variable declarations

    other C++ statements

    return value
}
```

A **function prototype** declares a function. The syntax for a function prototype, which provides the return data type of the function, the function's name, and a list of parameter data types (parameter names are optional), is

```
returnDataType functionName(list of parameter data types);
```

Thus the prototype, along with precondition and postcondition comments (see the Programming Note on page 233), should provide users with all the programming information they need to call the function successfully.

Generally, all function prototypes are placed at the top of the program, and all definitions are placed after the `main()` function. However, this placement can be changed. The only requirement in C++ is that a function cannot be called before it has been either declared or defined.

to a function from outside the function and that variables are declared and assigned values from within the function body.

Program 6.2 includes the `findMax()` function within the program code listed in Program 6.1.

FIGURE 6.6 *Structure of a Function Body*

```
{
    variable declarations and
    other C++ statements
}
```

Program 6.2

```cpp
#include <iostream>
using namespace std;
void findMax(int, int);        // the function prototype

int main()
{
  int firstnum, secnum;

  cout << "\nEnter a number: ";
  cin  >> firstnum;
  cout << "Great! Please enter a second number: ";
  cin  >> secnum;

  findMax(firstnum, secnum);  // the function is called here

  return 0;
}

// following is the function findMax()

void findMax(int x, int y)
{                    // start of function body
  int maxnum;        // variable declaration

  if (x >= y)        // find the maximum number
    maxnum = x;
  else
    maxnum = y;

  cout << "\nThe maximum of the two numbers is " << maxnum << endl;

  return 0;
}    // end of function body and end of function
```

Program 6.2 can be used to select and print the maximum of any two integer numbers entered by the user. A sample run using Program 6.2 follows.

```
Enter a number: 25
Great! Please enter a second number: 5

The maximum of the two numbers is 25
```

PROGRAMMING NOTE

Preconditions and Postconditions

Preconditions are any set of conditions that a function requires to be true if it is to operate correctly. For example, if a function uses the symbolic constant MAXCHARS, which must have a positive value, a precondition is that MAXCHARS must be declared with a positive value before the function is called.

Similarly, a postcondition is a condition that will be true after the function is executed, assuming that the preconditions are met.

Preconditions and postconditions are typically documented as user comments. For example, consider the following declaration and comments:

```
bool leapyr(int)
// Preconditions : the integers must represent a year in a four
//                : digit form, such as 2006
// Postcondition : a true is returned if the year is a leap year;
//                : otherwise a false will be returned
```

Precondition and postcondition comments should be included with both function prototypes and function definitions whenever clarification is needed.

The placement of the findMax() function after the main() function in Program 6.2 is a matter of choice. We will always list main() first, because it is the driver function that should give those who read the program an idea of what the complete program is about before they encounter the details of each function. However, in no case can the definition of findMax() be placed inside main(). This is true for all C++ functions, which must be defined by themselves outside any other function. Each C++ function is a separate and independent entity with its own parameters and variables; *nesting of functions is never permitted*.

Placement of Statements

C++ does not impose a rigid statement-ordering structure on the programmer. The general rule for placing statements in a C++ program is simply that all preprocessor directives, named constants, variables, and functions must be either declared or defined before they can be used. As we have noted previously, although this rule permits both preprocessor directives and declaration statements to be placed throughout a program, doing so results in a very poor program structure.

As a matter of good programming practice, the following statement ordering should form the basic structure around which all of your C++ programs are constructed.

```
            preprocessor directives

            function prototypes

            int main()
            {
              symbolic constants
              variable declarations

              other executable statements

              return value
            }

            function definitions
```

As always, comment statements can be freely intermixed anywhere within this basic structure.

Function Stubs

An alternative to completing each function required in a complete program is to write the main() function first and add the functions later, as they are developed. The problem that arises with this approach, however, is the same problem that occurred with Program 6.1—that is, the program cannot be run until all of the functions are included. For convenience, we have reproduced the code for Program 6.1 here.

```cpp
#include <iostream>
using namespace std;

void findMax(int, int); // the function declaration (prototype)

int main()
{
  int firstnum, secnum;

  cout << "\nEnter a number: ";
  cin  >> firstnum;
  cout << "Great! Please enter a second number: ";
  cin  >> secnum;

  findMax(firstnum, secnum); // the function is called here

  return 0;
}
```

This program would be complete if there were a function definition for findMax. But we really don't need a *correct* findMax function to test and run what has been written; we just need a function that *acts* as though it is. A "fake" findMax that accepts the proper number and types of parameters and returns values of the proper form for the function call is all we need for initial testing. This fake function is called a stub. A **stub** is the beginning of a final function that can be used as a placeholder for the final unit until the unit is completed. A stub for findMax() follows.

```
void findMax(int x, int y)
{
  cout << "In findMax()\n";
  cout << "The value of x is " << x << endl;
  cout << "The value of y is " << y << endl;
}
```

We can now compile this stub function and link it with the previously completed code to obtain an executable program. The code for the function can then be further developed, with the "real" code, when it is completed, replacing the stub portion.

The minimum requirement of a stub function is that it compile and link with its calling module. In practice, it is a good idea to have a stub display a message that it has been entered successfully and the value(s) of its received parameters, as in the stub for findMax().

As the function is refined, you let it do more and more, perhaps allowing it to return intermediate or incomplete results. This incremental, or stepwise, refinement is an important concept in efficient program development. It provides you with the means to run a program that does not yet meet all of its final requirements.

Functions with Empty Parameter Lists

Although useful functions that have an empty parameter list are extremely limited (one such function is provided in Exercise 10), they can occur. The function prototype for such a function requires writing either the keyword void or nothing at all between the parentheses following the function's name. For example, both prototypes

```
int display();
```

and

```
int display(void);
```

PROGRAMMING NOTE

Isolation Testing

One of the most successful software-testing principles is always to embed the code being tested within an environment of working code. For example, assume you have two untested functions that are called in the order shown below, and the result returned by the second function is incorrect.

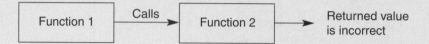

From the information shown in this figure, one or possibly both of the functions could be operating incorrectly. The first order of business is to isolate the problem to a specific function.

One of the most powerful methods of performing this code isolation is to decouple the functions. This is done either by testing each function individually or by testing one function first and then, when you know it is operating correctly, reconnecting it to the second function. Then, if an error occurs, you have isolated the error to either the transfer of data between functions or the internal operation of the second function.

This specific procedure is an example of the **basic rule of testing**, which states that each function should be tested only in a program in which all other functions are known to be correct. This means that one function must first be tested by itself, using stubs if necessary for any called functions, that a second tested function should be tested either by itself or with a previously tested function, and so on. This ensures that each new function is isolated within a test bed of correct functions, and the final program is effectively built up of tested function code.

indicate that the `display()` function takes no parameters and returns an integer. A function with an empty parameter list is called by its name with nothing written within the required parentheses following the function's name. For example, the statement `display();` correctly calls the `display()` function whose prototype is given above.

Default Arguments[3]

A convenient feature of C++ is its flexibility in providing default arguments in a function call. The primary use of default arguments is to extend the parameter list of existing functions without requiring any change in the calling argument lists already in place within a program.

---

[3] This topic may be omitted on first reading with no loss of subject continuity.

Default argument values are listed in the function prototype and are automatically transmitted to the called function when the corresponding arguments are omitted from the function call. For example, the function prototype

```
void example(int, int = 5, double = 6.78);
```

provides default values for the last two arguments. If any of these arguments are omitted when the function is actually called, the C++ compiler will supply these default values. Thus all of the following function calls are valid:

```
example(7, 2, 9.3)   // no defaults used
example(7, 2)        // same as example(7, 2, 6.78)
example(7)           // same as example(7, 5, 6.78)
```

Four rules must be followed when using default parameters. The first is that default values should be assigned in the function prototype.[4] The second is that if any parameter is given a default value in the function prototype, all parameters following it must also be supplied with default values. The third rule is that if one argument is omitted in the actual function call, then all arguments to its right must also be omitted. The second and third rules make it clear to the C++ compiler which arguments are being omitted and enable the compiler to supply correct default values for the missing arguments, starting with the rightmost argument and working in toward the left. The last rule specifies that the default value used in the function prototype may be an expression consisting of both constants and previously declared variables. If such an expression is used, it must pass the compiler's check for validly declared variables, even though the actual value of the expression is evaluated and assigned at run time.

Default arguments are extremely useful when extending an existing function to include more features that require additional arguments. Adding the new arguments to the right of the existing arguments and providing each new argument with a default value permit all existing function calls to remain as they are. Thus the effect of the new changes is conveniently isolated from existing code in the program.

Reusing Function Names (Overloading)[5]

C++ provides the capability of using the same function name for more than one function, which is referred to as **function overloading**. The only requirement in creating more than one function with the same name is that the compiler must be

---

[4] Some compilers accept default assignments in the function definition.

[5] This topic may be omitted on first reading with no loss of subject continuity.

able to determine which function to use on the basis of the data types of the parameters (not the data type of the return value, if any). For example, consider the three following functions, all named cdabs().

```
void cdabs(int x) // compute and display the absolute value of an integer
{
  if ( x < 0 )
    x = -x;
  cout << "The absolute value of the integer is " << x << endl;
}

void cdabs(float x) // compute and display the absolute value of a float
{
  if ( x < 0 )
    x = -x;
  cout << "The absolute value of the float is " << x << endl;
}

void cdabs(double x) // compute and display the absolute value of a double
{
  if ( x < 0 )
    x = -x;
  cout << "The absolute value of the double is " << x << endl;
}
```

Which of the three functions named cdabs() is actually called depends on the argument types supplied at the time of the call. Thus the function call cdabs(10); would cause the compiler to use the function named cdabs() that expects an integer argument, and the function call cdabs(6.28f); would cause the compiler to use the function named cdabs() that expects a double-precision argument.[6]

Note that overloading a function's name simply means using the same name for more than one function. Each function that uses the name must still be written, and each exists as a separate entity. The use of the same function name does not require that the code within the functions be similar, although good programming practice dictates that functions with the same name should perform essentially the same operations. All that is formally required in using the same function name is that the compiler be able to distinguish which function to select on the basis of the data types of the arguments when the function is called. Clearly, however, if all that is different about the overloaded functions is the argument types, a better programming solution is simply to create a function template. Employing overloaded functions, however, is extremely useful with constructor functions, a topic that is presented in Section 11.3.

---

[6] This is accomplished by a process referred to as **name mangling**. In name mangling, the function name actually generated by the C++ compiler differs from the function name used in the source code. The compiler appends information to the source code function name, depending on the type of data being passed, and the resulting name is said to be a mangled version of the source code name.

Function Templates[7]

In most high-level languages, including C++'s immediate predecessor, C, each function requires its own unique name. In theory this makes sense, but in practice it can lead to a profusion of function names, even for functions that perform essentially the same operations. For example, consider determining and displaying the absolute value of a number. If the number passed into the function can be an integer value, a single-precision value, or a double-precision value, three distinct functions must be written to handle each case correctly. Certainly, we could give each of these functions a unique name, such as abs(), fabs(), and dabs(), respectively, having the function prototypes

```
void abs(int);
void fabs(float);
void dabs(double);
```

Clearly, each of these three functions performs essentially the same operation, but on different parameter data types. A much cleaner and more elegant solution is to write a general function that handles all cases, but whose parameters, variables, and even return type can be set by the compiler on the basis of the actual function call. This can be done in C++ by using function templates.

A **function template** is a single, complete function that serves as a model for a family of functions. Which function from the family is actually created depends on subsequent function calls. To make this more tangible, consider a function template that computes and displays the absolute value of a passed argument. An appropriate function template is

```
template <class T>
void showabs(T number)
{
  if (number < 0)
    number = -number;
  cout << "The absolute value of the number "
       << " is " << number << endl;

  return;
}
```

For the moment, ignore the first line template <class T> and look at the second line, which consists of the function header void showabs(T number). Note that this header line has the same syntax that we have been using for all of our function definitions, except for the T where a data type is usually placed. For example, if the header line were void showabs(int number), you should rec-

---

[7] This topic may be omitted on first reading with no loss of subject continuity.

ognize this as a function named showabs that expects one integer argument to be passed to it and that returns no value. Similarly, if the header line were void showabs(float number), you should recognize it as a function that expects one floating-point argument to be passed when the function is called.

The advantage in using the T within the function template header line is that it represents a general data type that is replaced by an actual data type, such as int, float, or double, when the compiler encounters an actual function call. For example, if a function call with an integer argument is encountered, the compiler will use the function template to construct the code for a function that expects an integer parameter. Similarly, if a call is made with a floating-point argument, the compiler will construct a function that expects a floating-point parameter. As a specific example of this, consider Program 6.3.

Program 6.3

```cpp
#include <iostream>
using namespace std;

template <class T>
void showabs(T number)
{
  if (number < 0)
    number = -number;
  cout << "The absolute value of the number is "
       << number << endl;

  return;
}

int main()
{
  int num1 = -4;
  float num2 = -4.23F;
  double num3 = -4.23456;

  showabs(num1);
  showabs(num2);
  showabs(num3);

  return 0;
}
```

First note the three function calls made in the `main()` function shown in Program 6.3, which call the function `showabs()` with an integer, float, and double value, respectively. Now let's review the function template for `showabs()` and consider the first line `template <class T>`. This line, which is called a **template prefix**, is used to inform the compiler that the function immediately following is a template that uses a data type named `T`. Within the function template, the `T` is used in the same manner as any other data type, such as `int`, `float`, `double`, and so on. Then, when the compiler encounters an actual function call for `showabs()`, the data type of the argument passed in the call is substituted for `T` throughout the function. In effect, the compiler creates a specific function, using the template, that expects the argument type in the call. Because Program 6.3 makes three calls to `showabs`, each with a different argument data type, the compiler will create three separate `showabs()` functions. The compiler knows which function to use on the basis of the arguments passed at the time of the call. The output displayed when Program 6.3 is executed is

```
The absolute value of the number is 4
The absolute value of the number is 4.23
The absolute value of the number is 4.23456
```

The letter `T` used in the template prefix `template <class T>` is simply a placeholder for a data type that is defined when the function is actually invoked. Accordingly, any letter or non-keyword identifier can be used instead. Thus the `showabs()` function template could just as well have been defined as follows:

```
template <class DTYPE>
void showabs(DTYPE number)
{
  if (number < 0)
    number = -number;
  cout << "The absolute value of the number is "
       << number << endl;

  return;
}
```

In this regard, it is sometimes simpler and clearer to read the word *class* in the template prefix as the words *data type*. Thus, the template prefix `template <class T>` can be read as "We are defining a function template that has a data type named T." Then, within both the header line and the body of the defined function, the data type `T` (or any other letter or identifier defined in the prefix) is used in the same manner as any built-in data type, such as `int`, `float`, or `double`.

Now, suppose we would like to create a function template to include both a return type and an internally declared variable. For example, consider the following function template.

```
template <class T> // template prefix
T abs(T value)      // header line
{
  T absnum;          // variable declaration

  if (value < 0)
    absnum = -value;
  else
    absnum = value;

  return absnum;
}
```

In this template definition, we have used the data type T to declare three items: the return type of the function, the data type of a single function parameter named value, and one variable declared within the function. Program 6.4 illustrates how this function template could be used within the context of a complete program.

 Program 6.4

```
#include <iostream>
using namespace std;

template <class T> // template prefix
T abs(T value)      // header line
{
  T absnum;          // variable declaration

  if (value < 0)
    absnum = -value;
  else
    absnum = value;

  return absnum;
}
int main()
```

```
{
  int num1 = -4;
  float num2 = -4.23F;
  double num3 = -4.23456;

  cout << "The absolute value of " << num1
       << " is " << abs(num1) << endl;
  cout << "The absolute value of " << num2
       << " is " << abs(num2) << endl;
  cout << "The absolute value of " << num3
       << " is " << abs(num3) << endl;

  return 0;
}
```

In the first call to abs() made within main(), an integer value is passed as an argument. In this case, the compiler substitutes an int data type for the T data type in the function template and creates the following function:

```
int abs(int value) // header line
{
  int absnum; // variable declaration

  if (value < 0)
    absnum = -value;
  else
    absnum = value;

  return (absnum);
}
```

Similarly, in the second and third function calls, the compiler creates two more functions, one in which the data type T is replaced by the keyword float, and one in which the data type T is replaced by the keyword double. The output produced by Program 6.4 is

```
The absolute value of -4 is 4
The absolute value of -4.23 is 4.23
The absolute value of -4.23456 is 4.23456
```

The value of using the function template is that one function definition has been used to create three different functions, all of which use the same logic and operations but operate on different data types.

Finally, although both Program 6.3 and Program 6.4 define a function template that uses a single placeholder data type, function templates with more than one data type can be defined. For example, the template prefix

```
template <class DTYPE1, class DTYPE2, class DTYPE3>
```

can be used to create a function template that requires three different data types. As before, within the header and body of the function template, the data types DTYPE1, DTYPE2, and DTYPE3 would be used in the same manner as any built-in data type, such as int, float, double, and so on. Additionally, as we noted before, the names DTYPE1, DTYPE2, and DTYPE3 can be any non-keyword identifier. Conventionally, the letter T followed by nothing or by a digit such as T, T1, T2, T3, etc. would be used.

▮ EXERCISES 6.1

1. For the following function headers, determine the number, type, and order (sequence) of the values that must be passed to the function.
   a. void factorial(int n)
   b. void price(int type, double yield, double maturity)
   c. void yield(int type, double price, double maturity)
   d. void interest(char flag, double price, double time)
   e. void total(float amount, double rate)
   f. void roi(int a, int b, char c, char d, double e, double f)
   g. void getVal(int item, int iter, char decflag, char delim)

2. *a.* Write a function named check() that has three arguments. The first argument should accept an integer number, the second argument a double-precision number, and the third argument a double-precision number. The body of the function should just display the values of the data passed to the function when it is called. (Note: When tracing errors in functions, it is helpful to have the function display the values it has been passed. Quite frequently, the error is not in what the body of the function does with the data but, rather, in the data received and stored.)
   b. Include the function written in Exercise 2a in a working program. Make sure your function is called from main(). Test the function by passing various data to it.

3. *a.* Write a function named `findAbs()` that accepts a double-precision number passed to it, computes its absolute value, and displays the absolute value. The absolute value of a number is the number itself if the number is positive or zero and is the negative of the number if the number is negative.

   b. Include the function written in Exercise 3a in a working program. Make sure your function is called from `main()`. Test the function by passing various data to it.

4. *a.* Write a function called `mult()` that accepts two double-precision numbers as arguments, multiplies these two numbers, and displays the result.

   b. Include the function written in Exercise 4a in a working program. Make sure your function is called from `main()`. Test the function by passing various data to it.

5. *a.* Write a function named `square()` that computes the square of the value passed to it and displays the result. The function should be capable of squaring numbers with decimal points.

   b. Include the function written in Exercise 5a in a working program. Make sure your function is called from `main()`. Test the function by passing various data to it.

6. *a.* Write a function named `powfun()` that raises an integer number passed to it to a positive integer power and displays the result. The positive integer should be the second value passed to the function. Declare the variable used to store the result as a long-integer data type to ensure sufficient storage for the result.

   b. Include the function written in Exercise 6a in a working program. Make sure your function is called from `main()`. Test the function by passing various data to it.

7. *a.* Write a function that produces a table of the numbers from 1 to 10, their squares, and their cubes. The function should produce the same display as that produced by Program 5.10.

   b. Include the function written in Exercise 7a in a working program. Make sure your function is called from `main()`. Test the function by passing various data to it.

8. *a.* Modify the function written for Exercise 7 to accept the starting value of the table, the number of values to be displayed, and the increment between values. If the increment is not explicitly sent, the function should use a default value of 1. Name your function `selTable()`. A call to `selTable(6,5,2);` should produce a table of five lines, the first line starting with the number 6 and each succeeding number increasing by 2.

   b. Include the function written in Exercise 8a in a working program. Make sure your function is called from `main()`. Test the function by passing various data to it.

9. *a.* Write a C++ program that accepts an integer argument and determines whether the passed integer is even or odd. (*Hint:* Use the `%` operator.)

   b. Enter, compile, and execute the program written for Exercise 9a.

10. A useful function that uses no parameters can be constructed to return a value for π that is accurate to the maximum number of decimal places allowed by your computer. This value is obtained by taking the arcsine of 1.0, which is $\pi/2$, and multiplying the result by 2. In C++, the required expression is *2.0 * asin(1.0)*, where the `asin()` function is provided in the standard C++ mathematics library (remember to include `cmath`). Using this expression, write a C++ function named `Pi()` that calculates and displays the value of π.

11. *a.* Write a function template named `display()` that displays the value of the single argument that is passed to it when the function is called.

    b. Include the function template created in Exercise 11a within a complete C++ program that calls the function three times: once with a character argument, once with an integer argument, and once with a double-precision argument.

12. *a.* Write a function template named `whole()` that returns the integer value of any argument that is passed to it when the function is called.

    b. Include the function template created in Exercise 12a within a complete C++ program that calls the function three times: once with a character argument, once with an integer argument, and once with a double-precision argument.

13. *a.* Write a function template named `maximum()` that returns the maximum value of three arguments that are passed to the function when it is called. Assume that all three arguments will be of the same data type.

    b. Include the function template created for Exercise 13a within a complete C++ program that calls the function with three integers and then with three double-precision numbers.

14. *a.* Write a function template named `square()` that computes and returns the square of the single argument passed to the function when it is called.

    b. Include the function template created for Exercise 14a within a complete C++ program.

6.2   Returning a Single Value

When the method of passing data into a function presented in the previous section is used, the called function receives copies only of the values contained in the arguments at the time of the call (review Figure 6.3 if this is unclear to you). When a value is passed to a called function in this manner, the passed argument is referred to as a **pass by value** argument and is a distinct advantage of C++.[8] Because the called function does not have direct access to the variables used as arguments by the calling function, it cannot inadvertently alter the value stored in one of these variables.

The function receiving the passed by value arguments may process the values sent to it in any fashion desired and may directly return at most one, and only one, "legitimate" value to the calling function (see Figure 6.7). In this section we see how such a value is returned to the calling function. As you might expect in view of C++'s flexibility, there is a way of returning more than a single value, but that is the topic of the next section.

---

[8] This is also referred to as a **call by value**. The term, however, does not refer to the function call as a whole but, rather, to how an individual argument is passed when the call to a function is made.

FIGURE 6.7 *A Function Directly Returns at Most One Value*

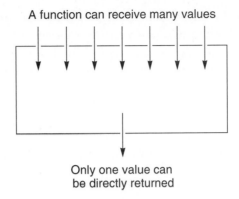

A function can receive many values

Only one value can
be directly returned

As with the calling of a function, directly returning a value requires that the interface between the called and calling functions be handled correctly. From its side of the return transaction, the called function must provide

- The data type of the returned value
- The actual value being returned

A function returning a value must specify, in its header line, the data type of the value that will be returned. Recall that the function header line is the first line of the function, which includes both the function's name and a list of parameter names. As an example, consider the findMax() function written in the last section. It determined the maximum value of two numbers passed to the function. For convenience, we will list the findMax() code again:

```
void findMax(int x, int y)
{                       // start of function body
  int maxnum;           // variable declaration

  if (x >= y)           // find the maximum number
    maxnum = x;
  else
    maxnum = y;

  cout  << "\nThe maximum of the two numbers is "
        << maxnum << endl;

} // end of function body and end of function
```

As written, the function's header line is

```
void findMax(int x, int y)
```

where x and y are the names chosen for the function's parameters.

If findMax() is now to return a value, the function's header line must be amended to include the data type of the value being returned. For example, if an integer value is to be returned, the proper function header line is

```
int findMax(int x, int y)
```

Similarly, if the function is to receive two floating-point values and return a floating-point value, the correct function header line is

```
float findMax(float x, float y)
```

and if the function is to receive two double-precision values and return a double-precision value, the correct header line is[9]

```
double findMax(double x, double y)
```

Let us now modify the function findMax() to return the maximum value of the two numbers passed to it. To do this, we must first determine the data type of the value that is to be returned and include this data type in the function's header line.

The maximum value determined by findMax() is stored in the integer variable maxnum, so it is the value of this variable that the function should return. Returning an integer value from findMax() requires that the function declaration be

```
int findMax(int x, int y)
```

Observe that this is the same as the original function header line for findMax() with the substitution of the keyword int for the keyword void.

Having declared the data type that findMax() will return, all we need to do is include a statement within the function to cause the return of the correct value. To return a value, a function must use a return statement, which has the form[10]

```
return expression;
```

---

[9] The return data type is related to the parameter data types only inasmuch as the returned value is computed from parameter values. In this case, because the function is used to return the maximum value of its parameters, it would make little sense to return a data type that did not match the function's parameter types.

[10] Many programmers place the expression within parentheses, yielding the statement return (expression);. Although either form can be used, for consistency only one should be adopted.

When the `return` statement is encountered, the expression is evaluated first. The value of the expression is then automatically converted to the data type declared in the function header before being sent back to the calling function. After the value is returned, program control reverts to the calling function. Thus, to return the value stored in `maxnum`, all we need to do is add the statement `return maxnum;` before the closing brace of the `findMax()` function. The complete function code is

These should be the same data type.

```
int findMax(int x, int y) // function header line
{                          // start of function body
  int maxnum;              // variable declaration

  if (x >= y)
    maxnum = x;
  else
    maxnum = y;

  return maxnum;                      // return statement
}
```

In this new code for the function `findMax()`, note that the data type of the expression contained in the `return` statement correctly matches the data type in the function's header line. It is up to the programmer to ensure that this is so for every function that returns a value. Failure to match the `return` value exactly with the function's declared data type may not result in an error when your program is compiled, but it may lead to undesired results because the `return` value is always converted to the data type declared in the function declaration. Usually this is a problem only when the fractional part of a returned floating-point or double-precision number is truncated because the function was declared to return an integer value.

Having taken care of the sending side of the `return` transaction, we must now prepare the calling function to receive the value sent by the called function. On the calling (receiving) side, the calling function must

- Be alerted to the type of value to expect
- Properly use the returned value

Alerting the calling function to the type of `return` value to expect is properly taken care of by the function prototype. For example, including the function prototype

```
int findMax(int, int);
```

before the `main()` function is sufficient to alert `main()` that `findMax()` is a function that will return an integer value.

To actually use a returned value we must either provide a variable to store the value or use the value directly in an expression. Storing the returned value in a variable is accomplished by using a standard assignment statement. For example, the assignment statement

```
max = findMax(firstnum, secnum);
```

can be used to store the value returned by `findMax()` in the variable named `max`. This assignment statement does two things. First the right-hand side of the assignment statement calls `findMax()`, and then the result returned by `findMax` is stored in the variable `max`. The value returned by `findMax()` is an integer, so the variable `max` must also be declared as an integer variable within the calling function's variable declarations.

The value returned by a function need not be stored directly in a variable but can be used wherever an expression is valid. For example, the expression `2 * findMax(firstnum, secnum)` multiplies the value returned by `findMax()` by 2, and the statement

```
cout << findMax(firstnum, secnum);
```

displays the returned value.

Program 6.5 illustrates the inclusion of both prototype and assignment statements for `main()` to correctly call and store a returned value from `findMax()`. As before, and in keeping with our convention of placing the `main()` function first, we have placed the `findMax()` function after `main()`.

In reviewing Program 6.5, it is important to note the four items we have introduced in this section. The first item is the prototype for `findMax()`. This statement, which ends with a semicolon as all declaration statements do, alerts `main()` and any subsequent functions that use `findMax()` to the data type that `findMax()` will be returning. The second item to notice in `main()` is the use of an assignment statement to store the returned value from the `findMax()` call into the variable `max`. We have also made sure to declare `max` correctly as an integer within `main()`'s variable declarations so that it matches the data type of the returned value.

The last two items of note concern the coding of the `findMax()` function. The first line of `findMax()` declares that the function will return an integer value, and the expression in the `return` statement evaluates to a matching data type. Thus `findMax()` is internally consistent in sending an integer value back to `main()`, and `main()` has been correctly alerted to receive and use the returned integer.

Program 6.5

```cpp
#include <iostream>
using namespace std;

int findMax(int, int); // the function prototype

int main()
{
  int firstnum, secnum, max;

  cout << "\nEnter a number: ";
  cin  >> firstnum;
  cout << "Great! Please enter a second number: ";
  cin  >> secnum;

  max = findMax(firstnum, secnum); // the function is called here

  cout << "\nThe maximum of the two numbers is " << max << endl;

  return 0;
}

int findMax(int x, int y)
{                       // start of function body
  int maxnum;           // variable declaration

  if (x >= y)           // find the maximum number
    maxnum = x;
  else
    maxnum = y;

  return maxnum;        // return statement
}
```

In writing your own functions, you must always keep these four items in mind. For another example, see whether you can identify these four items in Program 6.6.

In reviewing Program 6.6, let us first analyze the tempvert() function. The complete definition of the function begins with the function's header line and ends with the closing brace after the return statement. The function is declared as a double; this means the expression in the function's return statement must evaluate to a double-precision number, which it does. Because a function header line is not a statement but the start of the code defining the function, the function header line does not end with a semicolon.

For the receiving side, there is a prototype for the function `tempvert()` that agrees with `tempvert()`'s function definition. No variable is declared in `main()` to store the returned value from `tempvert()` because the returned value is immediately passed to `cout` for display.

One further point is worth mentioning here. One of the purposes of declarations, as we learned in Chapter 2, is to alert the compiler to the amount of internal storage to reserve for the data. The prototype for `tempvert()` performs this task and alerts the compiler to the type of storage needed for the returned value.

Program 6.6

```cpp
#include <iostream>
using namespace std;

double tempvert(double);   // function prototype

int main()
{
  const CONVERTS = 4;     // number of conversions to be made
  int count;              // start of variable declarations
  double fahren;

  for(count = 1; count <= CONVERTS; count++)
  {
  cout << "\nEnter a Fahrenheit temperature: ";
  cin  >> fahren;
  cout << "The Celsius equivalent is "
          << tempvert(fahren) << endl;
  }

  return 0;
}

// convert fahrenheit to celsius
double tempvert(double inTemp)
{
  return (5.0/9.0) * (inTemp - 32.0);
}
```

Had we placed the tempvert() function definition before main(), the function's header line would serve the same purpose and the function prototype could be eliminated. We have chosen always to list main() as the first function in a file, so we must include function prototypes for all functions called by main() and any subsequent functions.

Inline Functions[11]

Calling a function places a certain amount of overhead on a computer. This consists of placing argument values in a reserved memory region that the function has access to (this memory region is referred to as the **stack**), passing control to the function, providing a reserved memory location for any returned value (again, the stack region of memory is used for this purpose), and finally returning to the proper point in the calling program. Paying this overhead is well justified when a function is called many times because it can significantly reduce the size of a program. Rather than the same code being repeated each time it is needed, the code is written once, as a function, and called whenever it is needed.

For small functions that are not called many times, however, paying the overhead for passing and returning values may not be warranted. It still would be convenient, though, to group repeating lines of code together under a common function name and have the compiler place this code directly into the program wherever the function is called. This capability is provided by *inline functions*.

Telling the C++ compiler that a function is **inline** causes a copy of the function code to be placed in the program at the point where the function is called. For example, consider the function tempvert() defined in Program 6.6. This relatively short function is an ideal candidate to be an inline function. To make this, or any other function, an inline one, we simply place the reserved word inline before the function name and define the function before any calls are made to it. This is done for the tempvert() function in Program 6.7.

Observe in Program 6.7 that the inline function is placed ahead of any calls to it. This is a requirement of all inline functions and obviates the need for a function prototype before any subsequent calling function. Because the function is now an inline one, its code will be expanded directly into the program wherever it is called.

The advantage of using an inline function is an increase in execution speed. The inline function is directly expanded and included in every expression or statement calling it, so no loss of execution time results from the call and return overhead required by a non-inline function. The disadvantage is the increase in program size when an inline function is called repeatedly. Each time an inline function is referenced, the complete function code is reproduced and stored as an

---

[11] This section is optional and may be omitted on first reading without loss of subject continuity.

integral part of the program. A non-inline function, however, is stored in memory only once. No matter how many times the function is called, the same code is used. Therefore, inline functions should be used only for small functions that are not extensively called in a program.

Program 6.7

```
#include <iostream>
using namespace std;

inline double tempvert(double inTemp)  // an inline function
{
  return( (5.0/9.0) * (inTemp - 32.0) );
}

int main()
{
  const CONVERTS = 4;      // number of conversions to be made
  int count;               // start of variable declarations
  double fahren;

  for(count = 1; count <= CONVERTS; count++)
  {
    cout << "\nEnter a Fahrenheit temperature: ";
    cin  >> fahren;
    cout << "The Celsius equivalent is "
         << tempvert(fahren) << endl;
  }

  return 0;
}
```

▥ EXERCISES 6.2

1. Rewrite Program 6.5 to have the function findMax() accept two floating-point arguments and return a double-precision value to main(). Make sure to modify main() in order to pass two floating-point values to findMax() and accept and store the double-precision value returned by findMax().

2. For the following function headers, determine the number, type, and order (sequence) of values that should be passed to the function when it is called and the data type of the value returned by the function.

   a. `int factorial(int n)`
   b. `double price(int type, double yield, double maturity)`
   c. `double yield(int type, double price, double maturity)`
   d. `char interest(char flag, float price, float time)`
   e. `int total(float amount, float rate)`
   f. `float roi(int a, int b, char c, char d, float e, float f)`
   g. `void getVal(int item, int iter, char decflag)`

3. Write function headers for the following functions.

   a. A function named `check()`, which has three parameters. The first parameter should accept an integer number, the second parameter a floating-point number, and the third parameter a double-precision number. The function returns no value.

   b. A function named `findAbs()` that accepts a double-precision number passed to it and returns that number's absolute value.

   c. A function named `mult()` that accepts two floating-point numbers as parameters, multiplies these two numbers, and returns the result.

   d. A function named `square()` that computes and returns the square of the integer value passed to it.

   e. A function named `powfun()` that raises an integer number passed to it to a positive integer power (also passed as an argument) and returns the result as an integer.

   f. A function named `table()` that produces a table of the numbers from 1 to 10, their squares, and their cubes. No arguments are to be passed to the function, and the function returns no value.

4. *a.* Write a C++ function named `findAbs()` that accepts a double-precision number passed to it, computes that number's absolute value, and returns the absolute value to the calling function. The absolute value of a number is the number itself if the number is positive or zero; it is the negative of the number if the number is negative.

   b. Include the function written in Exercise 4a in a working program. Make sure your function is called from `main()` and correctly returns a value to `main()`. Have `main()` use `cout` to display the value returned. Test the function by passing various data to it.

5. *a.* Write a C++ function called `mult()` that accepts two double-precision numbers, multiplies these two numbers, and returns the result to the calling function.

   b. Include the function written in Exercise 5a in a working program. Make sure your function is called from `main()` and correctly returns a value to `main()`. Have `main()` use `cout` to display the value returned. Test the function by passing various data to it.

6. *a.* Write a C++ function named `powfun()` that raises an integer number passed to it to a positive integer power (also passed as an argument) and returns the result to the calling function. Declare the variable used to return the result as a long-integer data type to ensure sufficient storage for the result.

b. Include the function written in Exercise 6a in a working program. Make sure your function is called from `main()` and correctly returns a value to `main()`. Have `main()` use `cout` to display the value returned. Test the function by passing various data to it.

7. A second-degree polynomial in x is given by the expression $ax^2 + bx + c$, where a, b, and c are known numbers, and a is not equal to zero. Write a C++ function named `polyTwo(a,b,c,x)` that computes and returns the value of a second-degree polynomial for any passed values of a, b, c, and x.

8. *a.* Rewrite the function `tempvert()` in Program 6.6 to accept a temperature and a character as parameters. If the character passed to the function is the letter f, the function should convert the passed temperature from Fahrenheit to Celsius; otherwise, the function should convert the passed temperature from Celsius to Fahrenheit.

b. Modify the `main()` function in Program 6.6 to call the function written for Exercise 8a. Your `main()` function should ask the user for the type of temperature being entered and pass the type (f or c) into `tempvert()`.

9. *a.* Write a function named `rightTriangle()` that accepts the lengths of two sides of a right triangle as the parameters a and b, respectively. The subroutine should determine and return the hypotenuse, c, of the triangle. (*Hint:* Use the Pythagorean theorem, $c^2 = a^2 + b^2$.)

b. Include the function written for Exercise 9a in a working program. The `main()` function unit should correctly call `rightTriangle()` and display the value returned by the function.

10. *a.* Write a function named `totamt()` that uses four parameters named `quarters`, `dimes`, `nickels`, and `pennies`, which represent the number of quarters, dimes, nickels, and pennies in a piggybank. The function should determine the dollar value of the number of quarters, dimes, nickels, and pennies passed to it and return the calculated value.

b. Include the function written in Exercise 10a in a working program. Make sure your function is called from `main()` and correctly returns a value to `main()`. Have `main()` use a `cout` statement to display the value returned. Test the function by passing various data to it.

11. *a.* The volume, v, of a cylinder is given by the formula

$$v = \pi r^2 l$$

where r is the cylinder's radius and l is its length. Using this formula, write a C++ function named `cylvol()` that accepts the radius and length of a cylinder and returns its volume.

b. Include the function written in Exercise 11a in a working program. Make sure your function is called from `main()` and correctly returns a value to `main()`. Have `main()` use a `cout` statement to display the value returned. Test the function by passing various data to it.

12. *a.* An extremely useful programming algorithm for rounding a real number to n decimal places is

Step 1. Multiply the number by 10^n
Step 2. Add .5
Step 3. Delete the fractional part of the result
Step 4. Divide by 10^n

For example, using this algorithm to round the number 78.374625 to three decimal places yields

$$\text{Step 1:} \quad 78.374625 * 10^3 = 78374.625$$
$$\text{Step 2:} \quad 78374.625 + .5 = 78375.125$$
$$\text{Step 3:} \quad \text{Retaining the integer part} = 78375$$
$$\text{Step 4:} \quad 78375 \text{ divided by } 10^3 = 78.375$$

Using this algorithm, write a C++ function that accepts a user-entered value of money, multiplies the entered amount by an 8.675 percent interest rate, and displays the result rounded to two decimal places.

b. Enter, compile, and execute the program written for Exercise 12a.

13. *a.* Write a C++ function named `whole()` that returns the integer part of any number passed to the function. (*Hint:* Assign the passed argument to an integer variable.)

b. Include the function written in Exercise 13a in a working program. Make sure your function is called from `main()` and correctly returns a value to `main()`. Have `main()` use `cout` to display the value returned. Test the function by passing various data to it.

c. Write a C++ function named `fracpart()` that returns the fractional part of any number passed to the function. For example, if the number 256.879 is passed to `fracpart()`, the number 0.879 should be returned. Have the function `fracpart()` call the function `whole()` that you wrote in Exercise 13a. The number returned can then be determined as the number passed to `fracpart()` less the returned value when the same argument is passed to `whole()`. The completed program should consist of `main()` followed by `fracpart()` followed by `whole()`.

d. Include the function written in Exercise 13c in a working program. Make sure your function is called from `main()` and correctly returns a value to `main()`. Have `main()` use `cout` to display the value returned. Test the function by passing various data to it.

6.3   Pass by Reference

In a typical function invocation, the called function receives values from its calling function, stores and manipulates the passed values, and directly returns at most one single value. When data is passed in this manner, it is referred to as a **pass by value.**

Calling a function and passing arguments by value is a distinct advantage of C++. It allows functions to be written as independent entities that can use any variable or parameter name without concern that other functions may also be using the same name. It also alleviates any concern that altering a parameter or variable in one function may inadvertently alter the value of a variable in another function. Under this approach, parameters can be considered as either initialized variables or variables that will be assigned values when the function is executed. However, at no time does the called function have direct access to any variable defined in the calling function, even if the variable is used as an argument in the function call.

There are times when it is necessary to alter this approach by giving a called function direct access to the variables of its calling function. This allows one function, which is the called function, to use and change the values of variables that have been defined in the calling function. To do this requires that the address of the variable be passed to the called function. Once the called function has the variable's address, it "knows where the variable lives," so to speak, and can directly access and change the value stored there.

Passing addresses is referred to as a function *pass by reference*[12] because the called function can reference, or access, the variable whose address has been passed. C++ provides two types of address parameters: references and pointers. In this section we describe the method that uses reference parameters.

Passing and Using Reference Parameters

As always, in exchanging data between two functions, we must be concerned with both the sending side and the receiving side of the data exchange. From the sending side, however, calling a function and passing an address as an argument that will be accepted as a reference parameter on the receiving side is exactly the same as calling a function and passing a value; the called function is summoned into action by giving its name and a list of arguments. For example, the statement `newval(firstnum, secnum);` both calls the function named `newval` and passes two arguments to it. Whether a value or an address is actually passed depends on the parameter types declared for `newval()`. Let us now write the `newval()` function and prototype so that it receives the addresses of the variables `firstnum` and `secnum`, which we will assume to be double-precision variables, rather than their values.

One of the first requirements in writing `newval()` is to declare two reference parameters for accepting passed addresses. In C++ a reference parameter is declared using the syntax

$$dataType\& \quad referenceName;$$

For example, the reference declaration

```
double& num1;
```

declares that `num1` is a reference parameter that will be used to store the address of a `double`. Similarly, `int& secnum` declares that `secnum` is a reference to an integer, and `char& key` declares that `key` is a reference to a character.

---

[12] It is also referred to as a **call by reference**, where again the term applies only to the arguments whose addresses have been passed.

The ampersand, &, symbol in C++ means "the address of." Additionally, when an & symbol is used within a declaration, it refers to "the address of" the preceding data type. Thus, declarations such as `double& num1` and `int& secnum` are sometimes more clearly understood if they are read backward. Reading the declaration `double& num1` in this manner yields the information that "num1 is the address of a double-precision value."

Because we need to accept two addresses in the parameter list for `newval()`, the declarations `double& num1` and `double& num2` can be used. When we include these declarations within the parameter list for `newval()`, and assuming that the function returns no value (`void`), the function header for `newval()` becomes

```
void newval(double& num1, double& num2)
```

For this function header line, an appropriate function prototype is

```
void newval(double&, double&);
```

This prototype and header line are included in Program 6.8, which includes a completed `newval()` function body that both displays and directly alters the values stored in these reference parameters from within the called function.

In calling the `newval()` function within Program 6.8, it is important to understand the connection between the arguments, `firstnum` and `secnum`, used in the function call and the parameters, xnum and ynum, used in the function header. *Both refer to the same data items.* The significance of this is that the values in the arguments (`firstnum` and `secnum`) can now be altered from within `newval()` by using the parameter names (xnum and ynum). Thus the parameters xnum and ynum do not store copies of the values in `firstnum` and `secnum` but directly access the locations in memory set aside for these two arguments. The equivalence of argument and parameter names in Program 6.8, which is the essence of a pass by reference, is illustrated in Figure 6.8. As this figure shows, the argument names and their matching parameter names are simply different names referring to the same memory storage areas. In `main()` these memory locations are referenced by the names `firstnum` and `secnum`, respectively, whereas in `newval()` the same locations are referenced by the parameter names xnum and ynum, respectively.

The following sample run was obtained using Program 6.8:

```
Enter two numbers: 22.5 33.0

The value in firstnum is: 22.5
The value in secnum is: 33

The value in xnum is: 22.5
The value in ynum is: 33
```

```
                    The value in firstnum is now: 89.5
                    The value in secnum is now: 99.5
```

In reviewing this output, note that the values initially displayed for the parameters xnum and ynum are the same as those displayed for the arguments firstnum and secnum. Because xnum and ynum are reference parameters, however, newval() now has direct access to the arguments firstnum and secnum.

 Program 6.8

```cpp
#include <iostream>
using namespace std;

void newval(double&, double&);  // prototype with two reference parameters

int main()
{
  double firstnum, secnum;

  cout << "Enter two numbers: ";
  cin  >> firstnum >> secnum;
  cout << "\nThe value in firstnum is: " << firstnum << endl;
  cout << "The value in secnum is: " << secnum << "\n\n";

  newval(firstnum, secnum);    // call the function

  cout << "The value in firstnum is now: " << firstnum << endl;
  cout << "The value in secnum is now: " << secnum << endl;

  return 0;
}

void newval(double& xnum, double& ynum)
{
  cout << "The value in xnum is: " << xnum << endl;
  cout << "The value in ynum is: " << ynum << "\n\n";
  xnum = 89.5;
  ynum = 99.5;

  return;
}
```

FIGURE 6.8   *The Equivalence of Arguments and Parameters in Program 6.8.*

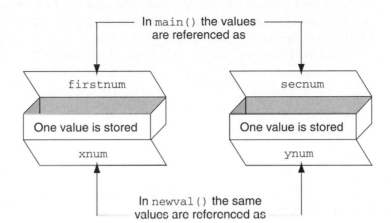

Thus any change to xnum within newval() directly alters the value of firstnum in main(), and any change to ynum directly changes secnum's value. As illustrated by the final displayed values, the assignment of values to xnum and ynum within newval() is reflected in main() as the altering of firstnum's and secnum's values.

The equivalence between actual calling arguments and function parameters illustrated in Program 6.8 provides the basis for returning multiple values from within a function. For example, assume that a function is required to accept three values, compute these values' sum and product, and return these computed results to the calling routine. Naming the function calc() and providing five parameters (three for the input data and two references for the returned values) enables us to use the following function:

```
void calc(double n1, double n2, double n3, double& sum, double& product)
{
  sum = n1 + n2 + n3;
  product = n1 * n2 * n3;
  return;
}
```

This function has five parameters, named n1, n2, n3, sum, and product, of which only the last two are declared as references. Thus the first three arguments are passed by value, and the last two arguments are passed by reference. Within the function, only the last two parameters are altered. The value of the fourth parameter, sum, is calculated as the sum of the first three parameters, and the last parameter, product, is computed as the product of the parameters n1, n2, and n3. Program 6.9 includes this function in a complete program.

Within main(), the function calc() is called using the five arguments firstnum, secnum, thirdnum, sum, and product. As required, these arguments agree in number and data type with the parameters declared by calc(). Of the five arguments passed, only firstnum, secnum, and thirdnum have been assigned values when the call to calc() is made. The remaining two arguments have not been initialized and will be used to receive values back from calc(). Depending on the compiler used in compiling the program, these arguments will initially contain either zeros or "garbage" values. Figure 6.9 illustrates the relationship between actual and parameter names and the values they contain after the return from calc().

Program 6.9

```cpp
#include <iostream>
using namespace std;

void calc(double, double, double, double&, double&); // prototype

int main()
{
  double firstnum, secnum, thirdnum, sum, product;

  cout << "Enter three numbers: ";
  cin  >> firstnum >> secnum >> thirdnum;

  calc(firstnum, secnum, thirdnum, sum, product); // function call

  cout << "\nThe sum of the numbers is: " << sum << endl;
  cout << "The product of the numbers is: " << product << endl;

  return 0;
}

void calc(double n1, double n2, double n3, double& sum, double& product)
{
  sum = n1 + n2 + n3;
  product = n1 * n2 * n3;
  return;
}
```

Once `calc()` is called, it uses its first three parameters to calculate values for `total` and `product` and then returns control to `main()`. Because of the order of its actual calling arguments, `main()` knows the values calculated by `calc()` as `sum` and `product`, which are then displayed. Following is a sample run using Program 6.9:

```
Enter three numbers: 2.5 6.0 10.0

The sum of the entered numbers is: 18.5
The product of the entered numbers is: 150
```

As a final example illustrating the usefulness of passing references to a called function, we will construct a function named `swap()` that exchanges the values of two of `main()`'s double-precision variables. Such a function is useful when we are sorting a list of numbers.

Because the value of more than a single variable is affected, `swap()` cannot be written as a pass by value function that returns a single value. The desired exchange of `main()`'s variables by `swap()` can be obtained only by giving `swap()` access to `main()`'s variables. One way of doing this is to use reference parameters.

FIGURE 6.9   *Relationship Between Argument and Parameter Names*

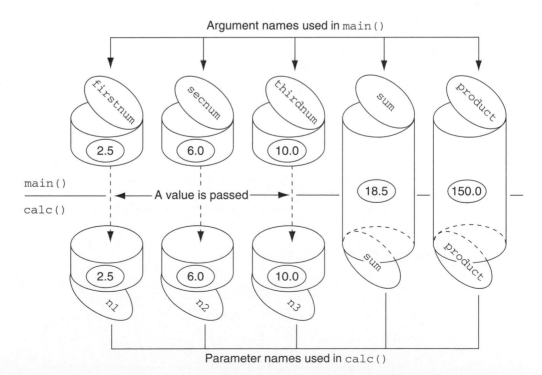

We have already seen, in Program 6.8, how to pass references to two variables. We will now construct a function to exchange the values in the passed reference parameters. Exchanging values in two variables is accomplished by using the three-step exchange algorithm

1. Save the first parameter's value in a temporary location (see Figure 6.10a)
2. Store the second parameter's value in the first variable (see Figure 6.10b)
3. Store the temporary value in the second parameter (see Figure 6.10c)

Following is the function swap() written according to these specifications:

```
void swap(double& num1, double& num2)
{
   double temp;

   temp = num1;        // save num1's value
   num1 = num2;        // store num2's value in num1
   num2 = temp;        // change num2's value

   return;
}
```

FIGURE 6.10a *Save the First Value*

FIGURE 6.10b *Replace the First Value with the Second Value*

FIGURE 6.10c *Change the Second Value*

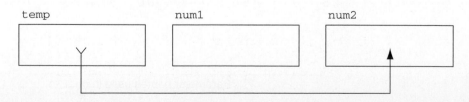

Note that the use of references in `swap()`'s header line gives `swap()` access to the equivalent arguments in the calling function. Thus any changes to the two reference parameters in `swap()` automatically change the values in the calling function's arguments. Program 6.10 contains `swap()` in a complete program.

Program 6.10

```cpp
#include <iostream>
using namespace std;

void swap(double&, double&);   // function receives 2 references

int main()
{
  double firstnum = 20.5, secnum = 6.25;

  cout << "The value stored in firstnum is: " << firstnum << endl;
  cout << "The value stored in secnum is: "<< secnum << "\n\n";

  swap(firstnum, secnum);    // call the function with references

  cout << "The value stored in firstnum is now: " << firstnum << endl;
  cout << "The value stored in secnum is now: " << secnum << endl;

  return 0;
}

void swap(double& num1, double& num2)
{
  double temp;

  temp = num1;      // save num1's value
  num1 = num2;      // store num2's value in num1
  num2 = temp;      // change num2's value

  return;
}
```

The following sample run was obtained using Program 6.10:

```
The value stored in firstnum is: 20.5
The value stored in secnum is: 6.25
```

```
The value stored in firstnum is now: 6.25
The value stored in secnum is now: 20.5
```

As the output illustrates, the values stored in `main()`'s variables have been modified from within `swap()`, which was made possible by the use of reference parameters. If a pass by value had been used instead, the exchange within `swap()` would affect only `swap()`'s parameters and would accomplish nothing with respect to `main()`'s variables. Thus a function such as `swap()` can be written only using references or some other means that provides access to `main()`'s variables (this other means is by pointers, the topic of Chapter 12).

There are two cautions to keep in mind when using reference parameters. The first is that the equivalent arguments *must* be variables (that is, they cannot be used to change constants). For example, calling `swap()` with two constants, such as in the call `swap(20.5, 6.5)`, passes two constants to the function. Although `swap()` may execute, it will not change the values of these constants.[13]

The second caution is that a function call itself gives no indication that the called function will be using reference parameters. The default in C++ is to make passes by value rather than passes by reference, precisely to limit a called function's ability to alter variables in the calling function. This calling procedure should be adhered to whenever possible, which means that reference parameters should be used only in very restricted situations that actually require multiple return values, such as in the `swap()` function illustrated in Program 6.10. The `calc()` function, included in Program 6.9, though it is useful for illustrative purposes, can also be written as two separate functions, each returning a single value.

▌ EXERCISES 6.3

1. Write parameter declarations for:

   a. A formal parameter named `amount` that will be a reference to a double-precision value
   b. A formal parameter named `price` that will be a reference to a double-precision number
   c. A formal parameter named `minutes` that will be a reference to an integer number
   d. A formal parameter named `key` that will be a reference to a character
   e. A formal parameter named `yield` that will be a reference to a double-precision number

2. Three integer arguments are to be used in a call to a function named `time()`. Write a suitable function header for `time()`, assuming that `time()` accepts these variables as the reference parameters `sec`, `min`, and `hours` and returns no value to its calling function.

---

[13] Most compilers will catch this error.

3. Rewrite the findMax() function in Program 6.5 so that the variable max, declared in main(), is used to store the maximum value of the two passed numbers. The value of max should be set directly from within findMax(). (*Hint:* A reference to max will have to be accepted by findMax().)

4. Write a function named change() that has an integer parameter and six integer reference parameters named hundreds, fifties, twenties, tens, fives, and ones. The function is to consider the integer passed value as a dollar amount and convert the value into the least number of equivalent bills. Using the references, the function should directly alter the respective arguments in the calling function.

5. Write a function named time() that has an integer parameter named seconds and three integer reference parameters named hours, min, and sec. The function is to convert the passed number of seconds into an equivalent number of hours, minutes, and seconds. Using the references, the function should directly alter the respective actual arguments in the calling function.

6. Write a function named yrCalc() that has an integer parameter representing the total number of days since the turn of the last century (1/1/1900) and reference parameters named year, month, and day. The function is to calculate the current year, month, and day for the given number of days passed to it. Using the references, the function should directly alter the respective actual arguments in the calling function. For this problem, assume that each year has 365 days and each month has 30 days.

7. Write a function named liquid() that has an integer number parameter and reference parameters named gallons, quarts, pints, and cups. The passed integer represents the total number of cups, and the function is to determine the numbers of gallons, quarts, pints, and cups in the passed value. Using the references, the function should directly alter the respective actual arguments in the calling function. Use the relationships of 2 cups to a pint, 4 cups to a quart, and 16 cups to a gallon.

8. The following program uses the same argument and parameter names in both the calling function and the called function. Determine whether this causes any problem for the computer.

```cpp
#include <iostream>
using namespace std;

int main()
{
  int min, hour;
  void time(int&, int&);      // function prototype

  cout << "Enter two numbers :";
  cin  >> min >> hour;
  time(min, hour);

  return 0;
}
```

(continued on next page)

(continued from previous page)

```
void time(int& min, int& hour)          // accept two references
{
  int sec;

  sec = (hour * 60 + min) * 60;
  cout << "The total number of seconds is " << sec << endl;

  return 0;
}
```

6.4   Variable Scope

Now that we have begun to write programs that contain more than one function, we can look more closely at the variables declared within each function and their relationship to variables in other functions.

By their very nature, C++ functions are constructed to be independent modules. As we have seen, values are passed to a function using the function's parameter list, and a value is returned from a function using a `return` statement. Seen in this light, a function can be thought of as a closed box, with slots at the top to receive values and a single slot at the bottom of the box to return a value (see Figure 6.11).

The metaphor of a closed box is useful because it emphasizes the fact that what goes on inside the function, including all variable declarations within the function's body, is hidden from the view of all other functions. Because the variables created inside a function are conventionally available only to the function itself, they are said to be local to the function, or **local variables**. This term refers to the scope of an identifier, where **scope** is defined as the section of the program where the identifier, such as a variable, is valid or "known." This section of the program is also referred to as where the variable is visible. A variable can have either a local scope or a global scope. A variable with a **local scope** is simply one that has had storage locations set aside for it by a declaration statement made within a function body. Local variables are meaningful only when used in expressions or statements inside the function that declared them. This means that the same variable name can be declared and used in more than one function. For each function that declares the variable, a separate and distinct variable is created.

All the variables that we have used until now have been local variables. This is a direct result of placing our declaration statements inside functions and using them as definition statements that cause the compiler to reserve storage for the declared variable. As we shall see, declaration statements can be placed outside functions, and they need not act as definitions that cause new storage areas to be reserved for the declared variable.

FIGURE 6.11   *A Function Can Be Considered a Closed Box*

Values into the function

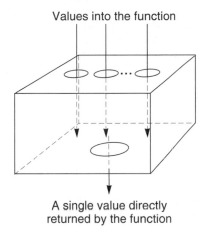

A single value directly
returned by the function

A variable with **global scope**, more commonly termed a **global variable**, is one whose storage has been created for it by a declaration statement located outside any function. These variables can be used by all functions that are physically placed after the global variable declaration. This is shown in Program 6.11, where we have purposely used the same variable name inside both functions contained in the program.

The variable `firstnum` in Program 6.11 is a global variable because its storage is created by a definition statement located outside a function. Because both functions, `main()` and `valfun()`, follow the definition of `firstnum`, both of these functions can use this global variable with no further declaration needed.

Program 6.11 also contains two separate local variables, both named `secnum`. Storage for the `secnum` variable named in `main()` is created by the definition statement located in `main()`. A different storage area for the `secnum` variable in `valfun()` is created by the definition statement located in the `valfun()` function. Figure 6.12 illustrates the three distinct storage areas reserved by the three definition statements found in Program 6.11.

All of the variables named `secnum` are local to the function in which their storage is created, and each of these variables can be used only from within the appropriate function. Thus when `secnum` is used in `main()`, the storage area reserved by `main()` for its `secnum` variable is accessed, and when `secnum` is used in `valfun()`, the storage area reserved by `valfun()` for its `secnum` variable is accessed. The following output is produced when Program 6.11 is run:

```
From main(): firstnum = 10
From main(): secnum = 20
```

Program 6.11

```cpp
#include <iostream>
using namespace std;

int firstnum;          // create a global variable named firstnum

void valfun();    // function prototype (declaration)

int main()
{
  int secnum;          // create a local variable named secnum

  firstnum = 10;       // store a value into the global variable
  secnum = 20;         // store a value into the local variable

  cout << "From main(): firstnum = " << firstnum << endl;
  cout << "From main(): secnum = " << secnum << endl;

  valfun();            // call the function valfun

  cout << "\nFrom main() again: firstnum = " << firstnum << endl;
  cout << "From main() again: secnum = " << secnum << endl;

  return 0;
}

void valfun()      // no values are passed to this function
{
  int secnum;      // create a second local variable named secnum

  secnum = 30;     // this only affects this local variable's value

  cout << "\nFrom valfun(): firstnum = " << firstnum << endl;
  cout << "From valfun(): secnum = " << secnum << endl;

  firstnum = 40;       // this changes firstnum for both functions

  return;
}
```

```
From valfun(): firstnum = 10
From valfun(): secnum = 30

From main() again: firstnum = 40
From main() again: secnum = 20
```

Let's analyze the output. Because firstnum is a global variable, both the main() function and the valfun() function can use and change its value. Initially, both functions print the value of 10 that main() stored in firstnum. Before returning, valfun() changes the value of firstnum to 40, which is the value displayed when the variable firstnum is next displayed from within main().

FIGURE 6.12   *The Three Storage Areas Created by Program 6.11*

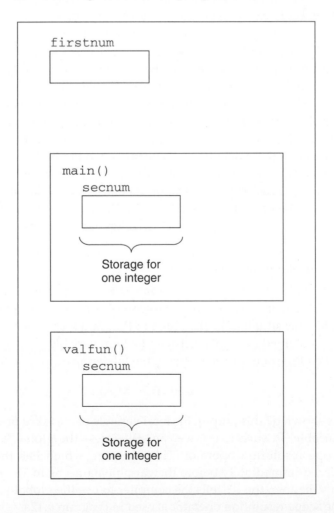

FIGURE 6.13   *Relating the Scope and Type of a Variable*

Scope

Local				Global			
char	int	bool	double	char	int	bool	double

Data type

Because each function "knows" only its own local variables, main() can send only the value of its secnum to the cout object, and valfun() can send only the value of its secnum to the cout object. Thus whenever secnum is obtained from main(), the value 20 is displayed, and whenever secnum is obtained from valfun(), the value 30 is displayed.

C++ does not confuse the two secnum variables because only one function can execute at a given moment. While a function is executing, only those variables and parameters that are "in scope" for that function (global and local) can be accessed.

The scope of a variable in no way influences or restricts the data type of the variable. Just as a local variable can be a character, integer, Boolean, double, or any of the other data types (long/short) that we have introduced, so can global variables be of these data types, as illustrated in Figure 6.13. The scope of a variable is determined by the placement of the definition statement that reserves storage for it and optionally by a declaration statement that makes it visible, whereas the data type of the variable is determined by using the appropriate keyword (char, int, bool, double, etc.) before the variable's name in a declaration statement.

Scope Resolution Operator

When a local variable has the same name as a global variable, all references to the variable name made within the scope of the local variable refer to the local variable. This situation is illustrated in Program 6.12, where the variable name number is defined as both a global and a local variable.

When Program 6.12 is executed, the following output is displayed:

```
The value of number is 26.4
```

As shown by this output, the local variable name takes precedence over the global variable. In such cases, we can still access the global variable by using C++'s scope resolution operator. This operator, which has the symbol ::, must be placed immediately before the variable name, as in :: number. When used in this manner, the :: tells the compiler to use the global variable. As an example, the scope resolution operator is used in Program 6.12a.

Program 6.12

```cpp
#include <iostream>
using namespace std;

double number = 42.8;       // a global variable named number

int main()
{
    double number = 26.4;     // a local variable named number

    cout << "The value of number is " << number << endl;

    return 0;
}
```

Program 6.12a

```cpp
#include <iostream>
using namespace std;

double number = 42.5;       // a global variable named number

int main()
{
    double number = 26.4;     // a local variable named number

    cout << "The value of number is " << ::number << endl;

    return 0;
}
```

The output produced by Program 6.12a is

```
The value of number is 42.5
```

As indicated by this output, the scope resolution operator causes the global, rather than the local, variable to be accessed.

Misuse of Globals

Global variables allow the programmer to "jump around" the normal safeguards provided by functions. Rather than passing variables to a function, it is possible to make all variables global ones. *Do not do this.* By indiscriminately making all variables global, you instantly destroy the safeguards that C++ provides to make functions independent and insulated from each other, including the necessity of carefully designating the type of parameters a function needs, the variables used in the function, and the value returned.

Using only global variables can be especially disastrous in larger programs that have many user-created functions. Because all variables in a function must be declared, creating functions that use global variables requires that you remember to write the appropriate global declarations at the top of each program that uses the function; they no longer come along with the function. More devastating than this, however, is the horror of trying to track down an error in a large program using global variables. A global variable can be accessed and changed by any function following the global declaration, so it is a time-consuming and frustrating task to locate the origin of an erroneous value.

Global definitions, however, are sometimes useful in creating variables and named constants that must be shared among many functions. Rather than passing the same value to each function, it is easier to define the variable or constant once as a global. Doing so also notifies anyone reading the program that many functions use the variable. Most large programs nearly always make use of a few global variables and/or constants. Smaller programs containing a few functions, however, should almost never contain global variables.

The misuse of globals does not apply to function prototypes, which typically are global. Note that all of the function prototypes we have used have been of global scope, which declares the prototype to all subsequent functions. Placing a function prototype within a function makes the prototype a local declaration, available only to the function within which it is declared.

EXERCISES 6.4

1. *a.* For the following section of code, determine the data type and scope of all declared constants and variables. To do this, use a separate sheet of paper and list the three column headings that follow (we have filled in the entries for the first variable).

Identifier	Data Type	Scope
PRICE	integer	global to `main()`, `roi()`, and `step()`

```cpp
#include <iostream>
using namespace std;

const int PRICE;
const long YEARS;
const double YIELD;
int main()
{
  int bondtype;
  double interest, coupon;

    .
    .
    .

  return 0;
}
double roi(int mat1, int mat2)
{
  int count;
  double effectiveRate;

    .
    .
    .

  return effectiveRate;
}
int step(double first, double last)
{
  int numofyrs;
  double fracpart;

    .
    .
    .

  return(10*numofyrs);
}
```

b. Draw boxes around the appropriate section of the above code to enclose the scope of each variable.

c. Determine the data type of the parameters that the functions `roi()` and `step()` expect and the data type of the value returned by these functions.

2. *a.* For the following section of code, determine the data type and scope of all declared constants and variables. To do this, use a separate sheet of paper and list the three column headings that follow (we have filled in the entries for the first variable).

Identifier	Data Type	Scope
KEY	char	global to `main()`, `func1()`, and `func2()`

```
#include <iostream>
using namespace std;

const char KEY;
const long NUMBER;
int func1(int, int);           // function prototype
double func2(double, double);  // function prototype
int main()
{
  int a,b,c;
  double x,y;

    .

    .

    .

  return 0;
}

double secnum;
int func1(int num1, int num2)
{
  int o,p;
  double q;

    .

    .

    .

  return p;
}

double func2(double first, double last)
{
  int a,b,c,o,p;
  float r;
  double s,t,x;

    .

    .

    .

  return s * t;
}
```

b. Draw a box around the appropriate section of the above code to enclose the scope of the variables key, secnum, y, and r.

c. Determine the data type of the parameters for the functions func1() and func2() and the data type of the value returned by these functions.

3. Besides speaking about the scope of a variable, we can also apply the term to a function's parameters. What do you think is the scope of all function parameters?

4. Determine the values displayed by each `cout` statement in the following program:

```cpp
#include <iostream>
using namespace std;

int firstnum = 10;   // declare and initialize a global variable
void display(void);   // function prototype
int main()
{
   int firstnum = 20; // declare and initialize a local variable

   cout << "\nThe value of firstnum is " << firstnum;
   display();

   return 0;
}
void display(void)
{
   cout << "\nThe value of firstnum is now " << firstnum;

   return;
}
```

6.5   Variable Storage Class

The scope of a variable defines the location within a program where that variable can be used. Given a program, you could take a pencil and draw a box around the section of the program where each variable is valid. The space inside the box would represent the scope of a variable. From this viewpoint, the scope of a variable can be thought of as the space within the program where the variable is valid.

In addition to the space dimension represented by its scope, variables also have a time dimension. The time dimension refers to the length of time that storage locations are reserved for a variable. This time dimension is referred to as the variable's "lifetime." For example, all variable storage locations are released back to the operating system when a program is finished running. However, while a program is still executing, interim variable storage areas also are reserved and subsequently released back to the operating system. Where and how long a variable's storage locations are kept before they are released can be determined by the **storage class** of the variable.

Besides having a data type and scope, every variable also has a storage class. The four available storage classes are called `auto`, `static`, `extern`, and `register`. If one of these class names is used, it must be placed before the variable's data type in a declaration statement. Examples of declaration statements that include a storage class designation are

```
auto int num;       // auto storage class and int data type
static int miles;   // static storage class and int data type
register int dist;  // register storage class and int data type
extern int volts;   // extern storage class and int data type
auto float coupon;  // auto storage class and float data type
static double yrs;  // static storage class and double data type
extern float yld;   // extern storage class and float data type
auto char inKey;    // auto storage class and char variable
```

To understand what the storage class of a variable means, we will consider first local variables (those variables created inside a function) and then global variables (those variables created outside a function).

Local Variable Storage Classes

Local variables can only be members of the `auto`, `static`, or `register` storage classes. If no class description is included in the declaration statement, the variable is automatically assigned to the `auto` class. Thus `auto` is the default class used by C++. Because the storage class designation was omitted, all the local variables that we have used have been `auto` variables.

The term `auto` is short for **automatic**. Storage for `auto` local variables is automatically reserved (that is, created) each time a function declaring `auto` variables is called. As long as the function has not returned control to its calling function, all `auto` variables local to the function are "alive"—that is, storage for the variables is available. When the function returns control to its calling function, its local `auto` variables "die"—that is, the storage for the variables is released back to the operating system. This process repeats itself each time a function is called. For example, consider Program 6.13, where the function `testauto()` is called three times from `main()`.

The output produced by Program 6.13 is

```
The value of the automatic variable num is 0
The value of the automatic variable num is 0
The value of the automatic variable num is 0
```

Each time `testauto()` is called, the `auto` variable num is created and initialized to zero. When the function returns control to `main()`, the variable num is destroyed, along with any value stored in num. Thus the effect of incrementing num in `testauto()`, before the function's `return` statement, is lost when control is returned to `main()`.

Program 6.13

```cpp
#include <iostream>
using namespace std;

void testauto();   // function prototype

int main()
{
  int count;              // count is a local auto variable

  for(count = 1; count <= 3; count++)
    testauto();

  return 0;
}

void testauto()
{
  int num = 0;     // num is a local auto variable
                   // that is initialized to zero
  cout << "The value of the automatic variable num is "
       << num << endl;
  num++;

  return;
}
```

For most applications, the use of `auto` variables works just fine. There are cases, however, where we would like a function to remember values between function calls. This is the purpose of the `static` storage class. A local variable that is declared as `static` causes the program to keep the variable and its latest value, even when the function that declared it is finished executing. Examples of `static` variable declarations are

```cpp
static int rate;
static double amount;
static char inKey;
```

A local `static` variable is not created and destroyed each time the function declaring the `static` variable is called. Once created, local `static` variables remain in existence for the life of the program. This means that the last value stored in the variable when the function is finished executing is available to the function the next time it is called.

Because local static variables retain their values, they are not initialized within a declaration statement in the same way as auto variables. To understand why, consider the automatic declaration int num = 0;, which causes the auto variable num to be created and set to zero each time the declaration is encountered. This is called a **run-time initialization** because initialization occurs each time the declaration statement is encountered. This type of initialization would be disastrous for a static variable because resetting the variable's value to zero each time the function is called would destroy the very value we are trying to save.

The initialization of static variables (both local and global) is done only once, when the program is first compiled. At compilation time, the variable is created and any initialization value is placed in it.[14] Thereafter, the value in the variable is kept without further initialization each time the function is called. To see how this works, consider Program 6.14.

Program 6.14

```cpp
#include <iostream>
using namespace std;

void teststat();    // function prototype

int main()
{
  int count;             // count is a local auto variable
  for(count = 1; count <= 3; count++)
    teststat();

  return 0;
}

void teststat()
{
  static int num = 0;    // num is a local static variable
  cout << "The value of the static variable num is now "
       << num << endl;
  num++;

  return;
}
```

---

[14] Some compilers initialize static local variables the first time the definition statement is executed rather than when the program is compiled.

The output produced by Program 6.14 is

```
The value of the static variable num is now 0
The value of the static variable num is now 1
The value of the static variable num is now 2
```

As illustrated by this output, the `static` variable num is set to zero only once. The function `teststat()` then increments this variable just before returning control to `main()`. The value that num has when leaving the function `teststat()` is retained and displayed when the function is next called.

Unlike `auto` variables that can be initialized by either constants or expressions using both constants and previously initialized variables, `static` variables can be initialized only by using constants or constant expressions, such as $3.2 + 8.0$. Also, unlike `auto` variables, all `static` variables are set to zero when no explicit initialization is given. Thus the specific initialization of num to zero in Program 6.14 is not required.

The remaining storage class available to local variables, the register class, is not used as extensively as either `auto` or `static` variables. Examples of `register` variable declarations are

```
register int time;
register double diffren;
register float coupon;
```

`Register` variables have the same time duration as `auto` variables; that is, a local `register` variable is created when the function declaring it is entered, and it is destroyed when the function completes execution. The only difference between `register` and `auto` variables is in where the storage for the variable is located.

Storage for all variables (local and global), except `register` variables, is reserved in the computer's memory area. Most computers have a few additional high-speed storage areas located directly in the computer's processing unit that can also be used for variable storage. These special high-speed storage areas are called **registers**. Because registers are physically located in the computer's processing unit, they can be accessed faster than the normal memory storage areas located in the computer's memory unit. Also, computer instructions that access registers typically require less space than instructions that access memory locations because there are fewer registers that can be accessed than there are memory locations. When the compiler substitutes the location of a register for a variable during program compilation, less space in the instruction is needed than is required to address a memory that has millions of locations.

Besides decreasing the size of a compiled C++ program, using register variables can also increase the execution speed of a C++ program, if the computer you are using supports this data type. Variables declared with the `register` storage class are automatically switched to the `auto` storage class if your compiler does not support `register` variables or if the declared `register` variables exceed the computer's register capacity. Applications programs that are intended to be executed on a variety of computers *should not* use registers.

The only restriction in using the `register` storage class is that the address of a `register` variable, using the address operator `&`, cannot be taken. This is easily understood when you realize that registers do not have standard memory addresses.

Global Variable Storage Classes

Global variables are created by definition statements external to a function. By their nature, these externally defined variables do not come and go with the calling of any function. Once a global variable is created, it exists until the program in which it is declared is finished executing. Thus global variables cannot be declared as either `auto` or `register` variables that are created and destroyed as the program is executing. Global variables may additionally be declared as members of the `static` or the `extern` storage class (but not both). Examples of declaration statements including these two class descriptions are

```
extern int sum;
extern double volts;
static double current;
```

The `static` and `extern` classes affect only the scope, not the time duration, of global variables. Like `static` local variables, all global variables are initialized to zero at compile time.

The purpose of the `extern` storage class is to extend the scope of a global variable beyond its normal boundaries. To understand this, we must first note that all of the programs we have written so far have been contained together in one file. Thus, when you have saved or retrieved programs, you have only needed to give the computer a single name for your program. This is not required by C++.

Larger programs typically consist of many functions that are stored in multiple files. An example of this is shown in Figure 6.14, where the three functions `main()`, `func1()`, and `func2()` are stored in one file and the two functions `func3()` and `func4()` are stored in a second file.

For the files illustrated in Figure 6.14, the global variables `volts`, `current`, and `power` declared in `file1` can be used only by the functions `main()`, `func1()`, and `func2()` in this file. The single global variable `factor` declared in `file2` can be used only by the functions `func3()` and `func4()` in `file2`.

PROGRAMMING NOTE

Storage Classes

Variables of type `auto` and `register` are always local variables. Only non-static global variables may be declared using the `extern` keyword. Doing so extends the variable's scope into another file or function.

Making a global variable `static` makes the variable private to the file in which it is declared. Thus, `static` variables *cannot* use the `extern` keyword. Except for `static` variables, all variables are initialized each time they come into scope. `static` variables are only initialized once, when they are defined.

FIGURE 6.14 *A Program May Extend Beyond One File*

```
file1

int volts;
double current;
static double power;
int main()
{
    func1();
    func2();
    func3();
    func4();
}
int func1()
{

    .
    .
    .

}
int func2()
{

    .
    .
    .

}
```

```
file2

double factor;
int func3()
{
    .
    .
    .
}
int func4()
{
    .
    .
    .
}
```

Although the variable `volts` has been created in `file1`, we may want to use it in `file2`. Placing the declaration statement `extern int volts;` in `file2`, as shown in Figure 6.15, allows us to do this. Putting this statement at the top of `file2` extends the scope of the variable `volts` into `file2` so that it may be used by both `func3()` and `func4()`. Thus the `extern` designation simply declares a global variable that is defined in another file. So placing the statement `extern` double `current;` in `func4()` extends the scope of this global variable, created in `file1`, into `func4()`, and the scope of the global variable `factor`, created in `file2`, is extended into `func1()` and `func2()` by the declaration statement `extern double factor;` placed before `func1()`. Notice that `factor` is not available to `main()`.

A declaration statement that specifically contains the word `extern` is different from every other declaration statement in that it does not cause the creation of a new variable by reserving new storage for the variable. An `extern` declaration statement simply informs the compiler that a global variable already exists and can now be used. The actual storage for the variable must be created somewhere else in the program using one, and only one, global declaration statement in which the word `extern` has not been used. Initialization of the global variable can, of course, be made with the original declaration of the global variable. Initialization within an `extern` declaration statement is not allowed and will cause a compilation error.

The existence of the `extern` storage class is the reason we have been so careful to distinguish between the creation and the declaration of a variable. Declaration statements that contain the word `extern` do not create new storage areas; they only extend the scope of existing global variables.

FIGURE 6.15   *Extending the Scope of Global Variables*

file1

```
int volts;
double current;
static double power;
int main()
{
    func1();
    func2();
    func3();
    func4();
}
extern double factor;
int func1()
{

    .
    .
    .

}
int func2()
{

    .
    .
    .

}
```

file2

```
double factor;
extern int volts;
int func3()
{

    .
    .
    .

}
int func4()
{
    extern double current;
    .
    .
    .

}
```

The last global class, `static` global variables, is used to prevent the extension of a global variable into a second file. Global `static` variables are declared in the same way as local `static` variables, except that the declaration statement is placed outside any function.

The scope of a global `static` variable cannot be extended beyond the file in which it is declared. This provides a degree of privacy for `static` global variables. Because they are only "known" and can be used only in the file in which they are declared, other files cannot access or change their values. Thus `static` global variables cannot subsequently be extended to a second file by using an `extern` declaration statement. Trying to do so will result in a compilation error.

▌ EXERCISES 6.5

1. a. List the storage classes available to local variables.
  b. List the storage classes available to global variables.

2. Describe the difference between a local `auto` variable and a local `static` variable.

3. What is the difference between the following functions?

```
void init1()
{
  static int yrs = 1;
  cout << "\nThe value of yrs is " << yrs;
  yrs = yrs + 2;

  return;
}

void init2()
{
  static int yrs;
  yrs = 1;
  cout << "\nThe value of yrs is " << yrs;
  yrs = yrs + 2;

  return;
}
```

4. a. Describe the difference between a `static` global variable and an `extern` global variable.
  b. If a variable is declared with an `extern` storage class, what other declaration statement must be present somewhere in the program?

5. The declaration statement `static double years;` can be used to create either a local or a global `static` variable. What determines the scope of the variable `years`?

FIGURE 6.16 *Files for Exercise 6*

file1

```
char choice;
int flag;
long date, time;
int main()
{
        .
        .
        .
}
double coupon;
double price()
{
        .
        .
        .
}
int yield()
{
        .
        .
        .
}
```

file2

```
char bondType;
double maturity;
int roi()
{
        .
        .
        .
}
int production()
{
        .
        .
        .
}
int bid()
{
        .
        .
        .
}
```

6. For the function and variable declarations illustrated in Figure 6.16, place an `extern` declaration to individually accomplish each of the following:

   a. Extend the scope of the global variable `choice` into all of `file2`.
   b. Extend the scope of the global variable `flag` into the function `production()` only.
   c. Extend the scope of the global variable `date` into `pduction()` and `bid()`.
   d. Extend the scope of the global variable `date` into `roi()` only.
   e. Extend the scope of the global variable `coupon` into `roi()` only.
   f. Extend the scope of the global variable `bondType` into all of `file1`.
   g. Extend the scope of the global variable `maturity` into both `price()` and `yield()`.

6.6   Common Programming Errors

An extremely common programming error related to functions is passing incorrect data types. The values passed to a function must correspond to the data types of the parameters declared for the function. One way to verify that correct values have been received is to display all passed values within a function's body before any calculations are made. Once this verification has taken place, the display can be dispensed with.[15]

Another common error can occur when the same variable is declared locally within both the calling function and the called function. Even though the variable name is the same, a change to one local variable *does not* alter the value in the other local variable.

Related to this error is the error that can occur when a local variable has the same name as a global variable. Within the function declaring it, the use of the variable's name affects only the local variable's contents unless the scope resolution operator, : :, is used.

Another common error is omitting the called function's prototype either before or within the calling function. The calling function must be alerted to the type of value that will be returned, and this information is provided by the function prototype. The prototype can be omitted if the called function is physically placed in a program before its calling function. Although it is also permissible to omit the prototype and return type for functions that return an integer, it is poor documenting practice to do so. The actual value returned by a function can be verified by displaying it both before and after it is returned.

The last two common errors are terminating a function's header line with a semicolon and forgetting to include the data type of a function's parameters within the function header line.

6.7   *Chapter Summary*

1. A function is called by giving its name and passing any data to it in the parentheses following the name. If a variable is one of the arguments in a function call, the called function receives a copy of the variable's value.

2. The commonly used form of a user-written function is

```
returnDataType functionName(parameter list)
{
   declarations and other C++ statements;
     return expression;
}
```

The first line of the function is called the **function header**. The opening and closing braces of the function and all statements in between these braces

---

[15] In practice, a good debugger program should be used.

constitute the function's **body**. When no returned data type is specified, the returned data type is, by default, an integer. The parameter list is a comma-separated list of parameter declarations.

3. A function's return type is the data type of the value returned by the function. If no type is declared, the function is assumed to return an integer value. If the function does not return a value, it should be declared as a `void` type.

4. Functions can directly return at most a single data type value to their calling functions. This value is the value of the expression in the `return` statement.

5. Using reference parameters, a function can be passed the address of a variable. If a called function is passed an address, it has the capability of directly accessing the respective calling function's variable. Using passed addresses permits a called function effectively to return multiple values.

6. Functions can be declared to all calling functions by means of a **function prototype**. The prototype provides a declaration for a function that specifies the data type returned by the function, its name, and the data types of the arguments expected by the function. Like all declarations, a function prototype is terminated with a semicolon and may be included within local variable declarations or as a global declaration. The most common form of a function prototype is

    ```
    dataType functionName(parameter-data-type-list);
    ```

   If the called function is placed physically above the calling function, no further declaration is required because the function's definition serves as a global declaration to all following functions.

7. Every variable used in a program has a *scope*, which determines where in the program the variable can be used. The scope of a variable is either local or global and is determined by where the variable's definition statement is placed. A local variable is defined within a function and can be used only within its defining function or block. A global variable is defined outside a function and can be used in any function following the variable's definition. All global variables that are not specifically initialized by the user are initialized to zero by the compiler and can be shared between files by using the keyword `extern`.

8. Every variable has a *class*. The class of a variable determines how long the value in the variable will be retained: `auto` variables are local variables that exist only while their defining function is executing; `register` variables are similar to automatic variables but are stored in a computer's internal registers rather than in memory; `static` variables can be either global or local and retain their values for the duration of a program's execution. All `static` variables are set to zero when they are defined if they are not explicitly initialized by the user.

6.8   Chapter Supplement: Generating Random Numbers

There are many business and engineering simulation problems in which probability must be considered or statistical sampling techniques must be used. For example, statistical models are required in simulating automobile traffic flow or telephone usage patterns. Additionally, applications such as simple computer games and more involved gaming scenarios can be described only statistically. All of these statistical models require the generation of **random numbers**—that is, a series of numbers whose order cannot be predicted.

In practice, there are no truly random numbers. Dice are never perfect; cards are never shuffled completely randomly; the supposedly random motions of molecules are influenced by the environment; and digital computers can handle numbers only within a finite range and with limited precision. The best one can do is generate **pseudorandom** numbers, which are sufficiently random for the task at hand.

Some computer languages contain a library function that produces random numbers; others do not. All C++ compilers provide two functions for creating random numbers: `rand()` and `srand()`. The `rand()` function produces a series of random numbers in the range $0 \le \mathtt{rand()} \le \mathtt{RAND\_MAX}$, where the constant `RAND_MAX` is defined in the `cstdlib` header file. The `srand()` function provides a starting "seed" value for `rand()`. If `srand()` or some other equivalent "seeding" technique is not used, `rand()` will always produce the same series of random numbers.

The general procedure for creating a series of *N* random numbers using C++'s library functions is illustrated by the following code:

```
srand(time(NULL)); // this generates the first "seed" value

for (int i = 1; i <= N; i++) // this generates N random numbers
{
  rvalue = rand();
  cout << rvalue << endl;
}
```

Here, the argument to the `srand()` function is a call to the `time()` function with a `NULL` argument. With this argument, the `time()` function reads the computer's internal clock time, in seconds. The `srand()` function then uses this time, converted to an unsigned `int`, to initialize the random number generator function `rand()`.[16] Program 6.15 uses this code to generate a series of ten random numbers.

---

[16] Alternatively, many C++ compilers have a `randomize()` routine that is defined using the `srand()` function. If this routine is available, the call `randomize()` can be used in place of the call `srand(time(NULL))`. In either case, the initializing "seed" routine is called only once, after which the `rand()` function is used to generate a series of random numbers.

Program 6.15

```cpp
#include <iostream>
#include <iomanip>
#include <cstdlib>
#include <ctime>
using namespace std;

// this program generates ten pseudo random numbers
// using C++'s rand() function

int main()
{
  const int NUMBERS = 10;

  double randvalue;
  int i;

  srand(time(NULL));
  for (i = 1; i <= NUMBERS; ++i)
  {
    randvalue = rand();
    cout << setw(20) << randvalue << endl;
  }

  return 0;
}
```

The following is the output produced by one run of Program 6.15:

```
               20203
               21400
               15265
               26935
                8369
               10907
               31299
               15400
                5074
               20663
```

Because of the srand() function call in Program 6.15, the series of ten random numbers will differ each time the program is executed. Without the randomizing "seeding" effect of this function, the same series of random numbers would always be produced. Note also the inclusion of the `cstdlib` and `ctime` header files. The `cstdlib` file contains the function prototypes for the `srand` and `rand()` functions, whereas the `ctime` header file contains the function prototype for the `time()` function.

Scaling

In practice, it is typically necessary to make one modification to the random numbers produced by the `rand()` function. In most applications, the random numbers are required to be either floating-point numbers within the range of 0.0 to 1.0 or integers within a specified range, such as 1 to 100. The method for adjusting the random numbers produced by a random number generator to reside within such ranges is called scaling.

Scaling random numbers to reside within the range of 0.0 to 1.0 is easily accomplished by dividing the returned value of `rand()` by RAND_MAX. Thus the expression `double(rand())/RAND_MAX` produces a double-precision random number between 0.0 and 1.0.

Scaling a random number as an integer value between 0 and N is accomplished using either the expression `rand() % (N+1)` or the expression `int(double(rand())/RAND_MAX * N)`. For example, the expression

```
int(double(rand())/RAND_MAX * 100)
```

produces a random integer between 0 and 100.

To produce an integer random number between 1 and N, we can use the expression `1 + rand() % N`. For example, in simulating the roll of a die, the expression `1 + rand() % 6` produces a random integer between 1 and 6. The more general scaling expression `a + rand() % (b + 1 - a)` can be used to produce a random integer between the numbers *a and b.*

Completing the Basics

The current ANSI/ISO standard for C++ introduced two new features that were not part of the original C++ specification: *exception handling* and a `string` class. Both of these new features are presented in this chapter.

Exception handling is a means of error detection and processing that has gained increasing acceptance in programming technology. It permits detecting an error at the point in the code where the error has occurred and providing a means of processing the error and returning control to the line in the code that generated the error. Although such error detecting and correcting code was always possible using `if` statements and functions, exception handling provides one more extremely useful programming tool specifically targeted to error detection and processing.

Additionally, with the new ANSI/ISO C++ standard, a class named `string` is provided as part of the standard C++ library. This class provides a greatly expanded set of class methods that include easy insertion and removal of characters from a string, automatic string expansion whenever a string's original capacity is exceeded, string contraction when characters are removed from the string, and range checking to detect invalid character positions.

In addition to presenting these two new C++ features, this chapter shows how exception handling, when applied to strings, provides a very useful means of validating user input.

7.1   The `string` Class

We have used the `iostream` class' `cout` object extensively throughout our programs, without really investigating this class or how the `cout` object is created. One of the advantages of object-oriented program design is that thoroughly tested classes can be used without knowing the internals of how the class is constructed. In this section we will use another class provided by C++'s standard library, the `string` class. However, in this case, we will actually create objects from the class before using them, rather than just use an existing object, such as `cout`.

A **class** is a user-created data type. Like the familiar built-in data types, a class defines both a valid set of data values and a set of operations that can be used on them. The difference between a class and a built-in type is simply how the class is constructed. Whereas a built-in data type is provided as an integral part of the compiler, a programmer constructs a class using C++ code. Other than that, and the terminology used, the two types are used in much the same manner. The key difference in terminology is that storage areas for built-in types are referred to as variables while storage areas declared for a class are referred to as objects.

The values permitted by the string class are referred to as string literals. A **string literal**, as we have already seen, is any sequence of characters enclosed in double quotation marks. As has also been noted, a string literal is also referred to as a string value, a string constant, and more conventionally, simply as a string. Examples of strings are "This is a string", "Hello World!", and "xyz 123 *!#@&". The double quotation marks are used to mark the beginning and ending points of the string and are never stored with the string.

Figure 7.1 shows the programming representation of the string Hello whenever this string is created as an object of the string class. By convention, the first character in a string is always designated as position 0. This position value is also referred to as both the character's index value and its offset value.

FIGURE 7.1   *The Storage of a string as a Sequence of Characters*

Character position:	0	1	2	3	4
	H	e	l	l	o

string Class Methods

The string class provides a number of methods for declaring, creating, and initializing a string. Formally, the process of creating a new object is referred to as instantiating an object, which in this case becomes instantiating a string object, or creating a string, for short. Table 7.1 lists the methods provided by the string class for creating and initializing a string object. In class terminology, methods that perform this task are referred to as constructor methods, or constructors, for short.

TABLE 7.1   string *Class Constructors (Required Header File Is* string*)*

Constructor	Description	Examples

string objectName = value	Creates and initializes a string object to value, which can be a string literal, previously declared string object, or an expression containing both string literals and string objects	string str1 = "Good Morning";
		string str2 = str1;
		string str3 = str1 + str2;

string objectName(string-value)	Produces the same initialization as above	string str1("Hot"); string str1(str1 + " Dog");

(continued on next page)

TABLE 7.1   *(continued)*

`string objectName(str, n)`	Creates and initializes a string object with a substring of string object `str`, starting at index position n of `str`	`string str1(str2, 5)` If `str2` contains the string `Good Morning`, then `str1` becomes the string `Morning`
`string objectName(str, n, p)`	Creates and initializes a string object with a substring of string object `str`, starting at index position n of `str` and containing p characters.	`string str1(str2, 5,2)` If `str2` contains the string `Good Morning`, then `str1` becomes the string `Mo`
`string objectName(n, char)`	Creates and initializes a string object and initializes it with n copies of `char`.	`string str1(5,'*')` This makes `str1 = "*****"`
`string objectName`	Creates and initializes a string object to represent an empty character sequence. Same as `string objectName = "";` The length of the string is `0`.	`string message;`

Program 7.1 illustrates examples of each of the constructor methods provided by the string class.

Program 7.1

```
#include <iostream>
#include <string>
using namespace std;

int main()
{
  string str1; // an empty string
  string str2("Good Morning");
  string str3 = "Hot Dog";
  string str4(str3);
  string str5(str4, 4);
  string str6 = "linear";
```

(continued on next page)

(continued from previous page)

```
                                       string str7(str6, 3, 3);

    cout << "str1 is: " << str1 << endl;
    cout << "str2 is: " << str2 << endl;
    cout << "str3 is: " << str3 << endl;
    cout << "str4 is: " << str4 << endl;
    cout << "str5 is: " << str5 << endl;
    cout << "str6 is: " << str6 << endl;
    cout << "str7 is: " << str7 << endl;

    return 0;
}
```

The output created by Program 7.1 is:

```
str1 is:
str2 is: Good Morning
str3 is: Hot Dog
str4 is: Hot Dog
str5 is: Dog
str6 is: linear
str7 is: ear
```

Although this output is straightforward, two comments are in order. First, notice that str1 is an empty string consisting of no characters. Next, because the first character in a string is designated as position 0, not 1, the character position of the D in the string Hot Dog is located at position 4, which is shown in Figure 7.2.

FIGURE 7.2 *The Character Positions of the string* Hot Dog

Character position:	0	1	2	3	4	5	6
	H	o	t		D	o	g

string Input and Output

In addition to initializing a string using the constructor methods listed in Table 7.1, strings can be input from the keyboard and displayed on the screen. Table 7.2 lists the basic methods and objects that can be used to input and output string values.

As listed in Table 7.2, in addition to the standard cout and cin streams, the string class provides the getline() method for string input. For example, the expression getline(cin, message) will continuously accept and store characters typed at the terminal until the Enter key is pressed. Pressing the Enter key at the terminal generates a newline character, '\n', which is interpreted by getline() as the end-of-line entry. All the characters encountered by getline(), except the newline character, are stored in the string named message, as illustrated in Figure 7.3.

TABLE 7.2 string *Input and Output Routines*

C++ Routine	Description
cout	General purpose screen output
cin	General purpose terminal input that stops reading when a whitespace is encountered
getline(cin, strObj)	General purpose terminal input that inputs all characters entered into the string named strObj and stops accepting characters when it receives a newline character (\n)

FIGURE 7.3 *Inputting a string with* getline()

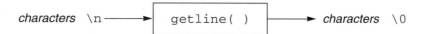

characters \n ⟶ getline( ) ⟶ *characters* \0

Program 7.2 illustrates using the getline() method and cout stream to input and output a string, respectively, that is entered at the user's terminal.

 Program 7.2

```
#include <iostream>
#include <string>
using namespace std;

int main()
{
  string message;      // declare a string object

  cout << "Enter a string:\n";

  getline(cin, message);

  cout << "The string just entered is:\n"
       << message << endl;

  return 0;
}
```

The following is a sample run of Program 7.2:

```
Enter a string:
This is a test input of a string of characters.
The string just entered is:
This is a test input of a string of characters.
```

Although the `cout` stream object is used in Program 7.2 for string output, the `cin` stream input object generally cannot be used in place of `getline()` for string input. This is because the `cin` object reads a set of characters up to either a blank space or a newline character. Thus, attempting to enter the characters `This is a string` using the statement `cin >> message;` only results in the word `This` being assigned to `message`. Entering the complete line using a `cin` object requires a statement such as

```
cin >> message1 >> message2 >> message3 >> message4;
```

Here the word `This` is assigned to the string `message1`, the word `is` is assigned to the string `message2`, and so on. The fact that a blank terminates a `cin` extraction operation restricts `cin`'s usefulness for entering string data and is the reason for using `getline()`.

In its most general form, the `getline()` method has the syntax

```
getline(cin, strObj, terminatingChar)
```

where *strObj* is a string variable name, and *terminatingChar* is an optional character constant or variable specifying the terminating character. For example, the expression `getline(cin, message, '!')` will accept all characters entered at the keyboard, including a newline character, until an exclamation point is entered. The exclamation point will not be stored as part of the string.

If the optional third argument is omitted when `getline()` is called, the default terminating character is the newline (`'\n'`) character. Thus, the statement `getline(cin, message,'\n');` can be used in place of the statement `getline(cin, message);`. Both of these statements stop reading characters when the Enter key is pressed. In all future programs we will assume that input is terminated by the Enter key, which generates a newline character. As such, the optional third argument passed to `getline()`, which is the terminating character, will be omitted.

Caution: The Phantom Newline Character

Seemingly strange results can be obtained when either the `cin` input stream and `getline()` method are used together to accept data, or when the `cin` input stream is used, by itself, to accept individual characters. To see how this can occur, consider Program 7.3, which uses `cin` to accept an integer entered at the keyboard, storing it in the variable named `value`, followed by a `getline()` method call.

Program 7.3

```cpp
#include <iostream>
#include <string>
using namespace std;

int main()
{
  int value;
  string message;

  cout << "Enter a number: ";
  cin  >> value;
  cout << "The number entered is:\n"
       << value << endl;

  cout << "Enter text:\n";
  getline(cin, message);
  cout << "The string entered is:\n"
       << message << endl;


  return 0;
}
```

When Program 7.3 is run, the number entered in response to the prompt Enter a number: is stored in the variable named `value`. At this point, everything seems to be working fine. Notice, however, that in entering a number, you actually enter a number and press the Enter key. On almost all computer systems this entered data is stored in a temporary holding area called a buffer immediately after the characters are entered, as illustrated in Figure 7.4.

The `cin` input stream in Program 7.3 first accepts the typed number, but leaves the `'\n'` in the buffer. The next input statement, which is a call to `getline()`, will automatically pick up the code for the Enter key as the next character, and immediately terminate any further input. Following is a sample run for Program 7.3:

```
Enter a number: 26
The number entered is 26
```

```
Enter text:
The string entered is
```

Notice in this output that no text is accepted in response to the prompt `Enter text:`. Text is not accepted because after the number 26 has been accepted by the program, the code for the Enter key, which is a newline escape sequence, remains in the buffer and is picked up and interpreted by the `getline()` method as the end of its input. This process will occur whether an integer, as in Program 7.3, or a string, or any other input is accepted by `cin`, and then followed by a `getline()` method call.

FIGURE 7.4 *Typed Keyboard Characters Are First Stored in a Buffer*

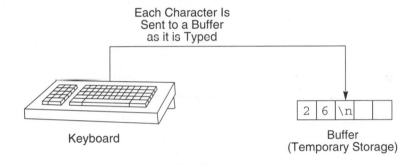

There are three separate solutions to this "phantom" Enter key problem. The three solutions follow:

- Do not mix `cin` with `getline()` inputs in the same program.
- Follow the `cin` input with the call to `cin.ignore()`
- Accept the Enter key into a character variable and then ignore it

The preferred solution is the first one. All solutions, however, center on the fact that the Enter key is a legitimate character input and must be recognized as such. We will encounter this problem again when we consider accepting `char` data types in the next section.

String Processing

Strings can be manipulated using either `string` class methods or the character-at-a-time methods described in the next section. Table 7.3 lists the most commonly used `string` class methods. The most commonly used methods include accessor and mutator methods, plus additional methods and operator functions that use the standard arithmetic and comparison operators.

The most commonly used method in Table 7.3 is the `length()` method. This method returns the number of characters in the string, which is referred to as the

TABLE 7.3 *The* `string` *Class Processing Methods (Require the Header File* `string`*)*

Method/Operation	Description	Example
`int length()`	Returns the length of the implicit string.	`string.length()`
`int size()`	Same as above.	`string.size()`
`at(int index)`	Returns the character at the specified index, and throws an exception if the index is non existent.	`string.at(4)`
`int compare(string)`	Compares two strings; returns a negative value if the implied string is less than `str`, `0` if they are equal, and a positive value if the implied string is less than `str`.	`string1.compare(string2)`
`c_str()`	Returns the string as a `null` terminated C-string	`string1.c_str()`
`bool empty`	Returns `true` if the implied string is empty; otherwise, returns `false`.	`string1.empty()`
`erase(ind,n)`	Remove n characters from the implied string, starting at index `ind`.	`string1.erase(2,3)`
`erase(ind)`	Remove all characters from the implied string, starting from index `ind` until the end of the string. The length of the remaining string becomes `ind`.	`string1.erase(4)`
`int find(str)`	Returns the index of the first occurrence of `str` within the implied object.	`string1.find("the")`
`int find(str, ind)`	Returns the index of the first occurrence of `str` within the implied object, with the search beginning at index `ind`.	`string1.find("the",5)`
`int find_first_of(str, ind)`	Returns the index of the first occurrence of any character in `str` within the implied object, with the search starting at index `ind`.	`string1.find_first_of("lt", 6)`

TABLE 7.3 *(continued)*

Method/Operation	Description	Example
int find_first_not_of(str, ind)	Returns the index of the first occurrence of any character not in str within the implied object, with the search starting at index ind.	string1.find_first_not_of("lt",6)
void insert(ind, str)	Insert the string str into the implied string, starting at index ind.	string.insert(4, "there")
void replace(ind, n, str)	Remove n characters in the implied object, starting at index position ind, and insert the string str at index position ind.	string1.replace(2,4,"okay")
string substr(ind,n)	Returns a string consisting of n characters extracted from the implied string starting at index ind. If n is greater than the remaining number of characters, the rest of the implied string is used.	string2 = string1.substr(0,10)
void swap(str)	Swaps characters in str with the implied object.	string1.swap(string2)
[ind]	Returns the character at index x, without checking if ind is a valid index.	string1[5]
=	Assignment (also converts a C-string to a string)	string1 = string
+	Concatenates two strings	string1 + string2
+=	Concatenation and assignment	string2 += string1
== != < <= > >=	Relational operators. Return true if the relation is satisfied; otherwise return false.	string1 == string2 string1 <= string2 string1 > string2

PROGRAMMING NOTE

The `string` *and* `char` *Data Types*

A string can consist of zero or more characters. When it has no characters, it is said to be an empty string and has a length of zero. A string with a single character, such as `"a"`, is a string of length one and is stored differently than a `char` data type such as `'a'`. Although for many practical purposes a string of length one and a `char` respond in the same manner; for example `cout >> "\n"` and `cout >> '\n'` both produce a new line on the screen, it is important to understand that they are different data types. For example, both declarations

```
string s1 = 'a';  // INVALID INITIALIZATION
char key = "\n"; // INVALID INITIALIZATION
```

produce a compiler error because they attempt to initialize one data type with literal values of another type.

string's length. For example, the value returned by the method call `"Hello World!".length()` is 12. As always, the double quotes surrounding a string value are not considered part of the string. Similarly, if the string referenced by `string1` contains the value `"Have a good day."`, the value returned by the call `string1.length()` is 16.

Notice that two string expressions may be compared for equality using the standard relational operators. Each character in a string is stored in binary using either the ASCII or Unicode code. Although these codes are different, they have some characteristics in common: In each of them, a blank precedes (is less than) all letters and numbers; the letters of the alphabet are stored in order from A to Z; and the digits are stored in order from 0 to 9. In both character codes, the digits come before (that is, are less than) the uppercase characters, which are then followed by the lowercase characters. Thus, the uppercase characters are mathematically less than the lowercase characters. When two strings are compared, their individual characters are compared a pair at a time (both first characters, then both second characters, and so on). If no differences are found, the strings are equal; if a difference is found, the string with the first lower character is considered the smaller string. Thus,

- `"Hello"` is greater than `"Good Bye"` because the first H in Hello is greater than the first G in Good Bye
- `"Hello"` is less than `"hello"` because the first H in Hello is less than the first h in hello
- `"SMITH"` is greater than `"JONES"` because the first S in SMITH is greater than the first J in JONES

- "123" is greater than "1227" because the third character, the 3 in 123 is greater than the third character, the 2 in 1227
- "Behop" is greater than "Beehive" because the third character, the h, in Behop is greater than the third character, the e, in Beehive.

Program 7.4 uses length() and several relational expressions within the context of a complete program.

 Program 7.4

```cpp
#include <iostream>
#include <string>
using namespace std;

int main()
{
  string string1 = "Hello";
  string string2 = "Hello there";

  cout << "string1 is the string: " <<  string1 << endl;
  cout << "The number of characters in string1 is " <<  string1.length()
       << endl << endl;

  cout << "string2 is the string: " <<  string2 << endl;
  cout << "The number of characters in string2 is " <<  string2.length()
       << endl << endl;

  if (string1 < string2)
    cout << string1 <<  " is less than " <<  string2 << endl << endl;
  else if (string1 == string2)
    cout << string1 <<  " is equal to " <<  string2 << endl << endl;
  else
    cout << string1 <<  " is greater than " <<  string2 << endl << endl;

  string1 = string1 + " there world!";
  cout << "After concatenation, string1 contains the characters: "
       << string1 << endl;
  cout << "The length of this string is " << string1.length() << endl;


  return 0;
}
```

Following is a sample output produced by Program 7.4:

```
string1 is the string: Hello
The number of characters in string1 is 5

string2 is the string: Hello there
The number of characters in string2 is 11

Hello is less than Hello there

After concatenation, string1 contains the characters:
Hello there world!
The length of this string is 18
```

In reviewing this output, refer to Figure 7.5, which shows how the characters in `string1` and `string2` are stored in memory. Note that the length of each string refers to the total number of characters in the string and that the first character in each string is located at index position 0. Thus, the length of a string is always one more than the index number of the last character's position in the string.

Although you will mostly use concatenation operator and `length()` method, at times you will find the other string methods in Table 7.3 are useful. One of the more useful is the `at()` method, which permits you to retrieve individual characters in a string. Program 7.5 uses this method to select one character at a time from the string, starting at string position 0 and ending at the index of the last character in the string. This last index value is always one less than the number of characters (that is, the string's length) in the string.

FIGURE 7.5   *The Initial Strings Used in Program 7.4*

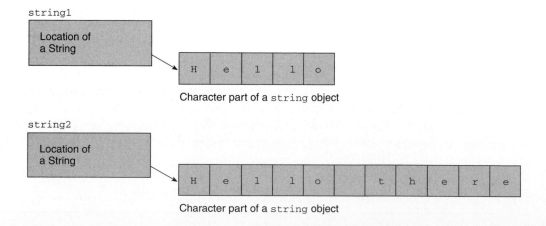

Program 7.5

```cpp
#include <iostream>
#include <string>
using namespace std;

int main()
{

  string str = "Counting the number of vowels";
  int i, numChars;
  int vowelCount = 0;

  cout << "The string: \"" << str << "\"";

  numChars = str.length();
  for (i = 0; i < numChars; i++)
  {
    switch(str.at(i))   // here is where a character is retrieved
    {
      case 'a':
      case 'e':
      case 'i':
      case 'o':
      case 'u':
         vowelCount++;
    }
  }
  cout << " has " << vowelCount << " vowels." << endl;


  return 0;
}
```

The expression str.at(i) in Program 7.5's switch statement retrieves the character at position i in the string. This character is then compared to five different character values. The switch statement uses the fact that selected cases "drop through" in the absence of break statements. Thus, all selected cases result in an increment to vowelCount. The output displayed by Program 7.5 is:

```
The string: "Counting the number of vowels" has 9 vowels.
```

As an example of insertion and replacement methods listed in Table 7.3, assume that we start with a string created by the statement

```
string str = "This cannot be";
```

Figure 7.6 illustrates how this string is stored in the buffer created for it. As indicated, the initial length of the string is 14 characters.

FIGURE 7.6   *Initial Storage of a* `string` *Object*

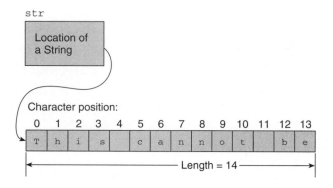

Now assume that the following statement is executed:

```
str.insert(4," I know");
```

This statement causes the designated seven characters, beginning with a blank, to be inserted starting at index position 4 in the existing string. The resulting string, after the insertion, is as shown in Figure 7.7.

FIGURE 7.7   *The String After the Insertion*

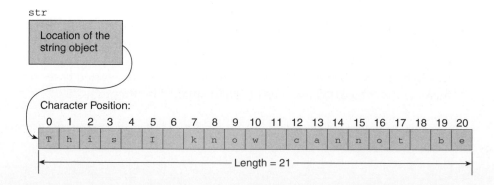

If the statement `str.replace(12, 6, "to");` is executed, the existing characters in index positions 12 through 17 will be deleted and the two characters `to` inserted starting at index position 12. Thus, the net effect of the replacement is as shown in Figure 7.8. It is worthwhile noting that the number of replacement characters, which in this particular case is two, can be less than, equal to, or greater than the characters that are being replaced, which in this case is six.

FIGURE 7.8   *The string after the Replacement*

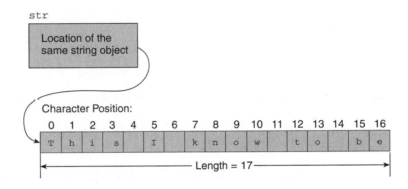

Finally, if we append the string `"correct"` to the string shown in Figure 7.8 using the concatenation operator, +, the string illustrated in Figure 7.9 is obtained.

Program 7.6 illustrates using the statements we have just examined within the context of a complete program.

FIGURE 7.9   *The String After the Append*

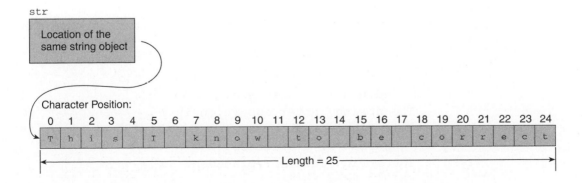

Program 7.6

```cpp
#include <iostream>
#include <string>
using namespace std;

int main()
{
  string str = "This cannot be";
  int i, numChars;

  cout << "The original string is: " << str << endl
       << "  and has " << str.length() << " characters." << endl;

  // insert characters
  str.insert(4," I know");
  cout << "The string, after insertion is : " << str << endl
       << "  and has " << str.length() << " characters." << endl;

  // replace characters
  str.replace(12, 6, "to");
  cout << "The string, after replacement is: " << str << endl
       << "  and has " << str.length() << " characters." << endl;

  // append characters
  str = str + " correct";
  cout << "The string, after appending is: " << str << endl
       << "  and has " << str.length() << " characters." << endl;

   return 0;
}
```

The following output, produced by Program 7.6, matches the strings shown in Figures 7.6 to 7.9.

```
The original string is: This cannot be
   and has 14 characters.
The string, after insertion is:
This I know cannot be
   and has 21 characters.
The string, after replacement is:
This I know to be
   and has 17 characters.
```

```
                    The string, after appending is:
                    This I know to be correct
                        and has 25 characters.
```

Of the remaining string methods listed in Table 7.3, the most common are those that are used to locate specific characters in a string and create substrings. Program 7.7 presents examples of how some of these other methods are used.

Program 7.7

```cpp
#include <iostream>
#include <string>
using namespace std;

int main()
{

  string string1 = "LINEAR PROGRAMMING THEORY";
  string s1, s2, s3;
  int j, k, l;

  cout << "The original string is " << string1 << endl;

  j = string1.find('I');
  cout << "  The first position of an 'I' is " << j << endl;

  k = string1.find('I', (j+1));
  cout << "  The next position of an 'I' is " << k << endl;

  j = string1.find("THEORY");
  cout << "  The first location of \"THEORY\" is " << j << endl;

  k = string1.find("ING");
  cout << "  The first index of \"ING\" is " << k << endl;

  s1 = string1.substr(2,5);
  s2 = string1.substr(19,3);
  s3 = string1.substr(6,8);

  cout << s1 + s2 + s3 << endl;


  return 0;
}
```

The output produced by Program 7.7 is:

```
The original string is LINEAR PROGRAMMING THEORY
   The first position of an 'I' is 1
   The next position of an 'I' is 15
   The first location of "THEORY" is 19
   The first index of "ING" is 15
NEAR THE PROGRAM
```

The main point illustrated in Program 7.7 is that both individual characters and sequences of characters can be located and extracted from a string.

▌ EXERCISES 7.1

1. Enter and execute Program 7.2 on your computer.

2. Determine the value of `text.at(0)`, `text.at(3)`, and `text.at(10)`, assuming that `text` is, individually, each of the following strings:
   a. `now is the time`
   b. `rocky raccoon welcomes you`
   c. `Happy Holidays`
   d. `The good ship`

3. Enter and execute Program 7.5 on your computer.

4. Modify Program 7.5 to count and display the individual numbers of each vowel contained in the string.

5. Modify Program 7.5 to display the number of vowels in a user-entered string.

6. Using the `at()` method, write and execute a C++ program that reads in a string using `getline()` and then displays the string out in reverse order. (*Hint:* Once the string has been entered and saved, retrieve and display characters starting from the end of the string.)

7. Write a C++ program that accepts both a string and a single character from the user. The program should then determine how many times the `char` is contained in the string. (*Hint:* Search the string using the `find(str, ind)` method. This method should be used in a loop that starts the index value at zero, and then changes the index to one value past the index of where the `char` was last found.)

8. Enter and execute Program 7.6 on your computer.

9. Enter and execute Program 7.7 on your computer.

10. Write a C++ program that accepts a string from the user and then replaces all occurrences of the letter e with the letter x.

11. Modify the program written for Exercise 10 to search for the first occurrence of a user entered sequence of characters and replace this sequence, when it is found in the string, with a second set of a user-entered sequence. For example, if the entered string is Figure

4-4 illustrates the output of Program 4-2 and the user enters that 4- is to be replaced by 3-, the resulting string will be Figure 3-4 illustrates the output of Program 4-2. (Note that only the first occurrence of the searched for sequence has been changed.)

12. Modify the program written for Exercise 11 to replace all occurrences of the designated sequence of characters with the new sequence of characters. For example, if the entered string is Figure 4-4 illustrates the output of Program 4-2 and the user enters that 4- is to be replaced by 3-, the resulting string will be Figure 3-4 illustrates the output of Program 3-2.

7.2   Character Manipulation Methods

In addition to the string methods provided by the string class, the C++ language provides a number of very useful character class functions. These functions are listed in Table 7.4. The function declarations (prototypes) for each of these routines are contained in the header files string and cctype, which must be included in any program that uses these functions.

Because all of the istype( ) functions listed in Table 7.4 return a nonzero integer (which is interpreted as a Boolean true value) when the character meets the desired condition, and a zero integer (or Boolean false value) when the condition is not met, these functions are typically used directly within an if statement.

TABLE 7.4   *Character Library Functions (Require Either the Header File* string *or* cctype*)*

Function Prototype	Description	Example
int isalpha(charExp)	Returns a true (nonzero integer) if charExp evaluates to a letter; otherwise, it returns false (zero integer).	isalpha('a')
int isalnum(charExp)	Returns a true (nonzero integer) if charExp evaluates to a letter or a digit; otherwise, it returns a false (zero integer).	char key; cin >> key; isalnum(key);
int isupper(charExp)	Returns a true (nonzero integer) if charExp evaluates to an uppercase letter; otherwise returns a false (zero integer).	isupper('a')

(continued)

TABLE 7.4 *(continued)*

Function Prototype	Description	Example
`int islower(charExp)`	Returns a `true` (nonzero integer) if `charExp` evaluates to a lowercase letter; otherwise it returns a `false` (zero integer).	`islower('a')`
`int isdigit(charExp)`	Returns a `true` (nonzero integer) if `charExp` evaluates to a digit (0 through 9);otherwise it returns a `false` (zero integer).	`isdigit('a')`
`int isascii(charExp)`	Returns a `true` (nonzero integer) if `charExp` evaluates to an ASCII character; otherwise returns a `false` (zero integer).	`isascii('a')`
`int isspace(charExp)`	Returns a `true` (nonzero integer) if `charExp` evaluates to a space; otherwise, returns a `false` (zero integer).	`isspace(' ')`
`int isprint(charExp)`	Returns a `true` (nonzero integer) if `charExp` evaluates to a printable character; otherwise, returns a `false` (zero integer).	`isprint('a')`
`int isctrl(charExp)`	Returns a `true` (nonzero integer) if `charExp` evaluates to a control character; otherwise, it returns a `false` (zero integer).	`isctrl('a')`
`int ispucnt(charExp)`	Returns a `true` (nonzero integer) if `charExp` evaluates to a punctuation character; otherwise, returns a `false` (zero integer).	`ispucnt('!')`
`int isgraph(charExp)`	Returns a `true` (nonzero integer) if `charExp` evaluates to a printable character other than whitespace; otherwise `false` (zero integer).	`isgraph(' ')`
`int toupper(charExp)`	Returns the uppercase equivalent if `charExp` evaluates to a lowercase character; otherwise it returns the character code without modification.	`toupper('a')`
`int tolower(charExp)`	Returns the lowercase equivalent if `charExp` evaluates to an uppercase character; otherwise it returns the character code without modification.	`tolower('A')`

For example, consider the following code segment, which assumes that ch is a character variable:

```
if(isdigit(ch))
  cout << "The character just entered is a digit" << endl;
else if(ispunct(ch))
  cout << "The character just entered is a punctuation mark" << endl;
```

Here, if ch contains a digit character, the first cout statement is executed; if the character is a letter, the second cout statement is executed. In both cases, however, the character to be checked is included as an argument to the appropriate method. Program 7.8 illustrates this type of code within a program that counts the number of letters, digits, and other characters in a string. The individual characters to be checked are obtained using the string class' at() method. Here, this method is used in a for loop that cycles through the string from the first character to the last.

The output produced by Program 7.8 is:

```
The original string is: This 123/ is 567 A ?<6245> Test!
This string contains 32 characters, which consist of
        11 letters
        10 digits
        11 other characters.
```

As indicated by this output, each of the 32 characters in the string has correctly been categorized as either a letter, digit, or other character.

 Program 7.8

```
#include <iostream>
#include <string>
#include <cctype>
using namespace std;

int main()
{
    string str = "This 123/ is 567 A ?<6245> Test!";
    char nextChar;
    int i;
    int numLetters = 0, numDigits = 0, numOthers = 0;

    cout << "The original string is: " << str
         << "\nThis string contains " << str.length()
```

(continued on next page)

(continued from previous page)

```
                    << " characters," << " which consist of" << endl;

        // check each character in the string
        for (i = 0; i < str.length(); i++)
        {
          nextChar = str.at(i);   // get a character
          if (isalpha(nextChar))
            numLetters++;
          else if (isdigit(nextChar))
            numDigits++;
          else
            numOthers++;
        }

        cout << "      " << numLetters << " letters" << endl;
        cout << "      " << numDigits << " digits" << endl;
        cout <<"      " << numOthers << " other characters." << endl;

        return 0;
}
```

Typically, as in Program 7.8, each of the functions in Table 7.4 is used in a character-by-character manner on each character in a string. This is again illustrated in Program 7.9, where each lowercase string character is converted to its uppercase equivalent using the `toupper()` function. This function only converts lowercase letters, leaving all other characters unaffecte. A sample run of Program 7.9 produced the following output:

```
Type in any sequence of characters: this is a test OF 12345.
The characters just entered, in uppercase are: THIS IS A TEST OF 12345.
```

Pay particular attention in Program 7.9 to the statement `for (i = 0; i < str.length(); i++)` that is used to cycle through each of the characters in the string. This method is typically how each element in a string is accessed, using the `length()` method to determine when the end of the string has been reached (review Program 7.8 to see that it is used in the same way). The only real difference is that in Program 7.9 each element is accessed using the subscript notation `str[i]`, while in Program 7.8 the `at()` method was used. Although these two notations are interchangeable, and which you use is a matter of choice, for consistency the two notations should not be mixed in the same program.

Program 7.9

```cpp
#include <iostream>
#include <string>
using namespace std;

int main()
{
  int i;
  string str;

  cout << "Type in any sequence of characters: ";
  getline(cin,str);

  // cycle through all elements of the string
  for (i = 0; i < str.length(); i++)
    str[i] - toupper(str[i]);

  cout << "The characters just entered, in uppercase, are: "
       << str << endl;

    return 0;
}
```

Character I/O

Although we have used `cin` and `getline()` to accept data entered from the keyboard in a more or less "cookbook" manner, it is useful to understand what data are actually being sent to the program and how the program must react to process the data correctly. At a very fundamental level, all input (as well as output), is done on a character-by-character basis as illustrated in Figure 7.10.

As illustrated in Figure 7.10, the entry of every piece of data, be it a string or a number, consists of typing individual characters. For example, the entry of the string `Hello` consists of pressing and releasing the six keys H, e, l, l, o, and the Enter key. Similarly, the output of the number `26.95` consists of the display of the five characters 2, 6, ., 9, and 5. Although the programmer typically doesn't think of data in this manner, the program is always restricted to this character-by-character I/O, and all of C++'s higher-level I/O methods and streams are based on lower-level character I/O methods. These more elemental character methods, which can also be used directly by a programmer, are listed in Table 7.5.

FIGURE 7.10   *Accepting Keyboard Entered Characters*

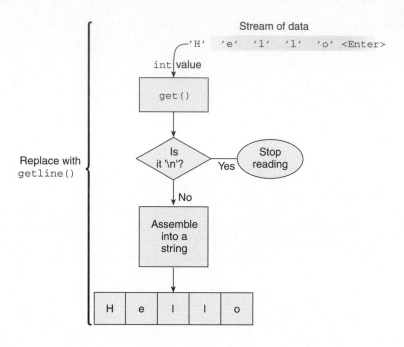

TABLE 7.5   *Basic Character I/O Methods (Require the Header File* `iostream`*)*

Method	Description	Example
`cout.put(charExp)`	Places the character value of `charExp` on the output stream	`cout.put('A');`
`cin.get(charVar)`	Extracts the next character from the input stream and assigns it to the variable `charVar`.	`cin.get(key);`
`cin.peek(charVar)`	Assigns the next character from the input stream to the variable `charVar` *without* extracting the character from the stream.	`cin.peek(nextKey);`
`cin.putback(charExp)`	Pushes a character value of `charExp` back onto the input stream.	`cin.putback(cKey);`
`cin.ignore(n, char)`	Ignores a maximum of the next n input characters, up to and including the detection of `char`. If no arguments are specified, ignores the next single character on input stream.	`cin.ignore(80,'\n');` `cin.ignore();`

PROGRAMMING NOTE

Why the `char` *Data Type Uses Integer Values*

In C++, a character is stored as an integer value, which is sometimes confusing to beginning programmers. The reason is, in addition to the standard English letters and characters, a program needs to store special characters that have no printable equivalents. One of these is the end-of-file sentinel, which all computer systems use to designate the end of a file of data. These end-of-file sentinels can also be transmitted from the keyboard. For example, on Unix-based systems it is generated using Ctrl-D, while on Windows-based systems it is generated using Ctrl-Z. Both of these sentinels are stored as the integer number −1, which has no equivalent character value. (You can check this by displaying the integer value of each entered character (see Program 7.9), and typing either Ctrl-D or Ctrl-Z, depending on the system you are using.)

Additionally, by using a 16-bit integer value, over 64,000 different characters can be represented. This provides sufficient storage for multiple character sets that can include Arabic, Chinese, Hebrew, Japanese, Russian, and virtually almost all known language symbols. Thus, storing a character as an integer value has a very practical value.

A very important consequence of using integer codes for string characters is that characters can easily be compared for alphabetical ordering. For example, as long as each subsequent letter in an alphabet has a higher value than its preceding letter, the comparison of character values is reduced to the comparison of numeric values. Additionally, if characters are stored in sequential numerical order, it ensures that adding one to a letter will produce the next letter in the alphabet.

The `get()` function reads the next character in the input stream and assigns it to the function's character variable. For example, a statement, such as,

```
cin.get(nextChar);
```

causes the next character entered at the keyboard to be stored in the character variable `nextChar`. This function is extremely useful in inputting and checking individual characters before they are assigned to a complete string or other C++ data type.

The character output function corresponding to `get()` is `put()`. This function expects a single character argument and displays the character passed to it on the terminal. For example, the statement `cout.put('A')` causes the letter A to be displayed on the screen.

Of the last three functions listed in Table 7.5, the `cin.ignore()` function is the most useful. This function permits skipping over input until a

PROGRAMMING NOTE

A Notational Inconsistency

Notice that all of the `character` class methods listed in Table 7.5 use the standard object-oriented notation of preceding the method's name with an object name, as in `cin.get()`. This is not the case with the `string` class `getline()` method, which uses the notation `getline(cin, strVar)`. In this notation the object, in this case `cin`, appears as an argument. For consistency's sake we would have expected `getline()` to be called as `cin.getline()`.

Unfortunately, this proper notation was already in use for a `getline()` method originally created for C-style strings (see Section 10.1). Hence, a notational inconsistency was created.

designated character, such as `'\n'` is encountered. For example, the statement `cin.ignore(80, '\n')` will skip up to a maximum of the next 80 characters, or stop the skipping if the newline character is encountered. Such a statement can be useful in skipping all further input on a line, up to a maximum of 80 characters, or until the end of the current line is encountered. Input would then begin with the next line.

The `peek()` function returns the next character on the stream, but does not remove it from the stream's buffer (see Figure 7.4). For example, the expression `cin.peek(nextChar)` returns the next character input by the keyboard, but leaves it in the buffer. This is sometimes useful for "peeking" ahead and seeing what the next character is, while leaving it in place for the next input.

Finally, the `putback()` function places a character back on the stream so that it will be the next character read. The argument passed to `putback()` can be any character expression that evaluates to a legitimate character value, and need not be the last input character.

The Phantom newline Revisited

As we saw in the previous section, seemingly strange results are sometimes obtained when a `cin` stream input is followed by a `getline()` method call. This same result can occur when characters are input using the `get()` character method. To see how this can occur, consider Program 7.10, which uses the `get()` method to accept the next character entered at the keyboard and stores the character in the variable `fkey`.

Program 7.10

```cpp
#include <iostream>
using namespace std;

int main()
{
  char fkey, skey;

  cout << "Type in a character: ";
  cin.get(fkey);
  cout << "The key just accepted is " << int(fkey) << endl;

  return 0;
}
```

When Program 7.10 is run, the character entered in response to the prompt `Type in a character:` is stored in the character variable `fkey` and the decimal code for the character is displayed by explicitly casting the character into an integer, to force its display as an integer value. The following sample run illustrates this:

```
Type in a character: m
The key just accepted is 109
```

At this point, everything seems to be working just fine, although you might be wondering why we displayed the decimal value of m rather than the character itself. The reason for this will soon become apparent.

In typing m, two keys are usually pressed, the m key and the Enter key. As was noted in the previous section, these two characters will be stored in a buffer immediately after they are pressed (see Figure 7.4).

The first key pressed, m in this case, is taken from the buffer and stored in `fkey`. This, however, still leaves the code for the Enter key in the buffer. Thus, a subsequent call to `get()` for a character input will automatically pick up the code for the Enter key as the next character. For example, consider Program 7.11.

Program 7.11

```cpp
#include <iostream>
using namespace std;

int main()
{
  char fkey, skey;

  cout << "Type in a character: ";
  cin.get(fkey);
  cout << "The key just accepted is " << int(fkey) << endl;

  cout << "Type in another character: ";
  cin.get(skey);
  cout << "The key just accepted is " << int(skey) << endl;

   return 0;
}
```

The following is a sample run for Program 7.11.

```
Type in a character: m
The key just accepted is 109
Type in another character: The key just accepted is 10
```

Let us review what has happened. In entering m in response to the first prompt, the Enter key is also pressed. From a character standpoint this represents the entry of two distinct characters. The first character is m, which is coded and stored as the integer 109. The second character also gets stored in the buffer with the numerical code for the Enter key. The second call to get() picks up this code immediately, without waiting for any additional key to be pressed. The last cout stream displays the code for this key. The reason for displaying the numerical code rather than the character itself is because the Enter key has no printable character associated with it that can be displayed.

Remember that every key has a numerical code, including the Enter, Spacebar, Escape, and Control keys. These keys generally have no effect when entering numbers, because the input methods ignore them as leading or trailing input with numerical data. Nor do these keys affect the entry of a single character requested as the first user data to be input, as is the case in Program 7.10. Only when a character is requested after the user has already input some other data, as in Program 7.11, does the usually invisible Enter key become noticeable.

In Section 7.1 you learned some ways to prevent the Enter key from being accepted as a legitimate character input when the `getline()` method was used. The following ways can be used when the `get()` method is used within a program:

- Follow the `cin.get()` input with the call `cin.ignore()`
- Accept the Enter key into a character variable and then don't use further

Program 7.12 applies the first solution to Program 7.11. Ignoring the Enter key immediately after the first character is read and displayed clears the buffer of the Enter key and gets it ready to store the next valid input character as its first character.

Program 7.12

```
#include <iostream>
using namespace std;

int main()
{
  char fkey, skey;

  cout << "Type in a character: ";
  cin.get(fkey);
  cout << "The key just accepted is " << int(fkey) << endl;
  cin.ignore();

  cout << "Type in another character: ";
  cin.get(skey);
  cout << "The key just accepted is " << int(skey) << endl;
  cin.ignore();

  return 0;
}
```

In reviewing Program 7.12, observe that when the user types an m and presses the Enter key, the m is assigned to `fkey` and the code for the Enter key is ignored. The next call to `get()` stores the code for the next key pressed in the variable skey. From the user's standpoint, the Enter key has no effect except to signal the end of each character input. The following is a sample run for Program 7.12.

```
Type in a character: m
The key just accepted is 109
Type in another character: b
The key just accepted is 98
```

A Second Look at User-Input Validation

As mentioned in our first look at user-input validation (Section 3.3), programs that respond effectively to unexpected user input are formally referred to as robust programs and informally as "bulletproof" programs. Code that validates user input and ensures that a program does not produce unintended results due to unexpected input is a sign of a well-constructed, robust program. One of your jobs as a programmer is to produce such programs. To see how such unintended results can occur, consider the following two code examples. First assume that your program contains the statements:

```
cout << "Enter an integer: ";
cin  >> value;
```

Now assume that, by mistake, a user enters the characters e4. On earlier versions of C++, this would cause the program to unexpectedly terminate, or **crash.** While crashes can still occur with the current ANSI/ISO standard (see, for example, Exercise 9), it will not occur in this case. Rather, a meaningless integer value will be assigned to the variable named value. This, of course, will invalidate any results obtained using this variable.

As a second example, consider the following code, which will cause an infinite loop to occur if the user enters a non-numeric value (the program can be halted by pressing the control and c keys at the same time)

```
double value;

  do
  {
    cout << "Enter a number (enter 0 to exit): ";
    cin  >> value;

    cout << "The square root of this number is: " << sqrt(value) <<
endl;
  }while (value !=0);
```

The basic technique for handling invalid data input and preventing seemingly innocuous code, such as that in our two simple examples from producing unintended results is referred to as **user-input validation.** Essentially this means validating the entered data either during or immediately after data entry and providing the user with a way of re-entering any invalid data. User-input validation is an essential part of any commercially viable program, and if done correctly, it will protect a program from attempting to process data types that can either cause a program to crash, create infinite loops, or produce more invalid results.

The central element in user-input validation is checking each entered character to verify that it qualifies as a legitimate character for the expected data type. For example, if an integer is required, the only acceptable characters are a leading plus or minus sign and the digits 0 through 9. These characters can be checked either as they are being typed, which means that the get() function is used to input a character at a time, or all of the characters can be accepted in a string, and then each string character checked for validity. Once all the entered characters have been validated, the entered string can then be converted into the correct data type.

There are two basic means of accomplishing the actual validity of the entered characters. Section 7.4 initially presents one of these ways, which uses character-by-character checking. A second technique, which encompasses a broader scope of data processing tasks using exception handling, is presented at the end of Section 7.4.

▍ EXERCISES 7.2

1. Enter and execute Program 7.8 on your computer.

2. Enter and execute Program 7.9 on your computer.

3. Write and execute a C++ program that counts the number of words in a string. A word is encountered whenever a transition from a blank space to a nonblank character is encountered. Assume that the string contains only words separated by blank spaces.

4. Generate 10 random numbers in the range 0 to 129. If the number represents a printable character print the character with an appropriate message that:

```
The character is a lowercase letter
The character is an uppercase letter
The character is a digit
The character is a space
```

If the character is none of these, display its value in integer format.

5. *a.* Write a function named length() that determines and returns the length of a string, without using the string class length() method.

b. Write a simple main() function to test the length() function written for Exercise 5a.

6. *a.* Write a function named `countlets()` that returns the number of letters in a string passed as an argument. Digits, spaces, punctuation, tabs, and newline characters should not be included in the returned count.

   b. Include the `countlets()` method written for Exercise 6a in an executable C++ program and use the program to test the method.

7. Write a program that accepts a string from the console and displays the hexadecimal equivalent of each character in the string.

8. Write a C++ program that accepts a string from the console and displays the string one word per line.

9. In response to the following code:

   ```
   cout << "Enter an integer: ";
   cin  >> value;
   ```

   suppose a user enters the data `12e4`. What value will be stored in the integer variable `value`?

10. *a.* Write a C++ program that stops reading a line of text when a period is entered and then displays the sentence with correct spacing and capitalization. For this program, correct spacing means that there should only be one space between words and that all letters should be in lowercase, except for the first letter of the first word. For example, if the user entered the text `i      am         going     to     Go     TO      THe moVies.` the displayed sentence should be `I am going to go to the movies.`

    b. Determine what characters, if any, are not correctly displayed by the program you created for Exercise 10a.

11. Write a C++ program that accepts a name as first name last name and then displays the name as last name, first name. For example, if the user entered Gary Bronson, the output should be Bronson, Gary.

12. Modify the program written for Exercise 11 to include an array of five names.

7.3   Exception Handling

One of the latest features added to C++ has been the introduction of exception handling for dealing with error conditions. The traditional approach that was initially used in C++, and is still available and used quite frequently, is that a function returns a specific value to indicate specific operations. Typically, a return value of 0 or 1 is used to indicate a successful completion of the function's task, while a negative value is used to indicate an error condition. For example, if a function were used to divide two numbers, a return value of –1 could be used to indicate that the denominator was 0, and the division could not be performed. When multiple error conditions can occur, different return values would be used to indicate specific errors.

A number of problems can occur with this traditional approach. First, it requires that the programmer actually checks the return value to detect if an error did occur. Next, the error handling code that checks the return value frequently becomes intermixed with normal processing code, so it sometimes can be very difficult to clearly determine which part of the code is handling errors as opposed to normal program processing. And finally, returning an error condition from a function means that the condition must be of the same data type as a valid returned value; hence, the error code must be a specific value that can be identified as an error alert. This means that the error code is effectively embedded as one of the possible non-error values that may be required from the function and is only available at the point where the method returns a value. Finally, a function that returns a Boolean value has no additional values that can be used to report an error condition.

None of this is insurmountable, and many times this approach is simple and effective. However, in its latest version C++ compilers have an additional technique specifically designed for error detection and handling, which is referred to as exception handling.

In **exception handling**, when an error occurs while a method is executing, the method creates either a value, variable, or object, which is referred to as an **exception**, at the point the error occurs, that contains information about the error. This exception is then immediately passed, again at the point it was generated, to code that is referred to as the **exception handler**, which is designed to correctly deal with the exception. The process of generating and passing the exception at the point the error was detected is referred to as **throwing an exception**. Notice that the exception is thrown from within the function while it is still executing. This permits handling the error and returning control back to the function so that it can complete its assigned task correctly.

In general, two fundamental types of errors can cause C++ exceptions: those that result from an inability of the program to obtain a required resource and those that result from flawed data. Examples of the first error type are attempts to obtain a system resource, such as locating and finding a file for input. These types of errors are the result of external resources over which the programmer has no control.

Examples of the second type of error can occur when a program prompts the user to enter an integer, and the user enters a string, such as e234, that cannot be converted to a numerical value. Another example is the attempt to divide two numbers when the denominator has a value of 0. This latter condition is referred to as a divide by zero error. Each of these errors can always be checked and handled in a manner that does not result in a program crash. Before seeing how this is accomplished using exception handling, review Table 7.6 to familiarize yourself with the terminology that is used in relation to the processing of exceptions.

TABLE 7.6 *Exception Handling Terminology*

Terminology	Description
Exception	A value, variable, or object that identifies a specific error that has occurred while a program is executing.
Throw an exception	Send the exception to a section of code that processes the detected error.
Catch or handle an exception	Receive a thrown exception and process it.
Catch clause	The section of code that processes the error.
Exception handler	The code used to throw and catch an exception.

The general syntax of the code required to throw and catch an exception is:

```
try
{
   // one or more statements,
   // at least one of which should
   // be capable of throwing an exception;
}
catch(exceptionDataType parameterName)
{
   // one or more statements
}
```

This code uses two new keywords: `try` and `catch`. Let's see what each of these words does.

The keyword `try` identifies the start of an exception handling block of code. At least one of the statements within the braces defining this block of code should be capable of throwing an exception. For example, the `try` block in the following section of code

```
try
{
  cout << "Enter the numerator (whole number only):";
  cin  >> numerator;
  cout << "Enter the denominator (whole number only):";
  cin  >> denominator;
  result = numerator/denominator;
}
```

contains five statements, three of which may result in an error that we want to catch. In particular, in a professionally written program we would want to ensure that valid integers were entered in response to both prompts, and that the second entered value was not a zero. For demonstration purposes we will initially only check that this second value entered is not zero (in Section 7.4 you will find the exception handling code that can be used to validate both inputs to ensure that both entered data are integers).

Thus, from the standpoint of the `try` block, it is only the value of the second number that is now of concern. Essentially, the `try` block will be altered to say "try all of the statements within me to see if an exception, which in this particular case is a zero second value, occurs." This is accomplished by adding a `throw` statement within the `try` block, as follows:

```
try
{
  cout << "Enter the numerator (whole number only):";
  cin  >> numerator;
  cout << "Enter the denominator (whole number only):";
  cin  >> denominator;
  if (denominator == 0)
    throw denominator;
  else
    result = numerator/denominator;
}
```

Two points need to be understood with respect to this `try` block. First, the item that is thrown is an integer value. We could just as easily have thrown a string or an object; but only one of these items can be thrown by any single throw statement. Secondly, the first four statements in the `try` block need not have been included in the code; however, doing so keeps all of the relevant statements together. This will also facilitate adding throw statements within the same `try` block to ensure that both input values are integer values, so it is more convenient to have all the relevant code available within the same `try` block.

A `try` block must be followed by one or more `catch` blocks, which serve as exception handlers for any exceptions thrown by the statements in the `try` block. Here is a `catch` block that appropriately handles the thrown exception, which is an integer.

```
catch(int e)
{
  cout << "A denominator value of " << e << " is invalid." << endl;
  exit (1);
}
```

The exception handling provided by this `catch` block is simply an output statement that identifies the particular exception that has been caught and terminates program execution. Notice the parentheses following the `catch` keyword. Listed within the parentheses is the data type of the exception that is thrown and a parameter name used to receive it, which we have named e. This identifier, which is programmer selected, but conventionally uses the letter e for exception, is used to hold the exception value generated when an exception is thrown.

Although we have provided a single `catch` block, multiple `catch` blocks can be provided, as long as each block catches a unique data type. All that is required is that at least one `catch` block be provided for each `try` block. Naturally, the more exceptions that can be caught with the same `try` block, the better. Program 7.13 provides a complete program that includes a `try` and `catch` block to detect a divide by zero error.

Program 7.13

```
#include <iostream>
using namespace std;

int main()
{
  int numerator, denominator;

  try
  {
    cout << "Enter the numerator (whole number only): ";
    cin  >> numerator;
    cout << "Enter the denominator(whole number only): ";
    cin  >> denominator;
    if (denominator == 0)
      throw denominator;  // an integer value is thrown
    else
      cout << numerator << '/' << denominator
           << " = " << double(numerator)/ double(denominator) << endl;
  }
  catch(int e)
  {
    cout << "A denominator value of " << e << " is invalid." << endl;
    exit (1);
  }

  return 0;
}
```

Following are two sample runs using Program 7.13. As seen, the second output indicates that an attempt to divide by a zero denominator has been successfully detected before the operation is performed.

```
Enter the numerator (whole number only): 12
Enter the denominator(whole number only): 3
12/3 = 4
```

and

```
Enter the numerator (whole number only): 12
Enter the denominator(whole number only): 0
A denominator value of 0 is invalid.
```

Having detected a zero denominator, rather than terminating program execution, a more robust program would provide the user with the opportunity to re-enter a nonzero value. This can be accomplished by including the `try` block within a `while` statement, and then having the `catch` block return program control to the `while` statement after informing the user that a zero value has been entered. Program 7.14 accomplishes this.

In reviewing this code, notice that it is the `continue` statement within the `catch` block that returns control to the top of the while statement (see Section 5.2 for a review of the `continue` statement). Following is a sample run using Program 7.14.

```
Enter a numerator (whole number only): 12
Enter a denominator (whole number only): 0
A denominator value of 0 is invalid.
Please re-enter the denominator (whole number only): 5
12/5 = 2.4
```

One caution should be mentioned when throwing string literals as opposed to numeric values. As an example, consider that rather than throwing the value of the `denominator` variable in both Programs 7.13 and 7.14, the following statement was used:

```
throw "***Invalid input - A denominator value of zero is not permitted***";
```

Whenever a string literal is thrown, it is a C-string, not a `string` class object that is thrown. This means that the `catch` statement must declare the received argument as a C-string, which is a character array, rather than as a string. Thus, a correct `catch` statement for the preceding `throw` statement is

```
                           catch(char e[])
```

An attempt to declare the exception as a `string` class variable will result in a compiler error.

Program 7.14

```cpp
#include <iostream>
using namespace std;

int main()
{
  int numerator, denominator;
  bool needDenominator = true;

  cout << "Enter a numerator (whole number only): ";
  cin  >> numerator;

  cout << "Enter a denominator (whole number only): ";
  while(needDenominator)
  {
    cin  >> denominator;
    try
    {
      if (denominator == 0)
        throw denominator;  // an integer value is thrown
    }
    catch(int e)
    {
      cout << "A denominator value of " << e << " is invalid." << endl;
      cout << "Please re-enter the denominator (whole number only): ";
      continue;  // this sends control back to the while statement
    }
    cout << numerator << '/' << denominator
         << " = " << double(numerator)/ double(denominator) << endl;
    needDenominator = false;
  }

  return 0;
}
```

▌EXERCISES 7.3

1. Define the following terms:
   exception
   `try` block
   `catch` block
   exception handler
   throw an exception
   catch an exception

2. Enter and execute Program 7.13.

3. Replace the statement

```
cout << numerator << '/' << denominator
      << " = " << double (numerator)/ double (denominator) << endl;
```

in Program 7.13 with the statement

```
        cout << numerator << '/' << denominator
              << " = " << numerator/denominator << endl;
```

and execute the modified program. Enter the values 12 and 5, and explain why the result is incorrect from the user's viewpoint.

4. Modify Program 7.13 so that it throws and correctly catches the message `***Invalid input - A denominator value of zero is not permitted***`. (*Hint:* Review the caution presented at the end of this section.)

5. Enter and execute Program 7.14.

6. Modify Program 7.14 so that it continues to divide two numbers until the user enters the characters `999` (either as a numerator or denominator) to terminate program execution.

7.4   Input Data Validation

One of the major uses of strings in professionally written programs is for user-input validation. The necessity for validating user input is the rather obvious fact that even though a program prompts the user to enter a specific type of data, such as an integer, this does not ensure that the user will comply. What a user enters is, in fact, totally out of the programmer's control. What is in your control is how you deal with the entered data.

It certainly does no good to tell a frustrated user that "The program clearly tells you to enter an integer and you entered a date." Rather, professional programmers understand that successful programs always anticipate invalid data and isolate such data from being accepted and processed. This is typically accomplished by first validating that the data is of the correct type; if it is, the data is accepted; otherwise, the user is requested to re-enter the data, with an explanation of why the entered data was invalid.

One of the most common methods of validating numerical input data is to accept all numbers as strings. Each character in the string can then be checked to ensure that it complies with the data type being requested. Only after the data is checked and verified for the correct type is the string converted to either an integer or floating-point value using the conversion functions listed in Table 7.7 (for data accepted using `string` class objects, the `c_str()` method must be applied to the string before the conversion functions listed in Table 7.7 are invoked).

TABLE 7.7 *C-string Conversion Functions*

Function	Description	Example
`int atoi(stringExp)`	Converts an ASCII string to an integer. Conversion stops at the first noninteger character.	`atoi("1234")`
`double atof(stringExp)`	Converts an ASCII string to a double precision number. Conversion stops at the first character that cannot be interpreted as a double.	`atof("12.34")`
`char[] itoa(stringExp)`	Converts an integer to an ASCII string. The space allocated for the returned string must be large enough for the converted value.	`itoa(1234)`

As an example, consider the input of an integer number. To be valid, the data entered must adhere to the following conditions.

- *The data must contain at least one character*
- *If the first character is a + or – sign, the data must contain at least one digit*
- *Only digits from 0 to 9 are acceptable following the first character*

The following function, named `isvalidInt()` can be used to check that an entered string complies with these conditions. This function returns the Boolean value of `true`, if the conditions are satisfied; otherwise, it returns a Boolean `false` value.

```
bool isvalidInt(string str)
{
  int start = 0;
  int i;
  bool valid = true;   // assume a valid
  bool sign = false;   // assume no sign

  // check for an empty string
  if (str.length() == 0)  valid = false;

  // check for a leading sign
  if (str.at(0) == '-'|| str.at(0) == '+')
  {
    sign = true;
    start = 1;  // start checking for digits after the sign
  }

  // check that there is at least one character after the sign
  if (sign && str.length() == 1) valid = false;

  // now check the string, which we know has at least one non-sign char
  i = start;
  while(valid && i < str.length())
  {
    if(!isdigit(str.at(i))) valid = false;   //found a non-digit character
    i++;  // move to next character
  }

  return valid;
}
```

In reviewing the code for the `isvalidInt()` method, pay attention to the conditions that are being checked. These are commented in the code and consist of checking that:

- The string is not empty
- The presence of a valid sign symbol (+ or −)
- If a sign symbol is present, that there is at least one digit following it
- That all of the remaining characters in the string are digits

Only if all of these conditions are met does the function return a Boolean `true` value. Once this value is returned, the string can be safely converted into an integer with the assurance that no unexpected value will result to hamper further data processing. Program 7.15 uses this method within the context of a complete program.

 Program 7.15

```cpp
#include <iostream>
#include <string>
using namespace std;

int main()
{
  bool isvalidInt(string);   // function prototype (declaration)
  string value;
  int number;

  cout << "Enter an integer: ";
  getline(cin, value);

  if (!isvalidInt(value))
   cout << "The number you entered is not a valid integer.";
  else
  {
     number = atoi(value.c_str());
   cout << "The integer you entered is " << number;
  }

  return 0;
}

  bool isvalidInt(string str)
  {
    int start = 0;
    int i;
    bool valid = true;   // assume a valid
    bool sign = false;   // assume no sign

    // check for an empty string
    if (str.length() == 0)  valid = false;
```

```
          // check for a leading sign
          if (str.at(0) == '-'|| str.at(0) == '+')
          {
             sign = true;
             start = 1;   // start checking for digits after the sign
          }

          // check that there is at least one character after the sign
          if (sign && str.length() == 1) valid = false;

          // now check the string, which we know has at least one non-sign char
          i = start;
          while(valid && i < str.length())
          {
             if(!isdigit(str.at(i))) valid = false;   //found a non-digit charac-
ter
             i++;   // move to next character
          }

          return valid;
       }
```

Two sample runs using Program 7.15 produced the following:

```
          Enter an integer: 12e45
          The number you entered is not a valid integer.
```

and

```
          Enter an integer: -12345
          The number you entered is -12345
```

As illustrated by this output, the program successfully determines that an invalid character was entered in the first run.

Rather than accepting and then checking a complete string, an alternative is to check each character as it is typed. This is an especially useful method when a GUI is used for data input, because it permits the user to correct the data as it is being entered, rather than after the complete number has been entered.

A second line of defense is to provide error processing code within the context of exception handling code. This type of code is typically provided to permit the user to correct a problem such as invalid data entry by re-entering a new value. The means of providing this in C++ is referred to as exception handling and is presented next.

Using exception handling, a complete means of ensuring that an integer number is entered by a user in response to a request for an integer value can be constructed. The technique we will use extends the isvalidInt() function included in Program 7.15 to ensure that an invalid integer value is not only detected, but that the program provides the user with the option of re-entering values until a valid integer is obtained. This technique can easily be applied to ensure the entry of a valid double-precision number, which is the other numerical data type frequently requested as user-entered data.

Using the isvalidInt() function provided in Program 7.15 we now develop a more comprehensive function, named getanInt() that uses exception processing to continuously accept a user input until a string that corresponds to a valid integer is detected. Once such a string is entered, the getanInt() function converts the string to an integer and returns the integer value. This ensures that the program requesting an integer actually receives an integer and prevents any unwarranted effects, such as a program crash due to an invalid data type being entered.

The algorithm that we will use to perform this task is:

Set a Boolean variable named notanint to true
while (notanint is true)
   try
      Accept a string value
      If the string value does not correspond to an integer throw an exception
   catch the exception
      Display the error message "Invalid integer - Please re-enter: "
      Send control back to the while statement
      Set notanint to false (this causes the loop to terminate)
End while
Return the integer corresponding to the entered string

The code corresponding to this algorithm is highlighted in Program 7.16.

Following is a sample output produced by Program 7.16

```
Enter an integer value: abc
Invalid integer - Please re-enter: 12.
Invalid integer - Please re-enter: 12e
Invalid integer - Please re-enter: 120
The integer entered is: 120
```

As verified by this output, the getanInt() function works correctly. It continuously requests input until a valid integer is entered.

Program 7.16

```cpp
#include <iostream>
#include <string>
using namespace std;

int main()
{
  int getanInt();  // function declaration (prototype)
  int value;

  cout << "Enter an integer value: ";
  value = getanInt();
  cout << "The integer entered is: " << value << endl;

  return 0;
}

int getanInt()
{
  bool isvalidInt(string);  // function declaration (prototype)
  bool notanint = true;
  string svalue;

  while (notanint)
  {
    try
    {
      cin >> svalue;  // accept a string input
      if (!isvalidInt(svalue)) throw svalue;
    }
    catch (string e)
    {
      cout << "Invalid integer - Please re-enter: ";
        continue; // send control to the while statement
    }
    notanint = false;
  }
  return atoi(svalue.c_str());  // convert to an integer
}

bool isvalidInt(string str)
{
  int start = 0;
  int i;
  bool valid = true;     // assume a valid
  bool sign = false;     // assume no sign
```

(continued on next page)

(continued from previous page)

```
                    // check for an empty string
                    if (str.length() == 0)  valid = false;

                    // check for a leading sign
                    if (str.at(0) == '-'|| str.at(0) == '+')
                    {
                      sign = true;
                      start = 1;  // start checking for digits after the sign
                    }

                    // check that there is at least one character after the sign
                    if (sign && str.length() == 1) valid = false;

                    // now check the string, which we know has at least one non-sign char
                    i = start;
                    while(valid && i < str.length())
                    {
                      if(!isdigit(str.at(i))) valid = false;  //found a non-digit character
                      i++;  // move to next character
                    }

                  return valid;
                }
```

▌ EXERCISES 7.4

1. Write a C++ program that prompts the user to type in an integer. Have your program accept the number, as an integer using `cin`, and using `cout` display the value your program actually accepted from the data entered. Run your program four times. The first time you run the program enter a valid integer number, the second time enter a double-precision number, and the third time enter a character. Finally, enter the value `12e34`.

2. Repeat Exercise 1 but have your program use a double-precision variable. Run the program four times. The first time enter an integer, the second time enter a decimal number, the third time enter a decimal number with an `f` as the last character entered, and the fourth time enter a character. Using the output display, keep track of what number your program actually accepted from the data you entered. What happened, if anything, and why?

3. *a.* Why do you think that successful application programs contain extensive data input validity checks? (*Hint:* Review Exercises 1 and 2.)

b. What do you think is the difference between a data type check and a data reasonableness check?

c. Assume that a program requests that a month, day, and year be entered by the user. What are some reasonable checks that could be made on the data entered?

4. *a.* Enter and execute Program 7.15.

   b. Run Program 7.15 four times, using the data referred to in Exercise 1 for each run.

5. Modify Program 7.15 to display any invalid characters that were entered.

6. Modify Program 7.15 to continually request an integer until a valid number is entered.

7. Modify Program 7.15 to remove all leading and trailing spaces from the entered string before it is checked for validity.

8. Write a function that checks each digit as it is entered, rather than checking the completed string, as is done in Program 7.15.

9. Enter and execute Program 7.16.

10. Modify the `isvalidInt()` function used in Program 7.16 to remove all leading and trailing blank spaces from its string argument before determining if the string corresponds to a valid integer.

11. Modify the `isvalidInt()` function used in Program 7.16 to accept a string that ends in a decimal point. For example, the input 12. should be accepted and converted to the integer number twelve.

12. *a.* Write and test a C++ function named `isvalidReal()` that checks for a valid floating point number. Such a number can have an optional + or − sign, at most one decimal point, which can also be the first character, and at least one digit between 0 and 9 inclusive. The function should return a Boolean value of `true` if the entered number is a real number; otherwise, it should return a Boolean value of `false`.

   b. Modify the `isvalidReal()` function written for Exercise 13a to remove all leading and trailing blank spaces from its string argument before determining if the string corresponds to a valid real number.

13. Write and test a C++ function named `getareal()` that uses exception handling to continuously accept an input string until a string that can be converted to a real number is entered. The function should return a double value corresponding to the string value entered by the user.

7.5   Namespaces and Creating a Personal Library

Until the introduction of personal computers in the early 1980s, with their extensive use of integrated circuits and microprocessors, both the speed of computers and their available memory were severely restricted. For example, the most advanced computers of the time had speeds measured in milliseconds (one-thousandth of a second), whereas current computers have speeds measured in nanoseconds (one-billionth of a second) and higher. Similarly, the memory capacity of early desk-top computers consisted of 32,000 locations, with each location consisting of 8 bits. Today's computer memories consist of millions of memory locations, each consisting of from 32 to 64 bits.

These early hardware restrictions made it imperative that programmers use every possible trick to save memory space and make programs run more efficiently. Almost every program was handcrafted and included what was referred to as "clever-code" to minimize run time and maximize the use of memory storage. Unfortunately, this individualized code, over time, became a liability. New programmers had to expend considerable time understanding existing code, and frequently even the original programmer had trouble figuring out code that was written only months before. This made modifications extremely time consuming and costly, and precluded cost-effective use of existing code for new installations.

The inability to reuse code efficiently combined with expanded hardware capabilities provided the incentive for discovering more efficient ways of programming. Initially this lead to the structured programming concepts incorporated into procedural languages such as Pascal, and currently to the object-oriented techniques that form the basis of C++. One of the early criticisms of C++, however, was that it did not provide a comprehensive library of classes. This has changed dramatically with the current ANSI/ISO standard and the inclusion of a rather extensive C++ library.

No matter how many useful classes and methods that are provided, however, each major type of programming application, such as financial, marketing, engineering, and scientific areas, always have their own specialized requirements. For example, C++ provides rather good date and time functions in its `ctime` header file. For specialized needs, such as those encountered in the financial industry, however, these functions must be expanded. Thus, a more complete set of functions would include finding the number of business days between two dates that takes into account both weekends and holidays. It would also require functions that implemented prior and next day algorithms that take into account leap years and the actual days in each month. These functions could either be provided as part of a more complete `Date` class or as non-class functions.

In these situations, professional programmers create and share their own libraries of classes and functions with other programmers working on the same or similar projects. Once the classes and functions have been tested, they can be incorporated into any program without further expenditures of coding time.

At this stage in your programming career you can begin to build your own library of specialized functions and classes . To show how this is accomplished in practice we will use Section 7.4's input validation functions, `isvalidInt()` and `getanInt()`, which are reproduced, for convenience, next.

```
int getanInt()
{
  bool isvalidInt(string);  // function declaration (prototype)
  bool notanint = true;
  string svalue;

  while (notanint)
  {
    try
    {
      cin >> svalue;  // accept a string input
      if (!isvalidInt(svalue)) throw svalue;
    }
    catch (string e)
    {
      cout << "Invalid integer - Please re-enter: ";
        continue; // send control to the while statement
    }
    notanint = false;
  }
  return atoi(svalue.c_str());  // convert to an integer
}

bool isvalidInt(string str)
{
  int start = 0;
  int i;
  bool valid = true;  // assume a valid
  bool sign = false;  // assume no sign

  // check for an empty string
  if (str.length() == 0)  valid = false;

  // check for a leading sign
  if (str.at(0) == '-'|| str.at(0) == '+')
  {
    sign = true;
    start = 1;  // start checking for digits after the sign
  }

  // check that there is at least one character after the sign
  if (sign && str.length() == 1) valid = false;
```

(continued on next page)

(continued from previous page)

```
   // now check the string, which we know has at least one non-sign char
   i = start;
   while(valid && i < str.length())
   {
     if(!isdigit(str.at(i))) valid = false;  //found a non-digit character
     i++;  // move to next character
   }

   return valid;
 }
```

The first step in creating a library is to optionally encapsulate all of the desired functions and classes into one or more namespaces and then store the complete code in one or more files. For our example we create one namespace named dataChecks and save it in the file named dataChecks.cpp. It is important to note that the file name under which the namespace is saved *need not* be the same as the namespace name used in the code.

The syntax for creating a namespace is

```
namespace name
{
   functions and/or classes in here
}   // end of namespace
```

Including the two functions getanInt() and isvalidInt() within a namespace named dataChecks and adding the appropriate include files and using declaration statement needed by the new namespace yields the following code. For convenience, the syntax required to create the namespace has been highlighted.

```
namespace dataChecks
{
  #include <iostream>
  #include <string>
  #include <cctype>
  using namespace std;

  int getanInt()
  {
    bool isvalidInt(string);  // function declaration (prototype)
    bool notanint = true;
    string svalue;
```

```cpp
    while (notanint)
    {
      try
      {
        cin >> svalue;  // accept a string input
        if (!isvalidInt(svalue)) throw svalue;
      }
      catch (string e)
      {
        cout << "Invalid integer - Please re-enter: ";
        continue; // send control to the while statement
      }
      notanint = false;
    }
    return atoi(svalue.c_str());  // convert to an integer
  }

  bool isvalidInt(string str)
  {
    int start = 0;
    int i;
    bool valid = true;  // assume a valid
    bool sign = false;  // assume no sign

    // check for an empty string
    if (str.length() == 0)  valid = false;

    // check for a leading sign
    if (str.at(0) == '-'|| str.at(0) == '+')
    {
      sign = true;
      start = 1;  // start checking for digits after the sign
    }

    // check that there is at least one character after the sign
    if (sign && str.length() == 1) valid = false;

    // now check the string, which we know has at least one non-sign char
    i = start;
    while(valid && i < str.length())
    {
      if(!isdigit(str.at(i))) valid = false; //found a non-digit character
      i++;  // move to next character
    }
    return valid;
  }

}  // end of dataChecks namespace
```

Once the namespace has been created and stored in a file, it can be included within another file by supplying a preprocessor directive informing the compiler where the desired namespace is to be found, and including a `using` directive instructing the compiler as to which particular namespace in the file to use. For our namespace, which has been stored in a file named `dataChecks.cpp` within a folder named `myLibrary`, this is accomplished by the statements:

```
#include <c:\\myLibrary\\dataChecks.cpp>
using namespace dataChecks;
```

The first statement provides the full path name for the source code file. Notice that a full path name has been used and that two slashes are used to separate path names. The double slashes are required whenever providing either a relative or full path name. The only time that slashes are not required is when the library code resides in the same directory as the program being executed. As indicated, on the author's computer the `dataChecks.cpp` source file has been saved within a folder named `myLibrary`. The second statement tells the compiler to use the `dataChecks` namespace within the designated file. Program 7.17 includes these two statements within an executable program.

 Program 7.17

```cpp
#include <c:\\myLibrary\\dataChecks.cpp>
using namespace dataChecks;

int main()
{
  int value;

  cout << "Enter an integer value: ";
  value = getanInt();
  cout << "The integer entered is: " << value << endl;

  return 0;
}
```

The only requirement for the `include` statement in Program 7.17 is that file name and location must correspond to an existing file having the same name in the designated path; otherwise a compiler error will occur. Should you wish to name the source code file using an extension, any extension can be used, as long as the following rules are maintained:

1. The file name under which the code is stored includes the extension
2. The same file name, including extension, is used in the `include` statement

Thus, if the file name used to store the functions were `dataLib.cpp`, the `include` statement in Program 7.17 would be `#include <c::\\myLibrary\\dataLib.cpp>`. Additionally, a namespace is not required within the file. Using a namespace lets us isolate class code into distinct areas and permits us to add additional namespaces to our file for code as the need arises. The designation of a namespace in the `using` statement tells the compiler to only include the code in the specified namespace, rather than all of the code in the file. If the data check functions were not enclosed within a namespace, the `using` statement for the `dataChecks` namespace in Program 7.17 would have to be omitted.

Including the previously written and tested data checking functions within Program 7.17 as a separate file allows you to focus on the code within the program that uses these functions, rather than being concerned with the function code itself. This permits you to concentrate on correctly using these functions as opposed to reexamining or even seeing the previously written and tested function code. In Program 7.17 the `main()` method simply exercises the data checking functions and produces the same output as Program 7.16. In creating the `dataChecks` namespace we have included source code for the two functions. This is not required and a compiled version of the source code can be saved instead. Finally, additions to a namespace defined in one file can be made in another file by using the same namespace name in the new file and including a using statement for the first file's namespace.

▌ EXERCISES 7.5

1. Enter and compile Program 7.17 (*Hint:* Both the namespace header file `dataChecks` and the program file are available with the source code provided on the Course Technology web site for this text.

2. Why would a programmer supply a namespace file in its compiled form rather than as source code?

3. *a.* What is an advantage of namespaces?
   b. What is a possible disadvantage of namespaces?

4. What types of classes and functions would you include in a personal library? Why?

5. *a.* Write a C++ function named `whole()` that returns the integer part of any number passed to the function. (*Hint:* Assign the passed argument to an integer variable.)

b. Include the function written in Exercise 5a in a working program. Make sure your function is called from `main()` and correctly returns a value to `main()`. Have `main()` use a `cout` statement to display the value returned. Test the function by passing various data to it.

c. When you are confident that the `whole()` function written for Exercise 5a works correctly, save it in a namespace and a personal library of your choice.

6. *a.* Write a C++ function named `fracpart()` that returns the fractional part of any number passed to the function. For example, if the number 256.879 is passed to `fracpart()`, the number 0.879 should be returned. Have the function `fracpart()` call the function `whole()` that you wrote in Exercise 5. The number returned can then be determined as the number passed to `fracpart()` less the returned value when the same argument is passed to `whole()`. The completed program should consist of `main()` followed by `fracpart()` followed by `whole()`.

b. Include the function written in Exercise 6a in a working program. Make sure your function is called from `main()` and correctly returns a value to `main()`. Have `main()` use a `cout` statement to display the value returned. Test the function by passing various data to it.

c. When you are confident that the `fracpart()` function written for Exercise 6a works correctly, save it in the same namespace and personal library selected for Exercise 6c.

7.6 Common Programming Errors

The common errors associated with defining and processing strings are:

1. Forgetting to include the `string` header file when using `string` class objects.
2. Forgetting that the newline character, `'\n'`, is a valid data input character.
3. Forgetting to convert a `string` class object using the `c_str()` method when converting `string` class objects to numerical data types.

7.7 Chapter Summary

1. A **string literal** is any sequence of characters enclosed in double quotation marks. A string literal is also referred to as a string value, a string constant, and more conventionally, simply as a string.
2. A string can be constructed as an object of the `string` class.

3. The `string` class is commonly used for constructing strings for input and output purposes, such as for prompts and displayed messages. In additionally, because of the provided capabilities, this class is also used when strings need to be compared, searched, or individual characters in a string need to be examined or extracted as a substring.

   It is also used in more advanced situations when characters within a string need to be replaced, inserted, or deleted on a relatively regular basis.

4. Strings can be manipulated using either the methods of the class they are objects of or by using general-purpose string and character methods.

5. The `cin` object, by itself, tends to be of limited usefulness for string input because it terminates input when a blank is encountered.

6. For `string` class data input use the `getline()` method.

7. The `cout` object can be used to display `string` class strings.

PART II

Data Structures

Arrays

The variables that we have used so far have all had a common characteristic: Each variable could be used to store only a single value at a time. For example, although the variables key, count, and grade declared in the statements

```
char key;
int count;
double grade;
```

are of different data types, each variable can store only one value of the declared data type. These types of variables are called atomic variables. An **atomic variable,** which is also referred to as a **scalar variable,** is a variable whose value cannot be further subdivided or separated into legitimate data types.

Frequently we may have a set of values, all of the same data type, that form a logical group. For example, Figure 8.1 illustrates three groups of items. The first group is a list of five integer grades, the second group is a list of four character codes, and the last group is a list of six floating-point prices.

A simple list containing individual items of the same data type is called a one-dimensional array. In this chapter we describe how one-dimensional arrays are declared, initialized, stored inside a computer, and used. We also explore the use of one-dimensional arrays with example programs and present the procedures for declaring and using multidimensional arrays.

FIGURE 8.1   *Three Lists of Items*

Grades	Codes	Prices
98	x	10.96
87	a	6.43
92	m	2.58
79	n	.86
85		12.27
		6.39

8.1   One-Dimensional Arrays

A **one-dimensional array,** which may also be referred to as a **single-dimensional array,** or a *vector*, is a list of related values with the same data type that is stored using a single group name.[1] In C++, as in other computer languages, the group name is referred to as the **array name.** For example, consider the list of grades shown in Figure 8.2.

[1] Note that lists can be implemented in a variety of ways. An array is simply one implementation of a list in which all of the list elements are of the same type and each element is stored consecutively in a set of contiguous memory locations.

FIGURE 8.2 *A List of Grades*

Grade
98
87
92
79
85

All the grades in the list are integer numbers and must be declared as such. However, the individual items in the list do not have to be declared separately. The items in the list can be declared as a single unit and stored under a common variable name called the array name. For convenience, we will choose `grade` as the name for the list shown in Figure 8.2. To specify that `grade` is to store five individual floating-point values requires the declaration statement `float grade[5]`. Note that this declaration statement gives the array (or list) name, the data type of the items in the array, and the number of items in the array. It is a specific example of the general array declaration statement that has the syntax

```
dataType arrayName[numberOfItems]
```

Common programming practice requires defining the number of items in the array as a constant before declaring the array. This constant is extremely useful later for processing all the items in an array. Thus the previous array declaration for `grade` would, in practice, be declared by using two statements, such as

```
const int NUMELS = 5;   // define a constant for the number of
                        // items
int grade[NUMELS];      // declare the array
```

Further examples of array declarations that use this two-line syntax are

```
const int ARRAYSIZE = 4;
char code[ARRAYSIZE];

const int NUMELS = 6;
double prices[NUMELS];

const int SIZE = 100;
double amount[SIZE];
```

In these declaration statements, each array is allocated sufficient memory to hold the number of data items given in the declaration statement. Thus the array named `code` has storage reserved for four characters, the array named `prices` has storage reserved for six double-precision numbers, and the array named `amount` has storage reserved for 100 double-precision numbers. The constant identifiers, `ARRAYSIZE`, `NUMELS`, and `SIZE`, are programmer-selected names.

Figure 8.3 illustrates the storage reserved for the `grade` and `code` arrays, assuming that an integer is stored using four bytes and a character is stored using one byte.

Each item in an array is called an **element** or **component** of the array. The individual elements stored in the arrays illustrated in Figure 8.3 are stored sequentially, the first array element being stored in the first reserved location, the second element in the second reserved location, and so on until the last element is stored in the last reserved location. This contiguous storage allocation for the list is a key feature of arrays; it provides a simple mechanism for easily locating any single element in the array.

FIGURE 8.3   *The* `grade` *and* `code` *Arrays in Memory*

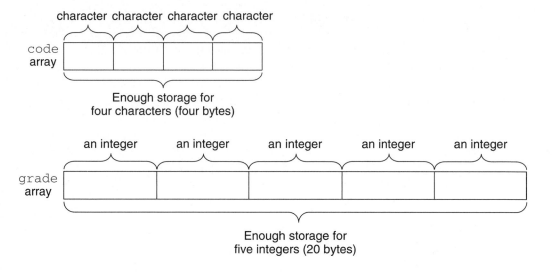

Because elements in the array are stored sequentially, any individual element can be accessed by giving the name of the array and the element's position. This position is called the element's **index** or **subscript value** (the two terms are synonymous). For a single-dimensional array, the first element has an index of 0, the second element has an index of 1, and so on. In C++, the array name and index of the desired element are combined by listing the index in braces after the array name. For example, given the declaration `double grade[5]`,

grade[0] refers to the first grade stored in the grade array
grade[1] refers to the second grade stored in the grade array
grade[2] refers to the third grade stored in the grade array
grade[3] refers to the fourth grade stored in the grade array
grade[4] refers to the fifth grade stored in the grade array

Figure 8.4 illustrates the grade array in memory with the correct designation for each array element. Each individual element is called an **indexed variable** or a **subscripted variable,** because both a variable name and an index or subscript value must be used to reference the element. Remember that the index or subscript value gives the *position* of the element in the array.

FIGURE 8.4 *Identifying Individual Array Elements*

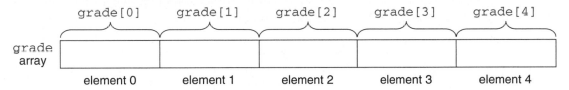

The subscripted variable grade[0] is read as both "grade sub zero" and "grade zero." This is a shortened way of saying "the grade array subscripted by zero." Similarly, grade[1] is read as "grade sub one" or "grade one," grade[2] as "grade sub two" or "grade two," and so on.

Although it may seem unusual to reference the first element with an index of zero, doing so increases the computer's speed when it accesses array elements. Internally, unseen by the programmer, the computer uses the index as an offset from the array's starting position. As illustrated in Figure 8.5, the index tells the computer how many elements to skip, starting from the beginning of the array, to get to the desired element.

FIGURE 8.5 *Accessing an Individual Array Element—Element 3*

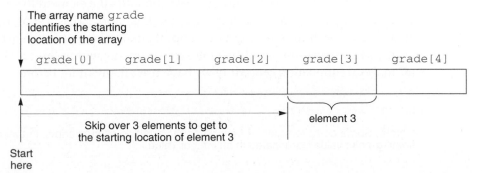

Subscripted variables can be used anywhere that scalar variables are valid. Here are some examples that use the elements of the grade array:

```
grade[0] = 95.75;
grade[1] = grade[0] - 11.0;
grade[2] = 5.0 * grade[0];
grade[3] = 79.0;
grade[4] = (grade[1] + grade[2] - 3.1) / 2.2;
sum = grade[0] + grade[1] + grade[2] + grade[3] + grade[4];
```

The subscript contained within brackets need not be an integer constant; any expression that evaluates to an integer may be used as a subscript.[2] In each case, of course, the value of the expression must be within the valid subscript range defined when the array is declared. For example, assuming that i and j are int variables, the following subscripted variables are valid:

```
grade[i]
grade[2*i]
grade[j-i]
```

One extremely important advantage of using integer expressions as subscripts is that it allows sequencing through an array by using a loop. This makes statements like

```
sum = grade[0] + grade[1] + grade[2] + grade[3] + grade[4];
```

unnecessary. The subscript values in this statement can be replaced by a for loop counter to access each element in the array sequentially. For example, the code

```
sum = 0;                          // initialize the sum to zero
for (i = 0; i < NUMELS; i++)
  sum = sum + grade[i];           // add in a value
```

sequentially retrieves each array element and adds the element to sum. Here the variable i is used both as the counter in the for loop and as a subscript. As i increases by 1 each time through the loop, the next element in the array is referenced. This procedure for adding the array elements within the for loop is similar to the accumulation procedure we have used many times before.

---

[2] Note: Some compilers permit floating-point variables as subscripts; in these cases, the floating-point value is truncated to an integer value.

The advantage of using a `for` loop to sequence through an array becomes apparent when we are working with larger arrays. For example, if the `grade` array contains 100 values rather than just 5, simply setting the constant NUMELS to 100 is sufficient both to create the larger array and to have the `for` statement sequence through the 100 elements and add each grade to the sum.

As another example of using a `for` loop to sequence through an array, assume that we want to locate the maximum value in an array of 1000 elements named `prices`. The procedure we will use to locate the maximum value is to assume initially that the first element in the array is the largest number. Then, as we sequence through the array, the maximum is compared to each element. When an element with a higher value is located, that element becomes the new maximum. The following code does the job:

```
const int NUMELS = 1000;

maximum = prices[0];               // set the maximum to element zero
for (int i = 1; i < NUMELS; i++)   // cycle through the rest of the array
   if (prices[i] > maximum)        // compare each element to the maximum
         maximum = prices[i];      // capture the new high value
```

In this code the `for` statement consists of one `if` statement. The search for a new maximum value starts with the element 1 of the array and continues through the last element. In a 1000-element array, the last element is 999. Each element is compared to the current maximum, and when a higher value is encountered, it becomes the new maximum.

Input and Output of Array Values

Individual array elements can be assigned values interactively by using a `cin` stream object. Examples of individual data entry statements are

```
cin >> grade[0];
cin >> grade[1] >> grade[2] >> grade[3];
cin >> grade[4] >> prices[6];
```

In the first statement, a single value will be read and stored in the variable named `grade[0]`. The second statement causes three values to be read and stored in the variables `grade[1]`, `grade[2]`, and `grade[3]`, respectively. The last `cin` statement can be used to read values into the variables `grade[4]` and `prices[6]`.

Alternatively, a `for` loop can be used to cycle through the array for interactive data input. For example, the code

```
const int NUMELS = 5;

for (int i = 0; i < NUMELS; i++)
{
   cout  << "Enter a grade: ";
   cin   >> grade[i];
}
```

prompts the user for five grades. The first grade entered is stored in `grade[0]`, the second in `grade[1]`, and so on until five grades have been input.

One caution should be mentioned about storing data or accessing in an array. Most implementations of C++ do not check the value of the index being used (called a **bounds check**). If an array has been declared as consisting of ten elements, for example, and you use an index of 12, which is outside the bounds of the array, C++ will not notify you of the error when the program is compiled. The program will attempt to access element 12 by skipping over the appropriate number of bytes from the start of the array. This usually results in a program crash—but not always. If the referenced location itself contains a data value, the program will simply access the value in the referenced memory locations. This leads to more errors, which are particularly troublesome to locate when the value legitimately assigned to the storage location is retrieved and processed. Using symbolic constants as we have done helps to eliminate this problem.

During output, individual array elements can be displayed by using the `cout` object, or complete sections of the array can be displayed by including a `cout` statement within a `for` loop. Here are some examples where `cout` is used to display subscripted variables:

```
cout << prices[5];
```

and

```
cout << "The value of element " << i << " is " << grade[i];
```

and

```
const int NUMELS = 20;

for (int k = 5; k < NUMELS; k++)
   cout << k << " " << amount[k];
```

The first `cout` statement displays the value of the subscripted variable `prices[5]`. The second `cout` statement displays the value of the subscript `i` and the value of `grade[i]`. Before this statement can be executed, `i` would have to have

PROGRAMMING NOTE

Structured Data Types

In contrast to atomic date types, such as integers and floating-point built-in types that cannot be decomposed into simpler types, structured types can be decomposed into simpler types that are related within a defined structure. Another term used for a structured type is a data structure. Because a structured type consists of one or more simpler types, operations must be available for retrieving and updating the individual types that make up a data structure.

Single-dimensional arrays are examples of a structured types. In a single-dimensional array, such as an array of integers, the array is composed of individual integer values. In an array, the values are related by their position in the array. For arrays, index numbers provide the means of accessing and modifying individual elements.

an assigned value. The last example includes a cout statement within a for loop. Both the value of the index and the value of the elements from 5 to 19 are displayed.

Program 8.1 illustrates these input and output techniques using an array named grade that is defined to store five integer numbers. Included in the program are

Program 8.1

```cpp
#include <iostream>
using namespace std;

int main()
{
  const int NUMELS = 5;

  int i, grade[NUMELS];

  for (i = 0; i < NUMELS; i++)      // Enter the grades
  {
    cout << "Enter a grade: ";
    cin  >> grade[i];
  }

  cout << endl;

  for (i = 0; i < NUMELS; i++)     // Print the grades
    cout << "grade [" << i << "] is " << grade[i] << endl;

  return 0;

}
```

two `for` loops. The first `for` loop is used to cycle through each array element and allows the user to input individual array values. After five values have been entered, the second `for` loop is used to display the stored values.

Following is a sample run using Program 8.1:

```
Enter a grade: 85
Enter a grade: 90
Enter a grade: 78
Enter a grade: 75
Enter a grade: 92

grade[0] is 85
grade[1] is 90
grade[2] is 78
grade[3] is 75
grade[4] is 92
```

In reviewing the output produced by Program 8.1, pay particular attention to the difference between the subscript value displayed and the numerical value stored in the corresponding array element. The subscript value refers to the *location* of the element in the array, whereas the subscripted variable refers to the *value* stored in the designated location.

In addition to simply displaying the values stored in each array element, the elements can also be processed by appropriately referencing the desired element. In Program 8.2, for example, the value of each element is accumulated in a total, which is displayed upon completion of the individual display of each array element.

Following is a sample run using Program 8.2:

```
Enter a grade: 85
Enter a grade: 90
Enter a grade: 78
Enter a grade: 75
Enter a grade: 92

The total of the grades  85  90  78  75  92  is 420
```

Note that in Program 8.2, unlike Program 8.1, only the values stored in each array element are displayed. Although the second `for` loop was used to accumulate the total of each element, the accumulation could also have been accomplished in the first loop by placing the statement `total = total + grade[i];` after the cin statement used to enter a value. Also note that the cout statement used to display the total is made outside the second for loop, so that the total is displayed only once, after all values have been added to the total. If this cout statement were placed inside the for loop, five totals would be displayed, with only the last displayed total containing the sum of all of the array values.

Program 8.2

```
#include <iostream>
using namespace std;

int main()
{
  const int NUMELS = 5;

  int i, grade[NUMELS], total = 0;

  for (i = 0; i < NUMELS; i++)    // Enter the grades
  {
    cout << "Enter a grade: ";
    cin  >> grade[i];
  }

  cout << "\nThe total of the grades";

  for (i = 0; i < NUMELS; i++) // Display and total the grades
  {
    cout << " " << grade[i];
    total = total + grade[i];
  }

  cout << " is " << total << endl;

  return 0;
}
```

■ EXERCISES 8.1

1. Write array declarations for the following:
  a. A list of 100 integer grades
  b. A list of 50 double-precision temperatures
  c. A list of 30 characters, each representing a code
  d. A list of 100 integer years
  e. A list of 32 double-precision velocities
  f. A list of 1000 double-precision distances
  g. A list of 6 integer code numbers

2. Write appropriate notation for the first, third, and seventh elements of the following arrays.
  a. `int grades[20]`
  b. `double prices[10]`
  c. `double amps[16]`
  d. `int dist[15]`
  e. `double velocity[25]`
  f. `double time[100]`

3. a. Using the `cin` object, write individual statements that can be used to enter values into the first, third, and seventh elements of each of the arrays declared in Exercises 2a through 2f.
  b. Write a `for` loop that can be used to enter values for the complete array declared in Exercises 2a–2f.

4. a. Write individual statements that can be used to display the values from the first, third, and seventh elements of each of the arrays declared in Exercises 2a through 2f.
  b. Write a `for` loop that can be used to display values for the complete array declared in Exercises 2a–2f.

5. List the elements that will be displayed by the following sections of code.
  a. `for (m = 1; m <= 5; m++)`
       `cout << a[m] << " ";`
  b. `for (k = 1; k <= 5; k = k + 2)`
       `cout << a[k] << " ";`
  c. `for (j = 3; j <= 10; j++)`
       `cout << b[j] << " ";`
  d. `for (k = 3; k <= 12; k = k + 3)`
       `cout << b[k] << " ";`
  e. `for (i = 2; i < 11; i = i + 2)`
       `cout << c[i] << " ";`

6. a. Write a program to input the following values into an array named `prices`: 10.95, 16.32, 12.15, 8.22, 15.98, 26.22, 13.54, 6.45, 17.59. After the data have been entered, have your program display the values.

b. Repeat Exercise 6a, but after the data have been entered, have your program display them in the following form:

```
10.95    16.32    12.15
 8.22    15.98    26.22
13.54     6.45    17.59
```

7. Write a C++ program to input eight integer numbers into an array named `grade`. As each number is input, add the numbers into a total. After all numbers are input, display the numbers and their average.

8. *a.* Write a C++ program to input ten integer numbers into an array named `fmax` and determine the maximum value entered. Your program should contain only one loop, and the maximum should be determined as array element values are being input. (*Hint:* Set the maximum equal to the first array element, which should be input before the loop used to input the remaining array values.)

   b. Repeat Exercise 8a, keeping track of both the maximum element in the array and the index number for the maximum. After displaying the numbers, display these two messages:

```
The maximum value is: _____
This is element number _____ in the list of numbers
```

   Have your program display the correct values in place of the underlines in the messages.

   c. Repeat Exercise 8b, but have your program locate the minimum value of the data entered.

9. *a.* Write a C++ program to input the following integer numbers into an array named `grades`: 89, 95, 72, 83, 99, 54, 86, 75, 92, 73, 79, 75, 82, 73. As each number is input, add the numbers to a total. After all numbers are input and the total is obtained, calculate the average of the numbers and use the average to determine the deviation of each value from the average. Store each deviation in an array named `deviation`. Each deviation is obtained as the element value less the average of all the data. Have your program display each deviation alongside its corresponding element from the `grades` array.

   b. Calculate the variance of the data used in Exercise 9a. The variance is obtained by squaring each individual deviation and dividing the sum of the squared deviations by the number of deviations.

10. Write a C++ program that specifies three one-dimensional arrays named `price`, `amount`, and `total`. Each array should be capable of holding ten elements. Using a `for` loop, input values for the `price` and `amount` arrays. The entries in the `total` array should be the product of the corresponding values in the `price` and `amount` arrays (thus, `total[i]` = `price[i]` * `amount[i]`). After all the data have been entered, display the following output:

```
total    price    amount
-----    -----    ------
```

Under each column heading, display the appropriate value.

11. *a.* Write a program that inputs ten double-precision numbers into an array named raw. After ten user-input numbers are entered into the array, your program should cycle through raw ten times. During each pass through the array, your program should select the lowest value in raw and place the selected value in the next available slot in an array named sorted. Thus, when your program is complete, the sorted array should contain the numbers in raw in sorted order from lowest to highest. (*Hint:* Be sure to reset the lowest value selected during each pass to a very high number so that it is not selected again. You will need a second for loop within the first for loop to locate the minimum value for each pass.)

b. The method used in Exercise 11a to sort the values in the array is very inefficient. Can you determine why? What might be a better method of sorting the numbers in an array?

8.2 Array Initialization

Array elements can be initialized within their declaration statements in the same manner as scalar variables, except that the initializing elements must be included in braces. Examples of such initializations are

```
int grade[5] = {98, 87, 92, 79, 85};
char code[6] = {'s', 'a', 'm', 'p', 'l', 'e'};
double width[7] = {10.96, 6.43, 2.58, 0.86, 5.89, 7.56, 8.22};
```

Initializers are applied in the order in which they are written, with the first value used to initialize element 0, the second value used to initialize element 1, and so on, until all values have been used. Thus, in the declaration

```
const NUMELS = 5;
int grade[NUMELS] = {98, 87, 92, 79, 85};
```

grade[0] is initialized to 98, grade[1] is initialized to 87, grade[2] is initialized to 92, grade[3] is initialized to 79, and grade[4] is initialized to 85.

Because white space is ignored in C++, initializations may be continued across multiple lines. For example, the declaration for gallons[] in the set of declarations

```
const int NUMGALS = 20;
int gallons[NUMGALS] = {19, 16, 14, 19, 20, 18, // initializing values
                        12, 10, 22, 15, 18, 17, // may extend across
                        16, 14, 23, 19, 15, 18, // multiple lines
                            21, 5};
```

uses four lines to initialize all of the array elements.

If the number of initializers is less than the declared number of elements listed in square brackets, the initializers are applied starting with array element zero. Thus, in the declarations

```
const int ARRAYSIZE = 7;
double length[ARRAYSIZE] = {7.8, 6.4, 4.9, 11.2};
```

only `length[0]`, `length[1]`, `length[2]`, and `length[3]` are initialized with the listed values. The other array elements are initialized to zero.

Unfortunately, there is no method of either indicating repetition of an initialization value or initializing later array elements without first specifying values for earlier elements.

A unique feature of initializers is that the size of an array may be omitted when initializing values are included in the declaration statement. For example, the declaration

```
int gallons[] = {16, 12, 10, 14, 11};
```

reserves enough storage room for five elements. Similarly, the following declarations are equivalent:

```
const int NUMCODES = 6;
char code[6] = {'s', 'a', 'm', 'p', 'l', 'e'};
```

and

```
char code[] = {'s', 'a', 'm', 'p', 'l', 'e'};
```

Both declarations set aside six character locations for an array named `code`. An interesting and useful simplification can also be used when initializing character arrays. For example, the declaration

```
char code[] = "sample";    // no braces or commas
```

uses the string `"sample"` to initialize the `code` array. Recall that a string is any sequence of characters enclosed in double quotes. This last declaration creates an array named `code` having seven elements and fills the array with the seven characters illustrated in Figure 8.6. The first six characters, as expected, are the letters s, a, m, p, l, and e. The last character, which is the escape sequence \0, is called the **Null character.** The `Null` character is automatically appended to all strings that are used to initialize an array of characters. This character has an internal storage code that is numerically equal to zero (the storage code for the zero character has a numerical

FIGURE 8.6   *A String Is Terminated with a Special Symbol*

code[0]	code[1]	code[2]	code[3]	code[4]	code[5]	code[6]
s	a	m	p	l	e	\0

value of decimal 48, so the two cannot be confused by the computer) and is used as a marker, or sentinel, to mark the end of a string. As we shall see in Chapter 10, this marker is invaluable when we are manipulating strings of characters.

Once values have been assigned to array elements, either through initialization within the declaration statement or by using interactive input, the array elements can be processed as described in the previous section. For example, Program 8.3 illustrates element initialization within the declaration of the array and then uses a for loop to locate the maximum value stored in the array.

Program 8.3

```cpp
#include <iostream>
using namespace std;

int main()
{
  const int MAXELS = 5;

  int i, max, nums[MAXELS] = {2, 18, 1, 27, 16};

  max = nums[0];

  for (i = 1; i < MAXELS; i++)
    if (max < nums[i])
      max = nums[i];

  cout << "The maximum value is " << max << endl;

  return 0;
}
```

The output produced by Program 8.3 is

```
The maximum value is 27
```

■ **EXERCISES 8.2**

1. Write array declarations, including initializers, for the following:
   a. A list of ten integer grades: 89, 75, 82, 93, 78, 95, 81, 88, 77, 82
   b. A list of five double-precision amounts: 10.62, 13.98, 18.45, 12.68, 14.76
   c. A list of 100 double-precision interest rates; the first six rates are 6.29, 6.95, 7.25, 7.35, 7.40, 7.42
   d. A list of 64 double-precision temperatures; the first ten temperatures are 78.2, 69.6, 68.5, 83.9, 55.4, 67.0, 49.8, 58.3, 62.5, 71.6
   e. A list of 15 character codes; the first seven codes are f, j, m, q, t, w, z

2. Write an array declaration statement that stores the following values in an array named prices: 16.24, 18.98, 23.75, 16.29, 19.54, 14.22, 11.13, 15.39. Include these statements in a program that displays the values in the array.

3. Write a program that uses an array declaration statement to initialize the following numbers in an array named slopes: 17.24, 25.63, 5.94, 33.92, 3.71, 32.84, 35.93, 18.24, 6.92. Your program should locate and display both the maximum and the minimum values in the array.

4. Write a program that stores the following numbers in an array named prices: 9.92, 6.32, 12.63, 5.95, 10.29. Your program should also create two arrays named units and amounts, each capable of storing five double-precision numbers. Using a for loop and a cin object, have your program accept five user-input numbers into the units array when the program is run. Your program should store the product of the corresponding values in the prices and units arrays in the amounts array (for example, amounts[1] = prices[1] * units[1]) and should display the following output (fill in the table appropriately).

```
    Price      Units     Amount
    -----      -----     ------

     9.92        .          .
     6.32        .          .
    12.63        .          .
     5.95        .          .
    10.29        .          .

                          ------

    Total:                   .
```

5. The string of characters "Good Morning" is to be stored in a character array named goodstr1. Write the declaration for this array in three different ways.

6. a. Write declaration statements to store the string of characters "Input the Following Data" in a character array named message1, the string "------------" in the array named message2, the string "Enter the Date:" in the array named message3, and the string "Enter the Account Number:" in the array named message4.
   b. Include the array declarations written in Exercise 6a in a program that uses the cout object to display the messages. For example, the statement cout << message1; causes

the string stored in the message1 array to be displayed. Your program will require four such statements to display the four individual messages. Using the cout object to display a string requires that the end-of-string marker \0 be present in the character array used to store the string.

7. *a.* Write a declaration to store the string "This is a test" into an array named strtest. Include the declaration in a program to display the message using the following loop:

```
for (int i = 0; i < NUMDISPLAY; i++)
    cout << strtest[i];
```

where NUMDISPLAY is a symbolic constant for the number 15.

b. Modify the for statement in Exercise 7a to display only the array characters t, e, s, and t.

c. Include the array declaration written in Exercise 7a in a program that uses the cout object to display characters in the array. For example, the statement cout << strtest; will cause the string stored in the strtest array to be displayed. Using this statement requires that the last character in the array be the end-of-string marker \0.

d. Repeat Exercise 7a using a while loop. (*Hint:* Stop the loop when the \0 escape sequence is detected. The expression while (strtest[i] != '\0') can be used.)

8.3   Arrays as Arguments

Individual array elements are passed to a called function in the same manner as individual scalar variables; they are simply included as subscripted variables when the function call is made. For example, the function call findMax(grades[2], grades[6]); passes the values of the elements grades[2] and grades[6] to the function findMax().

Passing a complete array of values to a function is in many respects an easier operation than passing individual elements. The called function receives access to the actual array, rather than a copy of the values in the array. For example, if grades is an array, the function call findmax(grades); makes the complete grades array available to the findMax() function. This is different from passing a single variable to a function.

You will recall that when a single scalar argument is passed to a function, the called function receives only a *copy* of the passed value, which is stored in one of the function's parameters. If arrays were passed in this manner, a copy of the complete array would have to be created. For large arrays, making duplicate copies of the array for each function call would be wasteful of computer storage and would frustrate the effort to return multiple element changes made by the called program (remember that a function directly returns at most one value). To avoid these problems, the called function is given direct access to the original array. Thus any changes made by the called function are made directly to the array itself. For the following specific examples of function calls, assume that the arrays nums, keys, units, and grades are declared as

```
int nums[5];                      // an array of five integers
char keys[256];                   // an array of 256 characters
double units[500], grades[500];   // two arrays of 500 doubles
```

For these arrays, the following function calls can be made:

```
findMax(nums);
findCharacter(keys);
calcTotal(nums, units, grades);
```

In each case, the called function receives direct access to the named array.

On the receiving side, the called function must be alerted that an array is being made available. For example, suitable function header lines for the previous functions are

```
int findMax(int vals[5])
char findCharacter(char inKeys[256])
void calcTotal(int arr1[5], double arr2[500], double arr3[500])
```

In each of these function header lines, the names in the parameter list are chosen by the programmer. However, the parameter names used by the functions still refer to the original array created outside the function. This is made clear in Program 8.4.

Program 8.4

```
#include <iostream>
using namespace std;

const int MAXELS = 5;
int findMax(int [MAXELS]);   // function prototype

int main()
{
  int nums[MAXELS] = {2, 18, 1, 27, 16};

  cout << "The maximum value is " << findMax(nums) << endl;

  return 0;
}

// find the maximum value
int findMax(int vals[MAXELS])
```

(continued on next page)

(continued from previous page)

```
   {
     int i, max = vals[0];

     for (i = 1; i < MAXELS; i++)
       if (max < vals[i])
         max = vals[i];

     return max;
   }
```

First, note that the named constant MAXELS has been declared globally, not within the main() function. This placement of the declaration means that this constant can be used in any subsequent declaration or within any subsequent function. Next, observe that the prototype for findMax() uses this named constant and declares that the function will return an integer and expects an array of five integers as an argument. It is also important to know that only one array is created in Program 8.4. In main() this array is known as nums, and in findMax() it is known as vals. As illustrated in Figure 8.7, both names refer to the same array. Thus in Figure 8.7, vals[3] is the same element as nums[3].

FIGURE 8.7 *Only One Array Is Created*

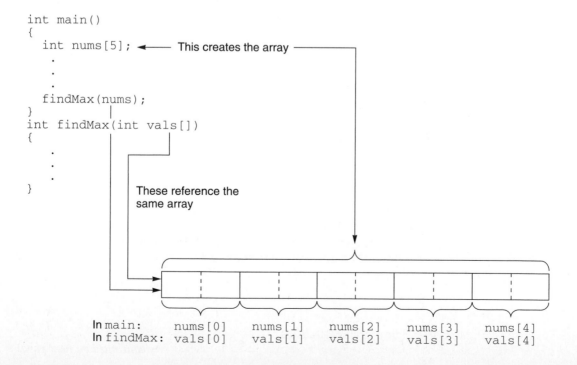

FIGURE 8.8   *The Starting Address of the Array Is Passed*

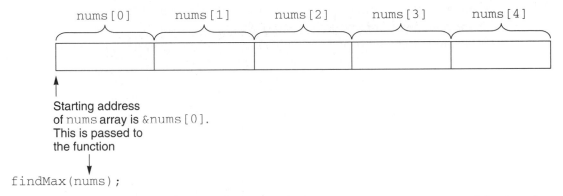

```
findMax(nums);
```

The parameter declaration in both the `findMax()` prototype and the function header line in Program 8.4 actually contains extra information that is not required by the function. All that `findMax()` must know is that the parameter `vals` references an array of integers. Because the array has been created in `main()` and no additional storage space is needed in `findMax()`, the declaration for `vals` can omit the size of the array. Thus an alternative function header line is

`int findMax(int vals[])`

This form of the function header makes more sense when you realize that only one item is actually passed to `findMax()` when the function is called, which is the starting address of the num array. This is illustrated in Figure 8.8.

Because only the starting address of `vals` is passed to `findMax()`, the number of elements in the array need not be included in the declaration for `vals`.[3] In fact, it is generally advisable to omit the size of the array in the function header line. For example, consider the more general form of `findMax()`, which can be used to find the maximum value of an integer array of arbitrary size:

```
int findMax(int vals[], int NUMELS)     // find the maximum value
{
  int i, max = vals[0];

  for (i = 1; i < NUMELS; i++)
    if (max < vals[i])
      max = vals[i];

  return max;
}
```

---

[3] An important consequence of this is that `findMax()` has direct access to the passed array. This means that any change to an element of the `vals` array actually is a change to the `nums` array. This is significantly different from the situation with scalar variables, where the called function does not receive direct access to the passed variable.

The more general form of findMax() declares that the function returns an integer value. The function expects the starting address of an integer array and the number of elements in the array as arguments. Then, using the number of elements as the boundary for its search, the function's for loop causes each array element to be examined in sequential order to locate the maximum value. Program 8.5 illustrates the use of findMax() in a complete program.

 Program 8.5

```cpp
#include <iostream>
using namespace std;

int findMax(int [], int);        // function prototype

int main()
{
  const int MAXELS = 5;
  int nums[MAXELS] = {2, 18, 1, 27, 16};

  cout << "The maximum value is " << findMax(nums, MAXELS) << endl;

  return 0;
}

// find the maximum value
int findMax(int vals[], int numels)
{
  int i, max = vals[0];

  for (i = 1; i < numels; i++)
    if (max < vals[i]) max = vals[i];

  return max;
}
```

The output displayed by both Program 8.4 and Program 8.5 is

```
The maximum value is 27
```

▓ EXERCISES 8.3

1. The following declarations were used to create the grades array:

```
const int NUMGRADES = 500;
double grades[NUMGRADES];
```

Write two different function header lines for a function named sortArray() that accepts the grades array as a parameter named inArray and returns no value.

2. The following declarations were used to create the keys array:

```
const int NUMKEYS = 256;
char keys[NUMKEYS];
```

Write two different function header lines for a function named findKey() that accepts the keys array as a parameter named select and returns a character.

3. The following declarations were used to create the rates array:

```
const int NUMRATES = 256;
double rates[NUMRATES];
```

Write two different function header lines for a function named prime() that accepts the rates array as a parameter named rates and returns a double-precision number.

4. *a.* Modify the findMax() function in Program 8.4 to locate the minimum value of the passed array.
   b. Include the function written in Exercise 4a in a complete program and run the program on a computer.

5. Write a program that has a declaration in main() to store the following numbers into an array named rates: 6.5, 7.2, 7.5, 8.3, 8.6, 9.4, 9.6, 9.8, 10.0. There should be a function call to show() that accepts the rates array as a parameter named rates and then displays the numbers in the array.

6. *a.* Write a program that has a declaration in main() to store the string "Vacation is near" into an array named message. There should be a function call to display() that accepts message in a parameter named strng and then displays the message.
   b. Modify the display() function written in Exercise 6a to display the first eight elements of the message array.

7. Write a program that declares three single-dimensional arrays named price, quantity, and amount. Each array should be declared in main() and should be capable of holding ten double-precision numbers. The numbers that should be stored in price are 10.62, 14.89, 13.21, 16.55, 18.62, 9.47, 6.58, 18.32, 12.15, 3.98. The numbers that should be stored in quantity are 4, 8.5, 6, 7.35, 9, 15.3, 3, 5.4, 2.9, 4.8. Your program should pass these three arrays to a function named extend(), which should calculate the elements in the amount array as the product of the corresponding elements in the price and quantity arrays (for example, amount[1] = price[1] * quantity[1]). After extend() has put values into the amount array, the values in the array should be displayed from within main().

8. Write a program that includes two functions named `calcAverage()` and `variance()`. The `calcAverage()` function should calculate and return the average of the values stored in an array named `testvals`. The array should be declared in `main()` and should include the values 89, 95, 72, 83, 99, 54, 86, 75, 92, 73, 79, 75, 82, 73. The `variance()` function should calculate and return the variance of the data. The variance is obtained by subtracting the average from each value in `testvals`, squaring the values obtained, adding them, and dividing by the number of elements in `testvals`. The values returned from `calcAverage()` and `variance()` should be displayed using `cout` statements activated from within `main()`.

8.4   Two-Dimensional Arrays

A **two-dimensional array,** which is also referred to as a table, consists of both rows and columns of elements. For example, the array of numbers

8	16	9	52
3	15	27	6
14	25	2	10

is called a two-dimensional array of integers. This array consists of three rows and four columns and thus is called a 3-by-4 array. To reserve storage for this array, both the number of rows and the number of columns must be included in the array's declaration. If we call the array `val`, the correct specification for this two-dimensional array is

```
int val[3][4];
```

Similarly, the declarations

```
double prices[10][5];
char code[6][26];
```

declare that the array `prices` consists of 10 rows and 5 columns of double-precision numbers and that the array `code` consists of 6 rows and 26 columns, with each element capable of holding one character.

In order to locate each element in a two-dimensional array, we identify an element by its position in the array. As illustrated in Figure 8.9, the term val[1][3] uniquely identifies the element in row 1, column 3. As with single-dimensional array variables, double-dimensional array variables can be used anywhere scalar variables are valid. Examples using elements of the val array are

```
price = val[2][3];
val[0][0] = 62;
newnum = 4 * (val[1][0] - 5);
sumRow = val[0][0] + val[0][1] + val[0][2] + val[0][3];
```

The last statement causes the values of the four elements in row 0 to be added and the sum to be stored in the scalar variable sumRow.

As with single-dimensional arrays, two-dimensional arrays can be initialized from within their declaration statements. This is done by listing the initial values within braces and separating them by commas. Additionally, braces can be used to separate individual rows. For example, the declaration

```
int val[3][4] = { {8,16,9,52},
                  {3,15,27,6},
                  {14,25,2,10} };
```

declares val to be an array of integers with three rows and four columns, with the initial values given in the declaration. The first set of internal braces contains the values for row 0 of the array, the second set of braces the values for row 1, and the third set of braces the values for row 2.

Although the commas in the initialization braces are always required, the inner braces can be omitted. Thus the initialization for val may be written as

```
int val[3][4] = {8,16,9,52,
                 3,15,27,6,
                 14,25,2,10};
```

FIGURE 8.9 *Each Array Element Is Identified by Its Row and Column Position*

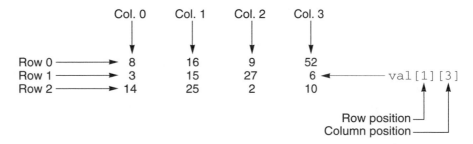

The separation of initial values into rows in the declaration statement is not necessary because the compiler assigns values beginning with the [0][0] element and proceeds row by row to fill in the remaining values. Thus the initialization

```
int val[3][4] = {8,16,9,52,3,15,27,6,14,25,2,10};
```

is equally valid but does not clearly tell another programmer where one row ends and another begins.

As illustrated in Figure 8.10, the initialization of a two-dimensional array is done in row order. First, the elements of the first row are initialized, then the elements of the second row are initialized, and so on, until the initializations are completed. This row ordering is also the same ordering used to store two-dimensional arrays. That is, array element [0][0] is stored first, followed by element [0][1], followed by element [0][2], and so on. Following the first row's elements are the second row's elements, and so on for all the rows in the array.

FIGURE 8.10   *Storage and Initialization of the* val[] *Array*

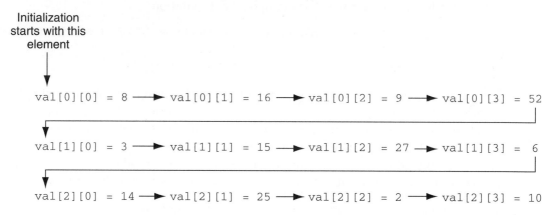

Like single-dimensional arrays, two-dimensional arrays may be displayed by individual element notation or by using loops (either while or for). This is illustrated by Program 8.6, which displays all the elements of a 3-by-4 two-dimensional array using two different techniques. Note in Program 8.6 that we have used symbolic constants to define the array's rows and columns.

Program 8.6

```cpp
#include <iostream>
#include <iomanip>
using namespace std;

int main()
{
  const int NUMROWS = 3;
  const int NUMCOLS = 4;

  int i, j
  int val[NUMROWS][NUMCOLS] = {8,16,9,52,3,15,27,6,14,25,2,10};

  cout << "\nDisplay of val array by explicit element"
       << endl << setw(4) << val[0][0] << setw(4) << val[0][1]
       << setw(4) << val[0][2] << setw(4) << val[0][3]
       << endl << setw(4) << val[1][0] << setw(4) << val[1][1]
       << setw(4) << val[1][2] << setw(4) << val[1][3]
       << endl << setw(4) << val[2][0] << setw(4) << val[2][1]
       << setw(4) << val[2][2] << setw(4) << val[2][3];

  cout << "\n\nDisplay of val array using a nested for loop";

  for (i = 0; i < NUMROWS; i++)
  {
    cout << endl;    // print a new line for each row
    for (j = 0; j < NUMCOLS; j++)
      cout << setw(4) << val[i][j];
  }

  cout << endl;

  return 0;
}
```

The display produced by Program 8.6 is

```
Display of val array by explicit element
    8    16     9    52
    3    15    27     6
   14    25     2    10

Display of val array using a nested for loop
    8    16     9    52
    3    15    27     6
   14    25     2    10
```

The first display of the val array produced by Program 8.6 is constructed by explicitly designating each array element. The second display of array element values, which is identical to the first, is produced by using a nested for loop. Nested loops are especially useful with two-dimensional arrays because they allow the programmer to designate and cycle through each element easily. In Program 8.6, the variable i controls the outer loop and the variable j controls the inner loop. Each pass through the outer loop corresponds to a single row, with the inner loop supplying the appropriate column elements. After a complete row is printed, a new line is started for the next row. The effect is a display of the array in a row-by-row fashion.

Once two-dimensional array elements have been assigned values, array processing can begin. Typically, for loops are used to process two-dimensional arrays because, as we have noted, they make it easy to designate and cycle through each array element. For example, the nested for loop illustrated in Program 8.7 is used to multiply each element in the val array by the scalar number 10 and display the resulting value.

Following is the output produced by Program 8.7:

```
Display of multiplied elements
    80   160    90   520
    30   150   270    60
   140   250    20   100
```

Passing two-dimensional arrays into functions is identical to passing single-dimensional arrays. The called function receives access to the entire array. For example, assuming that val is a two-dimensional array, the function call display(val); makes the complete val array available to the function named display(). Thus any changes made by display() will be made directly to the val array. As further examples, assume that the following two-dimensional arrays named test, code, and stocks are declared as

```
int test[7][9];
char code[26][10];
double stocks[256][52];
```

Program 8.7

```cpp
#include <iostream>
#include <iomanip>
using namespace std;

int main()
{
  const int NUMROWS = 3;
  const int NUMCOLS = 4;

  int i, j;
  int val[NUMROWS][NUMCOLS] = {8,16,9,52,
                               3,15,27,6,
                               14,25,2,10};

  // multiply each element by 10 and display it
  cout << "\nDisplay of multiplied elements";
  for (i = 0; i < NUMROWS; i++)
  {
    cout << endl;      // start each row on a new line
    for (j = 0; j < NUMCOLS; j++)
    {
      val[i][j] = val[i][j] * 10;
      cout << setw(5) << val[i][j];
    } // end of inner loop
  }   // end of outer loop
  cout << endl;

  return 0;
}
```

Then the following function calls are valid:

```cpp
findMax(test);
obtain(code);
price(stocks);
```

On the receiving side, the called function must be alerted that a two-dimensional array is being made available. For example, assuming that each of the previous functions returns an integer, suitable function header lines for these functions are

```
int findMax(int nums[7][9])
int obtain(char key[26][10])
int price(double names[256][52])
```

In each of these function header lines, the parameter names chosen are local to the function. However, the internal local names used by the function still refer to the original array created outside the function. Program 8.8 illustrates passing a two-dimensional array into a function that displays the array's values.

 Program 8.8

```
#include <iostream>
#include <iomanip>
using namespace std;

const int ROWS = 3;
const int COLS = 4;

void display(int [ROWS][COLS]);    // function prototype

int main()
{
  int val[ROWS][COLS] = {8,16,9,52,
                         3,15,27,6,
                         14,25,2,10};

  display(val);

  return 0;
}

void display(int nums[ROWS][COLS])
{
  int rowNum, colNum;
  for (rowNum = 0; rowNum < ROWS; rowNum++)
  {
    for(colNum = 0; colNum < COLS; colNum++)
      cout << setw(4) << nums[rowNum][colNum];
    cout << endl;
  }

  return;
}
```

Only one array is created in Program 8.8. This array is known as val in main() and as nums in display(). Thus val[0][2] refers to the same element as nums[0][2].

Note the use of the nested for loop in Program 8.8 for cycling through each array element. In Program 8.8, the variable rowNum controls the outer loop, and the variable colNum controls the inner loop. For each pass through the outer loop, which corresponds to a single row, the inner loop makes one pass through the column elements. After a complete row is printed, a new line is started for the next row. The effect is a display of the array in a row-by-row fashion:

```
 8   16    9   52
 3   15   27    6
14   25    2   10
```

The parameter declaration for nums in display() contains extra information that is not required by the function. The declaration for nums can omit the row size of the array. Thus an alternative function declaration is

```
display(int nums[][4]);
```

The reason the column size must be included, whereas the row size is optional, becomes obvious when you consider how the array elements are stored in memory. Starting with the element val[0][0], the succeeding elements are stored consecutively, row by row, as val[0][0], val[0][1], val[0][2], val[0][3], val[1][0], val[1][1], and so on, as illustrated in Figure 8.11.

FIGURE 8.11   *Storage of the* val[] *Array*

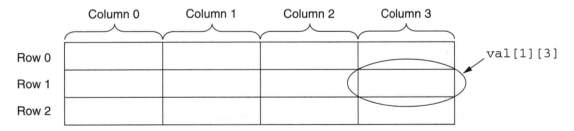

As with all array accesses, an individual element of the val array is obtained by adding an offset to the starting location of the array. For example, the element val[1][3] is located at an offset of 28 bytes from the start of the array (assuming four bytes for an int). Internally, the computer employs the row index, column index, and column size to determine this offset using the following calculation.

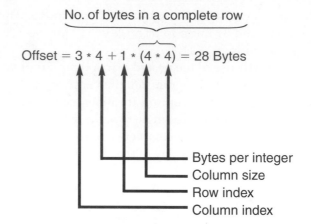

The number of columns is necessary in the offset calculation so that the computer can determine how many positions to skip over to get to the desired row.

Larger-Dimensional Arrays

Although arrays with more than two dimensions are not commonly used, C++ does allow any number of dimensions to be declared. This is done by listing the maximum size of all dimensions for the array. For example, the declaration `int response [4][10][6];` declares a three-dimensional array. The first element in the array is designated as `response [0][0][0]` and the last element as `response [3][9][5]`.

Conceptually, as illustrated in Figure 8.12, a three-dimensional array can be viewed as a book of data tables. Using this visualization, the first subscript, which is often called the "rank," can be thought of as the page number of the selected table, the second subscript value as the desired row in the table, and the third subscript value as the desired column.

Similarly, arrays of any dimension can be declared. Conceptually, a four-dimensional array can be represented as a shelf of books, where the first dimension is used to declare a desired book on the shelf, and a five-dimensional array can be viewed as a bookcase filled with books, where the first dimension refers to a selected shelf in the bookcase. Using the same analogy, a six-dimensional array can be considered as a single row of bookcases, where the first dimension references the desired bookcase in the row; a seven-dimensional array can be considered as multiple rows of bookcases, where the first dimension references the desired row, and so on. Alternatively, arrays of three-, four-, five-, and six-dimensional arrays can be viewed as mathematical n-tuples of order 3, 4, 5, and 6, respectively, and so on.

FIGURE 8.12   *Representation of a Three-Dimensional Array*

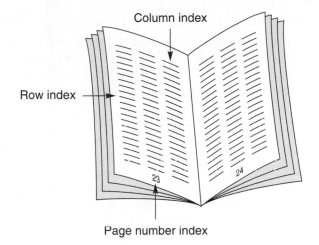

■ EXERCISES 8.4

1. Write appropriate specification statements for each of the following:
   a. An array of integers with 6 rows and 10 columns
   b. An array of integers with 2 rows and 5 columns
   c. An array of characters with 7 rows and 12 columns
   d. An array of characters with 15 rows and 7 columns
   e. An array of double-precision numbers with 10 rows and 25 columns
   f. An array of double-precision numbers with 16 rows and 8 columns

2. Determine the output produced by the following program:

```cpp
#include <iostream>
using namespace std;
int main()
{
  int i, j, val[3][4] = {8,16,9,52,3,15,27,6,14,25,2,10};

  for (i = 0; i < 3; i++)
    for (j = 0; j < 4; j++)
      cout << val[i][j] << " ";

  return 0;
}
```

3. a. Write a C++ program that adds the values of all elements in the `val` array used in Exercise 2 and displays the total.

b. Modify the program written for Exercise 3a to display the total of each row separately.

4. Write a C++ program that adds equivalent elements of the two-dimensional arrays named `first` and `second`. Both arrays should have two rows and three columns. For example, element `[1][2]` of the resulting array should be the sum of `first[1][2]` and `second[1][2]`. The `first` and `second` arrays should be initialized as follows:

First				Second		
16	18	23		24	52	77
54	91	11		16	19	59

5. a. Write a C++ program that finds and displays the maximum value in a two-dimensional array of integers. The array should be declared as a 4-by-5 array of integers and initialized with these data: 16, 22, 99, 4, 18, –258, 4, 101, 5, 98, 105, 6, 15, 2, 45, 33, 88, 72, 16, 3.

b. Modify the program written in Exercise 5a so that it also displays the maximum value's row and column subscript values.

6. Write a C++ program to select the values in a 4-by-5 array of integers in increasing order, and store the selected values in the single-dimensional array named `sort`. Use the data given in Exercise 5a to initialize the two-dimensional array.

7. a. A professor has constructed a 3-by-5 two-dimensional array of float numbers. This array currently contains the test grades of the students in the professor's advanced compiler design class. Write a C++ program that reads 15 array values and then determines the total number of grades in the ranges less than 60, greater than or equal to 60 and less than 70, greater than or equal to 70 and less than 80, greater than or equal to 80 and less than 90, and greater than or equal to 90.

b. Entering 15 grades each time the program written for Exercise 7a is run is cumbersome. What method is appropriate for initializing the array during the testing phase?

c. How might the program you wrote for Exercise 7a be modified to include the case of no grade being present? That is, what grade could be used to indicate an invalid grade, and how would your program have to be modified to exclude counting such a grade?

8. a. Write a function named `findMax()` that finds and displays the maximum value in a two-dimensional array of integers. The array should be declared as a 10-row-by-20-column array of integers in `main()`.

b. Modify the function written in Exercise 8a so that it also displays the row and column numbers of the element with the maximum value.

c. Can the function you wrote for Exercise 8a be generalized to handle a two-dimensional array of any size?

9. Write a function that can be used to sort the elements of a 10-by-20 two-dimensional array of integers. (*Hint:* Use the `swap()` function developed for Program 6.10 to exchange array elements.)

8.5 Common Programming Errors

Four common errors associated with using arrays are

1. Forgetting to declare the array. This error results in a compiler error message equivalent to "invalid indirection" each time a subscripted variable is encountered within a program.

2. Using a subscript that references a nonexistent array element—for example, declaring the array to be of size 20 and using a subscript value of 25. This error is not detected by most C++ compilers. It will, however, probably cause a run-time error that results in either a program "crash" or a value that has no relation to the intended element being accessed from memory. In either case, this is usually an extremely troublesome error to locate. The only solution to this problem is to make sure, either by specific programming statements or by careful coding, that each subscript references a valid array element. Using named constants for an array's size and for the maximum subscript value helps to eliminate this problem.

3. Not using a large enough counter value in a `for` loop counter to cycle through all the array elements. This error usually occurs when an array is initially specified to be of size n and there is a `for` loop within the program of the form `for (int i = 0; i < n; i++)`. The array size is then expanded, but the programmer forgets to change the interior `for` loop parameters. In practice, this error is eliminated by using the same `const` declaration for the array size and loop parameter.

4. Forgetting to initialize the array. Although many compilers automatically set all elements of integer-valued and real-valued arrays to zero and all elements of character arrays to blanks, it is up to the programmer to ensure that each array is correctly initialized before the processing of array elements begins.

8.6 Chapter Summary

1. A single-dimensional array is a data structure that can be used to store a list of values of the same data type. Such arrays must be declared by giving the data type of the values that are stored in the array and the array size. For example, the declaration

```
int num[100];
```

creates an array of 100 integers. A preferable approach is first to use a named constant to set the array size and then to use this constant in the definition of the array—for example,

```
const int MAXSIZE = 100;
```

and

```
int num[MAXSIZE];
```

2. Array elements are stored in contiguous locations in memory and referenced using the array name and a subscript—for example, `num[22]`. Any non-negative integer-value expression can be used as a subscript, and the subscript 0 always refers to the first element in an array.

3. A two-dimensional array is declared by listing both a row and a column size with the data type and name of the array. For example, the declarations

```
const int ROWS = 5;
const int COLS = 7;
int mat[ROWS][COLS];
```

creates a two-dimensional array consisting of five rows and seven columns of integer values.

4. Arrays may be initialized when they are declared. For two-dimensional arrays this is accomplished by listing the initial values, in a row-by-row manner, within braces and separating them with commas. For example, the declaration

```
int vals[3][2] = {{1, 2},
                  {3, 4},
                  {5, 6} };
```

produces the following 3-row-by-2-column array:

```
1 2
3 4
5 6
```

Because C++ uses the convention that initialization proceeds in rowwise order, the inner braces can be omitted. Thus an equivalent initialization is provided by the statement

```
int vals[3][2] = { 1, 2, 3, 4, 5, 6};
```

5. Arrays are passed to a function by passing the name of the array as an argument. The value actually passed is the address of the first array storage location. Thus the called function receives direct access to the original array, not a

copy of the array elements. Within the called function, a parameter must be declared to receive the passed array name. The declaration of the parameter can omit the row size of the array.

8.7   Chapter Supplement: Searching and Sorting Methods

Most programmers encounter the need to both sort and search a list of data items at some time in their programming careers. For example, experimental results may have to be arranged in either increasing (ascending) or decreasing (descending) order for statistical analysis, lists of names may have to be sorted in alphabetical order, or a list of dates may have to be rearranged in ascending date order. Similarly, a list of names may have to be searched to find a particular name in the list, or a list of dates may have to be searched to locate a particular date. In this section we introduce the fundamentals of both sorting and searching lists. Note that it is not necessary to sort a list before searching it, although, as we shall see, much faster searches are possible if the list is in sorted order.

Search Algorithms

A common requirement of many programs is to search a list for a given element. For example, in a list of names and telephone numbers, we might search for a specific name so that the corresponding telephone number can be printed, or we might wish to search the list simply to determine whether a name is there. The two most common methods of performing such searches are the linear and binary Search algorithms.

Linear Search

In a **linear search,** which is also known as a **sequential search,** each item in the list is examined in the order in which it occurs in the list until the desired item is found or the end of the list is reached. This is analogous to looking at every name in the phone directory, beginning with Aardvark, Aaron, until you find the one you want or until you reach Zzxgy, Zora. Obviously, this is not the most efficient way to search a long alphabetized list. However, a linear Search has these advantages:

1. The algorithm is simple.
2. The list need not be in any particular order.

In a linear Search, the search begins with the first item in the list and continues sequentially, item by item, through the list. The pseudocode for a function performing a linear Search is

For all the items in the list
  Compare the item with the desired item
  If the item was found
    Return the index value of the current item
  EndIf
EndFor
Return –1 because the item was not found

Note that the function's return value indicates whether the item was found or not. If the return value is –1, the item was not in the list; otherwise, the return value within the `for` loop provides the index of where the item is located within the list.

The function `linearSearch()` illustrates this procedure as a C++ function:

```
// this function returns the location of key in the list
// a -1 is returned if the value is not found
int linearSearch(int list[], int size, int key)
{
  int i;

  for (i = 0; i < size; i++)
  {
    if (list[i] == key)
      return i;
  }

  return -1;
}
```

In reviewing `linearSearch()`, note that the `for` loop is used simply to access each element in the list, from first element to last, until a match is found with the desired item. If the desired item is located, the index value of the current item is returned, which causes the loop to terminate; otherwise, the search continues until the end of the list is encountered.

To test this function, we have written a `main()` driver function to call it and display the results returned by `linearSearch()`. The complete test program is illustrated in Program 8.9.

Sample runs of Program 8.9 follow.

```
Enter the item you are searching for: 101
The item was found at index location 9
```

and

```
Enter the item you are searching for: 65
The item was not found in the list
```

Program 8.9

```cpp
#include <iostream>
using namespace std;

int linearSearch(int [], int, int);

int main()
{
  const int NUMEL = 10;
  int nums[NUMEL] = {5,10,22,32,45,67,73,98,99,101};
  int item, location;

  cout << "Enter the item you are searching for: ";
  cin  >> item;

  location = linearSearch(nums, NUMEL, item);

  if (location > -1)
   cout << "The item was found at index location " << location
        << endl;
  else
   cout << "The item was not found in the list\n";

  return 0;
}
// this function returns the location of key in the list
// a -1 is returned if the value is not found
int linearSearch(int list[], int size, int key)
{
  int i;

  for (i = 0; i < size; i++)
  {
    if (list[i] == key)
      return i;
  }
  return -1;

}
```

FIGURE 8.13   *The Binary Search Algorithm*

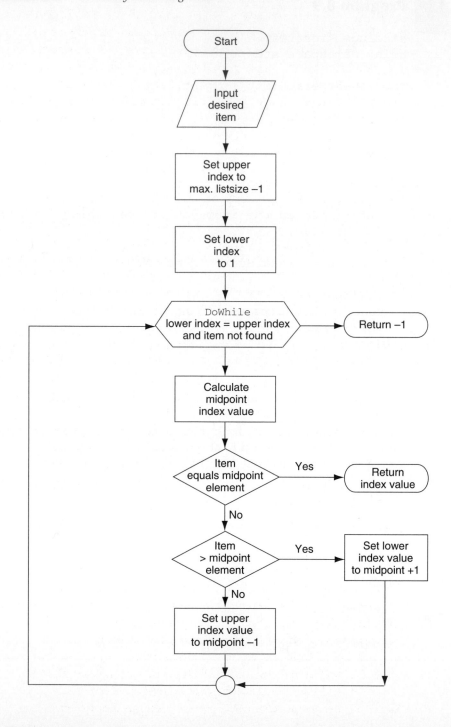

As has already been pointed out, an advantage of linear searches is that the list does not have to be in sorted order to perform the search. Another advantage is that if the desired item is toward the front of the list, only a small number of comparisons will be done. The worst case, of course, occurs when the desired item is at the end of the list. On average, however, and assuming that the desired item is equally likely to be anywhere within the list, the number of required comparisons will be $N/2$, where N is the list's size. Thus, for a 10-element list, the average number of comparisons needed for a linear Search is 5, and for a 10,000-element list, the average number of comparisons needed is 5000. As we show next, this number can be significantly reduced by using a binary Search algorithm.

Binary Search

In a **binary search,** the list must be in sorted order. Starting with an ordered list, the desired item is first compared to the element in the middle of the list (for lists with an even number of elements, either of the two middle elements can be used). Three possibilities present themselves once the comparison is made: The desired item may be equal to the middle element, it may be greater than the middle element, or it may be less than the middle element.

In the first case the search has been successful, and no further searches are required. In the second case, because the desired item is greater than the middle element, if it is found at all it must be in the second half of the list. This means that the front part of the list, consisting of all elements from the first to the midpoint element, can be discarded from any further search. In the third case, because the desired item is less than the middle element, if it is found at all it must be in the first half of the list. For this case the second half of the list, containing all elements from the midpoint element to the last element, can be discarded from any further search.

The algorithm for implementing this search strategy is illustrated in Figure 8.13 and defined by the following pseudocode:

Set the lower index to 0
Set the upper index to one less than the size of the list
Begin with the first item in the list
While the lower index is less than or equal to the upper index
  Set the midpoint index to the integer average of the lower and upper index values
  Compare the desired item to the midpoint element
    If the desired element equals the midpoint element
      Return the index value of the current item
    Else if the desired element is greater than the midpoint element
      Set the lower index value to the midpoint value plus 1
    Else if the desired element is less than the midpoint element

(continued on next page)

(continued from previous page)

> *Set the upper index value to the midpoint value less 1*
> *Endif*
> *EndWhile*
> *Return – 1 because the item was not found*

As illustrated by both the pseudocode and the flowchart of Figure 8.13, a `while` loop is used to control the search. The initial list is defined by setting the left index value to 0 and the right index value to one less than the number of elements in the list. The midpoint element is then taken as the integerized average of the left and right values. Once the comparison to the midpoint element is made, the search is subsequently restricted either by moving the left index to one integer value above the midpoint or by moving the right index to one integer value below the midpoint. This process is continued until the desired element is found or the left and right index values become equal. The function `binarySearch()` presents the C++ version of this algorithm.

```cpp
// this function returns the location of key in the list
// a -1 is returned if the value is not found
int binarySearch(int list[], int size, int key)
{
  int left, right, midpt;

  left = 0;
  right = size - 1;

  while (left <= right)
  {
    midpt = (int) ((left + right) / 2);
    if (key == list[midpt])
    {
      return midpt;
    }
    else if (key > list[midpt])
      left = midpt + 1;
    else
      right = midpt - 1;
  }

  return -1;
}
```

For purposes of testing this function, Program 8.10 is used.

Program 8.10

```cpp
#include <iostream>
using namespace std;

int binarySearch(int [], int, int);

int main()
{
  const int NUMEL = 10;
  int nums[NUMEL] = {5,10,22,32,45,67,73,98,99,101};
  int item, location;

  cout << "Enter the item you are searching for: ";
  cin >> item;
  location = binarySearch(nums, NUMEL, item);
  if (location > -1)
    cout << "The item was found at index location "
         << location << endl;
  else
    cout << "The item was not found in the list\n";
  return 0;
}

// this function returns the location of key in the list
// a -1 is returned if the value is not found
int binarySearch(int list[], int size, int key)
{
  int left, right, midpt;

  left = 0;
  right = size - 1;
  while (left <= right)
  {
    midpt = (int) ((left + right) / 2);
    if (key == list[midpt])
    {
      return midpt;
    }
    else if (key > list[midpt])
      left = midpt + 1;
    else
      right = midpt - 1;
  }

  return -1;
}
```

A sample run using Program 8.10 yielded the following:

```
Enter the item you are searching for: 101
The item was found at index location 9
```

The beauty of using a binary Search algorithm is that the number of elements that must be searched is cut in half each time through the `while` loop. Thus, the first time through the loop, N elements must be searched; the second time through the loop, $N/2$ of the elements have been eliminated and only $N/2$ remain. The third time through the loop, half of the remaining elements have been eliminated, and so on.

In general, after p passes through the loop, the number of values remaining to be searched is $N/(2^p)$. In the worst case, the search can continue until there is less than or equal to one element remaining to be searched. Mathematically, this can be expressed as $N/(2^p) \leq 1$. Alternatively, this may be rephrased as "p is the smallest integer such that $2^p \geq N$. For example, for a 1000-element array, N is 1000, and the maximum number of passes, p, required for a binary Search is 10. Table 8.1 shows the numbers of loop passes needed for a linear and a binary Search for various list sizes.

TABLE 8.1   *A Comparison of* `while` *Loop Passes for Linear and Binary Searches*

Array size	10	50	500	5,000	50,000	500,000	5,000,000	50,000,000
Average linear search passes	5	25	250	2,500	25,000	250,000	2,500,000	25,000,000
Maximum linear search passes	10	50	500	5,000	50,000	500,000	5,000,000	50,000,000
Maximum binary search passes	4	6	9	13	16	19	23	26

As illustrated, the maximum number of loop passes for a 50-item list is almost 10 times more for a linear Search than for a binary Search, and the difference is even more spectacular for larger lists. As a rule of thumb, 50 elements are usually taken as the switchover point: For lists smaller than 50 elements, linear searches are acceptable; for larger lists, a binary Search algorithm should be used.

Big O Notation

On average, over a large number of linear searches with N items in a list, we would expect to examine half ($N/2$) of the items before locating the desired item. In a binary Search, the maximum number of passes, p, occurs when $N/2^p = 1$. This relationship can be algebraically manipulated to $2^p = N$, which yields $p = \log_2 N$, which approximately equals $3.33 \log_{10} N$.

For example, finding a particular name in an alphabetical directory with $N = 1000$ names would require an average of 500 ($= N/2$) comparisons with a linear Search. With a binary Search, only about 10 ($\approx 3.33 \times \log_{10} 1000$) comparisons would be required.

A common way to express the number of comparisons required in any search algorithm using a list of N items is to give the order of magnitude of the number of comparisons required, on average, to locate a desired item. Thus the linear Search is said to be of order N, the binary Search of order $\log_2 N$. Notationally, this is expressed as $O(N)$ and $O(\log_2 N)$, where the O is read as "the order of."

Sort Algorithms

For sorting data, there are two major categories of sorting techniques. *Internal sorts* are used when the data list is not too large and the complete list can be stored within the computer's memory, usually in an array. *External sorts* are used for much larger data sets that are stored in large external disk or tape files and cannot be accommodated within the computer's memory as a complete unit. Here we present two internal sort algorithms that can be used effectively when sorting lists with less than approximately 50 elements. For larger lists, more sophisticated sorting algorithms are typically employed.

Selection Sort

One of the simplest sorting techniques is the selection sort. In a *selection sort*, the smallest value is initially selected from the complete list of data and exchanged with the first element in the list. After this first selection and exchange, the next smallest element in the revised list is selected and exchanged with the second element in the list. Because the smallest element is already in the first position in the list, this second pass need consider only the second through the last elements. For a list consisting of N elements, this process is repeated $N - 1$ times, with each pass through the list requiring one less comparison than the previous pass.

FIGURE 8.14   *A Sample Selection Sort*

Initial List	Pass 1	Pass 2	Pass 3	Pass 4
690	32	32	32	32
307	307	155	144	144
32	690	690	307	307
155	155	307	690	426
426	426	426	426	690

For example, consider the list of numbers shown in Figure 8.14. The first pass through the initial list results in the number 32 being selected and exchanged with the first element in the list. The second pass, made on the reordered list, results in the number 155 being selected from the second through the fifth elements. This value is then exchanged with the second element in the list. The third pass selects the number 307 from the third through the fifth elements in the list and exchanges this value with the third element. Finally, the fourth and last pass through the list selects the remaining minimum value and exchanges it with the fourth element. Although each pass in this example resulted in an exchange, no exchange would have been made in a pass if the smallest value had already been in the correct location.

In pseudocode, the selection sort is described as follows:

Set interchange count to zero (not required, but done just to keep track of the interchanges)
For each element in the list from first to next-to-last
   Find the smallest element from the current element being referenced to the last element by:
      Setting the minimum value equal to the current element
      Saving (storing) the index of the current element
   For each element in the list from the current element + 1 to the last element in the list
   If element[inner loop index] < minimum value
      Set the minimum value = element[inner loop index]
      Save the index of the new found minimum value
   EndIf
   EndFor
   Swap the current value with the new minimum value
   Increment the interchange count
EndFor
Return the interchange count

The function `selectionSort()` incorporates this procedure into a C++ function.

```
int selectionSort(int num[], int numel)
{
  int i, j, min, minidx, temp, moves = 0;

  for ( i = 0; i < (numel - 1); i++)
  {
    min = num[i];     // assume minimum is the first array element
    minidx = i;       // index of minimum element
    for(j = i + 1; j < numel; j++)
    {
      if (num[j] < min)      // if we've located a lower value
      {                      // capture it
```

```
      min = num[j];
      minidx - j;
    }
  }
  if (min < num[i])     // check if we have a new minimum
  {                     // and if we do, swap values
    temp = num[i];
    num[i] = min;
    num[minidx] = temp;
    moves++;
  }
}

return moves;
}
```

The selectionSort() function expects two arguments, the list to be sorted and the number of elements in the list. As specified by the pseudocode, a nested set of for loops performs the sort. The outer for loop causes one less pass through the list than the total number of data items in the list. For each pass, the variable min is initially assigned the value num[i], where i is the outer for loop's counter variable. Because i begins at 0 and ends at one less than numel, each element in the list, except the last, is successively designated as the current element.

The inner loop cycles through the elements below the current element and is used to select the next smallest value. Thus this loop begins at the index value i+1 and continues through the end of the list. When a new minimum is found, its value and position in the list are stored in the variables named min and minidx, respectively. Upon completion of the inner loop, an exchange is made only if a value less than that in the current position was found.

For purposes of testing selectionSort(), Program 8.11 was constructed. This program implements a selection sort for the same list of ten numbers that was previously used to test our search algorithms. For later comparison to the other sorting algorithms that will be presented, the number of actual moves made by the program to get the data into sorted order is counted and displayed.

Program 8.11

```cpp
#include <iostream>
using namespace std;

int selectionSort(int [], int);

int main()
{
  const int NUMEL = 10;
  int nums[NUMEL] = {22,5,67,98,45,32,101,99,73,10};
  int i, moves;

  moves = selectionSort(nums, NUMEL);

  cout << "The sorted list, in ascending order, is:\n";
  for (i = 0; i < NUMEL; i++)
    cout << " " << nums[i];

  cout << '\n' << moves << " moves were made to sort this list\n";

  return 0;
}
int selectionSort(int num[], int numel)
{
  int i, j, min, minidx, temp, moves = 0;

  for ( i = 0; i < (numel - 1); i++)
  {
    min = num[i]; // assume minimum is the first array element
    minidx = i;   // index of minimum element
    for(j = i + 1; j < numel; j++)
    {
      if (num[j] < min) // if we've located a lower value
      {                 // capture it
        min = num[j];
        minidx = j;
      }
    }
    if (min < num[i])      // check if we have a new minimum
    {                      // and if we do, swap values
      temp = num[i];
      num[i] = min;
      num[minidx] = temp;
      moves++;
    }
  }

  return moves;
}
```

The output produced by Program 8.11 is

```
The sorted list, in ascending order, is:
5    10    22    32    45    67    73    98    99    101
8 moves were made to sort this list
```

Clearly, the number of moves displayed depends on the initial order of the values in the list. An advantage of the selection sort is that the maximum number of moves that must be made is $N - 1$, where N is the number of items in the list. Further, each move is a final move that results in an element residing in its final location in the sorted list.

A disadvantage of the selection sort is that $N(N - 1)/2$ comparisons are always required, regardless of the initial arrangement of the data. This number of comparisons is obtained as follows: The last pass always requires one comparison, the next-to-last pass requires two comparisons, and so on, to the first pass, which requires $N - 1$ comparisons. Thus the total number of comparisons is

$$1 + 2 + 3 + \cdots + N - 1 = N(N - 1)/2 = N^2/2 - N/2$$

For large values of N, the N^2 dominates, and the order of the selection sort is $O(N^2)$.

Exchange (" Bubble") sort

In an **exchange sort,** or **bubble sort,** adjacent elements of the list are exchanged with one another in such a manner that the list becomes sorted. One example of such a sequence of exchanges is provided by the bubble sort, where successive values in the list are compared, beginning with the first two elements. If the list is to be sorted in ascending (from smallest to largest) order, the smaller value of the two being compared is always placed before the larger value. For lists sorted in descending (from largest to smallest) order, the smaller of the two values being compared is always placed after the larger value.

For example, assuming that a list of values is to be sorted in ascending order, if the first element in the list is larger than the second, the two elements are interchanged. Then the second and third elements are compared. Again, if the second element is larger than the third, these two elements are interchanged. This process continues until the last two elements have been compared and exchanged, if necessary. If no exchanges were made during this initial pass through the data, the data is in the correct order and the process is finished; otherwise, a second pass is made through the data, starting from the first element and stopping at the next-to-last element. The reason for stopping at the next-to-last element on the second pass is that the first pass always results in the most positive value "sinking" to the bottom of the list.

FIGURE 8.15 *The First Pass of an Exchange Sort*

690	307	307	307	307
307	690	32	32	32
32	32	690	155	155
155	155	155	690	426
426	426	426	426	690

As a specific example of this process, consider the list of numbers shown in Figure 8.15. The first comparison results in the interchange of the first two element values, 690 and 307. The next comparison, between elements two and three in the revised list, results in the interchange of values between the second and third elements, 690 and 32. This comparison and possible switching of adjacent values is continued until the last two elements have been compared and possibly switched. This process completes the first pass through the data and results in the largest number moving to the bottom of the list. As the largest value sinks to its resting place at the bottom of the list, the smaller elements slowly rise, or "bubble," to the top of the list. This bubbling effect of the smaller elements is what gave rise to the name *bubble sort* for this sorting algorithm.

Because the first pass through the list ensures that the largest value always moves to the bottom of the list, the second pass stops at the next-to-last element. This process continues, each pass stopping at one higher element than the previous pass, until either $N - 1$ passes through the list have been completed or no exchanges are necessary in any single pass. In both cases, the resulting list is in sorted order. The pseudocode describing this sort is

Set interchange count to zero (not required, but done just to keep track of the interchanges)
For the first element in the list to one less than the last element (i index)
   For the second element in the list to the last element (j index)
     If num[j] < num[j – 1]
     {
       swap num[j] with num[j – 1]
       increment interchange count
     }
   EndFor
EndFor
Return interchange count

This sort algorithm is coded in C++ as the function `bubbleSort()`, which is included within Program 8.12 for testing purposes. This program tests bubbleSort() with the same list of ten numbers used in Program 8.11 to test selectionSort(). For comparison to the earlier selection sort, the number of adjacent moves (exchanges) made by bubbleSort() is also counted and displayed.

Program 8.12

```cpp
#include <iostream>
using namespace std;

int bubbleSort(int [], int);

int main()
{
  const int NUMEL = 10;
  int nums[NUMEL] = {22,5,67,98,45,32,101,99,73,10};
  int i, moves;

  moves = bubbleSort(nums, NUMEL);

  cout << "The sorted list, in ascending order, is:\n";
  for (i = 0; i < NUMEL; i++)
    cout << " " << nums[i];

  cout << '\n' << moves << " moves were made to sort this list\n";

  return 0;
}

int bubbleSort(int num[], int numel)
{
  int i, j, temp, moves = 0;

  for ( i = 0; i < (numel - 1); i++)
  {
    for(j = 1; j < numel; j++)
    {
      if (num[j] < num[j-1])
      {
        temp = num[j];
        num[j] = num[j-1];
        num[j-1] = temp;
```

(continued on next page)

(continued from previous page)

```
            moves++;
        }
      }
   }

   return moves;
}
```

Here is the output produced by Program 8.12:

```
The sorted list, in ascending order, is:
   5   10   22   32   45   67   73   98   99   101
18 moves were made to sort this list
```

As with the selection sort, the number of comparisons using a bubble sort is $O(N^2)$, and the number of required moves depends on the initial order of the values in the list. In the worst case, when the data is in reverse sorted order, the selection sort performs better than the bubble sort. Here both sorts require $N(N-1)/2$ comparisons, but the selection sort needs only $N-1$ moves, whereas the bubble sort needs $N(N-1)/2$ moves. The additional moves required by the bubble sort result from the intermediate exchanges between adjacent elements to "settle" each element into its final position. In this regard the selection sort is superior, because no intermediate moves are necessary. For random data, such as that used in Programs 8.11 and 8.12, the selection sort generally performs as well as or better than the bubble sort.

Pointers

A fact not generally known to most programmers of high-level languages other than C and C++ is that memory addresses of variables are used extensively throughout the executable versions of their programs. The computer uses these addresses to keep track of where data and instructions are physically located inside of the computer.

One of C++'s advantages is that it provides the programmer access to the addresses of variables used in a program. This access enables a programmer to enter directly into the computer's inner workings and manipulate the computer's basic storage structure. It provides the C++ programmer with capabilities and programming power that are not typically available in other high-level languages.

This chapter presents the basics of declaring variables to store addresses. Such variables are referred to as **pointer variables**, or simply **pointers**. We also discuss methods of using pointer variables to access and use their stored addresses in meaningful ways.

9.1   Addresses and Pointers

Every variable has three major items associated with it: its data type, the actual value stored in the variable, and the address of the variable. As we have already seen, a variable's data type is declared with a declaration statement, and a value is stored in a variable by initialization when the variable is declared, by assignment, or by input. For the majority of applications, the variable's name is a simple and sufficient means of locating the variable's contents, and the translation of a variable's name to actual memory storage location is done by the computer each time the variable is referenced in a program.

Figure 9.1 illustrates the relationship among these three variable attributes (type, contents, and location). As this figure shows, the data type determines the number of memory bytes set aside for the variable, and the variable's name is a stand-in for the variable's actual memory address.

Programmers are usually concerned only with the value assigned to a variable (its contents) and pay little attention to where the value is stored (its address). For example, consider Program 9.1.

The output displayed when Program 9.1 is run is

```
The value stored in num is 22
4 bytes are used to store this value
```

FIGURE 9.1   *A Typical Variable*

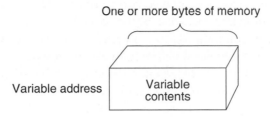

Program 9.1

```
#include <iostream>
using namespace std;

int main()
{
  int num;

  num = 22;
  cout << "The value stored in num is " << num << endl;
  cout << sizeof(num) << " bytes are used to store this value" << endl;

  return 0;
}
```

Program 9.1 displays both the number 22, which is the value stored in the integer variable num, and the amount of storage used for this number.[1] The information provided by Program 9.1 is illustrated in Figure 9.2.

FIGURE 9.2   *Somewhere in Memory*

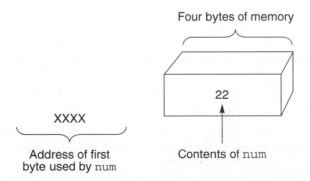

---

[1] The amount of storage allocated for each data type is compiler-dependent.

We can go further and obtain the address corresponding to the variable `num`. The address that is displayed corresponds to the address of the first byte set aside in the computer's memory for the variable.

To determine the address of `num`, we must use the address operator, `&`. We have seen this symbol before in declaring reference variables. Here it means *the address of* and when placed in front of a variable name is translated as *the address of the variable.*[2] For example, `&num` means *the address of* `num`, `&total` means *the address of* `total`, and `&price` means *the address of* `price`. Program 9.2 uses the address operator to display the address of the variable `num`.

 Program 9.2

```
#include <iostream>
using namespace std;

int main()
{
  int num;

  num = 22;
  cout << "num = " << num << endl;
  cout << "The address of num = " << &num << endl;

  return 0;
}
```

The output of Program 9.2 is

```
num = 22
The address of num = 0012FED4
```

Figure 9.3 illustrates the additional address information provided by the output of Program 9.2.

Clearly, the address output by Program 9.2 depends on the computer used to run the program. Every time Program 9.2 is executed, however, it displays the address of the first memory location used to store the variable `num`. As illustrated by the output of Program 9.2, the display of addresses is in hexadecimal notation.

---

[2] When used in the declaration of a reference variable, the `&` symbol has a similar meaning. For example, the declaration `int &num = factor;` can also be read as "num is the address of an `int`" (though it is more often read as "num is a reference to an `int`"). Because `num` is a reference variable, the compiler automatically assigns the address of `factor` to the address of `num`; both variables have the same memory address, so they both refer to the same variable.

FIGURE 9.3   *A More Comprehensive Picture of the Variable* num

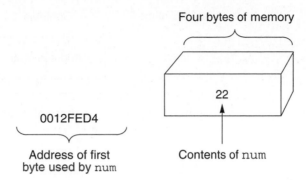

This display has no effect on how addresses are used within the program; it merely provides us with a means of displaying addresses that is helpful in understanding them. As we shall see, using addresses (as opposed to only displaying them) provides the C++ programmer with an extremely powerful programming tool.

Storing Addresses

Besides displaying the address of a variable, as was done in Program 9.2, we can also store addresses in suitably declared variables. For example, the statement

```
numAddr = &num;
```

stores the address that corresponds to the variable num in the variable numAddr, as illustrated in Figure 9.4. Similarly, the statements

```
d = &m;
tabPoint = &list;
chrPoint = &ch;
```

FIGURE 9.4   *Storing* num's *Address in* numAddr

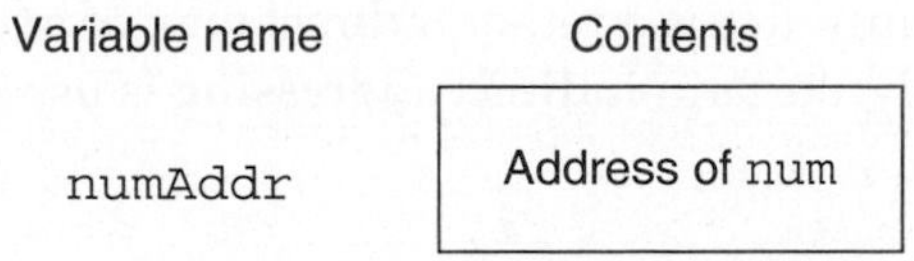

Variable name	Contents
numAddr	Address of num

FIGURE 9.5   *Storing More Addresses*

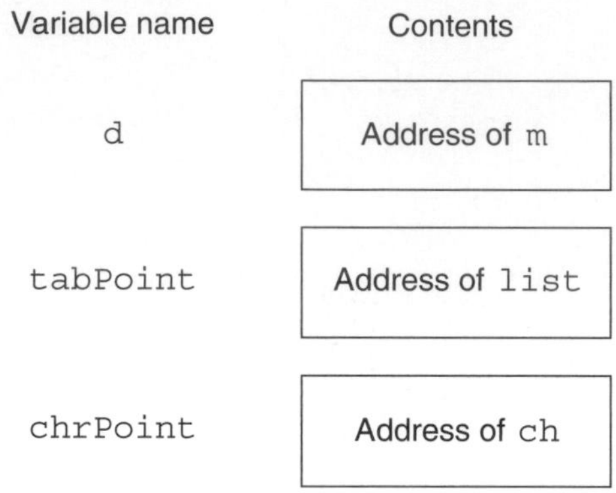

Variable name	Contents
d	Address of m
tabPoint	Address of list
chrPoint	Address of ch

store the addresses of the variables m, list, and ch in the variables d, tabPoint, and chrPoint, respectively, as illustrated in Figure 9.5.

The variables numAddr, d, tabPoint, and chrPoint are formally called *pointer variables*, or *pointers* for short. Pointers are simply variables that are used to store the addresses of other variables.

Using Addresses

To use a stored address, C++ provides us with an *indirection operator*, *. The * symbol, when followed by a pointer, means *the variable whose address is stored in*. Thus, if numAddr is a pointer (remember that a pointer is a variable that stores an address), then *numAddr means *the variable whose address is stored in* numAddr. Similarly, *tabPoint means *the variable whose address is stored in* tabPoint, and *chrPoint means *the variable whose address is stored in* chrPoint. Figure 9.6 shows the relationship between the address contained in a pointer variable and the variable ultimately addressed.

Although *d literally means *the variable whose address is stored in* d, this is commonly shortened to the statement *the variable pointed to by* d. Similarly, referring to Figure 9.6, *y can be read as *the variable pointed to by* y. The value ultimately obtained, as shown in Figure 9.6, is qqqq.

When we are using a pointer variable, the value that is finally obtained is always found by first going to the pointer variable (or pointer, for short) for an address. The address contained in the pointer is then used to get the desired contents. Certainly, this is a rather indirect way of getting to the final value, and not unexpectedly, the term **indirect addressing** is used to describe this procedure.

FIGURE 9.6 *Using a Pointer Variable*

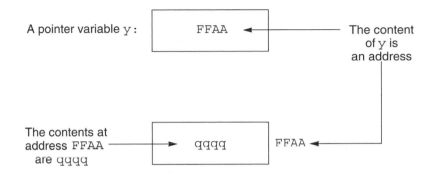

Because using a pointer requires the computer to do a double lookup (first the address is retrieved, and then the address is used to retrieve the actual data), a worthwhile question is, why would we want to store an address in the first place? The answer to this question rests on the intimate relationship between pointers and arrays and the ability of pointers to create and delete new variable storage locations dynamically, as a program is running. Both of these topics are presented later in this chapter. For now, however, given that each variable has a memory address associated with it, the idea of actually storing an address should not seem overly strange.

Declaring Pointers

Like all variables, pointers must be declared before they can be used to store an address. C++ requires that when we declare a pointer variable, we also specify the type of variable that is pointed to. For example, if the address in the pointer numAddr is the address of an integer, the correct declaration for the pointer is

```
int *numAddr;
```

This declaration is read as *the variable pointed to by* numAddr (from the *numAddr in the declaration) *is an integer.*[3]

---

[3] Pointer declarations may also be written in the form `dataType* pointerName;`, where a space is placed between the indirection operator symbol and the pointer variable name. This form, however, becomes error-prone when multiple pointer variables are declared in the same declaration statement and the asterisk symbol is inadvertently omitted after the first pointer name is declared. For example, the declaration `int* num1, num2;` declares `num1` as a pointer variable and `num2` as an integer variable. In order to accommodate multiple pointers in the same declaration more easily and clearly mark a variable as a pointer, we will adhere to the convention of placing an asterisk directly in front of each pointer variable name. This possible error rarely occurs with reference declarations, because references are almost exclusively used as parameters, and single declarations of parameters are mandatory.

Note that the declaration `int *numAddr;` specifies two things: first, that the variable pointed to by `numAddr` is an integer; second, that `numAddr` must be a pointer (because it is used with the indirection operator *). Similarly, if the pointer `tabPoint` points to (contains the address of) a double-precision number and `chrPoint` points to a character variable, then the required declarations for these pointers are

```
double *tabPoint;
char *chrPoint;
```

These two declarations can be read, respectively, as *the variable pointed to by* `tabPoint` *is a double* and *the variable pointed to by* `chrPoint` *is a char.* Consider Program 9.3.

Program 9.3

```cpp
#include <iostream>
using namespace std;

int main()
{
  int *numAddr;          // declare a pointer to an int
  int miles, dist;       // declare two integer variables

  dist = 158;            // store the number 158 into dist
  miles = 22;            // store the number 22 into miles
  numAddr = &miles;      // store the 'address of miles' in numAddr

  cout << "The address stored in numAddr is " << numAddr << endl;
  cout << "The value pointed to by numAddr is " << *numAddr << endl;

  numAddr = &dist; // now store the address of dist in numAddr
  cout << "\nThe address now stored in numAddr is " << numAddr << endl;
  cout << "The value now pointed to by numAddr is " << *numAddr << endl;

  return 0;
}
```

The output of Program 9.3 is

```
The address stored in numAddr is 0012FEC8
The value pointed to by numAddr is 22

The address now stored in numAddr is 0012FEBC
The value now pointed to by numAddr is 158
```

The only value of Program 9.3 is in helping us understand "what gets stored where." Let's review the program to see how the output was produced.

The declaration statement int *numAddr; declares numAddr to be a pointer variable used to store the address of an integer variable. The statement numAddr = &miles; stores the address of the variable miles into the pointer numAddr. The first cout statement causes this address to be displayed. The second cout statement in Program 9.3 uses the indirection operator to retrieve and print out *the value pointed to by* numAddr, which is, of course, the value stored in miles.

Because numAddr has been declared as a pointer to an integer variable, we can use this pointer to store the address of any integer variable. The statement numAddr = &dist illustrates this by storing the address of the variable dist in numAddr. The last two cout statements verify the change in numAddr's value and confirm that the new stored address does point to the variable dist. As illustrated in Program 9.3, only addresses should be stored in pointers.

It certainly would have been much simpler if the pointer used in Program 9.3 could have been declared as pointer numAddr;. Such a declaration, however, conveys no information about the storage used by the variable whose address is stored in numAddr. This information is essential when the pointer is used with the indirection operator, as it is in the second cout statement in Program 9.3. For example, if the address of an integer is stored in numAddr, then only four bytes of storage are typically retrieved when the address is used. If the address of a character is stored in numAddr, only one byte of storage would be retrieved, and a double typically requires the retrieval of eight bytes of storage.[4] The declaration of a pointer must therefore include the type of variable being pointed to. Figure 9.7 illustrates this concept.

FIGURE 9.7 *Addressing Different Data Types Using Pointers*

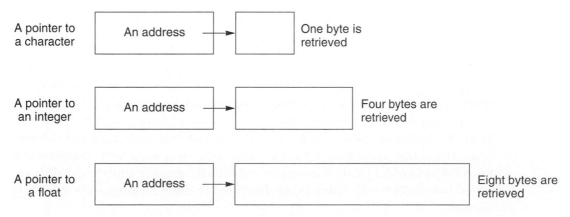

---

[4] The amount of storage used is compiler-dependent.

References and Pointers

At this point you might be asking what the difference is between a pointer and a reference. Essentially, a reference is a pointer with restricted capabilities that has the advantage of hiding a lot of internal pointer manipulations from the programmer. For example, consider these statements:

```
int b;        // b is an integer variable
int &a = b;   // a is a reference variable that stores b's address
a = 10;       // this changes b's value to 10
```

Here a is declared as a reference variable that contains the address of an integer—the address of b, in particular. Because the compiler knows, from the declaration, that a is a reference variable, it automatically assigns the address of b (rather than the contents of b) in the declaration statement. Finally, in the statement a = 10; the compiler uses the address stored in a to change the value stored in b to 10. The advantage of using the reference is that it automatically performs an indirect access of b's value without the need for explicitly using the indirection operator symbol, *. This type of access is referred to as an **automatic dereference**.

Implementing this same correspondence between a and b using pointers is done by the following sequence of instructions:

```
int b;         // b is an integer variable
int *a = &b;   // a is a pointer - store b's address in a
*a = 10;       // this changes b's value to 10
```

Here a is defined as a pointer that is initialized to store the address of b. Thus *a, which can be read either as "the variable whose address is in a" or as "the variable pointed to by a," is b, and the expression *a = 10 changes b's value to 10. Note that in the pointer case, the stored address can be altered to point to another variable; in the reference case, the reference variable cannot be altered to refer to any variable except the one to which it is initialized.

For simple cases, where an alias is required, using references is easier than using pointers and is clearly preferred. The same is true when we consider references to structures, which is the topic of Section 10.3. For other situations, such as dynamically allocating new sections of memory for additional variables as a program is running, or using alternatives to array notation (both topics of the next section), pointers are required. In other situations, such as passing addresses to a function, references provide a simpler notational interface and are usually preferred (see Section 9.4). Pointers are described in the remaining sections of this chapter.

▌ EXERCISES 9.1

1. If average is a variable, what does &average mean?

2. For the variables and addresses illustrated in Figure 9.8, determine &temp, &dist, &date, and &miles.

3. a. Write a C++ program that includes the following declaration statements. Have the program use the address operator and the cout object to display the addresses that correspond to each variable.

```
int num, count;
long date;
float yield;
double price;
```

b. After running the program written for Exercise 3a, draw a diagram of how your computer has set aside storage for the variables in the program. On your diagram, fill in the addresses displayed by the program.

c. Modify the program written in Exercise 3a to display the amount of storage your computer reserves for each data type (use the sizeof() operator). With this information and the address information provided in Exercise 3b, determine whether your computer set aside storage for the variables in the order in which they were declared.

FIGURE 9.8 *Memory Bytes for Exercise 2*

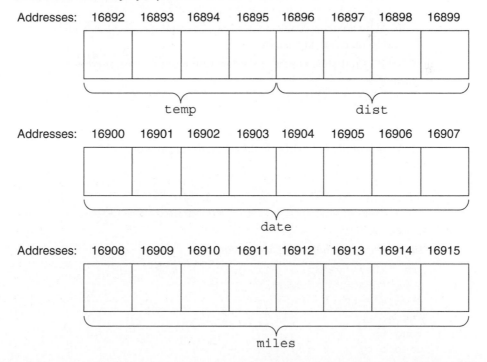

4. If a variable is declared as a pointer, what must be stored in the variable?

5. Using the indirection operator, write expressions for the following:
   a. The variable pointed to by xAddr
   b. The variable whose address is in yAddr
   c. The variable pointed to by ptYld
   d. The variable pointed to by ptMiles
   e. The variable pointed to by mptr
   f. The variable whose address is in pdate
   g. The variable pointed to by distPtr
   h. The variable pointed to by tabPt
   i. The variable whose address is in hoursPt

6. Write declaration statements for the following:
   a. The variable pointed to by yAddr is an integer.
   b. The variable pointed to by chAddr is a character.
   c. The variable pointed to by ptYr is a long integer.
   d. The variable pointed to by amt is a double-precision variable.
   e. The variable pointed to by z is an integer.
   f. The variable pointed to by qp is a floating-point variable.
   g. datePt is a pointer to an integer.
   h. yldAddr is a pointer to a double-precision variable.
   i. amtPt is a pointer to a floating-point variable.
   j. ptChr is a pointer to a character.

7. a. What are the variables yAddr, chAddr, ptYr, amt, z, qp, datePt, yldAddr, amtPt, and ptChr, used in Exercise 6, called?
   b. Why are the variable names amt, z, and qp, used in Exercise 6, not good choices for pointer variable names?

8. Write English sentences that describe what is contained in the following declared variables.

   a. `char *keyAddr;`   d. `long *yPtr;`
   b. `int *m;`   e. `double *pCou;`
   c. `double *yldAddr;`   f. `int *ptDate;`

9. Which of the following are declarations for pointers?

   a. `long a;`   f. `double w;`
   b. `char b;`   g. `float *k;`
   c. `char *c;`   h. `float l;`
   d. `int x;`   i. `double *z;`
   e. `int *p;`

10. Consider the following declarations.

```
int *xPt, *yAddr;
long *dtAddr, *ptAddr;
double *ptZ;
int a;
long b;
double c;
```

Given these declarations, determine which of the following statements are valid.

a. yAddr = &a;   *h.* dtAddr = &b;   *o.* ptAddr - &c;
b. yAddr = &b;   *i.* dtAddr = &c;   *p.* ptAddr = a;
c. yAddr = &c;   *j.* dtAddr = a;   *q.* ptAddr = b;
d. yAddr = a;   *k.* dtAddr = b;   *r.* ptAddr = c;
e. yAddr = b;   *l.* dtAddr = c;   *s.* yAddr = xPt;
f. yAddr = c;   *m.* ptZ = &a;   *t.* yAddr = dtAddr;
g. dtAddr = &a;   *n.* ptAddr = &b   *u.* yAddr = ptAddr;

11. For the variables and addresses illustrated in Figure 9.9, fill in the appropriate data as determined by the following statements.

a. ptNum = &m;   *e.* ptDay = zAddr;
b. amtAddr = &amt;   *f.* *ptYr = 1987;
c. *zAddr = 25;   *g.* *amtAddr = *numAddr;
d. k = *numAddr;

FIGURE 9.9   *Memory Locations for Exercise 11*

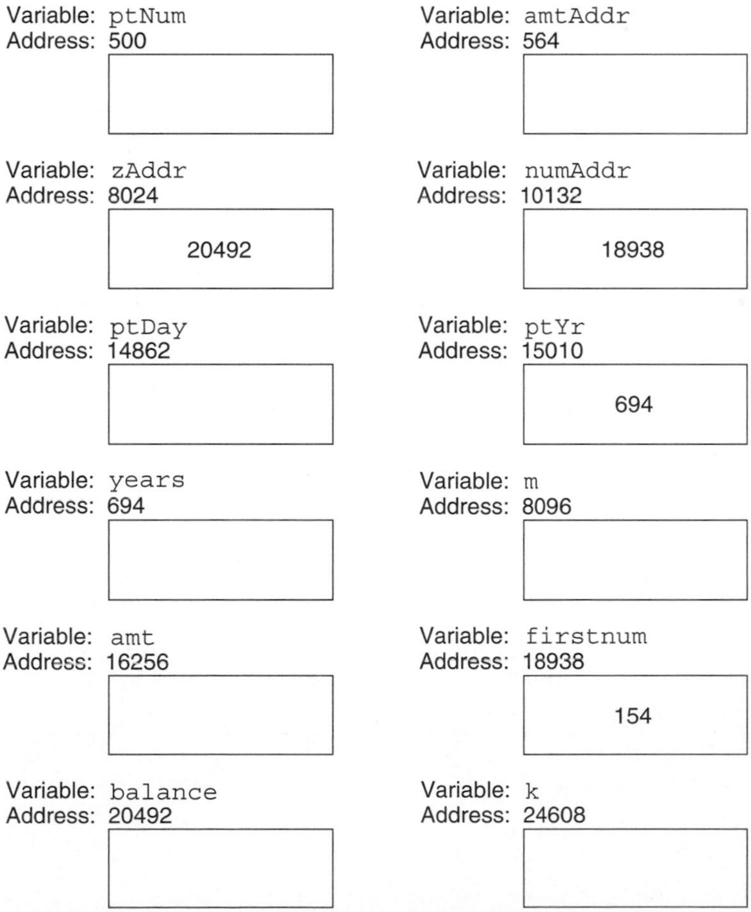

Variable: ptNum
Address: 500

Variable: amtAddr
Address: 564

Variable: zAddr
Address: 8024

20492

Variable: numAddr
Address: 10132

18938

Variable: ptDay
Address: 14862

Variable: ptYr
Address: 15010

694

Variable: years
Address: 694

Variable: m
Address: 8096

Variable: amt
Address: 16256

Variable: firstnum
Address: 18938

154

Variable: balance
Address: 20492

Variable: k
Address: 24608

12. Using the `sizeof()` operator, determine the number of bytes used by your computer to store the address of an integer, character, and double-precision number. (*Hint:* `sizeof(*int)` can be used to determine the number of memory bytes used for a pointer to an integer.) Would you expect the size of each address to be the same? Why or why not?

9.2   Array Names as Pointers

Although pointers are simply, by definition, variables used to store addresses, there is also a direct and intimate relationship between array names and pointers. In this section, we describe that relationship in detail.

Figure 9.10 illustrates the storage of a single-dimensional array named `grade`, which contains five integers. Assume that each integer requires four bytes of storage.

Using subscripts, the fourth element in the `grade` array is referred to as `grade[3]`. The use of a subscript, however, conceals the extensive use of addresses by the computer. Internally, the computer immediately uses the subscript to calculate the address of the desired element on the basis of both the starting address of the array and the amount of storage used by each element. Calling the third element `grade[3]` forces the compiler, internally, to make the address computation (assuming four bytes per integer)

$$\&grade[3] = \&grade[0] + (3 * 4)$$

Remembering that the address operator, &, means "the address of," we read this last statement "the address of `grade[3]` equals the address of `grade[0]` plus 12." Figure 9.11 illustrates the address computation used to locate `grade[3]`.

Remember that a pointer is a variable used to store an address. If we create a pointer to store the address of the first element in the `grade` array, we can mimic the operation used by the computer to access the array elements. Before we do this, let us consider Program 9.4.

FIGURE 9.10   *The* grade *Array in Storage*

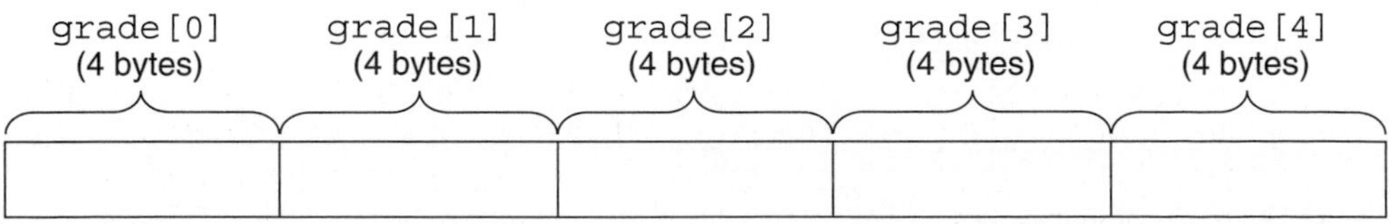

grade[0]   grade[1]   grade[2]   grade[3]   grade[4]
(4 bytes)   (4 bytes)   (4 bytes)   (4 bytes)   (4 bytes)

FIGURE 9.11 *Using a Subscript to Obtain an Address*

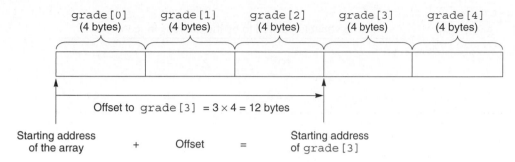

Program 9.4

```cpp
#include <iostream>
using namespace std;

int main()
{
  const int SIZE = 5;
  int i, grade[SIZE] = {98, 87, 92, 79, 85};

  for (i = 0; i < SIZE; i++)
    cout << "Element " << i << " is " << grade[i] << endl;

  return 0;
}
```

When Program 9.4 is run, the following display is obtained:

```
Element 0 is 98
Element 1 is 87
Element 2 is 92
Element 3 is 79
Element 4 is 85
```

Program 9.4 displays the values of the grade array using standard subscript notation. Now, let us store the address of array element 0 in a pointer. Then, using the indirection operator, *, we can use the address in the pointer to access each array element. For example, if we store the address of grade[0] in a pointer variable named gPtr (using the assignment statement gPtr = &grade[0];), then, as illustrated in Figure 9.12, the expression *gPtr, which means "the variable pointed to by gPtr," references grade[0].

FIGURE 9.12   *The Variable Pointed to by* *gPtr *Is* grade[0].

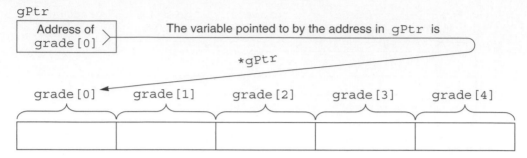

One unique feature of pointers is that offsets may be included in expressions using pointers. For example, the 1 in the expression *(gPtr + 1) is an offset. The complete expression references the integer that is one beyond the variable pointed to by gPtr. Similarly, as illustrated in Figure 9.13, the expression *(gPtr + 3) references the variable that is three integers beyond the variable pointed to by gPtr. This is the variable grade[3].

FIGURE 9.13   *An Offset of 3 from the Address in* gPtr

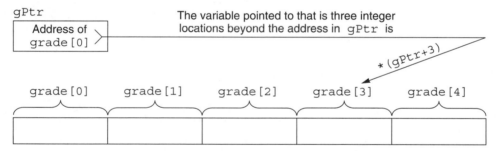

Table 9.1 lists the complete correspondence between elements referenced by subscripts and by pointers and offsets. The relationships listed in Table 9.1 are illustrated in Figure 9.14.

TABLE 9.1   *Array Elements May Be Referenced in Two Ways*

Array Element	Subscript Notation	Pointer Notation
Element 0	grade[0]	*gPtr and *(gPtr + 0)
Element 1	grade[1]	*(gPtr + 1)
Element 2	grade[2]	*(gPtr + 2)
Element 3	grade[3]	*(gPtr + 3)
Element 4	grade[4]	*(gPtr + 4)

FIGURE 9.14   *The Relationship Between Array Elements and Pointers*

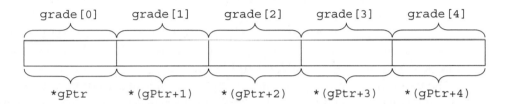

Using the correspondence between pointers and subscripts illustrated in Figure 9.14, we can now use pointers to access the array elements in Program 9.4 that we previously accessed using subscripts. This is done in Program 9.5.

 Program 9.5

```cpp
#include <iostream>
using namespace std;

int main()
{
    int *gPtr;            // declare a pointer to an int
    const int SIZE = 5;
    int i, grade[SIZE] = {98, 87, 92, 79, 85};

    gPtr = &grade[0];     // store the starting array address
    for (i = 0; i < SIZE; i++)
        cout << "Element " << i << " is " << *(gPtr + i) << endl;

    return 0;
}
```

The following display is obtained when Program 9.5 is run:

```
Element 0 is 98
Element 1 is 87
```

```
Element 2 is 92
Element 3 is 79
Element 4 is 85
```

This is the same display that Program 9.4 produced.

The method used in Program 9.5 to access individual array elements simulates the way the compiler internally references all array elements. Any subscript used by a programmer is automatically converted to an equivalent pointer expression by the compiler. In our case, because the declaration of gPtr included the information that integers are pointed to, any offset added to the address in gPtr is automatically scaled by the size of an integer. Thus *(gPtr + 3), for example, refers to the address of grade[0] plus an offset of twleve bytes (3 * 4). This is the address of grade[3] illustrated in Figure 9.11.

The parentheses in the expression *(gPtr + 3) are necessary to reference the desired array element correctly. Omitting the parentheses results in the expression *gPtr + 3. Because of the precedence of the operators, this expression adds 3 to "the variable pointed to by gPtr." Since gPtr points to grade[0], this expression adds the value of grade[0] and 3 together. Note also that the expression *(gPtr + 3) does not change the address stored in gPtr. Once the computer uses the offset to locate the correct variable from the starting address in gPtr, the offset is discarded, and the address in gPtr remains unchanged.

Although the pointer gPtr used in Program 9.5 was specifically created to store the starting address of the grade array, this was, in fact, unnecessary. When an array is created, the compiler automatically creates an internal pointer constant for it and stores the starting address of the array in this pointer. In almost all respects, a pointer constant is very similar to a pointer variable created by a programmer, but as we shall see, there are some differences.

For each array created, the name of the array becomes the name of the pointer constant created by the compiler for the array, and the starting address of the first location reserved for the array is stored in this pointer. Thus declaring the grade array in both Program 9.4 and Program 9.5 actually reserved enough storage for five integers, created an internal pointer named grade, and stored the address of grade[0] in the pointer. This is illustrated in Figure 9.15.

The implication is that every reference to grade using a subscript can be replaced by an equivalent reference using grade as a pointer. Thus, wherever the expression grade[i] is used, the expression *(grade + i) can also be used. This is illustrated in Program 9.6, where grade is used as a pointer to reference all of its elements.

Executing Program 9.6 produces the same output as that produced by Program 9.4 and Program 9.5. However, using grade as a pointer made it unnecessary to declare and initialize the pointer gPtr used in Program 9.5.

FIGURE 9.15   *Creating an Array Also Creates a Pointer*

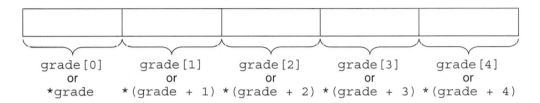

grade

&grade[0]

grade[0]   grade[1]   grade[2]   grade[3]   grade[4]
  or   or   or   or   or
*grade   *(grade + 1) *(grade + 2) *(grade + 3) *(grade + 4)

In most respects, an array name and a pointer can be used interchangeably. *A true pointer is a variable, however, and the address stored in it can be changed. An array name is a pointer constant, and the address stored in the pointer cannot be changed by an assignment statement.* Thus a statement such as grade = &grade[2]; is invalid. This should come as no surprise. The whole purpose of an array name is to locate the beginning of the array correctly, so allowing a programmer to change the address stored in the array name would defeat this purpose and lead to havoc whenever array elements were referenced. Also, expressions that take the address of an array name are invalid because the pointer created by the compiler is internal to the computer, not stored in memory as are pointer variables. Thus, trying to store the address of grade by using the expression &grade results in a compiler error.

Program 9.6

```cpp
#include <iostream>
using namespace std;

int main()
{
  const int SIZE = 5;
  int i, grade[SIZE] = {98, 87, 92, 79, 85};

  for (i = 0; i < SIZE; i++)
    cout << "Element " << i << " is " << *(grade + i) << endl;

  return 0;
}
```

An interesting sidelight to the observation that elements of an array can be accessed using pointers is that a pointer access can always be replaced using subscript notation. For example, if `numPtr` is declared as a pointer variable, the expression `*(numPtr + i)` can also be written as `numPtr[i]`. This is true even though `numPtr` is not created as an array. As before, when the compiler encounters the subscript notation, it replaces it internally with the pointer notation.

Dynamic Array Allocation

As each variable is defined in a program, sufficient storage for it is assigned from a pool of computer memory locations made available to the compiler. Once specific memory locations have been reserved for a variable, these locations are fixed for the life of that variable, whether they are used or not. For example, if a function requests storage for an array of 500 integers, the storage for the array is allocated and fixed from the point of the array's definition. If the application requires less than 500 integers, the unused allocated storage is not released back to the system until the array goes out of existence. On the other hand, if the application requires more than 500 integers, the size of the integer array must be increased and the function defining the array recompiled.

An alternative to this fixed, or static, allocation of memory storage locations is the dynamic allocation of memory. Under a **dynamic allocation** scheme, the amount of storage to be allocated is determined and adjusted as the program is run, rather than being fixed at compile time.

The dynamic allocation of memory is extremely useful when we are dealing with lists, because it allows the list to expand as new items are added and to contract as items are deleted. For example, in constructing a list of grades, we may not know the exact number of grades ultimately needed. Rather than creating a fixed array to store the grades, it is extremely useful to have a mechanism whereby the array can be enlarged and shrunk as necessary. Two C++ operators that provide this capability, `new` and `delete`, are described in Table 9.2.

TABLE 9.2 *Dynamic Allocation and Deallocation Operators*

Operator Name	Description
new	Reserves the number of bytes requested by the declaration. Returns the address of the first reserved location or returns NULL if sufficient memory is not available.
delete	Releases a block of bytes previously reserved. This operator requires the address of the first location of memory to be deallocated.

Explicit dynamic storage requests for scalar variables or arrays are made as part of either a declaration or assignment statement.[5] For example, the declaration statement `int *num = new int;` reserves an area sufficient to hold one integer and places the address of this storage area into the pointer `num`. This same dynamic allocation can be made by first declaring the pointer using the declaration statement `int *num;` and then subsequently assigning the pointer an address with the assignment statement `num = new int;`. In either case, the allocated storage area comes from the computer's free storage area.[6]

A similar (and more useful) process is the dynamic allocation of arrays. For example, the declaration

```
int *grade = new int[200];
```

reserves an area sufficient to store 200 integers and places the address of the first integer into the pointer `grade`. Although we have used the constant 200 in this example declaration, a variable dimension can be used. For example, consider the sequence of instructions

```
cout << "Enter the number of grades to be processed: ";
cin >> numgrades;
int *grade = new int[numgrades];
```

In this sequence, the actual size of the array that is created depends on the number input by the user. Because pointer and array names are related, each value in the newly created storage area can be accessed using standard array notation, such as `grade[i]`, rather than the equivalent pointer notation `*(grade + i)`. Program 9.7 illustrates this sequence of code in the context of a complete program.

Notice in Program 9.7 that the `delete` operator is used with braces whenever the `new` operator is used to create an array. The `delete[]` operator restores the allocated block of storage to the operating system while the programming is executing.[7] The only address required by `delete` is the starting address of the block of storage that was dynamically allocated. Thus any address returned by `new` can subsequently be used by `delete` to restore the reserved memory to the computer. The `delete` operator does not alter the address passed to it; rather, it simply removes the storage that the address references.

---

[5] Note that the compiler automatically provides this dynamic allocation and deallocation from the stack for all `auto` variables.

[6] The free storage area of a computer is formally referred to as the *heap*. The heap consists of unallocated memory that can be allocated to a program, as requested, while the program is running.

[7] The allocated storage would be returned automatically to the heap when the program completed execution. It is, however, good practice to restore the allocated storage formally to the heap, using `delete`, when the memory is no longer needed. This is especially true for larger programs that make numerous requests for additional storage areas.

Program 9.7

```cpp
#include <iostream>
using namespace std;

int main()
{
  int numgrades, i;

  cout << "Enter the number of grades to be processed: ";
  cin  >> numgrades;

  int *grade = new int[numgrades];     // create the array

  for(i = 0; i < numgrades; i++)
  {
    cout << " Enter a grade: ";
    cin  >> grade[i];
  }
  cout << "\nAn array was created for " << numgrades << " integers\n";
  cout << " The values stored in the array are:";
  for (i = 0; i < numgrades; i++)
    cout << "\n " << grade[i];

  delete []grade;  // return the storage to the heap
  cout << endl;

  return 0;
}
```

Following is a sample run using Program 9.7:

```
Enter the number of grades to be processed: 4
  Enter a grade: 85
  Enter a grade: 96
  Enter a grade: 77
  Enter a grade: 92

An array was created for 4 integers
  The values stored in the array are:
    85
    96
    77
    92
```

■ EXERCISES 9.2

1. Replace each of the following references to a subscripted variable with a pointer reference.
   a. `prices[5]`   *d.* `dist[9]`   *g.* `celsius[16]`
   b. `grades[2]`   *e.* `mile[0]`   *h.* `num[50]`
   c. `yield[10]`   *f.* `temp[20]`   *i.* `time[12]`

2. Replace each of the following references using a pointer with a subscript reference.
   a. `*(message + 6)`   *c.* `*(yrs + 10)`   *e.* `*(rates + 15)`
   b. `*amount`   *d.* `*(stocks + 2)`   *f.* `*(codes + 19)`

3. *a.* List the three things that the declaration statement `double prices[5];` causes the compiler to do.
   b. If each double-precision number uses eight bytes of storage, how much storage is set aside for the `prices` array?
   c. Draw a diagram similar to Figure 9.15 for the `prices` array.
   d. Determine the byte offset relative to the start of the `prices` array, corresponding to the offset in the expression `*(prices + 3)`.

4. *a.* Write a declaration to store the string `"This is a sample"` into an array named `samtest`. Include the declaration in a program that displays the values in `samtest` using a `for` loop that uses a pointer access to each element in the array.
   b. Modify the program written in Exercise 4a to display only array elements 10 through 15 (these are the letters `s`, `a`, `m`, `p`, `l`, and `e`).

5. Write a declaration to store the following values into an array named `rates`: 12.9, 18.6, 11.4, 13.7, 9.5, 15.2, 17.6. Include the declaration in a program that displays the values in the array using pointer notation.

6. Repeat Exercise 6 in Section 8.1, but use pointer references to access all array elements.

7. Repeat Exercise 7 in Section 8.1, but use pointer references to access all array elements.

8. As described in Table 9.2, the new operator either returns the address of the first new storage area allocated or returns NULL if insufficient storage is available. Modify Program 9.7 to check that a valid address has been returned before attempting to place values into the `grade` array. Display an appropriate message if sufficient storage is not available.

9.3   Pointer Arithmetic

Pointer variables, like all variables, contain values. The value stored in a pointer is, of course, an address. Thus, by adding numbers to and subtracting numbers from pointers, we can obtain different addresses. Additionally, the addresses in pointers can be compared by using any of the relational operators (==, !=, <, >, etc.) that are valid for comparing other variables. In performing arithmetic on pointers, we must be careful to produce addresses that point to something meaningful. In comparing pointers, we must also make comparisons that make sense. Consider these declarations:

```
int nums[100];
int *nPt;
```

To set the address of nums[0] into nPt, we can use either of the following two assignment statements:

```
nPt = &nums[0];
nPt = nums;
```

The two assignment statements produce the same result because nums is a pointer constant that is the address of the first location in the array. This is, of course, the address of nums[0]. Figure 9.16 illustrates the allocation of memory that results from the previous declaration and assignment statements, assuming that each integer requires four bytes of memory and that the location of the beginning of the nums array is at address 18934.

Once nPt contains a valid address, values can be added to and subtracted from the address to produce new addresses. When adding numbers to or subtracting numbers from pointers, the computer automatically adjusts the number to ensure that the result still "points to" a value of the correct type.

FIGURE 9.16 *The* nums *Array in Memory*

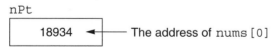

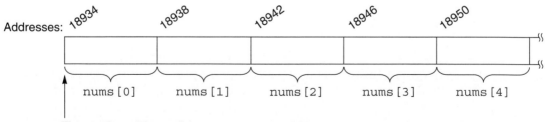

For example, the statement nPt = nPt + 4; forces the program to scale the 4 by the correct number to ensure that the resulting address is the address of an integer. Assuming that each integer requires four bytes of storage, as illustrated in Figure 9.16, the computer multiplies the 4 by 4 and then adds 16 to the address in nPt. The resulting address is 18950, which is the correct address of nums[4].

This automatic scaling by the program ensures that the expression nPt + i, where i is any positive integer, correctly points to the ith element beyond the one currently being pointed to by nPt. Thus, if nPt initially contains the address of nums[0], then nPt + 4 is the address of nums[4], nPt + 50 is the address of nums[50], and nPt + i is the address of nums[i]. Although we have used actual addresses in Figure 9.16 to illustrate the scaling process, the programmer normally does not know or need to know the actual addresses used by the computer. The manipulation of addresses using pointers generally does not require knowledge of the actual address.

Addresses can also be incremented or decremented using both prefix and postfix increment and decrement operators. Adding 1 to a pointer causes the pointer to point to the next element of the type being pointed to. Decrementing a pointer causes the pointer to point to the previous element. For example, if the pointer variable p is a pointer to an integer, the expression p++ causes the address in the pointer to be incremented to point to the next integer. This is illustrated in Figure 9.17.

In reviewing Figure 9.17, note that the increment added to the pointer is correctly scaled to account for the fact that the pointer is used to point to integers. It is, of course, up to the programmer to ensure that the correct type of data is stored in the new address contained in the pointer.

FIGURE 9.17 *Increments Are Scaled When Used with Pointers*

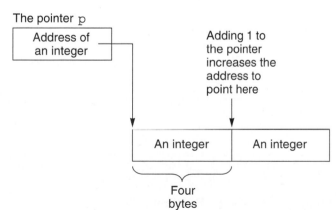

The increment and decrement operators can be applied as both prefix and postfix pointer operators. All of the following combinations using pointers are valid:

```
*ptNum++     // use the pointer and then increment it
*++ptNum     // increment the pointer before using it
*ptNum--     // use the pointer and then decrement it
*--ptNum     // decrement the pointer before using it
```

Of the four possible forms, the most commonly used is the form *ptNum++. This is because such an expression allows each element in an array to be accessed as the address is "marched along" from the starting address of the array to the address of the last array element. To see the use of the increment operator, consider Program 9.8. In this program, each element in the nums array is retrieved by successively incrementing the address in nPt.

Program 9.8

```
#include <iostream>
using namespace std;

int main()
{
  const int NUMPTS = 5;
  int nums[NUMPTS] = {16, 54, 7, 43, -5};
  int i, total = 0, *nPt;

  nPt = nums;    // store address of nums[0] in nPt
  for (i = 0; i < NUMPTS; i++)
    total = total + *nPt++;

  cout << "The total of the array elements is " << total <<
endl;

  return 0;
}
```

The output produced by Program 9.8 is

```
The total of the array elements is 115
```

The expression total = total + *nPt++ used in Program 9.8 is a standard accumulating expression. Within this expression, the term *nPt++ first causes the compiler to retrieve the integer pointed to by nPt. This is done by the *nPt part of the term. The postfix increment, ++, then adds one to the address in nPt so that nPt now contains the address of the next array element. The increment is, of course, scaled correctly by the computer so that the actual address in nPt is the correct address of the next array element.

Pointers may also be compared. This is particularly useful when we are dealing with pointers that point to elements in the same array. For example, rather than using a counter in a for loop to access each element in an array correctly, the address in a pointer can be compared to the starting and ending address of the array itself. The expression

$$nPt <= \&nums[4]$$

is true (nonzero) as long as the address in nPt is less than or equal to the address of nums[4]. Since nums is a pointer constant that contains the address of nums[0], the term &nums[4] can be replaced by the equivalent term nums + 4. Using either of these forms, we can rewrite Program 9.8 as Program 9.9 to continue adding array elements while the address in nPt is less than or equal to the address of the last array element.

Program 9.9

```
#include <iostream>
using namespace std;

int main()
{
  const int NUMPTS = 5;
  int nums[NUMPTS] = {16, 54, 7, 43, -5};
  int total = 0, *nPt;

  nPt = nums;     // store address of nums[0] in nPt

  while (nPt < nums + NUMPTS)
    total += *nPt++;

  cout << "The total of the array elements is " << total << endl;

  return 0;
}
```

Note that in Program 9.9 the compact form of the accumulating expression, `total +=  *nPt++`, was used in place of the longer form, `total  =  total  + *nPt++`. Also, the expression `nums  +  NUMPTS` does not change the address in `nums`. This expression retrieves the address in `nums`, adds 4 to this address (appropriately scaled), and uses the result for comparison purposes. Expressions such as `*nums++`, which attempt to change the address, are invalid because `nums` is an array name, not a pointer variable; as such, its value cannot be changed. Expressions such as `*nums` and `* (nums  +  i)`, which use the address without attempting to alter it, are valid.

Pointer Initialization

Like all variables, pointers can be initialized when they are declared. When initializing pointers, however, we must be careful to set an address in the pointer. For example, an initialization such as

```
int *ptNum = &miles;
```

is valid only if `miles` itself was declared as an integer variable prior to `ptNum`. Here we are creating a pointer to an integer and setting the address in the pointer to the address of an integer variable. Note that if the variable `miles` is declared subsequently to `ptNum`, as follows,

```
int *ptNum = &miles;
int miles;
```

an error occurs. This is because the address of `miles` is used before `miles` has even been defined. Because the storage area reserved for `miles` has not been allocated when `ptNum` is declared, the address of `miles` does not yet exist.

Pointers to arrays can also be initialized within their declaration statements. For example, if `prices` has been declared as an array of double-precision numbers, either of the following two declarations can be used to initialize the pointer named `zing` to the address of the first element in `prices`:

```
double *zing = &prices[0];
double *zing = prices;
```

The last initialization is correct because `prices` is itself a pointer constant containing an address of the proper type. (The variable name `zing` was selected in this example to reinforce the idea that any variable name can be selected for a pointer.)

▌ EXERCISES 9.3

1. Replace the `while` statement in Program 9.9 with a `for` statement.

2. a. Write a C++ program that initializes an array named `rates` with the following numbers: 6.25, 6.50, 6.8, 7.2, 7.35, 7.5, 7.65, 7.8, 8.2, 8.4, 8.6, 8.8, 9.0. Display the values in the array by changing the address in a pointer called `dispPt`. Use a `for` statement in your program.
b. Modify the program written in Exercise 2a to use a `while` statement.

3. a. Write a program that stores the string `Hooray for All of Us` into an array named `st.rng`. Use the declaration `strng[] = "Hooray for All of Us";`, which ensures that the end-of-string escape sequence `\0` is included in the array. Display the characters in the array by changing the address in a pointer called `messPt`. Use a `for` statement in your program.
b. Modify the program written in Exercise 3a to use the `while` statement `while (*messPt++ != '\0')`.
c. Modify the program written in Exercise 3a to start the display with the word `All`.

4. Write a C++ program that stores the following numbers in the array named `miles`: 15, 22, 16, 18, 27, 23, 20. Have your program copy the data stored in `miles` to another array named `dist` and then display the values in the `dist` array.

5. Write a C++ program that stores the following letters in the array named `message`: `This is a test`. Have your program copy the data stored in `message` to another array named `mess2` and then display the letters in the `mess2` array.

6. Write a C++ program that declares three single-dimensional arrays named `miles`, `gallons`, and `mpg`. Each array should be capable of holding ten elements. In the `miles` array store the numbers 240.5, 300.0, 189.6, 310.6, 280.7, 216.9, 199.4, 160.3, 177.4, 192.3. In the `gallons` array store the numbers 10.3, 15.6, 8.7, 14, 16.3, 15.7, 14.9, 10.7, 8.3, 8.4. Each element of the `mpg` array should be calculated as the corresponding element of the `miles` array divided by the equivalent element of the `gallons` array; for example, `mpg[0] = miles[0] / gallons[0]`. Use pointers when calculating and displaying the elements of the `mpg` array.

9.4   Passing Addresses

We have already seen one method of passing addresses to a function. This was accomplished using reference variables, as was described in Section 6.3. Although passing reference variables to a function provides the function with the address of the passed variables, it is an implied use of addresses because the function call does not reveal the fact that reference parameters are being used. For example, the function call `swap(num1, num2);` does not reveal whether `num1` or `num2` is passed by value or reference. Only when one looks at the function prototype for these variables or examines the function header line for swap() is the type of pass revealed.

In contrast to implicitly passing addresses using references, addresses can be explicitly passed using pointer variables. Let us see how this is accomplished.

To explicitly pass an address to a function, all we need to do is place the address operator, &, in front of the variable being passed. For example, the function call

```
swap(&firstnum, &secnum);
```

passes the addresses of the variables firstnum and secnum to swap(), as illustrated in Figure 9.18. Explicitly passing addresses using the address operator effectively is a **pass by reference** because the called function can reference, or access, variables in the calling function using the passed addresses. As we saw in Section 6.3, calls by reference are also accomplished using reference parameters. Here we will use the passed addresses and pointers to directly access the variables firstnum and secnum from within swap() and exchange their values—a procedure that was previously accomplished in Program 6.10 using reference parameters.

One of the first requirements in writing swap() is to construct a function header line that correctly receives and stores the passed values, which in this case are two addresses. As we saw in Section 9.1, addresses are stored in pointers, which means that the parameters of swap() must be declared as pointers. Assuming that firstnum and secnum are double-precision variables and that swap() returns no value, a suitable function header line for swap() is

```
void swap(double *nm1Addr, double *nm2Addr)
```

FIGURE 9.18 *Explicitly Passing Addresses to* swap()

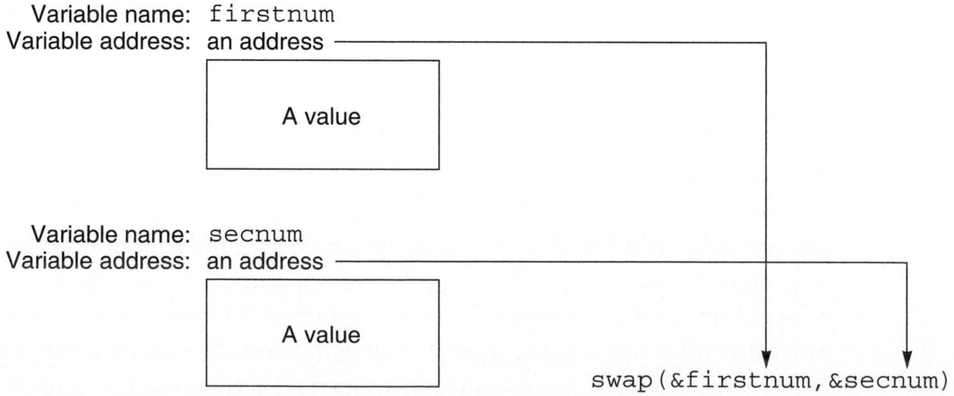

Variable name: firstnum
Variable address: an address ─────────────────────

A value

Variable name: secnum
Variable address: an address ─────────────────────

A value

swap(&firstnum,&secnum)

The choice of the parameter names nm1Addr and nm2Addr is, as with all parameter names, up to the programmer. The declaration double *nm1Addr, however, declares that the parameter named nm1Addr will be used to store the address of a double-precision value. Similarly, the declaration double *nm2Addr declares that nm2Addr will also store the address of a double-precision value.

Before writing the body of swap() to exchange the values in firstnum and secnum, let's first check that the values accessed using the addresses in nm1Addr and nm2Addr are correct. This is done in Program 9.10.

Program 9.10

```cpp
#include <iostream>
using namespace std;

void swap(double *, double *);    // function prototype
int main()
{
  double firstnum = 20.5, secnum = 6.25;

  swap(&firstnum, &secnum);        // call swap

  return 0;
}

void swap(double *nm1Addr, double *nm2Addr)
{
  cout << "The number whose address is in nm1Addr is "
       << *nm1Addr << endl;
  cout << "The number whose address is in nm2Addr is "
       << *nm2Addr << endl;

  return;
}
```

The output displayed when Program 9.10 is run is

```
The number whose address is in nm1Addr is 20.5
The number whose address is in nm2Addr is 6.25
```

In reviewing Program 9.10, note two things. First, the function prototype for swap(),

```
void swap(double *, double *)
```

declares that swap() returns no value directly and that its parameters are two pointers that "point to" double-precision values. Thus, when the function is called, it will require that two addresses be passed and that each address be the address of a double-precision value.

The second item to note is that within swap() the indirection operator is used to access the values stored in firstnum and secnum. swap() itself has no knowledge of these variable names, but it does have the address of firstnum stored in nm1Addr and the address of secnum stored in nm2Addr. The expression *nm1Addr used in the first cout statement means "the variable whose address is in nm1Addr." This is of course the variable firstnum. Similarly, the second cout statement obtains the value stored in secnum as "the variable whose address is in nm2Addr." Thus we have successfully used pointers to allow swap() to access variables in main(). Figure 9.19 illustrates the concept of storing addresses in parameters.

FIGURE 9.19   *Storing Addresses in Parameters*

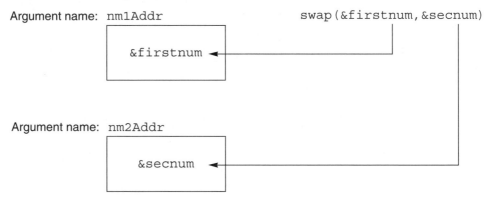

Having verified that swap() can access main()'s local variables firstnum and secnum, we can now expand swap() to exchange the values in these variables. The values in main()'s variables firstnum and secnum can be interchanged from within swap() using the three-step interchange algorithm described in Section 6.3, which for convenience we repeat here:

1. *Store* firstnum's *value in a temporary location.*
2. *Store* secnum's *value in* firstnum.
3. *Store the temporary value in* secnum.

Using pointers from within swap(), this takes the form:

1. Store the value of the variable pointed to by nm1Addr in a temporary location. The statement temp = *nm1Addr; does this (see Figure 9.20).
2. Store the value of the variable whose address is in nm2Addr in the variable whose address is in nm1Addr. The statement *nm1Addr = *nm2Addr; does this (see Figure 9.21).
3. Move the value in the temporary location into the variable whose address is in nm2Addr. The statement *nm2Addr = temp; does this (see Figure 9.22).

Program 9.11 contains the final form of swap(), written according to our description.

Program 9.11

```cpp
#include <iostream>
using namespace std;

void swap(double *, double *);    // function prototype

int main()
{
  double firstnum = 20.5, secnum = 6.25;

  cout << "The value stored in firstnum is: " << firstnum << endl;
  cout << "The value stored in secnum is: " << secnum << "\n\n";

  swap(&firstnum, &secnum);    // call swap

  cout << "The value stored in firstnum is now: " << firstnum << endl;
  cout << "The value stored in secnum is now: " << secnum << endl;

  return 0;
}

void swap(double *nm1Addr, double *nm2Addr)
{
  double temp;

  temp = *nm1Addr;             // save firstnum's value
  *nm1Addr = *nm2Addr;         // move secnum's value in firstnum
  *nm2Addr = temp;             // change secnum's value

  return;
}
```

FIGURE 9.20   *Indirectly Storing* firstnum*'s Value*

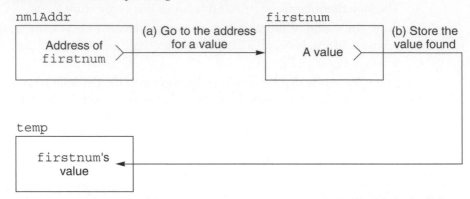

FIGURE 9.21   *Indirectly Changing* firstnum*'s Value*

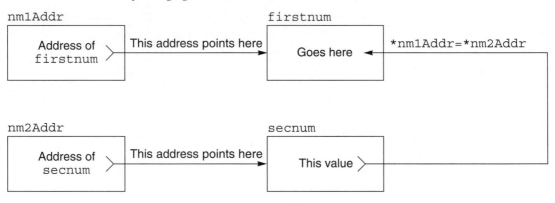

FIGURE 9.22   *Indirectly Changing* secnum*'s Value*

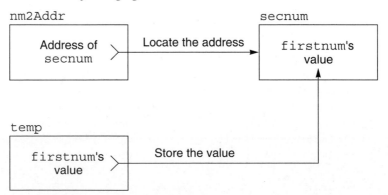

The following sample run was obtained using Program 9.11:

```
The value stored in firstnum is: 20.5
The value stored in secnum is: 6.25

The value stored in firstnum is now: 6.25
The value stored in secnum is now: 20.5
```

As illustrated in this output, the values stored in `main()`'s variables have been modified from within `swap()`, which was made possible by the use of pointers. The interested reader should compare this version of `swap()` with the version using references that was presented in Program 6.10. The advantage of using pointers rather than references is that the function call itself explicitly designates that addresses are being used, which directly alerts you that the function will probably alter variables of the calling function. The advantage of using references is that the notation is much simpler.

Generally, for functions such as `swap()`, the notational convenience wins out and references are used. In passing arrays to functions, however, which is our next topic, the compiler explicitly passes an address. This dictates that a pointer parameter be used to store the address.

Passing Arrays

When an array is passed to a function, its address is the only item actually passed. By this we mean the address of the first location used to store the array, as illustrated in Figure 9.23. Because the first location reserved for an array corresponds to element 0 of the array, the "address of the array" is also the address of element 0.

For a specific example in which an array is passed to a function, consider Program 9.12. In this program, the `nums` array is passed to the `findMax()` function using conventional array notation.

FIGURE 9.23   *The Address of an Array Is the Address of the First Location Reserved for the Array*

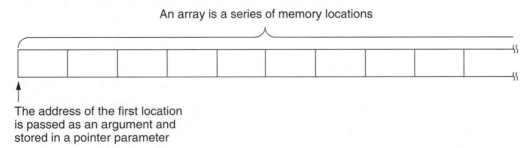

An array is a series of memory locations

The address of the first location
is passed as an argument and
stored in a pointer parameter

Program 9.12

```cpp
#include <iostream>
using namespace std;

int findMax(int [], int);            // function prototype

int main()
{
  const int NUMPTS = 5;
  int nums[NUMPTS] = {2, 18, 1, 27, 16};

  cout << "\nThe maximum value is "
       << findMax(nums,NUMPTS) << endl;

  return 0;
}
int findMax(int vals[], int numels) // find the maximum value
{
  int i, max = vals[0];

  for (i = 1; i < numels; i++)
    if (max < vals[i]) max = vals[i];

  return max;
}
```

The output displayed when Program 9.12 is executed is

```
The maximum value is 27
```

The parameter named vals in the header line declaration for findMax() actually receives the address of the array nums. Thus, vals is really a pointer, because pointers are variables (or parameters) used to store addresses. The address passed into findMax() is the address of an integer, so another suitable header line for findMax() is

```cpp
int findMax(int *vals, int NUMELS)  // here vals is declared as
                                    // a pointer to an integer
```

The declaration int *vals in the header line declares that vals is used to store an address of an integer. The address stored is, of course, the location of the beginning of an array.

The following rewritten version of the `findMax()` function uses a pointer declaration for `vals` but retains the use of subscripts to refer to individual array elements.

```
int findMax(int *vals, int NUMELS)    // find the maximum value
{
  int i, max = vals[0];

  for (i = 1; i < NUMELS; i++)
    if (max < vals[i]) max = vals[i];

  return max;
}
```

Regardless of how `vals` is declared in the function header or how it is used within the function body, it is truly a pointer. Thus the address in `vals` may be modified. This is not true for the name nums. Because nums is the name of the originally created array, it is a pointer constant. As described in Section 9.2, this means that the address in nums cannot be changed and that the address of nums itself cannot be taken. No such restrictions, however, apply to the pointer variable named `vals`. All the address arithmetic that we learned in the previous section can be legitimately applied to `vals`.

We shall write two additional versions of `findMax()`, both of which use pointers instead of subscripts. In the first version, we simply substitute pointer notation for subscript notation. In the second version, we use address arithmetic to change the address in the pointer.

As previously stated, access to an array element using the subscript notation `array_name[i]` can always be replaced by the pointer notation `*(array_name + i)`. In our first modification to `findMax()`, we use this correspondence by simply replacing all references to `vals[i]` with the equivalent expression `*(vals + i)`:

```
int findMax(int *vals, int NUMELS)    // find the maximum value
{
  int i, max = *vals;

  for (i = 1; i < NUMELS; i++)
    if (max < *(vals + i) ) max = *(vals + i);

  return max;
}
```

Our next version of findMax() uses the fact that the address stored in vals can be changed. After each array element is retrieved using the address in vals, the address itself is incremented by 1 in the altering list of the for statement. The expression max = *vals previously used to set max to the value of vals[0] is replaced by the expression max = *vals++, which adjusts the address in vals to point to the second element in the array. The element assigned to max by this expression is the array element pointed to by vals before vals is incremented. The postfix increment, ++, does not change the address in vals until after the address has been used to retrieve the array element.

```
int findMax(int *vals, int NUMELS)  // find the maximum value
{
  int i, max = *vals++;  // get the first element and increment
  for (i = 1; i < NUMELS; i++, vals++)
  {
    if (max < *vals) max = *vals;
  }

  return max;
}
```

Let us review this version of findMax(). Initially the maximum value is set to "the thing pointed to by vals." Because vals initially contains the address of the first element in the array passed to findMax(), the value of this first element is stored in max. The address in vals is then incremented by 1. The 1 that is added to vals is automatically scaled by the number of bytes used to store integers. Thus, after the increment, the address stored in vals is the address of the next array element. This is illustrated in Figure 9.24. The value of this next element is compared to the maximum, and the address is again incremented, this time from within the altering list of the for statement. This process continues until all the array elements have been examined.

FIGURE 9.24 *Pointing to Different Elements*

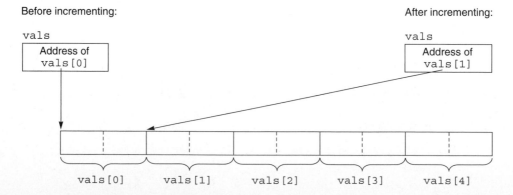

Before incrementing:

After incrementing:

Which version of `findMax()` appeals to you is a matter of personal style and taste. Generally, beginning programmers feel more at ease using subscripts than using pointers. Also, if the program uses an array as the natural storage structure for the application and data at hand, an array access using subscripts is more appropriate to indicate clearly the intent of the program. However, as we learn about strings and data structures, we will see that the use of pointers becomes an increasingly powerful tool in its own right. In these instances, there is no simple or equivalent way to use subscripts.

One further "neat trick" can be gleaned from our discussion. Because passing an array to a function really involves passing an address, we can just as well pass any valid address. For example, the function call `findMax(&nums[2],3)` passes the address of `nums[2]` to `findMax()`. Within `findMax()` the pointer `vals` stores the address, and the function starts the search for a maximum at the element corresponding to this address. Thus, from `findMax()`'s perspective, it has received an address and proceeds appropriately.

Advanced Pointer Notation[8]

Access to multidimensional arrays can also be made using pointer notation, although the notation becomes more and more cryptic as the array dimensions increase. An extremely useful application of this notation occurs with two-dimensional character arrays, one of the topics of the next chapter. Here we consider pointer notation for two-dimensional numeric arrays. For example, consider the declaration

```
int nums[2][3] = { {16,18,20},
                   {25,26,27} };
```

This declaration creates an array of elements and a set of pointer constants named `nums`, `nums[0]`, and `nums[1]`. The relationship between these pointer constants and the elements of the `nums` array is illustrated in Figure 9.25.

The availability of the pointer constants associated with a two-dimensional array enables us to access array elements in a variety of ways. One way is to consider the two-dimensional array as an array of rows, where each row is itself an array of three elements. Considered in this light, the address of the first element in the first row is provided by `nums[0]`, and the address of the first element in the second row is provided by `nums[1]`. Thus the variable pointed to by `nums[0]` is `num[0][0]`, and the variable pointed to by `nums[1]` is `num[1][0]`.

---

[8] This topic may be omitted without loss of subject continuity.

FIGURE 9.25   *Storage of the* nums *Array and Associated Pointer Constants*

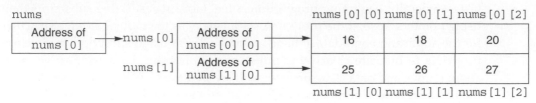

Once the nature of these constants is understood, each element in the array can be accessed by applying an appropriate offset to the appropriate pointer. Thus the following notations are equivalent:

Pointer Notation	Subscript Notation	Value
*nums[0]	nums[0][0]	16
*(nums[0] + 1)	nums[0][1]	18
*(nums[0] + 2)	nums[0][2]	20
*nums[1]	nums[1][0]	25
*(nums[1] + 1)	nums[1][1]	26
*(nums[1] + 2)	nums[1][2]	27

We can now go even further and replace nums[0] and nums[1] with their respective pointer notations, using the address of nums itself. As illustrated in Figure 9.25, the variable pointed to by nums is nums[0]. That is, *nums is nums[0]. Similarly, *(nums + 1) is nums[1]. Using these relationships leads to the following equivalences:

Pointer Notation	Subscript Notation	Value
*(*nums)	nums[0][0]	16
*(*nums + 1)	nums[0][1]	18
*(*nums + 2)	nums[0][2]	20
((nums + 1))	nums[1][0]	25
((nums + 1) + 1)	nums[1][1]	26
((nums + 1) + 2)	nums[1][2]	27

The same notation applies when a two-dimensional array is passed to a function. For example, assume that the two-dimensional array nums is passed to the function calc() using the call calc(nums);. Here, as with all array passes, an address is passed. A suitable function header line for the function calc() is

```
calc(int pt[2][3])
```

As we have already seen, the parameter declaration for pt can also be

```
calc(int pt[][3])
```

Using pointer notation, another suitable declaration is

```
calc(int (*pt)[3])
```

In this last declaration, the inner parentheses are required to create a single pointer to arrays of three integers. Each array is, of course, equivalent to a single row of the nums array. By suitably offsetting the pointer, we can access each element in the array. Note that without the parentheses, the declaration becomes

```
int *pt[3]
```

which creates an array of three pointers, each one pointing to a single integer.

Once the correct declaration for pt is made (any of the three valid declarations can be used), the following notations within the function calc() are all equivalent:

Pointer Notation	Subscript Notation	Value
*(*pt)	pt[0][0]	16
*(*pt+1)	pt[0][1]	18
*(*pt+2)	pt[0][2]	20
((pt+1))	pt[1][0]	25
((pt+1)+1)	pt[1][1]	26
((pt+1)+2)	pt[1][2]	27

The last two notations using pointers are encountered in more advanced C++ programs. The first of these occurs because functions can return any valid C++

scalar data type, including pointers to any of these data types. If a function returns a pointer, the data type being pointed to must be declared in the function's declaration. For example, the declaration

$$\text{int *calc()}$$

declares that `calc()` returns a pointer to an integer value. This means that an address of an integer variable is returned. Similarly, the declaration

$$\text{double *taxes()}$$

declares that `taxes()` returns a pointer to a floating-point value. This means that an address of a double-precision variable is returned.

In addition to declaring pointers to integers, floating-point numbers, and C++'s other data types, pointers can also be declared that point to (contain the address of) a function. Pointers to functions are possible because function names, like array names, are themselves pointer constants. For example, the declaration

$$\text{int (*calc)()}$$

declares `calc()` to be a pointer to a function that returns an integer. This means that `calc` will contain the address of a function, and the function whose address is in the variable `calc` returns an integer value. If, for example, the function `sum()` returns an integer, the assignment `calc = sum;` is valid.

▌ EXERCISES 9.4

1. The following declaration was used to create the `prices` array:

    double prices[500];

    Write three different header lines for a function named `sortArray()` that accepts the `prices` array as an argument named `inArray` and returns no value.

2. The following declaration was used to create the `keys` array:

    char keys[256];

    Write three different header lines for a function named `findKey()` that accepts the `keys` array as an argument named `select` and returns no value.

3. The following declaration was used to create the `rates` array:

`double rates[256];`

Write three different header lines for a function named `prime()` that accepts the `rates` array as an argument named `rates` and returns a double-precision value.

4. Modify the `findMax()` function to locate the minimum value of the passed array. Write the function using only pointers.

5. In the last version of `findMax()` presented, `vals` was incremented inside the altering list of the `for` statement. Instead, suppose that the incrementing was done within the condition expression of the `if` statement, as follows:

```
int findMax(int *vals, int NUMELS)    // incorrect version
{
  int i, max = *vals++;               // get the first element and increment
  for (i = 1; i < NUMELS; i++)
  {
    if (max < *vals++) max = *vals;
  }
  return max;
}
```

This version produces an incorrect result. Determine why.

6. a. Write a program that has a declaration in `main()` to store the following numbers into an array named `rates`: 6.5, 7.2, 7.5, 8.3, 8.6, 9.4, 9.6, 9.8, 10.0. There should be a function call to `show()` that accepts `rates` in a parameter argument named `rates` and then displays the numbers using the pointer notation `* (rates + i)`.
b. Modify the `show()` function written in Exercise 6a to alter the address in `rates`. Always use the expression `*rates` rather than `* (rates + i)` to retrieve the correct element.

7. a. Write a program that has a declaration in `main()` to store the string `Vacation is near` into an array named `message`. There should be a function call to `display()` that accepts `message` in an argument named `strng` and then displays the message using the pointer notation `* (strng + i)`.
b. Modify the `display()` function written in Exercise 7a to alter the address in `message`. Always use the expression `*strng` rather than `* (strng + i)` to retrieve the correct element.

8. Write a program that declares three single-dimensional arrays named `price`, `quantity`, and `amount`. Each array should be declared in `main()` and should be capable of holding ten double-precision numbers. The numbers to be stored in `price` are 10.62, 14.89, 13.21, 16.55, 18.62, 9.47, 6.58, 18.32, 12.15, 3.98. The numbers to be stored in `quantity` are 4, 8.5, 6, 7.35, 9, 15.3, 3, 5.4, 2.9, 4.8. Have your program pass these three arrays to a function called `extend()`, which calculates the elements in the `amount` array as the product of the equivalent elements in the `price` and `quantity` arrays (for example, `amount[1]` = `price[1] * quantity[1]`).

After `extend()` has put values into the `amount` array, display the values in the array from within `main()`. Write the `extend()` function using pointers.

9. *a.* Determine the output of the following program:

```cpp
#include <iostream>

const int ROWS = 2;
const int COLS = 3;
void arr(int [][COLS]);     // function prototype
int main()
{
   int nums[ROWS][COLS] = { {33,16,29},
                            {54,67,99}};

   arr(nums);

   return 0;
}

void arr(int (*val)[3])
{
   cout << *(*val) << endl;
   cout << *(*val + 1) << endl;
   cout << *(*(val + 1) + 2) << endl;
   cout << *(*val) + 1 << endl;

   return;
}
```

b. Given the declaration for `val` in the `arr()` function, would the notation `val[1][2]` be valid within the function?

9.5   Common Programming Errors

In using the material presented in this chapter, be aware of the following possible errors:

1. Attempting to explicitly store an address in a variable that has not been declared as a pointer.

2. Using a pointer to access nonexistent array elements. For example, if `nums` is an array of ten integers, then the expression `*(nums + 10)` points one integer location beyond the last element of the array. Most C++ compilers do not do

any bounds checking on array accesses, so this type of error is not caught by the compiler. This is the same error, disguised in pointer notation form, as using a subscript to access an out-of-bounds array element.

3. Incorrectly applying the address and indirection operators. For example, if pt is a pointer variable, the expressions

```
pt = &45
pt = &(miles + 10)
```

are both invalid because they attempt to take the address of a value. Note that the expression pt = &miles + 10, however, is valid. Here, 10 is added to the address of miles. Again, it is the programmer's responsibility to ensure that the final address "points to" a valid data element.

4. Taking addresses of a register variable. Thus, for the declarations

```
register int total;
int *ptTot;
```

the assignment

```
ptTot = &total;     // INVALID
```

is invalid. The reason is that register variables are stored in a computer's internal registers, and these storage areas do not have standard memory addresses.

5. Taking addresses of pointer constants. For example, given the declarations

```
int nums[25];

int *pt;
```

the assignment

```
pt = &nums;
```

is invalid. nums is a pointer constant that is itself equivalent to an address. The correct assignment is pt = nums.

6. Initializing pointer variables incorrectly. For example, the initialization

```
int *pt = 5;
```

is invalid. Because pt is a pointer to an integer, it must be initialized with a valid address.

7. Becoming confused about whether a variable *contains* an address or *is* an address. Pointer variables and pointer arguments contain addresses. Although a pointer constant is synonymous with an address, it is useful to treat pointer constants as pointer variables with two restrictions:

- The address of a pointer constant cannot be taken.
- The address "contained in" the pointer constant cannot be altered.

Except for these two restrictions, pointer constants and variables can be used almost interchangeably. Therefore, when an address is required, any of the following can be used:

- a pointer variable name
- a pointer argument name
- a pointer constant name
- a nonpointer variable name preceded by the address operator (such as, &variable)
- a nonpointer argument name preceded by the address operator (such as, &argument)

Some of the confusion surrounding pointers is caused by the cavalier use of the word *pointer*. For example, the phrase "a function requires a pointer argument" is more clearly understood when we realize that it really means "a function requires an address as an argument." Similarly, the phrase "a function returns a pointer" really means "a function returns an address."

If you are ever in doubt about what is really contained in a variable or how it should be treated, use the cout object to display the contents of the variable, the "thing pointed to," or "the address of the variable." Seeing what is displayed frequently helps sort out what is really in the variable.

8. Forgetting to use the bracket set, [], following the delete operator when dynamically deallocating memory that was previously allocated using the new [] operator

9.6   *Chapter Summary*

1. Every variable has a data type, an address, and a value. In C++ the address of a variable can be obtained by using the address operator, &.

2. A pointer is a variable that is used to store the address of another variable. Pointers, like all C++ variables, must be declared. The indirection operator, *, is used both to declare a pointer variable and to access the variable whose address is stored in a pointer.

3. An array name is a pointer constant. The value of the pointer constant is the address of the first element in the array. Thus, if `val` is the name of an array, `val` and `&val[0]` can be used interchangeably.

4. Any access to an array element using subscript notation can always be replaced using pointer notation. That is, the notation `a[i]` can always be replaced by the notation `*(a + i)`. This is true whether `a` was initially declared explicitly as an array or as a pointer.

5. Arrays can be dynamically created as a program is executing. For example, the sequence of statements

```
cout << "Enter the array size: ";
cin  >> num;
int *grades = new int[num];
```

creates an array named `grades` of size `num`. The area allocated for the array can be dynamically destroyed using the `delete` operator. For example, the statement `delete grades;` will return the allocated area for the `grades` array to the computer.

6. Arrays are passed to functions as addresses. The called function always receives direct access to the originally declared array elements.

7. When a single-dimensional array is passed to a function, the parameter declaration for the function can be either an array declaration or a pointer declaration. Thus the following parameter declarations are equivalent:

```
double a[];
double *a;
```

8. Pointers can be incremented, decremented, compared, and assigned. Numbers added to or subtracted from a pointer are automatically scaled. The scale factor used is the number of bytes required to store the data type originally pointed to.

CHAPTER 10

Strings as Character Arrays

C++ has two different ways of storing and manipulating strings. The second, and newer way, using the string class was presented in Chapter 7. The original procedure for storing a string in C++, and the one described in this chapter, is as an array of characters that is terminated by a sentinel value, which is the escape sequence `'\0'`. This representation permits strings to be manipulated using standard element-by-element array-processing techniques. Strings stored in this manner are now referred to as character strings, or C-strings, for short. Additionally, a `cstring` class was introduced with the latest ANSI/ISO standard that provides a number of useful methods, such as inserting, deleting, and extracting characters from a C-string. This class is also presented in this chapter. Finally, the character-based methods previously presented in Chapter 7, which can also be used to process individual elements of C-strings, are summarized in this chapter.

10.1   C-string Fundamentals

A string literal, informally referred to as a string, is any sequence of characters enclosed in double quotes. For example, `"This is a string"`, `"Hello World!"`, and `"xyz 123 *!#@&"` are all strings.

A string is stored as an array of characters terminated by a special end-of-string marker called the NULL character. The NULL character, represented by the escape sequence \0, is the sentinel marking the end of the string. For example, Figure 10.1 illustrates how the string `"Good Morning!"` is stored in memory. The string uses 14 storage locations, the last character in the string being the end-of-string marker \0. The double quotes are not stored as part of the string.

Because a string is stored as an array of characters, the individual characters in the array can be input, manipulated, or output using standard array-handling techniques that utilize either subscript or pointer notation. When we are handling strings in this fashion, the end-of-string NULL character is useful for detecting the end of the string.

FIGURE 10.1   *Storing a String in Memory*

G	o	o	d		M	o	r	n	i	n	g	!	\0

C-string Input and Output

Inputting a string from a keyboard and displaying a string requires using either a standard library function or class method. In addition to the standard input and output streams, `cin` and `cout`, Table 10.1 lists the commonly used library methods for both character-by-character and complete C-string input/output. These are contained in the `iostream` header file.

TABLE 10.1 *String and Character I/O Functions (Requires the iostream Header File)*

C++ Routine	Description	Example
`cin.getline(str, n, ch)`	C-string input from the keyboard	`cin.getline(str, 81,'\n');`
`cin.get()`	Character input from the keyboard	`nextChar = cin.get();`
`cin.peek()`	Return the next character from the input stream without extracting it from the stream.	`nextKey = cin.peek();`
`cout.put(charExp)`	Place the character on the output stream	`cout.put('A');`
`cin.putback(charExp)`	Push a character back onto the input stream.	`cin.putback(cKey);`
`cin.ignore(n, char)`	Ignore a maximum of the next n input characters, up to and including the detection of char. If no arguments are specified, ignore the next character on the input stream.	`cin.ignore(80,'\n');` `cin.ignore();`

As listed in Table 10.1, in addition to the `cout` and `cin` streams, C++ provides the methods, `cin.getline()`, `cin.get()`, and `cin.peek()` input (these are not the same as the methods defined for the string class having the same name). The character output functions, `put()` and `putback()`, however, are the same as those provided for the `string` class.

Program 10.1 illustrates using `cin.getline()` and `cout` to input and output a string entered at the user's terminal.

The following is a sample run of Program 10.1:

```
Enter a string:
This is a test input of a string of characters.
The string just entered is:
This is a test input of a string of characters.
```

The `cin.getline()` method used in Program 10.1 continuously accepts and stores characters typed at the terminal into the character array named `message` until either 80 characters are entered (the 81st character is then used to store the end-of string NULL character, \0), or the ENTER key is detected. Pressing the ENTER key at the terminal generates a newline character, \n, which is interpreted by `cin.getline()` as the end-of-line entry. All the characters encountered by `cin.getline()`, except the newline character, are stored in the `message` array.

Before returning, the `cin.getline()` function appends a NULL character, `'\0'`, to the stored set of characters, as illustrated in Figure 10.2. The `cout` object is then used to display the C-string.

Program 10.1

```
#include <iostream>
using namespace std;

int main ()
{
  const int MAXCHARS  =  81;
  char message [MAXCHARS];  // an array of characters large
                            // enough storage for a complete line

  cout << "Enter a string:\n";

  cin.getline(message,MAXCHARS,  '\n');

  cout << "The string just entered is:\n"
       << message << endl;

  cin.ignore();
  return 0;
}
```

FIGURE 10.2 *Inputting a C-string with* `cin.getline()`

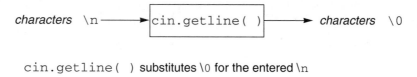

Although the `cout` object is used in Program 10.1 for C-string output, `cin` could not be used in place of `cin.getline()` for C-string input. This is because the `cin` object reads a set of characters up to either a blank space or a newline character. The `cin.getline()` function has the syntax.

```
cin.getline(str, terminatingLength, terminatingChar)
```

PROGRAMMING NOTE

Should You Use a string Class Object or a C-string?

The reasons for using a string class object are:
- The string class does an automatic bounds check on every index used to access string elements. This is not true for C-strings, and using an invalid C-string index can result in a system crash.
- The string class automatically expands and contracts storage as needed. C-strings are fixed in length and are subject to overrunning the allocated storage space.
- The string class provides a rich set of methods for operating on a string. C-strings almost always require a subsidiary set of functions.
- When necessary, it is easy to convert to a C-string using the string class' c_str () method. Conversely, a C-string can easily be converted to a string class object by assigning it to a string object.

The reasons for using a C-string are:
- The programmer has ultimate control over how the string is stored and manipulated.
- A large number of extremely useful functions exist to input, examine, and process C-strings.
- C-strings are an excellent way to explore advanced programming techniques using pointers (see Chapter 14).
- You will encounter them throughout your programming career, as they are embedded in almost all existing C++ code.
- They are fun to program.

where *str* is a C-string or character pointer variable (presented in Chapter 14), *terminatingLength* is an integer constant or variable indicating the maximum number of input characters that can be input, and *terminatingChar* is an optional character constant or variable specifying the terminating character. If this optional third argument is omitted, the default terminating character is the newline (' \n ') character. Thus, the statement

```
cin.getline(message, MAXCHARS);
```

can be used in place of the longer statement

```
cin.getline(message, MAXCHARS, '\n');
```

Both of these function calls stop reading characters when the ENTER key is pressed or until MAXCHARS characters have been read, whichever comes first. Since cin.getline() permits specification of any terminating character for the input stream a statement such as cin.getline(message, MAXCHARS, 'x'); is also valid. This particular statement will stop accepting character whenever the x key is pressed. In all future programs we will assume that input is terminated by the ENTER key, which generates a newline character. As such the optional third argument passed to `getline()`, which is the terminating character, will be omitted.

C-string Processing

C-strings can be manipulated by using either standard library functions or standard array-processing techniques. The library functions typically available for use are presented in the next section. For now, we will concentrate on processing a string in a character-by-character fashion. This will allow us to understand how the standard library functions are constructed and to create our own library functions. For a specific example, consider the function `strcopy()` that copies the contents of `string2` to `string1`.

```
// copy string2 to string1
void strcopy(char string1[], char string2[])
{
  int i = 0;                          // i will be used as a subscript

  while ( string2[i] != '\0')   // check for the end-of-string
  {
    string1[i] = string2[i];    // copy the element to string1
    i++;
  }
  string1[i] = '\0';              // terminate the first string
  return;
}
```

Although this string copy function can be shortened considerably and written more compactly, which is done in Section 10.2, it does illustrate the main features of string manipulation. The two strings are passed to `strcopy` as arrays. Each element of `string2` is then assigned to the equivalent element of `string1` until the end-of-string marker is encountered. The detection of the null character forces the termination of the `while` loop that controls the copying of elements. Because the NULL character is not copied from `string2` to `string1`, the last statement in `strcopy()` appends an end-of-string character to `string1`. Before calling `strcopy()`, the programmer must ensure that sufficient space has been allocated for the `string1` array to be able to store the elements of the `string2` array. Program 10.2 includes the `strcopy()` function in a complete program. Note that the function prototype for `strcopy()` in `main()` declares that the function expects to receive the addresses of the beginnings of the two character arrays.

Program 10.2

```cpp
#include <iostream>
using namespace std;

void strcopy(char [], char []);  // function prototype

int main()
{
  const int MAXCHARS = 81;
  char message[MAXCHARS];        // enough storage for a complete line
  char newMessage[MAXCHARS];   // enough storage for a copy of message
  int i;

  cout << "Enter a sentence: ";
  cin.getline(message,MAXCHARS);    // get the string
  strcopy(newMessage,message);      // pass two array addresses
  cout << newMessage << endl;

  return 0;
}

void strcopy(char string1[], char string2[])  // copy string2 to string1
{
  int i = 0;                        // i will be used as a subscript

  while (string2[i] != '\0')     // check for the end-of-string
  {
    string1[i] = string2[i];     // copy the element to string1
    i++;
  }
  string1[i] = '\0';               // terminate the first string

  return;
}
```

The following is a sample run of Program 10.2:

```
Enter a sentence: How much wood could a woodchuck chuck.
How much wood could a woodchuck chuck.
```

Character-by-Character Input

Just as C-strings can be processed by means of character-by-character techniques, they can also be entered and displayed in this manner. For example, consider Program 10.3, which uses the character input function `cin.get()` to accept a string one character at a time. The shaded portion of Program 10.3 essentially replaces the `cin.getline()` function previously used in Program 10.1.

 Program 10.3

```
#include <iostream>
using namespace std;

int main()
{
  const int MAXCHARS = 81;
  char message[MAXCHARS], c;

  cout << "Enter a sentence:\n";

  int i = 0;
  while(i < MAXCHARS && (c = cin.get()) ! = '\n')
  {
    message[i] = c;          // store the character entered
    i++;
  }
  message[i] = '\0';         // terminate the string a

  cout << "The sentence just entered is:\n";
  cout << message << endl;

  return 0;
}
```

The following is a sample run of Program 10.3:

```
Enter a sentence:
This is a test input of a string of characters.
The sentence just entered is:
This is a test input of a string of characters.
```

The `while` statement in Program 10.3 causes characters to be read. Provided that the number of characters entered is less than 81 and that the character returned by `cin.get()` is not the newline character, the entered characters will be correctly stored in the `message` array. The parentheses surrounding the expression `c = cin.get()` are necessary to assign the character returned by `cin.get()` to the variable `c` prior to comparing it to the newline escape sequence. Without the surrounding parentheses, the comparison operator, `!=`, which takes precedence over the assignment operator, causes the entire expression to be equivalent to

$$c = (cin.get() \ != \ '\backslash n')$$

which is an invalid application of `cin.get()`.[1]

Program 10.3 also illustrates a useful technique for developing functions. The shaded statements constitute a self-contained unit for entering a complete line of characters from a terminal. These statements can be removed from `main()` and placed together as a new function. Program 10.4 illustrates placing the shaded statements from Program 10.3 in a separate function named `getaline()`. Note that in the process the constant `MAXCHARS` has been placed above the `main()` function. This placement gives this constant a global scope, which makes it available to both the `main()` and the `getaline()` functions.

 Program 10.4

```
#include <iostream>
using namespace std;

const int MAXCHARS = 81;   // global symbolic constant
void getaline(char []);    // function prototype

int main()
{
  char message[MAXCHARS];  // enough storage for a complete line

  cout << "Enter a sentence:\n";
  getaline(message);
  cout << "The sentence just entered is:\n";
  cout << message << endl;
}
```

(continued on next page)

---

[1] The equivalent statement in C is `c= (getchar() != '\n')`, which is a valid expression that produces an unexpected result for most beginning programmers. Here the character returned by `getchar()` is compared to `'\n'`, and the value of the comparison is either 0 or 1, depending on whether or not `getchar()` received the newline character. This value, either 0 or 1, is then assigned to C.

(continued from previous page)

```
void getaline(char strng[])
{
  int i = 0;
  char c;
  while(i < MAXCHARS && (c = cin.get()) != '\n')
  {
    strng[i] = c;     // store the character entered
    i++;
  }
  strng[i] = '\0';    // terminate the string

  return;
}
```

■ **EXERCISES 10.1**

1. *a.* The following function can be used to select and display all vowels contained within a user-input string.

```
void vowels(char strng[])
{
  int i = 0;
  char c;
  while ((c = strng[i++]) != '\0')
    switch(c)
    {
      case 'a':
      case 'e':
      case 'i':
      case 'o':
      case 'u':
        cout << c;
    } // end of switch
  cout << endl;

  return;
}
```

Note that the switch statement in vowels() uses the fact that selected cases "drop through" in the absence of break statements. Thus, all selected cases result in a cout object call. Include vowels() in a working program that accepts a user-input string and then displays all vowels in the string. In response to the input How much is the little worth worth?, your program should display ouieieoo.

b. Modify vowels() to count and display the total number of vowels contained in the string passed to it.

2. Modify the `vowels()` function given in Exercise 1a to count and display the individual numbers of each vowel contained in the string.

3. *a.* Write a C++ function to count the total number of characters, including blanks, contained in a string. Do not include the end-of-string marker in the count.

    b. Include the function written for Exercise 3a in a complete working program.

4. Write a program that accepts a string of characters from a terminal and displays the hexadecimal equivalent of each character.

5. Write a C++ program that accepts a string of characters from a terminal and displays the string one word per line.

6. Write a function that reverses the characters in a string. (*Hint:* This can be considered as a string copy starting from the back end of the first string.)

7. Write a function called `delChar()` that can be used to delete characters from a string. The function should take three arguments: the string name, the number of characters to delete, and the starting position in the string where characters should be deleted. For example, the function call `delChar(strng,13,5)` , when applied to the string `all enthusiastic people`, should result in the string `all people`.

8. Write a function call `addChar()` to insert one string of characters into another string. The function should take three arguments: the string to be inserted, the original string, and the position in the original string where the insertion should begin. For example, the call `addChar("for all",message,6)` should insert the characters `for all` in `message` starting at `message[5]`.

9. *a.* Write a C++ function named `ToUpper()` that converts lowercase letters to uppercase letters. The expression `c - 'a' + 'A'` can be used to make the conversion for any lowercase character stored in `c`.

    b. Add a data input check to the function written in Exercise 9a to verify that a valid lowercase letter is passed to the function. A character in ASCII is lowercase if it is greater than or equal to a and less than or equal to z. If the character is not a valid lowercase letter, have the function `ToUpper()` return the passed character unaltered.

    c. Write a C++ program that accepts a string from a terminal and converts all lowercase letters in the string to uppercase letters.

10. Write a C++ program that accepts a string from a terminal and converts all uppercase letters in the string to lowercase letters.

11. Write a C++ program that counts the number of words in a string. A word is encountered whenever a transition from a blank space to a nonblank character is encountered. Assume that the string contains only words separated by blank spaces.

10.2   Pointers and C-string Library Functions

Pointers are exceptionally useful in constructing functions that manipulate C-strings (recall that the term C-string is short for character string, and consists of text stored in a character array whose last character is `'\0'`). When pointer notation is used in place of subscripts to access individual characters in a C-string, the resulting statements are both more compact and more efficient. In this section, we describe the equivalence between subscripts and pointers when accessing individual characters in a C-string.

Consider the strcopy() function introduced in the previous section. This function was used to copy the characters of one C-string to a second C-string. For convenience, this function is repeated below.

```
void strcopy(char string1[], char string2[])  // copy string2 to string1
{
  int i = 0;

  while (string2[i] != '\0')     // check for the end-of-string
  {
    string1[i] = string2[i];     // copy the element to string1
    i++;
  }
  string1[i] = '\0';             // terminate the first string

  return;
}
```

The function strcopy() is used to copy the characters from one array to another array, one character at a time. As currently written, the subscript i in the function is used successively to access each character in the array named string2 by "marching along" the string one character at a time. Before we write a pointer version of strcopy(), we will make two modifications to the function to make it more efficient.

The while statement in strcopy() tests each character to ensure that the end of the C-string has not been reached. Like all relational expressions, the tested expression, string2[i] != '\0', is either true or false. To take the string this is a string illustrated in Figure 10.3 as an example, as long as string2[i] does not access the end-of-C-string character, the value of the expression is nonzero and is considered to be true. The expression is false only when the value of the expression is zero. This occurs when the last element in the C-string is accessed.

Recall that C++ defines false as zero and true as anything else. Thus the expression string2[i] != '\0' becomes zero, or false, when the end of the string is reached. It is nonzero, or true, everywhere else. The NULL character has an internal value of zero by itself, so the comparison to '\0' is not necessary. When string2[i] accesses the end-of-C-string character, the value of string2[i] is zero. When string2[i] accesses any other character, the value of string2[i] is the value of the code used to store the character and is nonzero. Figure 10.4 lists the ASCII codes for the string this is a string. As the figure shows, each element has a nonzero value except for the NULL character.

FIGURE 10.3   *The* `while` *Test Becomes False at the End of the String*

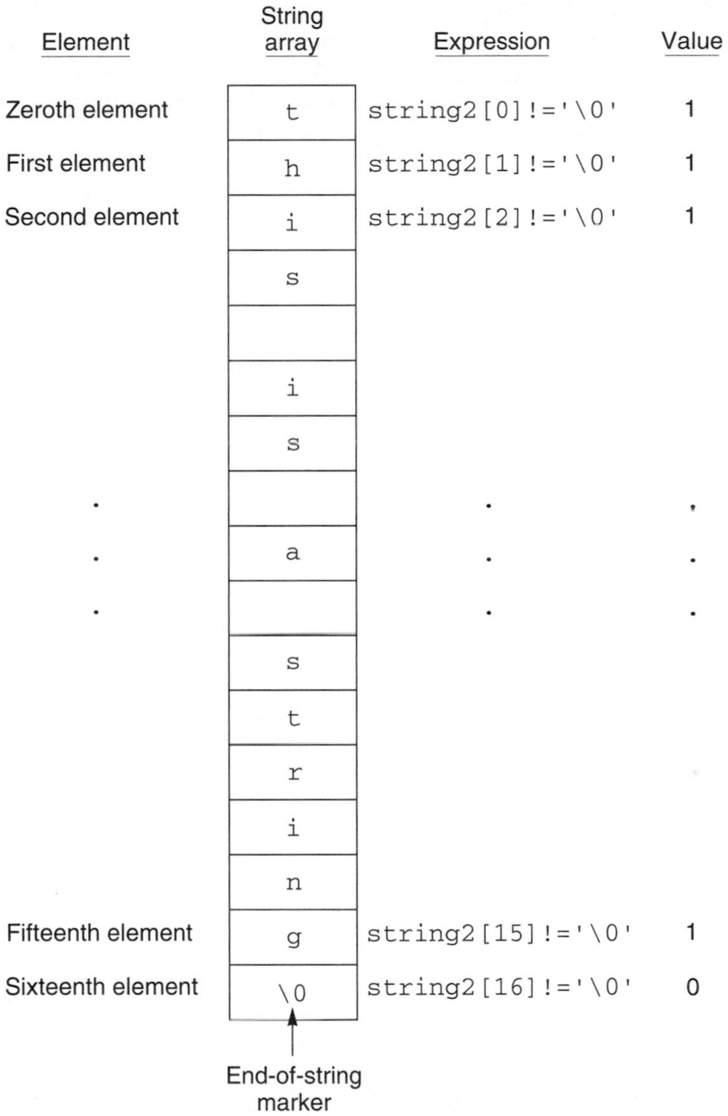

Element	String array	Expression	Value
Zeroth element	t	`string2[0]!='\0'`	1
First element	h	`string2[1]!='\0'`	1
Second element	i	`string2[2]!='\0'`	1
	s		
	i		
	s		
.		.	.
.	a	.	.
.		.	.
	s		
	t		
	r		
	i		
	n		
Fifteenth element	g	`string2[15]!='\0'`	1
Sixteenth element	\0	`string2[16]!='\0'`	0

End-of-string
marker

Because the expression `string2[i]` is zero only at the end of a C-string and is nonzero for every other character, the expression `while (string2[i] != '\0')` can be replaced by the simpler expression `while (string2[i])`. Although this may appear confusing at first, the revised test expression is certainly more compact than the longer version. End-of-C-string tests are frequently written by advanced C++ programmers in this shorter form, so it is worthwhile to be familiar with this expression. Including this expression in `strcopy()` results in the following version of `strcopy()`:

FIGURE 10.4 *The ASCII Codes Used to Store* this is a string

String array	Stored codes	Expression	Value
t	116	string2[0]	116
h	104	string2[1]	104
i	105	string2[2]	105
s	115		
	32		
i	105		
s	115		
	32	.	.
a	97	.	.
	32	.	.
s	115		
t	116		
r	114		
i	105		
n	110		
g	103	string2[15]	103
\0	0	string2[16]	0

```
void strcopy(char string1[], char string2[])  // copy string2 to string1
{
   int i = 0;

   while (string2[i])
   {
     string1[i] = string2[i];  // copy the element to string1
     i++;
   }
   string1[i] = '\0';                // terminate the first string

   return;
}
```

The second modification that can be made to this C-string copy function is to include the assignment inside the test portion of the while statement. Our new version of the C-string copy function is

```
void strcopy(char string1[], char string2[])   // copy string2 to string1
{
  int i = 0;

  while (string1[i] = string2[i])
    i++;

  return;
}
```

Note that including the assignment statement within the test part of the while statement eliminates the necessity of separately terminating the copied string with the null character. The assignment within the parentheses ensures that the null character is copied from string2 to string1. The value of the assignment expression becomes zero only after the NULL character is assigned to string1, at which point the while loop is terminated.

The conversion of strcopy() from subscript notation to pointer notation is now straightforward. Although each subscript version of strcopy() can be rewritten using pointer notation, the following is the equivalent of our last subscript version:

```
void strcopy(char *string1, char *string2)   // copy string2 to string1
{
  while (*string1 = *string2)
  {
    string1++;
    string2++;
  }

  return;
}
```

In both subscript and pointer versions of strcopy(), the function receives the name of the array being passed. Recall that passing an array name to a function actually passes the address of the first location of the array. In our pointer version of strcopy(), the two passed addresses are stored in the pointer parameters string1 and string2, respectively.

The declarations char *string1; and char *string2; used in the pointer version of strcopy() indicate that string1 and string2 are both pointers containing the address of a character, and they stress the treatment of the passed addresses as pointer values rather than array names. These declarations are equivalent to the declarations char string1[] and char string2[], respectively.

Internal to strcopy(), the pointer expression *string1, which refers to "the element whose address is in string1," replaces the equivalent subscript expression string1[i]. Similarly, the pointer expression *string2 replaces the equivalent subscript expression string2[i]. The expression *string1 = *string2 causes the element pointed to by string2 to be assigned to the element pointed to by string1. Because the starting addresses of both C-strings are passed to strcopy() and stored in string1 and string2, respectively, the expression *string1 initially refers to string1[0], and the expression *string2 initially refers to string2[0].

Consecutively incrementing both pointers in strcopy() with the expressions string1++ and string2++ simply causes each pointer to "point to" the next consecutive character in the respective C-string. As with the subscript version, the pointer version of strcopy() steps along, copying element by element, until the end of the string is copied. One final change to the C-string copy function can be made by including the pointer increments as postfix operators within the test part of the while statement. The final form of the C-string copy function is:

```
void strcopy(char *string1, char *string2)   // copy string2 to string1
{
  while (*string1++ = *string2++)
    ;

  return;
}
```

There is no ambiguity in the expression *string1++ = *string2++ even though the indirection operator, *, and the increment operator, ++, have the same precedence. Here the character pointed to is accessed before the pointer is incremented. Only after completion of the assignment *string1 = *string2 are the pointers incremented to point correctly to the next characters in the respective C-strings.

The C-string copy function included in the standard library supplied with C++ compilers is typically written exactly like our pointer version of strcopy().

Library Functions

C++ does not provide built-in operations for complete arrays, such as array assignment or array comparisons. Because a C-string is just an array of characters terminated with a '\0' character, this means that assignment and relational operations *are not* provided for C-strings. Extensive collections of C-string-handling functions and routines, however, that effectively supply C-string assignment, comparison, and other very useful C-string operations are included with all C++ compilers. The more commonly used of these are listed in Table 10.2.

TABLE 10.2 *String Library Routines (Required Header File Is* `cstring`*)*

Name	Description	Example
strcpy(stringVar, stringExp)	Copies `stringExp` to `stringVar`, including the `'\0'`.	strcpy(test, "efgh")
strcat(stringVar, stringExp)	Appends `str_exp` to the end of the string value contained in `stringVar`.	strcat(test, "there")
strlen(stringExp)	Returns the length of the string. Does not include the `'\0'` in the length count.	strlen("Hello World!")
strcmp(stringExp1, stringExp2)	Compares `stringExp1` to `stringExp2`. Returns a negative integer if `stringExp1 < stringExp2`, 0 if `stringExp1 == stringExp2`, and a positive integer if `stringExp1 > stringExp2`.	strcmp("Bebop","Beehive")
strncpy(stringVar, stringExp, n)	Copies at most *n* characters of `stringExp` to `stringVar`. If `stringExp` has fewer than *n* characters, it will pad `stringVar` with `'\0'`'s.	strncpy(str1, str2, 5)
strncmp(stringExp1, stringExp2, n)	Compare at most *n* characters of `stringExp1` to `stringExp2`. Returns the same values as `strcmp()` based on the number of characters compared.	strncmp("Bebop", "Beehive",2)
strchr(stringExp, character)	Locates the first occurrence of the character within the string. Returns the address of the character.	strchr("Hello", 'l')
strtok(string1, character)	Parses `string1` into tokens. Returns the next sequence of characters contained in `string1`, up to but not including the delimiter character `character`.	strtok("Hello there World!, '')

C-string library functions are called in the same manner as all C++ functions. This means that the appropriate declarations for these functions, which are contained in the standard header files <cstring>, must be included in your program before the function is called.

PROGRAMMING NOTE

Initializing and Processing C-strings

All of the following declarations produce the same result.

```
char test[5] = "abcd";
char test[] = "abcd";
char test[5] = {'a', 'b', 'c', 'd', '\0'};
char test[] = {'a', 'b', 'c', 'd', '\0'};
```

Each declaration creates storage for exactly five characters and initializes this storage with the characters 'a', 'b', 'c', 'd', and '\0'. A string literal is used for initialization in the first two declarations, so the compiler automatically supplies the end-of-string null character.

C-string variables declared in either of these ways preclude the use of any subsequent assignments, such as test = "efgh";, to the character array. In place of an assignment, you can use the strcpy() function, such as strcpy(test, "efgh"). The only restriction on using strcpy() is the size of the declared array, which in this case is five elements, cannot be exceeded. Attempting to copy a larger C-string value into test causes the copy to overflow the destination array, beginning with the memory area immediately following the last array element. This overwrites whatever was in these memory locations and typically causes a run-time crash when the overwritten areas are accessed via their legitimate identifier name(s).

The same problem can arise in using the strcat() function. It is your responsibility to ensure that the concatenated C-string will fit into the original string.

An interesting situation arises when C-string variables are defined using pointers (see the Programming Note in Section 10.3). In this situation, assignments can be made after the declaration statement.

The most commonly used functions listed in Table 10.2 are the first four. The strcpy() function copies a source C-string expression, which consists of either a string literal or the contents of a C-string variable, into a destination C-string variable. For example, in the function call strcpy(string1, "Hello World!") the source string literal "Hello World!" is copied into the destination C-string variable string1. Similarly, if the source string is a C-string variable named src_string, the function call strcpy(string1, src_string) copies the contents of src_string into string1. In both cases, it is the programmer's responsibility to ensure that string1 is large enough to contain the source C-string (see the Progamming Note above).

The strcat() function appends a string expression onto the end of a C-string variable. For example, if the contents of a C-string variable named dest_string is "Hello", then the function call strcat(dest_string, " there World!") results in the string value "Hello there World!" being assigned to dest_string. As with the strcpy() function, it is the programmer's responsibility to ensure that the destination C-string has been defined as large enough to hold the additional concatenated characters.

The `strlen()` function returns the number of characters in its C-string parameter but does not include the terminating `NULL` character in the count. For example, the value returned by the function call `strlen("Hello World!")` is 12.

Finally, two C-string expressions may be compared for equality using the `strcmp()` function. Each character in a string is stored in binary using either the ANSI or the UNICODE code. Although these codes are different, they have some characteristics in common: In each of them, a blank precedes (is less than) all letters and numbers; the letters of the alphabet are stored in order from A to Z; all upper-case letters precede the lower-case letters; and the digits are stored in order from 0 to 9. (It is important to note that ANSI uses 8 bits per character, while UNICODE uses 16 bits per character that supports multilingual characters.)

When two C-strings are compared, their individual characters are compared a pair at a time (both first characters, then both second characters, and so on). If no differences are found, the strings are equal; if a difference is found, the string with the first lower character is considered the smaller string. Thus,

> `"Hollo"` is greater than `"Good Bye"` because the first `'H'` in Hello is greater than the first `'G'` in Good Bye.
>
> `"Hello"` is less than `"hello"` because the first `'H'` in Hello is less than the first `'h'` in hello.
>
> `"Hello"` is less than `"Hello "` because the `'\0'` terminating the first string is less than the `' '` in the second string.
>
> `"SMITH"` is greater than `"JONES"` because the first `'S'` in SMITH is greater than the first `'J'` in JONES.
>
> `"123"` is greater than `"1227"` because the third character, the `'3'`, in 123 is greater than the third character, the `'2'`, in 1227.
>
> `"1237"` is greater than `"123"` because the fourth character, the `'7'`, in 1237 is greater than the fourth character, the `'\0'`, in 123.
>
> `"Behop"` is greater than `"Beehive"` because the third character, the `'h'`, in Behop is greater than the third character, the `'e'`, in Beehive.

Program 10.5 uses these C-string functions within the context of a complete program. Following is a sample output produced by Program 10.5:

```
Hello is less than Hello there

The length of string1 is 5 characters
The length of string2 is 11 characters

After concatenation, string1 contains the string value
Hello there World!
The length of this string is 18 characters

Type in a sequence of characters for string2: It's a wonderful day
After copying string2 to string1, the string value in string1 is:
It's a wonderful day
The length of this string is 20 characters
```

Program 10.5

```cpp
#include <iostream>
#include <cstring>  // required for the string function library
using namespace std;
int main()
{
  const int MAXELS = 50;
  char string1[MAXELS] = "Hello";
  char string2[MAXELS] = "Hello there";
  int n;

  n = strcmp(string1, string2);

  if (n < 0)
    cout << string1 << " is less than " << string2 << endl;
  else if (n == 0)
    cout << string1 << " is equal to " << string2 << endl;
  else
    cout << string1 << " is greater than " << string2 << endl;

  cout << "\nThe length of string1 is " << strlen(string1)
       << " characters" << endl;
  cout << "The length of string2 is " << strlen(string2)
       << " characters" << endl;

  strcat(string1," there World!");

  cout << "\nAfter concatenation, string1 contains "
       << "the string value\n" << string1
       << "\nThe length of this string is "
       << strlen(string1) << " characters" << endl;

  cout << "\nType in a sequence of characters for string2: ";
  cin.getline(string2, MAXELS);

  strcpy(string1, string2);

  cout << "After copying string2 to string1, "
       << "the string value in string1 is:\n" << string2
       << "\nThe length of this string is "
       << strlen(string1) << " characters" << endl;

  return 0;
}
```

Character Routines

In addition to C-string manipulation functions, all C++ compilers include the character-handling routines previously presented in Section 7.2 and repeated in Table 10.3 for convenience. The prototypes for each of these routines are contained in the header file `cctype`, which should be included in any program that uses these routines.

TABLE 10.3 *Character Library Routines (Required Header File Is* `cctype` *of* `iostream`*)*

Prototype	Description	Example
`int isalpha(char)`	Returns a nonzero number if the character is a letter; otherwise, returns a zero.	`isalpha('a')`
`int isupper(char)`	Returns a nonzero number if the character is uppercase; otherwise, returns a zero.	`isupper('a')`
`int islower(char)`	Returns a nonzero number if the character is lowercase; otherwise, returns a zero.	`islower('a')`
`int isdigit(character)`	Returns a nonzero number if the character is a digit (0 through 9); otherwise, returns a zero.	`isdigit('a')`
`int isascii(character)`	Returns a nonzero number if the character is an ASCII character; otherwise, returns a zero.	`isascii('a')`
`int isspace(character)`	Returns a nonzero number if the character is a space; otherwise, returns a zero.	`isspace(' ')`
`int isprint(character)`	Returns a nonzero number if the character is a printable character; otherwise, returns a zero.	`isprint('a')`
`int iscntrl(character)`	Returns a nonzero number if the character is a control character; otherwise, returns a zero.	`iscntrl('a')`
`int ispucnt(character)`	Returns a nonzero number if the character is a punctuation character; otherwise, returns a zero.	`ispucnt('!')`
`int toupper(char)`	Returns the uppercase equivalent if the character is lowercase; otherwise, returns the character unchanged.	`toupper('a')`
`int tolower(char)`	Returns the lowercase equivalent if the character is uppercase; otherwise, returns the character unchanged.	`tolower('A')`

Because all of the functions listed in Table 10.3 return a nonzero integer (that is, a True value) if the character meets the desired condition and a zero integer (that is, a False value) if the condition is not met, these functions can be used directly within an `if` statement. For example, consider the following code segment:

```
char ch;

ch = cin.get();  // get a character from the keyboard

if(isdigit(ch))
  cout << "The character just entered is a digit" << endl;
else if(ispunct(ch))
  cout << "The character just entered is a punctuation mark" << endl;
```

Note that the character function is included as a condition within the `if` statement because the function effectively returns either a True (nonzero) or a False (zero) value.

Program 10.6 on page 475 illustrates the use of the `toupper()` function within the function `ConvertToUpper()`, which is used to convert all lowercase string characters to their uppercase form.

The output produced when Program 10.6 is executed is

```
Type in any sequence of characters: this is a test OF 12345.
The characters just entered, in uppercase are: THIS IS A TEST OF 12345.
```

Note that the `toupper()` library function converts only lowercase letters and that all other characters are unaffected.

Conversion Routines

The last group of standard string library routines, which are listed in Table 10.4, are used to convert strings to and from integer and double-precision data types. The prototypes for each of these routines are contained in the header file `cstdlib`, which should be included in any program that uses these routines.

Program 10.6

```cpp
#include <iostream>
using namespace std;

void ConvertToUpper(char []);

int main()
{
  const int MAXCHARS = 100;
  char message[MAXCHARS];

  cout << "\nType in any sequence of characters: ";

  cin.getline(message,MAXCHARS);

  ConvertToUpper(message);

  cout << "The characters just entered, in uppercase are: "
       << message << endl;

  return 0;
}
// this function converts all lowercase characters to uppercase
void ConvertToUpper(char message[])
{
  for(int i = 0; message[i] != '\0'; i++)
    message[i] = toupper(message[i]);

  return;
}
```

TABLE 10.4 *String Conversion Routines (Required Header File Is* `cstdlib`)

Prototype	Description	Example
`int atoi(stringExp)`	Convert an ASCII string to an integer. Conversion stops at the first noninteger character.	`atoi("1234")`
`double atof(stringExp)`	Convert an ASCII string to a double-precision number. Conversion stops at the first character that cannot be interpreted as a double.	`atof("12.34")`
`char[] itoa(stringExp)`	Convert an integer to an ASCII string. The space allocated for the returned string must be large enough for the converted value.	`itoa(1234)`

Program 10.7 illustrates the use of the `atoi()` and `atof()` functions.

Program 10.7

```cpp
#include <iostream>
#include <cstring>
#include <cstdlib>
#include <iomanip>
using namespace std;

int main()
{
  const int MAXELS = 20;
  char string[MAXELS] = "12345";
  int num;
  double dnum;

  num = atoi(string);

  cout << "The string \"" << string << "\" as an integer number is: "
       << num;
  cout << "\nThis number divided by 3 is: " << num / 3 << endl;

  strcat(string, ".96");

  dnum = atof(string);

  cout << "The string \"" << string << "\" as a double number is: "
       << fixed << setprecision(2) << dnum;
  cout << "\nThis number divided by 3 is: " << dnum / 3 << endl;

  return 0;
}
```

The output produced when Program 10.7 is executed is

```
The string "12345" as an integer number is: 12345
This number divided by 3 is: 4115
The string "12345.96" as a double number is: 12345.96
This number divided by 3 is: 4115.32
```

As this output illustrates, once a string has been converted to either an integer or a double-precision value, mathematical operations on the numerical value are valid.

▍ EXERCISES 10.2

1. Determine the value of `*text`, `*(text + 3)`, and `*(text + 10)`, assuming that `text` is an array of characters and that the following has been stored in the array.

    a. `now is the time`
    b. `rocky raccoon welcomes you`
    c. `Happy Holidays`
    d. `The good ship`

2. a. The following function, `convert()`, "marches along" the C-string passed to it and sends each character in the string one at a time to the `ToUpper()` function until the null character is encountered.

```
void convert(char strng[])  // convert a string to uppercase letters
{
  int i = 0;
  while (strng[i] != '\0')
  {
    strng[i] = ToUpper(strng[i]);
    i++;
  }

  return;
}

char ToUpper(char letter) // convert a character to uppercase
{
  if( (letter >= 'a') && (letter <= 'z') )
    return (letter - 'a' + 'A');
  else
    return (letter);
}
```

The `ToUpper()` function takes each character passed to it and first examines it to determine whether the character is a lowercase letter (a lowercase letter is any character between a and z, inclusive). Assuming that characters are stored using the standard ASCII character codes, the expression `letter - 'a' + 'A'` converts a lowercase letter to its uppercase equivalent. Rewrite the `convert()` function using pointers.

    b. Include the `convert()` and `ToUpper()` functions in a working program. The program should prompt the user for a string and echo the string back to the user in uppercase letters.

3. Using pointers, repeat Exercise 1 from Section 10.1.

4. Using pointers, repeat Exercise 2 from Section 10.1.

5. Using pointers, repeat Exercise 3 from Section 10.1.

6. Write a function named `remove()` that returns nothing and deletes all occurrences of a character from a C-string. The function should take two arguments: the string name and the character to be removed. For example, if message contains the string `Happy Holidays`, the function call `remove(message, 'H')` should place the string `appy olidays` into `message`.

7. Using pointers, repeat Exercise 6 from Section 10.1.

8. Write a program using the `cin.get()`, and `toupper()` library routines, along with a `cout` stream object to echo back each entered letter in its uppercase form. The program should terminate when the digit 1 key is pressed.

9. Write a function that uses pointers to add a single character at the end of an existing C-string. The function should replace the existing `\0` character with the new character and append a new `\0` at the end of the string. The function returns nothing.

10. Write a function that uses pointers to delete a single character from the end of a C-string. This is effectively achieved by moving the `\0` character one position closer to the start of the string. The function returns nothing.

11. Determine what string-handling functions are available with your C++ compiler. For each available function, list the data types of the arguments expected by the function and the data type of any returned value.

12. Write a function named `trimfrnt()` that deletes all leading blanks from a C-string. Write the function using pointers. The function returns nothing.

13. Write a function named `trimrear()` that deletes all trailing blanks from a C-string. Write the function using pointers. The function returns nothing.

14. Write a function named `strlen()` that returns the number of characters in a C-string. Do not include the `\0` character in the returned count.

10.3   C-string Definitions and Pointer Arrays

The definition of a C-string automatically involves a pointer. For example, the definition `char message1[80];` both reserves storage for 80 characters and automatically creates a pointer constant, `message1`, that contains the address of `message1[0]`. As a pointer constant, the address associated with the pointer cannot be changed; it must always "point to" the beginning of the created array.

Instead of creating a C-string as an array, however, it is also possible to create a C-string using a pointer. For example, the definition `char *message2;` creates a pointer to a character. In this case, `message2` is a true pointer variable. Once a pointer to a character is defined, assignment statements, such as `message2 = "this is a string";`, can be made. In this assignment, `message2`, which is a pointer, receives the address of the first character in the string.

The main difference in the definitions of `message1` as an array and `message2` as a pointer is the way the pointer is created. Defining `message1` using the declaration char message1[80] explicitly calls for a fixed amount of storage for the array. This causes the compiler to create a pointer constant. Defining message2 using the declaration char *message2 explicitly creates a pointer variable first. This pointer is then used to hold the address of a C-string when the C-string is actually specified. This difference in definitions has both storage and programming consequences.

From a programming perspective, defining message2 as a pointer to a character allows C-string assignments, such as message2 = "this is a string";, to be made within a program. Similar assignments are not allowed for C-strings defined as arrays. Thus the statement message1 = "this is a string"; is not valid. Both definitions, however, allow initializations to be made using a string literal. For example, both of the following initializations are valid:

```
char message1[80] = "this is a string";
char *message2 = "this is a string";
```

From a storage perspective, the allocation of space for message1 is quite different from that for message2. As illustrated in Figure 10.5, both initializations cause the computer to store the same C-string internally. In the case of message1, a specific set of 80 storage locations is reserved, and the first 17 locations are initialized. For message1, different C-strings can be stored, but each string will overwrite the previously stored characters. The same is not true for message2.

FIGURE 10.5 *C-string Storage Allocation*

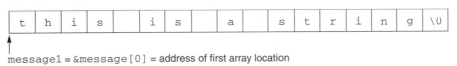

message1 = &message[0] = address of first array location

a. Storage allocation for a C-string defined as an array

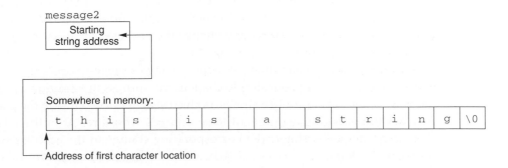

b. Storage of a C-string using a pointer

FIGURE 10.6   *Storage Allocation for Figure 10.5*

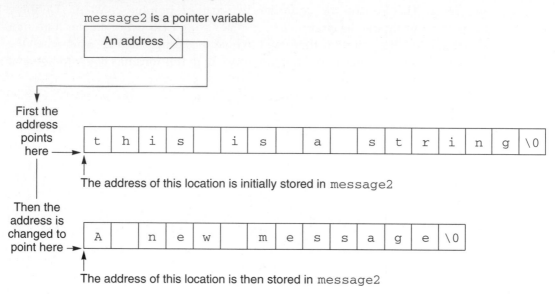

The definition of message2 reserves enough storage for one pointer. The initialization then causes the string literal to be stored in memory and the address of the string's first character, in this case the address of the t, to be loaded into the pointer. If a later assignment is made to message2, the initial C-string remains in memory, and new storage locations are allocated to the new C-string. For example, consider the sequence of instructions

```
char *message2 = "this is a string";
message2 = "A new message";
```

The first statement defines message2 as a pointer variable, stores the initialization string in memory, and loads the starting address of the string (the address of the t in this) into message2. The next assignment statement causes the computer to store the second string and change the address in message2 to point to the starting location of this new string.

It is important to realize that the second string assigned to message2 does not overwrite the first string but simply changes the address in message2 to point to the new string. As Figure 10.6 shows, both strings are stored inside the computer. Any additional string assignment to message2 would result in the additional storage of the new string and a corresponding change in the address stored in message2. Doing so also means that we no longer have access to the original C-string memory location.

Pointer Arrays

The declaration of an array of character pointers is an extremely useful extension to single string pointer declarations. For example, the declaration

```
char *seasons[4];
```

creates an array of four elements, where each element is a pointer to a character. As individual pointers, each pointer can be assigned to point to a string using string assignment statements. Thus the statements

```
seasons[0] = "Winter";
seasons[1] = "Spring";
seasons[2] = "Summer";
seasons[3] = "Fall";  // note: string lengths may differ
```

set appropriate addresses into the respective pointers. Figure 10.7 illustrates the addresses loaded into the pointers for these assignments.

As shown in Figure 10.7, the seasons array does not contain the actual strings assigned to the pointers. These strings are stored elsewhere in the computer in the normal data area allocated to the program. The array of pointers contains only the addresses of the starting location for each string.

FIGURE 10.7   *The Addresses Contained in the* seasons[] *Pointers*

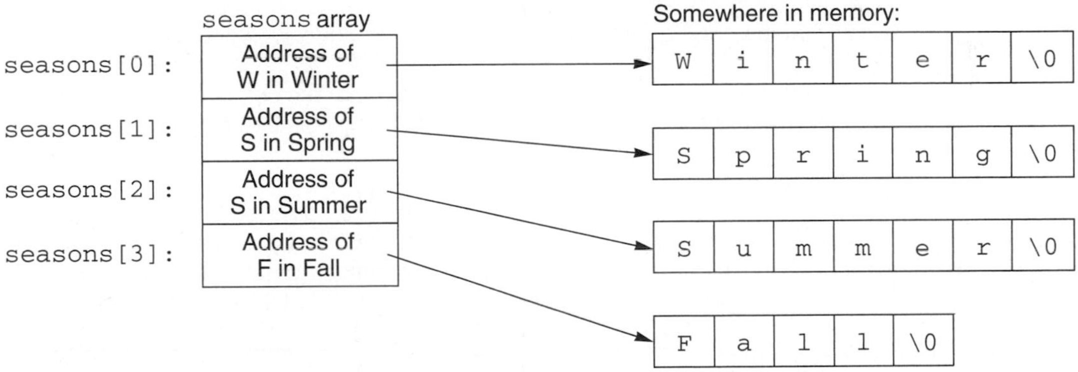

The initializations of the seasons array can also be incorporated directly within the definition of the array, as follows:

```
char *seasons[4] = {"Winter",
                    "Spring",
                    "Summer",
                    "Fall"};
```

Allocating Space for a String

Although the two declarations

```
char test[5] = "abcd";
```

and

```
char *test = "abcd";
```

both create storage for the characters `'a'`, `'b'`, `'c'`, `'d'`, and `'\0'`, there is a subtle difference between the two declarations and in how values can be assigned to `test`. An array declaration, such as `char test[5];`, precludes the use of any subsequent assignment expression, such as `test = "efgh"`, to assign values to the array. The use of a `strcpy`, such as `strcpy(test,"efgh")`, however, is subsequently valid. The only restriction on the `strcpy` is the size of the array, which in this case is five elements. This situation is reversed when a pointer is created. A pointer declaration, such as `char *test;`, precludes the use of a `strcpy` to initialize the memory locations pointed to by the pointer, but it does allow assignments. For example, the following sequence of statements is valid:

```
char *test;
test = "abcd";
test = "here is a longer string";
```

Once a C-string of characters has been assigned to `test`, a `strcpy` can be used, provided that the copy uses no more elements than are currently contained in the string.

The difference in usage is explained by the fact that the compiler automatically allocates sufficient new memory space for any C-string pointed to by a pointer variable but does not do so for an array of characters. The array size is fixed by the definition statement.

Formally, any expression that yields a value that can be used on the left side of an assignment expression is said to be an *lvalue*. (Similarly, any expression that yields a value that can be used on the right side of an assignment statement is said to be an *rvalue*). Thus a pointer variable can be an *lvalue*, but an array name cannot.

This declaration both creates an array of pointers and initializes the pointers with appropriate addresses. Once addresses have been assigned to the pointers, each pointer can be used to access its corresponding string. Program 10.8 uses the seasons array to display each season using a `for` loop.

Program 10.8

```cpp
#include <iostream>
using namespace std;
int main()
{
  const int NUMSEASONS = 4;
  int n;
  char *seasons[] = {"Winter",
                     "Spring",
                     "Summer",
                     "Fall"};

  for( n = 0; n < NUMSEASONS; n++)
  cout << "\nThe season is " << seasons[n];

  return 0;
}
```

The output obtained for Program 10.8 is

```
The season is Winter
The season is Spring
The season is Summer
The season is Fall
```

The advantage of using a list of pointers is that logical groups of data headings can be collected and accessed with one array name. For example, the months in a year can be collectively grouped in one array called months, and the days in a week can be collectively grouped in an array called days. The grouping of like headings allows the programmer to access and print an appropriate heading by simply specifying the correct position of the heading in the array. Program 10.9 uses the seasons array to correctly identify and display the season corresponding to a user-input month.

Program 10.9

```
#include <iostream>
using namespace std;
int main()
{
  int n;
  char *seasons[] = {"Winter",
                     "Spring",
                     "Summer",
                     "Fall"};

  cout << "\nEnter a month (use 1 for Jan., 2 for Feb., etc.): ";
  cin >> n;
  n = (n % 12) / 3;  // create the correct subscript
  cout << "The month entered is a "<< seasons[n] << " month.";

  return 0;
}
```

Except for the expression n = (n % 12) / 3, Program 10.9 is rather straightforward. The program requests the user to input a month and accepts the number corresponding to the month using a cin object to display the selected month. The expression n = (n % 12) / 3 uses a common programming "trick" to scale a set of numbers into a more useful set. Using subscripts, the four elements of the seasons array must be accessed via a subscript from 0 through 3. Thus the months of the year, which correspond to the numbers 1 through 12, must be adjusted to correspond to the correct season subscript. This is done by using the expression n = (n % 12) / 3. The expression n % 12 adjusts the month entered to lie within the range 0 through 11, with 0 corresponding to December, 1 to January, and so on. Dividing by 3 causes the resulting number to range between 0 and 3, corresponding to the possible seasons elements. The result of the division by 3 is assigned to the integer variable n. The months 0, 1, and 2, when divided by 3, are set to 0; the months 3, 4, and 5 are set to 1; the months 6, 7, and 8 are set to 2; and the months 9, 10, and 11 are set to 3. This is equivalent to the following assignments:

Months	Season
December, January, February	Winter
March, April, May	Spring
June, July, August	Summer
September, October, November	Fall

The following is a sample output obtained for Program 10.9:

```
Enter a month (use 1 for Jan., 2 for Feb., etc.): 12
The month entered is a Winter month.
```

▌ EXERCISES 10.3

1. Write two declaration statements that can be used in place of the declaration `char text[] = "Hooray!";`.

2. Determine the value of `*text`, `*(text + 3)`, and `*(text + 7)` for each of the following sections of code.

   a. `char *text;`
     `char message[] = "the check is in the mail";`
     `text = message;`

   b. `char *text;`
     `char formal[] = {'T','h','i','s',' ','i','s',' ','a','n',' ',`
                      `'i','n','v','i','t','a','t','i','o','n','\0'};`
     `text = &formal[0];`

   c. `char *test;`
     `char more[] = "Happy Holidays";`
     `text = &more[4];`

   d. `char *text, *second;`
     `char blip[] = "The good ship";`
     `second = blip;`
     `text = ++second;`

3. Determine the error in the following program:

```cpp
#include <iostream>
using namespace std;
int main()
{
  int i = 0;
  char message[] = {'H','e','l','l','o','\0'};

  for( ; i < 5; i++)
  {
    cout << *message;
    message++;
  }

  return 0;
}
```

4. *a.* Write a C++ function that displays the day of the week corresponding to a user-entered input number between 1 and 7. That is, in response to an input of 2, the program displays the name Monday. Use an array of pointers in the function.

   b. Include the function written for Exercise 4a in a complete working program.

5. Modify the function written in Exercise 4a so that the function returns the address of the character string containing the proper day to be displayed.

6. Write a function that will accept ten lines of user-input text and store the entered lines as ten individual C-strings. Use a pointer array in your function.

10.4 Common Programming Errors

Three errors are frequently made when pointers to C-strings are used. The most common is using the pointer to "point to" a nonexistent data element. This error is, of course, the same error we have already seen using subscripts. C++ compilers do not perform bounds checking on arrays, so it is the programmer's responsibility to ensure that the address in the pointer is the address of a valid data element.

The second common error lies in not providing sufficient space for the C-string to be stored. A simple variation of this is not providing space for the end-of-string NULL character when a C-string is defined as an array of characters, and not including the \0 character when the array is initialized. A more complicated variation of this error is declaring a character pointer, such as char *p, and then attempting to copy a C-string with a statement such as strcpy(p, "Hello"). Because no space has been allocated for the C-string, the C-string will overwrite the memory area pointed to by p.

The last commonly encountered error relates to a misunderstanding of terminology. For example, if text is defined as

```
char *text;
```

the variable text is sometimes referred to as a string. Thus the terminology "store the characters Hooray for the Hoosiers into the text C-string" may be encountered. Strictly speaking, calling text a string or a C-string variable is incorrect. The variable text is a pointer that contains the address of the first character in the C-string. Nevertheless, referring to a character pointer as a string occurs frequently enough that you should be aware of it.

10.5 Chapter Summary

1. A C-string is an array of characters that is terminated by the NULL character.

2. C-strings can always be processed using standard array-processing techniques. The input and display of a C-string, however, always require reliance on a standard library function.

3. The cin, cin.get(), and cin.getline() routines can be used to input a C-string. The cin object tends to be of limited usefulness for C-string input because it terminates input when a blank is encountered.

4. The cout object can be used to display C-strings.

5. In place of subscripts, pointer notation and pointer arithmetic are especially useful for manipulating C-string elements.

6. Many standard library functions exist for processing C-strings as a complete unit. Internally, these functions manipulate C-strings in a character-by-character manner, generally using pointers.

7. C-string storage can be created by declaring an array of characters. It can also be created by declaring and initializing a pointer to a character.

8. Arrays can be initialized using a string literal assignment of the form

   ```
   char *arr_name[ ] = "text";
   ```

   This initialization is equivalent to

   ```
   char *arr_name[ ] = {'t','e','x','t','\0'};
   ```

9. A pointer to a character can be assigned a string literal. String literal assignment to an array of characters is invalid except for initialization within a declaration statement.

Data Structures

FIGURE 11.1   *Typical Mailing List Components*

Name:
Street Address:
City:
State:
Zip Code:

An array makes it possible to access a list or table of data of the same data type by using a single variable name. At times, however, we may want to store information of varying types, such as a string name, an integer part number, and a real price, together in one structure. A data structure that stores different types of data under a single variable name is referred to in C++ as a structure.

To make this discussion more tangible, let's consider data items typically used in preparing mailing labels, as illustrated in Figure 11.1. Each of the individual data items listed in Figure 11.1 is an entity by itself that is referred to as a **data field**. Taken together, all the data fields form a single unit that is referred to as a **record**. In C++, a record is referred to as a **structure**.

Although there could be thousands of names and addresses in a complete mailing list, all the mailing labels are identical in form. In dealing with structures, then, it is important to distinguish between a structure's form and its contents.

A structure's form consists of the symbolic names, data types, and arrangement of individual data fields in the structure. The structure's contents are the actual data stored in the symbolic names. Figure 11.2 shows acceptable contents for the structure form illustrated in Figure 11.1.

FIGURE 11.2   *The Form and Contents of a Structure*

Name: Ronda Bronson-Karp
Street Address: 614 Freeman Street
City: Orange
State: NJ
Zip Code: 07052

In this chapter, we describe the C++ statements required to create, fill, and manipulate structures.

11.1   Structures

In its original form, and the one considered in this chapter, a structure can be considered as a class that has no methods and all of whose variables are public. In dealing with structures, as such, it is important to distinguish between form and content.

Creating and using a structure requires the same two steps needed for using any variable. First the structure must be declared. Then specific values can be assigned to the individual structure elements. Declaring a structure requires listing the data types, data names, and arrangement of data items. For example, the definition

```
struct
{
    int month;
    int day;
    int year;
}   birth;
```

gives the form of a structure called `birth` and reserves storage for the individual data items listed in the structure. The `birth` structure consists of three data items or fields, which are called **structure members**.

Assigning actual data values to the data items of a structure is referred to as **populating the structure**, and it is a relatively straightforward procedure. Each member of a structure is accessed by giving both the structure name and the individual data item name, separated by a period. Thus `birth.month` refers to the first member of the `birth` structure, `birth.day` refers to the second member of the structure, and `birth.year` refers to the third member. The period in each of these variable names is called the **member access operator** or the **dot operator** (the terms are used synonymously). Program 11.1 illustrates assigning values to the individual members of the `birth` structure.

 Program 11.1

```cpp
// a program that defines and populates a record
#include <iostream>
using namespace std;
int main()
{
  struct
  {
    int month;
    int day;
    int year;
  }   birth;

  birth.month = 12;
  birth.day = 28;
  birth.year = 86;

  cout << "My birth date is "
       << birth.month << '/'
       << birth.day   << '/'
       << birth.year  << endl;

  return 0;
}
```

The output produced by Program 11.1 is

```
My birth date is 12/28/86
```

As in most C++ statements, the spacing of a structure definition is not rigid. For example, the `birth` structure could just as well have been defined as

```
struct {int month; int day; int year;} birth;
```

Also, as with all C++ definition statements, multiple variables can be defined in the same statement. For example, the definition statement

```
struct
{
  int month;
  int day;
  int year;
} birth, current;
```

creates two structure variables that have the same form. The members of the first structure are referenced by the individual names `birth.month`, `birth.day`, and `birth.year`, whereas the members of the second structure are referenced by the names `current.month`, `current.day`, and `current.year`. Note that the form of this particular structure definition statement is identical to that used in defining any program variable: The data type is followed by a list of variable names.

The most commonly used modification for defining structure types is to list the form of the structure with no following variable names. In this case, however, the list of structure members must be preceded by a user-selected data type name. For example, in the declaration

```
struct Date
{
  int month;
  int day;
  int year;
};
```

the term `Date` is a structure type name: It defines a new data type that is a data structure of the declared form.[1] By convention, the first letter of a user-selected data type name is uppercase, as in the name `Date`; this practice helps us identify them

---

[1] For completeness, it should be mentioned that a C++ structure can also be declared as a class with no member functions and all public data members. Similarly, a C++ class can be declared as a structure that has all private data members and all public member functions. Thus C++ provides two syntaxes for both structures and classes. The convention, however, is not to mix notations and always to use structures for creating record types and classes for providing true information and implementation hiding.

when they are used in subsequent definition statements. Here, the declaration for the Date structure creates a new data type without actually reserving any storage locations. Thus it is not a definition statement. It simply declares a Date structure type and describes how individual data items are arranged within the structure. Actual storage for the members of the structure is reserved only when specific variable names are assigned. For example, the definition statement

```
Date birth, current;
```

reserves storage for two Date structure variables named birth and current, respectively. Each of these individual structures has the form previously declared for the Date structure.

The declaration of a structure data type, like all declarations, may be global or local. Program 11.2 illustrates the global declaration of a Date data type. Internal to main(), the variable birth is defined as a local variable of Date type.

 Program 11.2

```
#include <iostream>
using namespace std;
struct Date      // this is a global declaration
{
  int month;
  int day;
  int year;
};

int main()
{
  Date birth;

  birth.month = 12;
  birth.day = 28;
  birth.year = 86;

  cout << "My birth date is "
       << birth.month    << '/'
       << birth.day      << '/'
       << birth.year     << endl;

  return 0;
}
```

The output produced by Program 11.2 is identical to the output produced by Program 11.1.

The initialization of structures follows the same rules as the initialization of arrays: Global and local structures may be initialized by following the definition with a list of initializers. For example, the definition statement

```
Date birth = {12, 28, 86};
```

can be used to replace the first four statements internal to `main()` in Program 11.2. Note that the initializers are separated by commas, not semicolons.

The individual members of a structure are not restricted to integer data types, as in the `Date` structure. Any valid C++ data type can be used. For example, consider an employee record consisting of the following data items:

Name:
Identification Number:
Regular Pay Rate:
Overtime Pay Rate:

A suitable declaration for these data items is

```
struct PayRecord
{
  string name;
  int idNum;
  double regRate;
  double otRate;
};
```

Once the `PayRecord` data type is declared, a specific structure variable using this type can be defined and initialized. For example, the definition

```
PayRecord employee = {"H. Price",12387,15.89,25.50};
```

creates a structure named `employee` of the `PayRecord` data type. The individual members of `employee` are initialized with the respective data listed between braces in the definition statement.

Note that a single structure is simply a convenient method for combining and storing related items under a common name. Although a single structure is useful in explicitly identifying the relationship among its members, the individual members could be defined as separate variables. One of the real advantages of using structures is realized only when the same data type is used in a list many times over. Creating lists with the same data type is the topic of the next section.

Before we leave single structures, it is worth noting that the individual members of a structure can be any valid C++ data type, including both arrays and structures. An array of characters was used as a member of the employee structure defined previously. Accessing an element of a member array requires giving the structure's name, followed by a period, followed by the array designation.

To include a structure within a structure, we follow the same rules for including any data type in a structure. For example, assume that a structure is to consist of a name and a date of birth, where a Date structure has been declared as

```
struct Date
{
    int month;
    int day;
    int year;
};
```

A suitable definition of a structure that includes a name and a Date structure is

```
struct
{
    string name;
    Date birth;
} person;
```

In declaring the Date structure, note that the term Date is a data type name; thus it appears before the braces in the declaration statement. In defining the person structure variable, we note that person is a variable name; thus it is the name of a specific structure. The same is true of the variable named birth. This is the name of a specific Date structure. Individual members in the person structure are accessed by preceding the desired member with the structure name followed by a period. For example, person.birth.month refers to the month variable in the birth structure contained in the person structure.

▌ EXERCISES 11.1

1. Declare a structure data type named Stemp for each of the following records.
   a. A student record consisting of a student identification number, number of credits completed, and cumulative grade point average
   b. A student record consisting of a student's name, date of birth, number of credits completed, and cumulative grade point average
   c. A mailing list consisting of the items illustrated in Figure 11.1

d. A stock record consisting of the stock's name, the price of the stock, and the date of purchase

e. An inventory record consisting of an integer part number, a part description, the number of parts in inventory, and an integer reorder number

2. For the individual data types declared in Exercise 1, define a suitable structure variable name, and initialize each structure with the following data.

    a. Identification Number: 4672
       Number of Credits Completed: 68
       Grade Point Average: 3.01

    b. Name: Rhona Karp
       Date of Birth: 8/4/1960
       Number of Credits Completed: 96
       Grade Point Average: 3.89

    c. Name: Kay Kingsley
       Street Address: 614 Freeman Street
       City: Indianapolis
       State: IN
       Zip Code: 07030

    d. Stock: IBM
       Price Purchased: 134.5
       Date Purchased: 10/1/86

    e. Part Number: 16879
       Description: Battery
       Number in Stock: 10
       Reorder Number: 3

3. *a.* Write a C++ program that prompts a user to input the current month, day, and year. Store the data entered in a suitably defined record, and display the date in an appropriate manner.

    b. Modify the program written in Exercise 3a to use a record that accepts the current time in hours, minutes, and seconds.

4. Write a C++ program that uses a structure for storing the name of a stock, its estimated earnings per share, and its estimated price-to-earnings ratio. Have the program prompt the user to enter these items for five different stocks, each time using the same structure to store the entered data. When the data has been entered for a particular stock, have the program compute and display the stock price anticipated on the basis of the entered earnings and price-per-share values. For example, if a user entered the data XYZ 1.56 12, the anticipated price for a share of XYZ stock would be (1.56)*(12) = $18.72.

5. Write a C++ program that accepts a user-entered time in hours and minutes. Have the program calculate and display the time 1 minute later.

6. *a.* Write a C++ program that accepts a user-entered date. Have the program calculate and display the date of the next day. For purposes of this exercise, assume that all months consist of 30 days.

    b. Modify the program written in Exercise 6a to account for the actual number of days in each month.

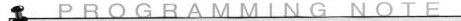

PROGRAMMING NOTE

Homogeneous and Heterogeneous Data Structures

Both arrays and records are structured data types. The difference between these two data structures is the types of elements they contain. An array is a *homogeneous* data structure, which means that each of its components must be of the same data type. A record is a *heterogeneous* data structure, which means that its components can be of different data types. Thus an array of records would be a homogeneous data structure whose elements are of the same heterogeneous type.

11.2 Arrays of Structures

The real power of structures is realized when the same structure is used for lists of data. For example, assume that the data shown in Figure 11.3 must be processed. Clearly, the employee numbers can be stored together in an array of integers, the names in an array of strings, and the pay rates in an array of double-precision numbers. In organizing the data in this fashion, we consider each column in Figure 11.3 as a separate list, which is stored in its own array. The correspondence between items for each individual employee is maintained by storing an employee's data in the same array position in each array.

FIGURE 11.3 *A List of Employee Data*

Employee Number	Employee Name	Employee Pay Rate
32479	Abrams, B.	6.72
33623	Bohm, P.	7.54
34145	Donaldson, S.	5.56
35987	Emst, T.	5.43
36203	Gwodz, K.	8.72
36417	Hanson, H.	7.64
37634	Monroe, G.	5.29
38321	Price, S.	9.67
39435	Robbins, L.	8.50
39567	Williams, B.	7.20

The separation of the complete list into three individual arrays is unfortunate, because all of the items related to a single employee constitute a natural organization of data into structures, as illustrated in Figure 11.4. Using a structure, we can make the program maintain and reflect the integrity of the data organization as a record. Under this approach, the list illustrated in Figure 11.4 can be processed as a single array of ten structures.

FIGURE 11.4   *A List of Structures*

	Employee Number	Employee Name	Employee Pay Rate
1st structure ⟶	32479	Abrams, B.	6.72
2nd structure ⟶	33623	Bohm, P.	7.54
3rd structure ⟶	34145	Donaldson, S.	5.56
4th structure ⟶	35987	Emst, T.	5.43
5th structure ⟶	36203	Gwodz, K.	8.72
6th structure ⟶	36417	Hanson, H.	7.64
7th structure ⟶	37634	Monroe, G.	5.29
8th structure ⟶	38321	Price, S.	9.67
9th structure ⟶	39435	Robbins, L.	8.50
10th structure ⟶	39567	Williams, B.	7.20

Declaring an array of structures is the same as declaring an array of any other variable type. For example, if the data type `PayRecord` is declared as

```
struct PayRecord
{
  int idNum;
  string name;
  double rate;
};
```

then an array of ten such structures can be defined as

```
PayRecord employee[10];
```

This definition statement constructs an array of ten elements, each of which is a structure of the data type `PayRecord`. Note that the creation of an array of ten structures has the same form as the creation of any other array. For example, creating an array of ten integers named `employee` requires the declaration

```
int employee[10];
```

In this declaration the data type is integer, whereas in the former declaration for `employee`, the data type is `PayRecord`.

Once an array of structures is declared, a particular data item is referenced by giving the position of the desired structure in the array, followed by a period and the appropriate structure member. For example, the variable `employee[0].rate` refers to the `rate` member of the first `employee` structure in the `employee` array. Including structures as elements of an array makes it possible to process a list of structures using standard array programming techniques. Program 11.3 displays the first five employee records illustrated in Figure 11.4.

 ## Program 11.3

```cpp
#include <iostream>
#include <iomanip>
using namespace std;

struct PayRecord          // this is a global declaration
{
  int id;
  string name;
  double rate;
};

int main()
{

const int NUMRECS = 5;    // maximum number of records

  int i;
  PayRecord employee[NUMRECS] = {
                               { 32479, "Abrams, B.", 6.72 },
                               { 33623, "Bohm, P.", 7.54},
                               { 34145, "Donaldson, S.", 5.56},
                               { 35987, "Ernst, T.", 5.43 },
                               { 36203, "Gwodz, K.", 8.72 }
                               };

  cout << endl;    // start on a new line
  cout << setiosflags(ios::left); // left justify the output
  for (i = 0; i < NUMRECS; i++)
    cout << setw(7)        << employee[i].id
         << setw(15)       << employee[i].name
         << setw(6)        << employee[i].rate << endl;

  return 0;
}
```

The output displayed by Program 11.3 is

```
32479    Abrams, B.        6.72
33623    Bohm, P.         7.54
34145    Donaldson, S.    5.56
35987    Ernst, T.        5.43
36203    Gwodz, K.        8.72
```

In reviewing Program 11.3, note the initialization of the array of structures. Although the initializers for each structure have been enclosed in inner braces, these are not strictly necessary because all members have been initialized. As with all external and static variables, in the absence of explicit initializers, the numeric elements of both static and external arrays or structures are initialized to zero, and their character elements are initialized to nulls. The `setiosflags(ios::left)` manipulator included in the `cout` object stream forces each name to be displayed left-justified in its designated field width.

▌ EXERCISES 11.2

1. Define arrays of 100 structures for each of the data types described in Exercise 1 of the previous section.

2. a. Using the data type

```
struct DaysInMonth
{
  string name;
  int days;
};
```

define an array of 12 structures of type `DaysInMonth`. Name the array `convert[]`, and initialize the array with the names of the 12 months in a year and the number of days in each month.

b. Include the array created in Exercise 2a in a program that displays the name of, and the number of days in, each month.

3. Using the data type declared in Exercise 2a, write a C++ program that accepts a month from a user in numeric form and displays the name of the month and the number of days in the month. Thus, in response to an input of 3, the program would display `March has 31 days`.

4. a. Declare a single-structure data type suitable for an employee structure of the type illustrated:

Number	Name	Rate	Hours
3462	Jones	4.62	40
6793	Robbins	5.83	38
6985	Smith	5.22	45
7834	Swain	6.89	40
8867	Timmins	6.43	35
9002	Williams	4.75	42

b. Using the data type declared in Exercise 4a, write a C++ program that interactively accepts the above data into an array of six structures. Once the data have been entered, the program should create a payroll report listing each employee's name, number, and gross pay. Include the total gross pay of all employees at the end of the report.

5. *a.* Declare a single-structure data type suitable for a car structure of the type illustrated below:

Car Number	Miles Driven	Gallons Used
25	1,450	62
36	3,240	136
44	1,792	76
52	2,360	105
68	2,114	67

b. Using the data type declared for Exercise 5a, write a C++ program that interactively accepts the above data into an array of five structures. Once the data have been entered, the program should create a report listing each car number and the miles per gallon achieved by the car. At the end of the report include the average miles per gallon achieved by the complete fleet of cars.

11.3   Structures as Function Arguments

Individual structure members may be passed to a function in the same manner as any scalar variable. For example, given the structure definition

```
struct
{
  int idNum;
  double payRate;
  double hours;
} emp;
```

the statement

```
display(emp.idNum);
```

passes a copy of the structure member `emp.idNum` to a function named `display()`. Similarly, the statement

```
calcPay(emp.payRate,emp.hours);
```

passes copies of the values stored in structure members `emp.payRate` and `emp.hours` to the function `calcPay()`. Both functions, `display()` and `calcPay`, must declare the correct data types for their respective parameters.

Complete copies of all members of a structure can also be passed to a function by including the name of the structure as an argument to the called function. For example, the function call

```
calcNet(emp);
```

passes a copy of the complete `emp` structure to `calcNet()`. Internal to `calcNet()`, an appropriate declaration must be made to receive the structure. Program 11.4 declares a global data type for an employee structure. This type is then used by both the `main()` and the `calcNet()` functions to define specific structures with the names `emp` and `temp`, respectively.

The output produced by Program 11.4 is

```
The net pay for employee 6782 is $361.66
```

In reviewing Program 11.4, observe that both `main()` and `calcNet()` use the same data type to define their individual structure variables. The structure variable defined in `main()` and the structure variable defined in `calcNet()` are two completely different structures. Any changes made to the local `temp` variable in `calcNet()` are not reflected in the `emp` variable of `main()`. In fact, because both structure variables are local to their respective functions, the same structure variable name could have been used in both functions with no ambiguity.

When `calcNet()` is called by `main()`, copies of `emp`'s structure values are passed to the temp structure. `calcNet()` then uses two of the passed member values to calculate a number, which is returned to `main()`.

Program 11.4

```cpp
#include <iostream>
#include <iomanip>
using namespace std;
struct Employee     // declare a global type
{
  int idNum;
  double payRate;
  double hours;
};

double calculateNet(Employee);     // function prototype

int main()
{
  Employee emp = {6782, 8.93, 40.5};
  double netPay;

  netPay = calculateNet(emp);     // pass copies of the values in emp

    // set output formats
  cout << setw(10)
       << setiosflags(ios::fixed)
       << setiosflags(ios::showpoint)
       << setprecision(2);

  cout << "The net pay for employee " << emp.idNum
       << " is $" << netPay << endl;

  return 0;
}

double calculateNet(Employee temp) // temp is of data type Employee
{
  return (temp.payRate * temp.hours);
}
```

An alternative to the pass by value function call illustrated in Program 11.4, in which the called function receives a copy of a structure, is a pass by reference that passes a reference to a structure. This permits the called function to directly access and alter values in the calling function's structure variable. For example, referring to Program 11.4, the prototype of calcNet() can be modified to

```cpp
double calcNet(Employee &);
```

If this function prototype is used and the `calcNet()` header line is rewritten to conform to it, the `main()` function in Program 11.4 may be used as is. Program 11.4a illustrates these changes within the context of a complete program.

 Program 11.4a

```
#include <iostream>
#include <iomanip>
using namespace std;
struct Employee     // declare a global type
{
  int idNum;
  double payRate;
  double hours;
};

double calculateNet(Employee&);     // function prototype

int main()
{
  Employee emp = {6782, 8.93, 40.5};
  double netPay;

  netPay = calculateNet(emp);     // pass a reference

    // set output formats
  cout << setw(10)
       << setiosflags(ios::fixed)
       << setiosflags(ios::showpoint)
       << setprecision(2);

  cout << "The net pay for employee " << emp.idNum
       << " is $" << netPay << endl;

  return 0;
}

double calculateNet(Employee& temp)     // temp is a reference variable
{
  return (temp.payRate * temp.hours);
}
```

Program 11.4a produces the same output as Program 11.4, except that the `calcNet()` function in Program 11.4a receives direct access to the `emp` structure rather than a copy of it. This means that the variable name `temp` within `calcNet()` is an alternative name for the variable `emp` in `main()`, and any changes to `temp` are direct changes to `emp`. Although the same function call, `calcNet(emp)`, is made in both programs, the call in Program 11.4a passes a reference, whereas the call in Program 11.4 passes values.

Passing a Pointer

Instead of passing a reference, we can use a pointer. Using a pointer requires that we modify the function's prototype and header line and also that the call to `calcNet()` in Program 11.4 be modified to

```
calcNet(&emp);
```

Here the function call clearly indicates that an address is being passed (which is not the case in Program 11.4a). The disadvantage, however, is in the dereferencing notation required internal to the function. However, pointers are widely used in practice, so it is worthwhile to become familiar with the notation used.

To store the passed address, `calcNet()` must declare its parameter as a pointer. A suitable function definition for `calcNet()` is

```
calcNet(Employee *pt)
```

Here, the declaration for `pt` declares this parameter as a pointer to a structure of type `Employee`. The pointer `pt` receives the starting address of a structure whenever `calcNet()` is called. Within `calcNet()`, this pointer is used to access any member in the structure. For example, `(*pt).idNum` refers to the `idNum` member of the structure, `(*pt).payRate` refers to the `payRate` member of the structure, and `(*pt).hours` refers to the `hours` member of the structure. These relationships are illustrated in Figure 11.5.

The parentheses around the expression `*pt` in Figure 11.5 are necessary to access initially "the structure whose address is in `pt`." This is followed by an identifier to access the desired member within the structure. In the absence of the parentheses, the structure member operator takes precedence over the indirection operator. Thus the expression `*pt.hours` is another way of writing `*(pt.hours)`, which would refer to "the variable whose address is in the `pt.hours` variable." This last expression clearly makes no sense, because there is no structure named `pt` and `hours` does not contain an address.

FIGURE 11.5 *A Pointer Can Be Used to Access Structure Members*

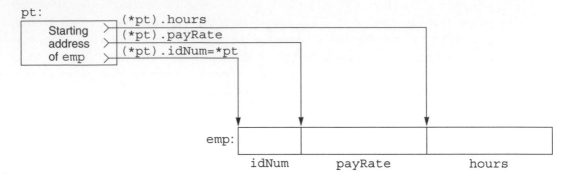

As illustrated in Figure 11.5, the starting address of the `emp` structure is also the address of the first member of the structure.

The use of pointers in this manner is so common that a special notation exists for it. The general expression *(*pointer).member* can always be replaced with the notation *pointer->member*, where the `->` operator is constructed using a minus sign followed by a right-facing arrow (greater-than symbol). Either expression can be used to locate the desired member. For example, the following expressions are equivalent:

`(*pt).idNum`	can be replaced by	`pt->idNum`
`(*pt).payRate`	can be replaced by	`pt->payRate`
`(*pt).hours`	can be replaced by	`pt->hours`

Program 11.5 illustrates passing a structure's address and using a pointer with the new notation to reference the structure directly.

The name of the pointer parameter declared in Program 11.5 is, of course, selected by the programmer. When `calcNet()` is called, `emp`'s starting address is passed to the function. Using this address as a starting point, individual members of the structure are accessed by including their names with the pointer.

As with all C++ expressions that access a variable, the increment and decrement operators can also be applied to them. For example, the expression

`++pt->hours`

adds one to the `hours` member of the `emp` structure. Because the `->` operator has a higher priority than the increment operator, the `hours` member is accessed first and then the increment is applied.

Program 11.5

```cpp
#include <iostream>
#include <iomanip>
using namespace std;

struct Employee  // declare a global type
{
  int idNum;
  double payRate;
  double hours;
};

double calcNet(Employee *);    //function prototype

int main()
{
  Employee emp = {6782, 8.93, 40.5};
  double netPay;

  netPay = calcNet(&emp);    // pass an address

     // set output formats
  cout << setw(10)
       << setiosflags(ios::fixed)
       << setiosflags(ios::showpoint)
       << setprecision(2);

  cout << "The net pay for employee " << emp.idNum
       << " is $" << netPay << endl;

  return 0;
}

double calcNet(Employee *pt)  // pt is a pointer to a
{                             // structure of Employee type
  return (pt->payRate * pt->hours);
}
```

Alternatively, the expression (++pt)->hours uses the prefix increment operator to increment the address in pt before the hours member is accessed. Similarly, the expression (pt++)->hours uses the postfix increment operator to increment the address in pt after the hours member is accessed. In both of these cases, however, there must be enough defined structures to ensure that the incremented pointers actually point to legitimate structures.

As an example, Figure 11.6 illustrates an array of three structures of type employee. Assuming that the address of emp[1] is stored in the pointer variable pt, the expression ++pt changes the address in pt to the starting address of emp[2], whereas the expression --pt changes the address to point to emp[0].

Returning Structures

In practice, most structure-handling functions receive direct access to a structure by receiving a structure reference or address. Then any changes to the structure can be made directly from within the function. If you want to have a function return a separate structure, however, you must follow the same procedures for returning complete data structures as for returning scalar values. These procedures include declaring the function appropriately and alerting any calling function to the type of data structure being returned. For example, the function getValues() in Program 11.6 returns a complete structure to main().

The following output is displayed when Program 11.6 is run:

```
The employee id number is 6789
The employee pay rate is $16.25
The employee hours are 38
```

FIGURE 11.6   *Changing Pointer Addresses*

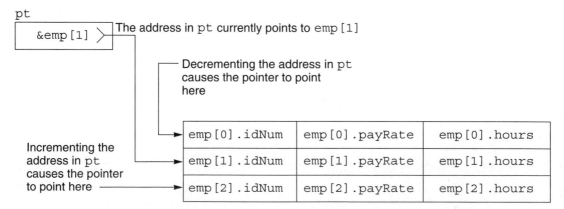

Program 11.6

```cpp
#include <iostream>
#include <iomanip>
using namespace std;

struct Employee    // declare a global type
{
  int idNum;
  double payRate;
  double hours;
};

Employee getValues();     // function prototype

int main()
{
  Employee emp;

  emp = getValues();
  cout << "\nThe employee id number is " << emp.idNum
       << "\nThe employee pay rate is $" << emp.payRate
       << "\nThe employee hours are " << emp.hours << endl;

  return 0;
}

Employee getValues() // return an employee structure
{
  Employee next;

  next.idNum = 6789;
  next.payRate = 16.25;
  next.hours = 38.0;

  return(next);
}
```

The getValues() function returns a structure, so the function header for getValues() must specify the type of structure being returned. Because getValues() does not receive any arguments, the function header has no parameter declarations and consists of the line

```cpp
Employee getValues();
```

Within getValues(), the variable next is defined as a structure of the type to be returned. After values have been assigned to the next structure, the structure values are returned by including the structure name within the parentheses of the return statement.

On the receiving side, main() must be alerted that the function getValues() will be returning a structure. This is handled by including a function declaration for getValues() in main(). Note that these steps for returning a structure from a function are identical to the normal procedures, described in Chapter 6, for returning scalar data types.

▌EXERCISES 11.3

1. Write a C++ function named days() that determines the number of days since January 1, 1900 for any date passed as a structure. Use the Date structure

```
struct Date
{
    int month;
    int day;
    int year;
};
```

In writing the days() function, use the convention that all years have 360 days and each month consists of 30 days. The function should return the number of days for any Date structure passed to it.

2. Write a C++ function named difDays() that calculates and returns the difference between two dates. Each date is passed to the function as a structure using the following global type:

```
struct Date
{
    int month;
    int day;
    int year;
};
```

The difDays() function should make two calls to the days() function written for Exercise 1.

3. *a.* Rewrite the days() function written for Exercise 1 to receive a reference to a Date structure, rather than a copy of the complete structure.
   b. Redo Exercise 3a, using a pointer rather than a reference.

4. *a.* Write a C++ function named `larger()` that returns the later of any two dates passed to it. For example, if the dates 10/9/2005 and 11/3/2005 were passed to `larger()`, the second date would be returned.

b. Include the `larger()` function that was written for Exercise 4a in a complete program. Store the `Date` structure returned by `larger()` in a separate `Date` structure and display the member values of the returned `Date`.

5. *a.* Modify the function `days()` written for Exercise 1 to account for the actual number of days in each month. Assume, however, that each year contains 365 days (that is, do not account for leap years).

b. Modify the function written for Exercise 5a to account for leap years.

11.4   Dynamic Structure Allocation

We have already encountered the concept of explicitly allocating and deallocating memory space using the `new` and `delete` operators (see Section 8.2). For convenience, the descriptions of these operators are repeated in Table 11.1.

TABLE 11.1   *Memory Allocation and Deallocation Operators*

Operator Name	Description
new	Reserves the number of bytes required by the requested data type. Returns the address of the first reserved location or returns NULL if sufficient memory is not available.
delete	Releases a block of bytes previously reserved. The address of the first reserved location is passed as an argument to the function.

This dynamic allocation of memory is especially useful when we are dealing with a list of structures, because it permits the list to expand as new records are added and to contract as records are deleted.

In requesting additional storage space, the user must provide the `new` operator with an indication of the amount of storage needed. This is done by requesting enough space for a particular type of data. For example, the expression `new(int)` or `new int` (the two forms may be used interchangeably) requests enough storage to store an integer number. A request for enough storage for a data structure is made in the same fashion. For example, using the declaration

```
struct TeleType
{
  string name;
  string phoneNo;
};
```

both the expressions new TeleType and new(TeleType) reserve enough storage for one TeleType data structure.

In allocating storage dynamically, we have no advance indication of where the computer system will physically reserve the requested number of bytes, and we have no explicit name to access the newly created storage locations. To provide access to these locations, new returns the address of the first location that has been reserved. This address must, of course, be assigned to a pointer. The return of an address by new is especially useful for creating a linked list of data structures. As each new structure is created, the address returned by new to the structure can be assigned to a member of the previous structure in the list.

Program 11.7 illustrates the use of new to create a structure dynamically in response to a user-input request.

 Program 11.7

```cpp
// a program illustrating dynamic structure allocation
#include <iostream>
#include <string>
using namespace std;

struct TeleType
{
  string name;
  string phoneNo;
};

void populate(TeleType *);  // function prototype needed by main()
void dispOne(TeleType *);   // function prototype needed by main()

int main()
{
  char key;
  TeleType *recPoint;  // recPoint is a pointer to a
                       // structure of type TeleType

  cout << "Do you wish to create a new record (respond with y or n): ";
  key = cin.get();
  if (key == 'y')
  {
    key = cin.get();      // get the Enter key in buffered input
    recPoint = new TeleType;
    populate(recPoint);
    dispOne(recPoint);
  }
```

```
   else
     cout << "\nNo record has been created.";

   return 0;
}
   // input a name and phone number
void populate(TeleType *record)   // record is a pointer to a
   {                              // structure of type TeleType
     cout << "Enter a name: ";
     getline(cin, record->name);
     cout << "Enter the phone number: ";
     getline(cin, record->phoneNo);

     return;
   }
   // display the contents of one record
void dispOne(TeleType *contents)   // contents is a pointer to a
{                                  // structure of type TeleType
     cout << "\nThe contents of the record just created is:"
          << "\nName: " << contents->name
          << "\nPhone Number: " << contents->phoneNo << endl;

     return;
}
```

A sample run produced by Program 11.7 is

```
Do you wish to create a new record (respond with y or n): y
Enter a name: Monroe, James
Enter the phone number: (555) 617-1817
The contents of the record just created is:
Name: Monroe, James
Phone Number: (555) 617-1817
```

In reviewing Program 11.7, note that only two variable declarations are made in main(). The variable key is declared as a character variable, and the variable recPoint is declared as being a pointer to a structure of the TeleType type. Because the declaration for the type TeleType is global, TeleType can be used within main() to define recPoint as a pointer to a structure of the TeleType type.

If a user enters y in response to the first prompt in main(), a call to new is made for the required memory to store the designated structure. Once recPoint has been loaded with the proper address, this address can be used to access the newly created structure. The function populate() is used to prompt the user for data needed in filling the structure and to store the user-entered data in the correct members of the structure. The argument passed to `populate()` in `main()` is the pointer `recPoint`. Like all passed arguments, the value contained in `recPoint` is passed to the function. The value in `recPoint` is an address, so `populate()` receives the address of the newly created structure and can directly access the structure members.

Within `populate()`, the value it receives is stored in the argument named `record`. Because the value to be stored in `record` is the address of a structure, `record` must be declared as a pointer to a structure. This declaration is provided by the statement `TeleType *record;`. The statements within `populate()` use the address in `record` to locate the respective members of the structure.

The `dispOne()` function in Program 11.7 is used to display the contents of the newly created and populated structure. The address passed to `dispOne()` is the same address that was passed to `populate()`. This passed value is the address of a structure, so the parameter name used to store the address is declared as a pointer to the correct structure type.

▮ EXERCISES 11.4

1. As described in Table 11.1, the `new` operator either returns the address of the first new storage area allocated or returns NULL if sufficient storage is not available. Modify Program 11.7 to check that a valid address has been returned before a call to `populate()` is made. Display an appropriate message if sufficient storage is not available.

2. Write a C++ function named `remove()` that removes an existing structure from linked list of structures consisting of names and telephone numbers. The argument passed to `remove()` should be the address of the structure preceding the record to be removed. In the removal function, make sure that the value of the pointer in the removed structure replaces the value of the pointer member of the preceding structure before the structure is removed.

3. Write a function named `insert()` that inserts a structure into a linked list of names and telephone numbers. The argument passed to `insert()` should be the address of the structure preceding the structure to be inserted. The inserted structure should follow this `current` structure. The `insert()` function should create a new structure dynamically, call the `populate()` function used in Program 11.7, and adjust all pointer values appropriately.

11.5   Common Programming Errors

There are three errors that are often made when using structures. The first error occurs because structures, as complete entities, cannot be used in relational expressions. For example, even if `TeleType` and `PhoneType` are two structures of the same type, the expression `TeleType == PhoneType` is invalid. Individual members of a structure or union can, of course, be compared, if they are of the same data type, by using any of C++'s relational operators.

The second common error is really an extension of a pointer error as it relates to structures and unions. Whenever a pointer is used to "point to" either of these data types, and whenever a pointer is itself a member of a structure or a union, take care to use the address in the pointer to access the appropriate data type. Should you be confused about just what is being pointed to, remember the saying: "If in doubt, print it out."

11.6   Chapter Summary

1. A structure allows individual variables to be grouped under a common variable name. Each variable in a structure is accessed by its structure variable name, followed by a period, followed by its individual variable name. Data structures are also called records. One form for declaring a structure is

```
struct
{
   individual member declarations;
} structure-name;
```

2. A data type can be created from a structure by using the declaration form

```
struct Data-type
{
   individual member declarations;
};
```

Individual structure variables may then be defined as this data type. By convention, the first letter of the `Data-type` name is always capitalized.

3. Structures are particularly useful as elements of arrays. Used in this manner, each structure becomes one record in a list of records.

4. Complete structures can be used as function arguments, in which case the called function receives a copy of each element in the structure. The address of a structure may also be passed, either as a reference or as a pointer, which provides the called function with direct access to the structure.

5. Structure members can be any valid C++ data type, including other structures, arrays, and pointers. When a pointer is included as a structure member, a linked list can be created. Such a list uses the pointer in one structure to "point to" (contain the address of) the next logical structure in the list.

PART III

Object-Oriented
Programming

CHAPTER 12

Introduction to Classes

Besides being an improved version of C, C++ is distinguished by its support of object-oriented programming. Central to this object orientation is the concept of an abstract data type, which is a programmer-defined data type. In this chapter, we explore the implications of permitting programmers to define their own data types and then present C++'s mechanism for constructing them. As we will see, the construction of a data type is based on both structures and functions; structures provide the means for creating new data configurations, and functions provide the means for performing operations on the structures. What C++ provides is a unique way of combining structures and functions in a self-contained, cohesive unit from which objects can be created.

12.1 Object-Based Programming

We live in a world full of objects—planes, trains, cars, telephones, books, computers, and so on. Until quite recently, however, programming techniques have not reflected this at all. The primary programming paradigm[1] has been procedural, where a program is defined as an algorithm written in a machine-readable language. The reasons for this emphasis on procedural programming are primarily historical.

When computers were developed in the 1940s, they were used by mathematicians for military purposes—for computing bomb trajectories, decoding enemy orders, and diplomatic transmissions. After World War II, computers were still used primarily by mathematicians for mathematical computations. This reality was reflected in the name of the first commercially available high-level language introduced in 1957. The language's name was FORTRAN, which was an acronym for FORmula TRANslation. In the 1960s, nearly all computer courses were taught in either engineering or mathematics departments. The term **computer science** was not yet in common use, and computer science departments were just being formed.

This situation has changed dramatically, primarily for two reasons. One of the reasons for disenchantment with procedural-based programs has been the failure of traditional procedural languages to provide an adequate means of containing software costs. Software costs include all costs associated with initial program development and subsequent program maintenance. As illustrated in Figure 12.1, the major cost of most computer projects today, whether technical or commercial, is for software.

Software costs contribute so heavily to total project costs because they are directly related to human productivity (they are labor-intensive), whereas the equipment associated with hardware costs is related to manufacturing technologies. For example, microchips that cost over $500 ten years ago can now be purchased for less than $1.

---

[1] A paradigm is a standard way of thinking about or doing something.

PROGRAMMING NOTE

Procedural, Hybrid, and Pure Object-Oriented Languages

Most high-level programming languages can be categorized into one of three main categories: procedural, hybrid, or object-oriented. FORTRAN, which was the first commercially available high-level programming language, is procedural. This makes sense because FORTRAN was designed to perform mathematical calculations that used standard algebraic formulas. These formulas were described as algorithms, and then the algorithms were coded using function and subroutine procedures. Other procedural languages that followed FORTRAN include BASIC, COBOL, and Pascal.

Currently there are only two pure object-oriented languages: Smalltalk and Eiffel. The first requirement of a pure object-oriented language is that it contain three specific features: classes, inheritance, and polymorphism (each of these features is described in this and the next two chapters). In addition to providing these features, however, a "pure" object-oriented language must always use classes. In a pure object-oriented language, all data types are constructed as classes, all data values are objects, all operators can be overloaded, and every data operation can be executed using only a class member function. *It is impossible, in a pure object-oriented language, not to use object-oriented features* throughout a program. This is not the case in a hybrid language.

In a hybrid language, such as C++, *it is impossible not to use elements of a procedural program.* This is because the use of any built-in data type or operation effectively violates the pure object-oriented paradigm. Although a hybrid language must have the ability to define classes, the distinguishing feature of a hybrid language is that it is possible to write a complete program using only procedural code. Furthermore, hybrid languages need not even provide inheritance and polymorphic features, but they must provide classes. Languages that use classes but do not provide inheritance and polymorphic features are referred to as *object-based* languages rather than *object-oriented*. All versions of Visual Basic prior to Version 4 are examples of object-based hybrid languages.

It is far easier, however, to increase manufacturing productivity a thousand-fold, with the resulting decrease in hardware costs, than it is for programmers to double either the quantity or the quality of the code they produce. Consequently, as hardware costs have plummeted, software productivity and its associated costs have remained relatively constant. Thus the ratio of software costs to total system costs (hardware plus software) has increased dramatically.

One way to increase programmer productivity significantly is to create code that can be reused without extensive revision, retesting, and revalidation. The inability of procedurally structured code to provide this type of reusability has led to the search for other software approaches.

FIGURE 12.1 *Software Is the Major Cost of Most Computer Projects*

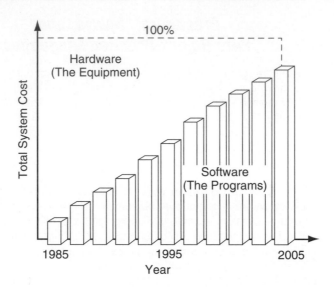

The second reason for disenchantment with procedural-based programming has been the emergence of graphical screens and the subsequent interest in window applications. Programming multiple windows on the same graphical screen is virtually impossible with standard procedural programming techniques.

The solution to producing programs that efficiently manipulate graphical screens and provide reusable windowing code was found in artificial intelligence–based and simulation programming techniques. The former area, artificial intelligence, contained extensive research on geometrical object specification and recognition. The latter area, simulation, contained considerable background on simulating items as objects with well-defined interactions between them. This object-based paradigm fit well in a graphical windows environment, where each window can be specified as a self-contained object.

An object is also well suited to a programming representation because it can be specified by two basic characteristics: a current **state**, which defines how the object appears at the moment, and a **behavior**, which defines how the object reacts to external inputs.

To make this more concrete, consider a geometric object, such as a rectangle. A rectangle's current state is defined by its shape and location. The shape is traditionally specified by its length and width, whereas its location can be specified in a number of ways. One simple way is to list the values of two corner positions. The behavior we provide a rectangle depends on what we are willing to have our rectangle do. For example, if we intend to display the rectangle on a screen, we might provide it with the ability to move its position and change either its length or its width.

It is worthwhile distinguishing here between an actual rectangle, which might exist on a piece of paper or a computer screen, and our description of it. Our description is more accurately termed a model. By definition, a model is only a representation of a real object; it is not the object itself. Very few models are ever complete; that is, a model typically does not reveal every aspect of the object it represents. Each model is defined for a particular purpose that usually requires representing only the part of an object's state or behavior that is of interest to us. To clarify this point further, let's consider another common object, an elevator.

Like all objects, an elevator can be modeled in terms of a state and a behavior. Its state might be given in terms of its size, location, interior decoration, or any number of attributes. Likewise, its behavior might be specified in terms of its reaction when one of its buttons is pushed. Constructing a model of an elevator, however, requires that we select those attributes and behaviors that are of interest to us. For purposes of a simulation, for example, we may be concerned only with the current floor position of the elevator and with how to make it move to another floor location. Other attributes and behaviors of the elevator may be left out of the model because they do not affect the aspects of the elevator that we are interested in studying. At the end of this chapter, we will see how to model an elevator in C++ and make our model elevator "move" using a very simple representation.

It is also important to distinguish between the attributes we choose to include in our model and the values that these attributes can have. The attributes and behavior together define a category, or type, of object out of which many individual objects can be designated. In object-based programming, the category of objects defined by a given set of attributes and behaviors is called a **class**. Only when specific values have been assigned to the attributes is a particular object defined.

For example, the attributes length and width can be used to define a general type of shape called a rectangle. Only when specific values have been assigned to these attributes have we represented a particular rectangle. This distinction carries over into C++: The attributes and behavior we select are said to define a general class, or type, of object. The object itself comes into existence only when we assign specific values to the attributes.

As you might expect, attributes in C++ are defined by variables, and behaviors are constructed from functions. The set of attributes and behavior defining a class is frequently referred to as the class's **interface**. Once the interface has been specified, creating a particular object is achieved by assigning specific values to the appropriate variables. How all of this is constructed is the topic of the remaining sections.

▌EXERCISES 12.1

1. Define the following terms.

   a. Attribute   *e.* Class

   b. Behavior   *f.* Object

   c. State   *g.* Interface

   d. Model

2. a. Instead of specifying a rectangle's location by listing the position of two diagonal corner points, what other attributes could we use?

   b. What other attributes, besides length and width, might be used to describe a rectangle if the rectangle were to be drawn on a color monitor?

   c. Describe a set of attributes that could be used to define circles that are to be drawn on a black-and-white monitor.

   d. What additional attributes would you add to those selected in response to Exercise 2c if the circles were to be drawn on a color monitor?

3. a. For each of the following, determine what attributes might be of interest to someone considering buying the item.

      i. A book

     ii. A can of soda

    iii. A pen

     iv. A cassette tape

      v. A cassette tape player

     vi. An elevator

    vii. A car

   b. Do the attributes you used in Exercise 3a model an object or a class of objects?

4. For each of the following items, what behavior might be of interest to someone considering buying the item?

   a. A car

   b. A cassette tape player

5. All of the examples of classes considered in this section have consisted of inanimate objects. Do you think that animate objects such as pets and even human beings could be modeled in terms of attributes and behavior? Why or why not?

6. a. The attributes of a class represent how objects of the class appear to the outside world. The behavior represents how an object of a class reacts to an external stimulus. Given this, what do you think is the mechanism by which one object "triggers" the designated behavior in another object? (*Hint:* Consider how one person typically gets another person to do something.)

   b. If behavior in C++ is constructed by defining an appropriate function, how do you think the behavior is activated in C++?

12.2   Classes

A **class** is a programmer-defined data type (more generally, a programmer-defined data type is also referred to as an **abstract data type**). To understand the full implications of this more clearly, consider three of the built-in data types supplied by C++: integers, reals, and characters. In using these data types, we typically declare one or more variables of the desired type, use them in their accepted ways, and avoid using them in ways that are not specified. Thus, for example, we would not use the modulus operator on two double-precision numbers. Because this operation makes no sense, it has not been supplied in C++.

In computer terminology, the combination of data and their associated operations is defined as a class. That is, a class defines *both* the types of data and the types of operations that may be performed on the data. Seen in this light, it is more accurate to speak of the built-in data types provided by C++ as the integer class, the double-precision class, the Boolean class, and the character class. Such a definition conveys that both a type of data and specific operational capabilities are being supplied. In a simplified form, this relationship can be described as

```
Class = Allowable Data Values + Operational Capabilities
```

Before seeing how to construct our own classes, let's take a moment to list some of the operational capabilities supplied with C++'s built-in classes. The reason for this is that we will have to provide the same capabilities as part of our own classes. The minimum set of the capabilities provided by C++'s built-in classes is listed in Table 12.1.

Although we don't normally think of these capabilities individually when we use them, the designers of C++ clearly had to when they created the C++ compiler. C++ allows us to create our own classes, so we must now be aware of these capabilities and provide them with the classes that we construct.

TABLE 12.1   *Built-in Data Type Capabilities*

Capability	Example
Define one or more variables of the class	`int a, b;`
Initialize a variable at definition	`int a = 5;`
Assign a value to a variable	`a = 10;`
Assign one variable's value to another variable	`a = b;`
Perform mathematical operations	`a + b`
Convert from one data type to another	`a = (int) 7.2;`

Construction of a class is inherently easy, and we already have all the necessary tools in variables and functions. In C++, various combinations of variables provide the means of defining new data types, and functions provide the means of defining operational capabilities. Using this information, we can now extend our equation definition of a class to its C++ representation:

$$C\text{++}\ Class\ =\ Data\ +\ Functions$$

Thus, in C++, a class provides a mechanism for packaging a data structure and functions together in a self-contained unit. In this chapter we describe how classes are constructed and how variables are declared and initialized. The assignment and mathematical capabilities listed in Table 12.1, as they apply to classes, are presented in Chapter 13. Type conversions are presented in Chapter 14.

Class Construction

A class defines both data and functions. This is usually accomplished by constructing a class in two parts, consisting of a declaration section and an implementation section. As illustrated in Figure 12.2, the declaration section declares both the data types and the functions for the class. The implementation section is then used to define the functions whose prototypes have been declared in the declaration section.[2]

FIGURE 12.2   *Format of a Class Definition*

```
// class declaration section
class classname
{
    data members    //    instance variables
       and
    function members   //   inline and prototypes
};
// class implementation section
function definitions
```

Both the variables and the functions listed in the class declaration section are collectively referred to as **class members**. Individually, the variables are referred to as both **data members** and **instance variables** (the terms are synonymous), and the functions are referred to as **member functions**. A member function name may not be the same as a data member name.

---

[2] This separation into two parts is not mandatory; the implementation can be included within the declaration section if inline functions are used.

As a specific example of a class, consider the following definition of a class named Date.

```cpp
//--- class declaration section

class Date
{
  private:
    int month;
    int day;
    int year;
  public:
    Date(int = 7, int = 4, int = 2006);  // constructor with defaults
    void setDate(int, int, int);   // member function to copy a Date
    void showDate(void);           // member function to display a Date
};

//--- class implementation section

Date::Date(int mm, int dd, int yyyy)
{
  month = mm;
  day = dd;
  year = yyyy;
}

void Date::setDate(int mm, int dd, int yyyy)
{
  month = mm;
  day = dd;
  year = yyyy;

  return;
}

void Date::showDate(void)
{
  cout << "The Date is ";
  cout << setfill('0')
       << setw(2) << month << '/'
       << setw(2) << day << '/'
       << setw(2) << year % 100; // extract the last 2 year digits
  cout << endl;
  return;
}
```

Because this definition may initially look overwhelming, first simply note that it does consist of two sections—a declaration section and an implementation section. Now let's consider each of these sections individually.

The class declaration section begins with the keyword `class` followed by a class name. Following the class name are the class's variable declarations and function prototypes, enclosed in a brace pair that is terminated with a semicolon. Thus the general structure of the form that we have used is[3]

```
class Name
{
   private:
      a list of variable declarations
   public:
      a list of function prototypes
};
```

Note that this format is followed by our `Date` class, which for convenience we have listed below with no internal comments:

```
//--- class declaration section

class Date
{
   private:
      int month;
      int day;
      int year;
   public:
      Date(int = 7, int = 4, int = 2006);
      void setDate(int, int, int);
      void showDate(void);
};   // this is a declaration - don't forget the semi-colon
```

The name of this class is `Date`. Although the initial capital letter is not required, it is conventionally used to designate a class. The body of the declaration section, which is enclosed within braces, consists of variable and function declarations. In this case the data members `month`, `day`, and `year` are declared as integers, and three functions named `Date()`, `setDate()`, and `showDate()` are declared via prototypes. The keywords `private` and `public` are access

---

[3] Other forms are possible. This form is one of the most commonly used and easily understood, so it will serve as our standard model throughout the text.

specifiers that define access rights. The `private` keyword specifies that the class members that follow—in this case the data members `month`, `day`, and `year`—may be accessed only by using the class functions (or friend functions, as we will see in Section 12.3).[4] The purpose of the `private` designation is to enforce data security by requiring all accesses to `private` data members through the provided member functions. This type of access, which restricts a user from seeing how the data is actually stored, is referred to as **data hiding**. Once a class category such as `private` is designated, it remains in force until a new category is listed.

Specifically, we have chosen to store a `Date` using three integers: one each for the month, day, and year. We will also always store the year as a four-digit number. Thus, for example, we will store the year 1998 as 1998, not as 98. Being sure to store all years with their correct century designation will eliminate a multitude of problems that can crop up if only the last two digits, such as 98, are stored. For example, the number of years between 2007 and 1999 can be quickly calculated as 2007 – 1999 = 8 years, but this same answer is not so easily obtained if only the year values 07 and 99 are used. Additionally, we are sure of what the year 2000 refers to, whereas a two-digit value such as 00 could refer to either 1900 or 2000.

Following the `private` class data members, the function prototypes listed in the `Date` class have been declared as `public`. This means that these class functions *can* be called by any objects and functions not in the class (outside). In general, all class functions should be public; thus they furnish capabilities to manipulate the class variables from outside of the class. For our `Date` class, we have initially provided three functions named `Date()`, `setDate()`, and `showDate()`. Note that one of these member functions has the same name, `Date`, as the class name. This particular function is referred to as a *constructor* function, and it has a specially defined purpose: It can be used to initialize class data members with values. The default values that are used for this function are the numbers `7`, `4`, and `2006`, which, as we will shortly see, are used as the default month, day, and year values, respectively. The only point to remember now is that the default year is correctly represented as a four-digit integer that retains the century designation. Also note that the constructor function has no return type, which is a requirement for this special function. The two remaining functions declared in our declaration example are `setDate()` and `showDate()`, both of which have been declared as returning no value (`void`). In the implementation section of the class, these three member functions will be written to permit initialization, assignment, and display capabilities, respectively.

---

[4] Note that the default membership category in a class is `private`, which means that this keyword can be omitted. In this text, we will explicitly use the `private` designation to reinforce the idea of access restrictions inherent in class membership.

The **implementation section** of a class is where the member functions declared in the declaration section are written.[5] Figure 12.3 illustrates the general form of functions included in the implementation section. This format is correct for all functions except the constructor, which, as we have stated, has no `return` type.

As shown in Figure 12.3, member functions defined in the implementation section have the same format as all user-written C++ functions, with the addition of the class name and the scope resolution operator, `::`, that identifies the function as a member of a particular class. Let us now reconsider the implementation section of our `Date` class, which is repeated below for convenience.

FIGURE 12.3 *Format of a Member Function*

```
return-type class-name::function-name(parameter list)
{
    function body
}
```

```
//--- class implementation section
Date::Date(int mm, int dd, int yyyy)
{
  month = mm;
  day = dd;
  year = yyyy;
}
void Date::setDate(int mm, int dd, int yyyy)
{
  month = mm;
  day = dd;
  year = yyyy;

  return;
}
void Date::showDate(void)
{
  cout << "The Date is ";
  cout << setfill('0')
       << setw(2) << month << '/'
       << setw(2) << day << '/'
       << setw(2) << year % 100; // extract the last 2 year digits
  cout << endl;
  return;
}
```

---

[5] It is also possible to define these functions within the declaration section by declaring and writing them as inline functions. Examples of inline member functions are presented in Section 12.3.

Note that the first function in this implementation section has the same name as the class, which makes it a constructor function. Accordingly, it has no return type. The `Date::` included at the beginning of the function header line identifies this function as a member of the `Date` class. The rest of the header line,

```
Date(int mm, int dd, int yyyy)
```

defines the function as having three integer parameters. The body of this function simply assigns the data members `month`, `day`, and `year` with the values of the parameters `mm`, `dd`, and `yyyy`, respectively.

The next function header line

```
void Date::setDate(int mm, int dd, int yyyy)
```

defines this as the `setDate()` function belonging to the `Date` class (`Date::`). This function returns no value (`void`) and expects three integer parameters, `mm`, `dd`, and `yyyy`. In a manner similar to the `Date()` function, the body of this function assigns the data members `month`, `day`, and `year` with the values of its parameters.

Finally, the last function header line in the implementation section defines a function named `showDate()`. This function has no parameters, returns no value, and is a member of the `Date` class. The body of this function, however, needs a little more explanation.

Although we have chosen to store all years internally as four-digit values that retain century information, users are accustomed to seeing `Date`s where the year is represented as a two-digit value, such as 12/15/99. To display the last two digits of the year value, the expression `year % 100` can be used. For example, if the year is 1999, the expression `1999 % 100` yields the value 99, and if the year is 2006, the expression `2006 % 100` yields the value 6. Note that if we had used an assignment such as `year = year % 100;`, we would actually be altering the stored value of `year` to correspond to the last two digits of the year. Because we want to retain the year as a four-digit number, we must be careful to manipulate only the displayed value using the expression `year % 100` within the `cout` stream. The `setfill` and `setw` manipulators are used to ensure that the displayed values correspond to conventionally accepted `Date`s. For example, the `Date` March 9, 2007 should appear as either 3/9/07 or 03/09/07. The `setw` manipulator forces each value to be displayed in a field width of 2. Because this manipulator remains in effect only for the next insertion, we have included it before the display of each `Date` value. The `setfill` manipulator, however, remains in effect until the `fill` character is changed, so we only have to include it once. We have used the `setfill` manipulator here to change the `fill` character from its default of a blank space to the character 0. Doing this ensures that a `Date` such as December 9, 2007 will appear as 12/09/07, not as 12/ 9/ 7.

To see how our `Date` class can be used within the context of a complete program, consider Program 12.1. To make the program easier to read, it has been shaded in light and darker areas. The lighter area contains the class declaration and implementation sections that we have already considered. The darker area contains the header and the `main()` function. For convenience, we will retain this shading convention for all programs that use classes.[6]

The declaration and implementation sections contained in the lightly shaded region of Program 12.1 should look familiar to you; they contain the class declaration and implementation sections that we have already discussed. Note, however, that this region only declares the class, it does not create any variables of this class type. This is true of all C++ types, including the built-in types such as integers and doubles. Just as a variable of an integer type must be defined, variables of a user-declared class must also be defined. Variables defined to be of a user-declared class are referred to as `objects`.

Using this new terminology, the first statement in Program 12.1's `main()` function, contained in the darker area, defines three objects, named a, b, and c, to be of class type `Date`. In C++, whenever a new object is defined, memory is allocated for the object and its data members are automatically initialized. This is done by an automatic call to the class constructor function. For example, consider the definition `Date  a, b, c(4,1,1998);` contained in `main()`. When the object named a is defined, the constructor function `Date` is automatically called. Because no parameters have been assigned to a, the default values of the constructor function are used, resulting in the initialization

$$a.month = 7$$
$$a.day = 4$$
$$a.year = 2006$$

---

[6] This shading is not accidental. In practice, the lightly shaded region containing the class definition would be placed in a separate file. A single `#include` statement would then be used to include this class declaration in the program. Thus the final program would consist of the two darkly shaded regions illustrated in Program 12.1 and one more `#include` statement in the first region.

Program 12.1

```cpp
#include <iostream>
#include <iomanip>
using namespace std;

// class declaration
class Date
{
  private:
    int month;
    int day;
    int year;
  public:
    Date(int = 7, int = 4, int = 2006); // constructor with defaults
    void setDate(int, int, int);   // member function to copy a date
    void showDate();               // member function to display a date
};

// implementation section
Date::Date(int mm, int dd, int yyyy)
{
  month = mm;
  day = dd;
  year = yyyy;
}

void Date::setDate(int mm, int dd, int yyyy)
{
  month = mm;
  day = dd;
  year = yyyy;

  return;
}

void Date::showDate()
{
  cout << "The date is ";
  cout << setfill('0')
       << setw(2) << month << '/'
       << setw(2) << day << '/'
       << setw(2) << year % 100; // extract the last 2 year digits
  cout << endl;
  return;
}
```

(continued on next page)

(continued from previous page)

```
int main()
{
    Date a, b, c(4,1,1998); // declare 3 objects

    b.setDate(12,25,2007);   // assign values to b's data members
    cout << endl;

    a.showDate();            // display object a's values
    b.showDate();            // display object b's values
    c.showDate();            // display object c's values

    cout << endl;

    return 0;
}
```

Note the notation that we have used here. It consists of an object name and an attribute name separated by a period. This is the standard syntax for referring to an object's attribute:

$$objectName.attributeName$$

where *objectName* is the name of a specific object and *attributeName* is the name of a data member defined for the object's class.

Thus the notation a.month = 7 refers to the fact that object a's month data member has been set to the value 7. Similarly, the notation a.day = 4 and a.year = 2006 refers to the fact that a's day and year data members have been set to the values 4 and 2006, respectively. In the same manner, when the object named b is defined, the same default parameters are used, resulting in the initialization of b's data members as

$$b.month = 7$$
$$b.day = 4$$
$$b.year = 2006$$

The object named c, however, is defined with the arguments 4, 1, and 1998. These three arguments are passed into the constructor function when the object is defined, resulting in the initialization of c's data members as

$$c.month = 4$$
$$c.day = 1$$
$$c.year = 1998$$

The next statement in `main()`, which is `b.setDate(12, 25, 2007)`, calls b's `setDate` function, which assigns the argument values 12, 25, and 2007 to b's data members, resulting in the assignment

```
b.month = 12
b.day = 25
b.year = 2007
```

Note the syntax for referring to an object's method. This syntax is

objectName.methodName(parameters)

where *objectName* is the name of a specific object and *methodName* is the name of one of the functions defined for the object's class. Because we have defined all class functions as `public`, a statement such as

```
b.setDate(12,25,2007)
```

is valid inside the `main()` function and is a call to the class's `setDate()` function. This statement tells the `setDate()` function to operate on the b object with the arguments 12, 25, and 2007. It is important to understand that because all class data members were specified as `private`, a statement such as `b.month = 12` would be invalid from within `main()`. We are therefore forced to rely on member functions to access data member values.

The last three statements in `main()` call the `showDate()` function to operate on the a, b, and c objects. The first call results in the display of a's data values, the second call in the display of b's data values, and the third call in the display of c's data values. Thus the output displayed by Program 12.1 is

```
The date is 07/04/06
The date is 12/25/07
The date is 04/01/98
```

Note that a statement such as `cout << a;` is invalid within `main()` because `cout` does not know how to handle an object of class `Date`. Thus we have supplied our class with a function that can be used to access and display an object's internal values.

Terminology

Confusion sometimes arises about the terms associated with object-oriented programming, so we will take a moment to clarify and review this terminology.

PROGRAMMING NOTE

Interfaces, Implementations, and Information Hiding

The terms **interface** and **implementation** are used extensively in object-oriented programming literature. Each of these terms can be equated to specific parts of a class's declaration and implementation sections.

An *interface* consists of a class's public member function declarations and any supporting comments. As such, the interface should be all that is required to tell a programmer how to use the class.

The *implementation* consists of both the class's implementation section, which is made up of both private and public member definitions, *and* the class's private data members that are contained in a class declaration section.

The implementation is the essential means of providing information hiding. In its most general context, **information hiding** refers to the principle that *how* a class is internally constructed is not relevant to any programmer who wishes to use the class. That is, the implementation can and should be hidden from all class users precisely to ensure that the class is not altered or compromised in any way. All that a programmer needs to know to use the class correctly should be provided by the interface.

A **class** is a programmer-defined data type out of which objects can be created. **Objects** are created from classes; they have the same relationship to classes as variables do to C++'s built-in data types. For example, in the declaration

```
int a;
```

a is said to be a variable, whereas in Program 12.1's declaration

```
Date a;
```

a is said to be an object. If it initially helps you to think of an object as a variable, do so.

Objects are also referred to as **instances** of a class, and the process of creating a new object is frequently referred to as an **instantiation** of the object. Each time a new object is instantiated (created), a new set of data members belonging to the object is created.[7] The particular values contained in these data members determines the object's **state**.

Seen in this way, a class can be thought of as a blueprint out of which particular instances (objects) can be created. Each instance (object) of a class will have its own set of particular values for the set of data members specified in the class declaration section.

---

[7] Note that only one set of class functions is created. These functions are shared between objects.

In addition to the data types allowed for an object, a class also defines *behavior*—that is, the operations that are permitted to be performed on an object's data members. Users of the object need to know *what* these functions can do and how to activate them through function calls, but unless run time or space implications are relevant, they do not need to know *how* the operation is done. The actual implementation details of an object's operations are contained in the class implementation, which can be hidden from the user. Other names for the operations defined in a class implementation section are **procedures**, **functions**, **services**, and **methods**. We will use these terms interchangeably throughout the remainder of the text.

▌ EXERCISES 12.2

1. Define the following terms.
   a. Class
   b. Object
   c. Declaration section
   d. Implementation section
   e. Instance variable
   f. Member function
   g. Data member
   h. Constructor
   i. Class instance
   j. Services
   k. Methods
   l. Interface

2. Write a class declaration section for each of the following specifications. In each case, include a prototype for a constructor and a member function named showdata() that can be used to display member values.

   a. A class named Time that has integer data members named secs, mins, and hours.

   b. A class named Complex that has double-precision data members named real and imaginary.

   c. A class named Circle that has integer data members named xcenter and ycenter and a double-precision data member named radius.

   d. A class named System that has character data members named computer, printer, and screen, each capable of holding 30 characters (including the end-of-string NULL), and double-precision data members named compPrice, printPrice, and scrnPrice.

3. a. Construct a class implementation section for the constructor and showData() function members corresponding to the class declaration created for Exercise 2a.

   b. Construct a class implementation section for the constructor and showData() function members corresponding to the class declaration created for Exercise 2b.

   c. Construct a class implementation section for the constructor and showData() function members corresponding to the class declaration created for Exercise 2c.

   d. Construct a class implementation section for the constructor and showData() function members corresponding to the class declaration created for Exercise 2d.

4. a. Include the class declaration and implementation sections prepared for Exercises 2a and 3a in a complete working program.

   b. Include the class declaration and implementation sections prepared for Exercises 2b and 3b in a complete working program.

c. Include the class declaration and implementation sections prepared for Exercises 2c and 3c in a complete working program.

d. Include the class declaration and implementation sections prepared for Exercises 2d and 3d in a complete working program.

5. Determine the errors in the following class declaration section:

```
class Employee
{
public:
  int empnum;
  char code;
private:
  class(int = 0);
  void showemp(int, char);
};
```

6. *a.* Add to Program 12.1 another member function named `convrt()` that does the following: The function should access the `month`, `year`, and `day` data members and should display and then return an integer that is calculated as *year * 10000 + month * 100 + day*. For example, if the Date is 4/1/2006, the returned value is `20060401` (dates in this form are useful when performing sorts, because placing the numbers in numerical order automatically places the corresponding dates in chronological order).

b. Include the modified `Date` class constructed for Exercise 6a in a complete C++ program.

7. *a.* Add to Program 12.1's class definition an additional member function named `leapyr()` that returns a true if the year is a leap year and a false if it is not a leap year. A leap year is any year that is evenly divisible by 4 but not evenly divisible by 100, with the exception that all years evenly divisible by 400 are leap years. For example, the year 1996 is a leap year because it is evenly divisible by 4 and not evenly divisible by 100. The year 2000 will be a leap year because it is evenly divisible by 400.

b. Include the class definition constructed for Exercise 7a in a complete C++ program. The `main()` function should display the message `The year is a leap year` or the message `The year is not a leap year`, depending on the `date` object's `year` value.

8. *a.* Add to Program 12.1's class definition a member function named `dayOfWeek()` that determines the day of the week for any `date` object. An algorithm for determining the day of the week, known as Zeller's algorithm, follows.

```
If mm is less than 3
  mm = mm + 12
  yyyy = yyyy - 1
Endif
Set century = Int(yyyy/100)
Set year = yyyy % 100
Set T = dd + int(26*(mm + 1)/10) + year + int(year/4)
          + int(century/4) - 2 * century
Set DayofWeek = T % 7
If DayofWeek is less than 0 then DayofWeek = DayofWeek + 7
```

Using this algorithm, the variable `DayofWeek` will have a value of 1 if the date is a Sunday, 2 if a Monday, etc.

b. Include the class definition constructed for Exercise 8a in a complete C++ program. The `main()` function should display the name of the day (`Sun`, `Mon`, `Tue`, etc.) for the `Date` object being tested.

9. *a.* Construct a class named `Rectangle` that has floating-point data members named `length` and `width`. The class should have a member function named `perimeter()` and `area()` to calculate the perimeter and area of a rectangle, a member function named `getdata()` to set a rectangle's length and width, and a member function named `showdata()` that displays a rectangle's length, width, perimeter, and area.

b. Include the `Rectangle` class constructed in Exercise 9a within a working C++ program.

10. *a.* Modify the `Date` class defined in Program 12.1 to include a `nextDay()` function that increments a date by one day. Test your function to ensure that it correctly increments days into a new month and into a new year.

b. Modify the `Date` class defined in Program 12.1 to include a `priorDay()` function that decrements a date by one day. Test your function to ensure that it correctly decrements days into a prior month and into a prior year.

11. Modify the `Date` class in Program 12.1 to contain a function that compares two `Date` objects and returns the larger of the two. The function should be written according to the following algorithm:

```
Comparison function
  Accept two Date values as parameters
  Determine the later date using the following procedure:
    Convert each date into an integer value having the form
    yyyymmdd.
    (This can be accomplished using the formula year * 10000 +
    month * 100 + day)
    Compare the corresponding integers for each date.
    The larger integer corresponds to the later date.
  Return the later date
```

12.3   Constructors

A **constructor** function is any function that has the same name as its class. Multiple constructors can be defined for each class as long as they are distinguishable by the numbers and types of their parameters (which is simply an example of function overloading).

The intended purpose of a constructor is to initialize a new object's data members. Thus, depending on the number and types of supplied arguments, one constructor function is automatically called each time an object is created. If no constructor function is written, the compiler supplies a default constructor. In addition to its initialization role, a constructor function may perform other tasks when it is called, and it can be written in a variety of ways. In this section we present the possible variations of constructor functions and introduce another function, the destructor, that is automatically called whenever an object goes out of existence.

Figure 12.4 illustrates the general format of a constructor. As shown in this figure, a constructor

- must have the same name as the class to which it belongs
- must have no return type (not even `void`)

If you do not include a constructor in your class definition, the compiler supplies a do-nothing default one for you. For example, consider the following class declaration:

```
class Date
{
  private:
    int month, day, year;
  public:
    void setDate(int, int, int);
    void showDate()
};
```

Because no user-defined constructor has been declared here, the compiler creates a default constructor. For our `Date` class, this default constructor is equivalent to the implementation `Date(void){}`—that is, the compiler-supplied default constructor expects no parameters and has an empty body. Clearly, this default constructor is not very useful, but it does exist if no other constructor is declared.

FIGURE 12.4 *Constructor Format*

```
classname::className(parameter list)
{
    function body
}
```

The term **default constructor** is used quite frequently in C++. It refers to any constructor that does not require any arguments when it is called. This can be because no parameters are declared, which is the case for the compiler-supplied default, or because all arguments have been given default values. For example, the constructor `Date(int = 7, int = 4, int = 2006)` is a valid prototype for a default constructor. Here, each argument has been given a default value, and an object can be declared as type `Date` without supplying any further arguments. Using such a constructor, the declaration `Date a;` initializes the a object with the default values 7, 4, and 2006.

Program 12.2

```cpp
#include <iostream>
#include <iomanip>
using namespace std;

// class declaration section

class Date
{
  private:
    int month;
    int day;
    int year;
  public:
    Date(int = 7, int = 4, int = 2006); // constructor with defaults
};

// implementation section

Date::Date(int mm, int dd, int yyyy)
{
  month = mm;
  day = dd;
  year = yyyy;
  cout << "Created a new data object with data values "
       << month <<", " << day << ", " << year << endl;
}

int main()
{
  Date a;                // declare an object
  Date b;                // declare an object
  Date c(4,1,2007);      // declare an object

  return 0;
}
```

To verify that a constructor function is automatically called whenever a new object is created, consider Program 12.2. Note that in the implementation section, the constructor function uses cout to display the message Created a new data object with data values. Thus, whenever the constructor is called, this message is displayed. Because the main() function creates three objects, the constructor is called three times, and the message is displayed three times.

The following output is produced when Program 12.2 is executed:

```
Created a new data object with data values 7, 4, 2006
Created a new data object with data values 7, 4, 2006
Created a new data object with data values 4, 1, 2007
```

Although any legitimate C++ statement can be used within a constructor function, such as the `cout` statement used in Program 12.2, it is best to keep constructors simple and to use them only for initializing purposes. One further point needs to be made with respect to the constructor function contained in Program 12.2. According to the rules of C++, object members are initialized in the order in which they are declared in the class declaration section, *not* in the order in which they may appear in the function's definition within the implementation section. Usually this will not be an issue, unless one member is initialized using another data member's value.

Calling Constructors

As we have seen, constructors are called whenever an object is created. The actual declaration, however, can be made in a variety of ways. For example, the declaration

```
Date c(4,1,2007);
```

used in Program 12.2 could also have been written as

```
Date c = Date(4,1,2007);
```

This second form declares c as being of type `Date` and then makes a direct call to the constructor function with the arguments `4`, `1`, and `2007`. This second form can be simplified when only one argument is passed to the constructor. For example, if only the `month` data member of the c object needed to be initialized with the value 8, and the `day` and `year` members can use the default values, the object can be created using the declaration

```
Date c = 8;
```

Because this resembles declarations in C, it and its complete form using the equals sign are referred to as the **C style of initialization**. The form of declaration used in Program 12.2 is referred to as the **C++ style of initialization**, and this is the form we will use most of the time throughout the remainder of the text.

Regardless of which initialization form you use, in no case should an object be declared with empty parentheses. For example, the declaration `Date a();` is not the same as the declaration `Date a;`. The latter declaration uses the default constructor values, whereas the former declaration results in no object being created.

Overloaded and Inline Constructors

The primary difference between a constructor and other user-written functions is how the constructor is called: Constructors are called automatically each time an object is created, whereas other functions must be explicitly called by name.[8] As a function, however, a constructor must still follow all of the rules applicable to user-written functions that were presented in Chapter 6. This means that constructors may have default arguments, as was illustrated in Programs 12.1 and 12.2, may be overloaded, and may be written as inline functions.

Recall from Section 6.1 that function overloading permits the same function name to be used with different parameter lists. On the basis of the argument types supplied, the compiler determines which function to use when the call is encountered. Let's see how this can be applied to our `Date` class. For convenience, the appropriate class declaration is repeated below:

```
// class declaration section
class Date
{
  private:
    int month;
    int day;
    int year;
  public:
    Date(int = 7, int = 4, int = 2006);   // constructor
};
```

Here, the constructor prototype specifies three integer parameters, which are used to initialize the `month`, `day`, and `year` data members.

An alternative method of specifying a `Date` is to use a long integer in the form *year* * *10000* + *month* * *100* + *day*. For example, the `Date` 12/24/2008 would be

---

[8] This is true for all functions except destructors, which are described later in this section. A destructor function is automatically called each time an object is destroyed.

20081224, and the date 2/5/2010 would be 20100205.[9] A suitable prototype for a constructor that uses dates of this form is

```
Date(long);  // an overloaded constructor
```

Here, the constructor is declared as receiving one long-integer argument. The code for this new `Date` function must, of course, correctly convert its single argument into a `month`, `day`, and `year` and would be included within the class implementation section. The actual code for such a constructor is

```
Date::Date(long yyyymmdd)       // a second constructor
{
  year = int(yyyymmdd/10000.0);      // extract the year
  month = int( (yyyymmdd - year * 10000.0) / 100.00 ); // extract the month
  day = int(yyyymmdd - year * 10000.0 - month * 100.0); // extract the day
}
```

Do not be overly concerned with the actual conversion code used within the function's body. The important point here is the concept of overloading the `Date()` function to provide two constructors. Program 12.3 contains the complete class definition within the context of a working program.

The output provided by Program 12.3 is

```
The date is 07/04/06
The date is 04/01/98
The date is 05/15/08
```

Three objects are created in Program 12.3's `main()` function. The first object, a, is initialized with the default constructor using its default arguments. Object b is also initialized with the default constructor but uses the arguments `4, 1`, and `1998`. Finally, object c, which is initialized with a long integer, uses the second constructor in the class implementation section. The compiler "knows" that it should use this second constructor because the argument specified, `20080515L`, is clearly designated as a long integer. It is worthwhile pointing out that a compiler error would occur if both `Date` constructors had default values. In such a case, a declaration such as `Date d;` would be ambiguous to the compiler, because it would not be able to determine which constructor to use. Thus, in each implementation section, only one constructor can be written as the default.

---

[9] The reasons for specifying dates in this manner are that only one number needs to be used per date and that sorting the numbers automatically puts the corresponding dates into chronological order.

Program 12.3

```cpp
#include <iostream>
#include <iomanip>
using namespace std;

// class declaration

class Date
{
 private:
    int month;
    int day;
    int year;
  public:
    Date(int = 7, int = 4, int = 2006);    // constructor with defaults
    Date(long);                     // another constructor
    void showDate();                // member function to display a date
};
// implementation section

Date::Date(int mm, int dd, int yyyy)
{
  month = mm;
  day = dd;
  year = yyyy;
}
Date::Date(long yyyymmdd)
{
  year = int(yyyymmdd/10000.0);    // extract the year
  month = int( (yyyymmdd - year * 10000.0)/100.00 ); // extract the month
  day = int(yyyymmdd - year * 10000.0 - month * 100.0); // extract the day
}
void Date::showDate()
{
  cout << "The date is " << setfill('0')
       << setw(2) << month << '/'
       << setw(2) << day << '/'
       << setw(2) << year % 100; // extract the last 2 year digits
  return;
}
```

(continued on next page)

(continued from previous page)

```
    int main()
    {
      Date a, b(4,1,1998), c(20080515L); // declare three objects
      cout << endl;
      a.showDate();           // display object a's values
      cout << endl;
      b.showDate();           // display object b's values
      cout << endl;
      c.showDate();           // display object c's values
      cout << endl << endl;
      return 0;
    }
```

Just as constructors may be overloaded, they may also be written as *inline member functions.*[10] Doing so simply means defining the function in the class declaration section. For example, making both of the constructors contained in Program 12.3 inline is accomplished by the declaration section

```
// class declaration
class Date
{
  private:
    int month;
    int day;
    int year;
  public:
    Date(int mm = 7, int dd = 4, int yyyy = 2006)
    {
      month = mm;
      day = dd;
      year = yyyy;
    }
    Date(long yyyymmdd)       // here is the overloaded constructor
    {
      year = int(yyyymmdd/10000.0);  // extract the year
      month = int( (yyyymmdd - year * 10000.0)/100.00 ); // extract the month
      day = int(yyyymmdd - year * 10000.0 - month * 100.0); // extract the day
    }
};
```

---

[10] A discussion of the advantages and disadvantages of inline functions was presented at the end of Section 6.2.

PROGRAMMING NOTE

Constructors

A **constructor** is any function that has the same name as its class. The primary purpose of a constructor is to initialize an object's member variables when an object is created. Thus, a constructor is automatically called when an object is declared.

A class can have multiple constructors, provided that each constructor is distinguishable by having a different formal parameter list. A compiler error results when unique identification of a constructor is not possible. If no constructor is provided, the compiler will supply a do-nothing default constructor.

Every constructor function must be declared *with no return type* (not even `void`). Because they are functions, constructors may also be explicitly called in nondeclarative statements. When used in this manner, the function call requires parentheses following the constructor name, even if no parameters are used. However, when the function is used in a declaration, parentheses *must not* be included for a zero parameter constructor. For example, the declaration `Date a();` is incorrect. The correct declaration is `Date a;`. When parameters are used, however, they must be enclosed within parentheses in both declarative and nondeclarative statements. Default parameter values should be included within the constructor's prototype.

The keyword `inline` is not required in this declaration, because member functions defined inside the class declaration are inline by default.

Generally, only functions that can be coded on a single line are good candidates for inline functions. This reinforces the convention that inline functions should be small. Thus the first constructor is more conventionally written as

```
Date(int mm = 7, int dd = 4, int yyyy = 2006)
{ month = mm; day = dd; year = yyyy; }
```

The second constructor, which extends over three lines, should not be written as an inline function.

Destructors

The counterparts of constructor functions are destructor functions. Destructors are functions that have the same class name as constructors but are preceded with a tilde (~). Thus, for our `Date` class, the destructor name is `~Date()`. Like constructors, a default do-nothing destructor is provided by the C++ compiler in the absence of an explicit destructor. Unlike constructors, however, there can be only one destructor function per class. This is because destructors take no arguments—they also return no values.

PROGRAMMING NOTE

Accessor and Mutator Functions

An **accessor function** is any nonconstructor member function that accesses a class's `private` data members. For example, the function `showDate()` in the `Date` class is an accessor function. Such functions are extremely important because they provide a means of displaying `private` data members' stored values.

When you construct a class make sure to provide a complete set of accessor functions. Each accessor function does not have to return a data member's exact value, but it should return a useful representation of the value. For example, assume that a `Date` such as 12/25/2002 is stored as a long-integer member variable in the form `20022512`. Although an accessor function could display this value, a more useful representation would typically be either 12/25/02, or December 25, 2002.

A mutator function, which is more commonly referred to as a mutator, for short, is any nonconstructor member function that changes an object's data values. Mutator methods are used to alter an object's data values after the object has been created and automatically initialized by a constructor method. A class can contain multiple mutators, as long as each mutator has a unique name or parameter list.

Destructors are automatically called whenever an object goes out of existence and are meant to "clean up" any undesirable effects that might be left by the object. Generally, such effects occur only when an object contains a pointer member, which is the topic of Section 13.2.

Arrays of Objects[11]

The importance of default constructors becomes evident when arrays of objects are created. Because a constructor is called each time an object is created, the default constructor provides an elegant way of initializing all objects to the same state.

Declaring an array of objects is the same as declaring an array of any built-in type. For example, the declaration

```
Date theDate[5];
```

will create five objects named `theDate[0]` through `theDate[4]`. Member functions for each of these objects are called by listing the object name followed by a dot (.) and the desired function. An example using an array of objects is provided by Program 12.4, which also includes `cout` statements within both the constructor

---

[11] This topic can be omitted with no loss of subject continuity.

and the destructor. As illustrated by the output of this program, the constructor is called for each declared object, followed by five member function calls to `showdate()`, followed by five destructor calls. The destructor is called when the objects go out of scope. In this case, the destructor is called when the `main()` function terminates execution.

Program 12.4

```cpp
#include <iostream>
#include <iomanip>
using namespace std;

// class declaration section
class Date
{
  private:
    int month;
    int day;
    int year;
  public:
    Date();    // constructor
    ~Date();   // destructor
    void showDate();
};
// class implementation
Date::Date()       // user-defined default constructor
{
  cout << "*** A Date object is being initialized ***\n";
  month = 1;
  day = 1;
  year = 2010;
}

Date::~Date()      // user-defined default destructor
{
  cout << "*** A Date object is going out of existence ***\n";
}

void Date::showDate()
{
  cout << "     The date is " << setfill('0')
       << setw(2) << month << '/'
       << setw(2) << day << '/'
       << setw(2) << year % 100; // extract the last 2 year digits
  return;
}
```

(continued on next page)

(continued from previous page)

```cpp
int main()
{
  const int NUMDATES = 5;
  Date thedate[NUMDATES];

  for(int i = 0; i < NUMDATES; i++)
  {
    thedate[i].showDate();
    cout << endl;
  }

  return 0;
}
```

The output produced by Program 12.4 is

```
*** A Date object is being initialized ***
*** A Date object is being initialized ***
*** A Date object is being initialized ***
*** A Date object is being initialized ***
*** A Date object is being initialized ***
        The Date is 01/01/2010
        The Date is 01/01/2010
        The Date is 01/01/2010
        The Date is 01/01/2010
        The Date is 01/01/2010
*** A Date object is going out of existence ***
*** A Date object is going out of existence ***
*** A Date object is going out of existence ***
*** A Date object is going out of existence ***
*** A Date object is going out of existence ***
```

▌ EXERCISES 12.3

1. Determine whether the following statements are true or false.
   a. A constructor function must have the same name as its class.
   b. A class can have only one constructor function.
   c. A class can have only one default constructor function.

d. A default constructor can be supplied only by the compiler.

e. A default constructor can have no parameters or all parameters must have default values.

f. A constructor must be declared for each class.

g. A constructor must be declared with a `return` type.

h. A constructor is automatically called each time an object is created.

i. A class can have only one destructor function.

j. A destructor must have the same name as its class, preceded by a tilde (~).

k. A destructor can have default arguments.

l. A destructor must be declared for each class.

m. A destructor must be declared with a `return` type.

n. A destructor is automatically called each time an object goes out of existence.

o. Destructors are not useful when the class contains a pointer data member.

2. For Program 12.3, what Date would be initialized for object c if the declaration `Date c(15);` were used in place of the declaration `Date c(20020515L);`?

3. Modify Program 12.3 so that the only data member of the class is a long integer named yyyymmdd. Do this by substituting the declaration

```
long yyyymmdd;
```

for the existing declarations

```
int month;
int day;
int year;
```

Then, using the same constructor function prototypes currently declared in the class declaration section, rewrite them so that the `Date(long)` function becomes the default constructor and the `Date(int, int, int)` function converts a month, day, and year into the proper form for the class data member.

4. *a.* Construct a `Time` class containing integer data members `seconds`, `minutes`, and `hours`. Have the class contain two constructors. The first should be a default constructor having the prototype `time(int, int, int)`, which uses default values of 0 for each data member. The second constructor should accept a long integer representing a total number of seconds and disassemble the long integer into hours, minutes, and seconds. The final function member should display the class data members.

b. Include the class written for Exercise 4a within the context of a complete program.

5. *a.* Construct a class named `Student` consisting of an integer student identification number, an array of five floating-point grades, and an integer representing the total number of grades entered. The constructor for this class should initialize all `Student` data members to zero. Included in the class should be member functions to (1) enter a student ID number, (2) enter a single test grade and update the total number of grades entered, and (3) compute an average grade and display the student ID followed by the average grade.

b. Include the class constructed in Exercise 5a within the context of a complete program. Your program should declare two objects of type `Student` and should accept and display data for the two objects to verify operation of the member functions.

6. *a.* In Exercise 4 you were asked to construct a `Time` class. For such a class, include a `tick()` function that increments the time by 1 second. Test your function to ensure that it correctly increments into a new minute and a new hour.

b. Modify the `Time` class written for Exercise 6a to include a `detick()` function that decrements the time by 1 second. Test your function to ensure that it correctly decrements time into a prior hour and into a prior minute.

12.4   Examples

Now that you have an understanding of how classes are constructed and the terminology used in describing them, let's apply this knowledge to construct two new examples using an object-oriented programming approach. In the first example we develop a class for determining the floor area of a rectangular shaped room. In the second example, we construct a single elevator object. We assume that the elevator can travel between the 1st and 15th floors of a building and that the location of the elevator must be known at all times.

Example 1: Constructing a Room Object

In this example we will create a class from which room type objects can be constructed. What is required is that a room's floor area will be calculated for any size room when its length and width are known. For modeling purposes we are to assume that every room is rectangular in shape, so that the area can be calculated as the room's length times its width.

Solution

In this application we have one type of object, which is a rectangular shaped room. Because of this, the floor of the room can be designated by its length and width. Once these values have been assigned to a room, its floor area can easily be calculated as the room's length times its width. Thus, a room can be represented by double-precision variables that we will name `length` and `width`. Additionally, we will need a constructor that allows us to specify an actual length and width value when a room is instantiated.

   In addition to the constructor, the services required are an accessor to display a room's length and width values, a mutator to change these values, and a function to calculate a room's floor area from its length and width values. To accomplish this, a suitable class declaration is:

```
class RoomType
{
  // data declaration section
  private:
    double length;  // declare length as a double variable
    double width;   // declare width as a double variable

  public:
    RoomType(); // the constructor's declaration statement
    void showRoomValues();  // an accessor function
    void setNewRoomValues();  // a mutator function
    void calculateRoomArea(); // a calculation function
};
```

Notice that we have declared two data members, length and width, and four class functions. The data members length and width will be to store a room's length and width, respectively. As private class members, they can only be accessed through the class' member function. These public member functions will be used to define the external services available to each RoomType object. Specifically, the RoomType() function, which has the same name as its class, becomes a constructor function that is automatically called when an object of type RoomType is created. We will use this function to initialize a room's length and width values. The function named showRoomValues() will be written as an accessor function to display a room's object's length and width values, the function setNewRoomValues() as a mutator function to change a room's length and width values, and finally, the function named calculateRoomArea() will be written to calculate and display a room's floor area.

To accomplish these services a suitable class implementation section is:

```
// methods implementation section
RoomType::RoomType(double l, double w)  // this is a constructor
{
  length = l;
  width = w;
  cout << "Created a new room object using the default constructor.\n\n";
}

void RoomType::showRoomValues()  // this is an accessor
{
  cout << "  length = " << length
       << "\n  width = " << width << endl;
}
```

(continued on next page)

(continued from previous page)

```
void RoomType::setNewRoomValues(double l, double w)  // this is a mutator
{
  length = l;
  width = w;
}
void RoomType::calculateRoomArea()  // this performs a calculation
{
  cout << (length * width);
}
```

Each of these functions is straightforward. When a room object is declared it will be initialized with a length and width of zero, unless specific values are provided in the declaration. The accessor function displays the values stored in length and width, while the mutator permits re-assigning values after a room object has been created. Finally, the calculation function displays the area of a room by multiplying its length times its width. Program 12.5 includes this class within a working program.

Program 12.5

```
#include <iostream>
using namespace std;
class RoomType
{
  // data declaration section
  private:
    double length; // declare length as a double variable
    double width;  // declare width as a double variable

  public:
    RoomType(double = 0.0, double = 0.0); // the constructor's declaration
                                          // statement
    void showRoomValues();
    void setNewRoomValues(double, double);
    void calculateRoomArea();
};
```

```cpp
// methods implementation section
RoomType::RoomType(double l, double w)  // this is a constructor
{
  length = l;
  width = w;
  cout << "Created a new room object using the default constructor.\n\n";
}
void RoomType::showRoomValues()    // this is an accessor
{
  cout << "  length = " << length
       << "\n   width = " << width << endl;
}


void RoomType::setNewRoomValues(double l, double w)    // this is a mutator
{
  length = l;
  width = w;
}


void RoomType::calculateRoomArea()  // this performs a calculation
{
  cout << (length * width);
}
```

```cpp
int main()
{
  RoomType roomOne(12.5, 18.2);  // declare a variable of type RoomType

  cout << "The values for this room are:\n";
  roomOne.showRoomValues();         // use a class method on this object
  cout << "\nThe floor area of this room is: ";
  roomOne.calculateRoomArea();     // use another class method on this object

  roomOne.setNewRoomValues(5.5, 9.3);    // call the mutator

  cout << "\n\nThe values for this room have been changed to:\n";
  roomOne.showRoomValues();
  cout << "\nThe floor area of this room is: ";
  roomOne.calculateRoomArea();

  cout << endl;
  return 0;
}
```

The lightly shaded portion of Program 12.5 contains the class construction that we have already described. To see how this class is used, concentrate on the darker shaded section of the program that contains the main() function.

This function creates one room object having a length of 12.5 and a width of 18.2. These room dimensions are displayed using the showRoomValues() function and the area is calculated and displayed using the calculateRoomArea() function. The room's dimensions are then reset, displayed, and the room's area recalculated. The output produced by Program 12.5 is:

```
Created a new room object using the default constructor.

The values for this room are:
  length = 12.5
   width = 18.2

The floor area of this room is: 227.5

The values for this room have been changed to:
  length = 5.5
   width = 9.3

The floor area of this room is: 51.15
```

The basic requirements of object-oriented programming are evident in even as simple a program as Program 12.5. Before the main() function can be written a useful class must be constructed. This is typical of programs that use objects. For such programs the design process is front-loaded with the requirement that careful consideration of the class—its declaration and implementation—be given. Code contained in the implementation section effectively removes code that would otherwise be part of main()'s responsibility. Thus, any program that uses the object does not have to repeat the implementation details within its main() function. Rather, the main() function and any function called by main() is only concerned with sending messages to its objects to activate them appropriately. How the object responds to the messages and how the state of the object is retained is not main()'s concern—these details are hidden within the class construction.

Example 2: Constructing an Elevator Object

In this example we will simulate the operation of an elevator. What is required is an output that describes the current floor that the Elevator is either stationed at or passing by and an internal elevator request button that is pushed as a request to move to another floor. The elevator can travel between the 1st and 15th floors of the building it is situated in.

Solution

For this application we have one object, which is an elevator. The only attribute of interest is the location of the elevator. The single requested service is the ability to request a change in the elevator's position (state). Additionally, we must be able to establish the initial floor position when a new elevator is put in service.

The location of the elevator, which corresponds to its current floor position, can be represented by an integer member variable. The value of this variable, which we will name currentFloor, effectively represents the current state of the elevator. The services that we will provide for changing the state of the elevator will be (1) an initialization function to set the initial floor position when a new elevator is put in service and (2) a request function to change the elevator's position (state) to a new floor. Putting an elevator in service is accomplished by declaring a single class instance (declaring an object of type Elevator), and requesting a new floor position is equivalent to pushing an elevator button. To accomplish this, a suitable class declaration is

```
// class declaration section
class Elevator
{
  private:
    int currentFloor;
  public:
    Elevator(int = 1);          // constructor
    void request(int);
};
```

Note that we have declared one data member, currentFloor, and two class functions. The data member, currentFloor, is used to store the current floor position of the elevator. As a private member, it can be accessed only through member functions. The two declared public member functions, Elevator() and request(), will be used to define the external services provided by each Elevator object. The Elevator() function, which has the same name as its class, becomes a constructor function that is automatically called when an object of type Elevator is created. We will use this function to initialize the starting floor position of the elevator. The request() function is used to alter the position of the elevator. To accomplish these services, a suitable class implementation section is

```
// class implementation section

Elevator::Elevator(int cfloor) // constructor
{
  currentFloor = cfloor;
}
```

(continued on next page)

(continued from previous page)

```cpp
void Elevator::request(int newfloor) // access function
{
  if (newfloor < 1 || newfloor > MAXFLOOR || newfloor == currentFloor)
    ; // do nothing
  else if (newfloor > currentFloor) // move elevator up
  {
    cout << "\nStarting at floor " << currentFloor << endl;
    while (newfloor > currentFloor)
    {
    currentFloor++;     // add one to current floor
    cout << " Going Up - now at floor " << currentFloor << endl;
  }
  cout << "Stopping at floor " << currentFloor << endl;
  }
  else // move elevator down
  {
    cout << "\nStarting at floor " << currentFloor << endl;
    while (newfloor < currentFloor)
    {
    currentFloor--;     // subtract one from current floor
    cout << " Going Down - now at floor " << currentFloor << endl;
  }
  cout << "Stopping at floor " << currentFloor << endl;
  }

  return;
}
```

The constructor function is straightforward. When an `Elevator` object is declared, it is initialized to the floor specified; if no floor is explicitly given, the default value of 1 will be used. For example, the declaration

<code>Elevator a(7);</code>

initializes the variable `a.currentFloor` to 7, whereas the declaration

<code>Elevator a;</code>

uses the default argument value and initializes the variable `a.currentFloor` to 1.

The `request()` function defined in the implementation section is more complicated and provides the class's primary service. Essentially, this function consists of an `if-else` statement that has three parts: If an incorrect service is requested, no action is taken; if a floor above the current position is selected, the elevator is moved up; and if a floor below the current position is selected, the elevator is moved down. For movement up or down, the function uses a `while` loop to increment the position one floor at a time and reports the elevator's movement using a cout object call. Program 12.6 includes this class in a working program.

Testing the Elevator class entails testing each class operation. To do this, we first include the Elevator class within the context of a working program, which is listed as Program 12.6.

The lightly shaded portion of Program 12.6 contains the class construction that we have already described. To see how this class is used, concentrate on the darkly shaded section of the program. At the top of the program, we have included the iostream header file and declared a named constant MAXFLOOR, which corresponds to the highest floor that can be requested.

Program 12.6

```
#include <iostream>
using namespace std;
const int MAXFLOOR = 15;

// class declaration
class Elevator
{
  private:
    int currentFloor;
  public:
    Elevator(int = 1);      // constructor
    void request(int);
};
// implementation section
Elevator::Elevator(int cfloor)
{
  currentFloor = cfloor;
}
void Elevator::request(int newfloor)
{

  if (newfloor < 1 || newfloor > MAXFLOOR || newfloor == currentFloor)
    ;   // do nothing
  else if (newfloor > currentFloor) // move elevator up
    {
      cout << "\nStarting at floor " << currentFloor << endl;
```

(continued on next page)

(continued from previous page)

```
            while (newfloor > currentFloor)
            {
              currentFloor++; // add one to current floor
              cout << " Going Up - now at floor " << currentFloor << endl;
            }
            cout << "Stopping at floor " << currentFloor << endl;
        }
        else // move elevator down
        {
            cout << "\nStarting at floor " << currentFloor << endl;
            while (newfloor < currentFloor)
            {
              currentFloor--;    // subtract one from current floor
              cout << " Going Down - now at floor " << currentFloor << endl;
            }
            cout << "Stopping at floor " << currentFloor << endl;
        }
        return;
}
```

```
int main()
{
    Elevator a;        // declare 1 object of type Elevator

    a.request(6);
    a.request(3);

    return 0;
}
```

Three class function calls are included within the `main()` function. The first statement creates an object named a of type `Elevator`. Because no explicit floor has been given, this elevator will begin at floor 1, which is the default constructor argument.

A request is then made to move the elevator to floor 6, which is followed by a request to move to floor 3. The output produced by Program 12.6 is

```
Starting at floor 1
  Going Up - now at floor 2
  Going Up - now at floor 3
  Going Up - now at floor 4
```

```
   Going Up - now at floor 5
   Going Up   now at floor 6
Stopping at floor 6

Starting at floor 6
   Going Down - now at floor 5
   Going Down - now at floor 4
   Going Down - now at floor 3
Stopping at floor 3
```

One further point should be made concerning Program 12.6, which is the control provided by the main() function. Notice that this control is sequential, with two calls made to the same object operation using different argument values. This control is perfectly correct for testing purposes. However, by incorporating calls to request() within a while loop and using the random number function rand() to generate random floor requests, a continuous simulation of the elevator's operation is possible (see Exercise 4).

▓ EXERCISES 12.4

1. Enter Program 12.5 on your computer and execute it.

2. Modify the main() function in Program 12.5 to create a second room having a length of 9 and a width of 12. have the program calculate this new room's floor area.

3. *a.* Modify the main() function in Program 12.5 to create four rooms named hall, kitchen, dining room, and living room. The dimensions for these rooms are as follows:

```
Hall: length = 12.40, width = 3.5
Kitchen: length = 14, width = 14
Living Room: length = 12.4, width = 20
Dining Room: length = 14, width = 9.5.
```

Your program should display the area of each room and the total area of all four rooms combined.

b. The total area of all rooms can be calculated and saved using a class variable. To do this, what type of variable do you think this class variable would have to be?

4. Enter Program 12.6 in your computer and execute it.

5. *a.* Modify the main() function in Program 12.6 to put a second elevator in service starting at the 5th floor. Have this second elevator move to the 1st floor and then move to the 12th floor.

b. Verify that the constructor function is called by adding, within the constructor, a message that is displayed each time a new object is created. Run your program to ensure its operation.

6. Modify the `main()` function in Program 12.6 to use a `while` loop that calls the elevator's request function with a random number between 1 and 15. If the random number is the same as the elevator 's current floor, generate another request. The while loop should terminate after five valid requests have been made and satisfied by movement of the elevator. (*Hint:* Review Section 6.8 for the use of random numbers.)

7. Construct a class named `Light` that simulates a traffic light. The color attribute of the class should change from `Green` to `Yellow` to `Red` and then back to `Green` by the class's `change()` function. When a new `Light` object is created, its initial color should be `Red`.

8. *a.* Construct a class definition that can be used to represent an employee of a company. Each employee is defined by an integer ID number, a floating-point pay rate, and the maximum number of hours the employee should work each week. The services provided by the class should be the ability to enter data for a new employee, the ability to change data for a new employee, and the ability to display the existing data for a new employee.

b. Include the class definition created for Exercise 8a in a working C++ program that asks the user to enter data for three employees and displays the entered data.

c. Modify the program written for Exercise 8b to include a menu that offers the user the following choices:

```
1. Add an Employee
2. Modify Employee data
3. Delete an Employee
4. Exit this menu
```

In response to a choice, the program should initiate appropriate action to implement the choice.

9. *a.* Construct a class definition that can be used to represent types of food. A type of food is classified as basic or prepared. Basic foods are further classified as either dairy, meat, fruit, vegetable, or grain. The services provided by the class should be the ability to enter data for a new food, the ability to change data for a new food, and the ability to display the existing data for a new food.

b. Include the class definition created for Exercise 9a in a working C++ program that asks the user to enter data for four food items and displays the entered data.

c. Modify the program written for Exercise 9b to include a menu that offers the user the following choices:

```
1. Add a Food Item
2. Modify a Food Item
3. Delete a Food Item
4. Exit this menu
```

In response to a choice the program should initiate appropriate action to implement the choice.

Encapsulation

The term **encapsulation** refers to the packaging of a number of items into a single unit. For example, a function is used to encapsulate the details of an algorithm. Similarly, a class encapsulates both variables and functions together in a single package.

Although the term *encapsulation* is sometimes used to refer to the process of information hiding, this usage is technically not accurate. The term *information hiding* refers to the encapsulation *and* hiding of all implementation details.

12.5   Common Programming Errors

The more common programming errors initially associated with the construction of classes are

1. Failing to terminate the class declaration section with a semicolon.
2. Including a return type with the constructor's prototype or failing to include a return type with the other functions' prototypes.
3. Using the same name for a data member as for a member function.
4. Defining more than one default constructor for a class.
5. Forgetting to include the class name and scope operator, : :, in the header line of all member functions defined in the class implementation section.

All of these errors will result in a compiler error message.

12.6   Chapter Summary

1. A *class* is a programmer-defined data type. *Objects* of a class may be defined and have the same relationship to their class as variables do to C++'s built-in data types.
2. A class definition consists of a declaration and an implementation section. The most common form of a class definition is

```
// class declaration section
class name
{
  private:
    a list of variable declarations;
  public:
    a list of function prototypes;
};

// class implementation section
class function definitions
```

The variables and functions declared in the class declaration section are collectively referred to as class members. The variables are individually referred to as class data members and the functions as class member functions. The terms `private` and `public` are access specifiers. Once an access specifier is listed, it remains in force until another access specifier is given.

The `private` keyword specifies that the class members following it are private to the class and can be accessed only by member functions. The `public` keyword specifies that the class members following may be accessed from outside the class. Generally all data members should be specified as `private` and all member functions as `public`.

3. Class functions listed in the declaration section may either be written inline or their definitions included in the class implementation section. Except for constructor and destructor functions, all class functions defined in the class implementation section have the header line syntax

```
returnType className::functionName(parameter list);
```

Except for the addition of the class name and scope operator, `::`, which are necessary to identify the function name with the class, this header line is identical to the header line used for any user-written function.

4. A constructor function is a special function that is automatically called each time an object is declared. It must have the same name as its class and cannot have any `return` type. Its purpose is to initialize each declared object.

5. If no constructor is declared for a class, the compiler will supply a default constructor. This is a do-nothing function that has the definition `className::className(){}`.

6. The term default constructor refers to any constructor that does not require any arguments when it is called. This can be because no parameters are declared (as is the case for the compiler-supplied default constructor) or because all parameters have been given default values.

7. Each class may only have one default constructor. If any constructor is user-defined, the compiler will not create its default constructor. Thus, if any class constructor is user-defined, a default class constructor should also be user-defined.

8. Objects are created using either the C++ or the C style of declaration. The C++ style of declaration has the form

```
className list-of-objectNames(list of initializers);
```

where the list of initializers is optional. An example of this style of declaration, including initializers, for a class named Date is

```
Date a, b, c(12,25,2002);
```

Here the objects a and b are declared to be of type Date and are initialized using the default constructor, and the object c is initialized with the values 12, 25, and 2002.

The equivalent C style of declaration, including the optional list of initializers, has the form

```
className objectName = className(list of initializers);
```

An example of this style of declaration for a class named Date is

```
Date c = Date(12,25,2006)
```

Here the object c is created and initialized with the values 12, 25, and 2006.

9. Constructors may be overloaded in the same manner as any other userwritten C++ function.

10. If a constructor is defined for a class, a user-defined default constructor should be written, because the compiler will not supply it.

11. A destructor function is called each time an object goes out of scope. Destructors must have the same name as their class, preceded by a tilde (~). There can be only one destructor per class.

12. A destructor function takes no arguments and returns no value. If a user-defined destructor is not included in a class, the compiler will provide a do-nothing destructor.

12.7   Chapter Supplement: Insides and Outsides

Just as the concept of an algorithm is central to procedures, the concept of encapsulation is central to objects. In this section, we present this encapsulation concept using an inside-outside analogy, which should help you understand what object-oriented programming is all about.

In programming terms, an object's attributes are described by data, such as the length and width of a rectangle, and the operations that can be applied to the attributes are described by procedures and functions.

As a practical example of this, assume that we will be writing a program that can deal a hand of cards. From an object-oriented approach, one of the objects that we must model is clearly a deck of cards. For our purposes, the attribute of interest for the card deck is that it contains 52 cards, divided into 4 suits (hearts, diamonds, spades, and clubs), each suit consisting of 13 pip values (ace to ten, Jack, Queen, and King).

Now consider the behavior of our deck of cards, which consists of the operations that can be applied to the deck. At a minimum, we will want the ability to shuffle the deck and to deal single cards. Let's now see how this simple example illustrates encapsulation using an inside-outside concept.

A useful visualization of the inside-outside concept is to consider an object as a boiled egg, such as shown in Figure 12.5. Note that the egg consists of three parts: a very inside yolk, a less inside white surrounding the yolk, and an outside shell, which is the only part of the egg visible to the outside world.

In terms of our boiled egg model, the attributes and behavior of an object correspond to the yolk and white, respectively, which are inside the egg. That is, the innermost protected area of an object, its data attributes, can be compared to the egg yolk.

FIGURE 12.5   *The Boiled Egg Object Model*

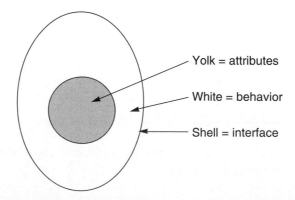

Yolk = attributes

White = behavior

Shell = interface

Surrounding the data attributes, much as an egg's white surrounds its yolk, are the operations that we choose to incorporate within an object. Finally, the interface to the outside world, which is analogous to the shell, represents the means by which a user invokes the object's internal procedures.

The egg model, with its egg shell interface separating the inside of the egg from the outside, is useful precisely because it so clearly depicts the separation between what should be contained inside an object and what should be seen from the outside. This separation is an essential element in object-oriented programming. Let's see why.

From an inside-outside perspective, an object's data attributes, the selected algorithms for the object's operations, and how these algorithms are actually implemented are always "inside" issues that are hidden from the view of an object user. How a user or another object can actually activate an inside procedure, by contrast, is an "outside" issue.

Now let's apply this concept to our deck of cards. First, consider how we might represent cards in the deck. Any of the following attributes (and there are others) could be used to represent a card:

1. Two integer variables, one representing a suit (a number from 1 to 4) and one representing a value (a number from 1 to 13).

2. One character value and one integer value. The character represents a card's suit, and the integer represents a card's value.

3. One integer variable having a value from 0 to 51. The expression `int(number / 13 + 1)` provides a number from 1 to 4, which represents the suit, and the expression `(number Mod 13 + 1)` represents a card value from 1 to 13.

Which attribute we select, however, is not relevant to the outside. The specific way we choose to represent a card is an inside issue to be decided by the designer of the deck object. From the outside, all that is of concern is that we have access to a deck consisting of 52 cards that have the necessary suits and pip values.

The same is true for the operations we decide to provide as part of our card deck object. Consider just the shuffling for now.

There are a number of algorithms for producing a shuffled deck. For example, we could use C++'s random number function, `Rand()`, or we could create our own random number generator. Again, the selected algorithm is an inside issue to be determined by the designer of the deck. Which algorithm is selected and how it is applied to the attributes we have chosen for each card in the deck are not relevant from the object's outside. For purposes of illustration, assume that we decide to use C++'s `Rand()` function to produce a randomly shuffled deck.

If we use the first attribute set previously given, each card in a shuffled deck is produced using `Rand()` at least twice: once to create a random number from 1 to 4 for the suit, and then again to create a random number from 1 to 13 for the card's pip value. This sequence must be done to construct 52 different attribute sets, with no duplicates allowed.

If, on the other hand, we use the second attribute set previously given, a shuffled deck can be produced in exactly the same fashion as above, with one modification: The first random number (from 1 to 4) must be changed into a character to represent the suit.

Finally, if we use the third representation for a card, we need to use Rand() once for each card to produce 52 random numbers from 0 to 51, with no duplicates allowed.

The important point here is that the selection of an algorithm and how it will be applied to an object's attributes are implementation issues, *and implementation issues are always inside issues.* A user of the card deck, who is outside, does not need to know how the shuffling is done. All the user of the deck must know is how to produce a shuffled deck. In practice, this means that the user is supplied with sufficient information to invoke the shuffle function correctly. This corresponds to the interface, or the outer shell of the egg.

Abstraction and Encapsulation

The distinction between insides and outsides is directly related to the concepts of abstraction and encapsulation. **Abstraction** means concentrating on what an object is and does before making any decisions about how the object will be implemented. Thus, abstractly, we define a deck and the operations we want to provide. (Clearly, if our abstraction is to be useful, it had better capture the attributes and operations of a real-world deck.) Once we have decided on the attributes and operations, we can actually implement, which means code, them.

Encapsulation in general usage means separating the implementation details of the chosen abstract attributes and behavior and hiding them from outside users of the object. The external side of an object should provide, to users of the object, only the interface necessary for activating internal procedures. Imposing a strict inside-outside discipline when creating objects is really another way of saying that the object successfully encapsulates all implementation details. In our deck-of-cards example, encapsulation means that users need never know how we have internally modeled the deck or how an operation, such as shuffling, is performed; they need only know how to activate the given operations.

Code Reuse and Extensibility

A direct advantage of an inside-outside object approach is that it encourages both code reuse and extensibility. This is a direct result of having all interactions between objects centered on the outside interface and hiding all implementation details within the object's inside.

FIGURE 12.6   *Using an Object's Interface*

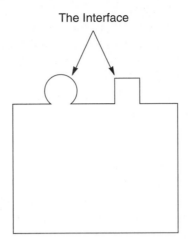

For example, consider the object shown in Figure 12.6. Here, each of the object's two operations can be activated by correctly stimulating either the circle or the square on the outside. In practice, the stimulation is simply a method call. We have used a circle and a square to emphasize that two different methods are provided for outside use. In our deck-of-cards example, activation of one method might produce a shuffled deck, whereas activation of another method might result in a card suit and pip value being returned from the object.

Now assume that we want to alter the implementation of an existing operation or add more functionality to our object. *As long as the existing outside interface is maintained, the internal implementation of any and all operations can be changed without the user ever being aware that a change took place.* This is a direct result of encapsulating the attribute data and operations within an object.

Furthermore, as long as the interface to existing operations is not changed, new operations can be added as they are needed. Essentially, from the perspective of the outside world, all that is being added is another function call that accesses the inside attributes and modifies them in a new way.

Additional Class Capabilities

The creation of a class requires that we provide the capability to declare, initialize, assign, manipulate, and display data members. In the previous chapter the declaration, initialization, and display of objects were presented. In this chapter we continue our construction of classes and see how to provide assignment between objects and include pointer members within a class declaration.

13.1   Assignment

In Chapter 3 we saw how C++'s assignment operator, =, performs assignment between variables. In this section we shall see how assignment works when it is applied to objects and how to define our own assignment operator to override the default provided for user-defined classes.

For a specific assignment example, consider the `main()` function of Program 13.1.

Note that the implementation section of the `Date` class in Program 13.1 contains no assignment function. Nevertheless, we would expect the assignment statement `a = b;` in `main()` to assign b's data member values to their counterparts in a. This is, in fact, the case and it is verified by the output produced when Program 13.1 is executed:

```
The date stored in a is originally 04/01/99
After assignment the date stored in a is 12/18/06
```

This type of assignment is called *memberwise assignment*. In the absence of any specific instructions to the contrary, the C++ compiler builds this type of default assignment operator for each class. If the class *does not* contain any pointer data members, this default assignment operator is adequate and can be used without further consideration. Before considering the problems that can occur with pointer data members, let's see how to construct our own explicit assignment operators.

Assignment operators, like all class members, are declared in the class declaration section and defined in the class implementation section. For the declaration of operators, however, the keyword `operator` must be included in the declaration. When we use this keyword, a simple assignment operator declaration has the form

```
void operator=(className& );
```

Program 13.1

```cpp
#include <iostream>
#include <iomanip>
using namespace std;

// class declaration

class Date
{
  private:
    int month;
    int day;
    int year;
  public:
    Date(int = 7, int = 4, int = 2006); // constructor prototype with defaults
    void showDate(); // member function to display a Date
};

// implementation section

Date::Date(int mm, int dd, int yyyy)
{
  month = mm;
  day = dd;
  year = yyyy;
}

void Date::showDate()
{
  cout << setfill ('0')
       << setw(2) << month << '/'
       << setw(2) << day << '/'
       << setw(2) << year % 100;
  return;
}

int main()
{
  Date a(4,1,1999), b(12,18,2006); // declare two objects

  cout << "\nThe date stored in a is originally ";
  a.showDate();      // display the original date
  a = b;             // assign b's value to a
  cout << "\nAfter assignment the date stored in a is ";
  a.showDate();      // display a's values
  cout << endl;

  return 0;
}
```

Here the keyword void indicates that the assignment returns no value, the operator= indicates that we are overloading the assignment operator with our own version, and the class name and ampersand within the parentheses indicate that the argument to the operator is a class reference. For example, to declare a simple assignment operator for our Date class, we can use the declaration

```
void operator=(Date& );
```

The actual implementation of the assignment operator is defined in the implementation section. For our declaration, a suitable implementation is

```
void Date::operator=(Date& newdate)
{
   day = newdate.day;       // assign the day
   month = newdate.month;   // assign the month
   year = newdate.year;     // assign the year
}
```

The use of the reference parameter in the definition of this operation is not accidental. In fact, one of the primary reasons for adding reference variables to C++ was to facilitate the construction of overloaded operators and make the notation more natural.[1] In this definition, newdate is defined as a reference to a Date class. Within the body of the definition, the day member of the object referenced by newdate is assigned to the day member of the current object, which is then repeated for the month and year members. Assignments such as a.operator=(b); can then be used to call the overloaded assignment operator and assign b's member values to a. For convenience, the expression a.operator=(b); can be replaced with a = b;. Program 13.2 contains our new assignment operator within the context of a complete program.

Except for the addition of the overloaded assignment operator declaration and definition, Program 13.2 is identical to Program 13.1 and produces the same output. Its usefulness to us is that it illustrates how we can explicitly construct our own assignment definitions. In the next section, when we introduce pointer data members, we will see how C++'s default assignment can cause troublesome errors that are circumvented by constructing our own assignment operators. Before moving on, however, we need to make two simple modifications to our assignment operator.

---

[1] Passing a reference is preferable to passing an object by value, because it eliminates the overhead required in making a copy of each object's data members.

Program 13.2

```cpp
#include <iostream>
#include <iomanip>
using namespace std;

// class declaration

class Date
{
  private:
    int month;
    int day;
    int year;
  public:
    Date(int = 7, int = 4, int = 2006); // constructor prototype with defaults
    void operator=(Date&);  // define assignment of a date
    void showDate();    // member function to display a date
};

// implementation section

Date::Date(int mm, int dd, int yyyy)
{
  month = mm;
  day = dd;
  year = yyyy;
}

void Date::operator=(Date& newdate)
{
  day = newdate.day;         // assign the day
  month = newdate.month;     // assign the month
  year = newdate.year;       // assign the year

  return;
}

void Date::showDate()
{
  cout << setfill('0')
       << setw(2) << month << '/'
       << setw(2) << day << '/'
       << setw(2) << year % 100;

  return;
}
```

(continued on next page)

(continued from previous page)

```
int main()
{
  Date a(4,1,1999), b(12,18,2006); // declare two objects

  cout << "\nThe date stored in a is originally ";
  a.showDate();      // display the original date
  a = b;             // assign b's value to a
  cout << "\nAfter assignment the date stored in a is ";
  a.showDate();      // display a's values
  cout << endl;

  return 0;
}
```

First, to preclude any inadvertent alteration to the object used on the right-hand side of the assignment, a constant reference parameter should be used. For our Date class, this takes the form

```
void Date::operator=(const Date& secdate);
```

The final modification concerns the operation's return value. As constructed, our simple assignment operator returns no value, which precludes our using it in multiple assignments such as a = b = c. The reason for this is that overloaded operators retain the same precedence and associativity as their equivalent built-in versions. Thus an expression such as a = b = c is evaluated in the order a = (b = c). As we have defined assignment, unfortunately, the expression b = c returns no value, making subsequent assignment to a an error. To provide for multiple assignments, a complete assignment operation would return a reference to its class type. Because the implementation of such an assignment requires a special class pointer, the presentation of this complete assignment operator is deferred until the material presented in the next chapter is introduced. Until then, our simple assignment operator will be more than adequate for our needs.

Copy Constructors

Although assignment looks similar to initialization, it is worthwhile noting that they are two entirely different operations. In C++ an initialization occurs every time a new object is created. In an assignment, no new object is created—the value of an existing object is simply changed. Figure 13.1 illustrates this difference.

FIGURE 13.1   *Initialization and Assignment*

$$c = a \qquad \longleftarrow \text{Assignment}$$

Type definition $\longrightarrow$ Date c = a; $\longleftarrow$ Initialization

One type of initialization that closely resembles assignment occurs in C++ when one object is initialized using another object of the same class. For example, in the declaration

```
Date b = a;
```

or its entirely equivalent form

```
Date b(a);
```

the b object is initialized to a previously declared a object. The constructor that performs this type of initialization is called a *copy constructor*, and if you do not declare one, the compiler will construct one for you. The compiler's *default copy constructor* performs in a similar manner as the default assignment operator by doing a memberwise copy between objects. Thus, for the declaration Date b = a; the default copy constructor sets b's month, day, and year values to their respective counterparts in a. Like default assignment operators, default copy constructors work just fine unless the class contains pointer data members. Before considering the complications that can occur with pointer data members and how to handle them, it will be helpful to see how to construct our own copy constructors.

Copy constructors, like all class functions, are declared in the class declaration section and defined in the class implementation section. The declaration of a copy constructor has the general form

```
className(const className&);
```

As with all constructors, the function name must be the class name. As further illustrated by the declaration, the parameter is a reference to the class, which is a characteristic of all copy constructors.[2] To ensure that the parameter is not inadvertently altered, it is always specified as a const. Applying this general form to our Date class, a copy constructor can be explicitly declared as

```
Date(const Date& );
```

---

[2] A copy constructor is frequently defined as a constructor whose first parameter is a reference to its class type, any additional parameters being defaults.

The actual implementation of this constructor, if it were to perform the same memberwise initialization as the default copy constructor, would take the form

```
Date::Date(const Date& olddate)
{
   month = olddate.month;
   day = olddate.day;
   year = olddate.year;
}
```

As with the assignment operator, the use of a reference parameter for the copy constructor is no accident: The reference parameter again facilitates a simple notation within the body of the function. Program 13.3 contains this copy constructor within the context of a complete program.

 Program 13.3

```
#include <iostream>
#include <iomanip>
using namespace std;

// class declaration
class Date
{
  private:
    int month;
    int day;
    int year;
  public:
    Date(int = 7, int = 4, int = 2006); // constructor with defaults
    Date(const Date&);      // copy constructor
    void showDate();   // member function to display a date
};
// implementation section
Date::Date(int mm, int dd, int yyyy)
{
  month = mm;
  day = dd;
  year = yyyy;
}
```

```
Date::Date(const Date& olddate)
{
  month = olddate.month;
  day = olddate.day;
  year = olddate.year;
}
void Date::showDate()
{
  cout << setfill('0')
       << setw(2) << month << '/'
       << setw(2) << day << '/'
       << setw(2) << year % 100;

return;
}

int main()
{
  Date a(4,1,1999), b(12,18,2002); // use the constructor
  Date c(a);      // use the copy constructor
  Date d = b;     // use the copy constructor

  cout << "\nThe date stored in a is ";
  a.showDate();
  cout << "\nThe date stored in b is ";
  b.showDate();
  cout << "\nThe date stored in c is ";
  c.showDate();
  cout << "\nThe date stored in d is ";
  d.showDate();
  cout << endl;

  return 0;
}
```

The output produced by Program 13.3 is

```
The date stored in a is 04/01/99
The date stored in b is 12/18/07
The date stored in c is 04/01/99
The date stored in d is 12/18/07
```

As illustrated by this output, c's and d's data members have been initialized by the copy constructor to a's and b's values, respectively. Although the copy constructor defined in Program 13.3 adds nothing to the functionality provided by the compiler's default copy constructor, it does provide us with the fundamentals of defining our own copy constructors. In the next section, we will see how to modify this basic copy constructor to handle cases that are not adequately taken care of by the compiler's default.

Base/Member Initialization[3]

Except for the reference names `olddate` and `secdate`, a comparison of Program 13.3's copy constructor to Program 13.2's assignment operator shows them to be essentially the same function. The difference between these functions is that the copy constructor creates an object's data members before the body of the constructor uses assignment to specify member values. Thus the copy constructor does not perform a true initialization, but rather a creation followed by assignment.

A true initialization would have no reliance on assignment whatsoever and is possible in C++ using a *base/member initialization list*. Such a list can be applied only to constructor functions and may be written in two ways.

The first way to construct a base/member initialization list is within a class's declaration section by using the form

```
className(parameter list) : list-of-data-members(initializing values) {}
```

For example, when we use this form, a default constructor that performs true initialization is

```
// class declaration section
public:
  Date(int mo = 7, int da = 4, int yr = 2006) : month(mo), day(da), year(yr) {}
```

The second way is to declare a prototype in the class's declaration section followed by the initialization list in the implementation section. For our `Date` constructor, this takes the form

---

[3] The material in this section is presented for completeness only and may be omitted without loss of subject continuity.

```
// class declaration section

public:
   Date(int = 7, int = 4, int = 2006);  // prototype with defaults

// class implementation section

Date::Date(int mo, int da, int yr) : month(mo), day(da), year(yr) {}
```

Note that in both forms, the body of the constructor function is empty. This is not a requirement, and the body can include any subsequent operations that you would like the constructor to perform. The interesting feature of this type of constructor is that it clearly differentiates among the initialization tasks performed in the member initialization list, contained between the colon and the braces, and any subsequent assignments that might be contained within the function's body. Although we will not be using this type of initialization subsequently, it is required whenever there is a `const` class instance variable.

EXERCISES 13.1

1. Describe the difference between assignment and initialization.

2. *a.* Construct a class named `Time` that contains three integer data members named `hrs`, `mins`, and `secs`, which will be used to store hours, minutes, and seconds. The function members should include a constructor that provides default values of 0 for each data member, a display function that prints an object's data values, and an assignment operator that performs a memberwise assignment between two `Time` objects.

   b. Include the `Time` class developed in Exercise 2a in a working C++ program that creates and displays two `Time` objects, the second of which is assigned the values of the first object.

3. *a.* Construct a class named `Complex` that contains two double-precision data members named `real` and `imag`, which will be used to store the real and imaginary parts of a complex number. The function members should include a constructor that provides default values of 0 for each member function, a display function that prints an object's data values, and an assignment operator that performs a memberwise assignment between two complex number objects.

   b. Include the class written for Exercise 3a in a working C++ program that creates and displays the values of two complex objects, the second of which is assigned the values of the first object.

4. *a.* Construct a class named `Car` that contains the following three data members: a double-precision variable named `engineSize`, a character variable named `bodyStyle`, an integer variable named `colorCode`. The function members should include a

constructor that provides default values of 0 for each numeric data member and an 'x' for each character variable; a display function that prints the engine size, body style, and color code; and an assignment operator that performs a memberwise assignment between two Car objects for each instance variable.

b. Include the class written for Exercise 4a in a working C++ program that creates and displays two Car objects, the second of which is assigned the values of the first object, except for the pointer data member.

5. *a.* Construct a class named Cartesian that contains two double-precision data members named x and y, which will be used to store the x and y values of a point in rectangular coordinates. The function members should include a constructor that initializes the x and y values of an object to 0, and functions to input and display an object's x and y values. Additionally, there should be an assignment function that performs a memberwise assignment between two Cartesian objects.

b. Include the class written for Exercise 5a in a working C++ program that creates and displays the values of two Cartesian objects, the second of which is assigned the values of the first object.

6. *a.* Construct a class named Savings that contains three double-precision data members named balance, rate, and interest and a constructor that initializes each of these members to 0. Additionally, there should be a member function that inputs a balance and rate and then calculates an interest. The rate should be stored as a percent, such as 6.5 for 6.5%, and the interest computed as *interest = balance × rate/100*. Additionally, there should be a member function to display all member values.

b. Include the class written for Exercise 6a in a working C++ program that tests each member function.

13.2   Pointers as Class Members

As we saw in Section 12.2, a class can contain any C++ data type. Thus the inclusion of a pointer variable in a class should not seem surprising. For example, the class declaration

```
// class declaration

class Test
{
  private:
    int idNum;
    double *ptPay;
  public:
    Test(int = 0, double * = NULL);    // constructor
    void setvals(int, double *);       // access function
    void display();                    // access function
};
```

declares a class consisting of two member variables and three member functions. The first member variable is an integer variable named idNum, and the second instance variable is a pointer named ptPay, which is a pointer to a double-precision number. We will use the setvals() member function to store values into the private member variables and the display() function for output purposes. The implementation of these two functions along with the constructor function Test() is contained in the class implementation section:

```cpp
// implementation section

Test::Test(int id, double *pt)
{
  idNum = id;
  ptPay = pt;
}

void Test::setvals(int a, double *b)
{
  idNum = a;
  ptPay = b;

  return;
}

void Test::display()
{
  cout << "\nEmployee number " << idNum << " was paid $"
       << setiosflags(ios::fixed)
       << setiosflags(ios::showpoint)
       << setw(6) << setprecision(2)
       << *ptPay << endl;

  return;
}
```

In this implementation the Test() constructor initializes its idNum data member to its first parameter and its pointer member to its second parameter; if no parameters are given, these variables are initialized to 0 and NULL, respectively. The display function simply outputs the value pointed to by its pointer member. As defined in this implementation, the setvals() function is very similar to the constructor and is used to alter member values after the object has been declared: the function's first parameter (an integer) is assigned to idNum, and its second parameter (an address) is assigned to ptPay.

P R O G R A M M I N G   N O T E

Values and Identities

Apart from any behavior that an object is supplied with, a characteristic feature of objects that they share with variables is that they always have a unique identity. It is an object's identity that permits distinguishing one object from another. This is not true of a value, such as the number 5, because all occurrences of 5 are indistinguishable from one another. Accordingly, values are not considered objects in object-oriented programming languages such as C++.

Another feature that differentiates an object from a value is that a value can never be a container whose value can change, whereas an object clearly can. A value is simply an entity that stands for itself.

Now consider a string such as `"Chicago"`. As a string, this is a value. However, because `Chicago` could also be a specific and identifiable object of type `City`, the context in which the name is used is important. Note that if the string `"Chicago"` were assigned to an object's `name` attribute, it would revert to being a value.

The `main()` function in Program 13.4 illustrates the use of the `Test` class by first creating one object, named `emp`, which is initialized using the constructor's default arguments. The `setvals()` function is then used to assign the value 12345 and the address of the variable `pay` to the data members of this `emp` object. Finally, the `display()` function is used to display the value whose address is stored in `emp.ptPay`. As illustrated by the program, the pointer member of an object is used like any other pointer variable.

Program 13.4

```
#include <iostream>
#include <iomanip>
using namespace std;

// class declaration

class Test
{
  private:
    int idNum;
    double *ptPay;
  public:
    Test(int = 0, double * = NULL);        // constructor
    void setvals(int, double *);           // access function
    void display();                        // access function
};
```

```
// implementation section

Test::Test(int id, double *pt)
{
  idNum = id;
  ptPay = pt;
}

void Test::setvals(int a, double *b)
{
  idNum = a;
  ptPay = b;

  return;
}

void Test::display()
{
  cout << "\nEmployee number " << idNum << " was paid $"
       << setiosflags(ios::fixed)
       << setiosflags(ios::showpoint)
       << setw(6) << setprecision(2)
       << *ptPay << endl;

  return
}

int main()
{
  Test emp;
  double pay = 456.20;

  emp.setvals(12345, &pay);
  emp.display();

  return 0;
}
```

The output produced by executing Program 13.4 is

```
Employee number 12345 was paid $456.20
```

Figure 13.2 illustrates the relationship between the data members of the `emp` object defined in Program 13.4 and the variable named `pay`. The value assigned to `emp.idNum` is the number 12345, and the value assigned to `pay` is 456.20. The address of the `pay` variable is assigned to the object member `emp.ptPay`. Because this member has been defined as a pointer to a double-precision number, placing the address of the double-precision variable `pay` in it is a correct use of this data member.

FIGURE 13.2 *Storing an Address in a Data Member*

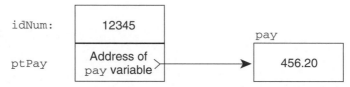

Although the pointer defined in Program 13.4 has been used in a rather trivial fashion, the program does illustrate the concept of including a pointer in a class.

Clearly, it would be more efficient to include the `pay` variable directly as a data member of the `Test` class, rather than using a pointer to it. In some cases, however, pointers are advantageous. For example, assume we need to store a list of book titles. Rather than use a fixed-length character array as a data member to hold each title, we could include a pointer member to a character array and then allocate the array of the correct size for each book title as it is needed. This arrangement is illustrated in Figure 13.3, which shows two objects, a and b, each of which consists of a single pointer data member. As depicted, object a's pointer contains the address of ("points to") a character array containing the characters `Windows Primer`, while object b's pointer contains the address of a character array containing the characters `A Brief History of Western Civilization`.

A suitable class declaration section for a list of book titles that are to be accessed as illustrated in Figure 13.3 is

```
// class declaration
class Book
{
  private:
    char *title;      // a pointer to a book title
  public:
    Book(char * = '\0');     // constructor
    void showtitle(void);    // display the title
};
```

FIGURE 13.3   *Two Objects that Contain Pointer Data Members*

Object a's data member:

Object b's data member:

The constructor function, Book(), and the display function, showtitle(), are defined in the implementation section as follows:

```
// class implementation

Book::Book(char *name)
{
   title = new char[strlen(name)+1];    // allocate memory
   strcpy(title,name);                  // store the string
}

void Book::showtitle(void)
{
   cout << title << endl;
}
```

The body of the Book() constructor contains two statements. The first statement, title = new char[strlen(name)+1];, performs two tasks. First, the right-hand side of the statement allocates enough storage for the length of the name parameter plus one, to accommodate the end-of-string null character, '\0'. Next, the address of the first allocated character position is assigned to the pointer variable title. These operations are illustrated in Figure 13.4. The second statement in the constructor copies the characters in the name argument to the newly created memory allocation. If no argument is passed to the constructor, then title is set to NULL. Program 13.5 uses this class definition within the context of a complete program.

Program 13.5

```cpp
#include <iostream>
#include <string>
using namespace std;

// class declaration

class Book
{
  private:
    char *title;   // a pointer to a book title
  public:
    Book(char * = '\0');  // constructor
    void showtitle(void); // display the title
};

// class implementation

Book::Book(char *strng)
{
  title = new char[strlen(strng)+1];        // allocate memory
  strcpy(title,strng);                      // store the string
}

void Book::showtitle(void)
{
  cout << title << endl;

  return;
}

int main()
{
  Book book1("Windows Primer");        // create 1st title
  Book book2("A Brief History of Western Civilization");  // 2nd title

  book1.showtitle();       // display book1's title
  book2.showtitle();       // display book2's title

  return 0;
}
```

FIGURE 13.4 *Allocating Memory for* `title = new char[strlen(name)+1]`

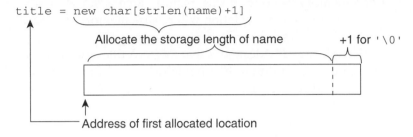

The output produced by Program 13.5 is:

```
Windows Primer
A Brief History of Western Civilization
```

Assignment Operators and Copy Constructors Reconsidered[4]

When a class contains no pointer data members, the compiler-provided defaults for the assignment operator and copy constructor adequately perform their intended tasks. Both of these defaults provide a member-by-member operation that produces no adverse side effects. This is not the case when a pointer member is included in the class declaration. Let's see why this is so.

Figure 13.5a illustrates the arrangement of pointers and allocated memory produced by Program 13.5 just before it completes execution. Let's now assume that we insert the assignment statement `book2 = book1;` before the closing brace of the `main()` function. Because we have not defined an assignment operation, the compiler's default assignment is used. As we know, this assignment produces a memberwise copy (that is, `book2.title = book1.title`) and means that the address in `book1`'s pointer is copied into `book2`'s pointer. Thus both pointers now "point to" the character array containing the characters `Windows Primer`, and the address of `A Brief History of Western Civilization` has been lost. This situation is illustrated in Figure 13.5b.

Because the memberwise assignment illustrated in Figure 13.5b results in the loss of the address of `A Brief History of Western Civilization`, there is no way for the program to release this memory storage (it will be cleaned up by the operating system when the program terminates). Worse, however, is the case where a destructor attempts to release the memory. Once the memory pointed to

---

[4] The material in this section pertains to the problems that occur when the default assignment, copy constructor, and destructor functions are used with classes that contain pointer members, and how to overcome these problems. On first reading, this section can be omitted without loss of subject continuity.

by `book2` is released (again, referring to Figure 13.5b), `book1` points to an undefined memory location. If this memory area is subsequently reallocated before `book1` is deleted, the deletion will release memory that another object is using. The results of this can wreck havoc on a program.

What is typically desired is that the book titles themselves be copied, as shown in Figure 13.5c, and that their pointers be left alone. This situation also removes all of the side effects of a subsequent deletion of any `book` object. To achieve the desired assignment, we must explicitly write our own assignment operator. A suitable definition for this operator is

```
void Book::operator=(Book& oldbook)
{
  if(oldbook.title != NULL)  // check that it exists
    delete(title);           // release existing memory
  title = new char[strlen(oldbook.title) + 1]; // allocate new memory
  strcpy(title, oldbook.title); // copy the title
}
```

FIGURE 13.5a *Before the Assignment* `book2 = book1;`

book1's pointer

book2's pointer

FIGURE 13.5b *The Effect Produced by Default Assignment*

book1's pointer

book2's pointer

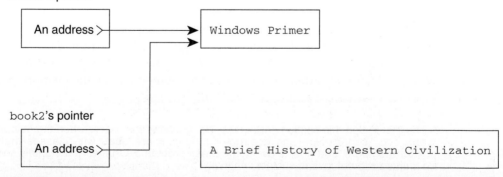

FIGURE 13.5c   *The Desired Effect*

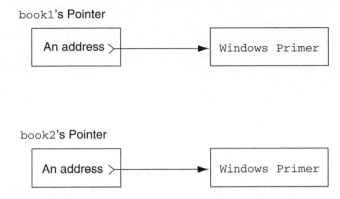

This definition cleanly releases the memory previously allocated for the object and then allocates sufficient memory to store the copied title.

The problems associated with the default assignment operator also exist with the default copy constructor, because it also performs a memberwise copy. As with assignment, we can avoid these problems by writing our own copy constructor. For our Book class, such a constructor is

```
Book::Book(Book& oldbook)
{

  title = new char[strlen(oldbook.title) + 1]; // allocate new memory
  strcpy(title, oldbook.title); // copy the title
}
```

Comparing the body of this copy constructor to the assignment operator's function body reveals they are identical except for the deallocation of memory performed by the assignment operator. This is because the copy constructor does not have to release the existing array before allocating a new one; none exists when the constructor is called.

▌ EXERCISES 13.2

1. Include the copy constructor and assignment operator presented in this section in Program 13.5 and run the program to verify their operation.

2. Write a suitable destructor function for Program 13.5.

3. *a.* Construct a class named Car that contains the following four data members: a double-precision variable named engineSize, a character variable named bodyStyle,

an integer variable named `colorCode`, and a character pointer named `vinPtr` to a vehicle identification code. The function members should include a constructor that provides default values of 0 for each numeric data member, an 'X' for each character variable, and a `NULL` for each pointer; a display function that prints the engine size, body style, color code, and vehicle identification number; and an assignment operator that performs a memberwise assignment between two `Car` objects that correctly handles the pointer member.

b. Include the class written for Exercise 3a in a working C++ program that creates two `Car` objects, the second of which is assigned the values of the first object.

4. Modify Program 13.5 to include the assignment statement b = a, and then run the modified program to assess the error messages, if any, that occur.

5. Using Program 13.5 as a start, write a program that creates five `Book` objects. The program should allow the user to enter the five book titles interactively and then display the titles entered.

6. Modify the program written in Exercise 5 so that the program sorts the entered book titles in alphabetical order before it displays them. (*Hint:* You will have to define a sort routine for the titles.)

13.3   Additional Class Features[5]

This section presents additional features pertaining to classes. These include the scope of a class, creating static class members, and granting access privileges to nonmember functions. Each of these topics may be read independently of the others.

Class Scope

We have already encountered local and global scope in Sections 6.4 and 6.5. As we saw, the scope of a variable defines the portion of a program where the variable can be accessed.

For local variables, this scope is defined by any block contained within a brace pair, { }. This includes both the complete function body and any internal subblocks. Additionally, all parameters of a function are considered as local function variables.

Global variables are accessible from their point of declaration throughout the remaining portion of the file containing them, with three exceptions:

---

[5] Except for the material on the `this` pointer, which is required for the material in Section 14.1, the topics in this section may be omitted on first reading with no loss of subject continuity.

1. If a local variable has the same name as a global variable, the global variable can only be accessed within the scope of the local variable by using the global resolution operator, `::`.

2. The scope of a global variable can be extended into another file by using the keyword `extern`.

3. The same global name can be reused in another file to define a separate and distinct variable by using the keyword `static`. Static global variables are unknown outside of their immediate file.

In addition to local and global scopes, each class also defines an associated **class scope**. That is, the names of the data and function members are local to the scope of their class. Thus, if a global variable name is reused within a class, the global variable is hidden by the class data member in the same manner as a local function variable hides a global variable of the same name. Similarly, member function names are local to the class they are declared in and can be used only by objects declared for the class. Additionally, local function variables hide the names of class data members that have the same name. Figure 13.6 illustrates the scope of the variables and functions for the following declarations:

```
double rate;    // global
// class declaration
class Test
{
  private:
    double amount, price, total;      // class scope
  public:
    double extend(double, double);    // class scope
};
```

`static` Members

As each class object is created, it gets its own block of memory for its data members. In some cases, however, it is convenient for every instantiation of a class to share the *same* memory location for a specific variable. For example, consider a class that consists of employee records, where each employee is subject to the same state sales tax. Clearly, we could make the sales tax a global variable, but this is not very safe. Such data could be modified anywhere in the program, could conflict with an identical variable name within a function, and certainly violates C++'s principle of data hiding.

This type of situation is handled in C++ by declaring a class variable to be `static`. Static data members share the same storage space for all objects of the class; accordingly, they act as global variables for the class and provide a means of communication between objects.

FIGURE 13.6 *Example of Scopes*

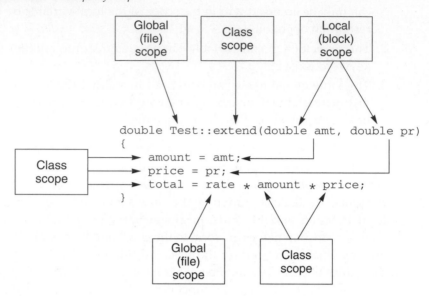

C++ requires that static variables be declared as such within the class's declaration section. Because a static data member requires only a single storage area, regardless of the number of class instantiations, it is defined in a single place outside of the class definition. This is typically done in the global part of the program where the class implementation section is provided. For example, assuming the class declaration

```
// class declaration

class Employee
{
  private:
    static double taxRate;
    int idNum;
  public:
    Employee(int);   //constructor
    void display();
};
```

the definition and initialization of the static variable taxRate are accomplished using a statement such as

```
double Employee::taxRate = 0.15;
```

Here the scope resolution operator, : :, is used to identify taxRate as a member of the class Employee, and the keyword static is not included. Program 13.6 uses this definition within the context of a complete program.

 Program 13.6

```cpp
#include <iostream>
using namespace std;

// class declaration

class Employee
{
  private:
    static double taxRate;
    int idNum;
  public:
    Employee(int = 0);      // constructor
    void display();         // access function
};

// static member definition
double Employee::taxRate = 0.15;

// implementation section

Employee::Employee(int num)
{
  idNum = num;
}

void Employee::display()
{
  cout << " Employee number " << idNum
       << " has a tax rate of " << taxRate << endl;

  return;
}

int main()
{
  Employee emp1(11122), emp2(11133);

  emp1.display();
  emp2.display();

  return 0;
}
```

The output produced by Program 13.6 is

```
Employee number 11122 has a tax rate of 0.15
Employee number 11133 has a tax rate of 0.15
```

Although it might appear that the initialization of taxRate is global, it is not. Once the definition is made, any other definition will result in an error. Thus the actual definition of a static member remains the responsibility of the class creator. The storage sharing produced by the static data member and the objects created in Program 13.6 is illustrated in Figure 13.7.

FIGURE 13.7   *Sharing the Static Data Member* taxRate

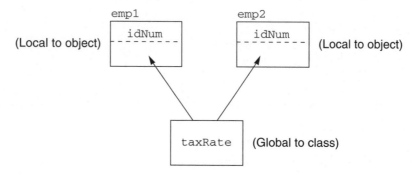

In addition to static data members, static member functions can also be created. Such functions apply to a class as a whole rather than to individual class objects and can access only static data members and other static member functions of the class.[6] An example of such a function is provided by Program 13.7.

 Program 13.7

```
#include <iostream>
using namespace std;

// class declaration

class Employee
{
  private:
    static double taxRate;
    int idNum;
```

---

[6] The reason for this is that the this pointer, discussed next, is not passed to static member functions.

```cpp
    public:
      Employee(int = 0);        // constructor
      void display();           // access function
      static void disp();       // static function
};
// static member definition
double Employee::taxRate = 0.15;

// implementation section

Employee::Employee(int num)
{
  idNum = num;
}

void Employee::display()
{
  cout << "Employee number " << idNum
       << " has a tax rate of " << taxRate << endl;

  return;
}

void Employee::disp()
{
  cout << "\nThe static tax rate is " << taxRate << endl;

  return;
}

int main()
{
  Employee::disp();    // call the static functions
  Employee emp1(11122), emp2(11133);

  emp1.display();
  emp2.display();

  return 0;
}
```

The output produced by Program 13.7 is

```
The static tax rate is 0.15
Employee number 11122 has a tax rate of 0.15
Employee number 11133 has a tax rate of 0.15
```

In reviewing Program 13.7, note that the keyword `static` is used only when static data and function members are declared; it is not included in the definition of these members. Also note that the static member function is called by using the resolution operator with the function's class name. Finally, because `static` functions access only `static` variables that are not contained within a specific object, static functions may be called before any instantiations are declared.

The `this` Pointer

Except for static data members, which are shared by all class objects, each object maintains its own set of member variables. This permits each object to have its own clearly defined state as determined by the values stored in its member variables.

For example, consider the `Date` class previously defined in Program 13.1 and repeated here for convenience:

```cpp
#include <iostream>
using namespace std;

// class declaration

class Date
{
  private:
    int month;
    int day;
    int year;
  public:
    Date(int, int, int); // constructor
    void showDate(); // member function to display a Date
};

// implementation section

Date::Date(int mm = 7, int dd = 4, int yyyy = 2006)
{
  month = mm;
  day = dd;
  year = yyyy;
}
void Date::showDate()
{
```

```
    cout << setfill('0')
          << setw(2) << month << '/'
          << setw(2) << day << '/'
          << setw(2) << year % 100;
    cout << endl;
    return;
}
```

Each time an object is created from this class, a distinct area of memory is set aside for its data members. For example, if two objects named a and b were created from this class, the memory storage for these objects would be as illustrated in Figure 13.8. Note that each set of data members has its own starting address in memory, which corresponds to the address of the first data member for the object.

FIGURE 13.8   *The Storage of Two* Date *Objects in Memory*

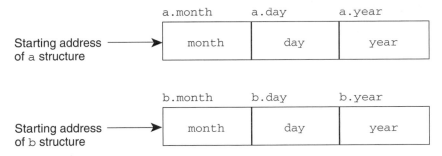

This replication of data storage is not implemented for member functions. In fact, for each class *only one copy of the member functions is retained in memory*, and each object uses these same functions.

Sharing member functions requires providing a means of identifying which specific data structure a member function should be operating on. This is accomplished by providing address information to the function indicating where in memory the particular data structure, corresponding to a specific object, is located. This address is provided by the name of the object, which is, in fact, a reference name. For example, again using our Date class and assuming that a is an object of this class, the statement a.showDate() passes the address of the a object into the showDate() member function.

An obvious question at this point is how this address is passed to showDate() and where it is stored. The answer is that the address is stored in a special pointer variable named this, which is automatically supplied as a hidden argument to each nonstatic member function when the function is called. For our `Date` class, which has two member functions, the actual parameter list of `Date()` is equivalent to

```
Date(Date *this, int mm = 7, int dd = 4, int yyyy = 2006)
```

and the actual parameter list of `showDate()` is equivalent to

```
showDate(Date *this)
```

That is, each member function actually receives an extra argument that is the address of a data structure. Although it is usually not necessary to do so, this pointer data member can be explicitly used in member functions. For example, consider Program 13.8, which incorporates the `this` pointer in each of its member functions to access the appropriate instance variables.

Program 13.8

```cpp
#include <iostream>
#include <iomanip>
using namespace std;

// class declaration

class Date
{
  private:
    int month;
    int day;
    int year;
  public:
    Date(int, int, int); // constructor
    void showDate(); // member function to display a Date
};

// implementation section

Date::Date(int mm = 7, int dd = 4, int yyyy = 2006)
{
  this->month = mm;
  this->day = dd;
  this->year = yyyy;
}
```

```
void Date::showDate()
{
  cout << setfill('0')
       << setw(2) << this->month << '/'
       << setw(2) << this->day << '/'
       << setw(2) << this->year % 100;
  return;
}

int main()
{
  Date a(4,1,1999), b(12,18,2007); // declare two objects

  cout << "\nThe date stored in a is originally ";
  a.showDate(); // display the original date
  a = b;          // assign b's value to a
  cout << "\nAfter assignment the date stored in a is ";
  a.showDate(); // display a's values
  cout << endl;

  return 0;
}
```

The output produced by Program 13.8 is

```
The date stored in a is originally 04/01/99
After assignment the date stored in a is 12/18/07
```

This is the same output produced by Program 13.1, which omits using the `this` pointer to access the data members. Clearly, using the `this` pointer in Program 13.8 is unnecessary and simply clutters up the member function code. There are times, however, when an object must pass its address on to other functions. In these situations, one of which we will see in Section 14.1, the address stored in the `this` pointer must be used explicitly.

`Friend` Functions

The only method we currently have for accessing and manipulating a class' private data members is through the class's member functions. Conceptually, this arrangement can be viewed as illustrated in Figure 13.9a. There are times, however, when it is useful to provide such access to selected nonmember functions.[7]

---

[7] In practice, this occurs when one class needs access to another class's private data members.

FIGURE 13.9a *Direct Access Is Provided to Member Functions*

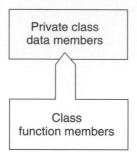

FIGURE 13.9b *Access Provided to Nonmember Functions*

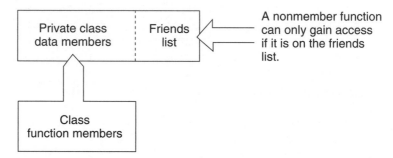

A nonmember function can only gain access if it is on the friends list.

The procedure for providing this external access is rather simple—the class maintains its own approved list of nonmember functions that are granted the same privileges as member functions. The nonmember functions on the list are called friend functions, and the list is referred to as a friends list.

Figure 13.9b conceptually illustrates the use of such a list for nonmember access. Any function attempting to get access to an object's private data members is first checked against the friends list. If the function is on the list, access is approved; otherwise, access is denied.

From a coding standpoint, the friends list is simply a series of function proto-type declarations that are preceded by the word `friend` and included in the class's declaration section. For example, if the functions named `addreal()` and `addimag()` are to be allowed access to the private members of a class named `Complex`, the following prototypes would be included within `Complex`'s declaration section:

```
friend double addreal(Complex&, Complex&);
friend double addimag(Complex&, Complex&);
```

Here the friends list consists of two declarations. The prototypes indicate that each function returns a double-precision number and expects two references to objects of type `Complex` as arguments. Program 13.9 includes these two friend declarations in a complete program.

In reviewing Program 13.9, note four things. The first is that because friends are not class members, they are unaffected by the access section in which they are declared; *they may be declared anywhere within the declaration section*. The convention we have followed is to include all friend declarations immediately following the class header. The second thing to notice is that the keyword `friend` (like the keyword `static`) is used only within the class declaration and not in the actual function definition. Third, because a friend function is intended to have access to an object's private data members, at least one of the friend's parameters should be a reference to an object of the class that has made it a friend. Finally, as illustrated by Program 13.9, it is the class that grants friend status to a function, not the other way around. The function can never confer friend status on itself, because to do so would violate the concepts of data hiding and access provided by a class.

Program 13.9

```
#include <iostream>
#include <cmath>
using namespace std;

// class declaration

class Complex
{
  // friends list
  friend double addreal(Complex&, Complex&);
  friend double addimag(Complex&, Complex&);
  private:
    V real;
    double imag;
  public:
    Complex(double = 0, double = 0); // constructor
    void display();
};
// implementation section

Complex::Complex(double rl, double im)
{
  real = rl;
  imag = im;
}
```

(continued on next page)

(continued from previous page)

```cpp
void Complex::display()
{
  char sign = '+';

  if(imag < 0) sign = '-';
  cout << real << sign << abs(imag) << 'i';

  return;
}

// friend implementations

double addreal(Complex &a, Complex &b)
{
  return(a.real + b.real);
}

double addimag(Complex &a, Complex &b)
{
  return(a.imag + b.imag);
}

int main()
{
  Complex a(3.2, 5.6), b(1.1, -8.4);
  double re, im;

  cout << "\nThe first complex number is ";
  a.display();
  cout << "\nThe second complex number is ";
  b.display();

  re = addreal(a,b);
  im = addimag(a,b);
  Complex c(re,im); // create a new Complex object
  cout << "\n\nThe sum of these two complex numbers is ";
  c.display();
  cout << endl;

  return 0;
}
```

The output produced by Program 13.9 is

```
The first complex number is 3.2+5.6i
The second complex number is 1.1-8.4i

The sum of these two complex numbers is 4.3-2.8i
```

▌ EXERCISES 13.3

1. **a.** Rewrite Program 13.7 to include an integer static data member named numemps. This variable should act as a counter that is initialized to zero and is incremented by the class constructor each time a new object is declared. Rewrite the static function disp() to display the value of this counter.

   b. Test the program written for Exercise 1a. Have the main() function call disp() after each Employee object is created.

2. **a.** Construct a class named Circle that contains two integer data members named xCenter and yCenter and a double-precision data member named radius. The class should also contain a static data member named scaleFactor. Here the xCenter and yCenter values represent the center point of a circle, radius represents the circle's actual radius, and scaleFactor represents a scale factor that will be used to scale the circle to fit on a variety of display devices.

   b. Include the class written for Exercise 2a in a working C++ program.

3. Rewrite the Date(), setDate(), and showDate() member functions in Program 12.1 to explicitly use the this pointer when referencing all data members. Run your program and verify that the same output as produced by Program 12.1 is achieved.

4. **a.** Indicate whether the following three statements in Program 13.9,

```
re = addreal(a,b);
im = addimag(a,b);
Complex c(re,im); // create a new complex object
```

   could be replaced by the single statement

```
Complex c(addreal(a,b), addimag(a,b));
```

   b. Verify your answer to Exercise 4a by running Program 13.9 with the suggested replacement statement.

5. Rewrite Program 13.9 to have only one friend function named addcomplex(). This function should accept two complex objects and return a Complex object. The real and imaginary parts of the returned object should be the sum of the real and imaginary parts, respectively, of the two objects passed to addcomplex().

6. *a.* Rewrite the program written for Exercise 2a, but include a `friend` function that multiplies an object's radius by the `static` scale factor and then displays the actual radius value and the scaled value.

   b. Include the class written for Exercise 6a in a working C++ program.

7. *a.* Construct a class named `Coord` that contains two double-precision data members named `xval` and `yval`, which will be used to store the x and y values of a point in rectangular coordinates. The function members should include appropriate constructor and display functions and a `friend` function named `convPol()`. The `convPol()` function should accept two double-precision numbers that represent a point in polar coordinates and convert them into rectangular coordinates. For conversion from polar to rectangular coordinates, use the formulas

$$x = r \cos \theta$$
$$y = r \sin \theta$$

   b. Include the class written for Exercise 7a in a working C++ program.

8. *a.* Construct two classes named `RecCoord` and `PolCoord`. The class named `RecCoord` should contain two double-precision data members named `xval` and `yval`, which will be used to store the x and y values of a point in rectangular coordinates. The function members should include appropriate constructor and display functions and a `friend` function named `convPol()`.

   The class named `PolCoord` should contain two double-precision data members named `dist` and `theta`, which will be used to store the distance and angle values of a point represented in polar coordinates. The function members should include appropriate constructor and display functions and a `friend` function named `convPol()`.

   The `friend` function should accept an integer argument named `dir`; two double-precision arguments named `val1` and `val2`; and two reference arguments named `recref` and `polref`, the first of which should be a reference to an object of type `RecCoord` and the second to an object of type `PolCoord`. If the value of `dir` is **1**, `val1` and `val2` are to be considered as x and y rectangular coordinates that are to be converted to polar coordinates; if the value of `dir` is any other value, `val1` and `val2` are to be considered as distance and angle values that are to be converted to rectangular coordinates. For conversion from rectangular to polar coordinates, use the formulas

$$r = \sqrt{x^2 + y^2}$$
$$\theta = tan^{-1}(y/x)$$

   For conversion from polar to rectangular coordinates, use the formulas

$$x = r \cos \theta$$
$$y = r \sin \theta$$

   b. Include the class written for Exercise 8a in a working C++ program.

13.4   Common Programming Errors

1. Using the default copy constructor and default assignment operators with classes that contain pointer members. These default functions do a member-wise copy, so the address in the source pointer is copied to the destination pointer. Typically, this is not what is wanted with both pointer members, because both pointers end up pointing to the same memory area.

2. Using a user-defined assignment operator in a multiple assignment expression when the operator has not been defined to return an object.

3. Using the keyword `static` when defining either a static data or function member. Here, the `static` keyword should be used only within the class declaration section.

4. Using the keyword `friend` when defining a friend function. The `friend` keyword should be used only within the class declaration section.

5. Failing to instantiate static data members before creating class objects that must access these data members.

6. Forgetting that `this` is a pointer that must be dereferenced using either `*this` or `this->`.

13.5   Chapter Summary

1. An *assignment operator* may be declared for a class with the function prototype

   ```
   void operator=(className& );
   ```

   Here, the argument is a reference to the class name. The `return` type of `void` precludes using this operator in multiple assignment expressions such as `a = b = c`.

2. A type of initialization that closely resembles assignment occurs in C++ when one object is initialized using another object of the same class. The constructor that performs this type of initialization is called a *copy constructor* and has the function prototype

   ```
   className(const className& );
   ```

   This is frequently represented using the notation X(X&).

3. Pointers may be included as class data members. A pointer member adheres to the same rules as a pointer variable.

4. The default copy constructor and default assignment operators are typically not useful with classes that contain pointer members. This is because these default functions do a memberwise copy in which the address in the source pointer is copied to the destination pointer, resulting in both pointers "pointing to" the same memory area. For these situations, you must define your own copy constructor and assignment operator.

5. Each class has an associated class scope, which is defined by the brace pair, { }, containing the class declaration. Data and function members are local to the scope of their class and can be used only by objects declared for the class. If a global variable name is reused within a class, the global variable is hidden by the class variable. Within the scope of the class variable, the global variable may be accessed using the scope resolution operator, : :.

6. For each class object, a separate set of memory locations is reserved for all data members, except those declared as static. A static data member is shared by all class objects and provides a means of communication between objects. Static data members must be declared as such within the class declaration section and are defined outside of the declaration section.

7. Static function members apply to the class as a whole, rather than individual objects. Thus a static function member can access only static data members and other static function members. Static function members must be declared as such within the class declaration section and are defined outside of the declaration section.

8. For each class, only one copy of the member functions is retained in memory, and each object uses the same function. The address of the object's data members is provided to the member function by passing a hidden argument reference, corresponding to the memory address of the selected object, to the member function. The address is passed in a special pointer argument named this. The this pointer may be used explicitly by a member function to access a data member.

9. A nonmember function may access a class's private data members if it is granted friend status by the class. This is accomplished by declaring the function as a friend within the class's declaration section. Thus it is always the class that determines which nonmember functions are friends; a function can never confer friend status on itself.

Class Functions, Conversions, and Inheritance

This chapter completes our introduction to classes. First we will see how to create operator and conversion capabilities similar to those inherent in C++'s built-in types. With these additions, our user-defined types will have all the functionality of built-in types.

This functionality is then extended by showing how a class designed by one programmer can be altered by another in a way that retains the integrity and design of the original class. This is accomplished using inheritance, a new feature that is central to object-oriented programming. Inheritance permits reusing and extending existing code in a way that ensures that the new code does not adversely affect what has already been written. It is the driving force behind the move to object-oriented programming.

14.1   Operator Functions

A simple assignment operator was constructed in Section 13.1. In this section we extend this capability and show how to broaden C++'s built-in operators to work with class objects. As we will discover, class operators are themselves either member or friend functions.

The only symbols permitted for user-defined purposes are the subset of C++'s built-in symbols listed in Table 14.1. Each of these symbols may be adopted for class use with no limitation as to its meaning.[1] This is done by making each operation a function that can be overloaded like any other function.

The operation of the symbols listed in Table 14.1 can be redefined as we see fit for our classes, subject to the following restrictions:

- Symbols that do not appear in Table 14.1 cannot be redefined. For example, the ., ::, and ?: symbols cannot be redefined.

- New operator symbols cannot be created. For example, because %% is not an operator in C++, it cannot be defined as a class operator.

- Neither the precedence nor the associativity of C++'s operators can be modified. Thus you cannot give the addition operator a higher precedence than the multiplication operator.

- Operators cannot be redefined for C++'s built-in types.

---

[1] The only limitation is that the syntax of the operator cannot be changed. Thus a binary operator must remain binary, and a unary operator must remain unary. Within this syntax restriction, an operator symbol can be used to produce any operation, whether or not the operation is consistent with the symbol's accepted usage. For example, we could redefine the addition symbol to provide multiplication. This, however, would violate the intent and spirit of making these symbols available to us. We shall be very careful to redefine each symbol in a manner consistent with its accepted usage.

- A C++ operator that is unary cannot be changed to a binary operator, and a binary operator cannot be changed to a unary operator.
- The operator must either be a member of a class or be defined to take at least one class member as an operand.

TABLE 14.1   *Operators Available for Class Use*

Operator	Description
( )	Function call
[ ]	Array element
->	Structure member pointer reference
new	Dynamically allocate memory
delete	Dynamically deallocate memory
++	Increment
--	Decrement
—	Unary minus
!	Logical negation
~	One's complement
*	Indirection
*	Multiplication
/	Division
%	Modulus (remainder)
+	Addition
—	Subtraction
<<	Left shift
>>	Right shift
<	Less than
<=	Less than or equal to
>	Greater than
>=	Greater than or equal to
==	Equal to
!=	Not equal to
&&	Logical AND
||	Logical OR
&	Bitwise AND
^	Bitwise exclusive OR
|	Bitwise inclusive OR
=	Assignment
+= −= *=	Assignment
/= %= &=	Assignment
^= |=	Assignment
<<= >>=	Assignment
,	Comma

The first step in providing a class with operators from Table 14.1 is to decide which operations make sense for the class and how they should be defined. As a specific example, we continue to build on the `Date` class introduced in Chapter 12. For this class a small, meaningful set of class operations is defined.

Clearly, the addition of two dates is not meaningful. The addition of a date with an integer, however, does make sense if the integer is taken as the number of days to be added to the date. Likewise, the subtraction of an integer from a date makes sense. Also, the subtraction of two dates is meaningful if we define the difference to mean the number of days between the two dates. Similarly, it makes sense to compare two dates and determine whether the dates are equal or one date occurs before or after another date. Let's now see how these operations can be implemented using C++'s operator symbols.

A user-defined operation is created as a function that redefines C++'s built-in operator symbols for class use. Functions that define operations on class objects and use C++'s built-in operator symbols are referred to as *operator functions*.

Operator functions are declared and implemented in the same manner as all member functions, with one exception: It is the function's name that connects the appropriate operator symbol to the operation defined by the function. An operator function's name is always of the form `operator<symbol>`, where `<symbol>` is one of the operators listed in Table 14.1. For example, the function name `operator+` is the name of the addition function, and the function name `operator==` is the name of the "equal to" comparison function.

Once the appropriate function name is selected, the process of writing the function amounts simply to having it accept the desired inputs and produce the correct returned value.[2] For example, in comparing two `Date` objects for equality, we would select C++'s equality operator. Thus the name of our function becomes `operator==`. We would want our comparison operation to accept two `Date` objects, internally compare them, and return a Boolean value indicating the result of the comparison, for example, true for equality and false for inequality. As a member function, a suitable prototype that could be included in the class declaration section is

```
bool operator==(const Date& );
```

This prototype indicates that the function is named `operator==`, that it returns an integer, and that it accepts a reference to a `Date` object.[3] Only one `Date`

---

[2] As previously noted, this implies that the specified operator can be redefined to perform any operation. Good programming practice, however, dictates avoiding such redefinitions.

[3] The prototype `bool operator==(const Date)` also works. Passing a reference, however, is preferable to passing an object, because it reduces the function call's overhead. This is because passing an object means that a copy of the object must be made for the called function, whereas passing a reference gives the function direct access to the object whose address is passed.

object is required here because the second Date object will be the object that calls the function. Let's now write the function definition to be included in the class implementation section. The const keyword ensures that the referenced Date object cannot be changed within the function. Assuming that our class is named Date, a suitable definition is

```cpp
bool Date::operator==(const Date& date2)
{
    if( day == date2.day && month == date2.month && year == date2.year)
        return true;
    else
        return false;
}
```

Once this function has been defined, it may be called by using the same syntax as for C++'s built-in types. For example, if a and b are objects of type Date, the expression if (a == b) is valid. Program 14.1 includes the if statement as well as the declaration and definition of this operator function within the context of a complete program.

The output produced by Program 14.1 is

```
Dates a and b are not the same.
Dates a and c are the same.
```

The first new feature to be illustrated in Program 14.1 is the declaration and implementation of the function named operator==(). Except for its name, this operator function is constructed in the same manner as any other member function: It is declared in the declaration section and defined in the implementation section. The second new feature is how the function is called. Operator functions may be called by using their associated symbols rather than in the way other functions are called. Because operator functions are true functions, however, the traditional method of calling them can also be used—specifying their name and including appropriate arguments. Thus, rather than calling the function using the expression a == b in Program 14.1, we could have used the call a.operator==(b).

Let's now create another operator for our Date class, an addition operator. As before, creating this operator requires that we specify three items:

1. The name of the operator function
2. The processing that the function is to perform
3. The data type, if any, that the function is to return

Program 14.1

```cpp
#include <iostream>
using namespace std;

// class declaration

class Date
{
  private:
    int month;
    int day;
    int year;
  public:
    Date(int = 7, int = 4, int = 2006);      // constructor
    bool operator==(const Date &);  // declare the operator== function
};

// implementation section

Date::Date(int mm, int dd, int yyyy)
{
  month = mm;
  day = dd;
  year = yyyy;
}

bool Date::operator==(const Date &date2)
{
  if(day == date2.day && month == date2.month && year == date2.year)
    return true;
  else
    return false;
}

int main()
{
  Date a(4,1,2008), b(12,18,2001), c(4,1,2008); // declare 3 objects

  if (a == b)
    cout << "\nDates a and b are the same." << endl;
  else
    cout << "\nDates a and b are not the same." << endl;

  if (a == c)
    cout << "Dates a and c are the same.\n" << endl;
  else
    cout << "Dates a and c are not the same.\n" << endl;

  return 0;
}
```

Clearly, for addition we will use the operator function named `operator+`. Having selected the function's name, we must now determine what we want this function to do, as it specifically relates to `Date` objects. As we noted previously, the sum of two dates makes no sense. Adding an integer to a date is meaningful, however, when the integer represents the number of days either before or after the given date. Here the sum of an integer to a `Date` object is simply another `Date` object, which should be returned by the addition operation. Thus a suitable prototype for our addition function is

`Date operator+(int);`

This prototype would be included in the class declaration section. It specifies that an integer is to be added to a class object and that the operation returns a `Date` object. Thus, if a is a `Date` object, the function call `a.operator+(284)`, or its more commonly used alternative, `a + 284`, should cause the number 284 to be correctly added to a's date value. We must now construct the function to accomplish this.

Constructing the function requires that we first select a specific date convention. For simplicity, we will adopt the financial date convention that considers each month to consist of 30 days and each year to consist of 360 days. Thus our function will first add the integer number of days to the `Date` object's day value and then adjust the resulting day value to lie within the range 1 to 30 and the month value to lie within the range 1 to 12. A function that accomplishes this is

```
Date Date::operator+(int days)
{
  Date temp;     // a temporary Date to store the result

  temp.day = day + days;     // add the days
  temp.month = month;
  temp.year = year;
  while (temp.day > 30)       // now adjust the months
  {
    temp.month++;
    temp.day -= 30;
  }
  while (temp.month > 12)     // adjust the years
  {
    temp.year++;
    temp.month -= 12;
  }
  return temp;     // the values in temp are returned
}
```

Program 14.2

```cpp
#include <iostream>
#include <iomanip>
using namespace std;

// class declaration

class Date
{
  private:
    int month;
    int day;
    int year;
  public:
    Date(int = 7, int = 4, int = 2006);    // constructor
    Date operator+(int);     // overload the + operator
    void showDate();          // member function to display a date
};

// implementation section

Date::Date(int mm, int dd, int yyyy)
{
  month = mm;
  day = dd;
  year = yyyy;
}

Date Date::operator+(int days)
{
  Date temp;     // a temporary date to store the result

  temp.day = day + days;    // add the days
  temp.month = month;
  temp.year = year;
  while (temp.day > 30)     // now adjust the months
  {
    temp.month++;
    temp.day -= 30;
  }
```

```
   while (temp.month > 12)     // adjust the years
   {
     temp.year++;
     temp.month -= 12;
   }
   return temp;      // the values in temp are returned
}

void Date::showDate()
{
   cout << setfill('0')
        << setw(2) << month << '/'
        << setw(2) << day << '/'
        << setw(2) << year % 100;

   return;
}

int main()
{
   Date a(4,1,1999), b;      // declare two objects

   cout << "\nThe initial date is ";
   a.showDate();
   b = a + 284;      // add in 284 days = 9 months and 14 days
   cout << "\nThe new date is ";
   b.showDate();
   cout << endl;

   return 0;
}
```

The important feature to note here is the use of the temp object. The purpose of this object is to ensure that none of the function's arguments, which become the operator's operands, are altered. To understand this, consider a statement such as b = a + 284; that uses this operator function, where a and b are Date objects. This statement should never modify a's value. Rather, the expression a + 284 should yield a Date value that is then assigned to b. The result of the expression is, of course, the temp Date object returned by the operator+() function. Program 14.2 uses this function within the context of a complete program.

The output produced by Program 14.2 is

```
The initial date is 04/01/99
The new date is 01/15/00
```

We can actually improve on the `operator+()` function contained in Program 14.2 by initializing the `temp` object with the value of its calling `Date` object. This is accomplished by using either of the following declarations:

```
Date temp(*this);
Date temp = *this;
```

Both of these declarations initialize the `temp` object with the object pointed to by the `this` pointer, which is the calling `Date` object. If the initialization is done, the first assignment statement in the function can be altered to

```
temp.day += days;
```

Operator Functions as Friends

The operator functions in both Programs 14.1 and 14.2 have been constructed as class members. An interesting feature of operator functions is that except for the operator functions =, (), [], and ->, they may also be written as friend functions. For example, if the `operator+()` function used in Program 14.2 were written as a friend, a suitable declaration section prototype would be

```
friend Date operator+(Date& , int);
```

Notice that the friend version contains a reference to a `Date` object that is not contained in the member function version. In all cases, the equivalent friend version of a member operator function *must* contain an additional class reference that is not required by the member function.[4] This equivalence is listed in Table 14.2 for both unary and binary operators.

TABLE 14.2 *Operator Function Argument Requirements*

	Member Function	Friend Function
Unary operator	1 implicit	1 explicit
Binary operator	1 implicit and 1 explicit	2 explicit

[4] This extra parameter is necessary to identify the correct object. This parameter is not needed when a member function is used, because the member function "knows" which object it is operating on. The mechanism of this "knowing" is supplied by an implied member function argument named `this`, which was presented in Section 13.3.

Program 14.2's `operator+()` function, written as a friend function, is

```
Date operator+(Date& op1, int days)
{
  Date temp;    // a temporary Date to store the result

  temp.day = op1.day + days;    // add the days
  temp.month = op1.month;
  temp.year = op1.year;
  while (temp.day > 30)    // now adjust the months
  {
    temp.month++;
    temp.day -= 30;
  }
  while (temp.month > 12)    // adjust the years
  {
    temp.year++;
    temp.month -= 12;
  }
  return temp;    // the values in temp are returned
}
```

The only difference between this version and the member version is the explicit use of a `Date` parameter named `op1` (the choice of this name is entirely arbitrary) in the friend version. This means that within the body of the friend function, the first three assignment statements explicitly reference `op1`'s data members as `op1.day`, `op1.month`, and `op1.year`, whereas the member function simply refers to its parameters as `day`, `month`, and `year`.

In making the determination to overload a binary operator as either a friend or a member operator function, the following convention can be applied: *friend functions are more appropriate for binary functions that modify neither of their operands, such as ==, +, and -, whereas member functions are more appropriate for binary functions, such as =, +=, and -= that are used to modify one of their operands.*

The Assignment Operator Revisited

In Section 13.1 a simple assignment operator function was presented. It is repeated here for convenience.

```
void Date::operator=(Date &newdate)
{
  day = newdate.day;       // assign the day
  month = newdate.month;   // assign the month
  year = newdate.year;     // assign the year
}
```

The drawback of this function is that it returns no value, which makes multiple assignments such as a = b = c impossible. Now that we have introduced operator functions with return types and have the this pointer at our disposal, we can fix our simple assignment operator function to provide an appropriate return type. In this case, the return value should be a Date. Thus an appropriate prototype for our operator is

```
Date operator=(const Date &);
```

Note that we have declared the function's parameter to be a const to ensure that this operand will not be altered by the function. A suitable function for this prototype is

```
Date Date::operator=(const Date &newdate)
{
  day = newdate.day;        // assign the day
  month = newdate.month;    // assign the month
  year = newdate.year;      // assign the year

  return *this;
}
```

In the case of an assignment such as b = c, or its equivalent form b.operator=(c), the function first alters b's member values from within the function and then returns the value of this object, which may be used in a subsequent assignment. Thus a multiple assignment expression such as a = b = c is possible; it is illustrated in Program 14.3.

Program 14.3

```
#include <iostream>
#include <iomanip>
using namespace std;

// class declaration
class Date
{
  private:
    int month;
    int day;
    int year;
  public:
    Date(int = 7, int = 4, int = 2006);    // constructor
    Date operator=(const Date &);    // define assignment of a date
    void showDate();            // member function to display a date
};
```

```cpp
// implementation section
Date::Date(int mm, int dd, int yyyy)
{
  month = mm;
  day = dd;
  year = yyyy;
}
Date Date::operator=(const Date& newdate)
{
  day = newdate.day;          // assign the day
  month = newdate.month;      // assign the month
  year = newdate.year;        // assign the year

  return *this;
}
void Date::showDate()
{
  cout << setfill('0')
       << setw(2) << month << '/'
       << setw(2) << day << '/'
       << setw(2) << year % 100;

  return;
}

int main()
{
  Date a(4,1,1999), b(12,18,2007), c(1,1,2009); // declare three objects

  cout << "Before assignment a's date value is ";
  a.showDate();
  cout << "\nBefore assignment b's date value is ";
  b.showDate();
  cout << "\nBefore assignment c's date value is ";
  c.showDate();

  a = b = c;     // multiple assignment

  cout << "\n\nAfter assignment a's date value is ";
  a.showDate();
  cout << "\nAfter assignment b's date value is ";
  b.showDate();
  cout << "\nAfter assignment c's date value is ";
  c.showDate();
  cout << endl;

  return 0;
}
```

The output produced by Program 14.3 is

```
Before assignment a's date value is 04/01/99
Before assignment b's date value is 12/18/07
Before assignment c's date value is 01/01/09

After assignment a's date value is 01/01/09
After assignment b's date value is 01/01/09
After assignment c's date value is 01/01/09
```

As we noted previously, the only restriction on the assignment operator function is that it can be overloaded only as a member function. It cannot be overloaded as a friend.

▌ EXERCISES 14.1

1. *a.* Define a *greater than* relational operator function named `operator>()` that can be used with the `Date` class declared in Program 14.1.

   b. Define a *less than* operator function named `operator<()` that can be used with the `Date` class declared in Program 14.1.

   c. Include the operator functions written for Exercises 1a and 1b in a working C++ program.

2. *a.* Define a subtraction operator function named `operator-()` that can be used with the `Date` class defined in Program 14.1. The subtraction should accept a long-integer argument that represents the number of days to be subtracted from an object's date and should return a date. In doing the subtraction, use the financial assumption that all months consist of 30 days and all years of 360 days. Additionally, an end-of-month adjustment should be made, if necessary, that converts any resulting day of 31 to a day of 30, except if the month is February. If the resulting month is February and the day is either 29, 30, or 31, it should be changed to 28.

   b. Define another subtraction operator function named `operator-()` that can be used with the `Date` class defined in Program 14.1. The subtraction should yield a long integer that represents the difference in days between two dates. In calculating the day difference, use the financial assumption that all months have 30 days and all years have 360 days.

   c. Include the overloaded operators written for Exercises 2a and 2b in a working C++ program.

3. *a.* Determine whether the following addition operator function provides the same result as the function used in Program 14.2:

```
Date Date::operator+(int days)    // return a date object
{
  Date temp;

  temp.day = day + days;    // add the days in
  temp.month = month + int(temp.day/30);   // determine total months
  temp.day = temp.day % 30;                // determine actual day
  temp.year = year + int(temp.month/12);   // determine total years
  temp.month = temp.month % 12;            // determine actual month

  return temp;
}
```

   b. Verify your answer to Exercise 3a by including the function in a working C++ program.

4. *a.* Rewrite the equality relational operator function in Program 14.1 as a friend function.

   b. Verify the operation of the friend operator function written for Exercise 4a by including it in a working C++ program.

5. *a.* Rewrite the addition operator function in Program 14.2 to account for the actual days in a month, neglecting leap years.

   b. Verify the operation of the operator function written for Exercise 5a by including it in a working C++ program.

6. *a.* Construct an addition operator for the `Complex` class declared in Program 13.9. This should be a member function that adds two complex numbers and returns a complex number.

b. Add a member multiplication operator function to the class used in Exercise 6a that multiplies two complex numbers and returns a complex number.

c. Verify the operation of the operator functions written for Exercises 6a and 6b by including them in a working C++ program.

7. *a.* Create a class named String and include an addition operator function that concatenates two strings. The function should return a string.

b. Include the overloaded operator written for Exercise 7a in a working C++ program.

14.2   Two Useful Alternatives—`operator()` and `operator[]`

There are times when it is convenient to define an operation having more than two arguments, which is the limit imposed on all binary operator functions. For example, each of our `Date` objects contains three integer data members: `month`, `day`, and `year`. For such an object, we might want to add an integer value to any of these three members, instead of just the `day` member as was done in Program 14.2. C++ provides for this possibility by supplying the parentheses operator function, `operator()`, which has no limits on the number of arguments that may be passed to it.

On the other end of the spectrum, the case illustrated by Program 14.2, where only a single nonobject argument is required, occurs so frequently that C++ also provides an alternative means of achieving it. For this special case, C++ supplies the subscript operator function, `operator[]`, which permits a maximum of one argument. The only restriction imposed by C++ on the `operator()` and `operator[]` functions is that they must be defined as member (not friend) functions. For simplicity, we consider the `operator[]` function first.

The subscript operator function, `operator[]`, is declared and defined in the same manner as any other operator function, but it is called differently from the normal function and operator call. For example, if we want to use this operator function to accept an integer argument and return a `Date` object, the following prototype is valid:

```
Date operator[](int);  // declare the subscript operator
```

Except for the operator function's name, this is similar in construction to any other operator function prototype. Assuming that we want this function to add its integer argument to a `Date` object, a suitable function implementation is

```
Date Date::operator[](int days)
{
   Date temp;     // a temporary date to store the result

   temp.day = day + days;    // add the days
   temp.month = month;
   temp.year = year;
   while (temp.day > 30)     // now adjust the months
   {
     temp.month++;
     temp.day -= 30;
   }
   while (temp.month > 12)   // adjust the years
   {
     temp.year++;
     temp.month -= 12;
   }
   return temp;    // the values in temp are returned
}
```

Again, except for the initial header line, this is similar in construction to other operator function definitions. Once the function is created, however, it can only be called by passing the required argument through the subscript brackets. For example, if a is a Date object, the function call a[284] calls the subscript operator function and causes the function to operate on the a object using the integer value 284. This call is illustrated in Program 14.4.

Program 14.4 is identical in every way to Program 14.2, except that we have used an overloaded subscript operator function in place of an overloaded addition operator function. Programs 14.4 and 14.2 produce identical output.

Although the expression a[284] used in Program 14.2 *appears* to indicate that a is an array, it is not. It is simply the notation that is required to call an overloaded subscript function.

The parentheses operator function, operator()(), is almost identical in construction and calling to the subscript function, operator[](), with the substitution of the parentheses, (), for the brackets, []. The difference between these two operator functions is in the number of allowable arguments. Whereas the subscript operator permits passing zero or one argument, the parentheses operator has no limit on the number of its arguments. For example, a suitable operator prototype to add an integer number of months, days, or years to a Date object is

```
Date operator()(int, int, int);
```

Program 14.4

```cpp
#include <iostream>
#include <iomanip>
using namespace std;

// class declaration

class Date
{
  private:
    int month;
    int day;
    int year;
  public:
    Date(int = 7, int = 4, int = 2006);    // constructor
    Date operator[](int);    // overload the subscript operator
    void showDate();         // member function to display a date
};

// implementation section

Date::Date(int mm, int dd, int yyyy)
{
  month = mm;
  day = dd;
  year = yyyy;
}

Date Date::operator[](int days)
{
  Date temp;    // a temporary date to store the result
  temp.day = day + days;    // add the days
  temp.month = month;
  temp.year = year;
  while (temp.day > 30)      // now adjust the months
  {
    temp.month++;
    temp.day -= 30;
  }
  while (temp.month > 12)    // adjust the years
  {
    temp.year++;
    temp.month -= 12;
  }
```

```
    return temp;     // the values in temp are returned
}

void Date::showDate()
{
  cout << setfill('0')
       << setw(2) << month << '/'
       << setw(2) << day << '/'
       << setw(2) << year % 100;

  return;
}

int main()
{
  Date a(4,1,1999), b; // declare two objects

  cout << "The initial date is ";
  a.showDate();
  b = a[284]; // add in 284 days = 9 months and 14 days
  cout << "\nThe new date is ";
  b.showDate();
  cout << endl;

  return 0;
}
```

Once such a function is implemented (which is left as an exercise) a call such as a(2,3,4) can be used to add 2 months, 4 days, and 3 years to the Date object named a.

These two extra functions provide a great deal of programming flexibility. In the case where only one argument is needed, they permit two different overloaded functions to be written, both of which have the same argument type. For example, we could use operator[] to add an integer number of days to a Date object and operator() to add an integer number of months. Because both functions have the same argument type, one function name could not be overloaded for both of these cases.

These two functions also permit us the flexibility to restrict the other operator functions to class member arguments and use these two functions for any other argument types or operations, such as adding an integer to a Date object.

▌ EXERCISES 14.2

1. Replace the subscript operator[] function in Program 14.4 with the parentheses operator() function.

2. *a.* Replace the subscript operator[] function in Program 14.4 with a member operator() function that accepts an integer month, day, and year count. Have the function add the input days, months, and years to the object's date and return the resulting date. For example, if the input is 3,2,1 and the object's date is 7/16/2006, the function should return the date 10/18/2007. Make sure that your function correctly handles an input such as 37 days and 15 months and that it adjusts the calculated day to be within the range 1 to 30 and the month to be within the range 1 to 12.

   b. Include the operator function written for Exercise 2a in a working C++ program and verify its operation.

3. *a.* Construct a class named Student consisting of the following private data members: an integer ID number, an integer count, and an array of four double-precision grades. The constructor for this class should set all data member values to zero. The class should also include a member function that displays all valid member grades, as determined by the grade count, and calculates and displays the average of the grades. Include the class in a working C++ program that declares three class objects named a, b, and c.

   b. Include, in the class constructed for Exercise 3a, a member operator[] function that has a double-precision grade count argument. The function should check the grade count data member, and if fewer than four grades have been entered, the function should store its argument into the grade array using the count as an index value. If four grades have already been entered, the function should return an error message indicating that the new grade cannot be accepted. Additionally, a new grade should force an increment to the count data member.

   c. Include, in the class constructed for Exercise 3a, a member operator() function that has a grade index and grade value as arguments. The function should force a change to the grade corresponding to the index value and should update the count if necessary. For example, an argument list of 4,98.5 should change the fourth test grade value to 98.5.

4. *a.* Add to Program 13.9 a member operator[] function that multiplies an object's complex number (both the real and the imaginary parts) by a real number and returns a complex number. For example, if the real number is 2 and the complex number is 3 + 4i, the result is 6 + 8i.

   b. Verify the operation of the operator function written for Exercise 4a by including it in a working C++ program.

14.3   Data Type Conversions

In Chapter 3, we discussed the conversion from one built-in data type to another. The introduction of user-defined data types expands the possibilities for conversion between data types to the following cases:

- Conversion from built-in type to built-in type
- Conversion from built-in type to class (user-defined) type
- Conversion from class (user-defined) type to built-in type
- Conversion from class (user-defined) type to class (user-defined) type

The first conversion is handled either by C++'s built-in implicit conversion rules or by its explicit cast operator. The second conversion type is made using a **type conversion constructor**. The third and fourth conversion types are made using a **conversion operator function**. In this section, we will examine the specific means of performing each of these conversions.

Conversion from Built-in to Built-in

The conversion from one built-in data type to another was presented in Section 3.2. To review this case briefly, recall that this type of conversion is either implicit or explicit.

An implicit conversion occurs in the context of one of C++'s operations. For example, when a double-precision value is assigned to an integer variable, only the integer portion of the value is stored. The conversion is implied by the operation and is performed automatically by the compiler.

An explicit conversion occurs whenever a cast is used. Two cast notations exist in C++. Using the older C notation, a cast has the form (dataType)expression; the newer C++ notation has the function-like form dataType(expression). For example, both of the expressions (int)24.32 and int(24.32) cause the double-precision value 24.32 to be truncated to the integer value 24.

Conversion from Built-in to Class

User-defined casts for converting a built-in to a user-defined data type are created by using constructor functions. A constructor whose first argument is not a member of its class and whose remaining arguments, if any, have default values is a **type conversion constructor**. If the first argument of a type conversion constructor is a built-in data type, the constructor can be used to cast the built-in data type to a class object. Clearly, one restriction of such functions is that, as constructors, they must be member functions.

Although this type of cast occurs when the constructor is invoked to initialize an object, it is actually a more general cast than might be evident at first glance. This is because a constructor function can be explicitly invoked after all objects have been declared, whether or not it was invoked previously as part of an object's declaration. Before exploring this further, let's construct a type conversion constructor. We will then see how to use it as a cast independent of its initialization purpose.

The cast we will construct will convert a long integer into a Date object. Our Date object will consist of dates in the form month/day/year and will use our now familiar Date class. The long integer will be used to represent dates in the form year * 10000 + month * 100 + day. For example, using this representation, the date 12/31/2001 becomes the long integer 20011231. Representing dates in this fashion is very useful for two reasons: First, it permits a date to be stored as a single integer, and second, such dates are in numerically increasing date order, which makes sorting extremely easy. For example, the date 01/03/2002, which occurs after 12/31/2001, becomes the integer 20020103, which is larger than 20011231. Because the integers that represent dates can exceed the size of a normal integer, the integers are always declared as longs.

A suitable constructor function for converting from a long-integer date to a date stored as a month, day, and year is

```
// type conversion constructor from long to Date

Date::Date(long findate)
{
  year = int(findate/10000.0);
  month = int((findate - year * 10000.0)/100.0);
  day = int(findate - year * 10000.0 - month * 100.0);
}
```

Program 14.5 uses this type conversion constructor both as an initialization function at declaration time and as an explicit cast later on in the program.

Program 14.5

```
#include <iostream>
#include <iomanip>
using namespace std;

// class declaration

class Date
{
  private:
    int month, day, year;
  public:
    Date(int = 7, int = 4, int = 2006); // constructor
    Date(long);               // type conversion constructor
    void showDate();
};
```

```cpp
// implementation section

// constructor
Date::Date(int mm, int dd, int yyyy)
{
  month = mm;
  day = dd;
  year = yyyy;
}

// type conversion constructor from long to date
Date::Date(long findate)
{
  year = int(findate/10000.0);
  month = int((findate - year * 10000.0)/100.0);
  day = int(findate - year * 10000.0 - month * 100.0);
}

// member function to display a date
void Date::showDate()
{
  cout << setfill('0')
       << setw(2) << month << '/'
       << setw(2) << day << '/'
       << setw(2) << year % 100;

  return;
}

int main()
{
  Date a, b(20101225L), c(4,1,1999); // declare 3 objects—initialize 2 of them

  cout << "\nDates a, b, and c are ";
  a.showDate();
  cout << ", ";
  b.showDate();
  cout << ", and ";
  c.showDate();
  cout << ".\n";

  a = Date(20110103L);   // cast a long to a date

  cout << "Date a is now ";
  a.showDate();
  cout << ".\n\n";

  return 0;
}
```

The output produced by Program 14.5 is

```
Dates a, b, and c are 07/04/06, 12/25/10, and 04/01/99.
Date a is now 01/03/11.
```

The change in a's date value illustrated by this output is produced by the assignment expression a = Date(20110103L), which uses a type conversion constructor to perform the cast from long to Date.

Conversion from Class to Built-in

Conversion from a user-defined data type to a built-in data type is accomplished using a conversion operator function. A **conversion operator function** is a member operator function that has the name of a built-in data type or class. When the operator function has a built-in data type name, it is used to convert from a class to a built-in data type. For example, a conversion operator function for casting a class object to a long integer would have the name operator long(). Here the name of the operator function indicates that a conversion to a long will take place. If this function were part of a Date class, it would be used to cast a Date object to a long integer. This usage is illustrated by Program 14.6.

 Program 14.6

```cpp
#include <iostream>
#include <iomanip>
using namespace std;

// class declaration

class Date
{
  private:
    int month, day, year;
  public:
    Date(int = 7, int = 4, int = 2006);    // constructor
    operator
    ;
};
```

```cpp
// implementation section

// constructor
Date::Date(int mm, int dd, int yyyy)
{
  month = mm;
  day = dd;
  year = yyyy;
}

// conversion operator function converting from Date to long
Date::operator long()     // must return a long
{
  long yyyymmdd;

  yyyymmdd = year * 10000.0 + month * 100.0 + day;

  return(yyyymmdd);
}

// member function to display a date
void Date::showDate()
{
  cout << setfill('0')
       << setw(2) << month << '/'
       << setw(2) << day << '/'
       << setw(2) << year % 100;

  return;
}

int main()
{
  Date a(4,1,2008);   // declare and initialize one object of type date
  long b;             // declare an object of type long

  b = a;              // a conversion takes place here

  cout << "\n a's date is ";
  a.showDate();
  cout << "\n This date, as a long integer, is " << b << "\n\n";

  return 0;
}
```

The output produced by Program 14.6 is

```
a's date is 04/01/08
This date, as a long integer, is 20080401
```

The change in a's date value to a long integer illustrated by this output is produced by the assignment expression b = a. This assignment, which also could have been written as b = long(a), calls the conversion operator function long() to perform the cast from Date to long. In general, because explicit conversion more clearly documents what is happening, its use is preferred to implicit conversion.

Note that the conversion operator has no explicit argument and no explicit return type. This is true of all conversion operators: Its implicit argument will always be an object of the class being cast from, and the return type is implied by the name of the function. Additionally, as previously indicated, a conversion operator function *must be* a member function.

Conversion from Class to Class

Converting from a user-defined data type to a user-defined data type is performed in the same manner as a cast from a user-defined to a built-in data type—it is done using a member conversion operator function. In this case, however, the operator function uses the class name being converted to rather than a built-in data name. For example, if two classes named Date and Intdate exist, the operator function named operator Intdate() could be placed in the Date class to convert from a Date object to an Intdate object. Similarly, the operator function named Date() could be placed in the Intdate class to convert from an Intdate to a Date.

Note that as before, in converting from a user-defined data type to a built-in data type, *the operator function's name determines the result of the conversion*; the class containing the operator function determines the data type being converted from.

Before we look at a specific example of a class-to-class conversion, we must note one additional point. Converting between classes clearly implies that we have two classes, one of which is always defined first and one of which is defined second. Having, within the second class, a conversion operator function with the name of the first class poses no problem, because the compiler knows of the first class's existence. However, including in the first class a conversion operator function with the second class's name does pose a problem, because the second class has not yet been defined. This is remedied by including a declaration for the second class prior to the first class's definition. This declaration, which is formally referred to as a **forward declaration**, is illustrated in Program 14.7, which also includes conversion operators between the two defined classes.

Program 14.7

```cpp
#include <iostream>
#include <iomanip>
using namespace std;

// forward declaration of class Intdate
class Intdate;

// class declaration for Date
class Date
{
  private:
    int month, day, year;
  public:
    Date(int = 7, int = 4, int = 2006);    // constructor
    operator Intdate();    // conversion operator Date to Intdate
    void showDate();
};
// class declaration for Intdate
class Intdate
{
  private:
    long yyyymmdd;
  public:
    Intdate(long = 0);    // constructor
    operator Date();  // conversion operator Intdate to Date
    void showInt();
};
// implementation section for Date
Date::Date(int mm, int dd, int yyyy)  // constructor
{
  month = mm;
  day = dd;
  year = yyyy;
}
// conversion operator function converting from Date to Intdate class
Date::operator Intdate()   // must return an Intdate object
{
  long temp;

  temp = year * 10000.0 + month * 100.0 + day;
  return(Intdate(temp));
}
// member function to display a Date
void Date::showDate()
{
  cout << setfill('0')
       << setw(2) << month << '/'
```

(continued on next page)

(continued from previous page)

```
                << setw(2) << day << '/'
            << setw(2) << year % 100;
    return;
}

// implementation section for Intdate
Intdate::Intdate(long ymd)   // constructor
{
    yyyymmdd = ymd;
}
// conversion operator function converting from Intdate to Date class
Intdate::operator Date()      // must return a Date object
{
    int mo, da, yr;

    yr = int(yyyymmdd/10000.0);
    mo = int((yyyymmdd - yr * 10000.0)/100.0);
    da = int(yyyymmdd - yr * 10000.0 - mo * 100.0);
    return(Date(mo,da,yr));
}
// member function to display an Intdate
void Intdate::showInt()
{
    cout << yyyymmdd;
    return;
}

int main()
{
    Date a(4,1,2008), b;        // declare two Date objects
    Intdate c(20111215L), d;    // declare two Intdate objects

    b = Date(c);        // cast c into a Date object
    d = Intdate(a);     // cast a into an Intdate object

    cout << "\n a's date is ";
    a.showDate();
    cout << "\n    as an Intdate object this date is ";
    d.showInt();

    cout << "\n c's date is ";
    c.showInt();
    cout << "\n    as a Date object this date is ";
    b.showDate();
    cout << "\n\n";

    return 0;
}
```

The output produced by Program 14.7 is

```
a's date is 04/01/08
    as an Intdate object this date is 20080401
c's date is 20111215
    as a Date object this date is 12/15/11
```

As illustrated by Program 14.7, the cast from `Date` to `Intdate` is produced by the assignment `b = Date(c)`, and the cast from `Intdate` to `Date` is produced by the assignment `d = Intdate(a)`. Alternatively, the assignments `b = c` and `d = a` would produce the same results. Note also the forward declaration of the `Intdate` class prior to the `Date` class's declaration. This is required so that the `Date` class can reference `Intdate` in its operator conversion function.

▌ EXERCISES 14.3

1. **a.** Define the four data type conversions available in C++ and the method of accomplishing each conversion.
   b. Define the terms *type conversion constructor* and *conversion operator function*, and describe how they are used in user-defined conversions.

2. Write a C++ program that declares a class named Time having integer data members named `hours`, `minutes`, and `seconds`. Include in the program a type conversion constructor that converts a long integer, representing the elapsed seconds from midnight, into an equivalent representation as `hours:minutes:seconds`. For example, the long integer 30336 should convert to the time 8:25:36. Use a military representation of time so that 2:30 p.m. is represented as 14:30:00. The relationship between time representations is

   elapsed seconds = hours * 3600 + minutes * 60 + seconds

3. A Julian date is a date represented as the number of days from a known base date. One algorithm for converting from a Gregorian date, in the form month/day/year, to a Julian date with a base date of 0/0/0 follows. All of the calculations in this algorithm use integer arithmetic, which means that the fractional part of all divisions must be discarded. In this algorithm, M = month, D = day, and Y = 4-digit year.

```
If M is less than or equal to 2
  set the variable MP = 0 and YP = Y-1
Else
  set MP = int(0.4 * M + 2.3) and YP = Y

T = int(YP/4) - int(YP/100) + int(YP/400)

Julian date = 365 * Y + 31 * (M - 1) + D + T - MP
```

Using this algorithm, modify Program 14.6 to cast from a Gregorian date object to its corresponding Julian representation as a long integer. Test your program by using the Gregorian dates 1/31/2005 and 3/16/2006, which correspond to the Julian dates 38381 and 38790, respectively.

4. Modify the program written for Exercise 2 to include a member conversion operator function that converts an object of type `time` into a long integer representing the number of seconds from twelve midnight.

5. Write a C++ program that has a `Date` class and a `Julian` class. The `Date` class should be the same `Date` class as that used in Program 14.7, whereas the `Julian` class should represent a date as a long integer. For this program, include a member conversion operator function within the `Date` class that converts a `Date` object to a `Julian` object, using the algorithm presented in Exercise 3. Test your program by converting the dates 1/31/2006 and 3/16/2007, which correspond to the Julian dates 38746 and 39155, respectively.

6. Write a C++ program that has a `Time` class and an `Ltime` class. The `Time` class should have integer data members named `hours`, `minutes`, and `seconds`, whereas the `Ltime` class should have a long data member named `elsecs`, which represents the number of elapsed seconds since midnight. For the `Time` class, include a member conversion operator function named `Ltime()` that converts a `Time` object to an `Ltime` object. For the `Ltime` class, include a member conversion operator function named `Time()` that converts an `Ltime` object to a `Time` object.

14.4   Class Inheritance and Polymorphism

The ability to create new classes from existing ones is the underlying motivation and power behind class and object-oriented programming techniques. Doing so facilitates reusing existing code in new ways without the need for retesting and validation. It permits the designers of a class to make it available to others for additions and extensions without relinquishing control over the existing class features.

Constructing one class from another is accomplished by using a capability called inheritance. Related to this capability is an equally important feature named polymorphism. Polymorphism provides the ability to redefine, on the basis of the class object being referenced, how member functions of related classes operate. In fact, for a programming language to be classified as an object-oriented language, it must provide the features of classes, inheritance, and polymorphism. In this section we describe the inheritance and polymorphism features provided in C++.

Inheritance

Inheritance is the capability of deriving one class from another class. The initial class that is used as the basis for the derived class is referred to as the **base class**, **parent class**, or **superclass**. The derived class is referred to as the **derived class**, **child class**, or **subclass**.

PROGRAMMING NOTE

Object-Based versus Object-Oriented Languages

An *object-based* language is one in which data and operations can be incorporated together in such a way that data values can be isolated and accessed through the specified class functions. The ability to bind the data members with operations in a single unit is referred to as *encapsulation*. In C++, encapsulation is provided by its class capability.

For a language to be classified as *object-oriented*, it must also provide inheritance and polymorphism. *Inheritance* is the capability to derive one class from another. A derived class is a completely new data type that incorporates all of the data members and member functions of the original class with any new data and function members unique to itself. The class used as the basis for the derived type is referred to as the *base* or *parent* class, and the derived data type is referred to as the *derived* or *child* class.

Polymorphism permits the same method name to invoke one operation in objects of a parent class and a different operation in objects of a derived class.

A derived class is a completely new class that incorporates all of the data and member functions of its base class. It can (and usually does), however, add its own additional new data and function members, and it can override any base class function.

As an example of inheritance, consider three geometric shapes: a circle, cylinder, and sphere. All of these shapes share a common characteristic, a radius. Thus, for these shapes, we can make the circle a base type for the other two shapes, as illustrated in Figure 14.1. By convention, arrows always point from the derived class to the base class. Reformulating these shapes as class types we would make the circle the base class and derive the cylinder and sphere classes from it.

FIGURE 14.1 *Relating Object Types*

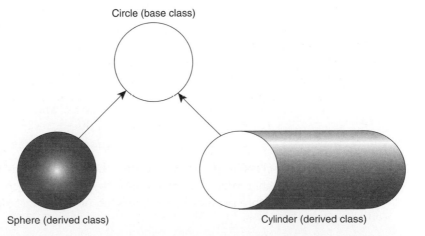

Circle (base class)

Sphere (derived class)

Cylinder (derived class)

The relationships illustrated in Figure 14.1 are examples of simple inheritance. In **simple inheritance**, each derived type has only one immediate base type. The complement to simple inheritance is multiple inheritance. In **multiple inheritance**, a derived type has two or more base types. Figure 14.2 gives an example of multiple inheritance. In this text we will only consider simple inheritance.

FIGURE 14.2 *An Example of Multiple Inheritance*

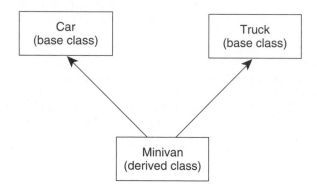

The class derivations illustrated in both Figure 14.1 and Figure 14.2 are formally referred to as **class hierarchies**, because they illustrate the hierarchy, or order, in which one class is derived from another. Let's now see how to derive one class from another.

A derived class has the same form as any other class in that it consists of both a declaration and an implementation. The only difference is in the first line of the declaration section. For a derived class, this line is extended to include an access specification and a base class name and has the form

```
class  derivedClassName : classAccess  baseClassName
```

For example, if `Circle` is the name of an existing class, a new class named `Cylinder` can be derived as follows:

```
class Cylinder : public Circle
{
    // add any additional data and
    // function members in here
}; // end of Cylinder class declaration
```

Except for the class-access specifier after the colon and the base class name, there is nothing inherently new or complicated about the construction of the `Cylinder` class. Before providing a description of the `Circle` class and adding data and function members to the derived `Cylinder` class, we will need to re-examine access specifiers and how they are related to derived classes.

Access Specifications

Until now we have used only private and public access specifiers within a class. Giving all data members private status ensured that they can be accessed only by class member functions or friends. This restricted access prevents access by any nonclass functions (except friends), *which also precludes access by any derived class functions*. This is a sensible restriction. If it did not exist, anyone could "jump around" the private restriction by simply deriving a class.

To retain a restricted type of access across derived classes, C++ provides a third access specification—protected. Protected access behaves identically to private access in that it permits only member or friend function access, but it permits this restriction to be inherited by any derived class. The derived class then defines the type of inheritance it is willing to take on, subject to the base class's access restrictions. This is done by the class-access specifier, which is listed after the colon at the start of its declaration section. Table 14.3 lists the resulting derived class member access based on the base class member specifications and the derived class-access specifier.

Table 14.3 shows (shaded region) that if the base class member has a protected access and the derived class specifier is public, then the derived class member will be protected to its class. Similarly, if the base class has a public access and the derived class specifier is public, then the derived class member will be public. Because this is the most commonly used type of specification for base class data and function members, respectively, it is the one we will use. This means that for all classes intended for use as a base class, we will use a protected data member access in place of a private designation.

TABLE 14.3 *Inherited Access Restrictions*

Base Class Member	Derived Class Access	Derived Class Member
private ⟶	: `private` ⟶	inaccessible
protected ⟶	: `private` ⟶	private
public ⟶	: `private` ⟶	private
private ⟶	: `public` ⟶	inaccessible
protected ⟶	: `public` ⟶	protected
public ⟶	: `public` ⟶	public
private ⟶	: `protected` ⟶	inaccessible
protected ⟶	: `protected` ⟶	protected
public ⟶	: `protected` ⟶	protected

An Example

To illustrate the process of deriving one class from another, we will derive a `Cylinder` class from a base `Circle` class. The definition of the `Circle` class is

```
// class declaration

class Circle
{
  protected:
    double radius;
  public:
    Circle(double = 1.0);    // constructor
    double calcval();
};

// class implementation

// constructor
Circle::Circle(double r)    // constructor
{
  radius = r;
}
// calculate the area of a circle
double Circle::calcval()
{
  return(PI * radius * radius);
}
```

Except for the substitution of the access specifier `protected` in place of the usual private specifier for the data member, this is a standard class definition. The only identifier not defined is PI, which is used in the `calcval()` function. We will define this as

```
const double PI = 2.0 * asin(1.0);
```

This is simply a "trick" that forces the computer to return the value of pi accurate to as many decimal places as allowed by your computer. This value is obtained by taking the arcsin of 1.0, which is $\pi/2$, and multiplying the result by 2.

Having defined our base class, we can now extend it to a derived class. The definition of the derived class is

```
// class declaration where
// Cylinder is derived from Circle

class Cylinder : public Circle
```

```
protected:
    double length;    // add one additional data member and
  public:             // two additional function members
    Cylinder(double r = 1.0, double l = 1.0) : Circle(r), length(l) {}
    double calcval();
};

// class implementation

double Cylinder::calcval()      // this calculates a volume
{
   return (length * Circle::calcval()); // note the base function call
}
```

This definition encompasses several important concepts related to derived classes. First, as a derived class, Cylinder contains all of the data and function members of its base class, Circle, plus any additional members that it may add. In this particular case, the Cylinder class consists of a radius data member, inherited from the Circle class, plus an additional length member. Thus each Cylinder object contains *two* data members, as is illustrated in Figure 14.3.

FIGURE 14.3 *Relationship Between Circle and Cylinder Data Members*

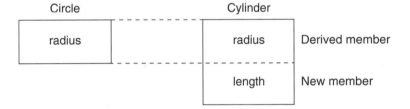

In addition to having two data members, the Cylinder class also inherits Circle's function members. This is illustrated in the Cylinder constructor, which uses a base member initialization list (see Section 13.1) that specifically calls the Circle constructor. It is also illustrated in Cylinder's calcval() function, which makes a call to Circle::calcval().

In both classes the same function name, calcval(), has been specifically used to illustrate the overriding of a base function by a derived function. When a Cylinder object calls calcval(), it is a request to use the Cylinder version of the function, and a Circle object call to calcval() is a request to use the Circle version. In this case the Cylinder class can only access the Circle class version of calcval() using the scope resolution operator, as is done in the call Circle::calcval(). Program 14.8 uses these two classes within the context of a complete program.

Program 14.8

```cpp
#include <iostream>
#include <cmath>
using namespace std;

const double PI = 2.0 * asin(1.0);

// class declaration

class Circle
{
  protected:
    double radius;
  public:
    Circle(double = 1.0);    // constructor
    double calcval();
};

// implementation section for Circle

// constructor
Circle::Circle(double r)
{
  radius = r;
}

// calculate the area of a circle
double Circle::calcval()
{
  return(PI * radius * radius);
}

// class declaration for the derived class
// Cylinder which is derived from Circle
class Cylinder : public Circle
{
  protected:
    double length;  // add one additional data member and
  public:            // two additional function members
    Cylinder(double r = 1.0, double l = 1.0) : Circle(r), length(l) {}
    double calcval();
};
```

```
// implementation section for Cylinder

double Cylinder::calcval()       // this calculates a volume
{
  return (length * Circle::calcval());  // note the base function call
}

int main()
{
  Circle circle_1, circle_2(2);  // create two Circle objects
  Cylinder cylinder_1(3,4);        // create one Cylinder object

  cout << "\nThe area of circle_1 is " << circle_1.calcval() << endl;
  cout << "The area of circle_2 is " << circle_2.calcval() << endl;
  cout << "The volume of cylinder_1 is " << cylinder_1.calcval() << endl;

  circle_1 = cylinder_1;     // assign a cylinder to a Circle

  cout << "\nThe area of circle_1 is now "
       << circle_1.calcval() << endl;

  return 0;
}
```

The output produced by Program 14.8 is

```
The area of circle_1 is 3.14159
The area of circle_2 is 12.5664
The volume of cylinder_1 is 113.097

The area of circle_1 is now 28.2743
```

The first three output lines are all straightforward and are produced by the first three cout statements in the program. As the output shows, a call to calcval() using a Circle object activates the Circle version of this function, whereas a call to calcval() using a Cylinder object activates the Cylinder version.

The assignment statement circle_1 = cylinder_1; introduces another important relationship between a base and derived class: *A derived class object can be assigned to a base class object.* This should not be surprising, because both base and derived classes share a common set of data member types. In this type of assignment, it is only this set of data members, which consists of all the base class data members, that are assigned. Thus, as illustrated in Figure 14.4, our `Cylinder` to `Circle` assignment results in the following memberwise assignment:

`circle_1.radius = cylinder_1.radius;`

FIGURE 14.4 *Assignment from Derived to Base Class*

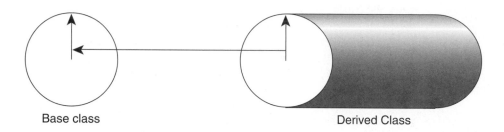

The `length` member of the `Cylinder` object is not used in the assignment because it has no equivalent variable in the `Circle` class. The reverse cast, from base to derived class, is not as simple and requires a constructor to correctly initialize the additional derived class members not in the base class.

Before leaving Program 14.8, we need to make one additional point. Although the `Circle` constructor was explicitly called using a base/member initialization list for the `Cylinder` constructor, an implicit call could also have been made. In the absence of an explicitly derived class constructor, the compiler will automatically call the default base class constructor first, before the derived class constructor is called. This works because the derived class contains all of the base class data members. In a similar fashion, the destructor functions are called in the reverse order—first derived class and then base class.

Polymorphism

The overriding of a base member function using an overloaded derived member function, as illustrated by the `calcval()` function in Program 14.8, is an example of polymorphism. **Polymorphism** permits the same function name to invoke one response in objects of a base class and another response in objects of a derived class. In some cases, however, this method of overriding does not work as one might desire. To understand why this is so, consider Program 14.9.

Program 14.9

```cpp
#include <iostream>
#include <cmath>
using namespace std;

// class declaration for the base class

class One
{
  protected:
    double a;
  public:
    One(double = 2);    // constructor
    double f1(double);    // a member function
    double f2(double);    // another member function
};

// class implementation for One

One::One(double val)    // constructor
{
  a = val;
}

double One::f1(double num)    // a member function
{
  return(num/2);
}
double One::f2(double num)    // another member function
{
  return( pow(f1(num),2) );    // square the result of f1()
}

// class declaration for the derived class

class Two : public One
{
  public:
    double f1(double);    // this overrides class One's f1()
};
```

(continued on next page)

(continued from previous page)

```
// class implementation for Two

double Two::f1(double num)
{
  return(num/3);
}

int main()
{
  One object_1;     // object_1 is an object of the base class
  Two object_2;     // object_2 is an object of the derived class

    // call f2() using a base class object call
  cout << "The computed value using a base class object call is "
       << object_1.f2(12) << endl;

    // call f2() using a derived class object call
  cout << "The computed value using a derived class object call is
"
       << object_2.f2(12) << endl;

  return 0;
}
```

The output produced by Program 14.9 is

```
The computed value using a base class object call is 36
The computed value using a derived class object call is 36
```

As this output shows, the same result is obtained no matter which object type calls the f2() function. This result is produced because the derived class does not have an override to the base class f2() function. Thus both calls to f2() result in the base class f2() function being called.

Once invoked, the base class f2() function will always call the base class version of f1() rather than the derived class override version. This behavior is due to a process referred to as **function binding**. In normal function calls, static binding is used. In **static binding**, the determination of which function is called is made at compile time. Thus, when the compiler first encounters the f1() function in the base class, it makes the determination that whenever f2() is called, either from a base class or a derived class object, it will subsequently call the base class f1() function.

In place of static binding, we would like a binding method that is capable of determining which function should be invoked at run time, on the basis of the object type making the call. This type of binding is referred to as **dynamic binding**. To achieve dynamic binding, C++ provides virtual functions.

A **virtual function** specification tells the compiler to create a pointer to a function but not to fill in the value of the pointer until the function is actually called. Then, at run time, *and on the basis of the object making the call*, the appropriate function address is used. Creating a virtual function is extremely easy—all that is required is that the keyword `virtual` be placed before the function's return type in the declaration section. For example, consider Program 14.10, which is identical to Program 14.9 except for the virtual declaration of the `f1()` function.

Program 14.10

```
#include <iostream>
#include <cmath>
using namespace std;

// class declaration for the base class

class One
{
  protected:
    double a;
  public:
    One(double = 2);     // constructor
    virtual double f1(double);     // a member function
    double f2(double);     // another member function
};

// class implementation for One

One::One(double val)     // constructor
{
  a = val;
}

double One::f1(double num)     // a member function
{
  return(num/2);
}

double One::f2(double num)     // another member function
{
  return( pow(f1(num),2) );     // square the result of f1()
}
```

(continued on next page)

(continued from previous page)

```
// class declaration for the derived class

class Two : public One
{
  public:
    virtual double f1(double);  // this overrides class One's f1()
};

// class implementation for Two

double Two::f1(double num)
{
  return(num/3);
}

int main()
{
  One object_1;    // object_1 is an object of the base class
  Two object_2;    // object_2 is an object of the derived class

    // call f2() using a base class object call
  cout << "The computed value using a base class object call is "
       << object_1.f2(12) << endl;

    // call f2() using a derived class object call
  cout << "The computed value using a derived class object call is "
       << object_2.f2(12) << endl;

  return 0;
}
```

The output produced by Program 14.10 is

```
The computed value using a base class object call is 36
The computed value using a derived class object call is 16
```

As illustrated by this output, the f2() function now calls different versions of the overloaded f1() function on the basis of the object type making the call. This selection, which is based on the object making the call, is the classic definition of polymorphic function behavior and is caused by the dynamic binding imposed on f1() because it is a virtual function.

Once a function is declared as virtual, *it remains virtual for the next derived class with or without a virtual declaration in the derived class.* Thus the second `virtual` declaration in the derived class is not strictly needed, but it should be included both for clarity and to ensure that any subsequently derived classes correctly inherit the function. Consider the inheritance diagram illustrated in Figure 14.5, where class C is derived from class B and class B is derived from class A.[5] In this situation, if function `f1()` is virtual in class A but is not declared in class B, it will not be virtual in class C. The only other requirement is that once a function has been declared as virtual, the return type and parameter list of all subsequent derived class override versions *must be* the same.

FIGURE 14.5   *Inheritance Diagram*

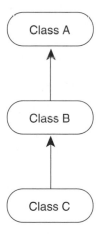

Class A

Class B

Class C

▌ EXERCISES 14.4

1. Define the following terms:
   - *a.* inheritance
   - *b.* base class
   - *c.* derived class
   - *d.* simple inheritance
   - *e.* multiple inheritance
   - *f.* class hierarchy
   - *g.* polymorphism
   - *h.* static binding
   - *i.* dynamic binding
   - *j.* virtual function

2. Describe the two methods that C++ provides for implementing polymorphism.

---

[5] By convention, as previously noted, arrows always point from the derived class to the base class.

3. What three features must a programming language provide for it to be classified as an object-oriented language?

4. Describe the difference between a private and a protected class member.

5. *a.* Modify Program 14.8 to include a derived class named `Sphere` from the base `Circle` class. The only additional class members of `Sphere` should be a constructor and a `calcval()` function that returns the volume of the sphere. (*Note:* volume = $(4/3)\pi$ radius³)

   b. Include the class constructed for Exercise 5a in a working C++ program. Have your program call all of the member functions in the `Sphere` class.

6. *a.* Create a base class named `Point` that consists of an x and a y coordinate. From this class, derive a class named `Circle` that has an additional data member named `radius`. For this derived class, the x and y data members represent the center coordinates of a circle. The function members of the first class should consist of a constructor, an area function named `area` that returns zero, and a distance function that returns the distance between two points, where

$$\text{distance} = \sqrt{(x_2 - x_1)^2 + (y_2 - y_1)^2}$$

Additionally, the derived class should have a constructor and an override function named `area` that returns the area of a circle.

   b. Include the classes constructed for Exercise 6a in a working C++ program. Have your program call all of the member functions in each class. In addition, call the base class `distance` function with two `Circle` objects, and explain the result returned by the function.

7. *a.* Using the classes constructed for Exercise 6a, derive a class named `Cylinder` from the derived `Circle` class. The `Cylinder` class should have a constructor and a member function named `area` that determines the surface area of the cylinder. For this function, use the algorithm

$$\textit{surface area} = 2\pi r\,(l + r)$$

where *r* is the radius of the cylinder and *l* is the length.

   b. Include the classes constructed for Exercise 7a in a working C++ program. Have your program call all of the member functions in the `Cylinder` class.

   c. What do you think might be the result if the base class `distance` function were called with two `Cylinder` objects?

8. *a.* Create a base class named `Rectangle` that contains `length` and `width` data members. From this class derive a class named `Box` that has an additional data member named `depth`. The function members of the base `Rectangle` class should consist of a constructor and an `area` function. The derived `Box` class should have a constructor and an override function named `area` that returns the surface area of the box and a `volume` function.

   b. Include the classes constructed for Exercise 8a in a working C++ program. Have your program call all of the member functions in each class and explain the result when the `distance` function is called using a `Box` object.

14.5   Common Programming Errors

The common programming errors associated with operator functions, conversions, and inheritance are the following:

1. Attempting to redefine an operator's meaning as it applies to C++'s built-in data types.
2. Redefining an overloaded operator to perform a function not indicated by its conventional meaning. Although this will work, it is extremely bad programming practice.
3. Attempting to make a conversion operator function a friend, rather than a member function.
4. Attempting to specify a return type for a member conversion operator function.
5. Attempting to override a virtual function without using the same type and number of parameters as the original function.
6. Using the keyword `virtual` in the class implementation section. Functions are declared as `virtual` only in the class declaration section.

14.6   Chapter Summary

1. User-defined operators can be constructed for classes by using member operator functions. An operator function has the form `operator<symbol>`, where `<symbol>` is one of the following:

```
() [] -> new delete ++ - ! ~ * / % + -
<< >> < <= > >= ++ != && || & ^ | = +=
-= *= /= %= &= ^= |= <<= >>= ,
```

For example, the function prototype `Date operator+(int);` declares that the addition operator will be defined to accept an integer and return a `Date` object.
2. User-defined operators may be called in either of two ways—as a conventional function with arguments or as an operator expression. For example, for an operator that has the header line

```
Date Date::operator+(int)
```

if `dte` is an object of type `Date`, the following two calls produce the same effect:

```
dte.operator+(284)
```

```
dte + 284
```

3. Operator functions may also be written as friend functions. The equivalent friend version of a member operator function will always contain an additional class reference that is not required by the member function.

4. The subscript operator function, `operator[]`, permits a maximum of one nonclass argument. This function can be defined only as a member function.

5. The parentheses operator function, `operator()`, has no limits on the number of arguments. This function can be defined only as a member function.

6. There are four categories of data type conversions. They are conversions from

   - Built-in types to built-in types
   - Built-in types to class (user-defined) types
   - Class (user-defined) types to built-in types
   - Class (user-defined) types to class (user-defined) types

   Conversions from built-in to built-in type are done by using C++'s implicit conversion rules or by explicitly using casts. Conversions from built-in to user-defined type are done using type conversion constructors. Conversions from user-defined types to either built-in or other user-defined types are done using conversion operator functions.

7. A *type conversion constructor* is a constructor whose first argument is not a member of its class and whose remaining arguments, if any, have default values.

8. A *conversion operator function* is a member operator function that has the name of a built-in data type or class. It has no explicit arguments or return type; rather, the return type is the name of the function.

9. *Inheritance* is the capability of deriving one class from another class. The initial class used as the basis for the derived class is referred to as the base class, parent class, or superclass. The derived class is referred to as the derived class, child class, or subclass.

10. Base class functions can be overridden by derived class functions with the same name. The override function is simply an overloaded version of the base class function defined in the derived class.

11. *Polymorphism* is the capability of having the same function name invoke different responses on the basis of the object making the function call. It can be accomplished by using either override functions or virtual functions.

12. In *static binding*, the determination of which function actually is invoked is made at compile time. In *dynamic binding*, the determination is made at run time.

13. A *virtual function* specification designates that dynamic binding should take place. The specification is made in the function's prototype by placing the keyword `virtual` before the function's return type. Once a function has been declared as `virtual` it remains so for all derived classes, so long as there is a continuous trail of function declarations through the derived chain of classes.

I/O File Streams and Data Files

The data for the programs we have used so far has either been assigned internally within the programs or entered by the user during program execution. This data is stored in the computer's main memory and ceases to exist once the program using it finishes executing. This type of data entry is fine for small amounts of data. But imagine a company having to pay someone to type in the names and addresses of hundreds or thousands of customers every month each time bills are prepared and sent.

As you'll learn in this chapter, it makes more sense to store such data outside of a program on a convenient storage medium. Data that is stored together under a common name on a storage medium other than the computer's main memory is called a data file. Typically data files are stored on disks, tapes, or CDs. Besides providing a permanent storage for the data, another advantage of data files is that they can be shared between programs, so that the data output by one program can be input directly to another program. You'll begin this chapter by learning how data files are created and maintained in C++. One major concern about using data files is ensuring that your programs open and connect correctly to them before any data processing begins. For this reason, you'll also learn how to use exception handling for this task. This type of error detection and correction is a major concern of all professionally written programs.

15.1   I/O File Stream Objects and Methods

To store and retrieve data outside a C++ program, you need two things:

- A file
- A file stream object

You'll learn about these important topics in the following two sections.

Files

A **file** is a collection of data that is stored together under a common name, usually on a disk, magnetic tape, or CD. For example, the C++ programs that you store on disk are examples of files. The stored data in a program file is the program code that becomes input data to the C++ compiler. In the context of data processing, however, the C++ program is not usually considered data, and the term **file**, or **data file**, is typically used to refer only to external files that contain the data used in a C++ program.

P R O G R A M M I N G   N O T E

Privacy, Security, and Files

Data files were around long before computers were used, but were primarily stored as paper records in filing cabinets. Terms such as *open*, *close*, *records*, and *lookup* that are used in handling computer files are reminders of these older techniques for accessing paper files stored in drawers.

Today most files are stored electronically, and the amount of information that is collected and stored proliferates wildly. The ease of sharing large amounts of data electronically has led to increasing problems with privacy and security.

Whenever a person fills out a government form or a credit application, submits a mail order, applies for a job, writes a check, or uses a credit card, an electronic data trail is created. Each time those files are shared among government agencies or private enterprises, the individual loses more of his or her privacy.

In order to help protect U.S. citizens' constitutional rights, the Fair Credit Reporting Act was passed in 1970, followed by the Federal Privacy Act in 1974. These acts specify that it is illegal for a business to keep secret files, that you are entitled to examine and correct any data collected about you, and that government agencies and contractors must show justification for accessing your records. Efforts continue to create mechanisms that will serve to preserve an individual's security and privacy.

A file is physically stored on an external medium such as a disk. Each file has a unique file name referred to as the file's **external name**. The external name is how the operating system knows the file . When you review the contents of a directory or folder (for example, in Windows Explorer) you see files listed by their external names. Each computer operating system has its own specification as to the maximum number of characters permitted for an external file name. Table 15.1 lists these specifications for the more commonly used operating systems.

TABLE 15.1 *Maximum Allowable File Name Characters*

Operating System	Maximum File Name Length
DOS	8 characters plus an optional period and 3 character extension
Windows 98, 2000, XP	255 characters

Unix
    Early Versions
    Current Versions
	
	14 characters
	255 characters

To ensure that the examples presented in this textbook are compatible with all of the operating systems listed in Table 15.1, we will generally, but not exclusively, adhere to the more restrictive DOS specifications. If you are using one of the other operating systems, however, you should take advantage of the increased length specification to create descriptive file names. Very long file names should be avoided, however, because they take more time to type and can result in typing errors. A manageable length for a file name is 12 to 14 characters, with an outside maximum of 25 characters.

Using the DOS convention then, the following are all valid computer data file names:

```
prices.dat     records        info.txt
exper1.dat     scores.dat     math.mem
```

Choose file names that indicate both the type of data in the file and the application for which it is used. Frequently, the first eight characters describe the data, and an extension (the characters after the period) describes the application. For example, the Excel spreadsheet program automatically applies an extension of "xls" to all spreadsheet files, Microsoft's Word and the WordPerfect word processing programs use the extensions "doc" and "wp$x$" (where x refers to the version number), respectively, and C++ compilers require a program file to have the extension "cpp." When creating your own file names, you should adhere to this practice. For example, using the DOS convention, the name "exper1.dat" is appropriate in describing a file of data corresponding to experiment number 1.

File Stream Objects

A **file stream** is a one-way transmission path that is used to connect a file stored on a physical device, such as a disk or CD, to a program. Each file stream has its own mode, which determines the direction of data on the transmission path—that is, whether the path will move data from a file into a program or whether the path will move data from a program to a file. A file stream that receives or reads data from a file into a program is referred to as an **input file stream**. A file stream that sends or writes data to a file is referred to as an **output file stream**. Notice that the direction, or mode, is always defined in relation to the program and not the file; data that go into a program are considered input data, and data sent out from the program are considered output data. Figure 15.1 illustrates the data flow from and to a file using input and output streams.

For each file that your program uses, a distinct file stream object must be created. If you are going to read and write to a file, both an input and output file stream object are required. There are two basic types of files: **text files**, which are also known as **character-based files**, and **binary-based** files. Both file types store data using a binary code; the difference is in what the codes represent. The default file type in C++ is a text file, and is the type presented in this chapter.

PROGRAMMING NOTE

Input and Output Streams

A *stream* is a one-way transmission path between a source and a destination. What gets sent down this transmission path is a stream of bytes. A good analogy to this "stream of bytes" is a stream of water that provides a one-way path for water to travel from a source to a destination.

Stream classes create stream objects. Two stream objects that we have used extensively are the input stream object named `cin` and the output stream object named `cout`. The `cin` object provides a transmission path from keyboard to program, while the `cout` object provides a transmission path from program to terminal screen. These two objects are created from the stream classes `istream` and `ostream`, respectively, which are parent classes to the `iostream` class. When the `iostream` header file is included in a program using the `#include <iostream>` directive, the `cin` and `cout` stream objects are automatically declared and opened by the C++ compiler for the compiled program.

File stream objects provide the same capabilities as the `cin` and `cout` objects, except they connect a program to a file rather than the keyboard or terminal screen. Also, file stream objects must be explicitly declared. File stream objects that will be used for input must be declared as objects of the class `ifstream`, while file stream objects that will be used for output must be declared as objects of the class `ofstream`. The classes `ifstream` and `ofstream` are made available to a program by inclusion of the `fstream` header file, using the directive `#include <fstream>`. The `fstream` class is derived from both the `ifstream` and `ofstream` classes (see Section 15.7).

For each file that your program uses, regardless of the file's type, a distinct file stream object must be created. If you want your program to both read and write to a file, both an input and output file stream object are required. Input file stream objects are declared to be of type `ifstream`, while output file streams are declared to be of type `ofstream`. For example, the declaration

```
ifstream inFile;
```

FIGURE 15.1   *Input and Output File Streams*

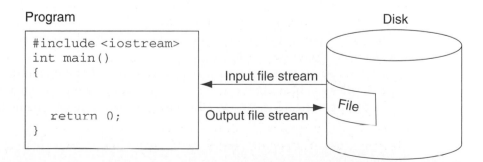

declares an input file stream object named `inFile` to be an object of the class `ifstream`. Similarly, the declaration

`ofstream outFile;`

declares an output file stream object named `outFile` to be an object of the class `ofstream`. Within a C++ program, a file stream is always accessed by its appropriate stream object name—one name for reading the file and one name for writing to the file. Object names, such as `inFile` and `outFile`, can be any programmer-selected names that conform to C++'s identifier rules.

Briefly, text-based files store each individual character, such as a letter, digit, dollar sign, decimal point, and so on, using an individual character code (typically ASCII or Unicode). The use of a character code allows such files to be displayed by a word processing program or text editor so that a person can read them. Binary-based files use the same code as your C++ compiler uses for its primitive data types. This means that numbers appear in their true binary form, while strings retain their ASCII or Unicode form. The advantage of binary-based files is compactness, because it takes less space to store most numbers using their binary code than as individual character values. In general, the vast majority of files programmers use are text files, simply because the file's data can be displayed by word processing programs and simple text editors.

File Stream Methods

Each file stream object has access to the methods defined for its respective `ifstream` or `ofstream` class. These methods include connecting a stream object name to an external file name (called **opening a file**), determining whether a successful connection has been made, closing a connection (called **closing a file**), getting the next data item into the program from an input stream, putting a new data item from the program onto an output stream, and detecting when the end of a file has been reached.

Opening a file connects each file stream object to a specific external file name. This is accomplished using a file stream's open method, which accomplishes two purposes. First, opening a file establishes the physical connecting link between a program and a file. Because details of this link are handled by the computer's operating system and are transparent to the program, the programmer normally doesn't need to consider them.

From a coding perspective, the second purpose of opening a file is more relevant. Besides establishing the actual physical connection between a program and a data file, opening a file connects the file's external computer name to the stream object name used internally by the program. The method that performs this task is named open() and is provided by both the ifstream and ofstream classes.

In using the open() method to connect the file's external name to its internal object stream name, only one argument is required, which is the external file name. For example, the statement

$$\text{inFile.open("prices.dat");}$$

connects the external text file named prices.dat to the internal program file stream object named inFile. This assumes, of course, that inFile has been declared as either an ifstream or ofstream object. If a file has been opened with the preceding statement, the program accesses the file using the internal object name inFile, while the computer saves the file under the external name prices.dat. Notice that the external file name argument passed to open() is a string contained between double quotes. Also notice that calling the open() method requires the standard object notation where the name of the desired method, in this case open(), is preceded by a period and an object name.

When an existing file is connecting to an input file stream, the file's data is made available for input, starting at the first data item in the file. Similarly, a file connected to an output file stream creates a new file and makes the file available for output. If a file exists with the same name as a file opened in output mode, the old file is erased and all its data is lost.

When opening a file, for input or output, good programming practice requires that you check that the connection has been established before attempting to use the file in any way. You can do this via the fail() method, which will return a true value if the file was unsuccessfully opened (that is, it is true the open failed), or a false value if the open succeeded. Typically the fail() method is used in code similar to the following, which attempts to open a file named prices.dat for input, checks that a valid connection was made, and reports an error message if the file was not successfully opened for input:

```
ifstream inFile;   // any object name can be used here
inFile.open("prices.dat");   // open the file

// check that the connection was successfully opened
if (inFile.fail())
{
  cout << "\nThe file was not successfully opened"
       << "\n Please check that the file currently exists."
       << endl;
  exit(1);
}
```

If the `fail()` method returns a `true`, which indicates that the open failed, a message is displayed by this code. In addition, the `exit()` function, which is a request to the operating system to end program execution immediately, is called. The `exit()` function requires inclusion of the `cstdlib` header function in any program that uses this function, and `exit()`'s single-integer argument is passed directly to the operating system for possible further operating system program action or user inspection. Throughout the remainder of the text we will include this type of error checking whenever a file is opened. (Section 15.3 shows how to use exception handling for the same type of error checking.)

In addition to the `fail()` method, C++ provides three other methods, all listed in Table 15.2, that can be used to detect a file's status. The use of these additional methods is presented at the end of the next section.

TABLE 15.2 *File Status Methods*

Prototype	Description
`fail()`	Returns a Boolean `true` if the file has not been successfully opened; otherwise returns a Boolean `false` value.
`eof()`	Returns a Boolean `true` if a read has been attempted past the end-of-file; otherwise returns a Boolean `false` value. The value becomes `true` only when the first character after the last valid file character is read.
`good()`	Returns a Boolean `true` value while the file is available for program use. Returns a Boolean `false` value if a read has been attempted past the end-of-file. The value becomes `false` only when the first character after the last valid file character is read.
`bad()`	Returns a Boolean `true` value if a read has been attempted past the end-of-file; otherwise returns a `false`. The value becomes `true` only when the first character after the last valid file character is read.

Program 15.1 illustrates the statements required to open a file for input, including an error checking routine to ensure that a successful open was obtained. A file opened for input is said to be in **read mode**.

Program 15.1

```cpp
#include <iostream>
#include <fstream>
#include <cstdlib>    // needed for exit()
using namespace std;

int main()
{
  ifstream inFile;

   inFile.open("prices.dat");   // open the file with the
                                // external name prices.dat
  if (inFile.fail())  // check for a successful open
  {
    cout << "\nThe file was not successfully opened"
         << "\n Please check that the file currently exists."
         << endl;
    exit(1);
  }

  cout << "\nThe file has been successfully opened for reading."
       << endl;

  // statements to read data from the file would be placed here

  return 0;
}
```

A sample run using Program 15.1 produced the output:

```
The file has been successfully opened for reading.
```

A slightly different check is required for output files, because if a file exists having the same name as the file to be opened in output mode, the existing file is erased and all its data is lost. To avoid this situation, the file is first opened in input mode to see if it exists. If it does, the user is given the choice of explicitly permitting it to be overwritten when it is later opened in output mode. The code used to accomplish this is highlighted in Program 15.2.

Program 15.2

```cpp
#include <iostream>
#include <fstream>
#include <cstdlib>    // needed for exit()
using namespace std;

int main()
{
  ifstream inFile;
  ofstream outFile;

  inFile.open("prices.dat");  // attempt to open the file for input

  char response;

  if (!inFile.fail())  // if it doesn't fail, the file exists
  {
   cout << "A file by the name prices.dat exists.\n"
        << "Do you want to continue and overwrite it\n"
        << " with the new data (y or n): ";
   cin >> response;
   if (tolower(response) == 'n')
   {
     cout << "The existing file will not be overwritten." << endl;
      exit(1);  //terminate program execution
   }
  }
  outFile.open("prices.dat");  // now open the file for writing

  if (inFile.fail())  // check for a successful open
  {
    cout << "\nThe file was not successfully opened"
         << endl;
    exit(1);
  }

  cout << "The file has been successfully opened for output."
       << endl;

  // statements to write to the file would be placed here

  return 0;
}
```

Following are two runs made with Program 15.2:

```
A file by the name prices.dat exists.
Do you want to continue and overwrite it
 with the new data (y or n): n
The existing file will not be overwritten.
```

and

```
A file by the name prices.dat exists.
Do you want to continue and overwrite it
 with the new data (y or n): y
The file has been successfully opened for output.
```

Although Programs 15.1 and 15.2 can be used to open an existing file for reading and writing, respectively, both programs lack statements to actually perform a read or write and close the file. These topics are discussed shortly. Before moving on, however, it is worthwhile noting that it is possible to combine the declaration of either an `ifstream` or `ofstream` object and its associated open statement into one statement. For example, the following two statements in Program 15.1

```
ifstream inFile;
inFile.open("prices.dat");
```

can be combined into the single statement

```
ifstream inFile("prices.dat");
```

Embedded and Interactive File Names

Two practical problems with Programs 15.1 and 15.2 are:

1. The external file name is embedded within the program code.
2. There is no provision for a user to enter the desired file name while the program is executing.

As both programs are written, if the file name is to change, a programmer must modify the external file name in the call to `open()` and recompile the program. Both of these problems can be alleviated by assigning the file name to a string variable.

A string variable as we have used it throughout the book (see especially Chapter 9) is a variable that can hold a string value, which is any sequence of zero or more characters enclosed within double quotes. For example,

"Hello World", "prices.dat", and "" are all strings. Notice that strings are always written with double quotes that delimit the beginning and end of a string, but are not stored as part of the string.

In declaring and initializing a string variable for use in an open() method, the string is always considered as a C-string. (See the Programming Note on the next page for precautions that must be understood when using a C-string.) A much safer alternative, and one that we will use throughout this book, is to use a string class object and then convert this object to a C-string using the c_str() method.

Once a string variable is declared to store a file name, it can be used in one of two ways. First, as shown in Program 15.3a, it can placed at the top of a program to clearly identify a file's external name, rather than embed it within an open() method call.

Program 15.3a

```
#include <iostream>
#include <fstream>
#include <cstdlib>    // needed for exit()
#include <string>
using namespace std;

int main()
{
  string filename = "prices.dat";  // place the file name up front
  ifstream inFile;

  inFile.open(filename.c_str());  // open the file

  if (inFile.fail())  // check for successful open
  {
    cout << "\nThe file named " << filename << " was not successfully opened"
        << "\n Please check that the file currently exists."
        << endl;
    exit(1);
  }

  cout << "\nThe file has been successfully opened for reading.\n";

  return 0;
}
```

PROGRAMMING NOTE

Using C-strings as File Names

If you choose to use a C-string to store an external file name, you must be aware of the following restrictions. The maximum length of the C-string must be specified within brackets immediately after it is declared. For example, in the declaration

```
char filename[21] = "prices.dat";
```

the number 21 limits the number of characters that can be stored in the C-string. The number in brackets, in this example 21, always represents one more than the maximum number of characters that can be assigned to the variable. This is because the compiler always adds a final end-of-string character to terminate the string. Thus, the string value `"prices.dat"`, which consists of 10 characters, is actually stored as 11 characters. The extra character is an end-of-string marker supplied by the compiler. In our example, the maximum string value assignable to the string variable file name is a string value consisting of 20 characters.

In reviewing Program 15.3a, notice that we have declared and initialized the string object named `filename` at the top of `main()` for easy file identification. Next, notice that when a string object is used, as opposed to a string literal, the variable name *is not* enclosed within double quotes in the `open()` method call. Also notice that within the `open()` call, the string object is converted to a C-string using the expression `filename.c_str()`. Finally, notice that in the `fail()` method code the file's external name is displayed by inserting the string object's name in the `cout` output stream. For these reasons, we will continue to identify the external names of files in this manner.

Another useful role string objects play is to permit the user to enter the file name as the program is executing. For example, the code

```
string filename;

cout << "Please enter the name of the file you wish to open: ";
cin  >> filename;
```

allows a user to enter a file's external name at run time. The only restriction in this code is that the user must not enclose the entered string value in double quotes and that the entered string value cannot contain any blanks. The reason for this is that when using `cin`, the compiler will terminate the string when it encounters a blank. Program 15.3b uses this code in the context of a complete program.

Program 15.3b

```cpp
#include <iostream>
#include <fstream>
#include <cstdlib>    // needed for exit()
#include <string>
using namespace std;

int main()
{
  string filename;
  ifstream inFile;

  cout << "Please enter the name of the file you wish to open: ";
  cin  >> filename;

  inFile.open(filename.c_str());  // open the file

  if (inFile.fail())  // check for successful open
  {
     cout << "\nThe file named " << filename << " was not successfully opened"
          << "\n Please check that the file currently exists."
          << endl;
     exit(1);
  }
  cout << "\nThe file has been successfully opened for reading.\n";

  return 0;
}
```

Following is a sample output provided by Program 15.3b.

```
Please enter the name of the file you wish to open: foobar

The file named foobar was not successfully opened
 Please check that the file currently exists.
```

Closing a File

A file is closed using the `close()` method. This method breaks the connection between the file's external name and the file stream object, which can then be used for another file. For example, the statement

```
inFile.close();
```

closes the `inFile` stream's connection to its current file. As indicated, the `close()` method takes no argument.

P R O G R A M M I N G   N O T E

Using `fstream` *Objects*

In using both `ifstream` and `ofstream` objects the input or output mode is implied by the object. Thus `ifstream` objects can only be used for input, and `ofstream` objects can only be used for output.

Another means of creating file streams is to use `fstream` objects that can be used for input or output, but this method requires an explicit mode designation. An `fstream` object is declared using the syntax

<code>fstream objectName;</code>

When using the `fstream` class's `open()` method, two arguments are required; a file's external name and a mode indicator. Permissible mode indicators are:

Indicator	Description
`ios::in`	Open a text file in input mode.
`ios::out`	Open a text file in output mode.
`ios::app`	Open a text file in append mode.
`ios::ate`	Go to the end of the opened file.
`ios::binary`	Open a binary file in input mode (default is text file).
`ios::trunc`	Delete file contents if it exists.
`ios::nocreate`	If file does not exist, open fails.
`ios::noreplace`	If file exists, open for output fails.

As with `ofstream` objects, an `fstream` object in output mode creates a new file and makes the file available for writing. If a file exists with the same name as a file opened for output, the old file is erased. For example, assuming that `file1` has been declared as an object of type `fstream` using the statement

<code>fstream file1;</code>

then the statement

<code>file1.open("prices.dat",ios::out);</code>

attempts to open the text file named `prices.dat` for output. Once this file has been opened, the program accesses the file using the internal object name `file1`, while the computer saves the file under the external name `prices.dat`.

An `fstream` file object opened in append mode means that an existing file is available for data to be added to the end of the file. If the file opened for appending does not exist, a new file with the designated name is created and made available to receive output from the program. For example, again assuming that `file1` has been declared to be of type `fstream`, the statement

<code>file1.open("prices.dat",ios::app);</code>

(continued on next page)

(continued from previous page)

attempts to open a text file named `prices.dat` and makes it available for data to be appended to the end of the file.

Finally, an `fstream` object opened in input mode means that an existing external file has been connected and its data is available as input. For example, assuming that `file1` has been declared to be of type `fstream`, the statement

```
file1.open("prices.dat",ios::in);
```

attempts to open a text file named `prices.dat` for input. The mode indicators can be combined by the bit `Or` operation (see Appendix D). For example, the statement

```
file1.open("prices.dat", ios::in | ios::binary)
```

opens the `file1` stream, which can be either an `fstream` or `ifstream`, as an input binary stream. If the mode indicator is omitted as the second argument for an `ifstream` object, the stream is, by default, opened as a text input file; if the mode indicator is omitted for an `ofstream` object, the stream is, by default, also opened as a text output file.

Because all computers have a limit on the maximum number of files that can be open at one time, closing files that are no longer needed makes good sense. The operating system will automatically close any open files existing at the end of normal program execution.

▌ EXERCISES 15.1

1. Write individual declaration and open statements that link the following external data file names to their corresponding internal object names. Assume that all the files are text based.

External Name	Object Name	Mode
coba.mem	memo	output
book.let	letter	output
coupons.bnd	coups	append
yield.bnd	yield	append
prices.dat	priFile	input
rates.dat	rates	input

PROGRAMMING NOTE

Checking for a Successful Connection

It is important to check that the `open()` method successfully established a connection between a file stream and an external file. Checking the connection is important because the `open()` call is really a request to the operating system that can fail for a variety of reasons. (Chief among these reasons are a request to open an existing file for reading that the operating system cannot locate, or attempting to open a file for output in a nonexistent folder.) If the operating system cannot satisfy the open request, you need to know about it and gracefully terminate your program. Failure to do so almost always results in abnormal program behavior or a subsequent program crash.

There are two styles of coding for checking the return value. The most common method for checking that a fail did not occur when attempting to use a file for input is the one coded in Program 15.1. It is used to clearly distinguish the `open()` request from the check made via the `fail()` call, and is repeated below for convenience:

```
inFile.open("prices.dat");  // request to open the file

if (inFile.fail())   // check for a failed connection
{
  cout << "\nThe file was not successfully opened"
       << "\n Please check that the file currently exists."
       << endl;
  exit(1);
}
```

Similarly, the check made in Program 15.2 is typically included when a file is being opened in output mode.

Alternatively, you may encounter programs that use `fstream` objects in place of both `ifstream` and `ofstream` objects (see the previous Programming note). When using `fstream`'s `open()` method, two arguments are required: a file's external name and an explicit mode indication. Using an `fstream` object, the open request and check for an input file typically appear as follows:

```
fstream inFile;

inFile.open("external file name", ios::in);
if (inFile.fail())
{
 cout << "\nThe file was not successfully opened"
      << "\n Please check that the file currently exists."
      << endl;
  exit(1);
}
```

Many times the conditional expression `inFile.fail()` is replaced by the equivalent expression `!inFile`. Although we will always use `ifstream` and `ofstream` objects, be prepared to encounter the styles that use `fstream` objects.

2. **a.** Write a set of two statements that first declares the following objects as `ifstream` objects and then opens them as text input files: `inData.txt`, `prices.txt`, `coupons.dat`, and `exper.dat`.

   b. Rewrite the two statements for Exercise 2a using a single statement.

3. **a.** Write a set of two statements that first declares the following objects as `ofstream` objects and then opens them as text output files: `outDate.txt`, `rates.txt`, `distance.txt`, and `file2.txt`.

   b. Rewrite the two statements for Exercise 3a using a single statement.

4. Enter and execute Program 15.1 on your computer.

5. Enter and execute Program 15.2 on your computer.

6. **a.** Enter and execute Program 15.3a on your computer.

   b. Add a `close()` method to Program 15.3a and then execute the program.

7. **a** Enter and execute Program 15.3b on your computer.

   b. Add a `close()` method to Program 15.3b and then execute the program.

8. Using the reference manuals provided with your computer's operating system, determine:

   a. The maximum number of characters that can be used to name a file for storage by the computer system.

   b. The maximum number of data files that can be open at the same time.

9. Would it be appropriate to call a saved C++ program a file? Why or why not?

10. **a.** Write individual declaration and open statements to link the following external data file names to their corresponding internal object names. Use only `ifstream` and `ofstream` objects.

External Name	Object Name	Mode
coba.mem	memo	binary and output
coupons.bnd	coups	binary and append
prices.dat	priFile	binary and input

   b. Redo Exercise 10a using only `fstream` objects.

   c. Write `close` statements for each of the files opened in Exercise 10a.

15.2   Reading and Writing Character-Based Files

Reading or writing character-based files involves almost the identical operations for reading input from a keyboard and writing data to a display screen. For writing to a file, the `cout` object is replaced by the `ofstream` object name declared in the program. For example, if `outFile` is declared as an object of type `ofstream`, the following output statements are valid:

```
outFile << 'a';
outFile << "Hello World!";
outFile << descrip << ' ' << price;
```

The file name in each of these statements, in place of `cout`, simply directs the output stream to a specific file instead of to the standard display device. Program 15.4 illustrates the use of the insertion operator, <<, to write a list of descriptions and prices to a file.

 Program 15.4

```
#include <iostream>
#include <fstream>
#include <cstdlib>    // needed for exit()
#include <string>
#include <iomanip>  // needed for formatting
using namespace std;

int main()
{
  string filename = "prices.dat";  // put the filename up front
  ofstream outFile;

  outFile.open(filename.c_str());

  if (outFile.fail())
  {
    cout << "The file was not successfully opened" << endl;
    exit(1);
  }

  // set the output file stream formats
  outFile << setiosflags(ios::fixed)
          << setiosflags(ios::showpoint)
          << setprecision(2);

  // send data to the file
  outFile << "Mats " << 39.95 << endl
          << "Bulbs " << 3.22 << endl
          << "Fuses " << 1.08 << endl;

  outFile.close();
  cout << "The file " << filename
       << " has been successfully written." << endl;

  return 0;
}
```

P R O G R A M M I N G   N O T E

Formatting Text File Output Stream Data

Output file streams can be formatted in the same manner as the `cout` standard output stream. For example, if an output stream named `fileOut` has been declared, the statement

```
fileOut << setiosflags(ios::fixed)
        << setiosflags(ios::showpoint)
        << setprecision(2);
```

formats all data inserted in the `fileOut` stream in the same way that these parameterized manipulators work for the `cout` stream. The first manipulator parameter, `ios::fixed`, causes the stream to output all numbers as if they were floating point values. The next parameter, `ios::showpoint`, tells the stream to always provide a decimal point. Thus, a value such as 1.0 will appear as 1.0, and not 1. Finally, the `setprecision` manipulator tells the stream to always display two decimal values after the decimal point. Thus, the number 1.0 for example, will appear as 1.00.

Instead of using manipulators, you can also use the stream methods `setf()` and `precision()`. For example, the previous formatting can also be accomplished using the code:

```
fileOut.setf(ios::fixed);
fileOut.setf(ios::showpoint);
fileOut.precision(2);
```

Which style you select is a matter of preference. In both cases the formats need only be specified once and remain in effect for every number subsequently inserted into the file stream.

When Program 15.4 is executed, a file named `prices.dat` is created and saved by the computer as a text file (which is the default file type). The file is a sequential file consisting of the following data:

```
Mats 39.95
Bulbs 3.22
Fuses 1.08
```

The actual storage of characters in the file depends on the character codes used by the computer. Although only 34 characters appear to be stored in the file—corresponding to the descriptions, blanks, and prices written to the file—the file actually contains 36 characters. The extra characters consist of the newline escape sequence at the end of each line that is created by the `endl` manipulator, which is created as a carriage return character (`cr`) and linefeed (`lf`). Assuming characters are stored using the ASCII code, the `prices.dat` file is physically stored as illustrated in Figure 15.2. For convenience, the character corresponding to each hexadecimal code is listed below the code. A code of 20 represents the blank character. Additionally, both C and C++ append the low-value

PROGRAMMING NOTE

The `put()` *Method*

All output streams have access to the `fstream` class's `put()` method, which permits character-by-character output to a stream. This method works in the same manner as the character insertion operator, `<<`. The syntax of this method call is:

```
ofstreamName.put(characterExpression);
```

where the *characterExpression* can be either a character variable or literal value. For example, the following code can be used to output an 'a' to the standard output stream:

```
cin.put('a');
```

In a similar manner, if `outFile` is an `ofstream` object file that has been opened, the following code outputs the character value in the character variable named keycode to this output:

```
char keycode;
      .
      .
outFile.put(keycode);
```

hexadecimal byte 0x00 as the end-of-file (EOF) sentinel when the file is closed. This end-of-file sentinel is never counted as part of the file.

FIGURE 15.2 *The* `prices.dat` *File as Stored by the Computer*

```
6D 61 74 73 20 33 39 2e 32 35 0D 0A 42 75 6c 62 73
 M  a  t  s     3  9  .  2  5 cr lf  B  u  l  b  s

20 33 2e 32 32 0D 0A 46 75 73 65 73 20 31 2e 30 38 0D 0A
    3  .  2  2 cr lf  F  u  s  e  s     1  .  0  8 cr lf
```

Reading from a Text File

Reading data from a character-based file is almost identical to reading data from a standard keyboard, except that the `cin` object is replaced by the `ifstream` object declared in the program. For example, if `inFile` is declared as an object of type `ifstream` that is opened for input, the input statement

```
inFile >> descrip >> price;
```

will read the next two items in the file and store them in the variables `descrip` and `price`.

The file stream name in this statement, in place of `cin`, simply directs the input to come from the file stream rather than the standard input device stream.

Other methods that can be used for stream input are listed in Table 15.3. Each of these methods must, of course, be preceded by a stream object name.

TABLE 15.3 `fstream` *Methods*

Method Name	Description
`get()`	Returns the next character extracted from the input stream as an `int`.
`get(charVar)`	Overloaded version of `get()` that extracts the next character from the input stream and assigns it to the specified character variable, `charVar`.
`getline(strObj, termChar)`	Extracts characters from the specified input stream, `strObj`, until the terminating character, `termChar`, is encountered. Assigns the characters to the specified string class object, `strObj`.
`peek()`	Returns the next character in the input stream without extracting it from the stream.
`ignore(int n)`	Skips over the next `n` characters. If n is omitted, the default is to skip over the next single character.

Program 15.5 illustrates how the `prices.dat` file created in Program 15.4 can be read. The program also illustrates one method of detecting the end-of-file (EOF) marker using the `good()` function (see Table 15.2). Because this function returns a Boolean `true` value before the EOF marker has been either read or passed over, it can be used to verify that the data just read is valid file data. Only after the EOF marker has been read or passed over does this function return a Boolean `false`. Thus, the notation `while(inFile.good())` used in Program 15.5 ensures that the data is from the file before the EOF has been read.

 Program 15.5

```
#include <iostream>
#include <fstream>
#include <cstdlib>      // needed for exit()
#include <string>
using namespace std;
```

```
int main()
{
  string filename = "prices.dat";   // put the filename up front
  string descrip;
  double price;

  ifstream inFile;

  inFile.open(filename.c_str());

  if (inFile.fail())  // check for successful open
  {
    cout << "\nThe file was not successfully opened"
         << "\n Please check that the file currently exists."
         << endl;
    exit(1);
  }

  // read and display the file's contents
  inFile >> descrip >> price;
  while (inFile.good())    // check next character
  {
    cout << descrip << ' ' << price << endl;
    inFile >> descrip >> price;
  }

  inFile.close();

  return 0;
}
```

The display produced by Program 15.5 is:

```
                     Mats 39.95
                     Bulbs 3.22
                     Fuses 1.08
```

Reexamine the expression inFile.good() used in the while statement. This expression is true as long as the EOF marker has not been read. Thus, as long as the item read was good, the loop continues to read the file. Within the loop, the items just read are first displayed and then a new string and a double-precision number are input to the program. When the EOF has been detected, the expression returns a Boolean value of false and the loop terminates. This ensures that data is read and displayed up to, but not including, the end-of-file marker.

A direct replacement for the statement `while(inFile.good())` is the statement `while(!inFile.eof())`, which is read as "while the end of file *has not* been reached." This works because the `eof()` function returns a `true` only after the EOF marker has been read or passed over. In effect then, the relational expression checks that the EOF *has not* been read—hence, the use of the NOT, `!`, operator.

Alternatively, another means of detecting the EOF is to use the fact that the extraction operation, `>>`, returns a Boolean value of `true` if data was extracted from a stream; otherwise, it returns a Boolean `false` value. Using this return value, the following code can be used within Program 15.5 to read the file.

```
// read and display the file's contents
  while (inFile >> descrip >> price) // check next character
    cout << descrip << ' ' << price << endl;
```

Although initially a bit cryptic, this code makes perfect sense when you understand that the expression being tested not only extracts data from the file, but returns a Boolean value to indicate if the extraction was successful or not.

Finally, in either the above `while` statement or in Program 15.5, the expression `inFile >> descrip >> price` can be replaced by a `getline()` method (see Section 7.1). For file input, this method has the syntax

```
getline(fileObject, strObj, terminatingChar)
```

where *fileObject* is the name of the `ifstream` file, *strObj* is a string class object , and *terminatingChar* is an optional character constant or variable specifying the terminating character. If this optional third argument is omitted, the default terminating character is the newline (`'\n'`) character. Program 15.6 illustrates using `getline()` within the context of a complete program.

 Program 15.6

```
#include <iostream>
#include <fstream>
#include <cstdlib>    // needed for exit()
#include <string>
using namespace std;

int main()
{
  string filename = "prices.dat";  // put the filename up front
```

```
string line;
ifstream inFile;

inFile.open(filename.c_str());

if (inFile.fail())  // check for successful open
{
  cout << "\nThe file was not successfully opened"
       << "\n Please check that the file currently exists."
       << endl;
  exit(1);
}

// read and display the file's contents
while (getline(inFile,line))
  cout << line << endl;

inFile.close();

return 0;
}
```

Program 15.6 is really a line-by-line text-copying program, which reads a line of text from the file and then displays it on the terminal. The output of Program 15.6 is:

```
Mats 39.95
Bulbs 3.22
Fuses 1.08
```

If it is necessary to obtain the description and price as individual variables, either Program 15.5 should be used or the string returned by getline() in Program 15.6 must be processed further to extract the individual data items (see Section 15.8 for parsing procedures).

Standard Device Files

The file stream objects we have used have all been logical file objects. A logical file object is a stream that connects a file of logically related data, such as a data file, to a program. In addition to logical file objects, C++ also supports physical file objects. A physical file object is a stream that connects to a hardware device, such as a keyboard, screen, or printer.

P R O G R A M M I N G   N O T E

A Way to Clearly Identify a File's Name and Location

During program development, test files are usually placed in the same directory as the program. Therefore, a method call such as `inFile.open("exper.dat")` causes no problems to the operating system. In production systems, however, it is not uncommon for data files to reside in one directory while program files reside in another. For this reason it is always a good idea to include the full path name of any file opened.

For example, if the `exper.dat` file resides in the directory `C:\test\files`, the `open()` call should include the full path name, `inFile.open("c:\\test\\files\\exper.dat")`. Then, no matter where the program is run from, the operating system will know where to locate the file. Note the use of double slashes, which is required.

Another important convention is to list all file names at the top of a program instead of embedding the names deep within the code. This can easily be accomplished by using string variables to store each file name.

For example, if the statements:

```
string filename = "c:\\test\\files\\exper.dat";
```

are placed at the top of a program file, the declaration statement clearly lists both the name of the desired file and its location. Then, if some other file is to be tested, all that is required is a simple one-line change at the top of the program.

Using a string variable for the file's name is also useful for the `fail()` method check. For example, consider the following code:

```
string filename;
    ifstream infile;

    inFile.open(filename.c_str());

    if (inFile.fail())
    {
      cout << "\n The file named " << filename
           << "was not successfully opened"
           << "\n Please check that this file currently exists."
           exit(1);
    }
```

In this code, the name of the file that failed to open is directly displayed within the error message without the name being embedded as a string value.

PROGRAMMING NOTE

The `get()` *and* `putback()` *Methods*

All input streams have access to the `fstream` class's `get()` method, which permits character-by-character input from an input stream. This method works in a similar manner to character extraction, using the `>>` operator with two important differences: If a newline character, `'\n'`, or a blank character, `' '`, are encountered, these characters are read in the same manner as any other alphanumeric character. The syntax of this method call is:

    istreamName.get(characterVariable);

For example, the following code can be used to read the next character from the standard input stream and store the character into the variable `ch`:

    char ch;
    cin.get(ch);

In a similar manner, if `inFile` is an `ifstream` object that has been opened to a file, the following code reads the next character in the stream and assigns it to the character `keycode`:

    char keycode;
    inFile.get(keycode);

In addition to the `get()` method, all input streams have a `putback()` method that can be used to put the last character read from an input stream back on the stream. This method has the syntax

    ifstreamName.putback(characterExpression);

where `characterExpression` can be any character variable or character value. The `putback()` method provides an output capability to an input stream. It should be noted that the putback character need not be the last character read; rather, it can be any character. All putback characters, however, have no effect on the data file but only on the open input stream. Thus, the data file characters remain unchanged, although the characters subsequently read from the input stream can change.

The actual physical device assigned to your program for data entry is formally called the **standard input file**. Usually this is the keyboard. When a `cin` object method call is encountered in a C++ program, it is a request to the operating system to go to this standard input file for the expected input. Similarly, when a `cout` object method call is encountered, the output is automatically displayed or "written to" a device that has been assigned as the **standard output file**. For most systems this is a computer screen, although it can be a printer.

When a program is executed, the standard input stream `cin` is automatically connected to the standard input device. Similarly, the standard output stream `cout` is automatically connected to the standard output device. These two object streams are always available for programmer use, as are the standard error stream, `cerr`, and the standard log stream, `clog`. Both of these streams also connect to the terminal screen.

Other Devices

The keyboard, display, error reporting, and logging streams are automatically connected to the stream objects named `cin`, `cout`, `cerr`, and `clog` respectively, when the `iostream` header file is included in a program. Additionally, other devices can be used for input or output if the name assigned by the system is known. For example, most personal computers assign the name `prn` to the printer connected to the computer. For these computers, a statement such as `outFile.open("prn")` connects the printer to the `ofstream` object named `outFile`. A subsequent statement, such as `outFile << "Hello World!";` would then cause the string `Hello World!` to be output directly on the printer. Notice that as the name of an actual file, `prn` must be enclosed in double quotes in the `open()` function call.

▌ EXERCISES 15.2

1. *a.* Enter and execute Program 15.5.
   b. Modify Program 15.5 to use the expression `!inFile.eof()` in place of the expression `inFile.good()`, and execute the program to see that it operates correctly.

2. *a.* Enter and execute Program 15.6.
   b. Modify Program 15.6 by replacing the identifier `cout` with `cerr`, and verify that the output for the standard error file stream is the screen.
   c. Modify Program 15.6 by replacing the identifier `cout` with `clog`, and verify that the output for the standard log stream is the screen.

3. *a.* Write a C++ program that accepts lines of text from the keyboard and writes each line to a file named `text.dat` until an empty line is entered. An empty line is a line with no text that is created by pressing the Enter (or Return) key.
   b. Modify Program 15.6 to read and display the data stored in the `text.dat` file created in Exercise 3a.

4. Determine the operating system command provided by your computer to display the contents of a saved file.

5. *a.* Create a text file named `employee.dat` containing the following data:

Anthony	A	10031	7.82	12/18/05
Burrows	W	10067	9.14	6/9/05
Fain	B	10083	8.79	5/18/04
Janney	P	10095	10.57	9/28/04
Smith	G	10105	8.50	12/20/03

b. Write a C++ program to read the `employee.dat file` created in Exercise 5a and produce a duplicate copy of the file named `employee.bak`.

c. Modify the program written in Exercise 5b to accept the names of the original and duplicate files as user input.

d. The program written for Exercise 5c always copies data from an original file to a duplicate file. What is a better method of accepting the original and duplicate file names, other than prompting the user for them each time the program is executed?

6. *a.* Write a C++ program that opens a file and displays the contents of the file with associated line numbers. That is, the program should print the number 1 before displaying the first line, then print the number 2 before displaying the second line, and so on for each line in the file.

b. Modify the program written in Exercise 6a to list the contents of the file on the printer assigned to your computer.

7. *a.* Create a text file containing the following data (without the headings):

Names	Social Security Number	Hourly Rate	Hours Worked
B. Caldwell	555-815-2222	7.32	37
D. Memcheck	555-77-4444	8.32	40
R. Potter	555-77-6666	6.54	40
W. Rosen	555-99-8888	9.80	35

b. Write a C++ program that reads the data file created in Exercise 7a and computes and displays a payroll schedule. The output should list the social security number, name, and gross pay for each individual, where gross pay is calculated as *Hourly Rate x Hours Worked*.

8. *a.* Create a text file containing the following: car numbers, miles driven, and gallons of gas used in each car (do not include the headings):

Car Number	Miles Driven	Gallons Used
54	250	19
62	525	38
71	123	6
85	1,322	86
97	235	14

b. Write a C++ program that reads the data in the file created in Exercise 8a and displays the car number, miles driven, gallons used, and the miles per gallon for each car. The output should also contain the total miles driven, total gallons used, and average miles per gallon for all the cars. These totals should be displayed at the end of the output report.

9. *a.* Create a text file with the following data (without the headings):

Part Number	Initial Amount	Quantity Sold	Minimum Amount
QA310	95	47	50
CM145	320	162	200
MS514	34	20	25
EN212	163	150	160

b. Write a C++ program to create an inventory report based on the data in the file created in Exercise 9a. The display should consist of the part number, current balance, and the amount that is necessary to bring the inventory to the minimum level.

10. *a.* Create a text file containing the following data (without the headings):

Name	Rate	Hours
Callaway, G.	6.00	40
Hanson, P.	5.00	48
Lasard, D.	6.50	35
Stillman, W.	8.00	50

b. Write a C++ program that uses the information contained in the file created in Exercise 10a to produce the following pay report for each employee:

```
Name   Pay Rate   Hours   Regular Pay   Overtime Pay   Gross Pay
```

Regular pay is to be computed as any hours worked up to and including 40 hours times the pay rate. Overtime pay is to be computed as any hours worked above 40 hours times a pay rate of 1.5 times the regular rate, and the gross pay is the sum of regular and overtime pay. At the end of the report, the program should display the totals of the regular, overtime, and gross pay columns.

11. *a.* Store the following data in a file:

```
5 96 87 78 93 21 4 92 82 85 87 6 72 69 85 75 81 73
```

b. Write a C++ program to calculate and display the average of each group of numbers in the file created in Exercise 11a. The data is arranged in the file so that each group of numbers is preceded by the number of data items in the group. Thus, the first number in the file, 5, indicates that the next five numbers should be grouped together. The number 4 indicates that the following four numbers are a group, and the 6 indicates that the last six numbers are a group. (*Hint:* Use a nested loop. The outer loop should terminate when the end-of-file has been encountered.)

15.3   Exceptions and File Checking[1]

Error detection and processing with exception handling is used extensively within C++ programs that use one or more files. For example, if a user deletes or renames a file using an operating system command, this action will cause a C++ program to fail when an `open()` function call attempts to open the file under its original name.

Recall from Section 7.3 that the code for general exception handling looks like this:

```
try
{
  // one or more statements,
  // at least one of which should
  // throw an exception
}
catch(exceptionDataType parameterName)
{
  // one or more statements
}
```

In this code, the `try` block statements are executed. If no error occurs, the `catch` block statements are omitted and processing continues with the statement following the `catch` block. However, if any statement within the `try` block throws an exception, the `catch` block whose exception data type matches the exception is executed. If no `catch` block is defined for a `try` block, a compiler error occurs. If no `catch` block exists that catches a thrown data type , a program crash occurs only if the exception is thrown. Most times, but not always, the `catch` block displays an error message and terminates processing with a call to the `exit()` function. Program 15.7 illustrates the statements required to open a file in read mode that includes exception handling.

 Program 15.7

```
#include <iostream>
#include <fstream>
#include <cstdlib>    // needed for exit()
#include <string>
```

(continued on next page)

---

[1] This section may be omitted on first reading without loss of subject continuity.

(continued from previous page)

```cpp
using namespace std;

int main()
{
  string filename = "prices.dat";  // put the filename up front
  string descrip;
  double price;

  ifstream inFile;

  try  // this block tries to open the file, read, and display the file's data
  {
    inFile.open(filename.c_str());

    if (inFile.fail()) throw filename; // this is the exception being checked

    // read and display the file's contents
    inFile >> descrip >> price;
      while (inFile.good())  // check next character
    {
        cout << descrip << ' ' << price << endl;
        inFile >> descrip >> price;
    }
        inFile.close();

    return 0;
  }
  catch (string e)
  {
    cout << "\nThe file " << e << " was not successfully opened"
         << "\n Please check that the file currently exists."
         << endl;
      exit(1);
  }
}
```

The exception message produced by Program 15.7 when the `prices.dat` file was not found is:

```
The file prices.dat was not successfully opened.
Please check that the file currently exists.
```

Although the exception handling code in Program 15.7 can be used to check for a successful file open for both input and output, a more rigorous check is usually required for output files. This check is required because, on output, the file is almost guaranteed to be found. If it exists, the file will be found, and if it does not exist, the operating system will create it (unless append mode is specified and the file already exists, or the operating system cannot find the indicated folder). Knowing that the file has been successfully found and opened, however, is insufficient for output

---

P R O G R A M M I N G   N O T E

Checking that a File was Opened Successfully

Using exception handling, the most common method for checking that the operating system successfully located the designated file is the one coded in Program 15.7, the key coding points of which are repeated here for convenience:

```
...try // this block tries to open the file, read, and display the file's data
  {
      // open the file, throwing an exception if the open fails
      // perform all required file processing
      // close the file
  }
catch (string e)
{
    cout << "\nThe file " << e << " was not successfully opened"
         << "\n Please check that the file currently exists."
            << endl;
    exit(1);
}
```

---

purposes when an existing output file *must not* be overwritten. For these cases, the file can first be opened for input, and then, if the file is found, a further check can be made to ensure that the user explicitly provides approval for overwriting it. How this is accomplished is illustrated in highlighted code within Program 15.8.

Program 15.8

```
#include <iostream>
#include <fstream>
#include <cstdlib>    // needed for exit()
#include <string>
#include <iomanip>   // needed for formatting
using namespace std;

int main()
{
  char response;
  string filename = "prices.dat";    // put the filename up front
  ifstream inFile;
  ofstream outFile;

  try  // open a basic input stream simply to check if the file exists
  {
    inFile.open(filename.c_str());
    if (inFile.fail()) throw 1;  // this means the file doesn't exist
      // only get here if the file was found;
      // otherwise the catch block takes control
    cout << "A file by the name " << filename << " currently exists.\n"
```

(continued on next page)

(continued from previous page)

```
        << "Do you want to overwrite it with the new data (y or n): ";
  cin >> response;
  if (tolower(response) == 'n')
  {
    inFile.close();
    cout << "The existing file has not been overwritten." << endl;
    exit(1);
  }
}
catch(int e) {};  // a do-nothing block that permits
                  // processing to continue
  try
  {
    // open the file in write mode and continue with file writes
    outFile.open(filename.c_str());
    if (outFile.fail()) throw filename;
    // set the output file stream formats
    outFile << setiosflags(ios::fixed)
            << setiosflags(ios::showpoint)
            << setprecision(2);
    // write the data to the file
    outFile << "Mats " << 39.95 << endl
            << "Bulbs " << 3.22 << endl
            << "Fuses " << 1.08 << endl;
    outFile.close();
    cout << "The file " << filename
         << " has been successfully written." << endl;

    return 0;
  }
  catch(string e)
  {
    cout << "The file " << filename
         << " was not opened for output and has not been written."
         << endl;
  }
}
```

Notice in Program 15.8 that the `try` blocks are separate. Because a `catch` block is affiliated with the closest previous `try` block, there is no ambiguity about unmatched `try` and `catch` blocks.

Opening Multiple Files

As an example of applying exception handling to the opening of two files at the same time, assume that we wish to read the data from a character-based file named `info.txt`, one character at a time, and write this data to a file named `backup.txt`. Essentially, this application is a file-copy program that reads the data from one file in a character-by-character manner and writes them to a second file. For purposes of illustration, assume that the characters stored in the input file are as shown in Figure 15.3.

FIGURE 15.3   *The Data Stored in the* `info.txt` *File*

```
Now is the time for all good people
   to come to the aid of their party.
Please call (555) 888-6666 for
   further information.
```

Figure 15.4 illustrates the structure of the streams that are necessary for producing our file copy. In this figure, an input stream object referenced by the variable `inFile` will read data from the `info.txt` file, and an output stream object referenced by the variable `outFile` will write data to the `backup.txt` file.

FIGURE 15.4   *The File Copy Stream Structure*

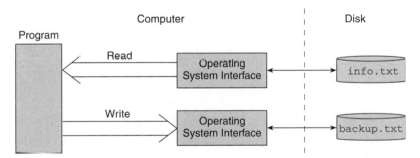

Now consider Program 15.9, which creates the `backup.txt` file as an exact duplicate of the `info.txt` file using the procedure illustrated in Figure 15.4.

Program 15.9

```cpp
#include <iostream>
#include <fstream>
#include <cstdlib>     // needed for exit()
#include <string>
using namespace std;

int main()
{
  string fileOne = "info.txt";   // put the filename up front
  string fileTwo = "info.bak";
  char ch;
  ifstream inFile;
  ofstream outFile;
```

(continued on next page)

(continued from previous page)

```cpp
try  //this block tries to open the input file
{
  // open a basic input stream
  inFile.open(fileOne.c_str());
    if (inFile.fail()) throw fileOne;
} // end of outer try block
catch (string in)  // catch for outer try block
{
  cout << "The input file " << in
       << " was not successfully opened." << endl
       << " No backup was made." << endl;
  exit(1);
}

try  // this block tries to open the output file and
{     // perform all file processing

  outFile.open(fileTwo.c_str());
  if (outFile.fail())throw fileTwo;
  while ((ch = inFile.get())!= EOF)
     outFile.put(ch);;

  inFile.close();
  outFile.close();
}
catch (string out)  // catch for inner try block
{
  cout < "The backup file " < out
       < " was not successfully opened." < endl;
  exit(1);
}

cout << "A successful backup of " << fileOne
     << " named " << fileTwo << " was successfully made." << endl;

return 0;
}
```

For simplicity, Program 15.9 attempts to open both the input and output files within separate and non-nested `try` blocks. More generally, the second file would be opened in a nested inner `try` block so that the attempt to open this second file would not be made if the opening of the first file threw an exception. (The Programming note on nesting `try` blocks explains how this is accomplished.)

In reviewing Program 15.9, pay particular attention to the statement:

```cpp
while((ch = inFile.get())!= EOF)
```

PROGRAMMING NOTE

Nesting `try` *Blocks*

When more than one file stream is involved, opening each file stream in its own `try` block permits exact isolation and identification of which file caused an exception, should one occur. The `try` blocks can be nested. For example, consider Program 15.9, which is rewritten here using nested `try` blocks. Notice that in this case the `catch` block for the inner `try` block must also be nested in the same block scope as its `try` block.

```
#include <iostream>
#include <fstream>
#include <cstdlib>   // needed for exit()
#include <string>
using namespace std;

int main()
{
  string fileOne = "info.txt";  // put the filename up front
  string fileTwo = "info.bak";
  char ch;
  ifstream inFile;
  ofstream outFile;

  try  //this block tries to open the input file
  {
    // open a basic input stream
    inFile.open(fileOne.c_str());
      if (inFile.fail()) throw fileOne;
    try  // this block tries to open the output file and
    {    // perform all file processing

        // open a basic output stream
      outFile.open(fileTwo.c_str());
      if (outFile.fail())throw fileTwo;
      while ((ch = inFile.get()) != EOF)
        outFile.put(ch);;

      inFile.close();
      outFile.close();
    }  // end of inner try block
    catch (string out)  // catch for inner try block
    {
      cout << "The backup file " << out
           << " was not successfully opened." << endl;
      exit(1);
    }
  }    // end of outer try block
```

(continued on next page)

(continued from previous page)

```
      catch (string in)  // catch for outer try block
      {
        cout << "The input file " << in
             << " was not successfully opened." << endl
             << " No backup was made." << endl;
        exit(1);
      }

      cout << "A successful backup of " << fileOne
           << " named " << fileTwo << "was successfully made." << endl;

      return 0;
    }
```

The important point to notice in this program is the nesting of the `try` blocks. If the two `try` blocks were not nested and the input stream declaration, `ifstream inFile;` was placed in the first block, it could not be used in the second `try` block without producing a compiler error. The reason is that all variables declared in a block of code, which is defined by an opening and closing brace pair, are local to the block in which they are declared.

This statement continually reads a value from the input stream until the EOF value is detected. As long as the returned value does not equal the EOF value, the value is written to the output object stream. The parentheses surrounding the expression `(ch = inFile.get())` are necessary to ensure that a value is first read and assigned to the variable `ch` before the retrieved value is compared to the EOF value. In their absence, the complete expression would be `ch = inFile.get() != EOF`. Due to the precedence of operations, the relational expression `inFile.get() != EOF` would be executed first. Because this is a relational expression, its result is either a Boolean `true` or `false` value based on the data retrieved by the `get(ch)` method. Attempting to assign this Boolean result to the character variable `ch` is an invalid conversion across an assignment operator.

▌ EXERCISES 15.3

1. List two conditions that will cause a fail condition when a file is opened for input.

2. List two conditions that will cause a fail condition when a file is opened for output.

3. If a file that exists is opened for output in write mode, what happens to the data currently in the file?

4. Modify Program 15.7 to use an identifier of your choice, in place of the letter e, for the catch block's exception parameter name.

5. Enter and execute Program 15.8.

6. Determine why the two try blocks in Program 15.8, which are not nested, cause no problems in either compilation or execution. (*Hint:* Place the declaration for the filename within the first try block and compile the program.)

7. a. If the nested try blocks in the Programming note on nested try blocks are separated into non-nested blocks the program will not compile. Determine why this is so.
    b. What additional changes would have to be made to the program in Exercise 7a that would allow it to be written with non-nested blocks? (*Hint:* See Exercise 6.)

8. Enter the data for the info.txt file in Figure 15.3 or obtain it from this text's web site (see Preface for the URL). Then enter and execute Program 15.9 and verify that the backup file was written.

9. Modify Program 15.9 to use a getline() method in place of the get() method currently in the program.

15.4   Random File Access

The term **file access** refers to the process of retrieving data from a file. There are two types of file access: sequential access and random access. To understand file access types, you first need to understand some concepts related to how data is organized within a file.

The term **file organization** refers to the way data is stored in a file. The files we have used, and will continue to use, all have a **sequential organization**. This means that the characters within the file are stored in a sequential manner, one after another.

In addition to being sequentially organized, we have also read each open file in a sequential manner. That is, we have accessed each character sequentially, one after another. This is referred to as **sequential access**. The fact that the characters in the file are stored sequentially, however, does not force us to access them sequentially. In fact, we can skip over characters and read a sequentially organized file in a nonsequential manner.

In **random access**, any character in the open file can be read directly, without first having to sequentially read all the characters stored ahead of it. To provide random access to files, each ifstream object automatically creates a file position marker. This marker is a long integer that represents an offset from the beginning of each file and keeps track of where the next character is to be read from or written to. The functions that are used to access and change the file position marker are listed in Table 15.4. The suffixes g and p in these function names denote get and put, respectively, where get refers to an input (get from) file and put refers to an output (put to) file.

TABLE 15.4 *File Position Marker Functions*

Name	Description
`seekg(offset, mode)`	For input files, move to the offset position as indicated by the `mode`.
`seekp(offset, mode)`	For output files, move to the offset position as indicated by the `mode`.
`tellg(void)`	For input files, return the current value of the file position marker.
`tellp(void)`	For output files, return the current value of the file position marker.

The `seek()` functions allow the programmer to move to any position in the file. To understand this method, you must first clearly understand how data is referenced in the file using the file position marker.

Each character in a data file is located by its position in the file. The first character in the file is located at position 0, the next character at position 1, and so on. A character's position is also referred to as its offset from the start of the file. Thus, the first character has a 0 offset, the second character has an offset of 1, and so on for each character in the file.

The `seek()` functions require two arguments: the offset, as a long integer, into the file; and where the offset is to be calculated from, as determined by the mode. The three possible alternatives for the mode are `ios::beg`, `ios::cur`, and `ios::end`, which denote the beginning, current position, and the end of the file, respectively. Thus, a mode of `ios::beg` means the offset is the true offset from the start of the file. A mode of `ios::cur` means that the offset is relative to the current position in the file, and an `ios::end` mode means the offset is relative to the end of the file. A positive offset means move forward in the file and a negative offset means move backward. Examples of `seek()` function calls are shown below. In these examples, assume that `inFile` has been opened as an input file and `outFile` as an output file. Notice, in these examples, that the offset passed to `seekg()` and `seekp()` must be a long integer.

```
inFile.seekg(4L,ios::beg);    // go to the fifth character in the input file
outFile.seekp(4L,ios::beg);   // go to the fifth character in the output file
inFile.seekg(4L,ios::cur);    // move ahead five characters in the input file
outFile.seekp(4L,ios::cur);   // move ahead five characters in the output file
inFile.seekg(-4L,ios::cur);   // move back five characters in the input file
outFile.seekp(-4L,ios::cur);  // move back five characters in the output file
inFile.seekg(0L,ios::beg);    // go to start of the input file
outFile.seekp(0L,ios::beg);   // go to start of the output file
```

```
inFile.seekg(0L,ios::end);     // go to end of the input file
outFile.seekp(0L,ios::end);    // go to end of the output file
inFile.seekg(-10L,ios::end);   // go to 10 characters before the input file's end
outFile.seekp(-10L,ios::end);  // go to 10 characters before the output file's end
```

As opposed to the `seek()` functions that move the file position marker, the `tell()` functions simply return the offset value of the file position marker. For example, if 10 characters have already been read from an input file named `inFile`, the function call

`inFile.tellg();`

returns the long integer 10. This means that the next character to be read is offset 10 byte positions from the start of the file, and is the eleventh character in the file.

Program 15.10 illustrates the use of `seekg()` and `tellg()` to read a file in reverse order, from last character to first. As each character is read it is also displayed.

 Program 15.10

```cpp
#include <iostream>
#include <fstream>
#include <string>
#include <cstdlib>
using namespace std;

int main()
{
  string filename = "test.dat";
  char ch;
  long offset, last;

  ifstream inFile(filename.c_str());

  if (inFile.fail())    // check for successful open
  {
    cout << "\nThe file was not successfully opened"
         << "\n Please check that the file currently exists"
         << endl;
    exit(1);
  }

  inFile.seekg(0L,ios::end);   // move to the end of the file
  last = inFile.tellg();       // save the offset of the last character
```

(continued on next page)

(continued from previous page)

```
for(offset = 1L; offset <= last; offset++)
{
  inFile.seekg(-offset, ios::end);
  ch = inFile.get();
  cout << ch << " : ";
}

inFile.close();

cout << endl;

return 0;
}
```

Assuming the file `test.dat` contains the following data,

```
The grade was 92.5
```

The output of Program 15.10 is:

```
5 : . : 2 : 9 :   : s : a : w :    : e : d : a : r : g :    : e : h : T :
```

Program 15.10 initially goes to the last character in the file. The offset of this character, which is the end-of-file character, is saved in the variable `last`. Because `tellg()` returns a long integer, `last` has been declared as a long integer.

Starting from the end of the file, `seekg()` is used to position the next character to be read, referenced from the end of the file. As each character is read, the character is displayed and the offset adjusted in order to access the next character. It should be noted that the first offset used is `-1`, which represents the character immediately preceding the EOF marker.

▌ EXERCISES 15.4

1. *a.* Create a file named `test.dat` that contains the data in the `test.dat` file used in Program 15.10. You can do this by using a text editor or by copying the file `test.dat` on the data disk provided with this book.

    b. Enter and execute Program 15.10 on your computer.

2. Rewrite Program 15.10 so that the origin for the `seekg()` function used in the `for` loop is the start of the file rather than the end.

3. Modify Program 15.10 to display an error message if `seekg()` attempts to reference a position beyond the end of the file.

4. Write a program that will read and display every second character in a file named `test.dat`.

5. Using the `seek()` and `tell()` functions, write a function named `fileChars()` that returns the total number of characters in a file.

6. *a.* Write a function named `readBytes()` that reads and displays *n* characters starting from any position in a file. The function should accept three arguments: a file object name, the offset of the first character to be read, and the number of characters to be read (*Note:* the prototype for `readBytes` should be `void readBytes(fstream&, long, int)`.
   b. Modify the `readBytes()` function written in Exercise 6a to store the characters read into a string or an array. The function should accept the address of the storage area as a fourth argument.

15.5   File Streams as Function Arguments

A file stream object can be used as a function argument. The only requirement is that the function's formal parameter be a reference (see Section 6.3) to the appropriate stream, either as `ifstream&` or `ofstream&`. For example, in Program 15.11 an `ofstream` object named `outFile` is opened in `main()` and this stream object is passed to the function `inOut()`. Notice that the function prototype and header line for `inOut()` both declare the formal parameter as a reference to an `ostream` object type. The `inOut()` function is then used to write five lines of user-entered text to the file.

 ## Program 15.11

```cpp
#include <iostream>
#include <fstream>
#include <cstdlib>
#include <string>
using namespace std;

int main()
{
  string fname = "list.dat";  // here is the file we are working with

  void inOut(ofstream&);     // function prototype

    ofstream outFile;
  outFile.open(fname.c_str());
  if (outFile.fail())    // check for a successful open
  {
```

(continued on next page)

(continued from previous page)

```cpp
        cout << "\nThe output file " << fname << " was not successfully opened"
            << endl;
        exit(1);
      }

   inOut(outFile);   // call the function

   return 0;
}

void inOut(ofstream& fileOut)
{

   const int NUMLINES = 5;   // number of lines of text
   string line;
   int count;

   cout << "Please enter five lines of text:" << endl;
   for (count = 0; count < NUMLINES; count++)
   {
     getline(cin,line);
     fileOut << line << endl;
   }

   cout << "\nThe file has been successfully written." << endl;
   return;
}
```

Within `main()` the file is an `ostream` object named `outFile`. This object is passed to the `inOut()` function and is accepted as the formal parameter named `fileOut`, which is declared to be a reference to an `ostream` object type. The function `inOut()` then uses its reference parameter `outFile` as an output file stream name in the same manner as `main()` would use the `fileOut` stream object. Notice also that Program 15.11 uses the `getline()` method introduced in Section 15.2 (see Table 15.3).

In Program 15.12, we have expanded on Program 15.11 by adding a `getOpen()` function to perform the open. Notice that `getOpen()`, like `inOut()`, accepts a reference argument to an `ofstream` object. After the `getOpen()` function completes execution, this reference is passed to `inOut()`, as it was in Program 15.11. Although you might be tempted to write `getOpen()` to return a reference to an `ofstream`, this will not work because it ultimately results in an attempt to assign a returned reference to an existing one.

Program 15.12

```cpp
#include <iostream>
#include <fstream>
#include <cstdlib>
#include <string>
using namespace std;

int main()
{
  int getOpen(ofstream&);   // pass a reference to an fstream
  void inOut(ofstream&);    // pass a reference to an fstream

  ofstream outFile;     // filename is an fstream object

  getOpen(outFile);     // open the file
  inOut(outFile);       // write to it

  return 0;
}

int getOpen(ofstream& fileOut)
{
  string name;

  cout << "\nEnter a file name: ";
  getline(cin,name);

  fileOut.open(name.c_str());       // open the file

  if (fileOut.fail())       // check for successful open
  {
    cout << "Cannot open the file" << endl;
    exit(1);
  }
  else
    return 1;
}

void inOut(ofstream& fileOut)
{
  const int NUMLINES = 5;   // number of lines
  int count;
  string line;
```

(continued on next page)

(continued from previous page)

```
      cout << "Please enter five lines of text:" << endl;
      for (count = 0; count < NUMLINES; ++count)
      {
        getline(cin,line);
        fileOut << line << endl;
      }
      cout << "\nThe file has been successfully written.";
      return;
    }
```

Program 15.12 is simply a modified version of Program 15.11 that now allows the user to enter a file name from the standard input device and then opens the `ofstream` connection to the external file. If the name of an existing data file is entered, the file will be destroyed when it is opened for output. A useful trick that you may employ to prevent this type of mishap is to open the entered file using an input file stream. If the file exists, the `fail()` method will indicate a successful open (i.e., the open does not fail), which indicates that the file is available for input. This can alert the user that a file with the entered name currently exists in the system, and to request confirmation that the data in the file can be destroyed and the file opened for output. Before the file is reopened for output, the input file stream should be closed. The implementation of this algorithm is left as an exercise.

▌EXERCISES 15.5

1. A function named `pFile()` is to receive a file name as a reference to an `ifstream` object. What declarations are required to pass a file name to `pFile()`?

2. Write a function named `fcheck()` that checks whether a file exists. The function should accept an `ifstream` object as a formal reference parameter. If the file exists, the function should return a value of 1, otherwise the function should return a value of 0.

3. Assume that a data file consisting of a group of individual lines has been created. Write a function named `printLine()` that will read and display any desired line of the file. For example, the function call `printLine(fstream& fName, 5);` should display the fifth line of the passed object stream.

4. Rewrite the function `getOpen()` used in Program 15.12 to incorporate the file checking procedures described in this section. Specifically, if the entered file name exists, an appropriate message should be displayed. The user should then be presented with the option of entering a new file name or allowing the program to overwrite the existing file. Use the function written for Exercise 2 in your program.

15.6   Common Programming Errors

The common programming errors with respect to files are:

1. Using a file's external name in place of the internal file stream object name when accessing the file. The only stream method that uses the data file's external name is the open() function. As always, all stream methods presented in this chapter must be preceded by a stream object name and the dot operator.

2. Opening a file for output without first checking that a file with the given name already exists. Not checking for a preexisting file name ensures that the file will be overwritten.

3. Not understanding that the end of a file is detected only after the EOF sentinel has either been read or passed over.

4. Attempting to detect the end of a file using character variables for the EOF marker. Any variable used to accept the EOF must be declared as an integer variable. For example, if ch is declared as a character variable, the expression

```
while ( (ch = in.file.peek()) != EOF )
```

produces an infinite loop.[2] This occurs because a character variable can never take on an EOF code. EOF is an integer value (usually–1) that has no character representation. This ensures that the EOF code can never be confused with any legitimate character encountered as normal data in the file. To terminate the loop created by the above expression, the variable ch must be declared as an integer variable.

5. Using an integer argument with the seekg() and seekp() functions. This offset must be a long integer constant or variable. Any other value passed to these functions can result in an unpredictable effect.

---

[2] This will not occur on Unix systems, where characters are stored as signed integers.

15.7   Chapter Summary

1. A data file is any collection of data stored together in an external storage medium under a common name.

2. A data file is connected to a file stream using `fstream`'s `open()` method. This function connects a file's external name with an internal object name. After the file is opened, all subsequent accesses to the file require the internal object name.

3. A file can be opened in input or output mode. An opened output file stream either creates a new data file or erases the data in an existing opened file. An opened input file stream makes an existing file's data available for input. An error condition results if the file does not exist and can be detected using the `fail()` method.

4. All file streams must be declared as objects of either the `ifstream` or `ofstream` classes. This means that a declaration similar to either

```
ifstream inFile;
ofstream outFile;
```

must be included with the declarations in which the file is opened. The stream object names `inFile` and `outFile` can be replaced with any user-selected object name.

5. In addition to any files opened within a function, the standard stream objects `cin`, `cout`, and `cerr` are automatically declared and opened when a program is run. `cin` is the object name of an input file stream used for data entry (usually from the keyboard), `cout` is the object name of an output file stream used for default data display (usually the computer screen), and `cerr` is the object name of an output file stream used for displaying system error messages (usually the computer screen).

6. Data files can be accessed randomly using the `seekg()`, `seekp()`, `tellg()`, and `tellp()` methods. The g versions of these functions are used to alter and query the file position marker for input file streams, while the p versions do the same for output file streams.

7. Table 15.5 lists the methods supplied by the `fstream` class for file manipulation.

TABLE 15.5 `fstream` *Methods*

Method Name	Description
`get()`	Extract the next character from the input stream and return it as an `int`.
`get(chrVar)`	Extract the next character from the input stream and assign it to `chrVar`.
`getline(fileObj, string, termChar)`	Extract the next string of characters from the input file stream object and assign them to `string` until the specified terminating character is detected. If omitted, the default terminating character is a newline.
`getline(C-stringVar,int n,'\n')`	Extract and return characters from the input stream until either `n-1` characters are read or a newline is encountered (terminates the input with a `'\0'`)
`peek()`	Return the next character in the input stream without extracting it from the stream.
`put(chrExp)`	Put the character specified by `chrExp` on the output stream.
`putback(chrExp)`	Push the character specified by `chrExp` back onto the input stream. Does not alter the data in the file.
`ignore(int n)`	Skip over the next `n` characters; if `n` is omitted, the default is to skip over the next single character.
`eof()`	Returns a Boolean `true` value if a read has been attempted past the end-of-file; otherwise returns a Boolean `false` value. The value becomes `true` only when the first character after the last valid file character is read.
`good()`	Returns a Boolean `true` value while the file is available for program use. Returns a Boolean `false` value if a read has been attempted past the end-of-file. The value becomes `false` only when the first character after the last valid file character is read.
`bad()`	Returns a Boolean `true` value if a read has been attempted past the end-of-file; otherwise returns a `false`. The value becomes `true` only when the first character after the last valid file character is read.
`fail()`	Returns a Boolean `true` if the file has not been opened successfully; otherwise returns a Boolean `false` value.

15.8   Chapter Supplement: The `iostream` Class Library

As we have seen, the classes contained within the `iostream` class library access files using entities called streams. For most systems, the data bytes transferred on a stream represent either ASCII characters or binary numbers.

The mechanism for reading a byte stream from a file or writing a byte stream to a file is always hidden when using a high-level language such as C++. Nevertheless, it is useful to understand this mechanism so that we can place the services provided by the `iostream` class library in their appropriate context.

File Stream Transfer Mechanism

The mechanism for transferring data between a program and a file is illustrated in Figure 15.5. As shown, transferring data between a program and a file involves an intermediate file buffer contained in the computer's memory. Each opened file is assigned its own file buffer, which is simply a storage area that the data uses as it is transferred between the program and the file.

FIGURE 15.5   *The Data Transfer Mechanism*

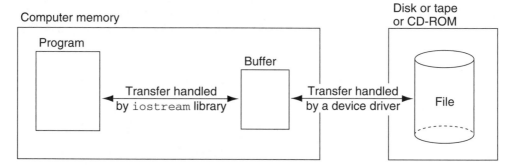

From its side, the program either writes a set of data bytes to the file buffer or reads a set of data bytes from the file buffer using a stream object. On the other side of the buffer, the transfer of data between the device storing the actual data file (usually a tape, disk, or CD) and the file buffer is handled by special operating system programs that are referred to as **device drivers**. Device drivers are not stand-alone programs but are an integral part of the operating system. Essentially a device driver is a section of operating system code that accesses a hardware device, such as a disk unit, and handles the data transfer between the device and the computer's memory. As such it must correctly synchronize the speed of the data transferred between the computer and the device sending or receiving the data. This is because the computer's internal data transfer rate is generally much faster than any device connected to it.

Typically a disk device driver will only transfer data between the disk and file buffer in fixed sizes, such as 1024 bytes at a time. Thus, the file buffer provides a convenient means of permitting a device driver to transfer data in blocks of one size while the program can access them using a different size (typically as individual characters or as a fixed number of characters per line).

Components of the iostream Class Library

The iostream class library consists of two primary base classes, the streambuf class and the ios class. The streambuf class provides the file buffer illustrated in Figure 15.5 and a number of general routines for transferring binary data. The ios class contains a pointer to the file buffers provided by the streambuf class and a number of general routines for transferring text data. From these two base classes a number of other classes are derived and included in the iostream class library.

Figure 15.6 illustrates an inheritance diagram for the ios family of classes as it relates to the ifstream, ofstream, and fstream classes. The inheritance diagram for the streambuf family of classes is shown in Figure 15.7. The convention adopted for inheritance diagrams is that the arrows point from a derived class to a base class.

FIGURE 15.6 *The Base Class ios and Its Derived Classes*

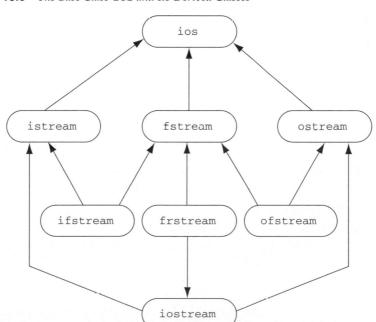

FIGURE 15.7   *The Base Class* streambuf *and Its Derived Classes*

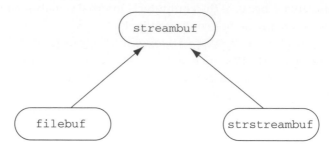

The correspondence between the classes illustrated in Figures 15.6 and 15.7, including the header files that define these classes, is listed in Table 15.6.

TABLE 15.6   *Correspondence between Classes Illustrated in Figures 15.6 and 15.7*

ios Class	streambuf Class	Header File
istream ostream iostream	streambuf	iostream or fstream
iftream oftream fstream	filebuf	fstream

Thus, the ifstream, ofstream, and fstream classes that we have used for file access all use a buffer provided by the filebuf class that is defined in the fstream header file. Similarly, the cin, cout, cerr, and clog iostream objects that we have been using throughout the book use a buffer provided by the streambuf class and defined in the iostream header file.

In-Memory Formatting

In addition to the classes illustrated in Figure 15.7, a class named strstream is also derived from the ios class. This class uses the strstreambuf class illustrated in Figure 15.7, requires the strstream header file, and provides capabilities for writing and reading strings to and from in-memory defined streams.

As an output stream, such streams are typically used to "assemble" a string from smaller pieces until a complete line of characters is ready to be written, either to cout or to a file. Attaching a strstream object to a buffer for this purpose is done in a similar manner as attaching an fstream object to an output file. For example, the statement

```
strstream inmem(buf, 72, ios::out);
```

attaches a strstream object to an existing buffer of 72 bytes in output mode.

Program 15.13 illustrates how this statement is used within the context of a complete program.

Program 15.13

```
#include <iostream>
#include <strstream>
#include <iomanip>
using namespace std;

int main()
{
  const int MAXCHARS = 81;  // one more than the maximum characters in a line
  int units = 10;
  double price = 36.85;
  char buf[MAXCHARS];

  strstream inmem(buf, MAXCHARS, ios::out);  // open an in memory stream

    // write to the buffer through the stream
  inmem << "No. of units = "
          << setw(3) << units
          << "  Price per unit = $"
          << setw(6) << setprecision(2) << fixed << price << '\0';

  cout << '|' << buf << '|';

  cout << endl;

  return 0;
}
```

The output produced by Program 15.13 is:

```
|No. of units =  10  Price per unit = $  36.85|
```

As illustrated by this output, the character buffer has been correctly filled in by insertions to the `inmem` stream (note that the end-of-string NULL, `'\0'`, which is the last insertion to the stream, is required to correctly close off the C-string). Once the desired character array has been filled, it would typically be written out to a file as a single string.

In a similar manner, a `strstream` object can be opened in input mode. Typically such a stream would be used as a working storage area, or buffer, for storing a complete line of text from either a file or standard input. Once the buffer has been filled, the extraction operator would be used to "disassemble" the string into component parts and convert each data item into its designated data type. Doing this permits inputting data from a file on a line-by-line basis prior to assigning individual data items to their respective variables.

The Standard Template Library

A driving force behind object-oriented programming was the desire to create easily reusable source code. For example, recreating source code each time an array or list is needed wastes both time and initial programming effort, which is added to by the time required for fully testing and verifying code that may have only been minimally modified.

Suppose, for example, that a program uses three arrays: an array of characters, an array of integers, and an array of double-precision numbers. Rather than code three different arrays, it makes more sense to implement each list from a single, fully tested, generic array class that comes complete with methods and algorithms for processing the array, such as sorting, inserting, finding maximum and minimum values, locating values, copying the list, comparing lists, and dynamically expanding and contracting the list, as needed. This generic type of list structure, referred to as a container, forms the basis of the Standard Template Library (STL).

This chapter is intended as an introduction to the STL, which provides seven types of generic list structures, and algorithms for manipulating the elements in each list type. A complete textbook would be required to cover the complete set of classes and capabilities provided by the STL. The applications presented in this chapter represent an extremely small subset of those that can be addressed using the STL. Typically, the second course in a computer science curriculum is specifically devoted to presenting the advanced applications that are programmed using either the STL or similarly constructed classes.

16.1   The Standard Template Library

You've already worked with one kind of list, an array, which is the list of choice for a fixed-length set of related data. Many programming applications, however, require variable-length lists that must constantly be expanded and contracted as items are added to and removed from the list. Although expanding and contracting an array can be accomplished by creating, copying, and deleting arrays, this solution tends to be costly in terms of both initial programming, maintenance, and testing time.

In all but the simplest of situations, it is almost always more efficient to use the STL to create and manipulate lists. Among other uses, one of the purposes of the STL is to provide a completely tested and generic set of easily used lists that can be maintained in various configurations. This is accomplished by calling either prewritten class methods or generalized algorithms applicable to all STL-created list types. The STL is one component of the larger Standard Library of header files and classes. It provides a broad range of generic capabilities for rapidly constructing and manipulating lists of objects—objects consisting of either built-in variables or objects. These STL capabilities allow you to maintain lists and perform operations on them, such as sorting and searching, without having to fully understand or program the advanced and frequently complicated underlying algorithms.

Currently the STL provides seven different types of lists, each supported by its own class. These seven list types are summarized in Table 16.1.

TABLE 16.1 *STL Lists*

List Type	Classification	Usage
vector	Sequence	Dynamic arrays
list	Sequence	Linked lists
deque	Sequence	Stacks and queues
set	Associative	Binary trees without duplicate objects
multiset	Associative	Binary trees that may have duplicate objects
map	Associative	Binary trees with a unique key that does not permit duplicate objects
multimap	Associative	Binary trees with a unique key that permits duplicate objects

As listed in the Classification column of Table 16.1, the seven different list types are categorized as either sequence or associative. A **sequence list** is one in which a list object is solely determined by its position in the list—that is, by where the object was placed in the list and how it may have been subsequently moved. For example, both arrays and vectors are sequence lists, where an object's position in the list is determined by the exact order in which it was added into the array or vector or subsequently moved. An **associative list** is automatically maintained in a sorted order. An object's position in an associative list depends on its value and a selected sorting criterion. For example, an alphabetical list of names depends on the name and a sorting criteria, rather than on the exact order that individual names were entered into the list. In this chapter you will only be concerned with STL's sequence types.

Before you begin working with lists and the STL, it's helpful to understand the difference between the lists provided by the STL and arrays. An array is a built-in list type. By contrast, the lists provided by the STL are class types. Although arrays are most often used to directly store built-in numerical data types, they still retain general characteristics common to the more advanced lists provided by the STL. For example, like an array, an STL list can be empty, which means that it currently holds no items. As it applies to both arrays and lists provided by the STL, a list is considered to be a container that can hold a collection of zero or more items, each of which is of the same type. For this reason, STL lists and arrays are referred to as both **containers** and **collections**, and in this text, these terms are used interchangeably. A list must also provide a means for accessing individual objects. When a list provides this individual data location capability, the list becomes a data structure. In an array, this location ability is provided by the position of each object in the array, which is designated using an integer index value.

Although STL lists can also store built-in data types, they are more commonly used to store and maintain objects. In commercial applications these objects are usually referred to as records. Once an object's structure has been defined, some means for collecting all of the objects into a single list is required. For example, the objects that may be stored could be students' academic records. In addition to the individual records, a means is needed to store all of the records in some order so that individual records can be located, displayed, printed, and updated.

Before describing specific types of applications in detail, however, it is worthwhile emphasizing that only objects—and not a class's methods—are stored in a list. The methods, which apply to the class as a whole, simply provide a means of initializing each object before it is placed into the list and reporting and modifying an object either before it is inserted into or after it has been extracted from the list. Figure 16.1 illustrates the complete process of creating and using both objects and lists.

FIGURE 16.1 *The List Creation Process*

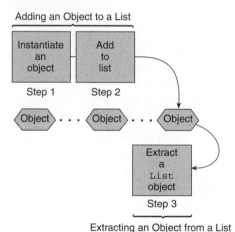

Each STL class provides its own set of methods. Additionally, the STL also provides a general set of methods, referred to as algorithms, that can be applied to any range of objects stored in any STL created list. These algorithms are listed in Table 16.2, for your convenience.

Finally, the last major set of components provided as part of the STL is iterators. Iterators provide the means of specifying the objects in a container and operate in a similar manner as indices do for arrays.

To create and use STL lists, you must do the following:

1. Use the STL class to construct the desired container type.
2. Store objects within the list.
3. Apply either the STL class's methods or the more general STL algorithms to the stored objects.

You will put these steps into practice in the following sections as you construct three commonly used lists: linked lists, stacks, and queues.

PROGRAMMING NOTE

Homogeneous and Heterogeneous Data Types

Lists and objects are both data structures. A data structure is a container of data organized in a way that facilitates the insertion, retrieval, and deletion of the data. The difference between a list and an object is in the types of objects they contain. A list is a **homogeneous** data structure, which means that its components must be of the same data type. An object is a **heterogeneous** data structure, which means that each of its internal objects can be of different data types. For example, an object could contain a name stored as a string data type, a pay rate stored as a double-precision data type, and an identification number stored as an integer data type. Because an object can be composed of different data types, it is a heterogeneous data structure. However, the list holding all of the objects is a homogeneous data structure, where each object has the same heterogeneous structure.

TABLE 16.2   *Commonly Used STL Algorithms*

Algorithm Name	Description
accumulate	Returns the sum of the numbers in a specified range.
binary_search	Returns a Boolean value of `true` if the specified value exists within the specified range; otherwise, returns `false`; can only be used on a sorted set of values.
copy	Copies objects from a source range to a destination range.
copy_backward	Copies objects from a source range to a destination range in a reverse direction.
count	Returns the number of objects in a specified range that match a specified value.
equal	Compares the objects in one range of objects, object by object, to the objects in a second range.
fill	Assigns every object in a specified range to a specified value.
find	Returns the position of the first occurrence of an object in a specified range having a specified value, if the value exists; performs a linear search, starting with the first object in a specified range and proceeds one object at a time until the complete range has been searched or the specified object has been found.
max_object	Returns the maximum value of the objects in the specified range.
min_object	Returns the minimum value of the objects in the specified range.
random_shuffle	Randomly shuffles object values in a specified range.
remove	Removes a specified value within a specified range without changing the order of the remaining objects.
replace	Replaces each object in a specified range having a specified value with a newly specified value.
reverse	Reverses objects in a specified range.
search	Finds the first occurrence of a specified value or sequence of values within a specified range.
sort	Sorts objects in a specified range into ascending order.
swap	Exchanges object values between two objects.
unique	Removes duplicate adjacent objects within a specified range.

■ EXERCISES 16.1

1. Define the following terms:
   a. container
   b. collection
   c. data structure
   d. iterator
   e. list
   f. STL

2. What sequential container types are supported in STL?

3. What associative container types are supported in STL?

4. For each of the following, define a class that contains only a data declaration section and can be used to create the following objects:
   a. an object, known as a student record, containing a student identification number, the number of credits completed, and a cumulative grade point average
   b. an object, known as a student record, capable of holding a student's name, date of birth, number of credits completed, and cumulative grade point average
   c. a mailing list containing a title field, last name field, first name field, two street address fields, a city field, a state field, and a zip code field
   d. a stock object containing the stock's name, the price of the stock, and the date of purchase
   e. an inventory object containing an integer part number, a string part description, an integer number of parts in inventory, and an integer re-order value

5. For each of the individual classes declared in Exercise 4, add a suitable constructor and accessor method. Test each method to initialize and display the following data:
   a. `Identification Number: 4672`
   `Number of Credits Completed: 68`
   `Grade Point Average: 3.01`
   b. `Name: Rhona Karp`
   `Date of Birth: 8/4/60`
   `Number of Credits Completed: 96`
   `Grade Point Average: 3.89`
   c. `Title: Dr.`
   `Last Name: Kingsley`
   `First Name: Kay`
   `Street Address: 614 Freeman Street`
   `City: Indianapolis`
   `State: IN`
   `Zip Code: 07030`
   d. `Stock: IBM`
   `Price Purchased: 134.5`
   `Date Purchased: 10/1/86`

e. `Part Number: 16879`
`Description: Battery`
`Number in Stock: 10`
`Reorder Number: 3`

6. *a.* Write a C++ program that prompts a user to input the current month, day, and year. Store the data entered in a suitably defined object and display the date in an appropriate manner.

b. Modify the program written in Exercise 6a to use an object that accepts the current time in hours, minutes, and seconds.

7. Define a class capable of creating objects that can store a business's name, description of the business's product or services, address, number of employees, and annual revenue.

8. Define a class capable of creating objects for various screw types held in inventory. Each object should contain a field for an integer inventory number, double-precision screw length, double-precision diameter, kind of head (Phillips or standard slot), material (steel, brass, other), and cost.

9. Write a C++ program that defines a class capable of creating objects for storing the name of a stock, its estimated earnings per share, and its estimated price to-earnings ratio. Have the program prompt the user to enter these items for five different stocks. When the data has been entered for a particular stock, have the program compute and display the anticipated stock price based on the entered earnings and price-per-earnings values. For example, if a user entered the data XYZ 1.56 12, the anticipated price for a share of XYZ stock is (1.56)*(12) = $18.72.

16.2 Linked Lists

A classic data-handling problem is making additions or deletions to existing objects that are maintained in a specific order. This is best illustrated by considering the alphabetical telephone list shown in Figure 16.2. Starting with this initial set of names and telephone numbers, assume that you now need to add new objects to the list such that the alphabetic ordering of the objects is always maintained.

FIGURE 16.2 *A Telephone List in Alphabetical Order*

Acme, Sam
(555) 898-2392
Dolan, Edith
(555) 682-3104
Lanfrank, John
(555) 718-4581
Mening, Stephen
(555) 382-7070
Zemann, Harold
(555) 219-9912

Although the insertion or deletion of ordered objects can be accomplished using an array or vector, these containers are not efficient representations for adding or deleting objects internal to the list, because deleting an object creates an empty slot that requires shifting up all objects below the deleted object to close the empty slot. Similarly, adding an object internally to the list requires that all objects after the addition be shifted down to make room for the new entry. Thus, either adding or deleting objects in an array or a vector requires restructuring objects within the container—an inherently inefficient practice even though it is automatically handled by the `vector` class.

A linked list provides a convenient method for maintaining a constantly changing list without the need for continually reordering and restructuring. In a **linked list** each object contains one variable that specifies the location of the next object in the list. Thus, with a linked list it is not necessary to physically store each object in the proper order; instead, each new object is physically stored in whatever memory space is currently free. If an object is added to the list, it's only necessary to update the variables for the objects immediately preceding and following the newly inserted object with the new location information. Therefore, from a programming standpoint, information is always contained within one object that permits location of the next object, no matter where this next object is actually stored.

A linked list is illustrated in Figure 16.3, where each object consists of a name and telephone number, plus an additional variable that stores the address of the next object in the list. Although the actual data for the Lanfrank object shown in the figure may be physically stored anywhere in the computer, the variable included at the end of the Dolan object maintains the proper alphabetical order and provides the location of the Lanfrank object. A variable used in this way is called a **pointer variable**. All that you need to know at this point, however, is that each object in a linked list must contain information to locate the next object.

FIGURE 16.3 *Using Pointer Variables to Link Structures*

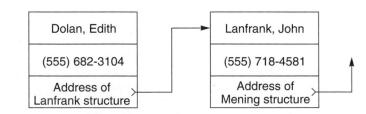

To see the usefulness of the pointer variable in the Dolan object, assume a telephone number for June Hagar has been added to the alphabetical list, as shown in Figure 16.4. The data for June Hagar is stored in a data object using the same type as that used for the existing objects. To ensure that the telephone number for Hagar is correctly displayed after the Dolan telephone number, the value in the pointer variable in the Dolan object must be altered to locate the Hagar object, and the pointer variable in the Hagar object must be set to the location of the Lanfrank object. As illustrated in Figure 16.4, the pointer variable in each object simply locates the object in the list, even if that object is not physically located in the correct order. Removal of an object from a linked list is the reverse process of adding an object. The actual object is logically removed from the list by simply changing the pointer variable's value in the object preceding it to the location of the object immediately following the deleted object.

FIGURE 16.4 *Adjusting Addresses to Point to Appropriate Objects*

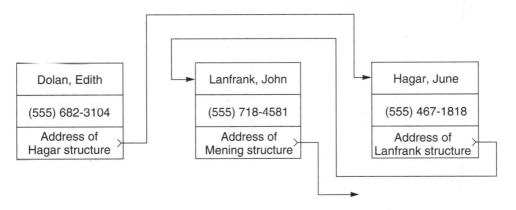

There are two fundamentally different approaches to actually constructing a linked list. The first approach is to use the STL list class; the second approach is to "make your own," in which the programmer provides a class that includes an object's declaration and the code for creating and maintaining the list.

The usefulness of the STL list class is that the linked list, as shown in Figure 16.4, can be constructed without the programmer having either to understand or to program the internal details of the pointer variables. The programmer doesn't even have to understand the details of how the STL list is created and maintained. This is, of course, the major benefit of object-oriented programming using existing classes. Thus, except for exceedingly specialized cases, you should almost always use the STL list class, which is described next. However, because it is useful to understand what is actually being provided by this class and the concepts underlying it, the basics of creating your own linked lists after the list class is also described.

STL `list` Class Implementation

Figure 16.5 presents the internal structure used by the STL `list` class to maintain a list of linked objects. The important point to notice is that the access through the list only occurs via variables in each object that contain location information for an object. These variables are referred to as **link variables**. This structure makes it possible to insert a new object into the list simply by storing the new object in any available memory location and adjusting the location information in at most two link variables. Unlike an array implementation, it is not necessary to store list objects in contiguous memory locations. Similarly, an object can be removed by adjusting the link information in two link variables. As explained earlier, this means that expansion and contraction of the list are more efficient than the same operations using a vector approach.

FIGURE 16.5 *Class Showing Four Link Variables*

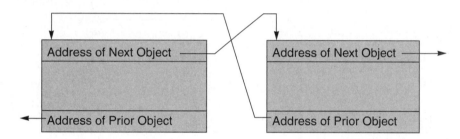

Table 16.3 lists the methods provided by the `list` class. These methods deal with adding, removing, and locating objects from the front and rear of the list. Note that linked lists provide no random access methods. To get to any internal object, the list must be sequentially traversed, object-by-object, starting at either the front or back of the list.

Also note that the `list` class provides no method for returning any object except the first and last objects. Instead, to access an internal object, not only must the list be traversed from one end, but all objects before the desired object must be removed from the list. Technically, when an item is removed in this fashion, it is referred to as "popping" the object from the list. Generally, not to lose the removed objects, a copy of the list is made, either as a complete list or object by object as each object is removed, or popped.

Now consider the following two example programs. Program 16.1 creates and displays a single linked list of names, stored as strings, whereas Program 16.2 shows how to store and retrieve user-created objects. Because of the STL's structure, the two applications are virtually the same. Later, in Program 16.3, we show how to construct your own linked list of objects without using the STL classes.

TABLE 16.3 *Summary of STL* `list` *Class Methods and Operations*

Methods and Operations	Type	Description
`list<DataType> name`	constructor	Creates an empty list named `name` with compiler-dependent initial size
`list<DataType> name(source)`	constructor	Creates a copy of the source list
`list<DataType> name(n)`	constructor	Creates a list of size `n`
`list<DataType> name(n, object)`	constructor	Creates a list of size `n` with each object initialized as `object`
`list<DataType> name(src.beg, src.end)`	constructor	Creates a list initialized with `objects` from a source container beginning at `src.beg` and ending at `src.end`
`~list<DataType>()`	destructor	Destroys the list and all objects it contains
`name.front()`	accessor	Returns the object at the front of the list (the first object) with no check for the existence of a first object
`name.pop_front()`	mutator	Removes, but does not return, the object at the front of the list
`name.push_front(object)`	mutator	Inserts `object` at the front of the list
`name.back()`	accessor	Returns the object at the back of the list with no check for the existence of a last object
`name.pop_back()`	mutator	Removes, but does not return, the object at the back of the list (the last object)
`name.push_back(object)`	mutator	Inserts `object` at the back of the list
`name.insert(itr, object)`	mutator	Inserts `object` at the iterator position `itr`
`name.insert(itr, src.beg, src.end)`	mutator	Inserts copies of objects from a source container, beginning at `src.beg` and ending at `src.end`, at iterator position `itr`
`name.insert(itr, n, object)`	mutator	Inserts n copies of `object` at iterator position `itr`
`name.assign(n, object)`	mutator	Assigns n copies of `object`
`name.(src.begin, src.end)`	mutator	Assigns the objects of the `src` container (need not be a list), between the range `src.begin` and `src.end`, to the named list
`name.erase(pos)`	mutator	Removes the object at the specified position
`name.erase(begin, end)`	mutator	Removes the objects within the specified range
`name.resize(value)`	mutator	Resizes the list to a larger size with new objects instantiated using the default constructor
`name.resize(value, object)`	mutator	Resizes the list to a larger size with new objects instantiated as `object`
`name.clear()`	mutator	Removes all objects from the list

(continued)

TABLE 16.3   *(continued)*

Methods and Operations	Type	Description
nameA.swap(nameB)	mutator	Swaps the objects of name and nameB lists; can be performed using the swap() algorithm
name.begin()	accessor	Returns an iterator to the first object in the list
name.end()	accessor	Returns an iterator to the position after the last object in the list
name.rbegin()	accessor	Returns a reverse iterator to the first object in the list
name.rend()	accessor	Returns a reverse iterator to the position after the last object in the list
name.unique()	mutator	Removes consecutive duplicate objects
name.merge(nameB)	mutator	Merges the sorted objects of nameB into the sorted objects of name, creating a final sorted list
name.reverse()	mutator	Reverses the objects in the list
name.splice(itr, nameB)	mutator	Inserts nameB objects into name at position itr
name.splice(itr, nameB, beg, end)	mutator	Inserts nameB objects in the position range from beg to end into name at position itr
name.sort()	mutator	Sorts the objects in the list
nameA == nameB	relational	Returns a Boolean true if nameA objects all equal nameB objects; otherwise, returns false
nameA != nameB	relational	Returns a Boolean false if nameA objects all equal nameB objects; otherwise, returns true; same as !(nameA == nameB)
nameA < nameB	relational	Returns a Boolean true if nameA is less than nameB; otherwise, returns false
nameA > nameB	relational	Returns a Boolean true if nameA is greater than nameB; otherwise, returns false; same as nameB < nameA
nameA <= nameB	relational	Returns a Boolean true if nameA is less than or equal to nameB
nameA >= nameB	relational	Returns a Boolean true if nameA is greater than or equal to nameB
name.size()	capacity	Returns the number of objects in the list as an integer
name.empty()	capacity	Returns a Boolean true if list is empty; otherwise, returns false
name.max_size()	capacity	Returns the maximum possible objects as an integer
name.capacity()	capacity	Returns the maximum possible objects as an integer without relocation of the list

Program 16.1

```cpp
#include <iostream>
#include <list>
#include <algorithm>
#include <string>
using namespace std;

int main()
{
  list<string> names, addnames;
  string n;

  // add names to the original list
  names.push_front("Dolan, Edith");
  names.push_back("Lanfrank, John");

  // create a new list
  addnames.push_front("Acme, Sam");
  addnames.push_front("Zemann, Frank");

  names.sort();
  addnames.sort();

  // merge the second list into the first
  names.merge(addnames);
  cout << "The first list size is: " <<  names.size() << endl;
  cout << "This list contains the names:\n";

  while (!names.empty())
  {
    cout << names.front() << endl;
    names.pop_front();  // remove the object
  }
}
```

The output produced by Program 16.1 is:

```
The first list size is: 4:
This list contains the names:
Acme,Sam
Dolan,Edith
Lanfrank,John
Zemann,Frank
```

PROGRAMMING NOTE

List Application Considerations

Vectors are the preferred list type whenever you need random access to objects without the need for many insertions or deletions. The reason is that an index value can be used to go directly to the desired object. Insertions and deletions require modifying the underlying array supporting the vector and can be costly in terms of overhead time required to perform these operations when many insertions and deletions are required.

Because the only way to get to an object in the middle of a list is by traversing all of the objects either before it or by traversing objects from the back of the list toward the desired object, attempts at random access tends to be costly in terms of access time. Thus, a list is the preferred list type whenever many object insertions and deletions need to be made *and* object access tends to be sequential.

Finally, if you only need to store primitive data types, such as integers or double-precision values, a simple array should be your first choice.

Using User-Defined Objects

In practice, the majority of real-life applications using linked lists require a user-defined object consisting of a combination of data types. For example, consider the problem of creating a linked list for the simplified telephone objects class illustrated in Figure 16.6.

FIGURE 16.6 *Class Description for a Telephone Directory Object*

```
              Class Name: NameTele

    Attributes
- - - - - - - - - - - - - - - - - - - - - - - - - - - -
        name: string
        phoneNum: string

    Methods
- - - - - - - - - - - - - - - - - - - - - - - - - - - -
        NameTele(name, phoneNum)
        string getName(): return name
        string getPhone(): return phoneNum
```

A suitable class definition corresponding to Figure 16.6 is:

Class 16.1

```
class NameTele
{
  // data declaration section
```

```
    private:
      string name;
      string phoneNum;
   // methods declaration and implementation section
   public:
      NameTele(string nn, string phone)   // constructor
      {
        name = nn;
        phoneNum - phone;
      }
      string getName(){return name;}
      string getPhone(){return phoneNum;}
};
```

This class permits constructing objects consisting of name and phoneNum instance variables using a constructor, as well as accessor methods for setting and retrieving these variables. Program 16.2 instantiates four objects of this class and stores them within a linked list. After it is created, the complete list is displayed.

 Program 16.2

```
#include <iostream>
#include <list>
#include <string>
using namespace std;

class NameTele
{
  // data declaration section
  private:
    string name;
    string phoneNum;

  // methods declaration and implementation section
  public:
    NameTele(string nn, string phone)   // constructor
    {
      name = nn;
      phoneNum = phone;
    }
    string getName(){return name;}
    string getPhone(){return phoneNum;}
  };
```

(continued on next page)

(continued from previous page)

```
int main()
{
  // instantiate a list and initialize the list
  // using the objects in the array
  list<NameTele> employee;

  employee.push_front(NameTele("Acme, Sam", "(555) 891-2392"));
  employee.push_back(NameTele("Dolan, Edith", "(555) 682-3104"));
  employee.push_back(NameTele("Mening, Stephen", "(555) 382-7070"));
  employee.push_back(NameTele("Zemann, Harold", "(555) 219-9912"));

  // retrieve all list objects
  // use accessor methods to extract the name and pay rate
  cout <<"The size of the list is " << employee.size() << endl;
  cout <<"\n     Name             Telephone";
  cout <<"\n-------------          -------------\n";

  while (!employee.empty())
  {
    cout << employee.front().getName()
         << "\t     " << employee.front().getPhone() << endl;
    employee.pop_front();  // remove the object
  }
}
```

The output produced by Program 16.2 is:

```
            The size of the list is 4

          Name                  Telephone
     ---------------          ---------------
     Acme, Sam                (555) 891-2392
     Dolan, Edith             (555) 682-3104
     Mening, Stephen          (555) 382-7070
     Zemann, Harold           (555) 219-9912
```

Notice in Program 16.2 that after each object is retrieved from the list, the underlying class's accessor methods extract individual name and telephone values. Because the dot operator has a left-to-right associativity, an expression such as employee.front().getName() is interpreted as (employee.front()).getName(). Thus, the STL's list class's front() method is used to return the front object from the list, which is then further processed by the NameTele class's getName() method.

Constructing a Programmer-Defined Linked List[1]

The key to constructing a linked list is to provide each object with at least one pointer variable. For example, to use the `NameTele` class (Class 16.1) in a user-created linked list, you first have to provide a link from one object to the next. This is accomplished by adding an extra variable to each object. As this variable must be capable of storing the address value of a `NameTele` object, a suitable declaration for the required instance variable is:

```
NameTele *link; // create a pointer variable to a NameTele object
```

The inclusion of a pointer variable in a data declaration section should not be surprising, because an object is permitted to contain any C++ data type. In this case, the variable named `link` will be used to locate an object of type `NameTele`. In addition to this new variable, you need to supply the class with a set of constructor, mutator, and accessor methods that include setting and retrieving the value stored in `link`. Class 16.2 provides a complete class definition to meet these additional requirements.

Class 16.2

```cpp
#include <iostream>
#include <string>
using namespace std;

class NameTele
{
  // data declaration section
  private:
    string name;
    string phoneNum;
    NameTele *link;

  // methods declaration and implementation section
  public:
    NameTele(string nn, string phone)  // constructor
    {
      name = nn;
      phoneNum = phone;
      link = NULL;
    }
```

---

[1] This topic can be omitted without loss of subject continuity.

```
      string getName(){return name;}
      string getPhone(){return phoneNum;}
      NameTele *getLink(){return link;}
      void setLink(NameTele *ll){link = ll;}
};
```

Because each object in a linked list has the same format, it is clear that the last object cannot have a pointer value that points to another object because there is none. To satisfy this requirement, the last object in the list will always have a Null value in its pointer variable. The Null value is interpreted as a sentinel indicating the end of the list has been reached. Similarly, an initial pointer variable must be available for storing the address of the first object in the list.

Program 16.3 illustrates using the NameTele class by specifically defining four objects having this form, which have been named head, r1, r2, and r3, respectively. The name and telephone members of three of these objects are initialized with actual name and telephone numbers when the objects are defined.

 Program 16.3

```
#include <iostream>
#include <string>
using namespace std;

class NameTele
{
  // data declaration section
  private:
    string name;
    string phoneNum;
    NameTele *link;

  // methods declaration and implementation section
  public:
    NameTele(string nn, string phone)  // constructor
    {
      name = nn;
      phoneNum = phone;
      link = NULL;
    }
    string getName(){return name;}
    string getPhone(){return phoneNum;}
    NameTele *getLink(){return link;}
    void setLink(NameTele *ll){link = ll;}
};
```

```
int main()
{
  NameTele head = NameTele("xx", "xx");  // create an empty object

  // create three objects
  NameTele r1 = NameTele("Acme, Sam", "(555) 898 2392");
  NameTele r2 = NameTele("Dolan, Edith", "(555) 682 3104");
  NameTele r3 = NameTele("Lanfrank, John", "(555) 718 4581");

  // link all of the objects
  head.setLink(&r1);  // have the head link point to the first object;
  r1.setLink(&r2);
  r2.setLink(&r3);

  // retrieve each object using the link from the prior object
  cout << head.getLink()->getName() << endl
       << r1.getLink()->getName() << endl
       << r2.getLink()->getName() << endl;
}
```

The output produced by executing Program 16.3 is:

```
Acme, Sam
Dolan, Edith
Lanfrank, John
```

The important concept illustrated by Program 16.3 is the use of a pointer variable in one object to access the next object in the list, as illustrated in Figure 16.7.

FIGURE 16.7   *The Relationship Between Objects in Program 16.3*

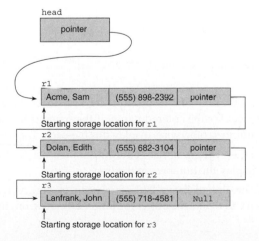

The initialization of the names and telephone numbers for each of the objects defined in Program 16.3 is straightforward. Although each object consists of three variables, only the first two variables in each are explicitly initialized when an object is instantiated. The remaining variable, which is a pointer, is only assigned an explicit address after the next object is placed in the list.

The three assignment statements in Program 16.3 perform the correct pointer assignments. The expression `head.setLink(&r1);` stores the address of the first telephone object in the pointer variable of the object named `head`. The expression `r1.setLink(&r2);` stores the address of the `r2` object in the pointer member of the `r1` object. Similarly, the expression `r2.setLink(&r3);` stores the address of the `r3` object in the pointer member of the `r2` object.

Once name and telephone values have been assigned to each object, and correct location information has been stored in the appropriate pointers, the pointers are then used to access each object's name member. For example, the expression `head.getLink()->getName()` is used to locate the `r1` object and then to extract its `name` value. Often the links in a linked list of objects can be used to loop through the complete list. As each object is accessed, it can be either examined to select a specific value or used to print out a complete list. Equally important is that a linked list can easily expand as new objects are added and contract as existing objects are deleted.

For objects that need to be inserted internally within a list, the new object's link would also have to be set to locate the next object in the list, and the prior object's link would also have to be adjusted to correctly locate the inserted object. Deleting an object is accomplished by removing the link to the object and adjusting the prior object's link to locate the next valid object in the list.

Programming all of the required insertion and deletion methods takes time and care. Using the STL's `list` class removes all of this programming effort from you, while providing a complete set of tested methods for performing all the maintenance tasks associated with a linked list.

▌ EXERCISES 16.2

1. Modify Program 16.2 to prompt the user for a name. Have the program search the existing list for the entered name. If the name is in the list, display the corresponding phone number; otherwise, display this message: The name is not in the current phone list.

2. Write a C++ program that contains a linked list of 10 integer numbers. Have the program display the numbers in the list.

3. Using the linked list of objects shown in Figure 16.4, write the sequence of steps necessary to delete the object for John Lanfrank from the list.

4. Generalize the description provided in Exercise 3 to describe the sequence of steps necessary to remove the nth object from a list of linked objects. The nth object is preceded by the (n − 1)st object and followed by the (n + 1)st object.

5. Determine the output of the following program:

```cpp
#include <iostream>
#include <list>
using namespace std;

int main()
{
  int intValue;
  double sum = 0.0;
  double average;

  // create an array of integer values
  int nums[] = {1, 2, 3, 4, 5 };

  // instantiate a list of ints using a
  // constructor that initializes the list with values from the array
  list<int> x(nums, nums + 4);

  cout <<"\nThe list x initially has a size of " << x.size()
          << "," << "\n and contains the objects: " ;

  while (!x.empty())
  {
    cout << x.front() << "   ";
    x.pop_front();
  }
  cout << endl;
}
```

16.3   Stacks

A **stack** is a special type of list in which objects can only be added to and removed from the top of the list. As such, it is a **last-in, first-out (LIFO)** list—that is, a LIFO list in which the last item added to the list is the first item that can be removed. An example of this type of operation is a stack of dishes in a cafeteria, where the last dish placed on top of the stack is the first dish removed. Another example is the "in basket" on a desk, where the last paper placed in the basket is typically the first one removed. In computer programming, stacks are used in all function calls to store and retrieve data to and from the function.

FIGURE 16.8   *A List of Names*

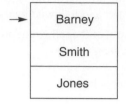

As a specific stack example, consider Figure 16.8, which illustrates an existing list of three last names. As shown, the top name on this list is Barney.

If you now restrict access to the list so that names can only be added and removed from the top of the list, then the list becomes a stack. This requires that you designate which end of the list is the top and which the bottom. Because the name Barney is physically placed above the other names, this is considered the top of the list. To explicitly signify this, an arrow has been used, so the list's top is clearly indicated.

Figure 16.9 (which consists of six parts, labeled a through f) illustrates how the stack expands and contracts as names are added and deleted. For example, in part b, the name Ventura has been added to the list. By part c, a total of two new names have been added and the top of the list has changed accordingly. By next removing the top name, Lanfrank, from the list in part c, the stack shrinks to that shown in part d, where Ventura now resides at the top of the stack. As names continue to be removed from the list (parts e and f), the stack continues to contract.

Although Figure 16.9 is an accurate representation of a list of names, it contains additional information that is not provided by a true stack object. When names are added to or removed from a stack, no count is kept of how many names have been added or deleted or of how many items the stack actually contains at any one time.

FIGURE 16.9   *An Expanding and Contracting List of Names*

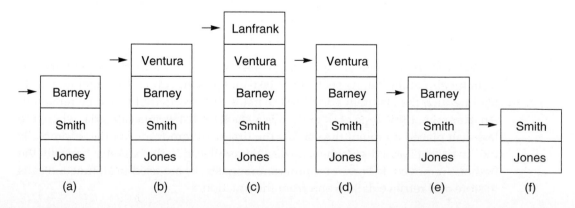

Dr. Lukasiewicz and RPN

Dr. Jan Lukasiewicz, born in 1878, studied and taught mathematics at the University of Lvov, in Poland, before becoming a respected professor at the University of Warsaw. He received an appointment in 1919 to the post of Minister of Education in Poland and, with Stanislaw Lesniewski, founded the Warsaw School of Logic.

After World War II, Dr. Lukasiewicz and his wife, Regina, found themselves exiled in Belgium. When he was offered a professorship at the Royal Academy in Dublin, they moved to Ireland, where they remained until his death in 1956.

In 1951 Dr. Lukasiewicz developed a new set of postfix algebraic notation, which was critical in the design of early microprocessors in the 1960s and 1970s.

The actual implementation of postfix algebra was done using stack arithmetic, in which data were pushed on a stack and popped off when an operation needed to be performed. Such stack handling instructions require no address operands and made it possible for very small computers to handle large tasks effectively.

Stack arithmetic, which is based on Dr. Lukasiewicz's work, reverses the more commonly known prefix algebra and became known as Reverse Polish Notation (RPN). Early pocket calculators developed by the Hewlett-Packard Corporation were especially notable for their use of RPN and made stack arithmetic the favorite of many scientists and engineers.

For example, by examining each part of Figure 16.9, you can determine how many names are on the list. In a true stack, the only item that can be seen and accessed is the top item on the list. To find out how many items the list contains would require continual removal of the top item until no more items exist.

Stack Class Implementation

Creating a stack requires the following four components:

- A container for holding items in the list
- A method of designating the current top stack item
- An operation for placing a new item on the stack
- An operation for removing an item from the stack

By convention, the operation of placing a new item on the top of a stack is called a **push**, and the operation of removing an item from a stack is called a **pop**. How each of these operations is actually implemented depends on the container type used to represent a stack. In C++, a stack can be easily created using the STL's deque class. This class creates a double-ended list, where objects can be pushed and popped from either end of the list. To create a stack, only the front end of the deque is used. A summary of the deque class's methods and operations are listed in Table 16.4.

TABLE 16.4 *Summary of* deque *Class Methods and Operations*

Methods and Operations	Type	Description
deque<DataType> name	constructor	Creates an empty deque named name with compiler-dependent initial size
deque<DataType> name(source)	constructor	Creates a copy of the source deque
deque<DataType> name(n)	constructor	Creates a deque of size n
deque<DataType> name(n, object)	constructor	Creates a deque of size n with each object initialized as object
deque<DataType> name(src.beg, src.end)	constructor	Creates a deque initialized with objects from a source container beginning at src.beg and ending at src.end
~deque(DataType>()	destructor	Destroys the deque and all objects it contains
name.at(index)	accessor	Returns the object at the designated index, and throws an exception if the index is out of bounds
name.front()	accessor	Returns the first object at the front of the deque with no check for the existence of a first object
name.pop_front()	mutator	Removes, but does not return, the first object at the front of the deque
name.push_front(object)	mutator	Inserts object at the front of the deque
name.back()	accessor	Returns the object at the back of the deque with no check for the existence of a last object
name.pop_back()	mutator	Removes, but does not return, the last object at the back of the deque
name.push_back(object)	mutator	Inserts object at the back of the deque
name.insert(itr, object)	mutator	Inserts object at iterator position itr
name.insert(itr, src.beg, src.end)	mutator	Inserts copies of objects from a source container, beginning at src.beg and ending at src.end at iterator position itr
name.insert(itr, n, object)	mutator	Inserts n copies of object at iterator position itr
name2.assign(n, object)	mutator	Assigns n copies of object
name2.(src.begin, src.end)	mutator	Assigns the objects of the src container (need not be a deque) between the range src.begin and src.end to name2
name.erase(pos)	mutator	Removes the object at the specified position

TABLE 16.4 *(continued)*

Methods and Operations	Type	Description
`name.erase(begin, end)`	mutator	Removes the objects within the specified range
`name.resize(value)`	mutator	Resizes the deque to a larger size with new objects instantiated using the default constructor
`name.resize(value, object)`	mutator	Resizes the deque to a larger size with new objects instantiated as `object`
`name.clear()`	mutator	Removes all objects from the deque
`name.swap(nameB)`	mutator	Swaps the objects of `name` and `nameB` deques; can be performed using the `swap()` algorithm
`name.begin()`	accessor	Returns an iterator to the first object in the deque
`name.end()`	accessor	Returns an iterator to the position after the last object in the deque
`name.rbegin()`	accessor	Returns a reverse iterator to the first object in the deque
`name.rend()`	accessor	Returns a reverse iterator to the position after the last object in the deque
`nameA == nameB`	relational	Returns a Boolean `true` if `nameA` objects all equal `nameB` objects; otherwise, returns `false`
`nameA != nameB`	relational	Returns a Boolean `false` if `nameA` objects all equal `nameB` objects; otherwise, returns `true`; same as `!(nameA == nameB)`
`nameA < nameB`	relational	Returns a Boolean true if `nameA` is less than `nameB`; otherwise, returns `false`
`nameA > nameB`	relational	Returns a Boolean `true` if `nameA` is greater than `nameB`; otherwise, returns `false`; same as `nameB < nameA`
`nameA <= nameB`	relational	Returns a Boolean `true` if `nameA` is less than or equal to `nameB`
`nameA >= nameB`	relational	Returns a Boolean `true` if `nameA` is greater than or equal to `nameB`
`name.size()`	capacity	Returns the number of objects in the deque as an `int`
`name.empty()`	capacity	Returns a Boolean `true` if deque is empty; otherwise, returns `false`
`name.max_size()`	capacity	Returns the maximum possible objects as an integer
`name.capacity()`	capacity	Returns the maximum possible objects as an integer without relocation of the deque

Stacking the Deque

Stacks and queues are two special forms of a more general data object called a *deque* (pronounced "deck"). Deque stands for *double-ended queue*.

In a deque object, data can be handled in one of four ways:

1. Insert at the beginning and remove from the beginning. This is the last-in, first-out (LIFO) stack.
2. Insert at the beginning and remove form the end. This is the first-in, first-out (FIFO) queue.
3. Insert at the end and remove from the end, which represents an inverted LIFO technique.
4. Insert at the end and remove from the beginning, which represents an inverted FIFO queue.

Implementation 1 (stack object) is presented in this section and implementation 2 (queue object) is presented in the next section. Implementations 3 and 4 are sometimes used for keeping track of memory addresses, such as when programming is done in machine language or when objects are handled in a file. When a high-level language, such as C++, manages the data area automatically, users may not be aware of where the data are being stored or of which type of deque is being applied.

Program 16.4 uses the deque class to implement a stack. The program is straightforward in that only one stack is instantiated and user-entered names are pushed to the front of the deque until the sentinel value of x is entered. Upon detection of this sentinel string value, the names are popped from the front of the deque as long as the deque is non-empty.

Program 16.4

```cpp
#include <iostream>
#include <deque>
#include <string>
#include <cctype>
using namespace std;

int main()
{
  string name;
  deque<string> stack;

  cout << "Enter as many names as you want, one per line" << endl;
  cout << "To stop enter a single x" << endl;
```

```
while(true)
{
  cout << "Enter a name (or x to stop): " ;
  getline(cin, name);
  if (tolower(name.at(0)) == 'x') break;
  stack.push_front(name);
}

  cout << "\nThe names in the stack are:\n";

  // pop names from the stack
  while(!stack.empty())
  {
    name = stack.front();   // retrieve the name
    stack.pop_front();   // pop name from the stack
    cout << name << endl;
  }
}
```

Following is a sample run using Program 16.4:

```
Enter as many names as you want, one per line
 To stop enter a single x
Enter a name (or x to stop): Jane Jones
Enter a name (or x to stop): Bill Smith
Enter a name (or x to stop): Jim Robinson
Enter a name (or x to stop): x

The names in the stack are:
Jim Robinson
Bill Smith
Jane Jones
```

▌ EXERCISES 16.3

1. State whether a stack is appropriate for each of the following tasks. Indicate why or why not.

a. A word processor must remember a line of up to 80 characters. Pressing the Backspace key deletes the previous character, and pressing CTRL and Backspace deletes the entire line. Users must be able to undo deletion operations.

b. Customers must wait one to three months for delivery of their new automobiles. The dealer creates a list that will determine the "fair" order in which customers should get their cars; the list is to be prepared in the order in which customers placed their requests for a new car.

c. You are required to search downward in a pile of magazines to locate the issue for last January. Each magazine was placed on the pile as soon as it was received.

d. A programming team accepts jobs and prioritizes them on the basis of urgency.

e. A line formed at a bus stop.

2. Modify Program 16.4 to implement a stack of integers rather than a stack of strings.

3. Modify Program 16.4 to instantiate three stacks of digits named `digits1`, `digits2`, and `digits3`. Initialize `digits1` to contain the digits 9, 8, 5, and 2, which is the number 2589 in reverse digit order. Similarly, the `digits2` stack should be initialized to contain the digits 3, 1, 5, and 7, which is the number 7513 in reverse digit order. Calculate and place the sum of these two numbers in the `digits3` stack. This sum should be obtained by popping respective objects from `digits1` and `digits2` and adding them together with a variable named `carry`, which is initialized to 0. If the sum of the two popped objects and carry does not exceed 10, the sum should be pushed onto `digits3` and the carry set to 0; otherwise, the carry should be set to 1, and the units digit of the sum pushed onto the `digits3` stack.

4. Write a C++ program that permits a user to enter a maximum of 100 integers into a stack object. Then have the program:

a. Reverse the stack contents into a second stack of integers.

b. Using two additional stacks, reverse the contents in the original stack. If the original stack contains the integers 1, 2, 3, and 4, it should contain the integers 4, 3, 2, and 1 at the end of the program.

5. Write a C++ program that permits a user to enter a maximum of 50 characters into a stack object. Then have the program sort the stack contents in increasing order. If the contents of the stack are initially D, E, A, and B, the final contents of the stack will be A, B, D, and E.

16.4 Queues

A **queue** (pronounced *cue*) is a list in which items are added to one end of the list, called the top, and removed from the other end of the list, called the bottom. This arrangement ensures that items are removed from the list in the exact order in which they were entered. This means that the first item placed on the list is the first item to be removed, the second item placed on the list is the second item to be removed, and so on. Thus, a queue is a **first-in, first-out (FIFO)** list—a list in which the first item added to the list is the first item that can be removed.

As an example of a queue, consider a list of people waiting to purchase season tickets to a professional football team. The first person on the list should be called when the first set of tickets becomes available, the second person should be called for the second available set, and so on. The names of the people currently on the list are shown in Figure 16.10.

FIGURE 16.10   *A Queue with Its Pointers*

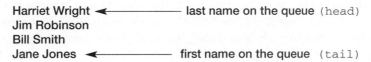

As illustrated in Figure 16.10, the names have been added in the same fashion as on a stack; that is, as new names are added to the list, they are stacked on top of the existing names. The difference in a queue relates to how the names are popped off the list. Clearly, the people on this list expect to be serviced in the order that they were placed on the list—that is, first in, first out. Thus, unlike a stack, the most recently added name to the list *is not* the first name removed. Rather, the oldest name still on the list is always the next name removed.

To keep the list in proper order, where new names are added to one end of the list and old names are removed from the other end, it is convenient to use two link variables: one that locates the front of the list for the next person to be serviced and one that locates the end of the list where new people will be added. The link variable that locates the front of the list where the next name is to be removed is referred to as the tail pointer, or tail, for short. The second link variable, which locates the last person in the list and indicates where the next person entering the list is to be placed, is called the head pointer, or head, for short. Thus, for the list shown in Figure 16.10, the tail points to Jane Jones and the head points to Harriet Wright. If Jane Jones were now removed from the list and Lou Hazlet and Teresa Filer were added, the queue and its associated position indicators would appear as in Figure 16.11.

FIGURE 16.11   *The Updated Queue Pointers*

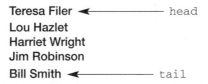

Deque Class Implementation

A queue is easily derived using the STL deque container. The operation of placing a new item on the queue is formally referred to as **enqueuing** and more causally referred to as a **push** operation, whereas removing an item from a queue is formally referred to as **serving** and casually as a **pop** operation. Operationally, enqueuing is an operation similar to pushing on one end of a stack, and serving from a queue is an operation similar to popping from the other end of a stack. How each of these operations is implemented depends on the list used to represent a queue.

Because you will use the deque class as the base class, you can easily create the push and pop operations using the deque class's push_front() and pop_back() methods (see Table 16.4). Program 16.5 illustrates using the deque class to construct a queue within the context of a complete program, where names are pushed onto the front of the deque and popped from the back. This creates the FIFO ordering that characterizes a queue.

Program 16.5

```cpp
#include <iostream>
#include <deque>
#include <string>
#include <cctype>
using namespace std;

int main()
{
  string name;
  deque<string> queue;

  cout << "Enter as many names as you want, one per line" << endl;
  cout << " To stop enter a single x" << endl;

  // push names on the queue
  while(true)
  {
    cout << "Enter a name (or x to stop): " ;
    getline(cin, name);
    if (tolower(name.at(0)) == 'x') break;
    queue.push_front(name);
  }

  cout << "\nThe names in the queue are:\n";

  // pop names from the queue
  while(!queue.empty())
  {
    name = queue.back();  // retrieve the name
    queue.pop_back();  // pop a name from the queue
    cout << name << endl;
  }
}
```

PROGRAMMING NOTE

Artificial Intelligence

One of the major steps toward creating programs that "learn" as they work is the development of dynamic data objects.

In 1950, Alan Turing proposed a test in which an expert enters questions at an isolated terminal. Presumably, artificial intelligence (AI) is achieved when the expert cannot discern whether the answers returned to the screen have been produced by a human or by a machine. Although there are problems with the Turing test, its concepts have spawned numerous research efforts.

By the mid-1960s, many AI researchers believed the efforts to create "thinking machines" were futile. Today, however, much lively research and development focus on topics such as dynamic problem solving, computer vision, parallel processing, natural language processing, and speech and pattern recognition—all of which are encompassed within the field of AI.

The development of techniques that allow machines to emulate humans have proliferated in recent years with the development of computers that are smaller, faster, more powerful, and less expensive. Most people agree that computers could never replace all human decision making. There is also general agreement that society must remain alert and in control of important decisions that require human compassion, ethics, and understanding.

A sample run using Program 16.5 produced the following:

```
Enter as many names as you want, one per line
 To stop enter a single x
Enter a name (or x to stop): Jane Jones
Enter a name (or x to stop): Bill Smith
Enter a name (or x to stop): Jim Robinson
Enter a name (or x to stop): x

The names in the queue are:
Jane Jones
Bill Smith
Jim Robinson
```

▌ EXERCISES 16.4

1. State whether a queue, a stack, or neither object would be appropriate for each of the following tasks. Indicate why or why not.

    a. A list of customers waiting to be seated in a restaurant

    b. A group of student tests waiting to be graded

c. An address book listing names and telephone numbers in alphabetical order

d. Patients waiting for examinations in a doctor's office

2. Modify Program 16.5 to use a queue of integers rather than a queue of strings.

3. Write a C++ program that permits a user to enter a maximum of 20 character values into a queue. Then have the program sort the queue contents in increasing order. If the contents of the queue are initially D, E, A, and B, the final contents of the queue will be A, B, D, and E.

4. Write a queue program that accepts an object consisting of an integer identification number and a double-precision hourly pay rate.

5. Add a menu method to Program 16.5 that gives the user a choice of adding a name to the queue, removing a name from the queue, or listing the contents of the queue without removing any objects from it.

6. A group of people have arrived at a bus stop and are lined up in this order:

1. Chaplin	4. Laurel	7. Oliver	10. Garland
2. West	5. Smith	8. Hardy	11. Wayne
3. Taylor	6. Grisby	9. Burton	12. Stewart

Read the names from an input file into a queue and display the order in which the passengers board the bus.

16.5   Common Programming Errors

Two common programming errors related to using STL's `list` and `deque` classes are:

1. Inserting objects instantiated from different classes into the same list.
2. Attempting to use indices rather than iterators when using STL class methods and algorithms.

The five most common programming errors related to linked lists, stacks, and queues, which occur when programmers attempt to construct their own lists. are:

1. Not checking the pointer provided by the `new` operator when constructing a non-STL list. If this operator returns a `NULL` value, the user should be notified that the allocation did not take place and the normal program operation must be altered in an appropriate way. You simply cannot assume that all calls to `new` will result in the requested allocation of memory space being successful.

2. Not correctly updating all relevant pointer addresses when adding or removing records from dynamically created stacks and queues. Unless extreme care is taken in updating all addresses, each of these dynamic data structures can quickly become corrupted.

3. Forgetting to free previously allocated memory space when the space is no longer needed. This is typically only a problem in a large application program that is expected to run continuously and can make many requests for allocated space based on user demand.

4. Not preserving the integrity of the addresses contained in the top-of-stack pointer when dealing with a stack and the queue-in and queue-out pointers when dealing with a queue. As each of these pointers locates a starting position in their respective data structures, the complete list will be lost if the starting addresses are incorrect.

5. Not correctly updating internal record pointers when inserting and removing records from a stack or queue. Once an internal pointer within these lists contains an incorrect address, it is almost impossible to locate and reestablish the missing set of objects.

16.6   Chapter Summary

1. An object permits individual data items to be stored under a common variable name. These objects can then be stored together in a list.

2. A linked list is a list of objects in which each object contains a pointer variable that locates the next object in the list. Each linked list must have a pointer to locate the first object in the list. The last object's pointer variable is set to NULL to indicate the end of the list.

3. Linked lists can be automatically constructed using the STL's list class.

4. A stack is a list consisting of objects that can only be added and removed from the top of the list. Such an object is a LIFO (last-in, first-out) list, which means the last object added to the list is the first object removed. Stacks can be implemented using the STL's deque class.

5. A queue is a list consisting of objects that are added to the top of the list and removed from the bottom of the list. Such an object is a FIFO (first-in, first-out) list, which means objects are removed in the order in which they were added. Queues can be implemented using the STL's deque class.

Appendixes

Appendix A   Operator Precedence Table

Table A.1 presents the symbols, precedence, descriptions, and associativity of C++'s operators. Operators toward the top of the table have a higher precedence than those toward the bottom. Operators within each box have the same precedence and associativity.

TABLE A.1   *Summary of C++ Operators*

Operator	Description	Associativity
() [] -> .	Function call Array element Structure member pointer reference Structure member reference	Left to right
++ -- - ! ~ (type) sizeof & *	Increment Decrement Unary minus Logical negation One's complement Type conversion (cast) Storage size Address of Indirection	Right to left
* / %	Multiplication Division Modulus (remainder)	Left to right
+ -	Addition Subtraction	Left to right
<< >>	Left shift Right shift	Left to right
< <= > >=	Less than Less than or equal to Greater than Greater than or equal to	Left to right
== !=	Equal to Not equal to	Left to right
&	Bitwise AND	Left to right
^	Bitwise exclusive OR	Left to right
|	Bitwise inclusive OR	Left to right
&&	Logical AND	Left to right
||	Logical OR	Left to right
?:	Conditional expression	Right to left
= += -= *= /= %= &= ^= |= <<= >>=	Assignment Assignment Assignment Assignment Assignment	Right to left
,	Comma	Left to right

Appendix B   ASCII Character Codes

Key(s)	Dec	Oct	Hex	Key	Dec	Oct	Hex	Key	Dec	Oct	Hex
Ctrl 1	0	0	0	+	43	53	2B	V	86	126	56
Ctrl A	1	1	1	,	44	54	2C	W	87	127	57
Ctrl B	2	2	2	-	45	55	2D	X	88	130	58
Ctrl C	3	3	3	.	46	56	2E	Y	89	131	59
Ctrl D	4	4	4	/	47	57	2F	Z	90	132	5A
Ctrl E	5	5	5	0	48	60	30	[	91	133	5B
Ctrl F	6	6	6	1	49	61	31	\	92	134	5C
Ctrl G	7	7	7	2	50	62	32	]	93	135	5D
Ctrl H	8	10	8	3	51	63	33	^	94	136	5E
Ctrl I	9	11	9	4	52	64	34	_	95	137	5F
Ctrl J (lf)	10	12	A	5	53	65	35	'	96	140	60
Ctrl K	11	13	B	6	54	66	36	a	97	141	61
Ctrl L	12	14	C	7	55	67	37	b	98	142	62
Ctrl M (Ret)	13	15	D	8	56	70	38	c	99	143	63
Ctrl N	14	16	E	9	57	71	39	d	100	144	64
Ctrl O	15	17	F	:	58	72	3A	e	101	145	65
Ctrl P	16	20	10	;	59	73	3B	f	102	146	66
Ctrl Q	17	21	11	<	60	74	3C	g	103	147	67
Ctrl R	18	22	12	=	61	75	3D	h	104	150	68
Ctrl S	19	23	13	>	62	76	3E	i	105	151	69
Ctrl T	20	24	14	?	63	77	3F	j	106	152	6A
Ctrl U	21	25	15	@	64	100	40	k	107	153	6B
Ctrl V	22	26	16	A	65	101	41	l	108	154	6C
Ctrl W	23	27	17	B	66	102	42	m	109	155	6D
Ctrl X	24	30	18	C	67	103	43	n	110	156	6E
Ctrl Y	25	31	19	D	68	104	44	o	111	157	6F
Ctrl Z	26	32	1A	E	69	105	45	p	112	160	70
Esc	27	33	1B	F	70	106	46	q	113	161	71
Ctrl <	28	34	1C	G	71	107	47	r	114	162	72
Ctrl /	29	35	1D	H	72	110	48	s	115	163	73
Ctrl =	30	36	1E	I	73	111	49	t	116	164	74
Ctrl -	31	37	1F	J	74	112	4A	u	117	165	75
Space	32	40	20	K	75	113	4B	v	118	166	76
!	33	41	21	L	76	114	4C	w	119	167	77
"	34	42	22	M	77	115	4D	x	120	170	78
#	35	43	23	N	78	116	4E	y	121	171	79
$	36	44	24	O	79	117	4F	z	122	172	7A
%	37	45	25	P	80	120	50	{	123	173	7B
&	38	46	26	Q	81	121	51			124	174	7C
'	39	47	27	R	82	122	52	}	125	175	7D
(	40	50	28	S	83	123	53	~	126	176	7E
)	41	51	29	T	84	124	54	del	127	177	7F
*	42	52	2A	U	85	125	55				

Appendix C   Bit Operations

C++ operates with data entities that are stored as one or more bytes, such as character, integer, and double-precision constants and variables. In addition, C++ provides for the manipulation of individual bits of character and integer constants and variables. Generally, these bit manipulations are used in engineering and computer science applications and are not required in commercial applications.

The operators that are used to perform bit manipulations are called **bit operators.** They are listed in Table C.1.

TABLE C.1   *Bit Operators*

Operator	Description
&	Bit-by-bit AND
|	Bit-by-bit inclusive OR
^	Bit-by-bit exclusive OR
~	Bit-by-bit one's complement
<<	Left shift
>>	Right shift

All the operators listed in Table C.1, except ~, are binary operators, requiring two operands. Each operand is treated as a binary number consisting of a series of individual 1s and 0s. The respective bits in each operand are then compared on a bit-by-bit basis, and the result is determined on the basis of the selected operation.

The AND Operator

The AND operator causes a bit-by-bit AND comparison between its two operands. *The result of each bit-by-bit comparison is a 1 only when both bits being compared are 1s; otherwise, the result of the AND operation is a 0.* For example, assume that the following two eight-bit numbers are to be ANDed:

```
1 0 1 1 0 0 1 1
1 1 0 1 0 1 0 1
---------------
```

To perform an AND operation, each bit in one operand is compared to the bit occupying the same position in the other operand. Figure C.1 illustrates the correspondence between bits for these two operands. As shown in the figure, when both bits being compared are 1s, the result is a 1; otherwise, the result is a 0. The result of each comparison is, of course, independent of any other bit comparison.

Program C.1 illustrates the use of an AND operation. In this program, the variable op1 is initialized to the octal value 325, which is the octal equivalent of the binary number 1 1 0 1 0 1 0 1, and the variable op2 is initialized to the octal value 263, which is the octal representation of the binary number 1 0 1 1 0 0 1 1. These are the same two binary numbers illustrated in Figure C.1.

 Program C.1

```
#include <iostream>
int main()
{
  int op1 = 0325, op2 = 0263;

  int op3 = op1 & op2;
  cout << oct << op1 << " ANDed with "<< op2 << " is " << op3 << endl;

  return 0;
}
```

Program C.1 produces the following output

```
325 ANDed with 263 is 221
```

The result of ANDing the octal numbers 325 and 263 is the octal number 221. The binary equivalent of 221 is the binary number 1 0 0 1 0 0 0 1, which is the result of the AND operation illustrated in Figure C.1.

FIGURE C.1   *A Sample AND Operation*

```
    1 0 1 1 0 0 1 1
&   1 1 0 1 0 1 0 1
    ---------------
    1 0 0 1 0 0 0 1
```

AND operations are extremely useful in **masking**, or eliminating, selected bits from an operand. This is a direct result of the fact that ANDing any bit (1 or 0) with a 0 forces the resulting bit to be a 0, whereas ANDing any bit (1 or 0) with a 1 leaves the original bit unchanged. For example, assume that the variable op1 has the arbitrary bit pattern x x x x x x x x, where each x can be either 1 or 0, independent of any other x in the number. The result of ANDing this binary number with the binary number 0 0 0 0 1 1 1 1 is

```
op1 =   x x x x x x x x
op2 =   0 0 0 0 1 1 1 1
        ---------------
Result =  0 0 0 0 x x x x
```

As can be seen from this example, the 0s in op2 effectively mask, or eliminate, the respective bits in op1, whereas the 1s in op2 filter the respective bits in op1, or pass them through, with no change in their values. In this example, the variable op2 is called a **mask.** By choosing the mask appropriately, any individual bit in an operand can be selected and filtered from an operand for inspection. For example, ANDing the variable op1 with the mask 0 0 0 0 0 1 0 0 forces all the bits of the result to be a 0, except for the third bit. The third bit of the result will be a copy of the third bit of op1. Thus, if the result of the AND is a 0, the third bit of op1 must have been a 0, and if the result of the AND is a nonzero number, the third bit must have been a 1.

Program C.2 uses this masking property to convert lowercase letters in a word into their uppercase form, assuming that the letters are stored using the ASCII code. The algorithm for converting letters is based on the fact that the binary codes for lowercase and uppercase letters in ASCII are the same except for bit five, which is a 1 for lowercase letters and a 0 for uppercase letters.[1] For example, the binary code for the letter a is 01100001 (hex 61), whereas the binary code for the letter A is 01000001 (hex 41). Similarly, the binary code for the letter z is 01111010 (hex 7A), whereas the binary code for the letter Z is 01011010 (hex 5A). (See Appendix B for the hexadecimal values of the uppercase and lowercase letters.) Thus, given a lowercase letter, it can be converted into its uppercase form by forcing the fifth bit to 0. This is accomplished in Program C.2 by masking the letter's code with the binary value 11011111, which has the hexadecimal value DF.

---

[1] This assumes the conventional numbering scheme starting with bit zero as the rightmost bit. Using this convention, the rightmost bit (or bit zero) is referred to as the least significant bit (LSB), and the leftmost bit is referred to as the most significant bit (MSB). Here the MSB is bit seven.

Program C.2

```cpp
#include <iostream>
const int TO_UP = 0xDF;
const int MAX = 80;
int main()
{
    char word[MAX];        // enough storage for a complete line
    void upper(char *);    // function prototype

    cout << "Enter a string of both upper and lowercase letters:\n";
    cin.getline(word,MAX,'\n');
    cout << "\nThe string of letters just entered is:\n"
         << word << endl;
    upper(word);
    cout << "\nThis string, in uppercase letters is:\n"
         << word << endl;
    return 0;
}
void upper(char *word)
{
  while (*word != '\0')
    *word++ &= TO_UP;
  return;
}
```

A sample run using Program C.2 follows.

```
Enter a string of both upper and lowercase letters:
abcdefgHIJKLMNOPqrstuvwxyz

The string of letters just entered is:
abcdefgHIJKLMNOPqrstuvwxyz

This string, in uppercase letters is:
ABCDEFGHIJKLMNOPQRSTUVWXYZ
```

Note that the lowercase letters are converted to uppercase form, whereas uppercase letters are unaltered. This is because bit five of all uppercase letters is a 0 to begin with, so forcing this bit to 0 using the mask has no effect. Only when bit five is a 1, as it is for lowercase letters, is the input character altered.

The Inclusive OR Operator

The inclusive OR operator, |, performs a bit-by-bit comparison of its two operands in a similar fashion to the bit-by-bit AND. The result of the OR comparison, however, is determined by the following rule:

The result of the comparison is a 1 if either bit being compared is a 1; otherwise, the result is a 0.

Figure C.2 illustrates an OR operation. As shown in the figure, when either of the two bits being compared is a 1, the result is a 1; otherwise the result is a 0. As with all bit operations, the result of each comparison is independent of any other comparison.

FIGURE C.2   *A Sample OR Operation*

```
  1 0 1 1 0 0 1 1
| 1 1 0 1 0 1 0 1
-----------------
  1 1 1 1 0 1 1 1
```

Program C.3 illustrates an OR operation, using the octal values of the operands illustrated in Figure C.2.

 Program C.3

```cpp
#include <iostream>
int main()
{
  int op1 = 0325, op2 = 0263;

  int op3 = op1 | op2;
  cout << oct << op1 << " ORed with " << op2 << " is " << op3 << endl;
  return 0;
}
```

Program C.3 produces the following output:

```
325 ORed with 263 is 367
```

The result of ORing the octal numbers 325 and 263 is the octal number 367. The binary equivalent of 367 is 1 1 1 1 0 1 1 1, which is the result of the OR operation illustrated in Figure C.2.

Inclusive OR operations are extremely useful in forcing selected bits to take on a 1 value or for passing through other bit values unchanged. This is a direct result of the fact that ORing any bit (1 or 0) with a 1 forces the resulting bit to be a 1, whereas ORing any bit (1 or 0) with a 0 leaves the original bit unchanged. For example, assume that the variable op1 has the arbitrary bit pattern x x x x x x x x, where each x can be either 1 or 0, independent of any other x in the number. The result of ORing this binary number with the binary number 1 1 1 1 0 0 0 0 is

```
   op1 =   x x x x x x x x
   op2 =   1 1 1 1 0 0 0 0
           ---------------
Result =   1 1 1 1 x x x x
```

As this example illustrates, the 1s in op2 force the resulting bits to 1, whereas the 0s in op2 filter the respective bits in op1, or pass them through, with no change in their values. Thus, using an OR operation, we can produce a masking operation similar to that produced with an AND operation, except the masked bits are set to 1s rather than cleared to 0s. Another way of looking at this is to say that ORing with a 0 has the same effect as ANDing with a 1.

Program C.4 uses this masking property to convert uppercase letters in a word into their respective lowercase form, assuming the letters are stored using the ASCII code. The algorithm for converting letters is similar to that used in Program C.2 and converts uppercase letters into their lowercase form by forcing the fifth bit in each letter to a 1. This is accomplished in Program C.4 by masking the letter's code with the binary value 00100000, which has the hexadecimal value 20.

A sample run using Program C.4 follows.

```
Enter a string of both upper and lowercase letters:
abcdefgHIJKLMNOPqrstuvwxyz

The string of letters just entered is:
abcdefgHIJKLMNOPqrstuvwxyz

This string, in lowercase letters is:
abcdefghijklmnopqrstuvwxyz
```

Program C.4

```cpp
#include <iostream>
const int MAX = 80;
const int TO_LOW = 0x20;
int main()
{
  char word[MAX];        // enough storage for a complete line
  void lower (char *); // function prototype
  cout << "Enter a string of both upper and lowercase letters:\n";
  cin.getline(word,MAX,'\n');
  cout << "\nThe string of letters just entered is:\n"
       << word << endl;
  lower(word);
  cout << "\nThis string, in lowercase letters is:\n"
       << word << endl;
  return 0;
}
void lower(char *word)
{
  while (*word != '\0')
    *word++ |= TO_LOW;
  return;
}
```

Note that the uppercase letters are converted to lowercase form, whereas lowercase letters are unaltered. This is because bit five of all lowercase letters is a 1 to begin with, so forcing this bit to 1 using the mask has no effect. Only when bit five is a 0, as it is for uppercase letters, is the input character altered.

The Exclusive OR Operator

The exclusive OR operator, ^, performs a bit-by-bit comparison of its two operands. The result of the comparison is determined by the following rule:

The result of the comparison is 1 if one and only one of the bits being compared is a 1; otherwise, the result is 0.

Figure C.3 illustrates an exclusive OR operation. As shown in the figure, when both bits being compared are the same value (both 1 or both 0), the result is a 0. Only when both bits have different values (one bit a 1 and the other a 0) is the result a 1. Again, each pair or bit comparison is independent of any other bit comparison.

FIGURE C.3 *A Sample Exclusive OR Operation*

```
      1 0 1 1 0 0 1 1
^     1 1 0 1 0 1 0 1
      ---------------
      0 1 1 0 0 1 1 0
```

An exclusive OR operation can be used to create the opposite value, or complement, of any individual bit in a variable. This is a direct result of the fact that exclusive ORing any bit (1 or 0) with a 1 forces the resulting bit to be of the value opposite that of its original state, whereas exclusive ORing any bit (1 or 0) with a 0 leaves the original bit unchanged. For example, assume that the variable op1 has the arbitrary bit pattern x x x x x x x x, where each x can be either 1 or 0, independent of any other x in the number. Using the notation that $\bar{x}$ is the complement (opposite) value of x, the result of exclusive ORing this binary number with the binary number 0 1 0 1 0 1 0 1 is

```
      op1 =   x x x x x x x x
      op2 =   0 1 0 1 0 1 0 1
              ---------------
   Result =   x x̄ x x̄ x x̄ x x̄
```

As can be seen from this example, the 1s in op2 force the resulting bits to be the complement of their original bit values, whereas the 0s in op2 filter the respective bits in op1, or pass through, with no change in their values.

Many encryption methods use the exclusive OR operation to code data by exclusive ORing each character in the string with a mask value. The choice of the mask value, which is referred to as the **encryption key,** is arbitrary, and any key value can be used.

Program C.5 uses an encryption key of 52 to code a user-entered message. A sample run using Program C.5 follows.

```
Enter a sentence:
Good morning

The sentence just entered is:
Good morning

The encrypted version of this sentence is:
s[[P¶Y[FZ]ZS
```

Program C.5

```cpp
#include <iostream>
const int MAX = 80;
int main()
{
  char message[MAX];     // enough storage for a complete line
  void encrypt(char *); // function prototype
  cout << "\nEnter a sentence:\n";
  cin.getline(message,MAX,'\n');
  cout << "\nThe sentence just entered is:\n"
       << message << endl;
  encrypt(message);
  cout << "\nThe encrypted version of this sentence is:\n"
       << message << endl;
  return 0;
}
void encrypt(char *message)
{
  while (*message != '\0')
     *message++ ^= 52;
  return;
}
```

Decoding an encrypted message requires exclusive ORing the coded message using the original encryption key.

The Complement Operator

The complement operator, ~, is a unary operator that changes each 1 bit in its operand to 0 and each 0 bit to 1. For example, if the variable op1 contains the binary number 11001010, ~op1 replaces this binary number with the number 00110101. The complement operator is used to force any bit in an operand to 0, independent of the actual number of bits used to store the number. For example, the statement

```cpp
        op1 = op1 & ~07;    // 07 is an octal number
```

and its shorter form,

```cpp
        op1 &= ~07;    // 07 is an octal number
```

both set the last three bits of `op1` to 0, regardless of how `op1` is stored within the computer. Either of these two statements can, of course, be replaced by ANDing the last three bits of `op1` with 0s, if the number of bits used to store `op1` is known. In a computer that uses 16 bits to store integers, the appropriate AND operation is

```
op1 = op1 & 0177770;    // in octal
```

or

```
op1 = op1 & 0xFFF8;     // in hexadecimal
```

For a computer that uses 32 bits to store integers, the above AND sets the leftmost or higher-order 16 bits to 0 also, which is an unintended result. The correct statement for 32 bits is

```
op1 = op1 & 027777777770;    // in octal
```

or

```
op1 = op1 & 0xFFFFFFF8;     // in hexadecimal
```

Using the complement operator in this situation frees the programmer from having to determine the storage size of the operand and, more important, makes the program portable between machines that use different integer storage sizes.

Different-Sized Data Items

When the bit operators `&`, `|`, and `^` are used with operands of different sizes, the shorter operand is always increased in bit size to match the size of the larger operand. Figure C.4 illustrates the extension of a 16-bit unsigned integer into a 32-bit number.

FIGURE C.4   *Extending 16-Bit Unsigned Data to 32 Bits*

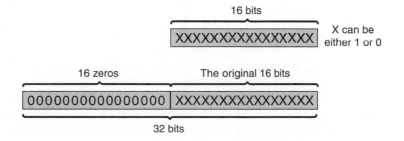

As the figure shows, the additional bits are added to the left of the original number and filled with 0s. This is the equivalent of adding leading 0s to the number, which has no effect on the number's value.

When extending signed numbers, the original leftmost bit is reproduced in the additional bits that are added to the number. As illustrated in Figure C.5, if the original leftmost bit is 0, corresponding to a positive number, 0 is placed in each of the additional bit positions. If the leftmost bit is 1, which corresponds to a negative number, 1 is placed in the additional bit positions. In either case, the resulting binary number has the same sign and magnitude as the original number.

FIGURE C.5   *Extending 16-Bit Signed Data to 32 Bits*

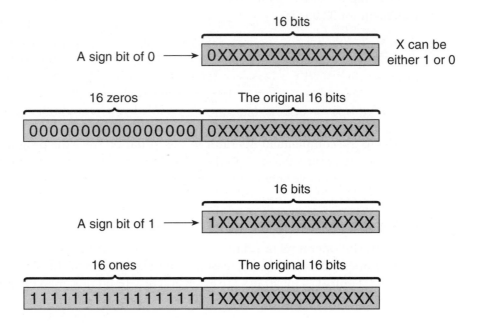

The Shift Operators

The left shift operator, <<, causes the bits in an operand to be shifted to the left by a given amount. For example, the statement

$$op1 = op1 << 4;$$

causes the bits in op1 to be shifted four bits to the left, filling any vacated bits with a 0. Figure C.6 illustrates the effect of shifting the binary number 1111100010101011 to the left by four bit positions.

FIGURE C.6   *An Example of a Left Shift*

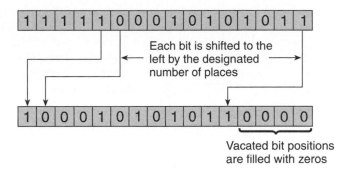

For unsigned integers, each left shift corresponds to multiplication by two. This is also true for signed numbers using twos complement representation, as long as the leftmost bit does not switch values. Because a change in the leftmost bit of a twos complement number represents a change in both the sign and the magnitude represented by the bit, such a shift does not represent a simple multiplication by two.

The right shift operator, >>, causes the bits in an operand to be shifted to the right by a given amount. For example, the statement

```
op2 = op1 >> 3;
```

causes the bits in op1 to be shifted to the right by three bit positions. Figure C.7a illustrates the right shift of the unsigned binary number 1111100010101011 by three bit positions. As illustrated, the three rightmost bits are shifted "off the end" and are lost.

For unsigned numbers, the leftmost bit is not used as a sign bit. For this type of number, the vacated leftmost bits are always filled with 0s. This is the case that is illustrated in Figure C.7a.

For signed numbers, what is filled in the vacated bits depends on the compiler. Most compilers reproduce the original sign bit of the number. Figure C.7b illustrates the right shift of a negative binary number by four bit positions, where the sign bit is reproduced in the vacated bits. Figure C.7c illustrates the equivalent right shift of a positive signed binary number C.7b and C.7c.

The type of fill illustrated in Figures C.7b and C.7c, where the sign bit is reproduced in vacated bit positions, is called an **arithmetic right shift**. In an arithmetic right shift, each single shift to the right corresponds to a division by two.

Instead of reproducing the sign bit in right-shifted signed numbers, some compilers automatically fill the vacated bits with 0s. This type of shift is called a **logical shift.** For positive signed numbers, where the leftmost bit is 0, both arithmetic and logical right shifts produce the same result. The results of these two shifts are different only when negative numbers are involved.

FIGURE C.7a   *An Unsigned Arithmetic Right Shift*

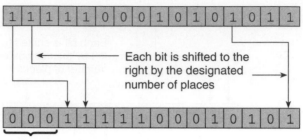

FIGURE C.7b   *The Right Shift of a Negative Binary Number*

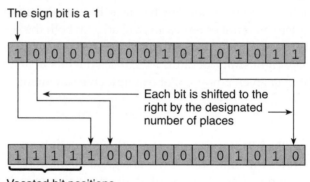

FIGURE C.7c   *The Right Shift of a Positive Binary Number*

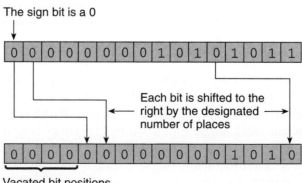

Appendix D Solutions

Solutions to all exercises can be found on the Course Technology Web site for this text. The URL for this Web site is www.course.com.

Index

Operators

(dot), 491
+, 49
++, 101–2, 611
– (negation), 50
– (subtraction), 49
––, 103, 429
*, 49, 410
/, 49
\, 38
%, 49
=, 71, 92, 572
==, 133
>, 133
>=, 133
<, 133
<=, 133
<< (insertion), 20, 53
<< (left shift) 611
>> (extraction), 116
>> (right shift), 611
–>, 611
&&, 134, 611
||, 134, 611
!, 134, 135, &, 78, 408
|, 59
^, 611
~, 547
( ), 624
[ ], 425, 624

A

abs( ) function, 108
abstract data type (ADT), 525
abstraction, 568
accessor function, 548
accessor method, 301
accumlating, 99–100
addition operator (+), 47, 49
address operator (&), 408
addresses, 87, 406–11, 451

incrementing/decrementing, 429
passing, 433–48
storing, 409–10, 586
using, 410–11
ADT (abstract data type), 525
algorithms, 6–8, 713
coding, 8, 10
search, 389
sort, 397
alias, 77
ampersand symbol (&), 78
AND operator (&&), 137
ANSI code, 471
ANSO standard, 144
argument(s), 18, 106
arrays as, 370–76
file streams as function
arguments, 697–701
structures as function
arguments, 501–11
arithmetic operators, 47–53
associativity, 51
integer division, 48
precedence, 50–51
array(s)
as arguments, 370–76, 388–89
array type, 98
default constructors and, 548
dynamic allocation of,
424–27, 451
elements or components of,
356, 388
input/output of array
values, 359–63
larger-dimensional, 384–85
of objects, 548–50
one-dimensional, 354–66, 387
passing, 439–43
pointer, 418–27, 451, 481
two-dimensional, 376–86, 388
array initialization, 366–70, 388
array names, 354

artificial intelligence, 522, 739
ASCII (American Standard
Code for Information
Interchange), 37–38
assignment, 572–82
base/member initialization,
580–81
copy constructors, 576–80
memberwise, 572
variations, 97–98
assignment operators, 95,
589–91, 619–20
assignment statements, 70,
92–95
accumulating statements,
99–100
counting statements, 101–4
associative list, 711
associativity, 51
atomic data, 37
auto storage class, 277, 278, 283
automatic dereference, 414

B

backslash character (\), 23, 38
bar symbol (|), 59
base class, 638, 645, 654
base member initialization list,
580–81
BASIC, 521
behavior, object, 522
big O notation, 396–97
binary operators, 47
binary search, 392, 393–96
binary-based files, 658, 660
bit, 86–87
block comments, 27
block scope, 145–46
body of a function, 229, 288
bool, 40, 144
boolalpha, 56
Boolean data type, 144–45